T0338242

Agricultural Risk Transfer

Founded in 1807, John Wiley & Sons is the oldest independent publishing company in the United States. With offices in North America, Europe, Australia and Asia, Wiley is globally committed to developing and marketing print and electronic products and services for our customers' professional and personal knowledge and understanding.

The Wiley Finance series contains books written specifically for finance and investment professionals as well as sophisticated individual investors and their financial advisors. Book topics range from portfolio management to e-commerce, risk management, financial engineering, valuation and financial instrument analysis, as well as much more.

For a list of available titles, visit our website at www.WileyFinance.com.

Agricultural Risk Transfer

Transfer

From Insurance to Reinsurance to Capital Markets

ROMAN MARCO HOHL

WILEY

Library of Congress Cataloging-in-Publication Data
Names: Hohl, Roman, author.
Title: Agricultural risk transfer : from insurance to reinsurance to capital
  markets / Roman Marco Hohl.
Description: Chichester, West Sussex, United Kingdom : John Wiley & Sons,
  [2019] | Series: Wiley finance series | Includes bibliographical
  references and index. |
Identifiers: LCCN 2018041509 (print) | LCCN 2018042300 (ebook) | ISBN
  9781119345640 (Adobe PDF) | ISBN 9781119345657 (ePub) | ISBN 9781119345633
  (hardcover)
Subjects: LCSH: Agricultural insurance. | Agriculture–Risk management. |
  Agriculture–Finance.
Classification: LCC HG9966 (ebook) | LCC HG9966 .H64 2019 (print) | DDC
  368.1/21–dc23
LC record available at https://lccn.loc.gov/2018041509

Cover Design: Wiley
Top Image: © WHYFRAME/Shutterstock,
Bottom Image: © Valentin Valkov/Shutterstock

Set in 10/12 Sabon LT Std by SPi Global, Chennai, India

Printed in Great Britain by TJ International Ltd, Padstow, Cornwall, UK

10 9 8 7 6 5 4 3 2 1

To Mark, Sayaka and Makiko

Contents

Foreword ix

Introduction xi

Acknowledgements xiii

Special Thanks xv

CHAPTER 1
Agricultural Markets and Risk Management 1

CHAPTER 2
Concepts of Insurance 21

CHAPTER 3
Agricultural Perils and Risk Modelling Concepts 45

CHAPTER 4
Agricultural Data and Proxies 103

CHAPTER 5
Agricultural Insurance 149

CHAPTER 6
Crop Insurance 189

CHAPTER 7
Livestock Insurance   271

CHAPTER 8
Aquaculture Insurance   311

CHAPTER 9
Forest Insurance   333

CHAPTER 10
Risk Transfer to Reinsurance Markets   363

CHAPTER 11
Risk Transfer to Capital Markets   393

ACRONYMS AND ABBREVIATIONS   407

INDEX   409

Foreword

Agriculture is an important industry segment of the global economy in terms of GDP contribution and employment, particularly in many low- and middle-income countries. At a time when population growth drives further demand for food and agricultural raw materials, and the producing sector faces supply challenges and uncertainties from potentially more natural disasters related to climate change, risk management is of ever-growing importance. As experienced in 2007/2008, and to a lesser extent in 2010, production shortfalls in key exporting countries cause immediate responses on global commodity markets and trigger food security crises for many net importers.

The agricultural insurance sector has been adapting to the increasing need for risk transfer and reached a premium volume of close to US$31 billion in 2017 – a threefold increase since 2006. While the large growth in our business allows for a better geographical diversification for global reinsurers and capital markets, it means at the same time higher exposure for specialised local insurers.

Agricultural Risk Transfer comes at the right time, when our industry is optimising covers in well-established markets and expanding in new territories where insurance penetration is low, demand is increasing but product development is challenging and requires high level of expertise. Underwriting agricultural risks has and will continue to be highly complex. Pure actuarial risk pricing methods that rely on limited historical claims data and loss proxies are not sufficient any more to quantify future loss expectations and they require catastrophe risk modelling skills. While learning by doing has largely been the main approach for all stakeholders in our industry, the systematic methods provided in this book form a common standard for risk transfer of crop, livestock, forestry and aquaculture assets in developed as well as in emerging markets.

As the theory is illustrated through comprehensive case studies from our industry, *Agricultural Risk Transfer* is of equal interest for (re)insurance underwriters, loss adjustors, risk assessors, corporate risk managers, actuaries, catastrophe modellers and fund managers as well as development agencies, government entities, funding and financing institutions, the agricultural supply chain and students in disciplines that relate to our industry. *Agricultural Risk Transfer* closes the knowledge gap between insurers and reinsurers as well as between academics and our industry. It therefore greatly supports the efforts of our professional associations to exchange experience and best practices among stakeholders in the agricultural risk transfer industry.

Arnaud de Beaucaron
President
International Association of Agricultural Production
Insurers (AIAG)
Paris, France

Dr Thomas Zacharias
President
National Crop Insurance Services (NCIS)
Overland Park, Kansas, USA

Introduction

This book is written for practitioners and researchers in agricultural development, risk transfer and risk management and aims to close the knowledge gap between mature and developing agricultural markets as well as between practitioners and academia. *Agricultural Risk Transfer* brings together the most important concepts and methods, from the fundamentals to specific products and modelling techniques, and demonstrates their applications through case studies from the industry.

This book has been a nearly two-year project, one that started on the suggestion of the (re)insurance industry to discuss the current risk transfer theory with practical examples. Based on the encouragement from (re)insurers, international development agencies and those in academia, and given that agricultural insurance is one of the fastest growing specialty lines, I started developing an outline for *Agricultural Risk Transfer*.

OVERVIEW OF CHAPTERS

While all chapters can be read alone, some references are made throughout the book to some of the technical chapters that define key concepts and practices. At the end of each chapter, a list of books and reports is provided for the interested reader.

Each chapter contains examples from the industry and numerical examples to highlight the main risk transfer products, which are intended to illustrate the concepts and methodologies and therefore do not suggest any particular price for the products described. To represent the growth of agricultural risk transfer by country and main types of products, I developed a detailed database for each country (2006–2017) based on market reports and in-depth discussions with leading (re)insurers and brokers.

Chapter 1 provides an overview of current trends and future constraints in the agricultural sector, which are discussed in more detail in subsequent chapters for crops, livestock, aquaculture and forestry. This chapter further provides an overview of risk transfer concepts and discusses the role of risk management at farm level, for the agricultural supply chain and for government entities. As risk transfer addresses mostly market and production risks, a special emphasis is put on these risks.

Chapter 2 presents the key concepts of insurance and actuarial as well as catastrophe risk pricing, with references as to how these concepts are applied in agriculture. This chapter forms the basis for Chapter 5 (Agricultural Insurance) and links to Chapter 10 (Risk Transfer to Reinsurance).

Chapter 3 discusses the main perils for agriculture, including drought, flood, hail, frost, snow, cyclones, wildfires and epidemic livestock and aquatic diseases. The chapter includes the main risk modelling concepts, and for most perils, a list of open source data and model outputs is provided.

Chapter 4 discusses the sources and statistical techniques to address agricultural data and proxies, including climate data, satellite data for vegetation monitoring and wildfire detection, crop yield data, and livestock/aquaculture as well as forestry datasets. These concepts form the basis of most of the following chapters.

Chapter 5 reveals specific concepts as well as benefits and challenges of agricultural insurance, and it includes an overview of different products and key markets. Agricultural insurance systems and the role of the government is discussed specifically.

Chapter 6 discusses all main crop insurance products, including named-peril covers, multi-peril insurance, revenue and income covers as well as index-based insurance through area-yield, weather-, satellite- and model-driven indices.

Chapter 7 is dedicated to livestock insurance and presents standard insurance covers and extensions to business interruption and epidemic livestock diseases. Revenue insurance and index-based structures are discussed separately.

Chapter 8 introduces insurance solutions for aquaculture risks and discusses indemnity-based as well as index-based products, with a view on the main insurance structures, pricing and loss adjustment.

Chapter 9 deals with forestry insurance, with a perspective on underwriting, pricing and loss adjustment for standard coverage and extensions to carbon sequestration and firefighting expenses for governments.

Chapter 10 reveals how agricultural risks are transferred to reinsurance markets and presents the concepts of the main reinsurance structures and particularities for agriculture.

Chapter 11 shows risk transfer concepts of capital markets which are gaining in importance and includes a discussion on how insurance-linked securities are or can be used for agriculture exposure.

Many colleagues and friends from the industry and academia have helped in reviewing the book's chapters and case studies – all remaining errors are my sole responsibility. I would appreciate if readers could report errors or inconsistencies to hohlroman@gmail.com or www.agriculturalrisktransfer.com.

Acknowledgements

I would like to sincerely thank the reviewers for their very helpful comments, including Prof Robert Finger (Swiss Federal Institute of Technology, Switzerland), Prof Barry Barnet (University of Kentucky, USA), Prof Yui Leong (National University of Singapore, Singapore), Dr Auguste Boissonnade (Risk Management Solutions, USA), Michael Owen (Guy Carpenter, Singapore), Claudio Busarello (Swiss Re, Switzerland), Randall Reese (Allianz ART, USA), Charles Stutley (World Bank, UK), Phil Cottle (Forest Re, UK), Dan Fairweather (Willis, UK) and Dr Hervé Castella (Partner Re, Switzerland).

I am equally grateful for the contributions and reviews of different case studies from colleagues and friends in the industry and academia, including Chen Peng (PICC, China), Zhao Wei (AXA Corporate Solutions, China), Prof Long (Ministry of Agriculture, China), Dr Chutatong Charumilind (Thai General Insurance Association), MK Poddar (Agriculture Insurance Company of India), Harini Kannan and Yu Deng (Swiss Re, Singapore), Sonia Rawal (Allianz Re, Singapore), Ulziibold Yadamsuren (National University of Mongolia), SVRK Prabhakar (Institute for Global Environmental Strategies, Japan), Mani Upadhyay (AFSC, Canada), Joseph Bradonisio (Guy Carpenter, Canada), Dr Oscar Vergara (AIR Worldwide, USA), Stefano Nicolini (Beach Group, USA), Gift Livata (Microensure, Malawi), Daisy Sabao (World Bank, Mozambique), Shadreck Mapfumo (IFC, South Africa), Roman Shynkarenko (Allianz, Australia), Chis Coe (Aon Benfield, UK), Dr Tom Osborne (Ironshore, UK), Julian Roberts (Willis, UK), Hansueli Lusti (Swiss Hail Insurance Company, Switzerland), Dr Olena Sosenko (Agricultural Reinsurance Specialist, Switzerland), Reto J. Schneider (Allianz Re, Switzerland), Maximilian Strobl and Dr Lambert Muhr (Munich Re, Germany), Luis Pulido (Hannover Re, Germany), Dr Juraj Balkovic (International Institute of Applied Systems Analysis, Austria), as well as Dr Marc Wueest, Dr Hans Feyen, Peter Welten, Dr Petra Winter and Lovemore Forichi (all Swiss Re, Switzerland).

Special Thanks

Special thanks go to Reto Zihlmann, a master student in agronomy at the Swiss Federal Institute of Technology, who helped me to generate most of the plots. I am also very grateful to Arnaud de Beaucaron (president of AIAG) and Dr Tom Zacharias (president of NCIS) for writing the foreword of *Agricultural Risk Transfer* and for all the encouragement. I wish to express my appreciation to my colleagues from the International Finance Corporation (World Bank Group), particularly Vijay Kalovakanda and Utako Saoshiro, for the understanding they showed over my limited ability to participate in field missions during the time writing the book. My sincere gratitude goes to Wiley as the publisher of *Agricultural Risk Transfer* and specifically, Emily Paul (project editor), Gemma Valler (commissioning editor), Gladys Ganaden (editorial executive), and Sharmila Srinivasan (production editor) for the great support and input to the manuscript.

Last but not least, special thanks go to my wife and children, who have lived with the book for two years, and to our golden retriever, who had shorter walks than usual at times.

Agricultural Risk Transfer

CHAPTER 1

Agricultural Markets and Risk Management

1.1 INTRODUCTION

Agriculture has always been a core human activity, and over the past century it has made enormous progress in increasing the production of food and agricultural raw materials. Much of the growth is due to specialisation, verticalisation, expansion in land use and water resources, the improvements in farming techniques and risk management. At the same time, food production has become globalised, is dominated by a few producing countries, and has managed to keep pace with population growth and increasing demand.

The large growth in production, verticalisation and industrialisation has led to increased stress on natural resources and a higher vulnerability to unexpected shocks, including natural disasters and epidemic diseases that impact local and global markets. Climate change, including more extreme weather events, and future economic developments are major factors that drive supply and demand for agricultural products and food security. Risk management, including risk transfer, has been an integral part of advancing agricultural production in coping, mitigating and transferring production risks. The (re)insurance industry and capital markets have been developing products to satisfy the growing need of farmers, agribusinesses and governments to transfer risks.

This chapter provides a brief introduction of the main trends that drives demand and supply in agriculture, while trends in the individual sectors are discussed in subsequent chapters. Key risks and risk management options are discussed for producers, agribusinesses and governments.

1.2 TRENDS AND CHALLENGES IN THE AGRICULTURAL SECTOR

At the change of the millennium, there was a reasonably high level of confidence that projected food demand could be met by improved crop production. In more recent years, the consensus is that future food production will struggle to keep up with growing demand. Part of the change in viewing future global food security is that (i) grain prices were initially assumed to decrease in future decades, (ii) rates of economic development in the most populated countries have exceeded initial projections, (iii) the demand for grain, energy and livestock products has increased more rapidly through higher than anticipated increases in purchasing power, (iv) increases in grain yields have been slowing, and (v) climate change is perceived to have larger impacts on most agricultural activities. The global 2017 World Economic Forum (WEF) risk survey revealed that (i) extreme weather events ranked as the likeliest of the 10 most likely risks and ranked as number 2 of the 10 risks with the largest impact and (ii) food security was ranked seventh among the 10 risks with the largest impact.[1]

Generally, a more sustainable approach to agriculture is needed to use land, water and input supplies more efficiently (conservation agriculture) and to increase farm incomes and food security while adapting to climate change through mixed crop–livestock systems and sustainable livestock production (climate-smart agriculture).[2] Producing more with fewer resources, reducing greenhouse gas (GHG) emissions (global warming) and enhancing the livelihoods of smallholders in low- and middle-income countries remain key challenges for the agricultural sector. Increasing investments that are backed by safety nets of more specialised and verticalised agriculture (risk transfer) is essential to increasing production.

RISING DEMAND

Recent projections on demand and supply conclude that the agricultural sector will need to produce almost 50% more food, feed and biofuel by 2050 compared with 2012.[3] This means global markets will need to produce on average one third more, while sub-Saharan Africa and South Asia will need to double production. There is a consensus that the additional food will need to come predominately from yield increases since expansion of arable land is challenging as it is not readily available due to a lack of infrastructure in remote locations and a concentration of available land in only a few countries.

A key driver of demand is a growing human population that is likely to reach 9.73 billion in 2050 and 11.2 billion in 2100. Demand is undergoing structural changes in that increasingly affluent middle classes in low- and middle-income countries can afford to change their dietary pattern towards more resource-intensive dairy and meat products. As the global demand for livestock products is projected to increase by 70% by 2050 relative to 2010, production of feed from grains and cereals has to increase substantially to satisfy demand for meat and dairy products.[4] Additionally, the demand for biofuels, which use the same grains and oilseeds as livestock feed, is projected to

---

[1] WEF, 2017: The Global Risks Report 2017. 12th edition, World Economic Forum Insight Report, Geneva, 78p.
[2] FAO, 2016: Managing Climate Risk Using Climate-Smart Agriculture. FAO Publication, Rome, 22p.
[3] FAO, 2017: The Future of Food and Agriculture – Trends and Challenges. FAO Publication, Rome, 180p.
[4] FAO, 2012: World Agriculture Towards 2030/2050: The 2012 Revision. ESA Working Paper 12-03, Rome, 154p.

continue growing and has increased the competition between food and non-food uses of biomass and created an interlinkage between food, feed and energy markets.

After peaks in 2008 and 2011, food prices have stabilised, but price volatility seems to have increased since 2000. Future food price levels are difficult to estimate and depend on how production systems will respond to resource constraints and climate change. On average, imports are 0–20% of domestic food supply, with some large agricultural economies exporting 50% of their domestic production while many African and Asian countries are among net food importers.

CHALLENGED SUPPLIES

While productivity in all agricultural sectors and key markets has significantly improved over the past 50 years, intensification and industrialisation put increased stress on natural resources, while the industry is going through structural changes. In a number of countries, faulty and distortionary government policy incentives led agriculture production to be highly inflexible to market demand. Global free trade and stringent domestic agricultural policies have added to the vulnerability of individual agricultural sectors and producers. A growing number of interrelated and longer-term trends that are likely to include more frequent natural disasters (climate change), rural transformation, stresses on natural resources and financial shocks in the global economy are difficult to estimate, but all have the potential to severely impact all agricultural sectors.

Structural Changes

The agricultural sector has undergone large structural changes, particularly in high-income countries where farming's share of gross domestic product (GDP) has decreased and where the industrial and service sectors have become multiple times larger. Under such changes, agriculture has become more efficient, specialised and verticalised, as well as more capital-intensive and better integrated into the wider economy. Consolidation of smaller farms into large operations has gained efficiency while entire supply chains have been developed and integrated. Although evidence is still limited, the same transformational processes seem to appear in agricultural sectors of low- and middle-income countries. As agricultural production bears large risks and low productivity, agriculture results in low income, most of any young rural population preferring to work in other sectors in cities, which leads to a lack of resources in agriculture, aging of farmers and rural–urban migration.

Productivity

The production of most main crop types has increased by more than 300% (1961–2016) as a function of greater arable land, higher yields and advanced production technology (Section 6.2). However, production of main crop types is concentrated in a few countries that dominate global markets, and while yields of key staple crops have doubled in the past 50 years, they have been stagnating since the 1990s at annual growth rates of 1%. While the area equipped for irrigation has increased at annual rates of 1.6% (1961–2009), it is projected to grow at 0.1% in future decades due to competition for water from other sectors.

Industrial-scale livestock production led the doubling of the global livestock population in 2016 compared with 1961. As grain and oilseeds are important components in livestock feed, a larger part in the increase of crop production is explained by the needs of the livestock industry. Increased livestock mobility, global trading and large differences in biosecurity plans of high- and low-income countries have resulted in a higher overall vulnerability to large-scale outbreaks of epidemic diseases (Section 7.2). Future increases in livestock production are thought to come from larger herds rather than from higher per-animal productivity, which in turn requires larger quantities of grains and oilseeds for feed.

Between 1960 and 2016, the production of aquatic animals increased 50 times based on the adaptation of new production methods and the expansion of aquaculture areas (Section 8.2). Aquaculture provided only 7% of fish for human consumption in 1974, which grew to 44% in 2014. However, intensified production has led to over-use of antibiotics in fish feed, polluted waste waters and environmental degradation. Growth rates in aquaculture production are expected to slow due to constraints in water availability and accessibility of high-quality broodstock.

Driven mainly by commercial agriculture in tropical environments, global forest land decreased by 3% between 1990 and 2015, while over the same time, forest plantations increased in size (Section 9.2). With strong demand for forest conversions from population growth and crop production, the global forest area is likely to continue to decrease.

Availability of Natural Resources and Investments

Agriculture production is highly water intensive and accounts for 70% of global water withdrawals. While the efficiency of irrigation has increased, water allocations to agriculture are shifting towards other industries and growing urban centres. Adaptation of production techniques is necessary to increase the efficiency of water usage, such as drop irrigation and alternate wetting and drying, which can reduce water use in rice cultivation by 25% without affecting yields. Today, over 33% of the global arable land is moderately to highly degraded, with particularly high levels in dryland production systems.

Investments in agriculture have increased over the past 15 years and low- and middle-income countries now invest, with US$190 billion annually, about the same as high-income countries. Government-driven investments into research and development rapidly reduced after the *green revolution* in the 1970s but are now growing, particularly in low- and middle-income countries. Agricultural trades closely follow global economic trends, with rapid increases since 2000 and a drop during the 2008–2009 financial crisis and a recovery thereafter, agriculture being one of the most protected sectors through import tariffs.[5] The use of biotechnology, including genetically modified organisms, which is thought to support production increases through higher-yielding crop species, remains controversial in Europe and Asia.

Supply Chains

Inefficient supply chains in harvesting, storing, transporting, processing, packaging and marketing agricultural products and changing consumer attitudes have led to

---

[5] FAO, 2015: The State of Agricultural Commodity Markets – Trade and Food Security. FAO Publication, Rome, 89p.

food waste in the range of 33%, which is a particularly severe problem in low- and middle-income countries. Improving supply chain efficiency and linking local food production systems to growing cities are thought to be key measures to reduce food losses and wastage.

Conflicts and Poverty

Civil conflicts have increased since the 2000s and are the cause of large-scale migration, which undermines agricultural development and can lead to humanitarian crises. Countries with the highest levels of undernourishment tend to have experienced conflicts, and the prevalence of hunger rises exponentially with the degree of fragility.[6] Poverty is closely linked to agricultural productivity as both are highly concentrated in rural areas. Population increases, growing income inequalities, resource stress and impacts of climate change are likely to aggravate poverty and food security in the next decades.

Climate Change

The agricultural sector contributes 21% of total global GHG emissions and if energy usage is included (e.g. fuel for tractors) the share of agriculture activities increases to 26%. With intensification of production, agriculture-related GHG emissions have nearly doubled in the past 50 years and projections foresee a further increase. Climate change is seen as a significant hunger-risk multiplier and projections anticipate that by 2050, an additional 120 million people, particularly in sub-Saharan Africa, will be at risk of undernourishment.

Climatological Disasters
Global warming is likely to change the frequency and severity of climatological and meteorological disasters with potentially more frequent and intensive events. Climate change through increasing temperatures can lead to an intensification of certain plant pests and diseases and these spreading to larger areas. This will make agricultural production more volatile and requires adaptation strategies in the most affected regions and an increase in humanitarian assistance. Through increasingly globalised markets, production shocks from severe weather events in major producing markets are immediately reflected in commodity prices, which can rapidly develop into food security crises such as the events of 2007–2008 and 2011. Many low- and middle-income countries are likely to continue to rely on grain imports for food security and are at the mercy of international markets and export bans in the case of low domestic supply of a key production country. For example, following a severe drought in 2010, the Russian government ordered a ban on grain exports, which increased global wheat prices significantly and caused grain shortages for large net importers such as Egypt.

Impacts on Crop Production
The latest Intergovernmental Panel on Climate Change (IPCC) report states that (i) crop production in low-latitude countries will be negatively affected by climate change with high confidence while impacts in northern latitudes are more uncertain,

---

[6] http://fundforpeace.org/fsi (accessed November 2017).

(ii) climate change will increase the inter-annual variability of crop yields in many regions with medium confidence, and (iii) agronomic adaptation can improve yields by 15–18% with moderate confidence. Rainfed smallholder production systems in highland areas and the tropics, which produce 60% of global agricultural output on 80% of the global arable land, will be most severely impacted through more volatile rainfall and temperature patterns.[7] Most studies of climate change impacts on crop yields show that crop yield variability will generally increase in the future (2030); however, this varies per crop type and by geography.[8] Potentially more frequent and severe extreme weather events increase yield variability and the volatility of staple food prices.[9] Past climate trends display yield volatilities of 20–24% and could increase to 43–53% in 2020–2040.[10]

Impacts on Livestock, Aquaculture and Forestry
Depending on the region, climate change has large impacts on livestock production through lower quantity and quality of feed, increased heat stress and limited water availability, potentially more frequent and extreme climate events (e.g. severe winters in Mongolia, El Niño-associated flooding in east Africa and droughts in southern Africa) and faster spread of certain livestock diseases. Poor livestock households in Africa and South Asia, and pastoralists in drylands in Africa and the Middle East, are most severely impacted by climate change due to limited water and forage availability, with a potential for political conflicts. Temperature increases in low-latitude regions are likely to cause local extinction of some fish species, while rising sea levels will threaten coastal aquaculture systems in river deltas and estuaries. Warming temperatures could prolong the wildfire season through heatwaves and fewer snowcaps in winter.

1.3 RISK MANAGEMENT IN AGRICULTURE

Risk management has been an integral part of agricultural industrialisation, which has led to significant production growth that is necessary to satisfy growing demand for food and agricultural raw materials. Sources of risk in agriculture are numerous and diverse and the sector is exposed to random (idiosyncratic) and highly systemic (co-variate) risks, which can impact an individual producer, a larger region, the wider supply chain, an entire country or global commodity markets. Production and market risk are some of the largest risks in the agricultural sector and are addressed through constantly evolving risk management approaches.

---

[7] FAO, 2011: The State of the World's Land and Water Resources for Food and Agriculture. FAO Publication, Rome, 308p.
[8] McCarl, B.A. et al., 2008: Climate change and future analysis: Is stationarity dying? *Amer. J. Agr. Econ.*, 90(5), 1241–7.
[9] Tadesse, G. et al., 2014: Drivers and triggers of international food price spikes and volatility. *Food Policy*, 47, 117–28.
[10] Diffenbaugh, N.S. et al., 2012: Response of corn markets to climate volatility under alternative energy futures. *Nat. Clim. Chang.*, 2, 514–18.

RISK MANAGEMENT STRATEGIES

Risks in agriculture are diverse and often interconnected and require different strategies to cope with the risk, mitigate the risk or transfer the risk, depending on its magnitude. Considering the risk and the impact on the economy and the wider society, government agencies and the private sector collaborate to develop adequate risk strategies. Holistic risk management approaches include a set of complex relations between the original sources of risk, the available strategies and interrelated tools from governments and markets.[11] The holistic framework supports a system where public policy enables market solutions and risk is managed at different levels, including (i) frequent and limited losses are part of the normal business environment and are managed at farm level, (ii) larger and infrequent risks that are beyond farm-based risk management are addressed by market mechanisms (e.g. financial and insurance products), and (iii) very large and rare risks that can lead to market failure require government intervention.[12]

Risk Strategies

Agricultural risk management strategies can be divided into (i) mitigation to limit the adverse impact of a disaster, including production diversification (e.g. growing different crop types), income diversification and management measures (e.g. soil drainage, mulching, optimal planting schedules, weather forecasts), (ii) transfer of the financial consequences to a third party through informal, formal and/or semi-formal approaches, (iii) coping to manage financial consequences in, for example, complementing farm income by other activities, contract farming, and (iv) prevention, through irrigation, flood water management, drainage and crop protection.

Risk strategies can further be distinguished as (i) informal approaches, which are ex-ante strategies and include diversification of income sources, risk-adopted agricultural production strategies (e.g. buffer stock accumulation, irrigation) and risk avoidance, (ii) formal approaches provided by governments (e.g. infrastructure development, establishment of social schemes and/or cash transfer schemes) or markets (e.g. financial products and insurance), and (iii) semi-formal approaches, including informal risk sharing and mutualisation. Risk strategies largely depend on the type of risk, the impact in terms of area affected and the available response measures and risk mitigation and transfer mechanisms that are in place (see Figure 1.1).

Risks are often classified according to severity on three levels, including (i) micro-level risks, where random (idiosyncratic) risks affect individual producers, (ii) meso-level risks, where systemic (covariate) risks affect larger communities and the agricultural supply chain, and (iii) macro-level risks, where systemic and highly systemic risks impact an entire country and can have global consequences (see Figure 1.1).

---

[11] OECD, 2010: Risk Management in Agriculture – A Holistic Conceptual Framework. OECD Publishing, Paris, 59p.

[12] Tangermann, S., 2011: Risk Management in Agriculture and the Future of the EU's Common Agricultural Policy. ICTSD, Issue Paper 34, Geneva, 50p.

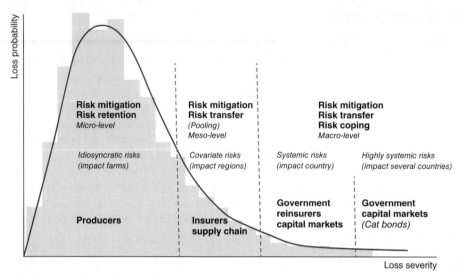

FIGURE 1.1 Layering of risks in function of loss probability/severity with typical risk management approaches.
Source: Adapted from World Bank (2016) and OECD (2009).

Risk Layering

Risk layering is a core analytical concept to develop a risk financing strategy to protect against events of different frequencies and severities; it includes different mechanisms to address needs for funds before or after a disaster. Risk layering assigns monetary levels at which risks can be retained, pooled or transferred through different levels of the agricultural sector while assuring that financial resources are optimised. Optimal risk layering contains probabilistic analyses where frequent low-consequence events and rare catastrophe-type events are assessed in terms of loss potential to develop disaster risk management strategies for each layer, which is particularly important in the wake of climate change.[13]

Risk Transfer

Risk transfer is one of the key risk strategies in agriculture and shifts identified risks or responsibilities from their source to a third party through mechanisms such as (re) insurance, capital market instruments and legislation. In a narrower sense, risk transfer instruments include financial derivatives, insurance and insurance-linked securities.[14]

Financial derivatives derive a value from one or more underlying assets, securities, prices or indices and differ according to (i) the type of the underlying value (e.g. equity, interest rate, exchange rate, commodity or credit), (ii) the structure of the derivative contract, (e.g. forward, swap, option), and (iii) the market in which they are offered.

[13] Linnerooth-Bayer, J. and Hochrainer-Stigler, S., 2015: Financial instruments for disaster risk management and climate change adaptation. *Clim. Change*, 133(1), 85–100.
[14] Anderson, P.R.D., 2014: Market Risk Transfer. Background Paper for the World Development Report 2014 on Opportunity and Risk. World Bank Report, Washington DC, 7p.

Insurance transactions are financial agreements that transfer losses against a cost (premium) and where insurers pool risks over different lines of businesses and geographical areas to absorb risks while maximising revenue from premiums and minimising the risk of payouts. While financial derivatives focus on transfer of market risk, insurance instruments cover production risks and some elements of market risks. Insurance-linked securities present an alternative to reinsurance with transfer of insurance risk to capital markets.

MARKET RISK MANAGEMENT

High price volatility is one of the main causes of volatile farm revenues and delayed or defaulted loan reimbursements and payments of input supplies. For low-income countries with large agricultural sectors and exports of a few leading commodities, commodity price volatilities have a large impact on export earnings, fiscal revenues and creditworthiness.

The international community and governments have tried to manage commodity price risks by stabilising price volatility through market interventions, including compensatory mechanisms (e.g. stabilisation funds, stockpiles, buffer stock), international commodity agreements and marketing boards. As set prices were often based on political bargains, market fundamentals were not accurately reflected and led to a failure of most stabilisation schemes and to the development of market-based commodity risk management mechanisms.[15] The main price risk management approaches for agriculture include financial instruments and contract farming.

Commodity Price Management Instruments

The main price hedging instruments include forward contracts, futures, options and swaps, which are available through standardised exchanges or are bilaterally negotiated between two parties. As price risks are spatially correlated, futures and options are efficient mechanisms to manage price risks as long as the basis risk is acceptable in that the volatility of price risks for a given area relates reasonably well to prices at a commodity exchange.

Forward Contracts
Forward contracts are private agreements (over the counter) for the seller (e.g. farmer) to deliver a specified quantity of a commodity to the buyer (e.g. a processor) at some time in the future for a specified price, with fix-priced contracts being the most common form.[16] Forward contracts are used to acquire physical delivery of the underlying commodity. While forward contracts buffer against negative price developments for the seller, the seller does not benefit from upsides when prices increase. Forward contracts contain (i) credit risk when the buyer fails to pay at maturity of the contract, and

---

[15] Varangis, P. et al., 2002: Agricultural Markets and Risks. World Bank Working Paper 2793, Washington DC, 34p.
[16] Other forms of forward contracts that allow for more flexibility in how prices at delivery are derived include price-to-be-fixed contracts, deferred pricing contracts, deferred payment contracts, minimum price contracts, reference price forward contracts, basis contracts and hedge-to-arrive contracts.

(ii) default risk when the seller is not able to deliver the commodity, in which case the seller is obliged to purchase the shortfall from another source.

Futures Contracts

Futures contracts are standardised contracts that trade forward through commodity exchanges and are mainly used to hedge price risk rather than acquiring physical delivery of the underlying commodity. Futures contracts allow producers who own a commodity to protect themselves from declining commodity prices by selling a futures contract. As futures are settled between the seller and the buyer through the clearing house of the exchange, there is no credit and default risk. Futures are based on approximate prices, with the effective costs varying with market conditions. In case a futures position is not closed before expiry, the position could either be physically delivered or settled for cash. Futures only exist for the most common and main agricultural commodities.

Call and Put Options

Options are used to provide the seller with a guarantee of obtaining a minimum selling price and the buyer to obtain a maximum price with downside protection while retaining some upside potential. The buyer of the option pays the seller a non-refundable cost (option premium). A put option (call option) gives the buyer of the put option (call option) the right to sell (buy) the underlying commodity at a specified price, while the seller of the put (call) has an obligation to buy the commodity on the exercise of the option. Farmers without an existing physical contract (e.g. contract farming) typically buy a put option for protection against declining prices. Producers with physical delivery contracts can gain a financial upside above the pre-agreed delivery price of the physical contract through call options.

While exchange-traded options are standardised, privately arranged options provide more flexibility but contain credit risk. Options are settled in (i) offsetting the trade by taking the opposite position where the buyer or seller sells the option, (ii) exercising the option by the buyer when the underlying commodity is physically bought or sold through the exchange, or (iii) letting the option expire. European-type options can be exercised at expiry only, while American-type options can be exercised at any time.

Swaps

A commodity swap contract obligates the hedger (e.g. a farmer) to pay a fixed price and receive a floating price for a predefined volume of a commodity over a certain time from the hedge provider (e.g. a processor). For agricultural commodities, the existence of liquid and well-established futures markets limits the need for swaps.

Contract Farming

For a producer, prices can be pre-agreed through a contract farming agreement with a processor that can take the form of (i) a marketing contract, which defines the price of the commodity to be delivered before harvest, or (ii) a production contract that specifies production input supplies, quality and quantity of the commodity to be delivered as well as the price. An out-grower scheme involves contract farming by small-scale farmers with a processor, which in turn supports production planning, provides input supply and technical expertise as well as transportation, and therefore assures guaranteed market access. Some cooperatives, associations and farmer groups operate under collective marketing plans to manage price risk through higher bargaining power with domestic and international markets.

PRODUCTION RISK MANAGEMENT

Production risks derive from adverse weather conditions, pests and diseases, and technological changes that impact production quantity and/or quality and, depending on the severity, can impact large areas and lead to temporary failure of markets. Forest fires and epidemic disease outbreaks are production risks that can impact a sector long-term until reestablishment has occurred and productivity is back to normal levels. Production risks are mostly managed through risk transfer to (re)insurance markets, while some efforts have been undertaken to develop financial instruments to hedge against crop yield volatility.

Financial Instruments

As financial instruments are widely used to manage commodity price risks, in some markets efforts were undertaken to develop financial solutions to manage crop yield volatility. In 1995, the Chicago Board of Trade (CBOT) introduced futures and options for crop yield to hedge against yield volatility in using state-based yield estimates by the United States Department of Agriculture (USDA) during the growing and harvest season for commodities such as corn, soybeans, rice and winter wheat.[17] A yield futures contract allows a producer to lock in a crop yield several months into the future and hedge the revenue through a combination of yield and price futures. Put and call options were available on the corn yield futures. Theoretical models were developed to simultaneously hedge price and yield risk through financial instruments.[18] However, limited interest from producers led to the CBOT yield futures and options being discontinued in 2000, which was probably related to the emergence of large-scale, government-subsidised area-yield index insurance.

Insurance

Agricultural insurance remains the main approach to managing production risks and mainly covers physical damage to an agricultural asset. Over time, specific products have been developed, including indemnity- and index-based covers that provide payouts for production volatility from physical damage, reduced revenue from production and price volatility, and low farm income from different commodities (Chapter 5). Compared with price management instruments, insurance products are more tailor-made and often benefit from government support through premium subsidies. As agricultural insurance covers systemic risks, insurers rely on government and private-sector reinsurance to prevent market failures.

---

[17] Vukina, T. et al., 1996: Crop yield futures: A mean–variance analysis. *Amer. J. Agr. Econ.*, 78, 1015–25.
[18] Nayak, G.N. and Turvey, C.G., 2000: The simultaneous hedging of price risk, crop yield risk and currency risk. *Can. J. Agric. Econ.*, 48(2), 123–40.

FARM RISK MANAGEMENT

Producers are exposed to a variety of constraints which depend on a farm's location, the agriculture production system, the climatic conditions and the market environment. Farm risk management is mostly a combination of formal and informal approaches, depending on available products and key constraints within an agricultural production system. Constraints are typically highest in low-income countries with limited financial services, underdeveloped infrastructure and a lack of regulation and market access.

Commonly, risks that affect agriculture production include (i) production risks driven by weather conditions, pests, diseases and technological changes, (ii) ecological risks, including climate change and management of natural resources such as water, (iii) market risks through volatility of output and input prices, relationships with the food chain with respect to quality and risks associated with the introduction of new products, and (iv) institutional risks from changes in agriculture policies, food safety and environmental regulations (see Table 1.1).[19] Often, personal risks, financial risks and human resources risks are added as risks for producers.

Farmers in high-income countries benefit from the greatest diversity of risk management options, while smallholders in low-income countries are limited in their ability to manage risk and often rely on government support in the case of disasters or are left alone to cope with various risks.

SUPPLY CHAIN RISK MANAGEMENT

Agricultural supply chains are networks that support the flow of (i) physical products (e.g. from input suppliers to producers, processors and consumers), (ii) finances from credit to lending, payment schedules and repayments, savings and insurance, and (iii) information related to products and finances.

Modern risk management theory states that risk reduction can add to a firm's value by (i) reducing the likelihood of raising expensive external capital, (ii) reducing expected tax liabilities due to different marginal tax rates at different income levels or general differences in taxation, or (iii) lowering the likelihood of financial distress. Enterprise risk management (ERM) aims at the holistic identification of risk exposures to increase the understanding of events that can prevent the firm from achieving its strategic objectives. Further, stock exchange rules and credit rating agencies increasingly require corporations to integrate ERM, with analysts and shareholders becoming more sensitive to deviations of earnings compared with projections.

Major risks for agribusinesses include weather and natural disasters, biological and environmental risks, market risks, logistical/infrastructural risks, managerial and operational risks, policy and institutional risks as well as political risks (see Table 1.1).[20] Further risks include product contamination and recall, loss of access to sites/people/suppliers, reduced capacity, contractual obligations, dual sourcing and general market forces.

---

[19] Hardaker, J.B. et al., 2015: Coping with Risk in Agriculture: Applied Decision Analysis. 3rd edition. CABI Publishing, Wallingford, 296p.

[20] Jaffee, S. et al., 2010: Rapid Agricultural Supply Chain Risk Assessment: A Conceptual Framework. World Bank Discussion Paper 47, Washington DC, 64p.

TABLE 1.1 Overview of the main risk types for an individual crop farmer and a grain processor with informal and formal risk management options.

	INDIVIDUAL OPERATOR (CROP FARMER)		AGRIBUSINESS (GRAIN PROCESSOR)	
Risk	Parameter	Risk Management (Non-Exhaustive)	Parameter	Risk Management (Non-Exhaustive)
Production risks	▪ Physical damage to crops leading to lower yield, unharvested areas ▪ Physical damage to farm infrastructure	*Informal:* ▪ Diversification of production by crop types and geography ▪ Vertical integration ▪ Use of irrigation, crop protection ▪ Early warning systems *Formal:* ▪ Government social/cash transfer and disaster compensation schemes ▪ Leasing agreements to manage production cycles ▪ Insurance for production, revenue or income volatility ▪ Weather derivatives	▪ Physical damage to regional/national crop production leading to lower production available for processing ▪ Physical damage to infrastructure, e.g. grain elevators and storage facilities ▪ Deteriorating grain quality in storage facilities/warehouses ▪ Physical damage during road and sea transport ▪ Non-delivery of grain by contractors due to production constraints	*Informal:* ▪ Diversification of sources of production ▪ Permanent monitoring/sampling of grain in storage ▪ Acquisition of processor in markets that are not exposed to the same perils at the same time *Formal:* ▪ Property and transport insurance ▪ Insurance (or weather derivative) for grain production volatility ▪ General liability insurance
Ecological/ environmental risks	▪ Uncertainties of production environment, e.g. management of natural resources (water grants) ▪ Impacts of climate change	*Informal:* ▪ Acquisition of water rights ▪ Climate change adaptation measures	▪ Uncertainties of production environment ▪ Impacts of climate change	*Informal:* ▪ Special storage facilities to reduce environmental risks ▪ ISO certifications *Formal:* ▪ Environmental liability insurance

(Continued)

TABLE 1.1 *(Continued)*

	INDIVIDUAL OPERATOR (CROP FARMER)		AGRIBUSINESS (GRAIN PROCESSOR)	
Risk	Parameter	Risk Management (Non-Exhaustive)	Parameter	Risk Management (Non-Exhaustive)
Market risks	▪ Volatility of input and output prices ▪ Foreign exchange rates ▪ Interest rates ▪ Risks in dealing with the food value chain (food quality, food safety)	*Informal:* ▪ Diversification and vertical integration *Formal:* ▪ Government minimum support prices ▪ Forward contracts, options and futures ▪ Contract farming, collective marketing plans ▪ Revenue or income insurance	▪ Volatility of commodity prices ▪ Volatility of freight costs ▪ Competitor behaviour (e.g. mergers and acquisitions) ▪ Restricted access to capital	*Informal:* ▪ Diversification and vertical integration *Formal:* ▪ Forward contracts, options and futures ▪ Contract farming with key producers ▪ Corporate revenue or income insurance
Institutional risks	▪ Changes in government actions/rules, e.g. pesticide usage, environmental/farm practices, tax provisions ▪ Restricted access to markets (e.g. closing of ports, export ban)	*Informal:* ▪ Lobby groups to obtain first-hand information	▪ Changes in fiscal and tax policies ▪ Changes in trade and market policy (e.g. foreign government subsidies, trade barriers) ▪ Strikes in harbours ▪ Political instability, corruption, nationalisation of assets	*Informal:* ▪ Lobby groups to obtain first-hand information on changing government rules *Formal:* ▪ Political risk insurance

Risk category	Risks	Management	Risks	Management
Financial/ infrastructure risks	■ Inability to pay interest rates for credit and loans, farmworkers' wages and leased machinery/ equipment	*Informal:* ■ Cash flow management/ planning ■ Off-farm work to complement farm income *Formal:* ■ Increase borrowing levels ■ Leasing of machinery/ equipment	■ Volatility in foreign currency exchange rates ■ Volatility in interest rates ■ Counter-party credit risk ■ Inability to pay debts and interest ■ Deteriorating transport infrastructure	*Informal:* ■ Cash flow management/ planning *Formal:* ■ Refinancing of debt ■ Liquidating assets ■ Interest rate swaps ■ Counter-party–credit risk derivatives
Operational risks	■ Machinery breakdown ■ Uncertain life events (e.g. death, disability) ■ Unavailable employees	*Informal:* ■ Regular health checks and inspection of machinery ■ Access to temporary employees *Formal:* ■ Life and disability insurance	■ Poor management decisions ■ Retention of key personnel ■ Pension and employment benefits schemes ■ Health and safety risks for employees ■ Contamination of produced grain (food safety) ■ Changes in reputation/ perception of supply chain and products	*Informal:* ■ Performance-based retention plan of key personnel ■ External evaluation of pension schemes and contributions ■ Audits of safety and health procedures ■ Tracking of input supplies and grain delivery to comply with food safety standards for domestic and export markets (e.g. HACCP and ISO 9000) *Formal:* ■ Directors & officers insurance ■ Workers' compensation insurance ■ Product liability insurance

Source: Adapted from OECD (2000) and various grain processors' annual reports.

Recently, green mandates oblige the supply chain to follow environmentally-friendly production processes, which bears additional risks.[21]

Most agribusinesses are well versed in the use of financial instruments to manage commodity prices and freight costs, interest and foreign exchange rates, and purchase insurance programmes to cover risks including general and product liability, environmental liability (where available), workers' compensation and transportation. Increasingly, production volatility risks related to natural perils and lower-than-expected volumes of agricultural commodities have become insurable and support agribusiness to manage fix costs and earnings volatility (Section 6.8).

GOVERNMENT RISK MANAGEMENT

Governments have different options for coping with the financial impact of natural disasters, depending on the severity of the disaster, geographical scope, and population directly and indirectly affected. Governments play a key role in providing agricultural assistance, including public food grain reserves, disaster assistance programmes, social protection schemes and disaster risk financing, most of which are anchored in the national disaster risk management strategy.

Depending on the scale and intensity of a natural disaster, a government has budgetary outflows for relief operations, recovery operations and reconstruction and therefore needs liquidity over several months, if not years. While for some low-loss events that occur frequently risk-reduction measures are appropriate, for low-probability but high-severity disasters, ex-ante and ex-post disaster financing strategies are necessary.

Disaster Assistance Programmes

Disaster assistance programmes include disaster risk management and/or disaster risk reduction programmes that aim to reduce the risk (e.g. early-warning systems, environmental protection) and mitigate impacts on livelihoods through response, recovery and reconstruction.

Disaster Risk Financing Programmes

Disaster risk financing aims to deal with the financial impact of disasters and includes (i) ex-post measures such as tax increases, reallocating funds from other budget items, and access to domestic and international credit and borrowing from multilateral finance institutions, and (ii) ex-ante measures including the building of financial reserves, contingent debt agreements and risk transfer to the (re)insurance industry or capital markets, typically through parametric products.

Ex-post Disaster Financing Instruments
Governments have several ex-post financing instruments available, which include both short-term and longer-term measures. Allocation of funds to cope with disasters from other priority development projects takes considerable time and often needs

---

[21] Enyinda, C.I. and Mbah, C.H., 2017: Quantifying sources of risk in global food operations and supply chain. *Thunderbird Int. Business Rev.*, 59(6), 653–61.

parliamentary approval. Equally, rising debt and obtaining credits from domestic and international sources after the occurrence of disaster are longer-term approaches. While appropriate to finance reconstruction efforts, debts and credits do typically not provide the required liquidity to finance immediate post-disaster needs and depending on the damage extent, post-disaster borrowing costs can be significantly higher compared with pre-disaster time and depend on a country's level of indebtedness and ability to service the debt. Obtaining assistance from international donor countries and multilateral financing institutions in the aftermath of a disaster is a common approach adopted by many low-income countries. However, donor funding largely depends on the level of visibility of a disaster in the international media and it can take time until funds are available. Increasing taxes over time to support reconstruction following a disaster are often used ex-post financing instruments; however, tax increases can discourage new private investments that are essential to redeveloping the economy after disaster impact.

Ex-ante Disaster Financing Instruments

Ex-ante instruments are considered more proactive risk financing strategies that provide faster funding than ex-post approaches. IPCC states that insurance and other financial instruments can play an important role in managing natural disaster risks in the framework of climate change adaptation.[22]

A reserve fund can be developed through borrowing or accumulating tax revenues to finance immediate post-disaster needs. Reserve funds are well established in high-income countries to smooth out peak financing requirements, but they are generally rare in low-income countries. Contingent debt provides immediate capital after disaster occurrence with interest rate and loan maturity defined on a pre-loss basis. For disbursement, contingent debt contracts can contain hard triggers (debt is disbursed only according to physical criteria of the intensity of the disaster) or soft triggers (debt is disbursed in the case of an emergency declaration being issued by the government).

Risks can be transferred to (re)insurance markets that provide adequate coverage for natural disasters. In high-income countries, compulsory insurance against natural disasters has proved effective for property assets, despite some political resistance. In low-income countries, insurance markets tend to be underdeveloped and inefficient without or with only limited coverage for natural perils, which leaves governments only with the option to transfer risks through indices directly to reinsurance and capital markets. Unlike contingent credit agreements, parametric risk transfer products are based on hard triggers where payouts are based on a disaster of a predefined intensity which is commonly defined through outputs of catastrophe risk models. As based on indices and model results, these products inherently contain basis risk and might not cover all types of natural disasters.

---

[22] IPCC, 2012: Summary for policymakers. In Fields, C.B. (ed): Managing the Risks of Extreme Events and Disasters to Advance Climate Change Adaptation. Cambridge University Press, 1–19.

Change of Paradigms
In the face of the rising frequency and intensity of losses in low- and middle-income countries, the old model of post-disaster financing and reliance on the donor community is increasingly inefficient. Ex-ante financial schemes that are based on optimal risk layering and an efficient disaster risk management framework can provide efficient solutions around immediate liquidity and reconstruction for low-income countries. International financing institutions and the donor community have been promoting proactive disaster risk management systems, including catastrophe risk financing models to reduce external assistance based on (i) assessing a government's contingent liability to natural disasters, (ii) enabling risk transfer to competitive (re)insurance markets, and (iii) financing sovereign risk.

In high-income countries, losses from natural disasters are typically funded through private risk financing agreements and an efficient public revenue system that relies on taxes. For low-income countries, which typically have low tax ratios and ongoing financial pressures, post-disaster funding comes mainly from international donors through multilaterally sourced infrastructure loans and relief aid. In low-income countries, the catastrophe insurance and risk transfer markets are clearly underdeveloped, which is demonstrated by the fact that while over 40% of the direct losses from natural disasters are insured in high-income countries, less than 10% of these losses are covered by insurance programmes in middle-income countries and less than 5% in low-income countries.[23] Post-disaster development lending from multilateral financing agencies is important for middle-income countries, while support from bilateral donors is typically more dominant in low-income countries.

Risk Layering
Optimal risk layering contains probabilistic analyses where frequent–low-consequence events and rare catastrophe-type events are assessed in terms of loss potential to develop disaster risk management strategies for each layer, which is particularly important in the wake of climate change (see Figure 1.1).[24] The optimal strategy to finance post-disaster liquidity for a government that has restrictions with budget reallocation and reserve funds is likely to include risk retention through reserving to cover small losses and contingent credit as well as risk transfer through reinsurance and/or capital markets to cover large losses.[25] While frequently used by governments or a group of governments to transfer risk to the (re)insurance industry and capital markets, such solutions in the form of insurance or financial instruments (derivatives) are becoming increasingly available for agricultural assets.

Government Risk Transfer for Agricultural Risks in Beijing, China
In 2007, the Beijing Municipal Government (BMG) implemented a new agricultural insurance policy to subsidise crop and livestock insurance premiums by up to 80%,

---

[23] Cummins, J.D. and Mahul, O., 2009: Catastrophe Risk Financing in Developing Countries: Principles for Public Intervention. World Bank Publication, Washington DC, 299p.

[24] Linnerooth-Bayer, J. and Hochrainer-Stigler, S., 2015: Financial instruments for disaster risk management and climate change adaptation. *Clim. Change*, 133(1), 85–100.

[25] Clarke, D. and Mahul, O., 2011: Disaster Risk Financing and Contingent Debt – A Dynamic Analysis. World Bank Policy Research Paper 5693, Washington DC, 31p.

with additional support for 10% of the administrative costs. The insurance programme covers field and horticultural crops against natural perils, livestock against diseases (including epidemics) and greenhouses for physical damage to contents and structures. In the first year, insured values of US$1.2 billion were covered through three insurers, which increased to US$1.6 billion in insured liabilities in 2017 with seven insurers.

Natural Disaster Fund

BMG established a protection fund for natural disaster losses to the underlying agricultural insurance portfolios of each insurer. The new agriculture policy framework works at three different levels that are based on combined loss ratios (CLRs) as (i) CLR is below 100% where insurers assume all losses with surpluses in good years to be put into the protection fund, (ii) CLR of 100–160% where insurers compensate losses from the protection fund and arrange for adequate reinsurance, and (iii) CLR above 160% when BMG assumes all losses. The 160% CLR has been established based on the advice of agricultural insurance experts and quantitative analyses of past calamity data by main peril and losses from previous agricultural insurance programmes in the province of Beijing.

A quantitative analysis that uses historical insurance experience through nonparametric information diffusion modelling shows that the probability of a loss over a CLR of 160% is 70%.[26] However, it has to be noted that past insurance claims stem from relatively small portfolios and different insurance terms and did not benefit from government premium support.

Sovereign Risk Transfer

In 2009, BMG decided to enter into an ex-ante sovereign risk transfer to proactively manage its liabilities above a CLR of 160%. Under the stop-loss reinsurance structure, the risks that are pooled by BMG are transferred to the national reinsurer and international markets for CLRs between 160% and 300%. The insurance regulator approved the risk transfer agreement and estimated the loss frequency at a CLR of 300% at a 50-year event. BMG has bought stop-loss reinsurance continuously since 2009, and in 2017, the stop-loss structure provided cover for US$125 million and incurred a payout in 2012 (excessive rainfall) and 2016 (rainstorm).

In China, province governments are becoming increasingly aware of potential financial liabilities from natural disasters in the agricultural sector and liabilities arising from the National Agricultural Insurance Program (Section 5.2). In 2016, the Heilongjiang government followed the example of Beijing and bought parametric reinsurance to cover income volatility of poor rural households from flood, excessive rainfall, drought and low temperature based on weather- and satellite-derived indices.

---

[26] Xing, L. and Lu, K., 2010: The importance of public–private partnerships in agricultural insurance in China: based on analysis for Beijing. *Agric. Agric. Sci. Procedia*, 1, 241–50.

BIBLIOGRAPHY

Barnard, F., Akridge, J., Dooley, F. et al. (2012). *Agribusiness Management*, 4e. Abingdon: Routledge, 481p.

Conforti, P. (2011). *Looking Ahead in World Food and Agriculture: Perspectives to 2050*. Rome: FAO Publication, 560p.

FAO (2009). *Climate Change Implications for Fisheries and Aquaculture: Overview of Current Scientific Knowledge*. FAO Publication 530. Rome: FAO, 218p.

FAO (2012). *World Agriculture towards 2030/2050 – The 2012 Revision*. ESA Working Paper 12-03. Rome: FAO Publication, 154p.

FAO (2013). *Tackling Climate Change through Livestock: A Global Assessment of Emissions and Mitigation Opportunities*. Rome: FAO Report, 139p.

FAO (2015). *The Impact of Disasters on Agriculture and Food Security*. Rome: FAO Publication, 54p.

FAO (2016). *The State of Food and Agriculture: Climate Change, Agriculture and Food Security*. Rome: FAO Publication, 194p.

GFS (2015). *Climate and Global Crop Production Shocks. Resilience Taskforce Sub-Report*. Global Food Security (GFS), UK Government, 30p.

Hertel, T.W. and Rosch, S.D. (2010). *Climate Change, Agriculture and Poverty*. Policy Research Paper 5468. Washington DC: World Bank, 55p.

Leal Filho, W. (2013). *Climate Change and Disaster Risk Management*. Heidelberg: Springer, 675p.

Nelson, G.C. et al. (2010). *Food Security, Farming, and Climate Change to 2050: Scenarios, Results, Policy Options*. Washington DC: IFPRI Publication, 155p.

OECD (2000). *Income Risk Management in Agriculture*. Paris: OECD Publishing, 147p.

OECD (2009). *Risk Management in Agriculture – A Holistic Conceptual Framework*. Paris: OECD Publishing, 59p.

OECD (2015). *Disaster Risk Financing: A Global Survey of Practices and Challenges*. Paris: OECD Publishing, 140p.

World Bank (2014). *Financial Protection Against Natural Disasters: From Products to Comprehensive Strategies*. Washington DC: World Bank Publication, 88p.

World Bank (2016). *Agricultural Sector Risk Assessment: Methodological Guidance for Practitioners*. Washington DC: World Bank Publication, 130p.

CHAPTER 2

Concepts of Insurance

2.1 INTRODUCTION

The global insurance industry is of fundamental importance in managing an increasing number of perils, hazards and risks. Risk transfer from individuals, corporations and government entities to (re)insurers and capital markets is a proven concept to sustainably manage systemic risks from natural and man-made disasters. Insurance is based on key concepts that evolved around the insurability of risks, risk management and risk pricing, including actuarial and catastrophe modelling concepts to facilitate and optimise risk transfer.

As one of the largest and fastest growing speciality lines of insurance, agricultural insurance follows the main concepts of insurance but includes specific approaches in underwriting and pricing that need to address trends in data and estimation of catastrophe loss potentials from a large number of different perils. As the agricultural risk transfer industry grows, specific methods have been developed to price and model risks based on historical claims and proxies that range from weather data to outputs of mechanistic models.

This chapter provides a brief overview of global insurance markets and introduces the main concepts of insurance with reference to agricultural insurance. Special emphasis is put on the insurability of risks, the management of liabilities, insurance pricing and the concept of catastrophe risk modelling, which is gaining importance for agricultural risks. As risk management is a fast-evolving concept, this chapter provides a snapshot of current methods and approaches. The chapter forms the basis for subsequent chapters and particularly Chapter 5 (Agricultural Insurance) and Chapters 6–9 on crop, livestock, aquaculture and forestry insurance.

2.2 GLOBAL INSURANCE MARKET

Insurance is a global business, with some of the largest insurers operating nearly in every country and offering multi-line insurance solutions. Gross written premium (GWP) of the global insurance industry reached US$4.7 trillion in 2016, split into US$2.6 trillion for life insurance and US$2.1 trillion for non-life insurance, representing 6.3% of global GDP.

OVERVIEW OF GLOBAL MARKETS

In 2016, the largest 10 insurance markets contributed 75.9% of the global GWP, with similar ratios for life and non-life insurance (Table 2.1). Large differences exist between insurance penetration ratios of developed countries (e.g. Taiwan 20%, South Korea 12.1% and Europe between 6.1% and 10.2%) and those of emerging markets (e.g. China at 4.2%). In Asia, the average non-life insurance penetration stands at 1.85%, with 1.84% in Latin America/Caribbean and 0.92% in Africa, and is low compared with the global average of 2.81%. Emerging and developing markets typically show large protection gaps and reveal growth opportunities for most insurance products. In most developed countries, the annual per capita non-life insurance premium reaches up to US$2000 while only US$125 is spent on insurance in developing countries.

AGRICULTURAL INSURANCE

With a GWP of US$28.8 billion in 2016, the agricultural insurance sector contributed 1.3% of the global non-life GWP and 0.6% of the total global insurance premium (Table 2.1). The largest 10 markets for general insurance contribute 72% to the global agricultural premium. While the general insurance industry grew by a compounded annual growth rate of 1% between 2010 and 2015, the agricultural GWP increased by 6.5% over the same time. In past years, Asia has contributed the majority of the large growth in agricultural insurance (Chapter 5).

TABLE 2.1   Overview of the largest 10 insurance markets in 2016 including agriculture.

	INSURANCE PREMIUM 2016 (US$ BILLION)					
Market	Total	Non-life	Life	Penetration[a] (%)	Agriculture	Ratio[b] (%)
USA	1352	794	558	7.5	10.35	1.30
Japan	471	117	354	9.5	0.76	0.65
China (mainland)	466	204	262	4.2	6.43	3.15
UK	304	105	199	10.2	0.06	0.06
France	237	85	152	9.2	0.55	0.65
Germany	215	121	94	6.1	0.35	0.29
South Korea	170	66	104	12.1	0.32	0.49
Italy	162	40	122	8.2	0.48	1.20
Canada	114	65	49	7.5	1.57	2.41
Taiwan	101	17	84	20.0	0.01	0.03
Top 10 markets	3592	1614	1978		20.88	1.29
Global market	4732	2115	2617	6.3	28.79	1.36
Ratio top 10	75.9%	76.3%	75.6%		72.5%	

[a] Total insurance premium as a percentage of GDP.
[b] Agriculture premiums as a percentage of the non-life insurance premiums.
Data source: Swiss Re World Insurance in 2016 (2017).

2.3 KEY CONCEPTS OF INSURANCE

The insurance industry operates on a number of key concepts which are fundamental for optimal and efficient risk transfer. The conditions of the insurability of a risk by an identifiable and measurable peril, the management of liabilities and efficient insurance operations as well as risk adequate pricing are part of the key concepts of insurance and highly relevant for agricultural insurance.

DEFINITION OF INSURANCE

Insurance is a technique to finance risks in combining a large number of loss exposure units to make losses more predictable. Insurance is also defined as a mechanism or a service for the transfer of risks to an insurer in exchange for the payment of an agreed monetary amount (premium) before the occurrence of a loss. Insurance reduces the adverse financial impact of random events that prevent the fulfilment of reasonable expectations. The general benefit of insurance is the exchange of the uncertainty concerning a potential loss for the certainty of indemnification in the case the insured suffers a loss against the payment of a premium. In a legal context, an insurance contract is an agreement where the insurer undertakes, for a premium, to pay the policyholder, or a known third party, an indemnity when an insured event occurs and causes a loss to an insured asset. From a risk management point of view, insurance pools a large number of similar loss exposures into risk classes that are priced according to the probability theory and the law of large numbers.

The insurer facilitates the risk transfer among individual policyholders in a way that is to be equitable and cost effective for customers while maintaining solvency and shareholder value for the insurer. The general understanding under an insurance contract is that the policyholder is not to make any profit out of the indemnity payment and is compensated only to the extent of the loss. Insurers are often allowed to select risks according to location (i.e. excluding high-risk areas) and can discontinue coverage in areas considered high risk. Depending on the regulation and assets insured, insurance can be voluntary or compulsory.

RISK TERMINOLOGIES

Risk is the foundation of insurance and is commonly defined as 'uncertainty as to the outcome of an event when two or more possibilities exist'. Different terminologies, definitions and classifications of risks are used in the risk transfer industry.

Risk Types

Risks are often divided into (i) static risks, which include sudden and often unforeseeable events that result in the destruction of assets, e.g. accidents and natural disasters, and (ii) dynamic risks, which result in changes of economic conditions and which can benefit societies in the long run, e.g. changes in price levels and consumer preferences. Risks can further be classified into (i) speculative risks that bear an upside and a downside (e.g. financial investments) and (ii) pure risks, which involve a downside only (e.g. natural disasters).

From a risk management point of view, risks can be (i) systemic (or covariate) in that most or all policyholders are simultaneously affected by the same event and with losses that cannot be mitigated through diversification (e.g. earthquake, drought, epidemic diseases), and (ii) non-systemic in that the impact is highly localised and randomly affects a limited number of policyholders (e.g. fire, hail). Although some typically non-systemic risks (e.g. hail) can affect larger areas, they are not considered to be systemic as not the entire policy pool is impacted. For an insurer, the ideal insurable risk is *static* in that it is a sudden and often unforeseeable event and *pure* in that it involves only downside risk.

Definition of Peril and Loss Events

Risks typically stem from a peril, which is an event or circumstance that can cause a loss and can be of natural, man-made or economic origin. A hazard is a behaviour, action or circumstance that increases the chance that a loss will realise from a specific peril. An exposure is a defined asset such as a person, a building, a tanker or a crop that is subjected to a defined peril and forms the basic unit of risk that underlies the insurance premium and coverage. A loss exposure is the potential financial loss on the exposure.

An event is the occurrence of a peril that leads to losses and is defined through time frames that, depending on the peril, can range from the entire policy period to several hours. Loss potentials can be characterised as (i) maximum foreseeable loss (MFL), which is the maximum loss that can occur assuming the failure of protective measures, e.g. sprinklers, flood defences, irrigation for agricultural risks, and (ii) probable maximum loss (PML) as the total loss assuming normal functioning of protective measures. For the insurer, the PML is an estimate of the maximum loss expected to incur on a single policy as the proportion of the limit of liability with a probability that is equal to or larger than any loss covered by the policy.

INSURANCE RISK MANAGEMENT FRAMEWORKS

Risk management is the core concept of sustainable (re)insurance and risk transfer in general. Insurance risk management involves (i) risk identification that includes the recognition of the existence of potential events that can cause severe financial losses, (ii) risk measurement through the development of analytics to quantify the potential size of a loss and the probability of occurrence, and (iii) risk assessment, which determines the seriousness of a hazard relative to frequency and severity.

Based on risk assessment, different measures to address risks include (i) risk control that aims at preventing a loss and targets the loss frequency, (ii) loss reduction that targets the loss severity, and (iii) risk financing through self-financing and/or risk transfer to a third party. It is often most economical to combine self-financing with risk transfer, which however requires precise risk measurement to determine the retention levels and cession rate for risk transfer.

Risk Perception and Risk Adversity

Risk perceptions vary greatly according to the experience of an individual or a corporation with a particular risk and determines how a risk is recognised, evaluated and/or mitigated.

The theory states that risk averse individuals strive to undertake a risky investment only if there is a strictly positive return. The utility theory provides the theoretical framework to assess an individual's action towards the maximisation of the expected utility (value for money), which in insurance terms means insurance is bought to maximise the benefits under conditions of uncertainty and general risk adversity. The level of risk aversion can be divided into (i) risk averters with a concave utility function, (ii) risk neutrality with a linear utility function, and (iii) risk lovers with a convex utility function and a large appetite for risks. The degree of risk aversion and utility function is an essential concept of insurance in understanding policyholders' behaviour and decisions regarding risks. The expected utility function when insurance protection is available at a fair price will predict an increased preference for insurance as the potential loss increases (concave utility function). The utility theory has been used in scientific studies to quantify the commercial value of different agricultural insurance products for producers that are generally assumed to be risk averse (Section 5.4).

Insurability of Risks

For a risk to be insurable, the following main conditions need to be fulfilled for insurance to be offered at reasonable and fair costs: (i) the existence of a large number of similar risks that allows risk diversification through the law of large numbers, (ii) individual risks to be preferably independent or with a low correlation with other risks, (iii) loss amounts to be measurable and to be reasonably estimated, (iv) loss distributions to be sufficiently stationary or predictable over time, (v) the ability to calculate the frequency and the severity of possible losses through judgement or the underlying probabilities of the risks, and (vi) moral hazard and adverse selection to be controllable.[1] Adverse selection includes policyholders' actions against buying insurance, while moral hazard relates to actions to influence loss extents. Additionally, insurable risks need to have an insurable interest and to be consistent with societal values at affordable premium rates for a typically risk-averse policyholder.

Insurability of Agricultural Risks

Agricultural insurance covers systemic risks such as drought, cyclone, epidemic diseases and wildfires, which have the potential to cause large-scale losses and make risk transfer for insurers to reinsurance and capital markets a necessity. Further, loss distributions of agricultural risks are often non-stationary and require special statistical treatment. Adverse selection has been a key issue in agricultural insurance and has been addressed through government premium subsidies to increase the affordability and penetration of insurance, improved methods to determine premium rates through risk classification, and the introduction of waiting periods before covers incept (Section 5.4). Moral hazard is typically addressed through loss-sharing structures, increased monitoring and multi-year policies (Section 5.4).

---

[1] Berliner, B., 1982: Limits of Insurability of Risks. 1st edition. Pearson College, London, 118p.

Insurable Interest

For insurance to be recognised as such, insurance regulators request the demonstration of an insurable interest, which is the financial interest a policyholder must possess for a legally enforceable insurance coverage. Further, insurable interest is required to prevent speculation and gambling. In case of a lack of an insurable interest, insurance regulators tend to classify the product as a financial product.

Insurance or Derivative?

Insurance and derivatives can be based on the same type of product (e.g. a weather index) that has very similar risk transfer benefits but with an execution form that involves entirely different regulations, accounting practices, tax implications and legal constraints. Under insurance law, the policyholder must have an interest in the subject matter of the policy and obtain some financial benefit from the preservation of the subject matter or sustain a pecuniary loss from its destruction or impairment when the risk insured against occurs. In contrast, derivatives simply base payouts on the performance of an index and are therefore not associated with any physical loss and can be bought for speculative purposes. In practice, most insurance policyholders have an exposure (and therefore an insurable interest) and index-based insurance products have been developed in a way that highly likely losses are indemnified.

In agriculture, weather- and area-yield insurances do not require the prove of loss of the policyholder as claims are settled directly on weather and yield data. Usually, insurance regulators accept these products as insurance, particularly if the payout occurs to individual producers (micro-level risk transfer) and premiums are government-subsidised. However, index-based insurance for agribusinesses could be seen by regulators as financial instruments rather than insurance and new products often require a legal opinion and regulatory approval.

KEY COMPONENTS OF AN INSURANCE POLICY

Insurance terms are captured in a policy wording which includes general insurance conditions. Risk-specific terms and conditions are listed in a schedule that attaches to the policy wording and changes in the schedule during the policy duration are captured in endorsements. The sum insured, loss-sharing structures and premium rates are key components of insurance contracts.

Sum Insured and Premium

The sum insured represents the amount of insurance purchased and the value at risk (VaR). The risk rate is expressed as a function of units of loss exposure and is typically derived by an actuary through quantitative analyses and probabilistic modelling of historical losses. Based on the risk rate, different costs are loaded, including underwriting, administration and loss adjustment expenses, to obtain the premium rate, which expressed in relation to the sum insured becomes the premium. Insurance regulators require the premium to be reasonable, not excessive, and not unfairly discriminatory. For the insurer, the premium calculation needs to satisfy the fundamental insurance equation where the premium (P) is defined as:

$$P = Losses + LAE + UWE + UWP$$

with *LAE* as the loss adjustment expenses, *UWE* as underwriting expenses and *UWP* as the underwriting profit. Actuarial methods use adjusted historical claims data and catastrophe risk modelling provides probabilistic views on the losses.

At renewal of the policy, insurers typically grant a no-claims bonus where the policyholder receives a return premium or a discount for a loss-free year. Bonus-malus systems rewards policyholders for each loss-free period with a premium reduction to the next lower category, while in turn, each claim increases the premium to the next higher level.

Deductibles, Franchises and Limits

Most policies include a deductible, which is the portion of the loss (a monetary amount and/or percentage) the policyholder will retain for each loss and/or in the aggregate over the policy period. Deductibles can be (i) simple (or flat or straight) in that the same deductible is applied independent of the loss extent, or (ii) flexible in that the deductible varies according to the loss extent, typically decreasing (or disappearing) with increasing loss levels. With a simple deductible, the premium rate reduces linearly with an increasing deductible, while flexible deductibles require the assessment of loss frequency and severity to determine the impact on the premium rate.

A franchise is used as a limit that is expressed either as a percentage of the sum insured or in monetary terms, below which no indemnity occurs. Franchises keep loss adjustment expenses low as only claims above a certain amount need to be inspected. The reduction of the premium rate in the presence of a franchise is typically a function of the level of the franchise and frequency and severity of past losses. To avoid unlimited liability, most insurance contracts include a monetary limit that is defined as a maximum amount per loss occurrence or as an aggregate limit up to which the insurer is liable.

LIABILITY MANAGEMENT

Depending on the size of the portfolio, the types of risks covered and the geographical spread, an insurer can carry significant liabilities, which require adequate funds to indemnify future claims. Insurance regulators provide guidance and models to determine appropriate funding levels (reserves) for (re)insurance portfolios. Liability management differs for (i) short-tail business, where losses are usually known shortly after the loss event, e.g. property catastrophe or crop insurance, and (ii) long-tail business, which requires longer-term funds as losses are likely to develop over years, e. g. general liability or workers' compensation insurance.

Unearned Premium and Loss Reserves

In non-life insurance, liabilities are defined as unearned premium reserves and loss reserves. Unearned premium reserves represent the portion of the premium that is not yet earned by the insurer at the end of the accounting, fiscal or calendar year. Loss reserves cover losses for known and unknown events and include (i) losses reported and adjusted but not yet paid, (ii) losses reported but not adjusted, (iii) losses incurred but not reported (IBNR), and (iv) loss adjustment expenses. The required loss reserves are determined through experience data and statistical models.

Unearned Premium Reserves in Agriculture

Most agricultural insurance is short-tail and does not require the establishment of unearned premium reserves, unless the insurance reporting cycle is very different from the policy coverage period. For example, winter crop insurance in the northern hemisphere extends over the calendar year on which insurers report and requires the estimation of the premium earning pattern, which is typically assumed to be uniform. As most agricultural insurance policies benefit from government premium subsidies, premium earning patterns can be distorted depending on the time at which the insurer receives the government subsidies, which can occur (i) around the same time policyholders pay premiums, (ii) in instalments during the policy period, (iii) at the end of the policy period, or (iv) several months after the expiration of the insurance period, which requires estimation of unearned premium reserves. Methods to establish unearned premium reserves in agriculture typically follow the concepts used for property insurance.

Loss Reserves in Agriculture

For crop insurance, methods to estimate loss extents and to develop loss reserves depend on the product. In markets where the government operates risk funds (e.g. the USA) and loss protection is provided (e.g. China, South Korea, USA), gross and net losses need to be differentiated when loss reserves are calculated. For crop hail and other named-peril policies, loss adjustment is undertaken within weeks of the loss and most losses are reported at the end of the crop season. Loss reserves, where necessary, can be estimated based on expected loss ratio (ELR) and historical reporting patterns. Loss reserves for multi-peril crop insurance (MPCI) require a regression of projected crop yields and loss ratios, which is typically non-linear as once yields are below the coverage level, loss amounts increase faster. This is addressed through exponential or quadric distributions at levels where yield projections are available (e.g. a county) and subsequently needs to be downward adjusted for individual policies at farm level. Loss reserving for revenue covers works in the same way as for MPCI but with the additional complexity that commodity prices need to be projected. The *ELR* for a revenue cover can be established through:[2]

$$ELR = a \times \frac{1}{(y \times p)^{b}} + if\left(y < 1, c \times (1 - y), 0\right)$$

with a, b, c as the regression coefficients solved by minimising the square error, y as the yield ratio, which is the current yield in relation to the average yield from past years, and p as the price change from harvest prices relative to planting prices. Reserving for income insurance is more complex as the income of different commodities, as a function of revenue and expenses, needs to be projected at a farm level.

INSURANCE OPERATIONS

Insurance is based on *uberrima fides* (utmost good faith) where the policyholder and the insurer are bound by fairness and where material facts must be disclosed. An efficient insurance market needs well-established operations that link and share information among different stakeholders, with solid financial infrastructure and clear regulations.

---

[2] Ashenbrenner, C.X., 2010: Crop Insurance Reserving. Casualty Actuarial Society E-Forum, 38p.

Information Flows

Insurance largely relies on information flows from the policyholder to an insurance agent, an insurer, the reinsurer and/or capital markets and across different (re)insurance intermediaries. Information passing across the insurance value chain gets aggregated and arrives at the reinsurance level on the basis of portfolios. While detailed policy-level information is proprietary to the insurer, aggregation increases costs to develop data and analytics that allows risk modelling at higher resolutions than those provided in reinsurance submissions. Interruptions in the information flow can lead to inefficient risk transfer, including incorrect pricing, under- or over-estimation of risk, inadequate loss reserves, insufficient equity and reinsurance protection.

The Importance of Technology

As insurance is data intensive, insurers have investigated and applied emerging technologies to automate certain processes and gain a higher cost efficiency. Some of the most recent adaptions include (i) robotic process automation to streamline underwriting, managing front-office operations and claims settlement, (ii) blockchain to develop contract systems that unite all parties in the insurance value chain on a platform with reduced documentation and fewer manual processes, (iii) tailor-made insurance covers based on lifestyle and customer behaviour such as *pay how you live* or *pay how you drive*, (iv) artificial intelligence for machine learning, and (v) general digitalisation of information. From having been a standalone sector, the insurance industry is gradually integrating into the wider service industry and is likely to evolve into larger InsurTech firms.

Special Forms of Insurance Operations

While most insurance is directly underwritten and administrated by insurers, highly specialised exposure and risks (including some agricultural business) are handled by a managing agency on behalf of the insurer. Large corporations have established in-house insurers (captives) to benefit from risk diversification through bundling and direct access to reinsurance and capital markets for risk transfer.

Managing General Agents

Insurers typically develop expertise in underwriting and managing risks; however, in some markets, and for highly specialised risks, insurers grant authority to managing general agents (MGAs) to administrate insurance programmes and negotiate contracts. In its most basic form, the insurer develops the insurance product and the MGA provides operational services and delivers the products. In a more advanced form, MGAs undertake risk surveys, underwriting and pricing, policy processing, customer services and claims adjustment. In agricultural insurance, MGAs are mainly used for highly specialised risks such as bloodstock, but used to be prominent for crop insurance in Australia and the USA.

Captives

Large corporations often have an in-house and wholly-owned insurance subsidiary (a captive), which pools and insures most of the corporation's risks at a global scale (master policies) and transfers peak risks to reinsurance markets. A captive is based on the concept of self-insurance and captives are often divided into (i) pure captive, which is a wholly owned subsidiary of a non-insurance organisation that funds all or a portion of the parent company's risks, (ii) senior captive, where the original parent company contributes less than 75% and third-party organisations contribute the remaining capital portion, (iii) profit centre captive, where the parent corporation funds up to 25% only, and (iv) group captive, which is financially supported or operated by more than two non-insurance corporations. Some captives can be rented (also called agency captive) where corporations unrelated to the parent organisation are insured. Most captives operate off-shore and are incorporated under a foreign jurisdiction compared with the location of the parent corporation. The advantage of a captive for a corporation is lower cost of insurance and broader coverage, premiums that reflect the experience (and not the bench market), certain tax advantages and generally more tailor-made risk transfer solutions. An example of a captive in the agricultural sector is Co-operative Bulk Handling (CBH) in Australia, which buys different insurances including coverage for grain volume volatility.

2.4 ACTUARIAL INSURANCE PRICING

Pricing establishes the technical premium the insurer should charge to cover costs and leave a certain profit margin, which is typically undertaken by an actuary. Costing is the process that establishes commercial terms based on the technical premium and is a different process to pricing. While pricing needs statistical expertise to extrapolate loss potentials from past claims data and benchmarks, costing requires an understanding of the competitive environment and the underwriting cycle. Actuarial pricing estimates premiums of individual risks and portfolios based on probabilities of loss occurrences from statistical distributions and historical claims information. Additionally, actuarial pricing addresses solvency ratios, risk retention levels and risk transfer through portfolio modelling.

PRICING APPROACHES

The pricing approach largely depends on the sophistication of the market, the line of insurance business, and the quantity and quality of historical claims and loss proxies. The conventional pricing approach is historical burning cost analyses, where the technical premium is based on the average of past losses that have been adjusted for current exposures, policy conditions and inflation. An extension to the burning cost analyses is the use of probability density functions (PDFs) to statistically describe a wider range of possible loss outcomes based on historical claims through expected loss calculations (ELCs).

A more complex approach is stochastic modelling, which establishes frequency–severity distributions from adjusted historical claims that are subsequently combined in an aggregated model through numerical techniques. With advanced computation, multivariate pricing allows the use of multiple variables that explain a certain risk to be included in pricings through generalised linear models. Machine learning and big data algorithms are increasingly used to identify factors that determine risk and correlations among risk parameters, which gradually leads to more tailored insurance terms and conditions for policyholders. Often several pricing approaches are combined to reflect future loss expectations in function of historical experience.

When historical claims data do not allow experience-based pricing, exposure modelling is an alternative to derive risk rates for individual and portfolio risks. For catastrophe-type risks, where actuarial methods have limitations as most severe events might not have been experienced in historical data, and loss potentials are driven by exposure and the physical nature of a peril, probabilistic catastrophe models are used as far as they are available (Section 2.5).

Credibility Theory

As insurance pricing relies on a sample of loss experiences, the statistical relevance of the sample and the confidence in the premium rates derived are evaluated through the concepts of the credibility theory. The law of large numbers states that as the sample becomes larger, the outcome of the sample becomes closer to the true value of the population. Credibility factors are used to weight the premium determined of the sample (e.g. 60%) and a weight of a common market rate for similar risks (e.g. 40%) is applied. Three methods are used to test the statistical significance of the sample – the classical credibility theory, the Bühlmann credibility method and Bayesian analysis, which introduces related experience into the actuarial estimate in a probabilistic measure but does not explicitly calculate a measure of credibility.

ADJUSTMENT OF HISTORICAL CLAIMS DATA

Historical insurance claims data form the basis of most actuarial pricing approaches and insurers have developed substantial databases that include key information on each underwritten policy and allow experience ratings at different aggregation levels. However, historical claims need to be adjusted (restated) to reflect changes in insurance rates and coverage levels, inflation and other changes that have an impact on past losses compared with the current environment. Extraordinary losses are typically removed from historical claims or capped below a certain threshold to avoid distorting effects to be reintroduced in the pricing process in the form of catastrophe loadings.

Often, insurers consider claims databases as proprietary and provide reinsurers and capital markets with aggregated data only. In some markets, insurers share loss information through an organisation that consolidates the data into industry loss databases (e.g. ZIP code or district resolution) or are mandated by the government to contribute and share loss data.

Adjustment of Historical Claims Data in Agriculture

Agricultural insurers in mature markets have developed comprehensive databases that include historical claims at the policyholder levels that are aggregated over administrative areas. Adjustments of historical claims in agriculture essentially include the removal of loss-sharing features (deductibles, franchises), the scaling of sum insured to a common basis, and adaptations of additional coverage such as replanting provisions (Section 6.4). For example, the *Statplan* in the USA contains standardised claims data for most crop types since 1975 (Section 6.5). The CIS broadacre hail loss cost database in Australia is an example of an industry loss database where insurers that are members obtain access to the market's historical loss costs.

SCHEDULE RATING

Schedule rating is one of the earliest forms of individual risk pricing. It uses a schedule which lists the average characteristics for a given type of risk with target premium rates and rebates for certain loss control measures. Schedule rating is used for insurance lines with large numbers of similar exposure, while the risk management standard that is applied to a particular risk is a key criterion that leads to increased or decreased premiums. Often, the maximum discount for well-managed risks is limited relative to the average premium rate (e.g. 25%).

Schedule Rating in Agriculture

Schedule rating is used for risks of a similar size and with standardised covers and perils in markets with long time experience in underwriting such risks. Individual animals under standard livestock insurance policies are often rated through schedules where for each peril a standard rate is available, and an upward or downward adjustment is applied to take into consideration factors such as risk management standards and animal numbers at a production site (Section 7.4). Similarly, smaller timber plantations that are insured in a facility are rated through schedules, with certain discounts granted in the presence of risk mitigation measures (Section 9.4). Bloodstock insurance is another example where schedule rates are applied based on the overall experience with race horses.

EXPERIENCE RATING

Experience rating uses experiences of an insured risk to derive the rate to be paid for future losses. The historical burn rate (HBR) method simply uses adjusted historical claims to directly derive risk rates on past experience, while the ELC method fits a statistical distribution function to adjusted historical claims underlying loss proxies (e.g. weather data for weather indices) to increase the possible loss range. Stochastic models simulate first loss frequency and severity distributions that are combined to obtain an aggregate loss model. All experience-based rating methods rely on some form of past claims data.

Historical Burn Rate Method

The HBR method, also called burning cost ratio or loss cost ratio, is commonly used to calculate losses above a certain threshold relative to the total subject premium over historical periods. In the most basic form, HBR uses aggregated losses over the period of insurance; however, this does not consider deductibles, franchises and limits of individual policies. HBR uses weighted exposure (BC_w) and unweighted exposure (BC) and is calculated for the available number of years of claims data (n) as:[3]

$$BC_w = \frac{\sum_{j=1}^{n} w_j \times \varepsilon_j \times BC_j}{\sum_{j=1}^{n} w_j \times BC_j}$$

$$BC = \frac{\sum_{j=1}^{n} w_j \times BC_j}{\sum_{j=1}^{n} w_j}$$

---

[3] Parodi, P., 2015: Pricing in General Insurance. CRC Press/Taylor & Francis, London, 594p.

with BC_j as the burning cost for a policy year j that, depending on the line of business and available data, includes adjustments made for (i) deductible, franchises and limits, (ii) development factors for IBNR, (iii) exposure, and (iv) large losses and catastrophe loadings. ε_j signifies the exposure in policy year j and w_j refers to a weighting factor for incurred losses or retained losses.

While relatively simple in its application, HBR has several shortcomings in that (i) long and consistent claims data are required, (ii) large and catastrophe-type losses are considered only as far as they are contained in the claims data, and (iii) the development of trends in the frequency and severity of losses is not specifically addressed.

Expected Loss Calculation

The ELC, also called the ELR method, is an extension to HBR in that PDFs are fitted to claims data to increase the spectrum of possible loss outcomes. The ELC is also used to model weather indices, through either distributions of the underlying parameters or the indices (Section 6.9). However, the ELC is highly sensitive to the type of PDF used and for parametric methods, the parameters chosen.

Loss Frequency and Loss Severity Modelling

Stochastic models are used to overcome the limitations of HBR methods in that a simplified mathematical model is developed to describe the loss frequency and the loss severity of historical adjusted claims. The frequency and severity distributions are subsequently combined into an aggregate loss model and are applicable for single as well as portfolio risks.

Loss Frequency Modelling

The frequency of losses is a measure of claim incidence, expressed per unit of exposure and defined as the number of claims divided by the number of exposures. The loss frequency can be directly determined from past claims or modelled through statistical functions. The number of claims during the policy period is typically modelled through a Poisson distribution when timing of an event is independent of the time of a previous event. In cases when the mean and variance in the number of claims are significantly different, either a binomial or a negative binomial distribution is used (Table 2.2).[4]

Loss Severity Modelling

The loss severity is a measure of the average loss per claim. It is defined as losses divided by the number of claims and is either determined from past losses or modelled with statistical functions. Most commonly used distributions include the normal, gamma, lognormal, Weibull, Pareto and Generalised Pareto (Table 2.2).[5] Statistical fitting tests are applied to determine the most suitable distribution. To assess trends in the tail of loss distributions, concepts of the extreme value theory are applied.

---

[4] Boucher, J.P. et al., 2008: Models of insurance claim counts with time dependence based on generalization of Poisson and negative binomial distributions. *Variance*, 2(1), 135–62.

[5] Pacakova, V. and Brebera, D., 2015: Loss distributions and simulations in general insurance and reinsurance. *Int. J. Comput. Math. Simmul.*, 9, 159–67.

TABLE 2.2 Examples of distribution functions used to model loss frequency and severity in (re)insurance.

Purpose	Distribution	Probability Density Dunction	Parameters
Loss frequency	Poisson	$f(x) = \dfrac{e^{-\lambda}\lambda^x}{x!}, x = 0,1,2,\ldots,\lambda > 0$	$Mean = \lambda$ $Variance = \lambda$
	Binomial	$f(x) = \dfrac{n!}{\left[x!(n-x)!\right]} p^x (1-p)^{(n-x)}$	$Mean = np$ $Variance = np(1-p)$
Loss severity	Gamma	$f(x) = \dfrac{\lambda^\alpha}{\Gamma(\alpha)} x^{\alpha-1} e^{-\lambda x}, x > 0$	$\alpha > 0$ $scale\ \lambda > 0$
	Lognormal	$f(x) = \dfrac{1}{\sigma x \sqrt{2\pi}} e^{-\frac{(ln(x)-\mu)^2}{2\sigma^2}}, x > 0$	$\mu = mean$ $scale\ \sigma > 0$
	Weibull	$f(x) = \dfrac{\alpha}{\beta^\alpha} x^{\alpha-1} e^{-(x/\beta)^\alpha}, x > 0$	$shape\ \alpha > 0$ $scale\ \beta > 0$
	Pareto	$f(x) = \dfrac{\alpha\lambda^\alpha}{(\lambda+x)^{\alpha+1}}$	$\alpha > 0$ $\lambda > 0$

Aggregate Loss Modelling (Combining Frequency and Severity)
The risk premium, also called pure premium or loss cost, is a measure of the average loss per exposure unit and is obtained by multiplying the loss frequency with the loss severity, which reflects the losses divided by the number of exposures. To obtain the risk premium, a joint distribution of the underlying frequency and severity distributions is developed through a collective risk model. The collective risk model describes the aggregate loss distribution that corresponds to the sum of the random number of events of various sizes, which is accomplished by direct calculation (e.g. by convolution or fast Fourier transformation) or using Monte Carlo simulations.

The most basic model is the standard risk theoretic model, which states that:

$$Aggregate\ Loss = X_1 + X_2 + \ldots + X_N$$

with N as a random variable representing the number of claims (events) and X_i as a random variable of the loss amount of a particular loss i. This standard model assumes that all X_i are independent and identically distributed while being reasonably independent of the number of claims, with the expected loss $E[L]$ and its variance $Var[L]$ written as:

$$E[L] = E[N] \times E[X]$$

$$Var[L] = E[N] \times Var[X] + (Var[N]) \times E[X^2]$$

If N is Poisson-distributed, then $E[N] = Var[N]$ and the formula simplifies to:

$$Var[L] = E[N] \times E[X^2]$$

However, the assumption of independence can be restrictive: often, loss frequency and severity are to some extent dependent and correlated. Approaches that allow correlations in loss frequency and/or severity include copula functions.[6]

Experience Rating in Agriculture

Experience rating is the most common approach to pricing agricultural risks for insurance and reinsurance. HBR is often used for (i) named peril crop insurance such as crop-hail covers, where long-adjusted claims series exist, and (ii) weather- and yield-based index insurance, when longer time series of area-yield data (Section 6.8) and weather data (Section 6.9) are available. Often, experience-based rating is supported by loss proxies, including calamity declarations, drought indices and fire weather indices, to understand regional trends in the occurrence of certain hazards and to address return periods of catastrophe-type events. To increase the range of possible losses, statistical distributions are commonly used, and particularly in the presence of short loss experience and with new insurance schemes. As most agricultural insurances cover a multitude of perils during the growing season or livestock rearing cycles, loss frequency and severity modelling are mostly applied when individual events are insured (e.g. fire or wind on forestry, epidemic disease outbreaks).

EXPOSURE RATING

Exposure rating approaches were developed originally by the reinsurance industry to derive premium amounts for specific layers of non-proportional property reinsurance agreements; however, the concepts are applied to price insurance risks and are often combined with loss frequency models. Exposure rating is based on exposure curves or loss curves and standardised loss severity distributions that are based on industry experiences. As similar risks tend to have similar characteristics, a normalised severity curve can be applied to derive expected losses and risk rates. The loss curves allow the allocation of insurance premiums to bands to price higher deductible policies. Over time, insurers have developed benchmarks through industry loss severity distributions that are based on the loss experience of similar portfolios of policies and allow the estimation of expected loss for entire portfolios.

Exposure Rating in Agriculture

Exposure rating in the stricter sense as it is used for property insurance is not used for agricultural risks and industry loss curves are therefore not available as such. However, agricultural insurance has developed pricing approaches that relate exposure (sum insured) through basic vulnerability functions to certain hazards, which is used particularly for products that rely on weather and yield indices. These exposure pricing models contain elements of catastrophe risk models (Section 2.5) and allow the simulation of losses based on current exposure and past weather or yield data.

---

[6] Krämer, N., Brechmann, E.C., Silvestrini, D. and Czado, C., 2013: Total loss estimation using copula-based regression models. *Insur. Math. Econ.*, 53(3), 829–39.

CATASTROPHE RISK MODELLING

Devastating insurance losses from natural disasters in the 1990s demonstrated that actuarial approaches in managing catastrophe risk from extrapolating past losses to the future were not sufficient. The development and use of catastrophe models was accelerated by the request of regulators and rating agencies for (re)insurers to model PMLs and capital requirements with science-based models. Earthquake and hurricane models were first developed for the USA and later expanded to other countries and other perils, including flood, severe convective storms, tornados and hail, winter storms, tsunamis, and man-made catastrophes such as pandemics and terrorism. Recently, agricultural and cyber risks have been included in catastrophe models for key markets and exposure.

MAIN MODULES OF CATASTROPHE MODELS

Catastrophe models rely on computer simulations that combine statistics, mathematics, physical science and economics to assess the financial risk posed by natural disasters and man-made hazards to insurance portfolios. The basis of these models is derived from the latest research findings on the physics of natural perils (Chapter 3) from disciplines such as atmospheric sciences, geosciences and geology, hydrology and structural engineering. Catastrophe models consist typically of four main modules that operate in coordination and require input of exposure at given geographical resolutions.

Event Module

The event module describes the occurrence of events at different locations through an event catalogue that is developed from data collected from government institutions and the research community. The event catalogue includes historical events as well as simulated (stochastic) events that are generated by algorithms that describe the physics of the peril and use spatial simulation techniques of underlying variables. The simulated events are based on realistic physical parameters that stem from historical observations. The event module defines the frequency and severity of a peril's intensity on a regular grid, ranging from $5 \times 5 \, km$ (low-resolution models) to $5 \times 5 \, m$ (high-resolution models).

Hazard Module

The hazard module assesses the level of physical hazards over a geographical area and includes typical features of the region such as the built environment, topography and risk mitigation measures.

Vulnerability Module

The vulnerability module contains vulnerability functions for each modelled risk type and class (e.g. building quality and age, construction materials, building type, occupancy type) describing loss expectation by function of event severity. Vulnerability functions are region-specific and include physical damage and consequential damage (e.g. business interruption). Damage is quantified as a mean damage ratio through a ratio of the average expected loss to the replacement value of the underlying exposure (e.g. a building). Vulnerability curves are typically developed from historical insurance claims, engineering models and laboratory experiments (e.g. wind tunnels).

Financial Module

The financial module translates physical losses into monetary losses and contains a database of insurance conditions (e.g. deductibles, franchises, limits) and reinsurance structures. The financial module typically produces (i) ground-up losses, which are the losses to the policyholder, (ii) gross losses, which are the losses to the insurer with loss reduction measures applied to ground-up losses, and (iii) net losses, which are the losses of the insurers net of reinsurance protection.

Input into Catastrophe Models

Catastrophe models require detailed exposure information (e.g. sum insured, type and age of building structures) and insurance terms and conditions as input. Depending on the model, exposure can be (i) entered for an administrative area (e.g. county or ZIP code) and is allocated by the model to individual model grids using detailed databases of building stocks, land use statistics and/or population densities, (ii) entered for a standardised insurance reporting area such as the Catastrophe Risk Evaluation and Standardizing Target Accumulations (CRESTA), or (iii) geo-coded for the individual exposure of underlying assets, which has become the standard input for the newer generation of high-resolution models.

Output of Catastrophe Models

Catastrophe models generate outputs as loss amounts in the form of event loss tables (ELTs) and exceedance probability (EP) curves. ELTs show modelled losses from historical and probabilistic events. EP curves reveal the annual probabilities or return periods of exceeding a certain level of loss and are built on risk metrics developed from thousands of simulated scenarios. The EP curve includes functions of (i) occurrence exceedance probability (OEP), which represents the probability of a single event within a predefined period (e.g. 72 hours) and a loss above a certain level, and (ii) aggregate exceedance probability (AEP), which reveals the probability of total annual losses above a certain amount. Based on EP curves, average annual losses (AALs) are determined, signifying the annual premium necessary to cover the losses under the assumption that the exposure remains constant and represents the pure risk premium. EP curves form the basis to calculate loss metrics that include (1) VaR for a return period in measuring a single point of a range of potential outcomes corresponding to a given confidence level, and (ii) tail value at risk (TVaR), which reveals the mean loss of all potential outcomes with losses above a certain level.

Uncertainties in Catastrophe Models

Catastrophe models include many assumptions and interpretations; different models can produce large differences in modelled losses on the same risks and geographies and compared with actual incurred losses. The reliability of catastrophe models is largely driven by the level of understanding of the underlying physical processes that determine the occurrence and behaviour of natural and man-made hazards. Further, model updates can significantly add to the volatility of loss estimates. Because of the proprietary nature of vendor models, it is difficult to make an assessment of the main assumptions in a model. Insurers deal with the inherent uncertainty in catastrophe models by using multiple vendor models, including in-house built and open source models. Additionally, insurers often apply adjustment factors to model outputs that are specific per market and insurance line of business. In recent times, European Union (EU) regulations require reinsurers to demonstrate that the main components of a catastrophe model are understood by users. Continued developments towards more open model platforms will allow all stakeholders to better understand model assumptions.[7]

Applications of Catastrophe Models

Catastrophe models are used by insurers to (i) gain a better understanding of catastrophe risks on insurance portfolios, (ii) derive catastrophe loss loadings per rating area from modelled AALs, (iii) determine risk rates at policy levels based on AALs, (iv) derive portfolio-level losses to determine capital- and risk-adequate retention levels and risk transfer requirements, and (v) comply with solvency and other regulatory or economic capital requirements where portfolio losses need to be determined at certain return periods. Reinsurers and capital markets use outputs of catastrophe models to price reinsurance structures and insurance-linked securities. Governments increasingly use catastrophe models to assess loss potentials on infrastructure portfolios and to develop sovereign disaster financing initiatives with risk transfer to reinsurance and capital markets.

CATASTROPHE MODELLING FOR AGRICULTURAL RISKS

Modelling agriculture risk relates to modelling biological systems which evolve dynamically over time and damage is often a function of a variety of environmental parameters, loss mitigation and risk management standards. Mechanistic models are used by government agencies and in the research domain to simulate damage from a range of natural perils and epidemic diseases affecting agricultural assets. While mechanistic models provide valuable estimates of frequencies and severities of extreme events, the outputs cannot directly be linked to insurance portfolios. Probabilistic catastrophe models as they exist for property exposure have only recently been adapted to include agricultural assets but are limited to the main agricultural insurance markets.

Challenges in Modelling Biological Systems

Agriculture production assets are biological systems that are non-static and evolve over time from the initial costs for input supplies (crops), saplings (forestry) and stock (livestock and aquaculture) to the commercial value at the end of the production cycle.

From a risk modelling point of view, damage degrees on crops are a function of the hazard severity and are typically narrow at field or farm level (i.e. total losses occur frequently) and therefore the total damage extent at a portfolio level is largely driven by the spatial and temporal extent of the event. Changing vulnerabilities during the production cycle, different risk management standards among producers and

---

[7] Recent initiatives for open model platforms include the Open Access Catastrophe Model (OASIS, www.oasislmf.org).

dynamic exposure changes are some of the main challenges in modelling agricultural risks.

Changing Vulnerabilities
Often, the vulnerability of agricultural assets increases over the production cycle, and losses towards the later part of the cycle can be significantly higher than during initial phases. Moreover, most crops have a potential for recovery after damage, particularly if losses occurred in early stages of the growth cycle or crops can be replanted. Damaged timber can have substantial salvage value in that although a log cannot be used for the initial purpose, a residual value remains for other usage. Vulnerability of agricultural assets is further driven by the level of risk management, access to early warning systems, and the use and availability of risk mitigation measures (e.g. irrigation, flood defences, frost sprinklers, hail nets, firefighting equipment for plantations, emergency vaccines for livestock).

Therefore, catastrophe risk models for agricultural risks need to contain different sets of vulnerability functions according to the time a loss occurs during the production cycle and a basic understanding of different risk management standards is required to validate the vulnerability functions.

Dynamic Exposure Changes
Crop areas can show large shifts in exposure between two productions due to natural crop rotation as well as government incentives and economic considerations leading, e.g. a preference to produce a certain crop in a given season. Crop planting dates can vary substantially due to soil moisture and weather forecasts and late planting increases exposure to late season frosts and reduced yield. Catastrophe models need to use frequently updated land use layers (crop masks), based on which, agricultural exposure is allocated to model grids. Equally, updated crop calendars need to be available to define risk periods based on the growth season.

Mechanistic Crop Models
While mechanistic crop models (Section 4.3) are capable of simulating crop growth on a daily basis, and livestock disease and forest fire models can provide probabilistic analyses, these models require extensive calibration and are mainly used by research institutions. Further, mechanistic crop models are run for research agendas, including the study of impacts of climate change and the optimisation of input supplies and crop management. The development of more open models and data provided by leading research institutes which operate mechanistic agricultural models (mainly for crops, livestock and forestry) should lead to a wider application in the insurance industry.

Stochastic and Probabilistic Risk Models
While stochastic and probabilistic risk modelling is widely used in property insurance, the first agriculture catastrophe models have emerged only within the last few years, based on the significant growth in agricultural insurance. Leading catastrophe modelling firms have developed models for agricultural risks for key insurance markets, including the USA (crop), Canada (crop), China (crop, livestock, forestry) and India (crop), with prospects to expand to other countries.

AIR Multi-Peril Crop Insurance (MPCI) Model for the USA

On the back of the growing agricultural insurance industry, AIR Worldwide, a leading catastrophe modelling and advisory firm, released the first probabilistic catastrophe model for agricultural crops in the USA in 2008 to provide a more accurate view of agricultural risk than that derived from historical data alone. The AIR MPCI Model for the USA provides portfolio-level loss estimates for (re)insurers, brokers, government agencies, risk managers, investors, regulatory and rating agencies as well as industry professionals.[8]

Hazard and Vulnerability Module

To explicitly account for the impact of weather events on crop yield, AIR developed an Agricultural Weather Index (AWI) using high-resolution temperature, precipitation and soil data as well as crop-specific phenological data. The result is a county-based yield probability distribution that reflects the effects of extreme weather events on crop yield. A total of 16 crop types are modelled using the AWI, which include most crops that are insured under various insurance policies: corn, soybean, wheat (winter, spring and durum), cotton, rice, barley, grain sorghum, peanut, sunflower, dry bean, potato, almond and grape (wine and table). Yearly AWI values are used to derive the influence of weather events on yield productivity and to determine trends from alternative influences (e.g. improved technology). Once a trend is established for a yield time series, it is used to detrend the data to the most current year in the series. Statistical distribution functions are fitted to the detrended yield data and stochastic simulations of correlated yields across crops and locations are performed to obtain 10000 potential yield outcomes that could occur in each county in the following year.

As revenue-based policies are the main products in the US crop insurance market (Section 6.6), modelling of price risks is additionally required. The AIR model includes a price module that relates historical price differentials between harvest and planting dates to national crop yields for the major crop types, providing county-level yield and associated price ratios, which are applied to insurance policy conditions to estimate insured losses. Pairing potential yield outcomes with four different sets of 10000 harvest price/planting price ratios allowed the development of four event catalogues that vary by price volatility and include historical, low, medium and high market volatilities. Containing the same yield events, the spread of the price distributions differs in each event catalogue to reflect differing market volatility in price behaviour from planting to harvest.

Financial Module

The financial module contains county-based insurance terms for all types of MPCI policies and includes guaranteed yields, coverage levels and guaranteed revenues as a function of expected yield and price differentials. Through the financial module, modelled gross losses are computed for each county, crop, coverage level and insurance product

---

[8] Vergara, O., Zuba, G., Doggett, T. and Seaquist, J., 2008: Modeling the potential impact of catastrophic weather on crop insurance industry portfolio losses. *Am. J. Agric. Econ.*, 90(5), 1256–62.

type and are aggregated at state level (e.g. buy-up, catastrophe, or revenue covers) and reflect an insurer's market share. To keep gross loss calculations consistent with changing insurance terms and conditions, the financial module is updated annually to reflect premium rate changes made by the Risk Management Agency (RMA). Besides modelled gross losses, the financial module computes modelled net losses, which are modelled gross losses less reinsurance protection levels provided by the US government under the Standard Reinsurance Agreement (SRA) for loss ratios above 500% at state level. The model uses an industry-wide fund designation component to determine post-SRA losses.

Model Validations
Modelled gross loss ratios for the historical years (1974–2015) are expected to differ from RMA reported losses because modelled losses are recasts that apply historic weather data to current market conditions and insurance terms, current exposure and crop mixes and today's industry exposure. Recasts reveal loss levels of past weather events on current market portfolios and insurance terms. While the magnitude of the recast and historical losses will differ for any specific location, there should be good spatial agreement between modelled and observed loss ratios to indicate that the model is responding correctly to weather variables (Figure 2.1).

For example, the recast analysis shows that in using the 2016 insurance terms, fund allocation levels and SRA agreement, the last years (2006–2015) would have experienced, on average, a lower gross loss ratio compared with reported gross loss ratios (Table 2.3). Further, the severe drought year of 2012 shows that at today's insurance terms, the observed gross loss ratio of 157% would have caused a gross loss ratio of 134%. Under the recast, Group 1 states, which account on average for over 40% of the liability in the US crop insurance industry and were particularly affected by the 2012 drought, would have a gross loss ratio of 189% (Table 2.3).

Model Applications
The AIR MPCI model allows several applications, including the quantification of (i) portfolio-level losses for insurers to optimise retentions and reinsurance protection, (ii) fund allocation, where insurers can optimise their allocation of policies to several government-operated funds with different retention levels for the insurer, and (iii) portfolio-level losses for reinsurers to determine risk-adequate reinsurance terms for both quota share and stop-loss agreements. A further application of the model is the estimation of year-end yields in real time considering growing conditions. AIR's CropAlert Growing Conditions Report contains monthly updates on key risk assessment data, from baseline yield, to recent weather impacts on crops, to loss estimates when warranted, to changes in policy conditions. This information can be used to evaluate the impact of these conditions on portfolio performance, evaluate the sufficiency of loss reserves or form the basis to procure additional in-season reinsurance for insurers or retrocession covers for reinsurers.

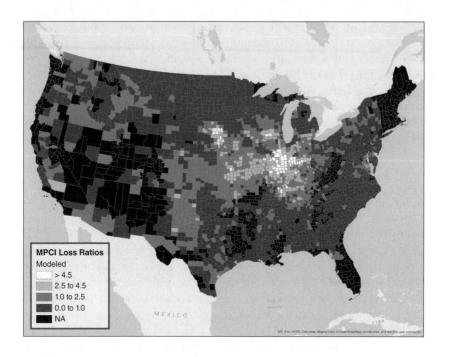

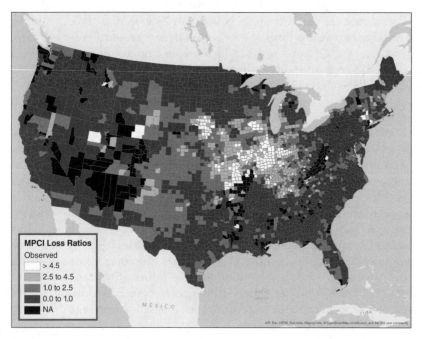

FIGURE 2.1   Above: Modelled (recast) MPCI loss ratios from the AIR Multiple Peril Crop Insurance (MPCI) Model. Bellow: Observed MPCI loss ratios as reported by RMA for the drought year 2012 at the resolution of a county. Note that a loss ratio of 4.5 signifies 450% loss ratio. *Source*: AIR with permission.

TABLE 2.3 Historical recast of gross loss ratios and post-SRA loss ratios from the AIR MPCI model (columns 2–5 at 2016 insurance terms and conditions) and observed gross loss ratios (column 6) for the US crop insurance industry, 2006–2015.

	Entire Industry		Group 1 States[a]		RMA
Year	Loss Ratio (Gross) (%)	Loss Ratio (Post SRA) (%)	Loss Ratio (Gross) (%)	Loss Ratio (Post SRA) (%)	Loss Ratio (Gross) (%)
2006	72	79	25	67	77
2007	63	72	41	69	54
2008	115	99	117	110	88
2009	57	70	25	67	58
2010	55	68	34	67	56
2011	82	81	48	70	91
2012	134	105	189	131	157
2013	81	79	91	88	102
2014	82	79	86	89	91
2015	67	74	44	72	65

[a] Includes Illinois, Indiana, Iowa, Minnesota and Nebraska.
Data source: AIR Worldwide with permission.

BIBLIOGRAPHY

Boland, P.J. (2007). *Statistical and Probabilistic Methods in Actuarial Science*. London: Chapman & Hall/CRC, 368p.

Dionne, G. (2013). *Handbook of Insurance*, 2e. New York: Springer, 1133p.

Gero, M. (2017). *Risk Modeling for Hazards and Disasters*, 1e. New York: Elsevier, 338p.

Gray, R.J. and Pitts, S.M. (2012). *Risk Modelling in General Insurance*. Cambridge: Cambridge University Press, 410p.

Grossi, P. and Kunreuther, H. (2005). *Catastrophe Modelling: A New Approach to Managing Risk*. Huebner International Series on Risk, Insurance, and Economic Security. Heidelberg: Springer, 256p.

Joe, H. (1997). *Multivariate Models and Dependence Concepts*. London: Taylor & Francis, 424p.

Kaas, R., Goovaerts, M., Dhaene, J., and Denuit, M. (2008). *Modern Actuarial Risk Theory. Using R*, 2e. Heidelberg: Springer, 393p.

Klugman, S.A., Panjer, H.H., and Willmot, G.E. (2008). *Loss Models, from Data to Decisions*, 3e. New York: Wiley, 726p.

Mitchell-Wallace, K., Jones, M., Hillier, J., and Foote, M. (2017). *Natural Catastrophe Risk Management and Modelling: A Practitioner's Guide*. New York: Wiley, 536p.

OECD (2005). *Catastrophic Risks and Insurance*. Policy Issues in Insurance 8. Paris: OECD Publishing, 424p.

Ohlsson, E. and Johansson, B. (2010). *Non-Life Insurance Pricing with Generalized Linear Models*. European Actuarial Academy Series. Heidelberg: Springer, 181p.

Olivieri, A. and Pitacco, E. (2015). *Introduction to Insurance Mathematics – Technical and Financial Features of Risk Transfers*, 2e. Heidelberg: Springer, 521p.

Parodi, P. (2015). *Pricing in General Insurance*. Chapman & Hall/CRC, 584p.

Swiss Re (2017): World Insurance in 2016. Zurich: Sigma 3/2017, 60p.

Thoyts, R. (2010). *Insurance Theory and Practice*. New York: Routledge, 340p.

Werner, G. and Moldin, C. (2016). *Basic Ratemaking*, 5e. Arlington: Publication of the Casualty Actuarial Society, 423p.

CHAPTER 3

Agricultural Perils and Risk Modelling Concepts

3.1 INTRODUCTION

Agricultural production is exposed to a wide range of perils that can affect an individual farm or a sub-region (e.g. hail or frost), an entire country (e.g. drought, cyclones) or several countries with global consequences (e.g. drought in a large grain-exporting market). The same disaster can simultaneously impact different agriculture sub-sectors, causing both direct (immediate) and indirect losses. Depending on the severity and scale of the losses, some agricultural production systems can take years to recover, with long-lasting impacts on the larger economy and society. Systemic perils such as droughts, floods, cyclones, wildfires and epidemic disease outbreaks cause the largest losses to the agricultural sector. While some perils are reoccurring under regular climate variability patterns, such as the El Niño Southern Oscillation (ENSO), others occur randomly in both space and time.

Risk transfer products and modelling concepts have been developed for most perils to facilitate risk transfer to (re)insurance and capital markets. The agricultural risk transfer industry relies mostly on past insurance claims data to structure and price products; however, historical claims often do not reveal the full range of possible loss expectations, which leads to over- or underestimation of risks and inadequate insurance conditions. Through outputs of physical models and climate indices, the research domain offers valuable loss proxies that are increasingly available through comprehensive open source websites and platforms.

This chapter provides first a general overview of the main perils for agricultural assets. The subsequent sections are dedicated to drought, flood, hail, frost, snow, cyclones, wildfires and epidemic livestock/aquatic diseases, for which an overview of the physical nature, data sources and key modelling concepts is presented. The chapter closely links to Chapter 4 (Agricultural Data and Proxies), which specifically discusses data sources and treatment techniques.

3.2 OVERVIEW OF MAIN PERILS FOR AGRICULTURE

Agriculture production assets are exposed to a large number of perils that can cause losses as a function of (i) intensity and duration, (ii) time of impact during the crop growth phase or the livestock rearing cycle, (iii) efficiency of national contingency plans (e.g. quarantine measures for epidemic diseases) for mitigation and availability of resources to contain the spread of certain perils (e.g. forest fires, diseases), and (iv) proficiencies of early warning systems for slowly on-setting perils (e.g. drought, flood, hurricane, livestock diseases).

CLASSIFICATION OF PERILS

In the risk transfer industry, perils are often grouped into: (i) geophysical perils, including earthquake, volcano and dry mass movement; (ii) meteorological perils, including different types of storms (tropical cyclones, extra-tropical cyclones, convective storms) and fog; (iii) hydrological perils, including flood, wet mass movements and wave action; (iv) climatological perils such as extreme temperature, cold waves, droughts and wildfires; (v) biological perils comprising viral and bacterial epidemics, insect infestations and animal stampede; and (vi) extra-terrestrial perils, including impact of space weather.[1] The agricultural sector is exposed to most of these perils, with a high vulnerability to meteorological, hydrological, climatological and biological perils.

Key Perils for Agriculture

Perils that cause high losses for agricultural production assets can be divided into natural perils and biological perils. The risk transfer industry has developed products to cover direct and, to some extent, indirect losses for most perils that can be insured through named-peril or multi-peril policies.

Natural Perils

Key perils that can affect different agricultural sub-sectors include drought, flood, cyclone and snow pressure. Drought is the main peril causing systemic losses for crop producers and can lead to heat stress and increased livestock mortality through reduced fodder and grazing opportunities. Flood impacts agriculture at a local to regional scale, typically along flood plains and major river systems. Tropical and extratropical cyclones (winter storms and thunderstorms) have caused significant losses to most agricultural production assets, particularly timber plantations and natural woodlands, through large-scale stem breakage and uprooting and disrupted timber markets. Severe snowstorms and freezing conditions cause high mortality among nomadic livestock thanks to starvation due to reduced access to grazing areas in winter. Hail is most damaging for crops; however, it can induce severe injuries to forest stands at local scale. Wildfires are a main risk for forest, with rare losses to livestock operations in areas impacted by uncontrollable fires. Winter crops and the horticultural sector are exposed to frost risk and winterkills have caused near total losses in winter wheat production

---

[1] IRDR, 2014: Peril Classification and Hazard Glossary. Integrated Research on Disaster Risk Publication, 28p.

in several countries. Earthquakes and tsunamis occasionally cause localised damage to agriculture through ground motion, saltwater intrusions and waves that overthrow off-shore aquaculture cage systems. Volcanic eruptions can cause damage to arable land through the deposition of toxic and solidifying ash layers, collapsing infrastructure and water contamination.

Biological Perils
The occurrence of pests and diseases is an integral part of farming. While crop protection is effective for most crop diseases, and vaccines contain widespread damage in animal and aquatic stock, epidemic diseases cause devastating losses, particularly when the impacted country has been declared disease free.

NATURAL DISASTERS AND AGRICULTURE

Natural disasters disrupt agricultural production, damage food production systems and, in severe cases, destabilise markets and threaten local and global food security. Low- and middle-income countries are most severely affected when rural household purchasing capacity is reduced, access to food is restricted, savings are depleted and forced selling of productive assets (e.g. livestock) is the consequence. Through further specialisation and verticalisation, necessary to increase food production, and potentially more frequent and extreme weather events through climate change, losses to agriculture are likely to increase further. Increasingly globalised food markets and the general transformation of the agricultural sector in low- and middle-income countries are likely to make food security less predictable.

Climate-change adaptation, improved disaster resilience frameworks, wider disaster financing and more risk transfer solutions are necessary to support the agricultural sector in producing more food and raw materials in a more sustainable way. The Intergovernmental Panel on Climate Change (IPCC) states that insurance and other financial instruments can play an important role in managing natural disaster risks in the framework of climate change adaptation.[2]

Trends in Global Disasters Relevant for Agriculture

Over 1980–2016, an increasing trend in the number of climatological disasters relevant for agriculture and economic losses was observed (Figure 3.1). Floods occurred most frequently, with an average of 113 events recorded per year, followed by storms with 86 events and drought with 15 occurrences. For all economic sectors, storms produced the highest average annual economic losses (US\$28.9 billion), followed by flood (US\$19.9 billion) and drought (US\$4.2 billion).

A recent study showed that (i) national cereal production during droughts decreased on average by 10.1% (1964–2007), (ii) 6.2% of global cereal production was lost due to extreme weather events and 3.2% from drought alone (2000–2007), (iii) cereal yield declined by 5.1% due to extreme weather events (2000–2007),

---

[2] IPCC, 2012: Summary for policymakers. In Fields C.B. (ed) Managing the Risks of Extreme Events and Disasters to Advance Climate Change Adaptation. A Special Report of Working Groups I and II of the Intergovernmental Panel on Climate Change. Cambridge University Press, Cambridge, 1–19.

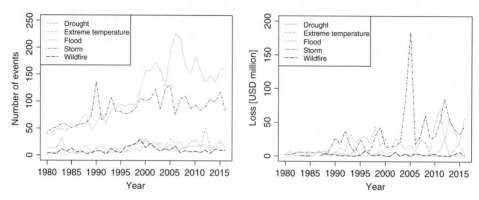

FIGURE 3.1 Left: Number of annual natural disasters relevant for agriculture, 1980–2016. Right: Economic losses relevant for agriculture, 1980–2016.
Data source: EM-DAT, with the last update on 27 September 2017.

(iv) the harvested area reduced by 4.1% during droughts (2000–2007), (v) well-developed production systems with monocultures in North America, Europe and Australasia showed a drought-related production deficit of 19.9% compared with 12.1% in Asia and 0.2% in Africa (2000–2007), and (vi) floods and extreme cold did not reduce production significantly.[3] In monetary terms, natural disasters caused US$1.5 trillion in economic damages worldwide, with more than a third occurring in developing countries and over US$80 billion in lost crop and livestock production in developing countries (2003–2013).[4]

CLIMATE VARIABILITY AND AGRICULTURE

Climate oscillations such as the ENSO, the Indian Ocean Dipole (IOD) and the North Atlantic Oscillation (NAO) strongly affect hydro-climatological processes that impact global crop yields. These oscillations and others may increase or weaken each other and produce combined climatological effects, and can have devastating effects on crop production on a global scale.

A recent study reveals that 67% of global cropland, which produces two-thirds of global food, is in areas where one or more climate oscillations show statistically significant changes in crop productivity during strong phases.[5] The same study further shows that (i) 27% of global crop production is sensitive to variations in ENSO, 5% to IOD variations and 20% to variations in NAO, (ii) crop productivity in Southeast Asia and many parts of Africa is especially sensitive to variations in the ENSO at sub-national level, and (iii) opposite phases of a climate oscillation do not necessarily produce crop productivity changes of opposite directions.

---

[3] Lesk, C., Rowhani, P. and Ramankutty, N., 2016: Influence of extreme weather disasters on global crop production. *Nature*, 529(7584), 84–7.
[4] FAO, 2015: The Impact of Natural Hazards and Disasters on Agriculture and Food Security and Nutrition. Rome, 16p.
[5] Heino, M., Puma, M.J., Ward, P.J. et al., 2018: Two-thirds of global cropland area impacted by climate oscillations. *Nat. Commun.*, 9(1257), 1–10.

El Niño Southern Oscillation (ENSO)

The ENSO is a local warming of sea surface waters in equatorial zones of the central and eastern Pacific Ocean. It affects global atmospheric circulation and reoccurs every 2–7 years, with a 12–18 month duration. Consistent positive anomalies (warming) in sea surface temperatures (SSTs) are referred to as El Niño events and negative anomalies (cooling) as La Niña. While El Niño and La Niña events change the likelihood of climate patterns, the outcomes of each event are never the same and there is always a potential for an event to generate serious impacts in some regions irrespective of the event's intensity. While El Niño phases are followed typically by neutral (SST) conditions or La Niña, two consecutive El Niño events can occur and may influence the climate for several years (e.g. 1986/87 and 1987/88).

Classifications of El Niño and La Niña Events
The standard for classifying the strength of El Niño and La Niña events is the Oceanic Niño Index (ONI), which is the running three-month mean SST anomaly in region 3.4 in the tropical Pacific. An event is defined as five consecutive overlapping three-month periods for an El Niño with an SST anomaly of $\geq+0.5°C$ and La Niña with $\leq-0.5°C$, with events classified according to the anomaly into weak (0.5–0.9°C anomaly), moderate (1.0–1.4), strong (1.5–1.9) and very strong (≥2.0). Very strong El Niño events occurred in 1982/83, 1997/98 and 2015/16 (Table 3.1) and caused large-scale damage to the agricultural sector at global scale.

Impact of ENSO on Crop Production
The ENSO has been shown to significantly influence maize, soybean, rice and wheat yields in larger parts of Latin America, South Asia and Southern Africa. A study of the impact of the ENSO on the production of the main crop types showed that

TABLE 3.1 Overview of El Niño and La Niña events classified into different intensities based on the Oceanic Niño Index, with numbers in brackets indicating the number of events, 1951–2018.

El Niño				La Niña		
Weak (10)	Moderate (7)	Strong (5)	Very Strong (3)	Weak (11)	Moderate (4)	Strong (7)
1952/53	1951/52	1997/58	1982/83	1954/55	1955/56	1973/74
1953/54	1963/64	1965/66	1997/98	1964/65	1970/71	1975/76
1958/59	1968/69	1972/73	2015/16	1971/72	1995/96	1988/89
1969/70	1986/87	1987/88		1983/84	2011/12	1998/99
1976/77	1994/95	1991/92		1984/85		1999/00
1977/78	2002/03			2000/01		2007/08
1979/80	2009/10			2005/06		2010/11
2004/05				2008/09		
2006/07				2016/17		
2014/15				2017/18		

Source: Adapted from NOOA.

(i) significant negative and positive impacts on the yields associated with El Niño appear in up to 22–24% and 30–36% of harvested areas worldwide respectively, and (ii) La Niña has negative impacts on up to 9–13% of harvested areas, while positive impacts occur in up to 2–4% of harvested areas.[6]

The most common climate impact of El Niño on the agricultural sector is reoccurring severe droughts or flash floods and intensified hurricanes, which leads to large impacts on agriculture including reduced crop production, more wildfires and reduced fish stocks especially along the Peruvian coast. Due to the random nature of atmospheric circulations and pre-conditions before the onset of an El Niño, the intensity expressed as the anomaly in SST does not directly relate to the global agricultural land under drought conditions. For example, the 1997/98 El Niño was one of the strongest on record (Table 3.1) but impacted only 80 million ha of agricultural land while the 1991/92 El Niño that was classified as strong impacted 350 million ha.[7]

Indian Ocean Dipole (IOD)
The IOD is defined as differences in SSTs between the Arabian Sea and the eastern Indian Ocean, and changes in SST gradients often lead to modified atmospheric circulations and rainfall variability in countries surrounding the Indian Ocean Basin. The IOD has a certain link to the ENSO and when in phase impacts of El Niño and La Niña events are often most extreme over Australia. The IOD has shown significant correlation with droughts in southern Australia[8] and has a strong influence on Australian wheat yields.[9]

North Atlantic Oscillation (NAO)
The NAO describes the difference in atmospheric pressure at sea level between the Icelandic low-pressure and the Azores high-pressure systems, which control the strength and direction of westerly winds and storm tracks across the North Atlantic. The NAO can affect crop yields in Northern and Eastern Europe and the eastern parts of the United States as well as northeast China.[10]

Early Warning and Forecast Systems
While global soft commodity markets facilitate trades and support countries that are impacted by low crop production, for countries that are not connected to global markets and/or did not have enough lead time to prepare for more food imports, low domestic production can have devastating effects for the population and for the economy.

---

[6] Iizumi, T., Luo J., Challinor, A.J. et al. 2014: Impacts of El Niño Southern Oscillation on the global yields of major crops. *Nat. Commun.*, 5(3712), 1–7.
[7] FAO, 2014: Understanding the Drought Impact of El Niño on the Global Agricultural Areas. Environment and Natural Resource Management Services Report 23, Rome, 52p.
[8] Ummenhofer, C.C., England, M.H., McIntosh, P.C. et al., 2009: What causes southeast Australia's worst droughts? *Geophys. Res. Lett.*, 36, 1–5.
[9] Yuan, C. and Yamagata, T., 2015: Impacts of IOD, ENSO and ENSO Modoki on the Australian winter wheat yields in recent decades. *Sci. Rep.*, 5(17252), 8p.
[10] Kim, M. and McCarl, B.A., 2005: The agricultural value of information on the North Atlantic oscillation: Yield and economic effects. *Clim. Change*, 71, 117–39.

To better prepare countries for ENSO's impact, early warning systems and forecasts have been established where international agencies work jointly in monitoring the ENSO system. Dynamical and statistical models are used to predict changes of the ENSO and expected climate variations several months ahead of anticipated impact, including the onset and intensities of El Niño and La Niña events.[11] While the accuracy in predicting onsets is relatively high, forecasts of intensities are less reliable due to random atmospheric disturbances that dampen or amplify the intensities and resulting impacts on weather patterns.

The early warning of El Niño events has supported governments in affected countries to prepare contingency plans and allowed global grain markets to expect increased volatility in core soft commodities in advance. The agricultural risk transfer industry has followed ENSO forecasts; however, as agricultural (re)insurance is often based on long-term business relationships, measures to limit exposure to drought and flash floods in El Niño and La Niña are not very common. For macro-level products with governments or the agribusiness industry, (re)insurers try to impose multiyear policies to limit the risk of adverse selection and to avoid the policyholder buying cover only in years with high loss expectations based on ENSO projections.

3.3 DROUGHT

Droughts and heatwaves cause some of the highest losses in the agricultural sector. They occur in both high- and low-rainfall areas and relate to the reduction of rainfall received over a certain area over an extended period of time. A typical drought time scale is months or even years, whereas a heatwave is typically in the order of a week. The onset and termination of a drought is driven by factors including high temperature, low relative humidity and the intensity, duration and spatial distribution of rainfall.

TYPES OF DROUGHT

There is a large range of definitions of drought, with the most commonly accepted being the extreme persistence of precipitation deficit over a specific region for a specific amount of time. The World Meteorological Organization (WMO) defines drought as 'sustained, extended deficiency of precipitation', while the Food and Agriculture Organization (FAO) describes drought as 'years when crops fail from the lack of moisture'.

As drought has different types of impact on the environment and on society, they are generally categorised into (i) meteorological drought resulting from a lack of precipitation for a period of time compared with average rainfall amounts, (ii) agricultural drought when declining soil moisture results in crop failure due to differences in actual and potential evapotranspiration (PET) and plant water demand which depends on weather conditions, biological characteristics of the plant at a certain growth stage and general soil properties, (iii) hydrological drought as a period with inadequate surface and sub-surface water resources, and (iv) social-economic drought from a failure of the water resource systems to meet demand.[12] Droughts typically occur in a particular

---

[11] ESCAP, 2017: Assessment of El Nino Associated Risks: The Step-Wise Process. Geneva, Publication of the Economic and Social Commission for Asia and the Pacific (ESCAP). 61p.

[12] Mishra, A.K. and Singh, V.P., 2010: A review of drought concepts. *J. Hydrol.*, 391, 202–16.

order, starting with precipitation deficiency (meteorological drought), which impacts soil moisture content (agricultural drought), and low recharges from the soil to streams and lakes causes low streamflow (hydrological drought), which can lead to a failure of the water resource systems (social–economic drought).

Drought Damage to Agriculture

For plants, drought stress occurs when water loss from the plant exceeds the ability of the plant's roots to absorb water and when the plant's water content is reduced enough to interfere with normal plant processes, including photosynthesis. Photosynthesis drives transpiration, where the plant moves water and nutrients from the root system and where water vapour is lost through the leaves, which allows the plant to cool. Drought conditions impact a plant in different ways, including (i) a direct effect as the top soil layer dries and reduces the plant's ability to absorb water through damaged root hairs, and (ii) indirect effects in that the plant becomes more susceptible to pests and diseases through increased stress. The time for drought damage to occur depends on the plant species, the water-holding capacity of the soil, environmental conditions and the stage of plant growth (nearly or poorly established plants with thin root systems are more susceptible to drought damage). Irrigation supplies water during dry periods; its efficiency in alleviating drought damage depends on the timing and amount of water provided as well as on the plant type, soil type and soil layering.

Drought can lead to heat stress for livestock and often forms the basis for increased wildfire activity due to dry fuel loads.

DROUGHT LOSSES

Droughts cause the highest losses in the agriculture sector, with a total of 549 drought events recorded (1980–2017) and damage reported for 154 of those events. The costs of the 10 most costly droughts amounted to US$74.6 billion (Table 3.2), which consists of 48% of the total drought-related damage (1980–2017), of which a major part

TABLE 3.2   Overview of the 10 costliest drought disasters ranked by total damage, 1980–2017.

Year	Country	Population Affected (Million)	Total Damage (US$ Million)
2012	USA	*Unknown*	20 000
1994	China	88.7	13 755
2011	USA	*Unknown*	8 000
2015	Vietnam	1.8	6 750
1981	Australia	0.1	6 000
2014	Brazil	27.0	5 000
1990	Spain	6.0	4 500
2014	China	27.7	3 680
2009	China	60.2	3 600
1999	Iran	37.0	3 300
Total		248.4	74 585

Data source: EM-DAT, with the last update on 5 December 2017.

is borne by the agricultural sector. The 2012 drought in the USA caused the highest losses, estimated at US$20 billion, followed by the 1994 drought in China at an estimated loss of US$13.7 billion.

Drought in the USA in 2012

The 2012 drought was one of the most severe events since recordings of weather parameters started in 1866 in the USA, with the agriculture sector being the industry worst affected. The drought in 2012 reached an extent similar to the droughts in the 1950s, covering nearly two-thirds of the continental USA, with 62% of the area classified in at least moderate drought conditions.

Development of the 2012 Drought
The drought developed rapidly in May over the central Great Plains and reached its peak in August. The Great Plains had experienced near normal winter rainfall (October 2011 to April 2012) and surface moisture was sufficient despite a warmer than usual winter and a very warm early spring. The warm spring, with near normal precipitation in most of the USA and strong commodity prices, led to early planting, with 53% of the area planted by the end of April, which was 26% higher compared with the previous five years. From May to August, weather stations in the Great Plains recorded an average rainfall of two standard deviations below normal and a rainfall deficit of 53% compared with the long-term average. At the same time, surface temperatures were recorded at two standard deviations above normal and soil moisture anomalies were in the lower deciles of the historical distribution. An intensive anti-cyclonic system caused a high extent of atmospheric stability and prevented the development of rain-bearing frontal systems, while a trough in August limited the inflow of moisture from the Gulf of Mexico.[13]

Drought Impact on Agriculture
The drought caused losses to the agricultural sector of over US$20 billion, the most expensive event after the 1988 drought that caused US$15 billion in agricultural losses.[14] As a result of the drought, yields and production of several crop types decreased significantly (Figure 3.2). Compared with 2011, yields of corn dropped by 16%, soybeans by 5% and barley by 2%, while wheat yields slightly increased and production grew by 14% due to favourable conditions in the southern and northern plains during spring. Crops outside the Great Plains, such as peanuts, cotton, rice, sunflower, beans, vegetables and citrus, experienced slight reductions relative to 2011. More than 76% of the cattle inventory was in the drought zone and 69% of the hay acreage was in drought areas in very poor to poor condition and resulted in the lowest production since 1964. In 2012, the demand for agricultural commodities remained strong and crop prices reached high levels in the USA. But the year saw a sharp decline in global grain production (wheat in Russia, Ukraine and Kazakhstan and US corn) and combined with low stock levels, grain markets tightened and resulted in increases in farmgate and future prices in the USA.

---

[13] Hoerling, M., Eischeid, J., Kumar, A. et al., 2014: Causes and predictability of the 2012 Great Plains drought. *Bull. Am. Meteorol. Soc.*, 95(2), 269–82.
[14] Steuer M. and Strobl, M., 2012: Drought in the US Midwest. In Natural Catastrophes 2012 Analyses, Assessments, Positions, Munich Re Publication, 17–19.

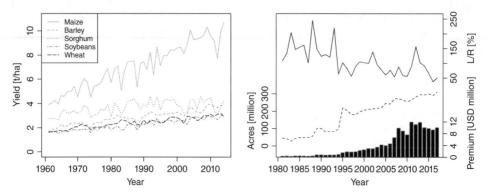

FIGURE 3.2   Left: Yield for maize, barley, sorghum, soybeans and wheat in the USA, 1961–2014. Right: Premium volume (right axis, columns), loss ratio (right axis, solid line) and insured area (left axis, dotted line) of the US Federal Crop Insurance Programs, 1981–2017.
Data source: FAOSTAT and RMA.

Drought Impact on Crop Insurance Programmes
Corn and soybean comprise 60% of the US crop insurance premium and the 2012 drought caused the second highest loss ratio in the history of the US crop insurance programmes. After above normal indemnities in 2011 (a loss ratio of 91%), 2012 saw a record enrolment for crop insurance among producers, with a 6.3% higher area insured and a total liability of US$117 billion. The 2012 drought caused an indemnity of US$17.4 billion and a loss ratio of 157%, which was the highest since the devastating flood year of 1993 (Figure 3.2). In comparison, the 1988 drought, when insurance density and liability levels were lower, caused indemnities of US$1 billion.

Highest payouts occurred in Illinois (US$3.38 billion), followed by Iowa (US$2 billion), Nebraska, (US$1.54 billion), Texas (US$1.41 billion) and Kansas (US$1.37 billion).[15] Around 90% of the indemnity payments went to just four crop types – corn (63%), soybeans (13%), cotton (8%) and wheat (6%). The underwriting loss reached US$6.3 billion and was by far the highest since modern crop insurance products were introduced in 1981.

Most crop insurance programmes incurred loss ratios above 100% with the exception of (i) gross revenue products that cover farm income, and (ii) dollar plans that compensate fix costs from yield reduction (Table 3.3). Of the 50 states which have both revenue and yield insurance plans, 36 states incurred higher loss ratios for revenue protection (RP) plans (e.g. actual revenue history (ARH), RP) than for yield plans (e.g. actual production history (APH), yield protection (YP)), driven by severe production losses, which caused harvest prices to increase for most crops and triggered larger indemnity as most revenue plans use the higher of the harvest or base price to establish payouts (Table 3.3). A rate review of the RMA during 2011 and 2012 led to a reduction in premium rates of 7% for corn and 9% for soybeans. In 2013, the RMA refined the rate methodology and increased the threshold above which large claims (now US$200 000) require a review.

---

[15] Collins, K. and Bulut, H., 2013: 2012 Year in Review. *Crop Ins. TODAY*, 16p.

TABLE 3.3 Overview of the main insurance plans (in alphabetical order), a description of the coverage, premium volume and loss ratios incurred in 2012.

Insurance Plan	Coverage	Premium Volume (US$ Million)	Loss Ratio (%)
Adjusted gross revenue (AGR)	Whole farm revenue insurance from crop production and to a limited extent from livestock and aquaculture based on tax filings	12.5	62
Adjusted gross revenue lite (AGRL)		4.5	60
Actual production history (APH)	Farm-based yield insurance with pre-set commodity prices and farm yield	895.9	70
Actual revenue history (ARH)	Farm-based revenue insurance	36.3	116
Dollar plan of insurance (DOL)	Farm-based yield insurance with compensation of production costs	98.1	80
Group risk income protection (GRIP)	Area-based revenue index insurance compensated at harvest price	17.0	193
Group risk income protection with harvest price exclusion (GRIP-HRO)	Area-based revenue index insurance compensated at the higher of the expected (projected) price and the harvest price	215.1	378
Group risk protection (GRP)	Area-based yield index insurance	24.0	375
Rainfall index 1 (RAINF)	Rainfall index for grassland	156.6	104
Rainfall index 2 (RAINF)	Rainfall index for apiculture (bees)	2.8	112
Revenue protection (RP)	Farm-based revenue insurance with prices as differences between planting prices (futures) and actual harvest prices	8614.5	167
Revenue protection with harvest price exclusion (RPHPE)	Farm-based revenue insurance with projected prices (futures)	168.5	158
Vegetation index 1 (VEGAT)	Satellite-based vegetation index (NDVI) for grassland	7.6	268
Vegetation index 2 (VEGAT)	Satellite-based vegetation index (NDVI) for apiculture	0.0025	106
Yield-based dollar amount insurance (YDO)	Farm-based yield insurance with pre-set commodity prices and standardised (not farm-based) yields	41.5	161
Yield protection (YP)	Farm-based yield insurance with projected prices from futures contracts	784.2	103
Total		11 079	157

Note that some of the insurance plans of 2012 were discontinued and/or integrated into other plans and renamed (see Chapter 6 for more information).
Data source: RMA (Summary of Business Reports).

DROUGHT INDICES

To monitor, forecast and model droughts, over 150 different drought indices have been developed.[16] Drought indices are quantitative measures that describe drought levels by assimilating data from one or several indicators, which include meteorological variables (e.g. temperature, precipitation, cloud cover), hydrological values (e.g. streamflow, ground water levels) and water-demand-and-supply data (e.g. reservoir storage levels).

The requirements for drought indices are that the index (i) needs to reflect developing short-term dry conditions, (ii) should not have any seasonality, and (iii) should be spatially comparable irrespective of climate zones being arid or humid. Drought indices can be categorised into meteorological indices, agricultural indices, hydrological indices, remote sensing-based indices and combined indices (also called hybrid or aggregated indices). The development of the Palmer Drought Severity Index (Table 3.4) was a major step in the quantification and monitoring of meteorological droughts as it measures dryness (negative values) and wetness (positive values) based on the supply and demand concept of the water balance equation. As long as reliable input parameters are available (precipitation and temperature in most agriculture markets are available for 40 years), drought indices can be developed to quantify regional drought frequency and severity. The suitability of a particular drought index depends on the characteristics of the production system, the data availability and the skills of the modeller.

Standard Precipitation Index (SPI)

The SPI is one of the most used multiscale indices for meteorological droughts and has shown good correspondences to variation in soil moisture, river discharge, reservoir storage, vegetation activity and crop production. The SPI, a probability index that considers only precipitation, reveals drought and excessive rainfall periods from a purely meteorological point of view. In a first step, the long-term precipitation records are fitted to a two-parameter Gamma probability distribution function (or a three-parameter Pearson III distribution), which, in a second step, is transformed to a normal distribution so that the median SPI is zero and with half of the observations being positive (negative), revealing drier (wetter) conditions compared with the median.[17] As the SPI is a standardised index, it allows the determination of the rarity of a current drought, the calculation of the probability of the precipitation necessary to end it and the comparison of historical and current droughts between different regions. The SPI can be calculated for a variety of time spans, typically one month, two months, three months, a year and multiple years. Recently, the SPI has been further developed into the Standardized Precipitation Evapotranspiration Index (SPEI) (Table 3.4) to include temperature-driven evapotranspiration.[18]

---

[16] Zargar, A., Sadiq, R., Naser, B. and Khan, F.I., 2011: A review of drought indices. *Environ. Rev.*, 19, 333–49.

[17] McKee, T.B., Doesken, N.J. and Kleist, J., 1993. The relationship of drought frequency and duration to time scales. In Proceedings of the 8th Conference on Applied Climatology, 17–22 January 1993. American Meteorological Society.

[18] Vicente-Serrano, S.M., Beguería, S. and López-Moreno, J.I., 2010: A multiscalar drought index sensitive to global warming: The standardized precipitation evapotranspiration index. *J. Clim.*, 23(7), 1696–718.

TABLE 3.4 Common drought indices per type (M = Meteorological Index, A = Agricultural Index, RS = Remote Sensing Index) and inputs (P = precipitation, T = temperature, SM = soil moisture, ET = evapotranspiration, SF = streamflow, NIR = near infrared, SWIR = short wave infrared).

Index	Type	Inputs							Notes
		P	T	SM	ET	SF	NIR	SWIR	
Percentage of normal precipitation	M	●							Non-standardised index describing rainfall deviation compared with normal but does not allow comparisons of droughts over seasons and regions; needs at least 30 years of data
Deciles of precipitation	M	●							Non-standardised index dividing rainfall distributions in 10% ranges (deciles)
Standard precipitation index (SPI)	M	●							Standardised index transforming rainfall into a normal distribution and expression of deficit/excess rainfall in standard deviations compared with long-term normal. Recommended as the main meteorological drought index by the WMO
Standard precipitation evapotranspiration index (SPEI)	M	●	●						Improved SPI index using temperature, water balance and evapotranspiration; in the absence of temporal temperature trends, produces similar results to SPI
Palmer drought severity index (PDSI)	M	●	●	●			●	●	Index based on soil moisture deficiencies (local available water content) through a water balance model; may not identify droughts as early as other indices and not well suited for mountainous land or areas of frequent climatic extremes
Crop moisture index (CMI)	A	●	●						Index developed on PDSI to monitor weekly crop development; analyses rainfall and temperature in water balance model

(Continued)

TABLE 3.4 (Continued)

Index	Type	Inputs							Notes
		P	T	SM	ET	SF	NIR	SWIR	
Soil moisture deficit index (SMDI)	A	●	●	●	●				Uses a crop model and hydrological model at high resolutions and different soil layer and depth; modelled data from a hydrological model with the Soil Water Assessment Tool (SWAT) are initially used to calculate soil water in the root zone; high complexity
Water requirement satisfaction index (WRSI) and geo-spatial WRSI	A	●	●	●	●				Crop-specific drought index that uses a water balance model and requires additionally soil type and irrigation extent
Normalised difference vegetation index (NDVI)	RS						●	●	Uses visible and near-infrared images, common vegetation health index including near-infrared and visible red spectral reflectance (Section 4.3)
Vegetation condition index (VCI)	RS						●	●	Based on thermal images, identifies drought situations and determines the onset, duration and severity of droughts for vegetation
US drought monitor (USDM)	M/A/RS	●	●	●	●	●	●	●	Composite drought index integrating SPI, PDSI and hydrological and vegetation indicators; uses percentile ranking in which indices and indicators from various periods are compared; used mainly in the USA but increasingly considered in other countries

Source: Adapted and expanded from Zargar et al. (2011).

Water Requirement Satisfaction Index (WRSI)

The WRSI is an indicator of crop performance based on the availability of water to the crop during a growing season. The WRSI is an agriculture drought index, with the most important inputs being precipitation and PET. Numerous studies have shown that the WRSI can be related to crop production using a crop-specific linear yield-reduction function.[19] The WRSI has been used widely in Africa, Central Asia and Central America for drought monitoring and crop performance.[20]

The WRSI for a crop season is based on the water supply and demand for a particular crop type over different growth phases that represent the entire growing season. The WRSI represents the ratio of seasonal actual crop evapotranspiration (*AETc*) to the water requirement over the entire growth season, equivalent to the potential crop evapotranspiration (*PETc*). The WRSI for a growth season is expressed as the sum of WRSIs over different growth phases *i*:

$$WRSI = \frac{\sum_i^n AETc}{\sum_i^n PETc} \times 100$$

PETc refers to the crop-specific PET after an adjustment relative to the crop PET through crop coefficients (Kc) using the Penman–Monteith equation. The FAO publishes Kc[21] which define crop-specific water usage over different growth phases, with values in between growth phases to be linearly interpolated. The WRSI requires the determination of the start and end of season, which is typically determined as (i) the rainfall amount for a certain time span being above a certain threshold, or (ii) the ratio between rainfall and PET being above a certain threshold. *AETc* represents the actual amount of water withdrawn from a soil water reservoir ('bucket') where shortfall relative to *PETc* is determined in function of the amount of available soil water in the 'bucket'. When the soil water content is above the maximum allowable depletion, *AET* remains the same as the water requirement (i.e. no water stress and crop yield reduction), resulting in a value of 100. If the soil water content is below the maximum allowable depletion, *AET* is lower than the water requirement, indicating water stress and a seasonal WRSI of less than 50 is considered a crop failure condition.

Use of Drought Indices for Risk Transfer

The agriculture risk transfer industry uses drought indices (particularly the SPI, WRSI, CMI and NDVI) to monitor crop growth conditions and to quantify impact of past droughts on current insurance portfolios. Drought indices have been used to set triggers for crop and livestock insurance products, including the NDVI (Section 6.10) and the WRSI (Section 6.11).

---

[19] Frère, M. and Popov, G.F., 1986: Early Agrometeorological Crop Yield Forecasting. FAO Plant Production and Protection Paper 73, Rome, 150p.

[20] Senay G.B. and Verdin, J., 2003: Characterization of yield reduction in Ethiopia using a GIS-based crop water balance model. *Can. J. Remote Sens.*, 29(6), 687–92.

[21] FAO, 1998: Crop Evapotranspiration - Guidelines for Computing Crop Water. FAO Irrigation and Drainage Paper 56, Rome, 15p.

DROUGHT MODELS

Based on inputs such as drought indices, hydro-meteorological parameters and climate variability indices, different drought models have been developed for the assessment and forecasting of droughts. The main models include, with increasing complexity, (i) regression analyses between hydro-meteorological parameters and crop yields, (ii) time series analyses including autoregressive methods (e.g. Autoregressive Integrated Moving Average, ARIMA), (iii) probability models such as Markov models to assess drought uncertainties from drought indices, (iv) artificial neural network models, and (v) hybrid models that combine different drought models.[22] Additionally, mechanistic crop models offer a possibility to model agricultural droughts (Section 4.4).

EXAMPLES OF OPEN SOURCE DROUGHT DATA

Increasingly, drought indices are made available open source and include on some occasions forecasts of drought indices, functionalities to analyse droughts and code to compute the indices.

- *Standard Precipitation Index (SPI)*. IRI provides SPIs at a global scale for 1-, 3-, 6-, 9- and 12-month intervals (since 1979) at different resolutions and similarly, the National Center for Atmospheric Research (NCAR) computes SPI values at 3-, 6- and 12-month scales for global land surface at a 1° resolution.
  http://iridl.ldeo.columbia.edu/SOURCES/.IRI/.Analyses/.SPI
  https://rda.ucar.edu/datasets/ds298.0
- *Standard Precipitation Evapotranspiration Index (SPEI)*. The Instituto Pirenaico de Ecología (IPE) provides global 0.5° gridded datasets for SPEI with time scales between one and 48 months (1901–2011) and 0.5° global real-time drought monitoring through SPEI indices. IPE further provides code to compute SPEI time series.
  http://sac.csic.es/spei
- *Water Requirement Satisfaction Index (WRSI)*. United States Geological Survey (USGS)/FEWSNET provides 10-day geospatial gridded WRSI values, WRSI maps, WRSI anomaly maps, start of the season maps, total AET and total water deficit for different parts of the world, time scales and resolutions.
  http://chg.geog.ucsb.edu/tools/geowrsi/index.html

3.4 FLOOD

Floods cause high losses to infrastructure and with some of the fertile soils in alluvial plains, the agriculture sector frequently suffers production shortfalls when floodwater systems fail. Irrigation schemes have been developed over time in alluvial plains to alleviate droughts but are frequently inundated through river floods. While reoccurring seasonal flooding is mostly addressed through engineering, watershed management and crop cycle management, catastrophic floods rely on ex-post government interventions. Agricultural production systems in flood-prone

---

[22] Mishra, A.K. and Singh, V.P., 2011: Drought modelling – A review. *J. Hydrol.*, 403, 157–75.

regions have evolved over time to reduce damage through specific cropping systems, planting schedules and the use of flood-resistant crop strains; however, severe and catastrophic floods are a key concern, particularly with global warming, where flash floods in particular are likely to occur more frequently. Severe floods (every 20 years) affect large areas and can cause significant damage to agriculture, and catastrophic floods (every 100 years) that inundate very large areas cause severe losses to agriculture and infrastructure.[23]

TYPES OF FLOODS

Generally, floods stem from severe rainfall events, short torrential rain, tropical cyclones, monsoon rainfalls and snowmelts, and often follow seasonal processes which vary by region. Floods are the result of physical processes which include (i) hydrological pre-conditions such as soil saturation and snow cover, (ii) meteorological conditions that determine the amount, intensity and spatial distribution of rainfall, and (iii) run-off driven by infiltration ratios into the soil and river routing.[24] Man-made structures including dams and flood water levies play an important role in the onset and development of floods. Significant changes in land use, the development of flood mitigation strategies and improved infrastructure can have severe impacts on future flood extents. For the agriculture sector, flood occurs mainly in the form of river flooding, flash floods and, to some extent, storm surge.

River Flooding

River flooding occurs as a function of prolonged rainfall that leads to soil saturation and increased run-off along topography through tributaries into the main river system. Run-off rates depend on the capacity of the river system, slope angles, soil permeability driven by land cover and land use, and controls of water flows through engineering structures (e.g. drainage, dams). River floods can originate from severe rainfall events or snow melt in upstream catchment areas. Due to shallow slopes in alluvial plains, river floods usually progress slowly and last days or weeks. The effect of inundation is enhanced when soils in the flood plain are saturated (waterlogged) from local excessive rainfall by the time river flooding occurs. Often agriculture land in designated areas is inundated through controlled flooding to prevent floods in urban areas. Farmers are warned by government agencies in advance of controlled flooding and typically receive financial compensation for lost production.

Flash Floods

Flash floods result from severe local rainfall events that are related to convective storms. The speed of movement of storms, rainfall duration and intensity as well as soil permeability, land cover and use determine the extent of inundation from flash floods. Depending on topographical features, residual ponds or shallow lakes form and last over days and weeks. Impacts are typically most severe in hilly or mountainous areas

---

[23] World Bank, 2010: Assessment of Innovative Approaches for Flood Risk Management and Financing in Agriculture. Discussion Paper 46, Washington DC, 122p.

[24] Nied, M., Pardowitz, T., Nissen, K. et al., 2014: On the relationship between hydro-meteorological patterns and flood types. *J. Hydrol.*, 519, 3249–62.

where impermeable soils and saturated soils on steep slopes lead to fast run-off and cause erosion and landslides in instable terrain.

Storm Surge

Storm surge is a result of tropical storms and cyclones, which, through differences in atmospheric pressure, produce temporary sea level rises that drive water onshore and inundate coastal plains and river deltas. The extent of flooding largely depends on the topography, tidal conditions, wind strength, wave action and water flow levels in rivers. Long-term effects of storm surge include increased soil salinity.

FLOOD LOSSES

Between 1980 and 2017, 2282 recorded flood events caused global losses of US$751 billion, with agriculture being one of the affected industries. The 10 most costly events reached US$219 billion. The 2011 Thailand flood caused the highest damage with US$40 billion and China has seen a series of severe floods amounting to overall total damage of US$231 billion (Table 3.5).

Flood Damage to Agriculture

Floods lead to direct losses to agricultural production, including crops, livestock, forestry and aquaculture, and indirect losses to farm property, equipment (e.g. machinery, irrigation systems) and stocks such as stored input supplies or feed and grain. Flood impacts crop quantity and quality and the loss extent is typically a function of (i) the crop type and cultivar, (ii) the time of flooding relative to the crop growth stage, with the flowering and ripening stages being the most vulnerable, (iii) the duration of flooding and water depth that leads to submergence, (iv) the flood water velocity, which can cause soil erosion and deposition of sediments (siltation) on farmland that limits the recovery of plants after flooding, and (v) the presence of flood mitigation measures. Floods and flood-related

TABLE 3.5 Overview of the 10 costliest flood disasters ranked by total damage, 1980–2017.

Year	Country	Population Affected (Million)	Total Damage (US$ Million)
2011	Thailand	10.2	40 317
2016	China	61.3	31 793
1998	China	242.7	31 744
1996	China	154.7	18 915
2010	China	140.2	18 171
2013	China	7.7	16 599
2014	India	5.2	16 465
2003	China	155.9	15 330
2016	USA	0.1	15 150
1995	South Korea	6.2	15 000
Total		784.2	219 484

Data source: EM-DAT, with the last update on 5 December 2017.

waterlogging at harvest time can lead to delayed harvests and rapidly decreasing quality of crops. Flood also impacts livestock through inundation and limited access to feed supplies, and flooding of on-shore pond aquaculture systems leads to disappearance of stock and/or mortality when water temperature changes abruptly through flood waters.

FLOOD MODELS

Earlier methods for assessing flood hazard relied on pure statistical analyses of streamflow data. Statistical models assume that historical data represent the overall possible flood peaks and that recurrence intervals are not changing systematically over time; however, that is rarely the case in dynamic river systems and the development of flood management infrastructure. More recent approaches to model floods include (i) physical parametric models that estimate the size and frequency of flood flows, inundation depths and in some occasions flood duration,[25] and (ii) remote sensing-based models.

Physical Flood Models

Key components of a physical flood model consist of (i) hydrological load based on historical and simulated rainfall patterns, (ii) catchment models that describe watershed processes through water infiltration into soils, (iii) hydraulic models where the hydrological load is routed through simplified river systems in a high-resolution topography model, (iv) simulations of breaches of levees and water release from dams and hydraulic outflow simulation, and (v) inundation and damage estimation through vulnerability functions (essentially flood depth and duration) on infrastructure.[26] Water flows are modelled with one-dimensional models for rivers and through two-dimensional models in flood plains. Physical models are highly data intensive and are generally as accurate as the available data. Physical flood models are operated by disaster risk management agencies and hydrological services, while catastrophe risk modelling companies have developed models to simulate flood losses on insurance portfolios.

Remote Sensing

Remote sensing-based models combine images of different sensors that measure flood extent, flood depth and estimate water velocity. Optical sensors provide good measurements of areal flood extents but can incur gaps in the presence of clouds and at night. Radar satellites use electromagnetic waves and provide estimates of flood extents and depth, even at night and with clouds. The temporal satellite coverage of an area and the image resolution are essential for consistent flood monitoring as river discharges can vary sometimes within a short period of time. Satellite images are often the only feasible approach in areas where historical streamflow data are missing and frequently

[25] Balica, S.F., Popescu, I., Beevers, L. and Wright, N.G., 2013: Parametric and physically based modelling techniques for flood risk and vulnerability assessment: A comparison. *Environ. Modell. Softw.*, 41, 84–92.

[26] Apel, H., Thieken, A.H., Merz, B. and Blöschl, G., 2006: A probabilistic modelling system for assessing flood risks. *Nat. Hazards*, 38, 79–100.

serve as inputs into physical models. Satellite data are increasingly used for the analysis of flood extent and damage to agricultural production.[27]

EXAMPLES OF OPEN SOURCE FLOOD INFORMATION

Historical and near real-time flood extent assessments are increasingly available at no or low cost from low- to medium-resolution satellite data, while high-resolution data (<30 m) remain costly.

- *Dartmouth Flood Observatory* (DFO) uses satellite data to map global floods and provides quasi-real-time information on flooding based on (i) satellite-based flood detection and magnitude assessment (8 km resolution since 2005), (ii) rapid flood mapping using Moderate Resolution Imaging Spectroradiometer (MODIS) data (250 m resolution with GIS polygons since 2000), and (iii) integration of mapped floods into quantitative flood hazard assessment at a resolution of 1° latitude and 2° longitude, including remote sensing data of floods since 2004. DFO also provides an interactive map of global flood events (1985–2002) and animations (1985–2007).
  http://floodobservatory.colorado.edu
- *Surface Dynamics Modeling Lab* (SDML) provides simulated global daily, monthly and yearly riverine water discharge data and global as well as USA-based flood inundation maps.
  https://sdml.ua.edu
- *European Flood Awareness System* (EFAS) contains an online flood mapper for Europe which includes return periods.
  https://www.efas.eu/efas-archive.html
- *Copernicus* provides the European Union with high-resolution flood layers for some historical flood events.
  http://emergency.copernicus.eu/mapping/list-of-components/EMSR069

3.5 HAIL

Agricultural crops are among the most exposed to hailfall as damage occurs through small hailstones and total losses occur frequently in areas that experience severe thunderstorms. As hail, unlike other meteorological perils, is not directly measured and hailfalls occur randomly, risk assessment typically relies on proxy data.

HAIL FORMATION

Hail is produced in thunderstorms and storm systems that contain one or several cells with vertical air motion (updraft). Thunderstorms are typically classified into (i) single-cell thunderstorms with shortlived updrafts where brief large hailfalls can occur,

---

[27]Tapia-Silva, F.-O., Itzerott, S., Foerster, S. et al., 2011: Estimation of flood losses to agricultural crops using remote sensing. *Phys. Chem. Earth.*, 36, 253–65.

(ii) multicell thunderstorms that can last over a few hours with several active cells at various stages of development and severe hailfalls in different areas, (iii) supercell thunderstorms with strong vertical wind shear and a rotating updraft region (out of which tornadoes can form), which produce very large hailstones, and (iv) mesoscale convective systems which contain non-severe and severe thunderstorms with a continuous precipitation area larger than 100 km in one direction that produce heavy rainfalls and hailfalls.

Severe convective storms contain deep convection that forms in the presence of (i) a moist air layer in the low or mid-troposphere, (ii) a steep lapse rate in the vertical temperature profile, and (iii) sufficient lifting from the moist layer to allow free convection. The formation of hail is a complex process and requires strong updrafts, large supercooled liquid water content and high cloud tops. Hail is defined by a diameter of at least 5 mm on ground and forms through movements of supercooled water droplets in updrafts of thunderstorms.

MEASUREMENT OF HAIL

Hailfalls show large spatial and temporal variations and are generally of short duration, while hail occurrence and intensity are difficult to measure.[28] Hail recordings are undertaken at a limited number of weather stations where observers report hail occurrence. Additionally, storm chasers, on their own initiative, document hail occurrence of some storms and newspapers sometimes report hail events. In research projects, hailpads, which are 0.1 m²-sized plates made from deformable materials, are used to record the impact of hailstones through dents. To overcome the limitation of ground-based hail measurement, weather radars and satellites are used to quantify the frequency and severity of hailfalls and to develop historical time series. Additionally, atmospheric stability indicators, lighting measurements and large-scale weather situations have been used to develop longer hail climatologies.[29] Satellite-based vegetation indices such as NDVI have been applied to assess hail damage through a change in the spectral characteristics of surface features in the visible and near-infrared radiation (Section 6.4).[30]

Hail Damage Time Series (Hail Days)

The number of days with hailfall (hail days) in an area where hailfalls are reported by observers at weather stations provide a valuable indication of hail frequency and show a good correspondence to loss costs for crop-hail insurance in the USA.[31] Through hail damage reports, some crop-hail insurers provide daily lists of administrative regions

[28] Punge, H.J. and Kunz, M., 2016: Hail observations and hailstorm characteristics in Europe: A review. *Atmos. Res.*, 159–84.

[29] Punge, H.J., Bedka, K.M., Kunz, M. and Werner, A., 2014: A new physically based stochastic event catalogue for hail in Europe. *Nat. Hazards*, 73, 1625–45.

[30] Bell, J.R. and Molthan, A.L., 2016: Evaluation of approaches to identifying hail damage to crop vegetation using satellite imagery. *J. Operational Meteor.*, 4(11), 142–59.

[31] Changnon, D. and Changnon, S.A., 1997: Surrogate data to estimate crop-hail loss. *J. Appl. Meteorol.*, 36, 1202–10.

(e.g. counties, districts) that have experienced hail damage, which allows hail tracks for a particular event to be established.

Weather Radars

Operational weather radars cover larger areas continously, with typical spatial resolution of 0.5–3 km every 5–15 minutes. Weather radars measure the backscatter of the emitted electromagnetic waves from cloud particles. The higher the backscatter, measured in decibel (dBZ), the larger the cloud particle. Hail signals are detected from radar reflectivity above the 55 dBZ level and show good correspondence with maximum hailstone sizes observed on the ground. Computing hail kinetic energy from radar reflectivity provides a measure of hail intensity and shows good correspondence with the extent of crop damage.[32]

Weather Satellites

Operational satellites provide information on cloud top temperatures that are estimated from (i) infrared measurements of overshooting convective cloud tops and cloud top mean vertical growth rates, and (ii) visual images to derive the thickness of a cloud. Cloud top temperatures above certain levels and overshooting cloud tops provide an indication of the height of a thunderstorm, which in turn can be linked through convective strength to the presence of hail. This is used to reconstruct tracks of hailstorm systems based on the frequency of the satellite images for large areas and resolutions of 30 km for the last 25 years. Hail tracks from satellites have detected around 50% of ground-verified hail events.[33]

HAIL DAMAGE TO CROPS

Hail impacts crops by reducing stand densities, breaking stalks, defoliation and damage to the grain-bearing part (ears). Stand reduction occurs mainly in the early growth stages where the impact of hailstones reduces the density of plants. Ear damage occurs at the final growth stages of the crop. Stalks are damaged through bruises but can still yield normal ears, particularly if damage occurred to young plants. Crippled plants are those that grow to average height but do not produce a normal ear. Defoliation is the loss of leaf area, which leads to lower photosynthetic activity and ability of the plant to produce dry matter and results in lower yield. Yield reductions are not directly proportional to reductions in the leaf area as increased dry matter production occurs in the remaining leaf area and forms other parts of the plant into the developing ear. Defoliation extents highly correlate to yield reductions of key phenological stages with coefficients of 0.60–0.89.[34] Besides losses of quantity, defoliation further leads to lower

---

[32] Schiesser, H.H., 1990: Hailfall: The relationship between radar measurements and crop damage. *Atmos. Res.*, 25, 559–82.
[33] Dworak, R., Bedka, K., Brunner, J. and Feltz, W., 2012: Comparison between GOES-12 overshooting-top detections, WSR-88D radar reflectivity, and severe storm reports. *Wea. Forecast*, 27(3), 684–99.
[34] Lauer, J.G., Roth, G.W. and Bertram, M.G., 2004: Impact of defoliation on corn forage yield. *Agron. J.*, 96, 1459–63.

quality, especially in the later stages of plant development.[35] With favourable weather conditions after hail damage, crops can recover to some extent and produce near normal yields depending on the number of surviving stalks and the extent of defoliation.

For fruits, the impact of a large hailstone causes deep depressions and deformations while smaller hailstones cause bruises and spots which lead to quality downgrades. Hailstones are known to defoliate trees on the windward side and, depending on the size of the hailstones, cause lesions and injuries to branches and stems, with increased susceptibility to diseases.

Examples of Severe Hail Losses in the USA

2014 saw some of the largest and most intense hailstorms in the US Midwest and caused a loss ratio of 122% on the cop-hail insurance portfolios (Section 6.4), which was the highest in history and only the third year since 1948 in which loss ratio exceeded 100%. In 2014, the crop-hail insurance premiums reached a record level of US$991.7 million, with an overall liability of US$39.6 billion in 42 states. Out of the 42 US states where crop-hail insurance was available, 12 states incurred a loss ratio above 100%, the highest being in Maryland (281%), followed by Nebraska (234%) and Arkansas (205%). Losses from the 10 most active hailstorm days reached US$420 million, which contributed 34% to the total loss amount. The single most expensive storm occurred in Nebraska on 3 June of that year, causing losses of US$145 million, or 12% of the total nationwide loss. Nebraska further experienced hail losses over US$63 million on 14 June (5.2% of the total nationwide losses), followed by Iowa with US$43 million on 30 June (3.6%).

HAIL MODELS

Hail models rely on a combination of weather radar data, satellite measurements and atmospheric stability indicators such as the Convective Available Potential Energy (CAPE) from radio soundings. While numerical weather prediction models in principle are able to simulate hail signatures, simulations are sensitive to the not well-known initial conditions and cloud microphysics scheme and do not reliably represent the climatology of convection and hail occurrence.

3.6 FROST

Frost and low-temperature events can lead to high damage to agricultural crops, particularly during phases when frost risk is typically unlikely to occur for summer crops and during extreme winter conditions (winterkill) for winter crops. Freezing conditions and significant snowfalls can lead to high mortality ratios among nomadic and semi-nomadic livestock populations (Section 7.6). Long-lasting freezing conditions have caused considerable losses to off-shore aquaculture farms, particularly in shallow fjords and lakes. Frost risk assessment is essentially based on low temperature recordings and lethal minimum temperatures for specific crop types.

---

[35] Roth, G.W. and Lauer, J.G., 2008: Impact of defoliation on corn forage quality. *Agron. J.*, 100, 651–7.

TYPES OF FROST

The term *frost* often refers to a meteorological event that causes plants to freeze with air temperatures below 0°C. Technically, frost relates to the deposit of soft white ice crystals or frozen dew drops on surfaces near the ground when the surface temperature falls below freezing point. *Freezing* refers to damages to plants with air temperatures below 0°C, while *chilling* occurs with temperatures above 0°C (e.g. for tropical fruits).

White frost forms when ice crystals deposit on objects that are exposed to air and when water vapour in the air freezes upon contact and air temperatures fall below 0°C. Black frost develops when the temperature is below freezing level but the air does not bear enough moisture to form white frost but causes an internal freezing of the vegetation that then leads to a characteristic black appearance. A killing frost forms when the frost period is so severe that it terminates the vegetation growing period and causes plant death, normally through black frosts. Black frosts that develop into killing frosts usually create the greatest damage to plants. Certain valleys are well known to be prone to frost (frost pockets and frost hollows) due to cold air drainage when air at hills cool at night, densifies and sinks to lower levels, which often results in frost while other areas remain frost free.

Frost occurs in two main forms: (i) advective frosts, which are caused by large-scale incursions of cold air that replaces warmer air with a well-mixed, windy atmosphere and sub-zero temperatures, and (ii) radiative frosts, which result from cooling near the ground due to energy losses to the atmosphere through radiant exchange during clear, calm nights in the presence of temperature inversions.[36] On some occasions, advective conditions bring a cold air mass into a region that results in an advection frost, which can be followed by several days of clear, calm conditions that are conductive for the development of radiation frosts.

FROST DAMAGE TO CROPS

Frost damage to crops occurs when the temperature falls below the melting point of water (0°C), which causes freezing of water in plant cells and the formation of ice crystals that puncture the cell walls (intercellular freezing) and the development of ice crystals inside the plant but outside the cells (extracellular freezing). With warming air temperature, the ice crystals melt and plant cells leak, causing the frozen plant to appear soggy, with a dark watery complexion.

Most plants can adjust to decreasing temperatures in a process called *hardening* (or acclimation), where plant cells accumulate more solutes that can lower the freezing point and develop freezing tolerance without significant damage. However, particularly severe frosts and alternative periods of freezing and thawing lead to black frosts and plant death. The severity of frost damage largely depends on the crop's sensitivity to freezing, the growth stage, the time and duration of the frost, and environmental conditions before and after the frost. Environmental conditions that contribute to lower frost damage include (i) cold and cloudy weather conditions before the frost event,

---

[36] Saulescu, N.N. and Braun, H.J., 2001: Cold tolerance. In Reynolds, M.P., Ortiz-Monasterio, J.I. and McNab, A. (eds): Application of Physiology in Wheat Breeding, CIMMYT, Mexico, 111–23.

which prepare the plant to harden, (ii) moist soils at the time of frost as temperature changes are slower in wet than in dry soils, and (iii) slow thawing that allows the plant cells to gradually defrost with increasing temperatures.

Lethal Minimum Temperature

The lethal minimum temperature is the critical temperature below which frost damage occurs; this varies among crop types and growth phases (Table 3.6). Crops are categorised according to freeze sensitivity as (i) tender, in lacking the ability to harden, e.g. tropical plants, (ii) slightly hardy with some ability to harden, e.g. sub-tropical trees, horticulture and vegetable crops that are sensitive to freezing of air temperatures of −5°C, (iii) moderately hardy, with the ability to harden to −10°C, and (iv) very hardy in avoiding intracellular freezing and related damage due to cell desiccation.

Frost Sensitivity of Summer Crops

Summer crops in the northern hemisphere are planted after the main spring frost period and harvested before autumn frost typically occurs; however, late spring and early autumn frosts can severely impact crops and lead to large yield reductions. Most summer crops have little to no hardening capacity; this decreases with plant growth, from higher hardening capacity at germination to low hardening during flowering and very low hardening at fruiting stage when cell regeneration is weak. Severe frosts can result in infertility at the flowering stage and total losses.

Frost Sensitivity of Winter Crops (Winterkill)

Winter crops in the northern hemisphere are sown in autumn and harvested in the summer of the following year. Winter crops such as winter wheat are exposed to phases of freezing and thawing during winter and can incur severe damage through *winterkill*. Winter survival is defined as the final integrated plant response to a multitude of stress factors involved during and after freezing, including external physical and biotic stresses.

TABLE 3.6 Lethal minimum temperature for some main crop types and three growth phases.

Crop type	Germination	Flowering	Fruiting
Spring wheat	−9 to −10°C	−1 to −2°C	−2 to −4°C
Barley	−7 to −8°C	−1 to −2°C	−2 to −4°C
Beans	−5 to −6°C	−2 to −3°C	−3 to −4°C
Sugar beet	−6 to −7°C	−2 to −3°C	−
Soybean	−3 to −4°C	−2 to −3°C	−2 to −3°C
Corn	−2 to −3°C	−1 to −2°C	−2 to −3°C
Sorghum	−2 to −3°C	−1 to −2°C	−2 to −3°C
Potato	−2 to −3°C	−1 to −2°C	−1 to −2°C
Cotton	−1 to −2°C	−1 to −2°C	−2 to −3°C
Peanut	−0.5 to −1°C	−	−
Tobacco	0 to −1°C	0 to −1°C	0 to −1°C

Source: After Snyder and Melo-Abreu (2005).

Winter Wheat
Winter wheat is grown in many regions that can experience severe winter conditions. After planting in autumn, winter wheat seedlings develop leaves and a root system in the first month after sowing to generate enough energy to endure hardening when temperatures decrease. Hardening typically starts at soil temperatures of 10°C and it takes 4–5 weeks at this soil temperature to full hardening, depending on the cultivar. Frost-resistant cultivars typically harden faster and de-harden slower than frost-susceptible cultivars. Damage from winterkill largely depends on (i) inadequate hardening due to late plant emergence in autumn or a sudden drop in temperature, (ii) prolonged periods of sub-zero temperatures, particularly in mid-winter with temperatures of –15°C and below, (iii) alternate freezing and thawing, (iv) ice encasement, which leads to suffocation of plants in the soil, and (v) absence of a snow cover of at least 2.5 cm on ground which serves as insulation and keeps soil temperatures above critical levels. Additionally, damage can occur through snow mold where fungi develop in long-lasting snow covers.

Winterkill in the Ukraine
Agriculture contributes 14% to Ukraine's GDP and the country is an important grain exporter, especially for wheat which is grown on some of the most fertile soils in the world. Around 95% of Ukraine's wheat is grown as a winter crop, with planting in autumn and harvest in July to August of the following year. On average, 15% of winter wheat fails to survive the winter due to low temperatures and other unfavourable weather conditions which can develop into total losses (winterkill). In Ukraine, the spatial extent and duration of snow covers determine the condition of crops at the end of winter and their development in early spring. Snow covers prevent frost and freeze damage through insulation and sufficient water released through snow melt in spring is critical for further development. In the past 100 years, most winterkill damage to winter wheat was caused by low temperatures (35% of cases), alternate freezing and thawing (26%) and ice encasement (22%).

Winterkill of 2002–2003
In the winter of 2002–2003, Ukraine and parts of Russia experienced the most severe winterkill in recent history. Temperature recordings revealed persisting low temperatures, and satellite images showed that most of the land surfaces in central and eastern Ukraine were snow-free. The freeze damage to crops in December 2002 was exacerbated by persistent ice crusting in February 2003 and led to 70% of all winter crop in Ukraine being affected by winterkill. The late and cold spring of 2003 delayed spring planting and drought occurrence affected the surviving winter wheat and the newly planted spring wheat. As a result, the 2003 wheat production in Ukraine reached only 3.6 million tons, a reduction of 78% compared with the 10-year average of 16.5 million tons (Figure 3.3) and in Central Ukraine the area lost from winterkill reached 61–88%. In 2003, Ukraine exported only 66 000 tons of wheat compared with the 10-year average of 2.3 million tons. To support farmers, the government provided disaster relief payments of US$74 million, with an average of US$13/ha, covering 30% of production costs.

Winterkill Insurance
In 2003, the crop insurance industry was in its infancy, with a premium volume of US$270 000, which was predominately written by former government insurer Oranta.

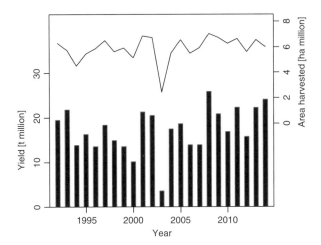

FIGURE 3.3 Wheat yields (left axis) and wheat area harvested (right axis) in Ukraine, 1991–2014. *Data source*: FAOSTAT.

The insurers offered coverage for winter freeze, defined as a drop in soil temperature below a crop's sensitivity threshold, with an average premium rate of 4% per region (oblast). The winterkill of 2002–2003 produced a loss ratio of 700% as nearly all those insured filed a claim. As the severe losses from winterkill were caused by ice crusting rather than by low temperature alone, policyholders obtained a limited indemnity as insurers maintained that crops perished from suffocation, which was not an insured peril, rather than from direct frost damage.

Following the winterkill losses and the negative experience for insurers and policyholders, a standalone winterkill insurance cover was developed for winter crops in 2003 and became a popular product. Insurance premiums were based on official area planted and harvested per district (rayon). Loss adjustment was based on sampling to determine stand reductions in function of the plant density at planting time compared with that of surviving plants in spring, with total losses defined as 70% stand reduction. To support farmers, the government provided 50% premium subsidies for crop insurance in 2005 and winterkill insurance as well as a newly introduced MPCI product, gained interest from producers. In 2006, 1200 producers were covered, with 3% of the area under field crops insured with a premium volume of US$5.4 million. A total of 37 insurers were actively providing crop insurance. In 2007, the premium volume increased to US$14.6 million, with 7.5% of area insured. With the withdrawal of government subsidies in 2008, the premium volume rapidly decreased to US$2.5 million in 2010, then increased to US$5 million by 2016 under private sector insurance.

In 2016, some 15 insurers offer winterkill insurance for the main winter crops as a standalone product, including compensation for (i) total losses if the stand reduction is over 70%; premium rates vary per crop type and rayon (district) and range between 3% and 12%, and (ii) partial losses in case at least 50% of stand reduction occurred, with an indemnity of 20% of sum insured and an increasing payout with higher damage extents up to 70%, after which total losses are recognised.

Additionally, crop producers have the option to buy a yield-based MPCI which includes all main natural perils and covers winterkill. Factors that limit growth of agriculture insurance include a lack of (i) stability in the political environment, (ii) strategy for agriculture, including a role for insurance to manage risks from adverse weather conditions, and (iii) linkage between banks and insurance companies despite insurers' efforts to provide crop insurance as part of the loan process. Additionally, a larger number of insurers service a small portfolio with high competition and low investment in product development, distribution and loss adjustment capabilities.

FROST MODELS

Modelling frost risk is complex as damage depends on the crop variety, planting and harvest dates, topography, lethal air temperatures, frost duration and the use of frost protection measures. The timing of the first frost day in spring and autumn in each year, the number of consecutive frost days from weather data and the duration of frost-free days within the growing season are common indicators that limit crop production and indicate frost frequencies and severities. Most mechanistic crop models (Section 4.4) include frost damage in daily crop growth simulations, including the aspects of crop death and reductions in seedling densities, biomasses and/or leaf areas that all result in reduced yield.[37] Although complex to operate with numerous input parameters and calibration, mechanistic crop models probably provide the most sophisticated approach to modelling frost risks on crops.

Minimum Temperature Models

A simple model to quantify the expected yield loss (EYL_i) from frost damage on a given day i in function of the minimum temperature is:[38]

$$EYL_i = \sum_{j=1}^{I} \left(\left[D\left(T_{ij}\right) \right] \cdot \left[P\left(T_{ij}\right) \right] \cdot S_i \right)$$

with day i as the first possible cold night over the frost period, T_{ij} as the minimum temperature j on day i, $D\left(T_{ij}\right)$ as the percentage damage given the minimum temperature, $P\left(T_{ij}\right)$ as the probability of the minimum temperature and S_i as the percentage of the crop area exposed to frost excluding the harvested and already frost-damaged areas. One of the main drawbacks of this model is that the duration of the minimum temperature, which besides the temperature level itself is a main loss driver, is not captured. Relating temperature measures at different atmospheric levels have shown a significant relationship to frost losses under the crop insurance in Greece.[39]

---

[37] Barlow, K.M., Christy, B.P. O'Leary, G.J. et al., 2015: Simulating the impact of extreme heat and frost events on wheat crop production: A review. *Field Crop Res.*, 171, 109–99.
[38] Venner, R. and Blank, S.C., 1995: Reducing Citrus Revenue Losses from Frost Damage: Wind Machines and Crop Insurance. Giannini Foundation Information Series 95–1, 61p.
[39] Piapagiannaki, K., Lagouvardos, K., Kotroni, V. and Papagiannakis, G., 2014: Agricultural losses related to frost events: Use of the 850 hPa level temperature as an explanatory variable of the damage cost. *Nat. Hazards Earth Syst. Sci.*, 14, 2375–86.

Frost Days

A frost day is a day within the period of the last frost day in spring and the first frost in autumn with a minimum air temperature (T_{min}) below a base temperature.[40] The base temperature is set as $T_{min} < 0°C$ for general studies on frost frequency or taken as the lethal minimum air temperature for crop-specific analyses. The number of frost days provides an indication of regional frost frequency at different time scales. Based on frost days, a crop-specific vulnerability function can be developed that takes into account the duration of a frost in terms of damage ratio per phenological stage. Historical temperature data from weather stations are used to determine the frequency and severity of losses for each crop growth phase over historical years.

3.7 SNOW

Snowstorms and blizzards can cause severe disruptions in traffic, energy shortages and infrastructure damage. For the agricultural sector, snowstorms and heavy snow events can lead to collapsing farm infrastructure, including greenhouses, damaged timber plantations, increased livestock mortality in nomadic or seminomadic systems (Section 7.6) and contribute to damage caused to crops by winterkill.

DEFINITION AND MEASUREMENT OF SNOW

Snow is defined as precipitation that is composed of white or translucent ice crystals that are snowflakes. Snowfall occurs on ground with air temperatures below 3°C and is most frequently observed between –2°C and +2°C. Snow covers influence the properties of soil surfaces, change reflectance ratios of sunlight (albedo) and alter soil water fluxes and runoff by reducing soil moisture recharges. During winter, snow covers insulate and therefore affect the time and depth of soil freezing and protect crops from winterkill, e.g. a snow cover of 50 cm keeps soil surface temperature within –10°C when air temperature drops below –30°C and therefore limits crop damage.

Measurement of Snow

Snow is manually measured by observers at weather stations and reported as (i) snowfall, (ii) snow depth which is established through snow rulers, (iii) total snow depth as measured with a stick or taken as the average of snow depth, (iv) water equivalent of snowfall where snow that has accumulated in rain gauges is melted and measured, and (v) snow water equivalent of total snow depth which is measured by extracting a snow core and reporting the melted water equivalent.

While the aerial extent of snow cover is one important parameter and is best assessed through remote sensing, modelling of snow melt rates and runoff requires an assessment of snow depth and water equivalent of snowfall, which is mostly determined from microwaves sensors. Additionally, snow depth is a prognostic variable of numerical weather prediction models.[41] Due to the high spatial variability and complexity of

---

[40] Anandhi, A., Perumal, S., Gowda, P.H. et al., 2013: Long-term spatial and temporal trends in frost indices in Kansas, USA. *Clim. Change*, 120, 169–81.

[41] Pullen, S., Jones, C. and Rooney, G., 2011: Using satellite-derived snow cover data to implement a snow analysis in the Met Office Global NWP Model. *J. Appl. Meteorol.*, 50, 958–73.

snowfalls, data of snow depths are often an assimilation of different types of data, with some data available publicly.

Snow Depth
Snow depth measurements have been projected on regular spatial grids to obtain more spatially coherent data[42] and have been derived from (i) satellites to determine the presence of snow covers, taking advantage of the fact that the presence of snow largely changes the albedo, and to approximate snow depths, (ii) Lidar (light detection and ranging) to measure snow depth through laser beams from ground or airborne devices,[43] (iii) radar satellites to assess the density and structure of snow covers through electromagnetic waves, and (iv) GPS interferometric reflectometry to measure snow depth and properties.[44]

SNOW DAMAGE TO AGRICULTURE

While many agricultural production systems are used to cope with snowfalls during winter months, particularly intensive and long-lasting snow storms can generate considerable damage to crops, semi-nomadic livestock populations and forests. For winter crops, the lack of a snow cover in combination with abnormally low temperatures can lead to winterkill (Section 3.6). Particularly thick snow covers and cold temperatures can develop into life-threating situations for livestock under nomadic and semi-nomadic conditions (Section 7.6).

Snow Damage to Forests
Freezing conditions in early and late winter months can induce physiological damage such as cold injuries to young branches and leaves, while unusually wet and heavy snow can cause structural damage to trees through bending and breakages of branches, crowns and stems as well as uprooting. Stem breakage is the most common snow damage, particularly for mature stands, and is a function of diameter and height as well as wood density and root anchorage strength. While damage depends on the type of snow, topography, stand density and age profile, coniferous trees typically suffer damage from snow loads of above $50\,kg\,m^{-2}$ while deciduous trees show damage at $25\,kg\,m^{-2}$.

The 2008 China Snow Disaster
Snow storms of various severities occur almost every year in the pastoral areas of China and especially in northern and north-eastern provinces. On rare occasions, severe snow storms that occur over central and southern provinces lead to large-scale disruptions and damage, as during the 2008 snow disaster.

[42] Dyer, J.L. and Mote, T.L., 2006: Spatial variability and trends in observed snow depth over North America. *Geophys. Res. Lett.*, 33, 6.
[43] Deems, J.S., Painter, T.H. and Finnegan, D.C., 2013: Lidar measurement of snow depth: A review. *J. Glaciol.*, 59(215), 467–79.
[44] Gutmann, E.D., Larson, K.M., Williams, M.W. et al., 2011: Snow measurement by GPS interferometric reflectometry: An evaluation at Niwot Ridge, Colorado. *Hydrol. Process.*, 26(19), 2951–61.

Development of the Disaster

From 10 January to 2 February 2008, a total of five snow weather systems impacted most of China, but particularly southern China. These events were unique through (i) 20 provinces affected with 10–20 frost days in central China, (ii) long duration, with average temperatures well below 1°C in central China, which was last observed in 1955, (iii) highest rainfall amounts since 1951 in central and western China, and (iv) record snow depths of 30–50 cm in Anhui and Jiangsu, with 90% of southern China covered in snow.[45] Overall, the return period of the events is estimated at 50 years (100 years in some areas). The direct economic losses reached US$24 billion, which was close to 0.8% of China's 2007 GDP and was the largest loss since the devastating floods of 1998 that caused US$33 billion in losses. Agriculture was one of the most affected sectors.

Damage to Agriculture

Over 11.8 million ha of crop areas were affected, of which 1.7 million ha incurred total losses in southern, central and eastern China. While winter wheat was fully dormant in north and west China and was not impacted, rapeseed grown over the winter months in the central and southern provinces were most affected through snow pressure and cold temperatures. Snow pressure damaged greenhouses and nurseries, which provide fresh vegetables to the main cities during the winter. As a result, vegetable prices increased by up to 300% in some markets due to lower supplies. A total of 69 million head of livestock perished, including 14 million poultry (snow pressure on houses and low temperatures) and 386 000 pigs (cold temperatures and delays in feed supplies). Heavy snow and freezing temperatures clogged transportation lines, causing delays in deliveries, and increased prices for meat, eggs and cooking oil at a time when demand was highest due to the Chinese Lunar New Year (celebrated in early February). Over 9300 km^2 of fish farms were damaged in 13 provinces in southern China.

Damage to Forests

More than 20 million ha of state-owned forest farms and natural woodlands were severely damaged, affecting 10% of the forest areas, with 3 million ha of destruction. The provinces of Hunan, Jiangxi, Yunnan, Hubei and Guangxi suffered the highest losses, with Masson's pine, Chinese fir and bamboo being the most affected tree species. In terms of destroyed forestland in Hunan, Yunnan, Guangdong, Sichuan and Guangxi, 28% showed severe losses (>60% damaged), 35% moderate losses (31–60%) and 36% low loss extents (10–30%).[46] Damage resulted mainly from stem breakage, stem bending, branch breakage, snapping, and uprooting. Losses under forestry insurance programmes were minimal as the scheme grew to current levels only in 2010. While damage from snow pressure is excluded in northern China, where snow storms frequently occur, it is insured in central and southern China under current policies.

---

[45] Wen, M., Yang, S., Kumar, A. and Zhang, P., 2009: An analysis of the large-scale climate anomalies associated with the snowstorms affecting China in January 2008. *Mon. Wea. Rev.*, 137, 1111–31.

[46] Forest Resources Management Department, 2008: Assessment Report of Forest Resources Loss Due to the 2008 Ice Storm and the 2008 Sichuan Earthquake. Beijing, 129p.

SNOW MODELS

Snow cover modelling relies on indicators such as air temperature, humidity, precipitation (amount and type), short-and long-wave radiation from satellites as well as wind speed and direction. Models of different complexities such as SnowFrost[47] and snowMAUS[48] have been developed to (i) relate snow accumulation and densification of snow covers and snow melt, and (ii) link freeze and thawing processes in the soil with weather parameters. Mechanistic crop models (Section 4.4) do not differentiate between solid and liquid precipitation, and winter soil moisture, and therefore do not consider snow cover effects on plant growth.

EXAMPLES OF OPEN SOURCE SNOW COVER DATA

Several research laboratories provide snow cover data that are assimilated from ground measurements, satellite data and/or numerical weather forecast models.

- *National Snowfall Analysis* from NOAA's National Operational Hydrologic Remote Sensing Center provides snow accumulations for 24, 48 and 72 hours for the USA since 2003 until near real time on a 1 km resolution.
  http://www.nohrsc.noaa.gov/snowfall_v2
- *Snow Cover Product (MODIS)* provides fractional snow cover data and snow albedos at resolutions between 500 m to 0.25° and from days to months since 2000.
  https://nsidc.org/data/mod10a1
- *MEaSUREs* from NASA's National Snow and Ice Data Center provides daily snow cover information on a 25 km grid for the northern hemisphere from 1999 to 2012.
  http://nsidc.org/data
- *Snow Cover Extent* from Rutgers University provides weekly and monthly snow cover extents for the northern hemisphere since 1966 at a resolution of 190.5 km.
  https://climatedataguide.ucar.edu/climate-data/snow-cover-extent-northern-hemisphere-climate-data-record-rutgers

3.8 CYCLONES

Cyclones, and particularly tropical cyclones (hurricanes, typhoons and cyclonic storms), cause large-scale damage to infrastructure through high wind speeds, flooding and storm surge. Large-scale losses have been reported to forest stands from both tropical and extratropical cyclones, leading to long-lasting effects in timber markets. Crops are vulnerable to high wind speed and flooding, with high losses in countries that are prone to impacts of tropical cyclones. High wind speeds and storm surge can

---

[47] Thorsen, S.M. and Haugen, L.E., 2007: Development of the SnowFrost model for the simulation of snow fall and soil frost. *Bioforsk Fokus*, 2(9), 23.
[48] Trnka, M., Kocmánková, E., Balek, J. et al., 2010: Simple snow cover model for agrometeorological applications. *Agric. For. Meteorol.*, 150(7), 1115–27.

lead to physical damage to aquaculture infrastructure and disappearance of stock from overturned cages in offshore production systems.

TYPES OF CYCLONES

Depending on the geographical area of development and occurrence, low-pressure systems that develop into cyclones are categorised into extratropical and tropical cyclones.

Extratropical Cyclones

Extratropical cyclones form at mid-latitudes (generally between 30° and 60° latitude), with the primary source of energy from temperature differences between warm and cold air masses. An extratropical cyclone typically contains several storm fronts and strong winds that can exceed 64 knots h⁻¹. Extratropical storms that occur in summer are referred to as thunderstorms and can produce hail and tornadoes; storms in winter are called winter storms or blizzards, with strong wind, freezing temperatures and significant snowfall.

Tropical Cyclones

Tropical cyclones are intense storms of tropical origin, with strong winds, substantial rainfall and coastal storm surge. Tropical cyclones go through various stages of development, starting as a mass of thunderstorms that develops into a tropical disturbance, a tropical depression (sustained winds of 20–34 knots), a tropical storm (35–64 knots), to which a name is usually given, and finally a tropical cyclone (>64 knots).

Development Conditions
Environmental conditions for the formation of tropical cyclones include (i) warm ocean waters of at least 26.5°C, extending to at least 50 m depths, (ii) an atmosphere that is unstable to moist convection and allows thunderstorm formation through a transformation of heat in ocean waters, (iii) moist mid-troposphere layers, (iv) a minimum distance of 500 km from the equator to allow for a minimum amount of Coriolis force to provide near-gradient wind balance, (v) a near-surface atmospheric disturbance with sufficient spin, convergence and low-level inflow, and (vi) low vertical wind shears of below 10 m s⁻¹.[49] An average tropical cyclone is around 550 km in diameter and contains an area of broken clouds (eye) of 20–50 km diameter where air pressure is lowest. The clouds align in rain bands that swirl towards the eye and wrap themselves around the eye. The eyewall is a characteristic ring of intense thunderstorms that extends up to 15 km and where wind and rainfall are strongest, decreasing towards the outer parts of the storm system. Tropical cyclones often transform into extratropical cyclones at the end of their existence at mid latitudes.

    Tropical cyclones are known as (i) hurricanes in the North Atlantic Ocean, the Northeast Pacific Ocean east of the dateline, and the South Pacific Ocean, (ii) typhoons in the Northwest Pacific Ocean west of the dateline, (iii) tropical cyclones in the Southwest Pacific Ocean west of 160°E or the Southeast Indian Ocean east of 90°E, and (iv) cyclonic storms in the North and Southwest Indian Ocean.

---

[49] www.aoml.noaa.gov/hrd/tcfaq/A15.html (accessed December 2017).

Intensity Scales
Hurricane intensity and potential damage are measured through the Saffir–Simpson Scale. The scale includes (i) tropical storms with wind speeds of 39–73 miles h^{-1} with minor wind and water-related damages, (ii) Category 1 with wind speeds of 74–95 miles h^{-1} and damage to mobile homes and with some coastal flooding, (iii) Category 2 (96–110 miles h^{-1}) causing some damage to roofs of buildings and uprooted trees, (iv) Category 3 (111–129 miles h^{-1}) with some structural damage to residential and utility buildings and uprooting of larger trees, (v) Category 4 (130–156 miles h^{-1}) with roofs of buildings destroyed, inland flooding and some coastal erosion, and (vi) Category 5 (>157 miles h^{-1}) with large-scale damage destruction of buildings, extensive flooding and power outages.

CYCLONE LOSSES

Between 1980 and 2017, a total economic loss of US$785 billion was recorded for 899 tropical cyclones, with the 10 costliest events causing damage totalling US$486 billion (Table 3.7). Over the same time, 100 extratropical cyclones caused economic losses of US$65 billion, with US$46 billion from the 10 costliest events.

Super Typhoon Haiyan in the Philippines
In 2013 the western north Pacific tropical cyclone season was very active, with four out of five typhoons of the highest intensity (category 5) worldwide occurring in this area. Super Typhoon Haiyan, also called Yolanda in the Philippines, developed into one of the strongest typhoons and with a maximum 1-minute wind speed of 315 km h^{-1} was the fourth highest ever observed with tropical cyclones. The maximum wind gust of Haiyan was 379 km h^{-1} and was very close to the highest ever measured gust of 408 km h^{-1} from Cyclone Olivia (1996).

Development of Super Typhoon Haiyan
Haiyan developed in Micronesia on 3 November 2013 and the storm system rapidly intensified from a tropical depression into a tropical storm following a west-north-westerly track. On 4 November it was named a typhoon and rapidly grew into category 5 within 36 hours. Warm waters with temperatures above 26°C with depths of over 100 m, low wind shear and favourable upper-level outflow conditions allowed the typhoon to remain at maximum intensity for a long time. Even after landfall in the central Philippines on 6 and 7 November, Haiyan kept its intensity at category 5 until 8 November, bringing maximum wind speeds of 300 km h^{-1} and sustained wind of 250 km h^{-1} to the Philippines, with high storm surge and torrential rainfall. The Philippine provinces of Eastern Samar, Samar and Leyte were most affected. Over the South China Sea, Haiyan followed a more northerly track and lost intensity, with the storm centre passing over Hainan island (China) until landfall occurred near Haiphong (northeast Vietnam) on 10 November. After landfall in Vietnam, Haiyan quickly weakened and transformed into a tropical depression on 11 November over southern China (Figure 3.4).

Impact on the Philippines
The Philippines were most impacted by Haiyan, with 16 million people affected, 4.1 million displaced and a death toll of 6300.[50] Economic losses were estimated at

---

[50] USAID, 2014: Philippines: Typhoon Yolanda/Haiyan. USAID Factsheet 22, 7p.

TABLE 3.7 Overview of the 10 costliest tropical cyclone and extratropical cyclone disasters, 1980–2017.

	Tropical cyclones				Extratropical cyclones		
Year	Country	Population Affected (Million)	Total Damage (US$ Million)	Year	Country	Population Affected (Million)	Total Damage (US$ Million)
2005	USA	0.83	157 530	1999	France	3.400	12 000
2017	USA	0.55	108 250	2016	USA	Unknown	10 000
2004	USA	5.07	53 063	2007	Germany	0.000	5 500
2012	USA	0.08	52 210	2010	France	0.500	4 230
2008	USA	2.30	38 540	2009	France	Unknown	3 200
1992	USA	0.30	31 500	2005	Sweden	Unknown	2 800
2004	Japan	0.33	15 144	1999	Denmark	Unknown	2 605
2013	Philippines	17.94	10 137	2016	Cuba	0.190	2 600
2013	China	9.64	10 106	2016	Haiti	2.100	2 000
1991	Japan	0.09	10 087	2009	Spain	Unknown	1 900
Total		37.13	486 567			6.190	46 835

Data source: EM-DAT, with the last update on 5 December 2017.

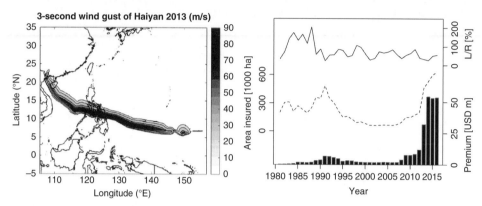

FIGURE 3.4   Left: Modelled three-second wind gusts of Super Typhoon Haiyan with different intensities (grey scales), 3–11 November 2013 over Asia. Right: Premium volumes (right axis, columns), loss ratios (right axis, solid line) and area insured (left axis, dotted line) for rice insured by the Philippine Crop Insurance Corporation (PCIC), 1981–2016.
Source: Swiss Re with permission (left plot) and data from PCIC Annual Reports (right plot).

US$14 billion, representing close to 5% of the country's economic output. Insured losses reached around US$1.5 billion, which was low considering the intensity of Haiyan and mainly was due to low insurance penetration in the poorer regions of central Philippines where the typhoon was most intense.

Typhoon Losses to Agriculture in the Philippines
In the Philippines around 32% of the land is dedicated to agricultural production and the sector contributes 15% to GDP while employing over a third of the labour force. Typhoons and droughts cause most damage to the agriculture sector and for rice alone reached over US$1.2 billion in 2007–2011. Haiyan caused a US$225 million loss to agriculture, including US$110 million for rice, corn and high-value crops such as coconut, banana, cassava, mangos and vegetables. As a result of lower rice production in the typhoon-affected regions, rice imports increased by 20% to 1.2 million tons in 2013. Aquaculture infrastructure, including oyster rafts, crab, shrimp and mussel farms, inland tilapia cages, hatcheries and fish ponds, was severely damaged by Haiyan. As agricultural insurance has low penetration ratios, households impacted by typhoon Haiyan were forced to rely on disaster assistance from government funds and international assistance.

Crop Insurance in the Philippines
Frequent losses from natural disasters led the government to invest in risk mitigation and disaster financing. The government-owned Philippine Crop Insurance Corporation (PCIC) was established in 1978 to implement agricultural insurance with a focus on subsistence farmers. PCIC started offering crop insurance for rice and corn in 1981 and added livestock covers in 1988. Since 2005, PCIC has been providing cover for credit and life term risks for farmers and fishermen, adding aquaculture insurance in 2011. In 2016, PCIC's five main agricultural insurance products were rice, corn, high-value commercial crops, livestock and fisheries.

For distribution, PCIC relies mainly on the Land Bank of the Philippines (LBP), the main provider of formal credit for rice and corn production, where agricultural insurance is bundled with credits. The government made crop insurance compulsory for borrowing rice farmers and the success of agricultural insurance is highly dependent on the issued loan amounts, particularly through LBP. Government premium subsidies vary per type of insurance and reach 48–63% for rice, with lending institutions such as LBP contributing premium subsidies for rice of 16–21%. Crop insurance applies per farm and is based on yield (MPCI) – premium rates vary per location, insured perils, product and the level of borrowing, e.g. for premium rates for rice range from 1.46% to 5.9% (borrowing farmers) and from 4.46% to 5.9% (non-borrowing farmers) at coverage levels of 90%.

To increase insurance with smallholders and fishermen, the government created the Registry System for Basic Sectors in Agriculture (RSBSA) in 2012, which is a comprehensive database on household income levels of subsistence farmers. A separate crop insurance programme was developed for RSBSA farmers, with government premium subsidies of 100% of premium. PCIC is currently the only insurer that benefits from government premium subsidies. RSBSA insurance is intended as a welfare insurance programme and its sustainability has been challenged in political debates.

Performance of PCIC

In 2016, PCIC produced a premium volume of US$53.7 million, with rice contributing 61%, corn 22%, high-value crops and livestock each 8% and other products, including credit insurance, 2%. The average weighted loss ratio of PCIC amounts to 52.2% (1981–2016), which has been driven by larger premium volumes and good underwriting results in recent years (Figure 3.4). Yet the insured area and insurance penetration ratios for rice and corn are below 10% despite the implementation of RSBSA. To overcome the high costs related to MPCI coverage, several pilot insurance programmes were established, including weather and area-yield index insurance.

Cyclone Damage to Agriculture

Agricultural assets are highly vulnerable to tropical cyclones and countries prone to landfalls frequently record damages. Extratropical storms have caused extensive damage to forest stands.

Damage to Crops

Crops are among the most vulnerable to strong wind from extratropical storms, tropical depressions, tropical storms and tropical cyclones. Depending on the intensity of wind gusts, damage to crops includes defoliation, leaf tearing and shredding, stem breakage, stem bruising and wounding to different extents. Stem breakage leads to high losses and can cause additional damage through sunburn. Horticulture crops typically experience losses of flowers and fruits as well as fruit bruising and wounding, which all lead to a reduction in quantity and/or quality (downgrades and unmarketable fruits). Recovery of storm-damaged crops depends on the crop type, the extent of defoliation and the ability of damaged plants to develop new leaves, the growth stage when damage occurred, and the prevalence of diseases and weather conditions that generally determine growth and outbreak of bacterial diseases. Increasingly, tropical cyclone models are used to understand the vulnerability of crops and to derive estimates of loss amounts.[51]

---

[51] Tillman, C.W., Sivillo, J.K. and Frolov, S.A., 2010: Managing typhoon related crop risk at WPC. *Agric. Agric. Sci. Procedia*, 1, 204–11.

Damage to Forests

Wind damage to tree stands is typically a function of the tree species and stand height, particularly the relationship between diameter and height, stand density, crown length, topography, soil structures and soil moisture content.[52]

In Europe, storms cause on average 51% of the damaged timber in Europe (1950–2010), with an annual loss of 0.12% of the standing timber, which is equivalent to 38 million m³ or the annual felling of timber in Poland.[53] In 1999, winter storms Lothar and Martin caused over 190 m³ of damaged timber, with an overall loss amount of US$6 billion, and a series of snowstorms caused losses of US$8.4 billion to China's forestry sector in 2008 (Table 3.8). Following large-scale disturbances, an oversupply of timber typically leads to decreasing prices, e.g. winter storm Lothar (1999) caused a 25% price decrease of Norway spruce saw logs in Germany. In Europe, the extent of damage caused by extratropical cyclones to forests is now 3–4 times larger than in the time between the 1950s and the 1970s.[54]

TABLE 3.8 Overview of recent severe winter storms with large losses to forests.

			Forestry Loss		Overall Loss	
Country	Year	Storm	Damage[a] (Mm³)	Loss Amount (US$ Million)	Total Damage (US$ Million)	Insured Loss (US$ Million)
France, Spain, Italy	2009	Klaus	44	700–1000	5100	3000
China (central and southern provinces)	2008	Winter (ice) storms	340	8400	24000	278
UK, Germany, France, Benelux	2007	Kyrill	49	1000	10000	5800
Scandinavia, Baltic	2005	Erwin (Gudrun)	83	2300–3500	6000	2600
Central Europe, France	1999	Lothar and Martin	190	6000	11500	6200
UK, Scandinavia, Baltic	1999	Anatol	8	*Unknown*	3100	2400

[a] Reported in million cubic meters (Mm³).

---

[52] Hanewinkel, M., Hummel, S. and Albrecht, A., 2011: Assessing natural hazards in forestry for risk management: A review. *Eur. J. Forest Res.*, 130, 329–51.

[53] Gardiner, B., Schuck, A., Schelhaas, M.-J. et al., 2013: Living with Storm Damage to Forests. European Forest Institute, Joensuu, 132p.

[54] Gregow, H., Laaksonen, A. and Alper, M.E., 2017: Increasing large scale windstorm damage in Western, Central and Northern European forests, 1951–2010. *Sci. Rep.*, 7, 7p.

TROPICAL CYCLONE MODELS

The basis of tropical cyclone models for risk analysis and early warning are wind and pressure measurements by weather stations, reconnaissance aircraft flights, dropsondes and satellite as well as radar observations.

Air Pressure Models

Most pressure-wind models derive the maximum wind of a cyclone (v_m) from the change of pressure from the minimum pressure (eye) as a function of distance as:

$$v_m = a\left(p_n - p_c\right)^x$$

with $p_n - p_c$ as the pressure drop from an external pressure (p_n) to the minimum central pressure (p_c) and with a and x as empirical constants. The Atkinson–Holiday model uses empirical values of $a = 3.4$, $p_n = 1010\,hPa$ and $x = 0.644$ to determine v_m as:

$$v_m = 3.4\left(1010 - p_c\right)^{0.644}$$

An extension to the Atkinson–Holiday model, known as the Holland Formula, includes the addition of the parameter b which allows variations in the degree of the pressure gradient near the maximum winds to determine v_m as:[55]

$$v_m = \left(\frac{b}{\rho e}\Delta p\right)^{0.5}$$

with ρ as the surface air density $(kg\,m^{-3})$, Δp as the drop in the pressure relative to the minimum central pressure and e as the natural logarithm. The Holland Formula has seen some further additions and modifications and has become the standard to derive wind fields for hurricanes.

Models Using Satellite Imagery

The Dvorak pressure-wind model uses visible and infrared satellite imagery to determine the hurricane centre, evaluate the cloud structure and create an estimate of intensity.[56] Based on a large collection of measurements from historical hurricanes, a statistical model was developed and subsequently updated based on wind speeds that are a function of return periods from track and intensity simulations based on the Holland Formula and a function that describes the decay of the hurricane after landfall.[57] These models allow the development of hazard maps for areas and points along coastal regions and include estimates of uncertainties in wind speeds that were obtained by propagating the

---

[55] Holland, G., 2008: A Revised Hurricane Pressure–Wind Model. *Mon. Wea. Rev.*, 136, 3432–45.
[56] Velden, C., Harper, B., Wells, F. et al., 2006: The Dvorak tropical cyclone intensity estimation technique: A satellite-based method that has endured for over 30 years. *B. Am. Meteorol. Soc.*, 87(9), 1195–210.
[57] Vickery, P.J., Wadhera, D., Twisdale, L.A. and Lavelle, F., 2009: US hurricane wind speed risk and uncertainty. *J. Struct. Eng.*, 135(3), 301–20.

uncertainties in the input parameters that drive wind speed modelling (mainly central pressure and the parameter b in the Holland Formula). The models were refined in modelling boundary layer air movement (low-level jet streams) that has an influence on the propagation of the hurricane and topographic features (roughness) at landfall.

WINDSTORM MODELS FOR FORESTRY

Based on tree vulnerability to wind speed from wind tunnel experiments using aerodynamical properties of tree canopies and airflows as a function of tree species, height and soil properties, mechanistic models such as HWIND[58] and ForestGales[59] have been developed. Mechanistic models use physical processes that lead to stem breakage and uprooting from critical wind speeds in combination with meteorological parameters (wind speed and airflow modelling). A key equation in mechanistic forest models is the mean wind force on trees $F(z)$, which is defined through[60]

$$F(z) = 0.5 \times C_d \times \rho \times U(z)^2 \times A(z)$$

with z the height of the stem, $U(z)$ the mean wind speed (m s^{-1}) and $A(z)$ the area of the tree projected against the wind (m^2), C_d as a drag coefficient and ρ the air density (kg m^{-3}). To determine the overall wind damage to a forest stand, assumptions are taken on the average stand height and tree species.

Mechanistic wind models first calculate the above-canopy wind speed (CWS) required to break or uproot trees as a function of resistive forces of the roots and stems and soil type, soil moisture, stem diameter and height. In a second phase, wind climatologies are used to determine the probability of CWS at a given location through statistical approaches and airflow modelling and outputs of numerical weather prediction models.[61] Analytical models use logistic regression analyses to derive wind damage as a function of tree height, tree species, height/diameter ratios and site-specific conditions based on large inventory data and historical storm events that caused damage to entire forests.[62] Several studies have shown reasonably good correspondences between observed storm damage to forest stands and modelled damaged with mechanistic models.[63]

---

[58] Peltola, H., Kellomäki, S., Väisänen, H. and Ikonen, V.P., 1999: A mechanistic model for assessing the risk of wind and snow damage to single trees and stands of Scots pine, Norway Spruce and birch. *Can. J. For. Res.*, 29, 647–61.

[59] Gardiner, B. and Quine, C., 2000: Management of forests to reduce the risk of abiotic damage – a review with particular reference to the effects of strong winds. *For. Ecol. Manag.*, 135, 261–77.

[60] Päätalo, M.J., Peltola, H. and Kellomäki, S., 1999: Modelling the risk of snow damage to forests under short-term snow loading. *For. Ecol. Manag.*, 116, 51–70.

[61] Gardiner, B., Byrne, K., Hale, S., et al., 2008: A review of mechanistic modelling of wind damage risk to forests. *Forestry*, 81, 447–61.

[62] Schütz, J.P., Götz, M., Schmid, W. and Mandallaz, D., 2006: Vulnerability of spruce *(Picea abies)* and beech *(Fagus sylvatica)* forest stands to storms and consequences for silviculture. *Eur. J. For. Re*, 125, 291–302.

[63] Hale, S.E., Gardiner, B., Peace, A.J. and Pizzirani, S., 2015: Comparison and validation of three versions of a forest wind risk model. *Environ. Modell. Softw.*, 69, 27–41.

EXAMPLES OF OPEN SOURCE TROPICAL CYCLONE TRACK DATA

Several meteorological agencies and hurricane centres publish tropical cyclone tracks in real time and contain extensive archives of historical cyclones. Cyclone tracks can vary for the same storm according to the source and the cyclone track forecasting system that has been used to generate the track.

- *HURricane DATabase (HURDAT)* from NOAA's National Hurricane Center provides a large number of datasets including maximum sustained surface wind, minimum pressure and radii of different wind strengths for hurricanes in the Atlantic basin since 1851.
  http://www.aoml.noaa.gov/hrd/data_sub/re_anal.html
- *Best Track Data* from the Japan Meteorological Agency (JMA) provides track data for tropical cyclones in the western North Pacific and the South China Sea since 1951.
  http://www.jma.go.jp/jma/jma-eng/jma-center/rsmc-hp-pub-eg/RSMC_HP.htm
- *UNISYS* lists and maps tracks of historical hurricanes from HURDAT and other sources, including the Joint Typhoon Warning Center (JTWC) for the Atlantic (since 1995), the East Pacific (1997), the West Pacific (1996), the South Pacific (2000) and South Indian (2000) as well as North Indian territories (2000).
  http://weather.unisys.com/hurricanes/search
- *International Best Track Archive for Climate Stewardship (IBTrACS)* is a recent initiative that consolidates global tropical cyclone track data from 12 different sources in a centralised location.
  https://www.ncdc.noaa.gov/ibtracs/index.php

3.9 WILDFIRES

Wildfires have caused significant damage to infrastructure, urban–wildland interfaces and forest areas, with both short- and long-term consequences. Increasing costs to suppress particularly large wildfires are a concern to many government agencies; possible impacts of climate change can lead to increased fire activity as fire seasons are prolonged and the distribution of rainfall and snow covers could be more extreme. The use of remote sensing supports early fire detection and wildfire models support near real-time estimations of areas impacted by a spreading wildfire and the evacuation of affected populations in high-danger zones.

DEFINITION AND CAUSE OF WILDFIRES

A wildfire is an unplanned and uncontrolled fire in wildland or brushland, which regardless of the source of ignition may require suppression or other responses. Wildfires can ignite by (i) natural causes, which are mostly lightning during dry thunderstorms, or (ii) human causes related to negligence (e.g. open fire cooking, accidents with fire spreads into wildland) or intention through arson. Key conditions that favour the development of large wildfires include (i) rainfall deficit and high temperatures, as typically experienced during heatwaves and droughts, (ii) low moisture levels in the soil as a result of deficit rainfall and/or reduced snowpack in winter, (iii) high wind, which favours the propagation of fires, iv) topography, with fires spreading fastest uphill, and

(vi) dry vegetation (fuel load), with trees that contain oily sap (e.g. eucalyptus) being particularly conductive for fires. Forest management strategies (e.g. fire gaps), the status and management of the urban–wildland interface as well as early warning system and response plans are important factors that define wildfire spread.

Wildfire Indices

Due to the importance of meteorological conditions for the onset and propagation of wildfires, Fire Weather Indices (FWI) have been developed to forecast periods of high wildfire activities. The FWI of the Canadian Forest Service is one of the most used indices and contains (i) three components that represent daily changes in moisture contents of three classes of forest fuel with different drying rates, and (ii) three components related to fire behaviour representing the rate of spread, fuel weight consumed and fire intensity, with temperature, relative humidity, wind speed and rainfall during the previous 24 hours as key parameters.[64] Government contingency plans relate to FWI where with an FWI above a certain severity level, additional resources and equipment are mobilised and stationed in an area that shows a high FWI.

WILDFIRE LOSSES

Wildfires can cause significant direct losses through burning of infrastructure and forest areas as well as indirect losses through river silting. Between 1980 and 2017, 283 reported wildfire events caused a global economic loss of US$65 billion, with the 10 costliest events amounting to US$33 billion in damages; the 1997 wildfires in Indonesia caused the highest damage at US$8 billion.[65] 2017 was a high wildfire activity year in many countries – large areas were burnt in Canada (e.g. British Columbia with 855 000 ha), the USA, with over 3.2 million ha burnt (particularly in Oregon, Washington and California), Chile (601 000 ha) and Portugal (520 000 ha).

Wildfire Damage to Forests

Among all agricultural assets, timber plantations and natural woodlands are most affected by wildfires. Vulnerability of a forest to fire depends on the combustibility, distribution and availability of alive biomass (foliage, lichen, shrubs) and dead biomass (including litter and humus), which determines the spread velocity of a fire through a forest. A permanent presence of easily ignitable fuel in the vertical direction (tall shrubs, dead branches and lichens) supports a ground fire to develop into a crown fire. Generally, coniferous species burn more easily than broadleaved species. The fire management approach in timber plantations (e.g. fuel management, fire watching towers, fire gaps) has a significant impact on the potential ignition of a fire, its development and its containment. Annual areas burnt typically differ in function of climate, tree stand compositions, fire management standards and fire prevention measures and range in Europe from 0.001% (Baltics) to 0.8% (Spain), in Latin America from 0.09% (Uruguay) to 1.2% (parts of Chile), from 0.05% to 0.3% in North America, from 0.01% to 1.2% in China, and average around 0.09% in New Zealand and 0.4% in

---

[64] Van Wagner, C.E., 1987: Development and Structure of a Canadian Forest Fire Weather Index System. Canadian Forestry Service Technical Report 35, Ottawa, 48p.
[65] Based on wildfire damage data of EM-DAT: *The Emergency Events Database, Université Catholique de Louvain.*

TABLE 3.9 Overview of some of the most severe wildfires that caused large losses to forests.

			Forestry Loss		Overall Loss	
Country	Year	Fire	Damaged Area (Ha)	Loss Amount (US$ Million)	Total Loss Amount (US$ Million)	Insured Loss (US$ Million)
Australia	2009	Black Saturday bushfire	400 000	*Unknown*	3500	930
USA (Georgia)	2007	Wildfire	228 000	65	*Unknown*	*Unknown*
Australia	2003	Canberra bushfires	10 000	50	234	200
China	1987	Black Dragon fire	1 900 000	700	*Unknown*	*Unknown*
Australia	1983	Ash Wednesday fires	400 000	400	*Unknown*	*Unknown*
Australia	1939	Black Friday fires	2 000 000	750	*Unknown*	*Unknown*

Australia. In southern Europe (including Portugal, Spain, France, Italy and Greece), wildfires destroy an annual surface of 445 000 ha with an average number of 48 000 individual fires (1980–2016).[66]

Wildfires have the potential to cause losses of US$1 billion to forests, as experienced in Australia and China (Table 3.9). In the USA, the annualised losses from wildfires are estimated to be between US$63.5 billion and US$285 billion, with annualised costs in the range of US$7.6 billion to US$62.8 billion.[67] Under climate projections, future wildfire potential has been found to increase significantly in the USA, South America, Central Asia, southern Europe, southern Africa and Australia and will require increased resources and management efforts for disaster prevention and recovery.[68]

WILDFIRE MODELS

Research on fire occurrence forms the basis for quantifying spatial and temporal factors that cause wildfire ignitions as a function of location and time.[69] Remote sensing technology, such as infrared and visual satellite images, largely supports the detection of wildfires (hot spots) and monitoring of propagation, based on which burnt areas are established after a wildfire (Section 4.3).

---

[66] European Commission, 2017: Forest Fires in Europe, Middle East and North Africa 2016. JRC report, 126p.

[67] Thomas, D., Butry, D., Gilbert, S. et al., 2017: The Costs and Losses of Wildfires – A Literature Survey. NIST Special Publication 1215, 72p.

[68] Liu, Y., Stanturf, J. and Goodrick, S., 2010: Trends in global wildfire potential in a changing climate. *For. Ecol. Manag.*, 259, 685–97.

[69] Plucinksi, M., 2012: A Review of Wildfire Occurrence Research. Report of the Bushfire Cooperative Research Centre, Australia. 28p.

Spatial and Temporal Fire Models

Spatial fire models describe the likelihood of ignition through natural causes (lightning) and human activity expressed in function of population density, distance to infrastructure (roads and towns) and accessibility to forests (risk of arson), land use and fire management standards. As the underlying mechanisms are fundamentally different, occurrence modelling is undertaken separately for lightning-triggered and human-induced fires. While lightning-ignited fires can smoulder for days and are detectable only above a certain size, fires caused by humans are rapidly detected and reported.

Temporal fire models assess the ignition frequency in a given area and at a given time (e.g. a day) based on meteorological parameters or FWI and the status of biomass (fuel). While burn probabilities for smaller fires (e.g. 0.1–5 ha) are similar to occurrence probabilities, large fires are far less frequent and require fire spread models to derive burn probabilities through simulations of fire behaviour.[70]

Statistical Fire Models

A statistical fire spread model involves the estimation of the probability of large fire ignition at a given time from historical relationships between weather patterns and large fires and the simulation of ignitions in function of fuel, weather and topography. Catastrophe risk modelling firms have been developing statistical wildfire models that include probabilistic features based on simulated weather patterns for different building classes. Such models are mainly available in markets such as the USA, Canada and Australia that frequently incur high economical and insured losses from wildfires.

Physical Fire Models

Physical (or mechanistic) fire spread models such as FarSite[71] and Prometheus[72] assume spreading of a fire through an elliptical region or a vector wave front and include surface and crown fire spreading rates. Combining the FarSite or LANDFIRE data layers that include data such as crown base height and bulk density, current weather projections, historical weather patterns, fuel moisture classifications, fire history, wind speed and direction. Fire effect models are used to simulate fuel management in terms of dynamics, tree mortality, carbon and soil as well as other ecosystem services. Physical forest fire models are operated by research and forest management departments for the purpose of tactical and strategic planning of fire risks.

EXAMPLES OF OPEN SOURCE WILDFIRE DATA

Wildfire monitoring centres and environmental agencies provide data on historical as well as developing wildfires, but the type, resolution and format of historical wildfires vary largely.

---

[70] Preisler, H.K. and Weise, D.R., 2013: Forest Fire Models. Encyclopedia of Environmetrics. 2nd edition. Wiley, Hoboken, NJ, 7p.

[71] http://www.firelab.org/project/farsite (accessed November 2017).

[72] https://www.firegrowthmodel.ca/prometheus/overview_e.php (accessed November 2017).

- *Global Fire Monitoring Center (GFMC)* monitors wildfires globally and provides early warnings, fire management advisory, data including burnt area globally (based on MODIS 1 km data, 2000–2007) and links to statistical databases. http://gfmc.online/
- *Earthdata* from NASA provides downloadable georeferenced products of active fires (last seven days) and past fires from MODIS at 1 km (since 2000) and 500 m (2000–2013) and VIRIS at 375 m (since 2012). https://earthdata.nasa.gov/earth-observation-data/near-real-time/firms/active-fire-data
- *LANDFIRE* from the US Forest Service produces geospatial data products that describe existing vegetation composition and structure, surface and canopy fuel characteristics, historical fire regimes/conditions on a 30 m resolution for the USA since 1999. www.landfire.gov
- *Federal Fire Occurrence Website* contains over 599 000 wildfire occurrences (geo-referenced polygons and fire points) for the USA that have been compiled by federal land management agencies since 1980. https:/wildfire.cr.usgs.gov/firehistory/data.html
- *Canadian Wildland Fire Information System* provides georeferenced (polygons) historical wildfires, ignition points and fire perimeters since 2004. http://cwfis.cfs.nrcan.gc.ca/ha/nfdb
- *Copernicus Emergency Management Service* provides for Europe access to hotspot data and area burnt analyses from MODIS (1 km) and VIIRS (375 m); the fire history product provides online mapping of area burnt and number of fires since 1980 at different geographical resolutions. http://effis.jrc.ec.europa.eu/applications/data-and-services

3.10 EPIDEMIC LIVESTOCK DISEASES

Outbreaks of epidemic livestock diseases can affect multiple livestock types and may cause large economic losses to livestock producers, export markets and the society. Epidemic livestock diseases are often classified into those with (i) low externalities which are moderately infectious (e.g. brucellosis, bovine tuberculosis) and require limited public involvement, and (ii) high externalities which are highly infectious (e.g. foot and mouth disease, avian influenza) and are notifiable under national and international regulations and require substantial government involvement and disaster risk financing strategies. While some diseases are eradicated in high-income countries (disease-free status), they remain endemic in many low- and middle-income countries. With global trade in livestock products increasing, the risk of re-infection in countries with a disease-free status grows accordingly.

GOVERNMENT RESPONSE TO EPIDEMIC DISEASES

National veterinary services require adapted legislation as well as the necessary human and financial resources to control and prevent outbreaks and re-emergences of livestock diseases through early detection (surveillance through field services and sample diagnostics), rapid response and timely information dissemination. Animal health is controlled at borders and ports and import bans are imposed in function of the animal health status of the exporting country following disseminated information of international organisations such as the World Organisation for Animal Health (OIE). Traceability of animals within the livestock supply chain and certification of disease-free livestock herds are fundamental measures to monitor the domestic livestock population. Veterinary services and animal health laboratories provide the framework for identifying and diagnosing livestock diseases.

Biosecurity plans and monitoring the movement of animals and animal products are essential to control and prevent outbreaks of epidemic livestock diseases. Diseases that spread rapidly across borders can impact several countries and require regional or international cooperation for transboundary animal diseases (TADs).[73]

Biosecurity Plans and Disease Response

Biosecurity plans vary among countries with a disease-free status (without vaccinations) like most high-income countries and countries with endemic diseases that typically include low- and some middle-income countries. Biosecurity plans typically include preventative culling, movement restrictions on livestock, emergency and preventative vaccinations, and some form of government compensation for direct losses. In general, culling programmes are used when no vaccine is available or known, the disease has reached a low level of incidence following other forms of control, and a country wants to maintain its access to export markets that require certification of being disease-free without vaccination.

Preventative Culling
High-income countries often follow preventative culling to contain the disease by removing susceptible herds within a certain radius (ring culling) of infected farms and infection probability. Government biosecurity plans include responses and mitigation measures that are a function of the distance between a given farm and a farm with a confirmed infection and include different zones as (i) infected zone (a 500 m radius of the infection), where livestock is culled and the premises are disinfected, (ii) buffer zone (within 3 km), with no movement of livestock (standstill) and emergency vaccinations, and (iii) surveillance zone (within 10 km), with restricted livestock movement to an approved slaughterhouse within the same zone.[74]

Vaccination Programmes
Vaccinations are a preventative measure and are often used to control diseases, particularly in countries where the disease is present in the livestock population (endemic disease). However, preventative vaccination does not lead to the eradication of the disease as vaccinated animals can still spread the disease.

---

[73] FAO, 2016: Economic Analysis of Animal Diseases. FAO Animal Production and Health Guidelines 18, Rome, 94p.
[74] OIE, 2018: Terrestrial Animal Health Code. Paris, 508p.

Government Compensation

For diseases with high externalities, biosecurity plans often include provisions to compensate livestock producers for direct losses that result from government-ordered slaughter (depopulation) due to epidemic diseases (Section 7.5). Government compensation schemes can additionally include payments of costs arising from the disposal of carcasses, the destruction of related products (e.g. feed, milk), emergency control measures (e.g. vaccinations), laboratory analytics, transportation and/or disinfection of facilities. Compensation is generally based on full market value or a certain percentage of market value, or is limited to a predefined amount per animal. Indirect losses including business interruption, movement restrictions and/or repopulation expenses are typically excluded from government compensation schemes but are covered in some markets by insurance programmes (Section 7.5).

International Monitoring of Diseases

As animal diseases are of global importance, and some diseases such as avian influenza and brucellosis have the potential to cause infection in humans (zoonotic diseases), the OIE was formed in 1924 to monitor animal diseases on a global scale. The OIE has 181 member countries and is responsible to (i) ensure transparency in the global animal disease situation where member countries report diseases, (ii) collect, analyse and disseminate veterinary scientific information through collaborating centres and reference laboratories, (iii) encourage international solidarity in the control of animal diseases, (iv) safeguard world trade by publishing health standards for international trade in animals and animal products, (v) improve the legal framework and resources of national veterinary services, and (vi) promote animal welfare through a science-based approach.

Disease Reporting and Sanitary Statuses

The OIE has developed a procedure for the official recognition of a country's sanitary status for six priority animal diseases: foot and mouth disease (FMD), contagious bovine pleuropneumonia, bovine spongiform encephalopathy (BSE), African horse sickness, peste des petits ruminants and classical swine fever. FMD is considered by far the most serious of all the six priority diseases as it affects several livestock types.

In 2017, the OIE listed 119 terrestrial and aquatic animal diseases of great importance for animal and public health (Table 3.10). It used to report diseases and infections under a List A and a List B, which were merged into a single list of notifiable terrestrial and aquatic animal diseases in 2006. The OIE standards are binding relative to international animal trade under the World Trade Organization (WTO) and guide national regulations on animal health and biosecurity plans to address outbreaks of epidemic diseases.

WAHIS and WAHIS-Wild

Given that 60% of the pathogens that affect humans are of animal origin, and 75% of emerging animal diseases can be transmitted to humans, the OIE developed the World Animal Health Information System (WAHIS), which connects all member countries and contains animal disease status data since 1996. The OIE has recently added WAHIS-Wild, which contains disease statuses of wild animals which have the potential to be reservoirs, hosts or victims of certain livestock diseases.

TABLE 3.10 Overview of some well-documented epidemic livestock disease outbreaks ranked by total damage.

Year	Country	Epidemic Disease	Impact	Total Damage (US$ Million)
2001	UK (with spread to other European countries)	FMD[a]	230 outbreaks, 12 million cows, cattle and sheep culled, 0.2% reduction in GDP	14 000
1997	Taiwan	FMD	4 million animals culled (mainly pigs), reduction in GDP by 0.28%	6 600
2013	China	Avian influenza	20 000 poultry culled	6 500
2015	USA	Avian influenza	48 million poultry culled, 80% increase in egg prices, import bans of 40 countries, 14% reduction in exports	3 300
2010/11	South Korea	FMD	3.4 million animals culled	2 780
1997	Netherlands	Classical swine fever	429 outbreaks, 7 million pigs culled	2 750
1990s	UK	BSE[b]	36 700 cases, 1.3 million cattle culled, import bans (30 months), 40% reduction in domestic beef sales and 25% reduction in domestic beef prices	1 545
2005	Brazil	FMD	Culling of 33 000 animals (mainly cattle), 156 000 animals vaccinated, import bans (mainly Russia as a key importer), 12% export price decrease	1 500
2003	Canada	BSE	Culling of 100 000 livestock, import ban by 40 countries	774[c]
2012	Mexico	Avian influenza	22 million poultry culled, temporary import bans	760
2010	Japan	FMD	290 000 animals culled	748
2001	Uruguay	FMD	20 000 animals culled	730
1983	USA	Avian influenza	17 million chickens culled	310
2004	Canada	Avian influenza	17 million poultry culled	300
2003	Netherlands	Avian influenza	30 million poultry culled	183[c]
2007	China	PRRS[d]	Over 2 million pigs infected, 400 000 pigs died, 100 million pigs vaccinated (1 million pigs died in 2006 from PRRS)	*Not available*

[a] Foot and mouth disease.
[b] Bovine spongiform encephalopathy (mad cow disease).
[c] Government spending only.
[d] Porcine reproductive and respiratory syndrome.

EPIDEMIC DISEASE LOSSES

Countries with a disease-free status experience the highest financial losses in case of an epidemic disease outbreak. For example, FMD outbreaks have caused losses of US$20 billion (1996–2011) in countries that were previously free of the disease, which is equivalent to 0.2–0.6% of GDP.[75]

The extent of economic losses from disease outbreaks is typically a function of (i) the location and size of the affected area, (ii) animal densities and species, (iii) the degree of mobility of affected animals and verticalisation of the production, and (iv) government contingency and biosecurity plans to contain and respond to the outbreak, particularly the duration between the initial outbreak and the response. Bioterrorism, which involves the intentional dissemination of biological agents through bacteria, viruses, fungi or toxins, is of increasing concern, particularly in the case of double agent pathogens (e.g. anthrax) which affect human and livestock populations.

Epidemic diseases cause direct and indirect losses, and while livestock producers are first impacted, losses gradually spread to the upstream and downstream livestock businesses, including processors, input suppliers and supporting industries (e.g. trading, transport). For example, direct losses caused by FMD include loss of milk production, lower weight gains, dead animals, lower fertility, changes in herd structures, and delay in sales of animals and products. Indirect losses of an FMD outbreak often include additional costs (e.g. vaccines, movement of livestock, diagnostic tests, culled animals) and loss of revenues (e.g. using sub-optimal breeds, denied access to domestic and international markets).[76] Depending on the type of disease and livestock affected, consumer attitudes can change dramatically, often leading to reduced domestic and international demand.

Reinfections are common, especially in smallholder livestock production systems (backyard farming) in low-income countries, where diagnostic capabilities and control programmes are less developed. Further, the proximity of small producers to larger-scale operations creates a potential for constant reinfection despite best efforts to manage and control diseases.

Large Historical Losses from Epidemic Diseases

FMD, BSE and avian influenza have caused some of the highest mortalities among livestock populations and some of the greatest economic losses (Table 3.10). Although FMD is rarely fatal for adult livestock, it causes large declines in milk production and very slow weight gains, and through fast transmission between a wide range of livestock species, it is considered to be the most serious infectious disease. One of the largest losses in recent times occurred in the 2001 FMD outbreak in the UK, with an economic loss of US$14 billion and 12 million culled livestock (Table 3.10).

---

[75] Knight-Jones, T.J.D. and Rushton, J., 2013: The economic impacts of foot and mouth disease – what are they, how big are they and where do they occur? *Prev. Vet. Med.*, 112(3), 161–73.
[76] Rushton, J., 2009: The Economics of Animal Health and Production. Cabi Publishing, Wallingford, p364.

EPIDEMIC DISEASE MODELS

Epidemic disease models have been developed for risk assessments of control measures, to support policy decisions during outbreaks, and to quantify economic and epidemiological impacts. Model development has focused on disease spread as a function of time and distance, with control functions applied for animal movements and disease control measures including quarantine, vaccination and destruction. FMD, classical swine fever, pseudorabies, avian influenza and Newcastle disease are the most modelled diseases at the scale of specific regions or countries. Empirical data from recent outbreaks including the 2011 UK FMD event have improved the models considerably. Model outputs include daily losses such as direct costs as a function of destruction and vaccination and indirect costs, as well as economic losses. Model results largely depend on user inputs that need to reflect the situation on the ground as closely as possible; even if all mechanisms are encoded, models remain limited on the available data and assumptions.

Key challenges of livestock disease modelling include the assessment of disease transmission rates, tracking animal movements, quantifying effects of disease control options and mapping wildlife populations as hosts of diseases.[77] Efforts have been made to provide open source disease spread models such as the Spatiotemporal Epidemiological Modeler[78] to support scientists and public health officials to better understand the risk and potential spread of emerging diseases.

Livestock State-Transition Models

The most widely used models are state-transition models such as the North American Animal Disease Spread Model[79] and AusSpread.[80] State-transition models are spatially explicit and stochastic in that a disease spread occurs between animal units (a group of animals with similar disease transmission ratios) at specified locations in function of distance.[81] With the occurrence of a disease within a unit, a state-transition model follows natural, predictable cycles over time through different disease states, unless it is altered by interventions such as disease controls.

Disease Stages
Without disease control, a susceptible unit becomes latent with infection, transitions to sub-clinically infectious to clinically infectious and to destruction or to a natural immune state are assumed, after which it will reach a susceptible state again. A stochastic process is used to simulate the duration of each disease stage for each unit and the spread is modelled through daily contacts as (i) direct contact where the disease spreads among animals and animal species per unit in function of distance, (ii) indirect

---

[77] Brooks-Pollock, E., de Jong, M.C.M., Keeling, M.J. et al., 2015: Eight challenges in modelling infectious livestock diseases. *Epidemics*, 10, 1–5.
[78] http://www.eclipse.org/stem (accessed December 2017).
[79] www.naadsm.org (accessed December 2017).
[80] www.agriculture.gov.au/animal/health/modelling/fmd (accessed December 2017).
[81] Harvey, N., Reeves, A., Schoenbaum, M.A. et al., 2007: The North American Animal Disease Spread Model: A simulation model to assist decision making in evaluating animal disease incursions. *Prev. Vet. Med.*, 82(3), 176–97.

contact through movement of people, equipment and/or animal products in sub-clinically and clinically infectious units, and (iii) airborne spread from quarantined units with sub-clinically and clinically infectious units. Empirical evidence shows that farms which are 0.5 km, 1 km and 1.5 km away from an FMD-infected farm have probabilities of 0.26, 0.06 and 0.02 of becoming infected, respectively.[82]

Infection Rates
The infection rate (*IR*) at which newly infected units are produced in the model is defined through

$$IR = \tau [SI] - \frac{p\beta SI}{N}$$

with *SI* as the number of locally connected, susceptible and infectious units, τ as the transmission rate across units, *p* as the proportion of long-range contacts and βSI as the random transmission of infection, with β as the transmission rate and *S* as the number of susceptible units, *I* the number of infectious units and *N* the total number of units. The speed of spread of the disease is further a function of the timing of disease detection and reporting to authorities. A disease control function is applied for (i) quarantine where after one day from an infection, the unit is quarantined, (ii) destruction through a maximum daily destruction rate, including the priority of destruction, and (iii) vaccination after a certain number of infected units occur, including maximum daily vaccination rates and priorities.

3.11 EPIDEMIC AQUACULTURE DISEASES

Outbreaks of epidemic diseases cause severe losses to the aquaculture industry and particularly large outbreaks can disrupt markets and local economies. Epidemic aquatic diseases transmit mainly through water, while high stock densities, the introduction of new species in aquaculture production systems and unrestricted movement of stock and equipment increase the risk of an outbreak. As with epidemic livestock diseases, some diseases that have national and international importance are notifiable under international regulations and governments have established biosecurity plans for epidemic diseases that affect aquaculture production.

TYPES OF EPIDEMIC DISEASES FOR AQUACULTURE

Wild stock supports infectious agents, which enter aquaculture farms through water inflows from surrounding waters, feed or infected broodstock. Aquatic diseases occur in the form of (i) metabolic diseases that result from improper feeding and malnutrition, (ii) stress-related diseases that occur through weak immune systems, and (iii) introduced diseases which can be highly contagious. While metabolic- and

---

[82] Ferguson, N.M., Donnelly, C.A. and Anderson, R.M., 2001: The foot-and-mouth epidemic in Great Britain: Pattern of spread and impact of interventions. *Science*, 292, 1155–60.

stress-related diseases are controlled through regular monitoring and adequate management practices, introduced diseases are generally beyond the control of aquaculture operators and lead to high stock mortality. New species in aquaculture farms are often not co-evolved with local infectious agents, which can lead to high and unpredictable losses.[83] Industry-wide losses from aquatic animal diseases are estimated to exceed US$6 billion annually.

To reduce the risk of disease outbreaks, the aquaculture industry has been investing in disease prevention, disease diagnostics and treatments including pesticides, antibiotics and vaccines. Vaccines for viruses and bacteria have been found particularly effective for finfish, which possess an adaptive immune response. Further, aquaculture operators have increased the use of frozen or dried feed to reduce feed-borne disease transmission. Separating wild-caught stock from cultured offspring and developing disease-resistant genetic stocks have further contributed to a reduction in disease outbreaks. The OIE provides standards for the reportable epidemic diseases that affect aquatic stocks to monitor different countries and limit the spread of aquatic diseases (Table 3.11).

EPIDEMIC DISEASE LOSSES

The white spot syndrome virus (WSSV), which affects crustaceans including shrimp, and infectious salmon anaemia (ISA) are two of the most important aquatic fish diseases that have affected the aquaculture industry in several countries (Table 3.12). With a loss of US$2 billion, the ISA events in Chile (2007–2010) caused one of the highest reported losses to the global aquaculture industry and it took several years for the Chilean salmon stock to recover.

White Spot Disease in Shrimp

Shrimps are among the seafoods most in demand and due to a drop in wild catches, the aquaculture industry started intensive farming in the 1980s, particularly in Thailand, China, India, Vietnam and Ecuador. Modern intensive shrimp farming uses large ponds, dry feeds, antibiotics and pumping aerator systems with high stock densities. Shrimp farms have frequently been impacted by infectious diseases such as WSSV, yellow-head virus, hepatopancreatic parvovirus, monodon baculovirus, Taura syndrome virus and infectious hypodermal and hematopoietic viruses, which are notifiable diseases under OIE standards (Table 3.11). It is estimated that 40% of tropical shrimp production is lost annually because of viral pathogens for which vaccination is not feasible and this will therefore limit future supplies.[84]

WSSV is one of the most damaging diseases in shrimp farming as the virus directly transmits and infects aquatic crustaceans including crabs, crayfish, lobsters and shrimp. WSSV owes its name to the white spots of 0.5–3.0 µm in diameter that are embedded in the exoskeleton of infected shrimp. WSSV transmits from wild shrimp that are captured for broodstock to intensive shrimp farming systems with high stock densities. Mortality ratio from WSSV easily reaches 100% within a week of infection, with rapid

[83] Lafferty, K.D., 2015: Infectious diseases affect marine fisheries and aquaculture economics. *Annu. Rev. Mar. Sci.*, 7, 471–96.
[84] Stentiford, G.D., Neil, D.M., Peeler, E.J. et al., 2017: Disease will limit future food supply from the global crustacean fishery and aquaculture sectors. *J. Invertebr. Pathol.*, 110, 141–57.

TABLE 3.11 Overview of diseases and infections of the OIE but excluding diseases for equine, lagomorphs (hares and rabbits), bees and amphibians.

Multiple species	Cattle	Sheep and goat	Swine	Avian	Fish	Mollusc	Crustacean
Anthrax	Bovine anaplasmosis	Caprine arthritis/encephalitis	African swine fever	Avian chlamydiosis	Epizootic haematopoietic necrosis disease	Abalone herpesvirus	Acute hepatopancreatic necrosis disease
Bluetongue	Bovine babesiosis	Contagious agalactia	Classical swine fever virus	Avian infectious bronchitis	Aphanomyces invadans (epizootic ulcerative syndrome)	Bonamia exitiosa	Crayfish plague
Crimean Congo haemorrhagic fever	Bovine genital campylobacteriosis	Contagious caprine pleuropneumonia	Taenia solium (Porcine cysticercosis)	Avian infectious laryngotracheitis	Gyrodactylus salaris	Bonamia ostreae	Yellow head virus
Epizootic haemorrhagic disease	Bovine spongiform encephalopathy (BSE)	Chlamydophila abortus	Nipah virus encephalitis	Avian mycoplasmosis	HPR-deleted or HPR0 infectious salmon anaemia virus	Marteilia refringens	Infectious hypodermal and haematopoietic necrosis
Equine encephalomyelitis (Eastern)	Bovine tuberculosis	Peste des petits ruminants virus	Porcine reproductive and respiratory syndrome	Avian mycoplasmosis	Salmonid alphavirus	Perkinsus marinus	Infectious myonecrosis
Heartwater	Bovine viral diarrhoea virus	Maedi-visna	Transmissible gastroenteritis	Duck virus hepatitis	Infectious haematopoietic necrosis	Perkinsus olseni	Necrotising hepatopancreatitis
Aujeszky's disease virus	Enzootic bovine leukosis	Nairobi sheep disease	African swine fever	Fowl typhoid	Koi herpesvirus disease	Xenohaliotis californiensis	Taura syndrome
Brucella abortus, Brucella melitensis and Brucella suis	Haemorrhagic septicaemia	Ovine epididymitis (Brucella ovis)		Avian influenza viruses	Red sea bream iridoviral disease		White spot disease

(Continued)

TABLE 3.11 (Continued)

Multiple species	Cattle	Sheep and goat	Swine	Avian	Fish	Mollusc	Crustacean
Echinococcus granulosus	Infectious bovine rhinotracheitis	Salmonellosis (S. abortusovis)		Influenza A viruses of high pathogenicity in birds other than poultry including wild birds	Spring viraemia of carp		White tail disease
Echinococcus multilocularis	Contagious bovine pleuropneumonia	Scrapie		Newcastle disease virus	Viral haemorrhagic septicaemia		
Foot and mouth disease virus	Lumpy skin disease	Sheep pox and goat pox		Infectious bursal disease (Gumboro disease)			
Rabies virus	Theileriosis			Pullorum disease			
Rift valley fever virus	Trichomonosis			Turkey rhinotracheitis			
Rinderpest virus	Trypanosomosis (tsetse-transmitted)						
Trichinella spp.							
Japanese encephalitis							
New & Old world screwworm							
Paratuberculosis							
Q fever							
Surra (Trypanosoma evansi)							
Tularemia							
West Nile fever							

Source: Adapted from OIE.

TABLE 3.12   Overview of some well-documented epidemic aquatic disease outbreaks.

Year	Country	Disease	Species	Total Damage (US$ Million)
2007–2010	Chile	ISA[a]	Salmon	2000
1997	Thailand	WSSV[b]	Shrimps	600
1995–1999	Malaysia	WSSV	Shrimps	400
2000	Ecuador	WSSV	Shrimps	400
1999	Ecuador	WSSV	Shrimps	280
1993	China	WSSV	Shrimp	250
1996	Thailand	WSSV	Shrimps	210
1994–1995	India	WSSV	Shrimps	120
2004–2005	Australia	Marteilia	Oysters	30
1998–1999	Scotland	ISA	Salmon	28
2003	Taiwan	Abalone disease	Abalones	11
1995	Bangladesh	WSSV	Shrimps	10

[a] Infectious salmon anaemia.
[b] White spot syndrome virus.
Source: Updated based on Alday (2010).

changes in water salinity and temperatures below 30°C being conductive for outbreaks. As vaccination of crustaceans is only partly effective and of short duration, frequent controls and immediate eradication remain the main response measures to WSSV.

White Spot Disease Outbreaks
WSSV was first reported in northern Taiwan in 1992 and spread globally within a decade. WSSV has been identified in crustaceans in China, Japan, South Korea, Southeast Asia, South Asia, the Indian Continent, the Mediterranean, the Middle East, Africa (Mozambique and Madagascar) and the Americas. WSSV outbreaks in Southeast Asia in 1992 caused an estimated loss of US$6 billion and shorter rotation cycles, where earthen ponds are used for seven years only, after which the ponds are contaminated and new ponds are established in mangrove forests, led to lower outbreaks but caused considerable degradation of coastal environments. In 1999, WSSV occurred in Ecuador where shrimp production decreased by 65% and caused losses of US$1 billion. The outbreaks in the 1990s changed shrimp farm management to using more closed systems, culturing shrimp larvae from resistant stocks, using more domestic stocks and reducing stress related to water salinity and temperature.

Infectious Salmon Anaemia
ISA is a serious viral disease of marine-farmed Atlantic salmon and causes paling of gills, liver swelling and internal haemorrhaging, which can lead to death. ISA can cause 90% mortality over several months. The first registered outbreak of ISA was in Norway in 1984 in Atlantic salmon juveniles; several countries have experienced outbreaks of the diseases and significant financial losses over past decades when salmon farming intensified in new territories.

ISA Outbreak in Chile

Over recent decades, Chile advanced to become the world's second largest salmon producer, with more than 500 production sites in operation today. While salmon production only reached 10 000 tons in 1991, it rapidly increased to 350 000 tons in 2005 and to 500 000 tons in 2015, worth US$3.8 billion. In 2007, Marine Harvest, the global leading salmon producer, reported the discovery of ISA at a salmon farm in Chile. ISA rapidly infected many salmon farms and caused economic losses of US$2 billion, with 20 000 jobs lost and around 400 000 tons of salmon destroyed. ISA-related mortality and culling led to a reduction in Atlantic salmon production in Chile of 33% in 2010 and 29% in terms of export value. It took several years for the country's salmon industry to recover.

The cause of the ISA outbreak in Chile is not entirely known but could have been from egg imports from Norway. The fast spread of ISA in Chile was related to several factors, including (i) high stock densities within distances of below 5 km between sites, (ii) high levels of sea lice that move among sites and can carry ISA, (iii) frequent movement of fish among sites and sharing of equipment such as nets, boats and barges among sites, (iv) weak biosecurity regulations, including imports of fish eggs, fallowing periods, disinfection procedures and zone management programmes, (v) inadequate diagnostic laboratory capacity to detect health issues in aquatic stock, and (vi) long lag times between the diagnosis of ISA and eliminating infected stock.[85] The control of ISA in Chile took over 3.5 years and was a joint effort between the aquaculture industry and the government. It led to (i) immediate measures, including mandatory testing of fish and broodstock samples every three months, mandatory reporting of ISA, biosecurity protocols with culling orders and surveillance areas and regular sea lice reporting, and (ii) longer-term measures through licences that are restricted to 25 years and zoning based on biological carrying capacity.

EPIDEMIC DISEASES MODELS

Modelling the spread of epidemic aquatic diseases is highly complex and follows the spatial-temporal approach (state-transition) models used for livestock diseases. Mechanistic epidemiological models have been developed to account for known, likely or potential transmission pathways between aquaculture farms with infection at stocking or being infected during the production process at different probabilities driven by external factors.[86] The distance of infected to non-infected but susceptible farms is an important factor that drives the spatial-temporal spread of a disease. Additionally, the stock density in aquaculture systems drives the probability of susceptible animals as in high-density production systems, physical contact between susceptible animals and an infected animal or an agent carrying the infection is more likely. The threshold stock density below which a disease cannot persist is an important condition for

---

[85] World Bank, 2014: Reducing Disease Risks in Aquaculture. World Bank Report 88 257-GLB, Washington, 119p.

[86] Aldrin, M., Huseby, R.B. and Jansen, P.A., 2015: Space-time modelling of the spread of pancreas disease (PD) within and between Norwegian marine salmonid farms. *Prev. Vet. Med.*, 121, 132–41.

disease spreads and empirical data have been used in disease models. The environmental transmission from disease agents in open-cage cultures (e.g. Atlantic salmon) has been addressed through hydrodynamical models that reproduce water movements coupled with a particle-tracking models of the spreading diseases at different locations and intensities.[87] To investigate the insurability of epidemic aquatic diseases, statistical models for disease spreads between ponds and within ponds have been developed for catfish in the USA.[88]

BIBLIOGRAPHY

Alday, V. (2010). Aquaculture insurance: The need for evaluation of disease risk for the sustainability of a company. *Trébol* 53, 10p.

Galina, J. (2017). *Fish Diseases: Prevention and Control Strategies.* Academic Press, 597p.

Inamura, M., Rushton, R., and Antón, J. (2015). *Risk Management of Outbreaks of Livestock Diseases.* Paris: OECD Food, Agriculture and Fisheries Papers 91, 37p.

Kalma, J.D., Laughlin, G.P., Caprio, J.M., and Hamer, P.J.C. (1992). *The Bioclimatology of Frost. Its Occurrence, Impact and Protection.* Vol. 2 of Advances in Bioclimatology. Springer, 144p.

Kumar, P. (2017). *Hailstorms – Prediction, Control and Damage Assessment,* 2e. CRC Press, 350p.

Longshore, D. (2008). *Encyclopedia of Hurricanes, Typhoons, and Cyclones.* Checkmark Books, 468p.

Nagarajan, R. (2010). *Drought Assessment.* Netherlands: Springer, 429p.

Neild, J., O'Flaherty, P., Hedley, P., and Underwood, R. (1998). *Impact of a Volcanic Eruption on Agriculture and Forestry in New Zealand.* MAF Policy Technical Paper 99/2. MAF. 92p.

Noga, E.J. (2010). *Fish Disease: Diagnosis and Treatment,* 2e. Wiley-Blackwell, 536p.

Pender, G. and Faulkner, H. (2010). *Flood Risk Science and Management.* Wiley-Blackwell, 544p.

Scarfe, D.A., Lee, C.-S., and O'Bryen, P.J. (2006). *Aquaculture Biosecurity Prevention, Control, and Eradication of Aquatic Animal Disease.* Wiley-Blackwell, 182p.

Sen, Z. (2015). *Applied Drought Modeling, Prediction, and Mitigation.* Elsevier Science Publishing, 484p.

Sheffield, J. and Wood, E.F. (2012). *Drought: Past Problems and Future Scenarios.* Routledge, 224p.

Shroder, J.F. and Paton, D. (2014). *Wildfire Hazards, Risks, and Disasters.* Elsevier, 284p.

Sivakumar, M.V.K., Motha, R.P., and Das, H.P. (2005). *Natural Disaster and Extreme Events in Agriculture.* Springer, 367p.

Snyder, R.L. and Melo-Abreu, J.P. (2005). *Frost Protection: Fundamentals, Practice and Economics.* Rome: FAO Publication, Environment and Natural Resources Series 10, 126p.

WMO (2016). *Handbook of Drought Indicators and Indices.* Geneva: WMO Publication 1173, 52p.

Zargar, A., Sadiq, R., Naser, B. and Khan, F.I., (2011): *A review of drought indices.* Environ. Rev., 19.

---

[87] Salama, N.K.G. and Rabe, B., 2013: Developing models for investigating the environmental transmission of disease-causing agents within open-cage salmon aquaculture. *Aquacult. Environ. Interact.,* 4, 91–115.

[88] Zagmutt, F.J. et al., 2014: Disease spread models to estimate highly uncertain emerging diseases losses for animal agriculture insurance policies: An application to the U.S. farm-raised catfish industry. *Risk Anal.,* 33(10), 1924–37.

CHAPTER 4

Agricultural Data and Proxies

4.1 INTRODUCTION

Exposure analysis, underwriting and pricing of agricultural risk transfer products require a large amount of data, including historical insurance claims, climate data, crop yield data, mortality statistics, satellite imageries and outputs from physical models. Data from different sources need to be combined to obtain meaningful estimates of past and future risks for a single risk and for entire portfolios of risks.

However, agricultural data and proxies often include inconsistencies and limited time spans, and show trends over time so that historical data do not necessarily reflect future loss potentials. Most agricultural production systems have gone through industrialisation and verticalisation in recent decades, which typically decreases the vulnerability to localised losses but increases the loss potential from systemic events. Trends in production statistics are often driven through improved technology, specialisation and verticalisation, changing weather patterns and new biosecurity regulations for epidemic diseases.

This chapter first introduces different sources of climate data and statistical methods to examine and remove data consistency and trends. Data from satellites and other remote sensing devices are discussed with a focus on vegetation indices (VI) and forest area burnt. Different sources of crop yield data are presented thereafter, including the main statistical concepts to prepare the data for pricing and underwriting. As data from government calamity declarations are valuable proxies for damage frequency and severity and form the basis of some crop insurance programmes, these data are briefly discussed. The last sections are dedicated to livestock, aquaculture and forestry production statistics.

4.2 CLIMATE DATA

Most agricultural production systems are exposed to adverse weather conditions. For crops, weather parameters directly relate to crop yield variability, and in many cases, up to 60% of crop yield variability can be explained through rainfall and/or temperature. In the risk transfer industry, the terms weather and climate are used interchangeably; however, *weather* relates to current and short-term atmospheric conditions while *climate* describes the average weather conditions over longer time periods. Data relating to past weather conditions are therefore referred to as climate data.

The continuous availability of high-quality climate data is essential for weather indices which directly settle on underlying weather parameters. Further, climate data are important to cross-validate crop yield data, prolong historical insurance claims series and form an integral part of data required to operate crop models. Typically, climate data are available for 40–60 years and are easier to access than crop yield and remote sensing data.

4.2.1 SOURCES OF CLIMATE DATA

While weather stations are the main source of climate data, increasingly climate data are available from satellites, reanalyses from numerical weather forecasting models and climate models, and are used for both risk analyses and risk transfer products.

Weather Station Data

The main source of weather station data is typically the National Weather Service (NWS), and on some occasions, universities, military organisations and private sector companies. An NWS typically operates an automatic weather station network and provides synoptic and climate data that include temperature, rainfall, humidity, wind speed and direction, solar radiation, surface pressure, cloud cover and visibility at different time intervals. Data reporting standards, quality assessment and cleaning methods vary among countries.[1]

Synoptic Weather Data

Synoptic data are collected in real time at weather stations and are immediately disseminated for weather forecasting purposes. Synoptic data typically include temperature (minimum and maximum) and rainfall, provided four times a day at standard times. Synoptic data are not quality controlled and the longest time series exist since the 1970s. SYNOP data are synoptic weather data that are reported at 8000 weather stations on a six-hourly basis, are exchanged among NWSs and include temperature, barometric pressure and visibility. The use of synoptic data for risk transfer products is limited as time series are short, data quality is low and the data need to be integrated over reporting times to obtain daily meteorological parameters.

Climate Data

Climate data are quality controlled by the provider, which is typically an NWS, and are available for most countries for at least 40 years. Climate data are available within weeks or months as quality control is time consuming; however, as the demand for weather data is increasing, many NWSs provide preliminary climate data before the official release. Climate data can be difficult and expensive to access, with data user agreements varying from very restrictive to free distribution of data. In some countries, climate data are available online at no or low costs (e.g. USA, Canada), require

---

[1] Boissonnade, A., Heitkemper, L.J. and Whitehead, D., 2002: Weather data: cleaning and enhancement. In Dischel, R.S. (ed.): *Climate Risk and the Weather Market*, Risk Books, London, 300p.

government pre-approval (e.g. Europe) or are classified and generally not accessible (e.g. China). To provide affordable or free climate datasets, research centres have developed comprehensive catalogues and platforms that contain the most commonly used climate datasets.[2] As the weather insurance and derivative industry is expanding, industry associations and the private sector have made agreements with NWSs to redistribute weather data for certain countries and regions.

Examples of Open Source Climate Data
- *Global Surface Summary of the Day (GSOD)* from NOAA is derived from the integrated surface hourly data from over 9000 weather stations and provides daily temperature (mean, maximum, minimum), rainfall, dew point, wind speed (mean, maximum, peak gust), air pressure, visibility and snow depth at a global scale since 1929, with the most complete series since 1973.
  https://data.noaa.gov/dataset/dataset/global-surface-summary-of-the-day-gsod.
- *Global Historical Climatology Network (GHCN)* from NOAA uses data from over 30 sources, including 90 000 weather stations, and provides globally daily rainfall since 1880 and daily maximum and minimum temperature. GHCN data are widely used as a reference, but many records contain inhomogeneities related to shifts in observation times, station location and type of instruments used. .
  https://www.ncdc.noaa.gov/data-access/land-based-station-data/land-based-datasets/global-historical-climatology-network-ghcn
- *European Climate Assessment Dataset (ECAD)* from the Royal Netherlands Meteorological Institute contains 12 daily climate variables (including rainfall and temperature) from 10 576 weather stations in Europe for various time lengths.
  https://www.ecad.eu/.
- *Tropical Ocean Global Atmosphere Program (TOGA)* from the World Climate Research Programme provides sub-daily and daily rainfall data with a special focus on sub-tropical and tropical regions (including Japan, Brazil, Indonesia, China) for 1992–2013.
  https://www.wcrp-climate.org.

Gridded Climate Data

Gridded climate data are based on spatial interpolation of data from weather stations, satellite- and reanalysis data on regular spatial grids of various resolutions and time intervals, ranging from daily to monthly and annual. Gridded climate data are typically provided by NWSs and are more affordable than data from weather stations while providing weather variables in areas that are not covered by weather stations (e.g. in mountainous regions). Initially, gridded climate datasets had coarse resolutions (>50 km) and could not accurately represent local climate features such as coastal effects, elevation gradients or temperature inversions. With denser weather stations networks, increased computing power and advanced data gridding methods, daily gridded climate data are now available at 10 km or finer resolutions at global scale. Gridded data are extensively

---

[2] NCAR has developed a *Climate Data Guide* that includes references, information on data reliability, data, tools and methodologies for 191 datasets that are used to evaluate earth system models and to understand the climate system, https://climatedataguide.ucar.edu (accessed February 2017).

used by the risk transfer industry for risk analyses but only regularly updated datasets can be used for risk transfer products such as weather index insurance.

Gridding Techniques
Commonly used spatial interpolation techniques to generate gridded climate datasets include inverse distance weighting (IDW), kriging, thin-plate smoothing splines, Daymet and the Parameter-elevation Regressions on Independent Slopes Model (PRISM).[3] With abundant station data and the absence of a coastline, IDW and kriging offer a good approach to grid weather data. PRISM is often used in regions with topography. Most gridded climate datasets contain a detailed description of the gridding methodology and rationale used.

Gridded climate data can show biases that are driven by (i) the quality and consistency of the weather station data, (ii) the density of the weather station network, (iii) the extent to which it represents climate-forcing factors, and (iv) the most adequate spatial interpolation method for the context and dataset. Biases can be high for daily gridded data, particularly for more extreme values of maximum and minimum temperature and daily rainfall in arid and mountainous regions.

Examples of Open Source Gridded Climate Data
A large collection of open source gridded climate data is available; however, not all time series are continuous for all meteorological parameters and often, two or more series need to be assembled to obtain a consistent time series.

- *Unified Gauge-Based Analysis of Global Daily Precipitation* from NOAA's Climate Prediction Center uses rain gauge data from over 30 000 stations to generate daily gridded global precipitation data at 0.125° resolution, which are released at a 0.5° resolution since 1979. The dataset includes a retrospective version which uses 30 000 stations and covers 1979–2005 and a real-time version with 17 000 stations since 2006. https://climatedataguide.ucar.edu/climate-data/cpc-unified-gauge-based-analysis-global-daily-precipitation.
- *Climatic Research Unit (CRU)* from the University of East Anglia (UK) provides various monthly gridded temperature and rainfall time series at global scale on a 0.5° resolution, typically for 1901–2015. https://crudata.uea.ac.uk/cru/data/hrg.
- *Berkeley Earth Surface Temperature (BEST)* from Berkeley University (USA) contains global surface temperatures from 37 000 stations, with the longest records dating back to 1701 at a resolution of 1° and equal-area grids with 0.25° for the USA and Europe. http://berkeleyearth.org/data.
- *Asian Precipitation – Highly-Resolved Observational Data Integration Towards Evaluation of Water Resources (Aphrodite)* from the Japan Meteorological Agency (JMA) provides for Northern Eurasia, Asia and the Mid-East gridded daily rainfall at 0.25° and 0.5° resolutions with assimilations from various sources including

---

[3] Daily, C., 2006: Guidelines for assessing the suitability of spatial climate data sets. *Int. J. Climatol.*, 26, 707–21.

12 000 weather stations for 1951–2007; for Japan gridded daily rainfall is available at 0.05° for 1900–2011 and gridded daily mean temperature from various sources for 1951–2007.
www.chikyu.ac.jp/precip/english/index.html.

- *Daily Surface Weather and Climatological Summaries (Daymet)* from NASA provides for North America daily gridded rainfall and temperature (minimum and maximum) on a 1 km grid for 1980–2013.
https://daymet.ornl.gov.
- *European Climate Assessment Dataset (ECAD)* from the Royal Netherlands Meteorological Institute provides daily rainfall and temperature at 0.1° grids for Europe for 1950–2006.
http://www.ecad.eu/download/ensembles/ensembles.php.
- *PRISM High-Resolution Spatial Climate Data* from Oregon State University (USA) provides for the USA monthly gridded temperature (maximum and minimum), dew point and precipitation at 4 km and 0.8 km since 1895.
http://prism.oregonstate.edu.
- *Bureau of Meteorology (BoM)* computes for Australia daily gridded rainfall and temperature at 0.25° (national data) and 0.05° grids (regional data) since 1900 with regular updates.
www.bom.gov.au/climate.
- *India Meteorological Department (IMD)* provides for India daily gridded (i) mean temperature from 395 weather stations at 1° grids, 1969–2005, and (ii) rainfall from 6955 rain gauge stations at 0.25° grids, 1901–2012. The time lag in updating the gridded datasets can be several years.
www.imd.gov.in.

Apiculture Insurance in the USA

The USA produces around 73 tons of honey each year and bees contribute to pollination of crops. To compensate the apiculture industry for fluctuations in plant growth and related losses in honey production, the RMA developed a Rainfall Index Insurance Plan (RIIP) in 2009, which is also available for forage and pasture production. RIIP is an area plan that compensates against declines in gridded precipitation from NOAA/ CPC compared with long-term averages on 0.25° grids in 11 intervals that contain 2-month periods. Average gridded precipitation is defined as the average since 1984 up to two years prior to the crop year. A final grid index is computed based on current precipitation and is expressed as a percentage above/below average precipitation.

Insurance Options Under RIIP

The policyholder selects a minimum of two index intervals in function of factors such as farm location and pollination times. RIIP uses productivity factors that allow the insured to individualise the insurance in selecting factors ranging from 60% to 150% in 1% increments based on the sum insured (base value) per area unit. If the insured believes that the intended production has a higher (lower) area-unit value than the base value in the county, a factor above (below) 100% is applied. Additionally, the insured can allocate a percentage of the total value to a certain index interval (e.g. 70% of total value for the April–May index interval and 30% of total value for the June–July index interval) to reflect its risk profile. The RMA website provides the insured with

(i) historical precipitation for each index interval and each grid cell since 1948, which allows the insured to determine whether its production history correlates well to the rainfall index pattern, and (ii) a grid locator that permits the insured to allocate the area insured to the individual grids.

Performance of RIIP
While RIIP stated as a pilot programme in 2009 with 90 410 bee colonies insured, it became available in all states in 2016 and expanded to 853 320 colonies, generating a premium volume of US$25.8 million in 2017. The overall performance of RIIP for apiculture stands at a loss ratio of 93% (2009–2017). In comparison, RIIP for pasture and forage land produced a premium volume of US$414.2 million in 2017, with over 33 000 policies sold and an average loss ratio of 85% (2007–2017).

4.2.2 SATELLITE-BASED CLIMATE DATA

Meteorological satellites provide a range of atmospheric parameters that include rainfall, temperature, soil moisture, evapotranspiration and vegetation extents at high spatial and temporal resolutions, with the earliest data available since 1978.[4] Climate data from satellites are widely used for forecasting purposes, risk analysis and input into climate and crop models. A general issue with weather parameters from satellites is that time series are built over time from non-identical sensors, sensors deteriorate over time, and different spatial and temporal resolutions limit the development of comparable and consistent time series. Considerable differences can exist between satellite- and ground-measured temperature due to atmospheric friction, which alters the track and altitude of the satellites. Underestimation of satellite rainfall amounts has been observed over terrain and along coastal areas.[5]

For risk transfer products, climate data from weather station networks and gridded data are preferred to satellite-derived data; however, these are often the only alternative in countries with low station densities and significant data gaps.

Estimation of Meteorological Parameters

Weather parameters are not directly measured by satellites but are derived from radiances within atmospheric layers and the ground from which meteorological variables are computed through complex models based on calibration with weather station data. Temperature measurements are based on microwave emissions of oxygen molecules in vertical atmospheric layers. Rainfall is estimated from a combination of visible and infrared radiation upwelling from the earth into the atmosphere. The higher the reflection coefficient (albedo) of a cloud, the more water droplets and/or ice crystals it contains and the deeper the cloud, which is a measure of the likeliness of rainfall on ground. Additionally, the lower the infrared brightness temperature, the higher the cloud top and the higher the likelihood of rainfall. The rate of change of cloud-top temperature indicates the cloud growth and areas of heavy rainfall.

---

[4] Tan, S.Y., 2014: Meteorological Satellite Systems. Springer Briefs in Space Development, 145p.
[5] Mendelsohn, R., Kurukulasuriya, P., Basist, A. et al., 2007: Climate analysis with satellite versus weather station data. *Clim. Change*, 81, 71–83.

Examples of Open Source Satellite-Based Climate Data

Open source satellite climate data are continuously expanding and result from research projects that aim at providing near real-time meteorological parameters that are used in a growing number of applications. Unless a research project is continued, satellite-based climate time series are discontinued but are still used for model validation purposes.

- *CICS High-Resolution Optimally Interpolated Microwave Precipitation from Satellites (CHOMPS)* from the Cooperative Institute for Climate Studies uses multiple satellite microwave sensors and provides daily rainfall at 0.25° grids at global scale for 1998–2007.
  https://climatedataguide.ucar.edu/climate-data/chomps-cics-high-resolution-optimally-interpolated-microwave-precipitation-satellites.
- *CMORPH (CPC MORPHing technique)* from NOAA uses rainfall estimates from low-orbit satellite microwave observations and provides sub-daily and daily rainfall globally at a resolution of 8–12 km since 2002 to near present.
  http://www.cpc.ncep.noaa.gov/products/janowiak/cmorph_description.html.
- *Climate Hazards Group InfraRed Precipitation with Station data (CHIRPS)* from the United States Geological Survey (USGS) provides daily global precipitation data using high-resolution satellite data with station data at 0.25° and 0.05° grids since 1981.
  http://chg.geog.ucsb.edu/data/chirps/index.html.
- Moderate resolution imaging spectroradiometer (*MODIS*) provides globally land surface temperatures and rainfall amounts at various spatial resolutions down to 1 km spatial grids through the Aqua sensor (since July 2002) and the Terra sensor (since 2000).
  https://lpdaac.usgs.gov/dataset_discovery/modis.
- *Monsoon Asia Integrated Regional Study (MAIRS)*, uses the MODIS Terra and Aqua sensors to compute 8-day temperature at a resolution 1 km grids for the Asia monsoon region since 2000 and 8-day temperature at a resolution of 5.6 km globally since 2000.
  http://lcluc.umd.edu/content/data-initiatives.
- *NASA Power* from NASA provides global daily solar insolation at 1° grids since 1983, global daily temperature (average, minimum, maximum) at 1° since 1983 and daily rainfall at 1° since 1997 with updates every two months.
  http://power.larc.nasa.gov.
- *Tropical Rainfall Measuring Mission (TRMM)*, provides from three-hourly to monthly rainfall at 27 km grids for latitudes between 50°N and 50°S, 1998–2015..
  http://pmm.nasa.gov/data-access/downloads/trmm
- *Precipitation Estimation from Remotely Sensed Information using Artificial Neural Networks-Climate Data Record (PERSIANN-CDR)* from the Center for Hydrometeorology and Remote Sensing uses artificial neural networks (ANN) to grid infrared satellite data to provide global sub-daily and daily rainfall on 0.25° grids since 1983.
  https://catalog.data.gov/dataset/noaa-climate-data-record-cdr-of-precipitation-estimation-from-remotely-sensed-information-using.
- *Africa Rainfall (RFE2)* from NOAA uses over 1000 rain gauges, satellite-based rainfall and infra-red cloud-top temperatures to provide daily rainfall for Africa at 0.1° grids since 2001. Daily data are aggregated to compute decadal (10 days), monthly and seasonal rainfall amounts.

https://catalog.data.gov/dataset/climate-prediction-center-cpc-africa-rainfall-climatology-version-2-0-arc2.

- *Africa Rainfall Climatology Version 2.0 (ARC2)* from NOAA uses rain gauge stations over Africa and satellite-based infrared data to provide daily rainfall estimates for Africa on 0.1° grids since 1983.
  www.cpc.ncep.noaa.gov/products/fews/AFR_CLIM/AMS_ARC2a.pdf.
- *Tropical Applications of Meteorology (TAMSAT)* established by the University of Reading (UK) uses satellite and ground-based observations to provide daily, decadal (10 days) and monthly rainfall estimates for Africa at a 4 km resolution since 1983.
  www.tamsat.org.uk.

Weather Index Insurance in Mozambique

In Mozambique (East Africa), agriculture accounts for 32% of GDP and involves over 81% of the population. Only 45% of the land surface is suitable for agriculture and less than 10% is currently cultivated, with only 3% of the arable land being irrigated. Mozambique, one of the poorest countries, went through a civil war that started in the 1970s and ended in 1992. The country is frequently affected by severe droughts that occur every 7–11 years, with flooding in some parts of the country in other years.

Mozambique covers a surface of 801 000 km². It has 69 districts but only 33 synoptic weather stations, 13 agrometeorological stations, 48 climatological stations and 7 automatic weather stations, leaving some regions uncovered. Climatological stations report precipitation only and many records ended in the 1990s, while weather station data show large gaps between 1975 and 1992, related to low maintenance during the civil war. Crop yield data are only consistently available since 2000 and show increasing trends with a high degree of uncertainties. Agribusinesses in Mozambique generally doubt the quality and reliability of the official crop yield records.

Development of Insurance Solutions
Following several feasibility studies to improve ex-ante risk management, the International Finance Corporation (IFC), which is part of the World Bank Group, in 2012 provided a grant for technical assistance to develop a weather index insurance pilot for cotton farmers in the districts of Lalaua and Monapo. The general lack of insurance infrastructure and smallholder structure prevented the implementation of indemnity-based insurance. The short and unreliable yield time series did not allow for area-yield indices to be developed. Similarly, the low density of weather stations and the large data gaps did not form an ideal basis for weather index insurance. As an alternative, the use of reanalysis climate data and satellite-based climate data was examined. While reanalysis data cover larger regions at fine spatial resolution for up to 50 years, one constraint for insurance purposes is that updates are irregular and would not allow for claims settlement after the crop season. Therefore, satellite data remained the only viable data source to develop weather indices for cotton in Mozambique.

Satellite-Based Weather Index Insurance
Ten-day (dekad) rainfall data at 10 km grids were used from Water Requirement Satisfaction Index (WRSI) precipitation estimates from the USAID Famine Early Warning Systems Network, available for Mozambique since 1995. Additionally, eight-day temperature data at 5.6 km grids were obtained from the MAIRS, which were available

for Mozambique since 2000. Both time series are frequently updated and allow the calculation of indemnities during and after the cotton season. For each district, the gridded rainfall and temperature data were allocated to the crop growth phases that, for the purpose of index development, were divided in each district into an initial phase, a vegetative phase, a flowering phase and a ripening phase. Daily average rainfall was computed from dekad rainfall using the number of days in each dekad for each grid cell and were subsequently averaged over the grids that cover a district. Temperature was calculated for each grid cell covering the district and the minimum for each dekad was determined.

Weather indices were structured for each district, including (i) deficit rainfall with different triggers depending on the phases, (ii) number of dry days with a digital payout during the initial and flowering phases, (iii) excess rainfall in the initial phase, and (iv) low temperature during the ripening phase. The sum insured was determined to cover production costs.

Performance of the Weather Indices

In 2012/2013, the weather indices were sold in the districts of Lalaua and Monapo to cotton production companies and cooperatives, which covered farmers with a total of 37 700 ha insured and a premium volume of US$680 000. In 2013, a drought caused a loss ratio over 100% and in 2014, the scheme was not renewed due to a lack of funding to support premiums and limited awareness of the product among cotton farmers. However, there are plans to restart the weather index scheme with a commitment from the government of Mozambique of US$1 million in premium subsidies and with IFC providing the technical assistance to support the implementation, with a focus on cotton, maize, soybeans and pigeon peas in the provinces of Nampula and Zambezi.

REANALYSIS CLIMATE DATA

Weather and climate forecast centres provide reanalysis climate data at various spatial resolutions and time frames. Reanalysis products are used extensively in climate research to monitor current climate conditions, analyse causes of climate variations and predict the climate. Reanalysis is based on historical and actual atmospheric observations from various sources and a numerical weather forecast model (NWFM) that coherently simulates one or several aspects of the atmosphere's layers, which are combined to generate a synthesised estimate of the state of the atmosphere. A reanalysis typically extends over several decades and covers the entire globe on a regular grid from the surface up to the stratosphere.

Numerical Weather Forecast Models

NWFMs use weather observations from various sources, including ground observations, airplanes, radio soundings, satellites and radars. NWFMs provide a large range of meteorological parameters, including temperature, humidity, precipitation, soil moisture and soil temperature, snow, and ocean waves at different atmospheric levels.

The observations are assimilated to produce an analysis of the initial state of the atmosphere on a particular day, based on which the NWFM is initialised. The NWFM is based on algorithms that describe the atmosphere through fluid- and thermo-dynamics equations and determine how the climate system evolves from an initial state over time.[6] The forecast model equations allow the extrapolation of information from the observed parameters to unobserved parameters in a physically meaningful way and a projection forward in time. A typical grid of an NWFM ranges from 5 km (high resolution) to 300 km (low resolution). The NWFM provides estimates of a wide range of physical parameters such as precipitation, turbulent fluxes, radiation fields, cloud properties, soil moisture at different atmospheric levels and geographical resolutions. Unlike archived weather analyses from operational NWFMs, a *reanalysis* is produced with a single version of assimilated data and therefore shows a consistent methodology.

Use of Reanalysis Data

One of the key advantages of reanalysis data is physical coherence in that estimated parameters must be consistent with the laws of physics and output data cover longer time periods of at least 30 years in a uniform way. The accuracy of reanalysis data naturally depends on the quality of the NWFM and the observations. For agricultural risk analysis and modelling purposes, outputs of NWFM were initially with 250 km grids too low in resolution. With advanced NWFMs, outputs are now available at a global scale on 25–50 km grids, which is considered an appropriate spatial scale for regional crop yield modelling and forecasting. Since crop modelling and forecasting rely on steady historical time series, an initial problem was that with frequent upgrades of the NWFM, biases in time series occurred. This has largely been addressed by the providers of reanalysis data and coherent and consistent time series are now available. While seasonal and monthly modelled variables are well reproduced in the reanalysis datasets relative to station data, daily values can differ largely. Precipitation has been found to create some of the largest inconsistencies, particularly in highly arid regions where daily rainfall levels are critical for crop growth. Similarly, extreme daily rainfall events (e.g. flash floods) are difficult to reproduce in a NWFM. As updates of reanalysis data are not undertaken at a frequency required for the risk transfer industry, most applications of these data in agricultural insurance have been in risk assessment and pricing.

Examples of Open Source Reanalysis Climate Data
- *ERA-Interim*, operated by the European Centre for Medium-Range Weather Forecasts (ECMWF) provides meteorological parameters at 60 vertical atmospheric levels, including three-hourly, daily and monthly surface temperature and precipitation at 0.75° grids at global scale since 1979 to near present with monthly updates. http://rda.ucar.edu/datasets/ds627.0.
- *Modern-Era Retrospective Analysis for Research and Applications (MERRA)* from NASA provides from sub-daily to monthly temperature and rainfall data on 0.5° grids on a global scale since 1979 to near real time. https://gmao.gsfc.nasa.gov/reanalysis/MERRA.
- *North American Regional Reanalysis (NARR)* generated by NOAA provides for North America a variety of parameters including daily precipitation, temperature, snow cover/height, plant canopy surface water and soil moisture at 0.3° grids since 1979 until near real time. http://www.esrl.noaa.gov/psd/data/gridded/data.narr.html.

---

[6] Dee, D.P., Uppala, S.M., Simmons, A.J. et al., 2011: The ERA-Interim reanalysis: Configuration and performance of the data assimilation system. *Q. J. R. Meteorol. Soc.*, 137, 553–97.

CLIMATE MODELS

Climate models are mathematical representations of the climate system on numerical grids expressed through physical, biological and chemical principles. Complex equations characterise how energy and matter interact in the ocean, atmosphere and land over thousands of three-dimensional grid cells that represent the globe at some 20 different atmospheric layers. Processes are first modelled in each grid cell and passed on to neighbouring cells to compute the exchange of matter and energy over different time dimensions. A climate model includes several coupled sub-models to (i) represent the oceans, atmosphere, land and continental ice as well as the fluxes between each other, and (ii) model sea ice mechanisms and evapotranspiration over land. The numerical grid of climate models of the highest resolution (100 km) is typically still too large to present small-scale processes such as turbulence in the atmosphere–ocean boundary layers and impact of topography on thunderstorm development. Therefore, climate models need to be parameterised based on empirical evidence and/or theoretical assumptions to account for the large-scale influence of processes that are not explicitly included in the climate models.

Outputs of climate models can be useful for risk analyses that involve a future perspective and to validate weather indices through forward-looking data.

Climate Scenarios

Most climate models are developed for climate projections where changes in climates are simulated in response to emissions of greenhouse gases and aerosols. Climate models then perform experiments out of which scenarios are constructed of how the climate will evolve. Initially, standard scenarios such as A1, A2, B1 and B2 were developed based on complex relationships between socio-economic forces driving greenhouse gas and aerosol emissions. Projections can be made from a single model run or from an ensemble of forecasts in slightly altering the initial conditions. Uncertainties of climate prediction are driven by uncertainties in chemical, physical and social models.

Climate Model Outputs

The size of the grid cells ranges from 100 km to 500 km and the number of time steps varies from hours to days. Typical outputs include daily or weekly paraments such as temperature (minimum, maximum, average), rainfall and solar radiation for a projection time of the next 30–100 years. If outputs are required to be below the standard resolution, downscaling is required. Dynamical downscaling uses a limited-area model to simulate physical processes at the sub-regional level, while statistical downscaling involves statistically determined relationships between the observed local response and the observed large-scale climate state.

TREATMENT OF CLIMATE DATA

Climate data form an essential part of risk analysis and are the basis for weather index insurance. The analysis of the extent of missing and erroneous data and potential discontinuities is essential to obtain a complete set of climate data. Climate data often show trends over time and when extreme realisations in weather parameters are judged not to be adequately represented in historical observations, probability density functions (PDFs) and weather pattern simulations are used to increase the range of possible realisations of different weather variables. The use of incomplete climate data and ignoring trends can lead to severe over- or underestimation of risk and inadequate insurance products.

DISCONTINUITIES, ERRONEOUS AND MISSING CLIMATE DATA

NWSs quality-control weather station data, clean climate data and replace erroneous data and fill missing values. Further, NWSs provide an overview of the methodology used to clean data and often make the original data (metadata) available. However, as some data cleaning processes are standardised and automated, climate data time series can show discontinuities, errors and missing values.

Discontinuities in Climate Data

Discontinuities or *jumps* often arise from changes in the location of the meteorological instrument including its surroundings and upgrades or replacement of the sensors with newer models (Figure 4.1). Discontinuities can lead to biases in the mean and standard deviation of weather variables, which are essential parameters for risk transfer products. As temperature is spatially more consistent than precipitation, biases in temperature recordings that relate to a shift of a weather station can be detected more easily than for precipitation. A simple way to detect inhomogeneity in temperature is to plot temperature differentials among several weather stations over time.

The magnitude of the discontinuities determines the approach as to how to deal with the data: (i) very small discontinuities that do not have any statistical relevance can be ignored, (ii) data before large discontinuities in earlier years should be ignored, and (iii) large discontinuities in recent years must be corrected or alternative data be used.

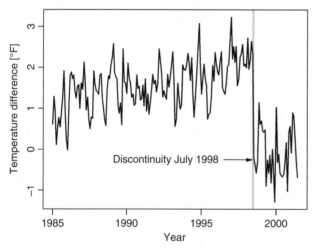

FIGURE 4.1   Monthly difference in temperature between the weather stations of Charlotte (NC, USA) and Greensboro Piedmont Triad International Airport (NC, USA) which lies 160 km apart for January 1985 to June 2001. The instrument in Charlotte was relocated in 1998 from an area near concrete to a low grassy area which lead to a discontinuity of 2°F. The same discontinuity was detected from other weather stations compared to Charlotte.
Data source: GHCN.

Erroneous Climate Data

Erroneous data such as incorrectly reported values typically stem from poorly calibrated meteorological instruments and from incorrect digitisation of data from hard copies. Errors in climate data can be visually detected in plotting the time series, checking whether minimum values are larger than the maximum values, and controlling that the magnitude of daily observations corresponds to the location and the time of year. Error rates in climate data of countries with rigorous quality control systems reach only 1–2%.

Missing Climate Data

Missing weather variables typically arise from malfunctioning instruments or a break in the transmission of the data. Missing daily temperature values at an individual station can be filled by averages, e.g. using values of the same day in other years. For rainfall which is spatially more variable than temperature, missing daily values can be filled with data from nearby stations or from SYNOP reports. For gaps over several days at several stations, spatial and temporal interpolations are required. For risk transfer products, the amount of missing data should be less than 10%.

Spatial Interpolation of Missing Climate Data

Spatial interpolation uses methods that directly interpolate data from observations (direct method) or through corrective iteration processes, which require a second predictor in addition to the observations (indirect method).[7] The use of an interpolation methodology depends on the density of weather stations and the strength of the point-to-point correlation.

Direct methods include the method of Cressman and its expansion under the Barnes approach using linear combinations of meteorological observations to generate a first-guess interpolation field. Alternatively, IDW uses the distance between weather stations and assumes that each measured point has a local influence that diminishes in proportion to the distance between the observed and predicted location. IDW works well for relatively homogenous datasets and particularly for daily temperatures which show a relatively uniform spatial distribution. Kriging is used for spatial interpolation for high spatial variation in weather parameters.[8] Kriging is similar to IDW in that it uses a linear combination of weights at known points to estimate the value at an unknown point. Indirect spatial interpolation techniques are used when the weather station density is too low for direct spatial interpolation. Increasingly, artificial neural networks (ANN) are used to fill non-linear statistical data to model complex relationships between inputs and outputs to reconstruct missing climate data.[9]

---

[7] Sluiter, R., 2008: Interpolation Methods for Climate Data – Literature Review. KNMI, R&D Information and Observation Technology, De Bilt, 24p.

[8] Hartwig, D., Dumolard, P. and Dyras, I., 2007: Spatial Interpolation for Climate Data – The Use of GIS in Climatology and Meteorology. ISTE, London, 284p.

[9] Kim, J.W. and Pachepsky, Y.A., 2010: Reconstructing missing daily precipitation data using regression trees and artificial neural networks for SAWT streamflow simulations. *J. Hydrol.*, 394, 305–14.

DETRENDING CLIMATE DATA

Trends in climate data are often driven by changes in the environment of the weather station (e.g. warming effect in temperature through increased urbanisation) and changing weather patterns. Detrending aims to obtain a time series from observation that is representative of today's environment. Detrending minimises the sum of the square of the errors of the residuals and optimises the bias and variance. The variance is largely driven by the influence of a given data point on the slope of the regression and a regression is considered *robust* if the influence of outliers is minimal.

Detrending climate data is essential for risk analyses and risk transfer products such as weather index insurance where weather parameters or the indices are detrended. Generally, when the trend in climate data stems from (i) random internal climate variability, trends are ignored and the observations are used, and (ii) changes in the environment of the weather station and in weather patterns, trends are removed through parametric and non-parametric detrending methods. Generally, parametric detrending methods tend to have a smaller variance but a higher bias, while non-parametric methods often show a smaller bias but a higher variance.

Parametric Detrending

Parametric methods include linear, piecewise-linear, quadratic and exponential functions which are characterised by a fixed shape that is adjusted through a small number of parameters that are derived from the observations. The type of trend in the underlying data must be assumed a priori.

A simple and commonly used method is to determine a linear trend in fitting a line to the observation, written as:

$$Trend_t = a_0 + a_1 t$$

with a_0 as the intercept and a_1 as the slope coefficient in the linear regression. The significance level of the linear trend is determined using t-statistics based on standard errors. The t-statistics are tested against a Student-t distribution with n-2 degrees of freedom to reveal the probability that the true value of the coefficient is zero.

In cases where clearly two distinct linear trends are present in the time series, a piecewise linear trend is used with one or several breakpoints, written for one breakpoint t_0 as:

$$Trend_t = \begin{cases} a_1 + b_1 t & t \leq t_0 \\ a_2 + b_2 t & t \geq t_0 \end{cases}$$

with a_1 and a_2 as the intercepts of each of the two trend segments and b_1 and b_2 as the corresponding slope coefficients. Parametric methods are mainly used for short time series. However, in cases of very short series and highly random observations, it can be difficult to determine a trend at all.

Non-Parametric Detrending

Non-parametric methods are used if parametric methods cannot accurately describe the shape of the trend but require longer time series. A simple non-parametric method uses moving averages that smooth the time series with a trend defined for a weather variable Y and p samples as:

$$Trend_t = \frac{1}{p} \sum_{i=-m}^{m} Y(t+i)$$

with $p = 2m = 1$ determining the number of observations.

More sophisticated methods include the Loess regression and kernel estimators, which fit simple models to localised subsets of the weather data to derive a function that describes the deterministic part of the variation in the data on a point-by-point basis. As an alternative, autoregressive integrated moving average (ARIMA) can be used to determine trends in weather time series.[10] In an autoregression, a variable of interest is forecasted through a linear combination of past values of the same variable.

Seasonality in Temperature Data

For temperature data, diurnal and seasonal cycles typically represent over 80% of the total variance. A simple approach to remove cyclicity in temperature is to average all observations in daily values and remove remaining noises through moving averages. Alternatively, temperature seasonality $S(t)$ can be modelled in fitting a single sinusoid to the data as:[11]

$$S(t) = a\sin\left(2\pi\left(t+\varphi\right)/365\right)$$

adjusted for the amplitude a and the phase φ, with the amplitude revealing the difference between the highest and the mean temperature and the phase specifying where the cycle in the oscillation begins.

PROBABILITY DENSITY FUNCTIONS FOR CLIMATE DATA

PDFs are used to statistically generate more extreme realisations of a weather parameter than has been observed, which is particularly relevant for shorter time series. PDFs are used over an entire weather station network to examine spatial distribution of meteorological parameters. When different types of distributions are used for the same weather variable at different stations, Copula functions provide joint distributions.

Temperature Data

Daily maximum, minimum and average temperature is often assumed to be normal distributed, with the gamma distribution used alternatively for daily maximum temperature. Monthly and annual temperature are typically normal distributed while temperature extremes are often best described through the Gumbel, the generalised extreme value or the generalised skew logistic distribution.

---

[10] Rank, E., 2003: Application of Bayesian trained RBF Networks to nonlinear time-series modeling. *Signal Process.*, 83, 1393–410.

[11] Schiller, F., Seidler, G. and Wimmer, M., 2012: Temperature models for pricing weather derivatives. *Quant. Financ.*, 12(3), 489–500.

Precipitation Data

For daily rainfall amounts, the gamma or lognormal distribution is used and wet days (excessive rainfall events) are often modelled through the gamma or Weibull distribution. Annual maximum precipitation is best described through the gamma or the Gumbel distribution. The kappa distribution has been used to statistically generate extreme precipitation events from long historical rainfall observations.

SIMULATION OF PRECIPITATION AND TEMPERATURE FIELDS

Multivariate statistical methods are used to simulate temperature and/or precipitation fields that show a high temporal and spatial dependence based on historical observations from a large number of weather stations. Principal component analyses (PCA) are often used to simulate rainfall and temperature fields and to obtain patterns of the simultaneous variations that reflect statistically plausible outcomes which are not included in the observations. PCA tries to simplify parameter estimation in decoupling multivariate time series into single-variable (univariate) models and requires high computing power, particularly if wider geographical areas are analysed.[12] Simulated rainfall and temperature fields have been used to examine historical extreme events and form the basis of many probabilistic catastrophe risk models (Section 2.5).

4.3 SATELLITE DATA

With increasing precision, spatial resolution and temporal coverage, remote sensing provides valuable data that support the mapping, classification and detection of natural disasters in agriculture, including drought, flood and water logging, low temperature as well as crop pests and diseases.[13] Satellite imagery is used for land use classification, vegetation monitoring, crop-yield assessments, crop forecasting, wildfire detection, area burnt mapping and monitoring of algal blooms. International research projects have contributed a large amount of past and current remote sensing data that are increasingly used by the risk transfer industry for risk analyses and products where data are directly used to define triggers for index-based insurance. Further, satellite data have been supporting loss adjustment efforts in classifying areas according to damage extents.

4.3.1 VEGETATION MONITORING

Satellite data are operationally used for vegetation monitoring, crop area, yield estimation and as inputs into crop forecast models. For risk transfer, vegetation indices (VI) and biophysical indices have been used for pasture land insurance (Section 6.10) and drought-related livestock mortality (Section 7.6).

Satellite measurements contain uncertainties and biases that include clouds and aerosols in the atmosphere that partially or entirely block a satellite's view of the earth

---

[12] Westra, S., Brown, C., Lall, U. and Sharma, A., 2007: Modelling multivariable hydrological series: principal component analysis or independent component analysis? *Water Resour. Res.*, 43(6), 1–11.

[13] Pan, Z., Huang, J. and Zhang, H., 2017: Remote sensing of agricultural disasters monitoring: Recent advances. *Int. J. Remote Sens.*, 10(13), 1–16.

surface and glare from the sun that saturates pixels. Further, soil background colours influence absorption and reflection in certain wavelengths and changes in the sensor's view angle as well as temporary malfunctions in satellite instruments can distort images. Although correction algorithms are used, satellite-based vegetation maps and area classifications can show inaccuracies, gaps and biases. In cases of significant changes in a dominant vegetation type in a pixel over time (e.g. through crop rotations), a recalibration of the VI is required to define the average VI (i.e. normal conditions) for the most prevailing vegetation type. A delay in crop planting by several weeks and, similarly, the use of high yielding and faster growing cultivars can lead to an underestimation of vegetation through VIs.

VEGETATION INDICES

Various approaches have been developed to monitor plant growth based on measurements of visual light and red and near-infrared from different wavelengths of satellites.[14] Spectral measurement of light reveals pigments in plant leaves (chlorophyll) which strongly absorb visible light from 0.4 to 0.7 μm, while the cell structure of leaves strongly reflects near-infrared light from 0.7 to 1.1 μm. The intensity of absorption in the visible bands and the reflection in the infrared bands allows the quantification of photosynthetic capacity of vegetation in a given pixel of land surface. A high rate of reflection in the near-infrared wavelengths indicates dense vegetation (e.g. forests), while scarce vegetation (e.g. grassland, desert) shows little difference in the intensity of visible and near-infrared wavelengths.

The reflection and absorption at different wavelengths have led to the development of VIs that use spectral measurements in the visible light and differences between near-infrared and visible radiation to quantify plant growth. Numerous VIs have been used in agricultural research and in the operational environment, with the Normalised Difference Vegetation Index (NDVI) as one of the most commonly used indices.

Normalised Difference Vegetation Index (NDVI)

The NDVI is calculated as the difference between near-infrared (*NIR*) and visible (*VIS*) wavelength measurements at different resolutions and time spans through:

$$NDVI = \frac{NIR - VIS}{NIR + VIS}$$

Healthy vegetation absorbs a large amount of visible light and reflects a large portion of the near-infrared light. Unhealthy or scarce vegetation reflects more visible light and less near-infrared light. NVDI values range from –1 to +1, with 0 in the absence of vegetation (e.g. bare soil, water, snow covers), and values of 0.8–0.9 reveal a high density of green leaves. Vegetation under stress or with a small leaf area produces lower positive NDVI values. Temporal changes in the NDVI are closely related to net primary production, which allows vegetation monitoring and estimations of crop yields.

Several studies have shown that NDVI and precipitation have a strong linear or log-linear relationship when monthly and annual precipitation is a limiting factor

---

[14] Wójtowicz, M., Wójtowicz, A. and Piekarczyk, J., 2016: Application of remote sensing methods in agriculture. *Comm. Biometry Crop Sci.*, 11, 31–50.

for vegetation growth. When precipitation is not the main limiting factor, soil moisture appears to become the dominant climate variable affecting NDVI values. A high variability in the relationship between NDVI values and yield as well as meteorological parameters such as cumulative precipitation and extreme heat has been found.[15] In the USA, NDVI values have shown reasonable correlations (0.65) with rangeland productivity at the resolution of a county but weak correlations at the level of farms.[16]

Examples of Open Source Vegetation Indices
Operational and research missions increasingly provide VIs that are placed in the open domain, with most data from MODIS, Satellite Pour l'Observation de la Terre (SPOT VEGETATION) and Advanced Very High Resolution Radiometer (AVHRR) at different resolutions and time spans. AVHRR provides the longest time series (since 1979) but a relatively low spatial resolution in the initial time periods. NOAA has established a website[17] that provides a comprehensive overview of different satellite-based products including a mapping functionality.

- *Center for Satellite Applications and Research (STAR)* from NOAA provides a large range of VIs including seven-day AVHRR NDVI at 16 km and 4 km since 1981 at global scale and allows online computation and animation of different time series.
  http://www.star.nesdis.noaa.gov/smcd/emb/vci/VH/index.php.
- *eMODIS* from USGS provides for the USA seven day-rolling MODIS NDVI composites at 250 m, 500 m and 1 km since 2000 (Terra satellite) and 2002 (Aqua satellite).
  http://www.foodsec.org/tools_gaul.htm.
- *Global Agricultural Monitoring Production System* from NASA provides the same data as *eMODIS* but additionally includes an online application to visualise data with crop masks at different resolutions.
  http://glam1.gsfc.nasa.gov.

Land Use Classification from Vegetation Indices
VIs are used for classification of land covers and to estimate surfaces through pixel counting. Regression estimators integrate and improve land use types and area from satellite images with data from ground surveys. Initially, the relationship between a land use class and the satellite signal needs to be established for each region to accommodate soil background and current crop growing patterns, with a readjustment when crop mixtures change significantly (e.g. through crop rotations). An image classification error of 20–30% is considered a good result in relatively homogenous areas and when the classification nomenclature is simple, including 4–6 main crop types and

---

[15] Turvey, C. and McLaurin, M.K., 2012: Applicability of the Normalized Difference Vegetation Index (NDVI) in index-based crop insurance design. *Weather Clim. Soc.*, 4, 271–84.
[16] Rowley, R.J., Price, K.P. and Kastens, J.H., 2007: Remote sensing and the rancher: Linking rancher perception and remote sensing. *Rangeland Ecol. Manag.*, 6, 359–68.
[17] https://earthdata.nasa.gov (accessed October 2017).

another 6–8 land cover categories.[18] The use of MODIS 250 m VIs was judged adequate for large-scale crop classification in the USA.[19]

Crop Yield Estimations from Vegetation Indices

A simple approach to estimate crop yields from VIs is to establish an empirical relationship between ground-measured crop yield at different growth phases and deviations of corresponding VI levels relative to normal. VIs have been found to explain 80% of the observed variation in yields within individual fields in certain regions.

A more complex approach is based on the light-use efficiency, which states that total biomass production is directly proportional to the total absorption of photosynthetically active radiation (PAR) over the course of the growing season. The ratio of biomass to PAR, known as radiation use efficiency (RUE), is relatively constant as plants adjust the total leaf area in response to other growth constraints such as nutrient or temperature stress. The interpolation of daily PAR fractions allows more flexibility in the timing of images relative to a crop growth stage. A more recent approach is to integrate satellite data into crop models that rely on numerous input parameters and use leaf area indices to obtain yield on a high-resolution grid.[20]

Generally, accuracies of satellite-based yield estimates are higher over larger areas (e.g. a county or sub-district) rather than an individual field. A common source of error in yield estimations with satellites stems from misclassifications of crop types in a pixel, which often occurs in mixed cropping systems. Further, high-resolution satellite data (e.g. from MODIS or SPOT) typically have 16-day gaps between individual images and parameters need to be estimated for days in between, which can lead to misinterpretation.

BIOPHYSICAL INDICES

Biophysical indices rely on radiation of vegetation in the visible light, PAR, and are used to calculate the rate of photosynthesis from the amount of absorbed PAR and the photosynthesis–light response of individual leaves. Photosynthesis rates have been used to develop the fraction of absorbed PAR (fAPAR), which depends on the geometry of illumination based on the angular position of the sun. Further, the vegetation cover fraction (fCover), which corresponds to the portion of ground-covered active vegetation and requires information on leaf area and plant canopy structures, has been used to monitor crop growth rates. In contrast to VIs, biophysical indices provide physically meaningful measures of the vegetation and have been proposed to monitor green vegetation in grassland areas. fCover is used for index-based pasture insurance in France (Section 6.10).

---

[18] Gallego, J., Carfagna, E. and Baruth, B., 2010: Accuracy, objectivity and efficiency of remote sensing for agricultural statistics. In *Agricultural Survey Methods*, Wiley, 193–211.

[19] Wardlow, B.D., Egbert, S.L. and Kastens, J.H., 2007: Analysis of time-series MODIS 250 m vegetation index data for crop classification in the U.S. Central Great Plains. *Remote Sens. Environ.*, 108(3), 290–310.

[20] Lobell, D., 2013: The use of satellite data for crop yield gap analysis. *Field Crop Res.*, 143, 56–64.

REMOTE SENSING-BASED CROP INSURANCE IN EMERGING ECONOMIES

In 2012, the Remote Sensing-Based Information and Insurance for Crops in Emerging Economies (RIICE) project was initiated to reduce vulnerability of smallholder rice producers in Southeast Asia through accurate production monitoring. RIICE further aims to develop more efficient agricultural insurance products such as area-yield indices with insurance terms determined from government yield data but loss calculations based on satellite-derived rice yields at a resolution of a district with a focus on drought and flood risk.[21]

Several studies have shown that rice produces characteristic backscatters over different growth stages from different wavelengths that can be used for area mapping and estimation of rice yield through empirical growth models. As most rice is grown in Southeast Asia during the monsoon season with considerable cloud coverage, RIICE uses synthetic aperture radar (SAR) imagery complemented by optical sensors. The spatial complexity of rice production, different establishment practices (e.g. direct seeding or transplanting), irrigation extents, growth cycles and spacing between rice plants require remote sensing data at a high spatial resolution. For test purposes of rice area mapping, RIICE uses SAR data at a resolution of 3 m (40 km × 40 km footprint per image) and 15 m (100 km × 140 km), with an average of two images per month.[22]

In the first phase (2012–2015), RIICE focused on monitoring and mapping of rice production on test sites and satellite-mapped rice areas were found to be within 85–93% accuracy compared with ground validations. In a second phase (2015–2018), RIICE planned the integration of satellite technology into national crop insurance programmes. In November 2016, the government of Tamil Nadu (India) introduced the RIICE technology into its new crop insurance initiative. RIICE has significant potential to improve access to more accurate rice area data and yield estimates, which in turn can support insurance loss adjustment. However, using satellite-based yield estimates for area-yield index insurance is highly challenging as (i) detailed crop calendars and site-specific information are necessary for each season for an empirical growth model that uses SAR data to estimate crop yields, (ii) misclassifications in rice areas can lead to inaccurate area-based yield estimates, (iii) historical yield data are necessary to price the area-yield indices as satellite-derived yield data would be available for 15 years at best, and (iv) farmers are likely to trust government-measured yields more than remote-sensed yields. The implementation of RIICE into crop insurance products will show to what extent satellite-based area-yield index insurance products are feasible for smallholder structures in Southeast Asia.

4.3.2 WILDFIRE MONITORING

Satellites provide data that are used for monitoring, management, modelling and damage assessments of wildfires. Often, satellites are the only way to detect wildfires in remote and inaccessible areas with dense forests. Individual active wildfires (hotspots) can be detected and monitored to obtain information on the spatial distribution, temporal evolution and size in terms of number of pixels, while area burnt analyses reveal

---

[21] www.asean-agrifood.org/projects/riice (accessed December 2017).
[22] Nelson, A., Setiyono, T., Rala, A.B. and Ninh, N.H., 2014: Towards an operational SAR-based rice monitoring system in Asia: Examples from 13 demonstration sites across Asia in the RIICE project. *Remote Sens.*, 6(10), 773–812.

the extent of burnt surfaces. Through reanalyses of archived data with the most current fire-detection algorithms, area burnt time series have been established for most fire-active regions and have improved fire management and risk analyses.

Several satellites contain sensors that allow wildfire detection at different resolutions, coverage areas and revisiting times. These include (i) NOAA-AVHRR for detection of hotspots, (ii) MODIS to identify hotspots, mapping of land surfaces/vegetation and burnt areas, (iii) LANDSAT to classify vegetation and map burnt areas, and (iv) SPOT for the identification of hotspots, assessment of vegetation and burnt areas. Sensors used for fire detection have varying spatial resolutions ranging from 1–2 km (coarse resolution) to 250–500 m (medium) and <30 m (high). With increasing resolution, the swath width narrows, and high-resolution data are therefore available for certain regions of special interest only.

The risk transfer industry has been using satellite-based area burnt data to assess regional risk levels in combination with government wildfire statistics for infrastructure and forest plantation assets. The usability of area burnt products from satellites has been investigated as a trigger for index-based wildfire insurance for fire exposure of industrialised timber companies (Section 9.7).

WILDFIRE DETECTION (HOTSPOTS)

During a wildfire, the emitted heat can be detected by satellites through thermal infrared radiation, while smoke plumes of large fires are visible on optical images. Algorithms compare the thermal radiation measured in Kelvin (K) with pixels of the surrounding areas and recognise abrupt changes above a certain temperature threshold as potential fire or *hotspot*. The amount of thermal radiation that is emitted at a particular wavelength from warm surfaces depends on the temperature. For a surface at a brightness temperature of around 300 K (26.85°C), spectral radiance peaks at a wavelength 10 μm, while temperatures of fires range from about 500 K (smouldering fire) to over 1000 K (flaming fire), with peak radiance occurring around 3.8 μm, which coincides with band wavelengths of several satellites such as AVHRR and MODIS.[23] Additionally, active fire detection algorithms use one or more bands at longer wavelengths (10–12 μm) to eliminate false detections.

The generalised nature of the detection algorithms may decrease detection accuracy in climatologically and geographically unique areas such as Southeast Asia. Depending on the region and the sensor, there have been low detection rates of small fires that cover only a fraction of a pixel and very large fires where substantial smoke plumes are interpreted by the detection algorithms as thick clouds. The adjustment of detection algorithms to local conditions has improved detection accuracy, but temporal sampling and fixed overpass times of polar-orbiting satellites remain key issues.

MODIS Hotspot Product

MODIS is one of the most used sensors for wildfire detection and area burnt mapping as the bands were specifically designed for fire monitoring and active fire detection. The MODIS sensor saturates at higher temperatures than other sensors with 450 K at

---

[23] Miettinen, J., Hyer, E.J., Chia, A.S. and Liew, S.C., 2013: Detection of vegetation fires and burnt areas by remote sensing in insular Southeast Asian conditions: Current status of knowledge and future challenges. *Int. J. Remote Sens.*, 34(12), 4344–66.

3.7 μm and 400 K at 11 μm bands, which improves the accuracy of fire detection. MODIS products are available since 2000 and the fire detection algorithms have been updated several times, with Collection 6 (2015) as the most recent version that includes improved fire detection thresholds and additional rejection tests of potential fire pixels. A potential fire in a pixel at the 4-μm band is defined at a brightness temperature (T_4) through:[24]

$$T_4 > \begin{cases} 360\,K\,(day\,time) \\ 320\,K\,(night\ time) \end{cases}$$

An identified potential fire pixel undergoes several false-alarm rejection tests that include sun-glint, with a special examination in desert boundaries (hot arid and barren soils), coastal regions and new forest clearings.

AREA BURNT ANALYSES

Recent fire scars suppress the reflectance in the visible and near infrared bands and appear dark due to the deposition of black char and ash. Burnt areas generally show a higher reflectance in the 1.6 μm band compared with the surrounding unaffected forest areas. Area burnt detection algorithms have been adjusted to climate zones and while in boreal forests NDVI supports the detection of burnt vegetation, near infrared and shortwave infrared are used in tropical areas in combination with algorithms that remove cloud shadows. Hybrid algorithms use surface reflectance and fire masks (hotspots) that serve as indicators of burn scars. Over the past 15 years, burnt area maps have been created in most fire-active regions using both coarse and medium-resolution sensors and show considerable discrepancies depending on the sensor used.

MODIS Area Burned Product

The MODIS Area Burned Product uses a hybrid detection algorithm that is based on (i) persistent changes in daily vegetation-index time series of surface reflectance and (ii) active fire data (hotspots). The daily burn-sensitive vegetation index (VI_i) is calculated from daily reflectance time series for each pixel as:[25]

$$VI_i = \frac{\rho_{5,i} - \rho_{7,i}}{\rho_{5,i} + \rho_{7,i}}$$

with $\rho_{5,i}$ and $\rho_{7,i}$ as daily reflectance with an index i of individual days of valid observations $i = 1, 2, 3, \ldots N$. In practice, cloud obscuration and coverage gaps often require double the number of satellite observations to reliably detect area burnt and avoid large omissions. VI_i shows a significant decrease after fire occurrence and provides good burn–unburned discrimination ratios. The MODIS detection algorithm identifies the date of burn to the nearest day at 250 m, 500 m and 1 km resolution at global scale from the Terra and Aqua sensors. A comparison of area burnt from 500 m MODIS

[24] Giglio, L., Schroeder, W. and Justice, C.O., 2016: The collection 6 MODIS active fire detection algorithm and fire products. *Remote Sens. Environ.*, 178, 31–41.
[25] Giglio, L., Loboda, T., Roy, D.P. et al., 2009: An active-fire based burned area mapping algorithm for the MODIS sensor. *Remote Sens. Environ.*, 113, 408–20.

data and high-resolution LANDSAT imagery revealed that mapped burnt areas were within 10% of all regions, except in parts of Africa where areas were underestimated, which could be related to overstory vegetation that obscured the view of the satellite.[26]

Examples of Open Source Hotspot and Area Burnt Data
Different satellite operators, research institutions and the Global Fire Monitoring Centre (GFMC)[27] led by Freiburg University (Germany) provide access to some forest fire products that include active fires and area burnt at different temporal and spatial resolutions. Some projects have focused on a specific year only, for example GLOBSCAR (2000), and time periods such as Global Burnt Surfaces (1982–1999) and Global Burnt Areas (2000–2007).

- *MODIS Area Burned Product* computed by the University of Maryland (USA) provides data on (i) active fires that are burning at the time of satellite overpass (1 km) for the last 24/48 hours and seven days, an eight-day summary (1 km) and a daily global summary (5 km and 20 km) since 2000, and (ii) area burnt including the approximate day of burning (500 m) for most land areas since 2000 and higher-resolution data (250 m) for some regions for 2001–2016; data are available in different formats including shapefiles and geotiff.
http://modis-fire.umd.edu/index.php.
- *Global Fire Emissions Database (GFED)* funded by different organisations to estimate global atmospheric CO_2 and produces global monthly area burnt at 0.25° grids since 1997 to near real time; higher-resolution data are available for some regions since 2000 and GFED provides comprehensive online analytical and mapping functions.
http://www.globalfiredata.org.

4.4 CROP YIELD DATA

High-quality crop yield data are fundamental to (i) assess crop production volatility in function of different causes, (ii) develop risk transfer products that are directly based on yield such as multi-peril crop insurance (MPCI) and area-yield indices, and (iii) validate payout functions and assess basis risk of weather indices. Different definitions of yield are used in the industry and most yield-based crop insurance products are based on data from government agricultural surveys at different spatial resolutions. In some cases, yield measurements from large grain producers and production managed by investment funds are used for risk transfer products. Additional sources of yield data include grain harvesters, elevators, satellites and outputs of crop models, which are so far used for validation purposes of government-reported yield.

Often, crop yield data are non-stationary and reveal trends that are often driven by improved technology and changes in weather patterns. Systematic and abrupt changes in yield levels can occur with privatisations of agriculture systems, the breakup of traditional farming production systems and economic aspects such as government incentives

---

[26] Ibid.
[27] www.fire.uni-freiburg.de (accessed January 2018).

to plant a certain crop type. Accurate detrending and representation of possible yield variability is essential to develop adequate insurance products and ignoring trends can lead to over- or underestimation of risk and to failure of crop insurance markets.

DEFINITION OF YIELD

Depending on the application, *yield* is defined differently and can lead to considerable confusion. The most common definitions of yield include crop yield, farm yield, potential yield and economic yield.[28] Crop insurance and risk transfer are based on crop yields at farm level but as these are often not consistently available, area-aggregated farm yields are used.

Crop Yield

Crop yield is the weight of grain at an agreed standard moisture content (e.g. 8–16%) reported at fresh weight basis per unit of land area harvested. Reporting standards vary by crop type and among countries. For example, paddy yield is typically reported with the husk attached, but in some countries (e.g. Japan), the husk is removed to determine the yield while in other countries (e.g. India), paddy yield is reported on a milled basis where the husk and the seed coat are removed. Crop yield is a function of dynamic, non-linear interactions between weather, soil water and nutrient dynamics, crop management practices and the physiology of the crop. Temporal and spatial variability of rainfall and temperature are among the key factors that determine yield variability.

Farm Yield

Farm yield is crop yield reported based on measurements at a farm by manual assessments or through equipment mounted on harvesters. Manual yield assessments are undertaken by government agencies at regular intervals on predefined or random plots. Agriculture surveys rely on the active participation of a selected number of representative farmers who report agricultural variables including farm yields on the basis of area harvested or area planted. Area-harvested yields are most common and can differ significantly from yields based on area planted as these contain area abandoned during the growing season due to crop failure. Official organisations such as the FAO mainly report yields on area harvested.

Potential Yield

Potential yield is the yield that is to be expected without manageable abiotic and biotic stresses and the use of the best adopted crop variety and management practices. Potential yield is determined from designated plots which are surveyed by crop physiologists or sampled from field experiments. Potential yields are calculated for optimum or recommended sowing dates, cultivar and planting densities in accordance with the dominant cropping system. Crop models are used to generate potential yields over wider areas, including different sowing dates, irrigation extent and management practices. Differences between simulated potential yield and actual yield reveal the *yield gap*, which is an important parameter in the analysis of food security and future production potential.[29]

---

[28] Fischer, R.A., 2015: Definitions and determination of crop yield, yield gaps, and of rates of change. *Field Crops Res.*, 182, 9–18.

[29] van Ittersum, M.K., Cassman, K.G., Grassini, P. et al., 2013: Yield gap analysis with local to global relevance – a review. *Field Crops Res.*, 143, 4–17.

Economic Yield

Economic yield is the yield obtained by farmers with average natural resources using economically optimal practices and inputs. In well-established cropping systems without competition among farmers for resources, prices and transportation costs, the economic yield typically reaches 70–80% of the potential yield. In less developed cropping systems, economic yields are typically well below potential yields.

4.4.1 SOURCES OF CROP YIELD DATA

The main source of agricultural production statistics are government surveys and censuses that include crop yield data at different geographical resolutions. In highly mechanised production systems, combine harvesters measure directly yield during harvesting and grain elevators aggregate production data at grain delivery stations. Satellites provide yield estimates through vegetation indices, which are frequently used for crop monitoring and forecasting. Crop models simulate yields based on daily input parameters and allow the assessment of past yields at current production conditions and systems.

AGRICULTURAL SURVEYS

The systematic measurement of agriculture production is mostly undertaken by government agencies and is based on statistical samples of farmers conducted through questionnaires or phone interviews. Objective yield surveys are conducted by assessors through plant counts and fruit measurements within a sample of representative parcels. Yield surveys follow standardise methods and approaches but can vary largely among countries.[30] Most yield surveys rely on multi-stage stratified sampling where plots are selected at farm level within a homogenous region to develop a statistically representative population through area sampling frames. Yield surveys are conducted at regular intervals, ranging from monthly to seasonal time frames, and are typically based on a set of selected farms or randomly chosen farms or a combination of both. Depending on the survey methodology and the efficiency of reporting the measurements within government organisations, it can take several months for official yield data to be available. In markets that contain heterogenous farm sizes, surveys tend to be biased towards larger farms, which typically produce higher yields, with better access to input supplies and finance compared with small farms.

In some cases, agriculture production data are available through surveys that focus on accounting and microeconomic data (e.g. FADN[31] in Europe) where crop yields can be derived from farm-based revenues, which divided by the price results in yield proxies.

Yield Surveys in the USA

The National Agricultural Statistics Service (NASS) is part of United States Department of Agriculture (USDA) and publishes agriculture reports that are based on surveys. NASS reports include production and supplies of food and fibre, prices paid and received by farmers, farm labour and wages, farm finances, chemical use, area

---

[30] Benedetti, R., Piersimoni, F. Bee, M. and Espa, G., 2010: Agricultural Survey. Wiley, Chichester, 434p.

[31] http://ec.europa.eu/agriculture/rica/concept_en.cfm (accessed June 2017).

planted, cost of production, farm expenditures, grain yield and production, livestock numbers and other agricultural variables. NASS provides regular updates and forecasts for the main crop types, including area planted, area harvested and yields.[32] To conduct surveys and collect data from statistically meaningful samples in a cost-efficient way, NASS uses area sampling frames. An area frame is a collection of all land parcels of an area of interest from which a sample is drawn.

Development of Strata
A first step is stratification where the land within a county is divided into homogenous groups (strata) through land use criteria to reduce the sampling variability. Satellite imagery is used to assist the delineation of the strata. The strata are further divided into substrata by grouping areas that are similar from an agricultural point of view. Multi-stage sampling is applied for each stratum to calculate the number of segments to sample. NASS uses approximately 11 000 segments in 49 states that are visited by data collection personnel, representing around 0.6% of the total segments. Each year, some 3000 segments are rotated and around 27% of the national area frame sample is based on newly selected segments each year. Frames are generally used for 15–20 years, after which a new frame is constructed, particularly in case of large land use changes.

Yield Surveys
NASS conducts an Agricultural Yield Survey that provides monthly farmer-reported data of crop yields and area planted throughout the growing season for all main field crops in all states except Alaska and Hawaii. Most farmers are interviewed by phone or in person. In the first month, area planted, area for harvest and expected yield are collected from each farmer in the sample for each crop type. In the following months, expected yields are updated. Sample sizes range from 5500 in June to 27 000 in August. NASS further undertakes an Objective Yield Survey that provides monthly farm-based yield measurements for wheat, corn, soybeans, cotton and potatoes. The survey is based on a sample of fields in which qualified personnel count plants and fruits in random plots until the crop is mature or harvested. Sampled ears, pods, bolls, heads or tubers are sent to a laboratory to determine weight, threshed grain weight and moisture content. Post-harvest visits are made to assess fruit left on some of the sampled fields to estimate harvest losses, which are subtracted from the gross yield to determine the net yield. NASS provides the survey data at different geographical resolutions down to county level and provides online tools to visualise and download the data.[33]

Aggregation Issues
Most governments report agricultural data at aggregated levels such as village, township, county, sub-district, district, prefecture, province and/or state, with yield being computed by weighting production and area planted or harvested. However, the aggregation of yields over administrative areas can severely reduce random and systematic variations in yields at farm level.[34] The variability of yield, as measured by the standard

---

[32] Schnepf, R., 2017: NASS and U.S. Crop Production Forecasts: Methods and Issues. Congressional Research Service 7-5700, 41p.
[33] https://quickstats.nass.usda.gov (accessed July 2017).
[34] Claassen, R. and Just, R.E., 2011: Heterogeneity and distributional form of farm-level yields. *Am. J. Agric. Econ.*, 93(1), 144–60.

deviation, typically decreases with increasing geographical aggregation, as farm-based yields are not perfectly correlated and are driven by local weather conditions, different soil types and management practices as well as the presence of pests and diseases. Numerous studies have shown that while the mean crop yield remains comparable at aggregated geographical level, such as a county compared with a farm, the standard deviation and coefficient of variance can decrease up to five times with a usual aggregation bias of factor two.[35]

Quality of Yields from Agricultural Surveys

The quality, resolution and ease of access to agricultural production statistics vary largely among countries. Yield data in most high-income countries are quality-controlled, distributed by a dedicated organisation and available online at little or no cost. In most low-income countries, agricultural statistics are available at national level, but regional statistics requires a collaboration with the relevant government agency to access the data and often require an effort for digitising from hard copies and quality control. In some countries, a special permission is required before yield data can be used for commercial purposes. Depending on the legal framework and the government use of yield measurements, a certain degree of smoothing in yield time series can occur at different administrative levels. The reason for smoothing is often thought to be driven by local governments aiming to obtain larger financial support from the central government. Further, smoothing might be politically motivated, particularly in election years, where the local government might want to be seen to contribute to the well-being of the farming community. Smoothing is difficult to detect and can be assessed only by regressing yield time series to weather data or using crop models if other random and systematic factors such as changes in farming technology can be ruled out.

COMBINE HARVESTERS AND ELEVATORS

Increasingly, crop yield data are available in highly mechanised production systems through combine harvesters that record yields during the harvesting process. Additionally, grain aggregators and elevators maintain records of delivered crop volumes, which allows the establishment of approximate regional and farm yields. However, yields from harvesters and aggregators are available only in some markets and for the main crop types.

Combine Harvesters

Most modern combine harvesters include equipment that measures the flow of granular material at constant velocity through grain mass flow sensors. The instantaneous yield is calculated continuously based on the quotient of grain mass flow and area productivity, which in turn is derived in multiplying velocity with actual cutting width of the combine harvester.[36] Besides grain flows, the sensors measure grain moisture contents while the positioning system permanently records the location of the

---

[35] Finger, R., 2012: Biases in farm-level yield risk analysis due to data aggregation. *Ger. J. Agric. Econ.*, 61(1), 30–43.

[36] Reitz, F. and Kutzbach, H.D., 1996: Investigations on a particular yield mapping system for combine harvesters. *Comput. Electron. Agr.*, 14, 137–50.

harvester. As grain losses occur during harvesting, dropped ears and cutter bar losses need to be estimated and added to the instantaneous yields to obtain gross yields. Based on the geo-coordinates and the instantaneous yields, high-resolution yield maps are established through statistical interpolation techniques (e.g. kriging) to display spatial yield variability as a function of soil type, nutrient availability, drainage status and slope. Some farming associations maintain large databases of yield maps from combine harvesters, which could be explored ultimately for agricultural insurance purposes in markets with a high level of mechanisation in harvesting. Errors in yield measurements typically stem from the flow sensor system, the position computation and abrupt changes in the forward velocity of the harvester.

Grain Elevators

Grain elevators, processors and logistics companies typically measure the quantity through weighing and quality through examining samples from individual grain providers such as farmers or producer groups. In cases where most farmers deliver grain to an exclusive elevator, which is typically the case with cooperatives with contract framing agreements, farm yields can be approximated in relating the production delivered to the elevator to the area of production. However, yields derived from elevators can only be approximative as farmers often retain some of the grain at the farm for cattle feed or seed production.

SATELLITES

Satellite-derived vegetation indices have been used to determine crop yields at high resolution and are used for crop monitoring and forecasting (Section 4.3). While crop yields based on vegetation indices provide valuable estimates and increasingly support traditional survey techniques at low costs, they cannot substitute for surveyed yields due to high spatial variability. Further, changes in crop planting patterns require recalibration of the vegetation indices and crop masks that identify areas where a certain crop is grown (Section 4.3).

CROP MODELS

Crop growth models simulate crop yields in a dynamic system as a function of the main biological, physical and chemical processes that define crop growth in response to environmental and management conditions. Statistical and mechanistic crop models have been used for a large number of applications, including (i) evaluation of the performance of new crop cultivars in function of genetic characteristics and environmental conditions, (ii) assessment of physiological processes where observations are lacking, (iii) analysis of the best crop rotation cycles as a response to input supplies, (iv) analysis of spatial yield variability, (v) assessments of impacts of management practices on yield, (vi) forecasting crop yields in function of current growth conditions, (vii) determination of potential yield under optimal growing conditions and management practices, (viii) risk analysis of extreme events such as droughts and excessive rainfall, and (ix) impact analysis of climate change on future yield and estimations of yield gaps.[37]

---

[37] Holzworth, D.P., Snow, V., Janssen, S. et al., 2015: Agricultural production systems modelling and software: Current status and future prospects. *Environ. Modell. Softw.*, 72, 276–86.

Types of Crop Models

Crop models can be divided into statistical, mechanistic and functional models. Statistical models use mathematical equations (regressions) to describe crop growth in function of input parameters such as weather parameters and basic soil–water equations. These models require long historical yield time series and often operate over large areas to identify broad trends. Mechanistic models use dynamic and deterministic equations of plant and soil processes to simulate crop growth in time steps (often daily) as a function of environmental factors. Functional models use simplified closed functional forms to simulate complex processes such as soil–water balance models to derive water-limited crop yields with fixed planting dates, 10-day time steps and a seasonally integrated ratio of actual to potential evapotranspiration.

The choice of a particular type of crop model depends largely on the purpose of the analysis, the required resolution and precision, and the availability of input data. There is always a trade-off between the reduction of uncertainty from capturing additional determinants of yield and the need to estimate an increasing number of model parameters.

Mechanistic Crop Models

Mechanistic models include dynamic components that address time-dependent changes in the crop growth and deterministic components that define the state of the crop growth system at a given time. These models require up to 30 different input parameters and need intensive calibration. While initially only used by researchers, mechanistic crop models are increasingly applied for precision farming, yield forecasts, projection of yields under future climate and yield-gap analyses, with data becoming increasingly available in the open domain.[38] Outputs of mechanistic crop models have been investigated for crop insurance purposes (Section 6.11).

Types of Mechanistic Crop Models

The most used models include the Decision Support System for Agrotechnology Transfer (DSSAT), the Agricultural Production Systems Simulator (APSIM), the Environmental Policy Integrated Climate (EPIC) model, the World Food Studies (WOFOST) model, the CROPSYS model, the Soil Plant System Simulation Model (DAISY) and Aquacrop. While most models contain the same or very similar dynamic and deterministic equations, large differences in simulated yields can occur for the same location, driven by mathematical functions that control plant growth and changes of soil water and nitrogen over time. To overcome the reliance on and potential bias of one particular model, the use of multi-model ensembles has been suggested.[39]

DSSAT

DSSAT is an open source software application that is under continuous development and includes a set of independent models that jointly simulate crop growth for 42 crop types, with applications in over 100 countries.[40] The proficient use of DSSAT requires an understanding of the basic physical process in plant growth relative to soil,

---

[38] For example, http://www.agmip.org/agmip-data (accessed July 2017).

[39] Martre, P., Wallach, D., Asseng, S. et al., 2015: Multimodel ensembles of wheat growth: many models are better than one. *Glob. Chan. Biol.*, 21, 911–25.

[40] https://dssat.net (accessed March 2017).

water, evapotranspiration and transpiration, nutrient fluxes and phenology. Expertise is required to derive parameters for sites where not all necessary data are available. DSSAT contains databases that describe weather, soil, experiment conditions and measurements as well as genotype information. The crop models require daily weather data, soil surface and profile information, and detailed crop management plans. While crop genetic information is defined in a crop species file within DSSAT, cultivar information needs to be provided by the user. The Cropping System Model (CSM) forms the core part of DSSAT. It simulates crop yields using data from the databases and relies on different modules that describe changes over time in soil and crop growth that occur on a single land unit. CSM allows sensitivity analyses and comparison of simulated and observed yields, simulations over several crop seasons using the same soil conditions, which supports trend and risk analyses, and simulations of crop rotations. DSSAT provides crop yields at a single point (which is often the location of the weather station) or on a regular grid in case gridded input data are used.

Performance of Mechanistic Crop Models

Generally, correlation coefficients between modelled and observed yields reach 0.7–0.9 if (i) the best suitable crop model is chosen and the capabilities and limitations of the model are understood, including the accuracy needed relative to the input parameters, (ii) weather data and soil water properties are available at the location where yields are measured, (iii) cultivar parameters are measured experimentally or calibrated with adequate data, and (iv) production is managed properly and damage from pests and diseases is measurable and included in the simulations.

A recent study examined the performance of four mechanistic crop models for winter wheat in Spain and found that yield outputs at field level were comparable when water was not a limiting factor; however, modelled yields can vary considerably under rainfed conditions, which is related to differences in how soil water availability is simulated.[41] Modelled yields with the EPIC crop model have shown good results with observed yields for winter wheat, rainfed and irrigated corn and spring barley in different European regions, including (i) modelled winter-wheat yields are significantly related to observed yields in 30% of the regions, with correlation coefficients ranging between 0.64–0.81, (ii) modelled corn yields show correlation coefficients of 0.29–0.64 with significance in 40% of the regions, and (iii) modelled spring barley yields reach correlation coefficients between 0.73 and 0.89 (Figure 4.2).[42]

4.4.2 TREATMENT OF YIELD DATA

Yield time series often include a variety of inconsistencies that includes errors, outliers and missing values, which are often related to inaccurate reporting or errors during geographical aggregation. Yield series typically show negative skewness in that crops have biological constraints that limit the maximum observed yield and yields near the

---

[41] Castaneda-Vera, A., Leffelaar, P.A., Álvaro-Fuentes, J. et al., 2015: Selecting crop models for decision making in wheat insurance. *Eur. J. Agron.*, 68, 97–116.
[42] Balkovic, J., van der Velde, M., Schmid, E. et al., 2013: Pan-European crop modelling with EPIC: Implementation, up-scaling and regional crop yield validation. *Agric. Sys.*, 120, 61–75.

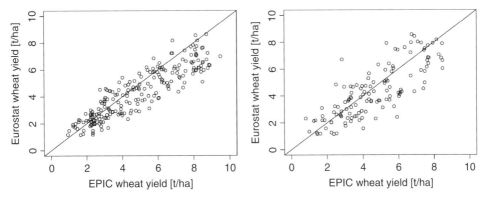

FIGURE 4.2   Left: Simulated winter wheat yield with EPIC and observed winter wheat yield (EUROSTAT) for NUTS2 resolution for 276 regions in Europe in 2007 including 130 data points and a correlation coefficient of 0.8 and Right: same as Left but for 214 data points and for 1997–2007 and a correlation coefficient of 0.89.

Data source: International Institute for Applied System Analysis (IASSA).

maximum are more frequently observed than yields near the minimum. Additionally, yield time series can show cycles that are related to climate oscillations such as the El Niño Southern Oscillation.[43]

Detrending of yield data is of fundamental importance for risk analysis and risk transfer products, and ignoring a yield trend can lead to severe over- or under-estimation of risk and inadequate insurance conditions. PDFs are used to increase the possible outcome of yield realisations, which is of particular interest for yield-based insurance products which cover low yields relative to an average expected yield.

DISCONTINUITIES AND MISSING YIELD DATA

As yield is typically recorded on paper during the field assessment and subsequently entered manually or through digitisation into an electronic format, errors can occur at different levels. Larger gaps in data can make yield time series unsuitable for risk analysis and transfer. Additionally yield time series often show outliers, particularly low yields, due to impacts of adverse weather conditions or pests and diseases, and heteroscedasticity as the error terms in regressions are non-homogeneous.

Discontinuities

Various discontinuities can occur in yield data, including errors and outliers that are wrongly reported or recorded when data are digitised or manually entered from hard copies. Errors in crop yield data are usually flagged and corrected by the data provider during quality control processes. Changes in reporting formats can lead to discontinuity, including units for which yields are reported, splitting or merging administrative areas, and crop seasons for which yield is reported (e.g. reporting yields of winter wheat separately from spring wheat). Large discontinuities often become evident from

---

[43] Nadolnyak, D., Vedenov, D. and Novak, J., 2008: Information value of climate-based yield forecasts in selecting optimal crop insurance coverage. *Am. J. Agric. Econ.*, 90(5), 1248–55.

plotting yield series (Figure 4.3) and over-regional comparisons of yields of the same crop type.

Missing Yield Data

Missing yield data are relatively common and are often related to a shortage of questionnaires during surveys, a lack of personnel to undertake the surveys or data that got lost after yield recordings. Data providers often flag missing values (e.g. –999 or a blank value), but in cases where zero yield is reported, it is important to understand whether the measurement is missing or yield was indeed zero. Statistical approaches used to fill gaps in crop yield data are similar to the spatial interpolation methods used to fill missing weather data (Section 4.2) and include Kernel smoothing, kriging and regressions.[44] In cases where yields of several seasons are missing, statistical filling of the gaps from the observations alone is challenging and requires the use of alternative data from satellites or crop models.

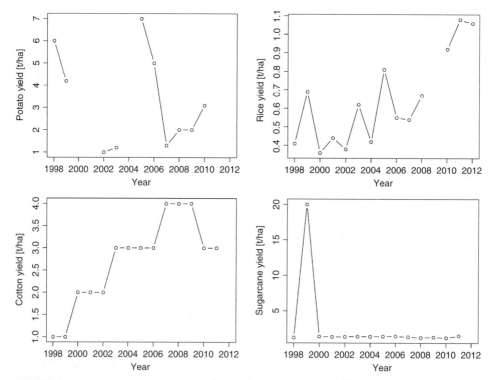

FIGURE 4.3 Top Left: Annual potato yield in the district of Sikar (Rajasthan, India), 1998–2010 with missing values in 2000, 2001 and 2004. Top Right: Rice yield in the district of Umaria (Madhya Pradesh, India), 1998–2012 with a missing value in 2009. Bottom Left: Cotton yield in the district of Patiala (Punjab, India) for the Kharif season, 1998–2011 with yields jumping after 2–4 seasons abruptly to a next level. Bottom Right: Sugarcane yield in the district of Rajnandgaon (Chhattisgarh, India), 1998–2011 with an erroneous value in 1999 where probably sugarcane biomass instead of yield was reported.
Data source: http://aps.dac.gov.in.

[44] Lokupitiya, R.S., Lokupitiya, E. and Paustian, K., 2006: Comparison of missing value imputation methods for crop yield data. *Environmetrics*, 17, 339–49.

TIME TRENDS IN CROP YIELDS

In many parts of the world, yields have undergone substantial changes due to the variability of weather conditions, improved input supplies (crop genetics, fertiliser, crop protection), better management practices, access to irrigation and soil drainage, and generally improved access to agricultural information, such as optimum planting dates in function of pre-sowing soil moisture. In many production systems these improvements have led to an increase in crop yield over time. The fast distributions of new agriculture technology and input supplies in developped agricultural markets lead to a relatively homogeneous pattern of yield increases over farms and regions and a consistent trend in farm-level yields, which is less the case in developing agricultural systems, where within a small area, positive and negative yield trends can occur (Figure 4.4). In countries where the agricultural production system went through restructuring with several phases of investment and de-investment, trends in crop

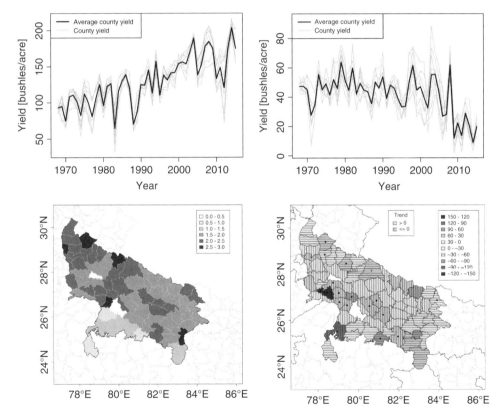

FIGURE 4.4 Top Left: Corn yield for 9 counties in Illinois, USA (thin lines) and the average county yield (solid line), 1968–2015 showing a positive trend over time (increasing yields); Top Right: Winter wheat yields for 9 counties in Oklahoma, USA (thin line) and the average county yield (solid line), 1968–2015 revealing a negative trend over time (decreasing yields); Bottom Left: Average district rice yields [t/ha] in the Kharif season in Uttar Pradesh, India, 1998–2010 and Bottom Right: Linear trends in district rice yields [kg/ha] in the Kharif season in Uttar Pradesh, India, 1998–2010 with the level of the trend (shading).
Data source: NASS (top left and top right plot) and http://aps.dac.gov.in (bottom left and bottom right plot).

yields can be complex and misleading. Often, yield time series show certain carry-over effects in that past seasons influence the next season and create additional noise in yield trends, e.g. a severe drought can impact soil moisture level in the next season.

Detrending Methods

Detrending methods for yield time series need to address outliers, heteroscedasticity and skewed distributions to produce reliable estimations in yield trends. The choice of a detrending method is often a trade-off between the complexity and number of data and practical consideration, particularly when large datasets are involved. Additional parameters can always be introduced but increase the risk of under- or over-fitting yield trends. Non-parametric methods generally tend to more over-fit trends than parametric models.

For many applications related to risk assessment and insurance, observed yield (y) is decomposed into two components, written as:[45]

$$y = \bar{y} + \varepsilon$$

where $\bar{y}$ is the technical yield achieved under average weather and growth conditions and ε is the residual (error) term that includes random impacts which typically stem from adverse weather conditions or pests and diseases. For the development of risk transfer products, detrending of yield series serves to (i) obtain $\bar{y}$ that is the basis to define the sum insured through the average yield, (ii) extrapolate the trend to the next growing season, and (iii) obtain ε which represents the insured risk, with negative values of ε being treated as damage which is compensated under crop insurance policies.

Deterministic trends in yield time series are generally addressed by regression techniques with linear or non-linear trends using splines, log-linear trending, higher-order polynomials and nonparametric smoothing. The predicted yield (y_t) is generally computed as a function of:

$$y_t = X_t \alpha + e_t$$

where X_t is a linear or non-linear function of time, α is the slope parameter and e_t is the deviation from the trend. Often, a linear detrending method is applied and ordinary least squares (OLS) are used to derive the parameters of the linear regression by minimising the sum of the squares of the differences between the observed dependent variable and those predicted by the linear function. The significance level of a linear trend is determined through standard errors (t-statistics), which are tested against a Student-t distribution with n-2 degrees of freedom to reveal the probability that the true value of the coefficient is zero.

In case the standard deviation does not depend on yield levels, the detrended yield in year t (Y_t) is obtained by simply adding all residuals (e_t) to the last year of yield observation (e.g. 2017) through:

$$Y_t = y_{2017} + e_t$$

---

[45] Goodwin, B.K. and Ker, A.P., 1998: Nonparametric estimation of crop yield distributions: implications for rating group-risk crop insurance contracts. *Am. J. Agric. Econ.*, 80, 139–53.

In case the standard deviation is proportional to the yield, Y_t becomes:

$$Y_t = y_{2017} + \left(1 + \frac{e_t}{Y_t}\right)$$

Both detrending approaches described above are used in practice, whereas the case that the standard deviation is proportional to the yield finds more empirical support.[46] However, this violates a precondition of OLS that error terms are to be uncorrelated with the underlying variable. Due to likely spatial correlation of yields and the presence of outliers, OLS-based detrending methods are considered as *non-robust*, particularly for short time series; however, there are arguments that ultimately, the correlation between yield data and errors decreases over distance and that OLS is therefore a justified approach. Detrending approaches that are based on MM estimators have shown to be efficient for both small outlier-uncontaminated samples and outlier-contaminated crop yield time series.[47]

In cases where large and abrupt changes have occurred in yield series and with time series that are outlier-contaminated, weather data have been proposed as regressors.[48] Alternatively, the quantile regression has been suggested as a robust regression method to allow more weight to more extreme values of crop yields.[49] As OLS methods are known to be biased in the presence of consistent carry-over effects from previous seasons, the ARIMA models are better suited to detrend yield series with carry-over effects.[50]

Piecewise Linear Trends
When several stage-wise trends exist in yield series over different time periods, piecewise linear splines are used for detrending through non-linear least squares to estimate parameters and breakpoints (Figure 4.5). For one breakpoint t_0 the predicted yield (y_t) is defined as:[51]

$$y_t = \begin{cases} X_t\alpha_1 + e_1t & t \leq t_0 \\ X_t\alpha_2 + e_2t & t \geq t_0 \end{cases}$$

[46] Goodwin, B.K. and Ker, A.P., 1998: Nonparametric estimation of crop yield distributions: implications for rating group-risk crop insurance contracts. *Am. J. Agric. Econ.*, 80, 139–53.

[47] Finger, R., 2010: Revisiting the evaluation of robust regression techniques for crop yield data detrending. *Am. J. Agric. Econ.*, 92, 205–11.

[48] Breustedt, G., Bokusheva, R. and Heidelbach, O., 2008: Evaluating the potential of index insurance schemes to reduce crop yield in an arid region. *J. Agric. Econ.*, 59(2), 312–28.

[49] Conradt, S., Finger, R. and Bokusheva, R., 2015: Tailored to the extremes: quantile regression for index-based insurance contract design. *Agric. Econ.*, 46, 537–47.

[50] Ker, A.P. and Goodwin, B.J., 2000: Nonparametric estimation of crop insurance rates revisited. *Am. J. Agric. Econ.*, 81(2), 287–304.

[51] Rondanini, D.P., Gomez, N.V., Agosti, M.B. and Miralles, D.J., 2012: Global trends of rapeseed grain yield stability and rapeseed-to-wheat yield ratio in the last four decades. *Eur. J. Agron.*, 37(1), 56–65.

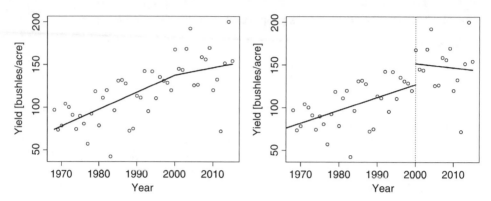

FIGURE 4.5 Piecewise linear trends in corn yields in Adams County (Illinois, USA), 1968–2015 with Left: 1 knot in the year 2000 and an average yield of 144.3 bushels/acre (2000–2015) and Right: 1 knot with a breaking point in the year 2000 (dotted line) and an average yield of 148.2 bushels/acre (2000–2015).
Data source: NASS.

When detrending yield observations, the degree of variance according to yield levels needs to be assessed, particularly to understand whether the variance systematically increases, decreases or remains constant in function of yield levels.

The Importance of Detrending for Risk Transfer Products

The correct identification of trends in yield series is essential for the development of risk transfer products, while failures and errors in detrending have been shown to lead to inefficient crop insurance products.[52] When yield series show a statistically significant positive trend and yields are not detrended, yield-based crop insurance products will be over-priced as yields in earlier years used to be well below current levels (Figure 4.6). Meanwhile, strong negative trends lead to an underestimation of risk as historical yields are well above current levels on which triggers for yield-based insurance are defined.

YIELD DISTRIBUTIONS

The residuals, which are the observed yields minus the estimated trend, that result from detrending show for each year of historical observation how much the yield has deviated from the trend, with positive (negative) values revealing seasons with above (below) normal yield relative to the trend. The density or probabilities of the residuals is described through a PDF and both parametric and non-parametric methods are used to generate yield distributions from observed yields. Parametric methods such as the beta distribution are typically used for shorter yield time series, while nonparametric methods like the kernel estimator are preferred when long data series are available.

---

[52] Just, R.E. and Weninger, Q., 1999: Are crop yields normally distributed? *Am. J. Agric. Econ*, 81(2), 287–304.

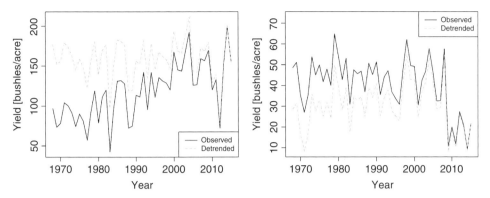

FIGURE 4.6 Left: Observed and linearly de-trended corn yields in Adams County (Illinois, USA), 1968–2015 with an average yield of 118 bushels/acre (observed) and a higher yield of 158 bushels/acre (detrended) due to a positive trend and Right: Observed and linearly de-trended winter wheat yields in Blaine County (Oklahoma, USA), 1968–2015 with an average yield of 40.7 bushels/acre (observed) and a lower yield of 30.7 bushels/acre (detrended) due to a negative trend. *Data source*: NASS.

Parametric Methods

With parametric methods, the parameters of the PDF are derived from the observed yields while the correct family of functions that fits best to the observed yield data has to be known a priori. Initially, the normal distribution was used, but this has been considered inappropriate as crop yields often show a tendency towards a negative skewness.[53] In the literature, several distributions, including log-normal, gamma, logistic, beta, Weibull and versions of the Burr distributions, have been used to describe yield densities for a variety of crop types and regions. Of these distributions, only the gamma, beta and Burr distributions can accommodate negative skewness in crop yields.

The four-parametric beta distribution is the most commonly used for yield data and the PDF takes the following form:[54]

$$\hat{f}(y) = \frac{1}{B(\alpha, \beta)} y^{\alpha-1} (1-y)^{\beta-1}$$

where α and β are shape parameters, B is defined through the gamma function Γ and is a normalisation constant to assure that the total probability sums to 1. B is defined through:

$$B(\alpha, \beta) = \frac{\Gamma(\alpha)\,\Gamma(\beta)}{\Gamma(\alpha + \beta)}$$

While α and β are determined from the data, the minimum and maximum yields need to be predetermined. While the minimum yield is typically set to zero, the

[53] Atwood, J., Shaik, S. and Watts, M., 2002: Can normality of yields be assumed for crop insurance? *Can. J. Agric. Econ.*, 50, 171–84.
[54] Nelson, C.H. and Preckel, P.V., 1989: The conditional beta distribution as a stochastic production function. *Am. J. Agric. Econ.*, 71, 370–7.

maximum yield is determined through (i) the maximum value or slightly increased value from the observations, or (ii) the potential yield, which is available from field experiences or crop models.

Non-Parametric Methods

Unlike parametric methods that require a particular functional form, non-parametric methods use the yield observations to select the appropriate representation of the yield distribution. The simplest non-parametric method is a histogram where all yield observations are divided into bins with predefined widths and where the number of observations in each bin determines the shape of the density function. More complex nonparametric models are based on kernel density estimators where the estimation of the density at a given point is the sum of the individual kernels at that point. The kernel estimator at a given point y is written as:[55]

$$\hat{f}(y) = n^{-1} \sum_{i=1}^{n} K_h(y - y_i)$$

with $K_h(u) = 1/hK(u/h)$, K as the kernel function and $h(h > 0)$ as the bandwidth or smoothing parameter, which determines the weight to assign to neighbouring observations in constructing the density. A larger bandwidth will smooth more and results in a flatter density function, while a small bandwidth size will generate a more irregular density. Methods to determine the bandwidth include the Silverman rule of thumb or mean integrated squared errors.[56]

The Importance of Detrending for Risk Transfer Products

The choice to derive yield densities through parametric or non-parametric methods largely defines the payout function of yield-based crop insurance products and determines the level of the premium rates. Inadequate density functions can lead to under- or over-estimation of risk (Figure 4.7) and results in increased adverse selection as producers evaluate the efficiency of insurance coverage.

4.5 DISASTER AND CALAMITY DATA

In most countries, government agencies maintain records of officially declared disasters and calamities, including magnitude, duration, severity and spatial extents. Procedures and contingency measures are defined in a country's disaster declaration processes and response plans. Although criteria to report disasters may vary over time, and improved irrigation schemes and flood water mitigation reduce vulnerability, disaster-affected areas provide valuable proxies to assess spatial dimensions of past disasters. Disaster declaration processes form the basis of calamity-based crop insurance such as the national rice insurance programme in Thailand (Section 6.4). Further, areas affected by

---

[55] Ker, A.P. and Coble, K., 2003: Modelling conditional yield densities. *Am. J. Agric. Econ.*, 85(2), 291–304.
[56] Goodwin, B.K. and Ker, A.P., 1998: Nonparametric estimation of crop yield distributions: implications for rating group-risk crop insurance contracts. *Am. J. Agric. Econ.*, 80, 139–53.

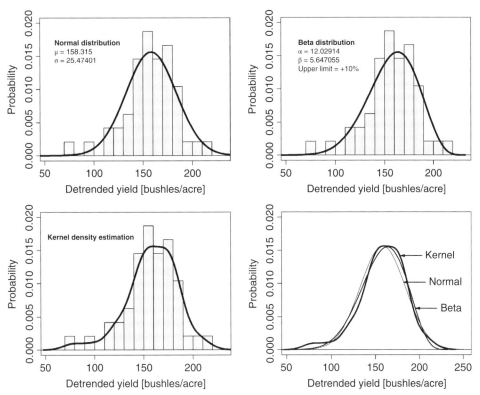

FIGURE 4.7 Probability density functions for linearly de-trended corn yields in Adams county (Illinois, USA), 1968–2015 with Top Left: Normal function with all parameters determined from the observations; Top Right: Beta function with the shape parameters determined from the observations, the minimum yield set as zero and the maximum yield as 10% above the highest observed yield; Bottom Left: Non-parametric Kernel function and Bottom Right: the three probability density functions in comparison.
Data source: NASS.

past disasters have been used to establish the initial premium rates for crop insurance in China (see Disaster Declaration Processes).

DISASTER DECLARATION PROCESSES

A disaster declaration is a mechanism through which governments acknowledge that response resources are overwhelmed and announce that additional assistance is necessary. The legal procedures to declare a disaster depend on a country's form of government and rules set in the emergency operations planning.[57] Disaster declaration processes, hazard identification processes and formats of risk reports vary largely among countries and can change over time. In countries with low regulation and loose

---

[57] Coppola, D.P., 2015: Introduction to International Disaster Management. 3rd edition. Elsevier, Amsterdam, 760p.

disaster risk management frameworks, there is a risk that local governments use disaster declarations to gain popularity with the population affected by a disaster through the release of ad-hoc payments, despite the fact that the disaster did not necessarily fulfil the declaration criteria in terms of severity and area affected. Further, it is often not clear to what extent quantitative parameters (e.g. a certain percentage of the total arable land needs to be affected to a certain extent) are included in the declaration process.

Government Response

In countries with centralised government, the entire disaster declaration process is handled centrally, while in the case of decentralised governing authorities (e.g. in provinces), disaster declaration takes a step-by-step approach, with local governments having the primary responsibility to respond. The local government first attempts to manage the hazard impact up to a point where resources and means are exhausted and a disaster is declared with an appeal to the next level of government (e.g. province or national level) for assistance. Based on an assessment of the extent and severity by the higher-level government (up to the level of the national government), the disaster declaration triggers a dedicated response including financial support. In case a national disaster is declared, various national government resources are mobilised with funds from a dedicated disaster response budgets. In case the disaster reaches a dimension with which the national government cannot cope any longer, an international appeal for assistance is issued to which governments of other countries, non-governmental organisations and multilateral finance institutions might respond.

Key Indicators for Disasters

Monitoring and early warning systems based on reliable triggers are a key component in disaster risk management. Typically, impacts of natural disasters that qualify for declaration are defined as exceptional circumstances. For drought, key elements that lead to a disaster declaration through exceptional circumstances include (i) meteorological conditions, (ii) agronomic and stock conditions, (iii) water supplies, (iv) environmental impacts, (v) farm income levels, and (vi) the general scale of the event.[58] Indicators that characterise a disaster describe magnitude, duration, severity and spatial extent, which are derived from measurements (e.g. hydrological and meteorological parameters) and include usage rates of resources (e.g. water levels in reservoirs). For drought, indicators for meteorological conditions often include drought indices such as the Standard Precipitation Index (SPI) or the Palmer Drought Index (Section 3.3), and the scale of the event is expressed as a percentage of the arable land affected. Triggers are threshold values that are based on indicators and determine the timing and level of response. Often, different triggers are combined in an ad-hoc fashion and can compromise a response plan.

Risk Statements

A competent government agency's identification of a hazard at the place of occurrence is an integral part of disaster risk management and forms the basis of risk analyses,

---

[58] Botterill, L.C. and Hayes, M.J., 2012: Drought triggers and declarations: Science and policy considerations for drought risk management. *Nat. Hazards*, 64, 139–51.

hazard profiling and response to address the disaster. Local disaster managers create risk statements and reports that include information such as type of hazard, description of the hazard, frequency and intensity of hazard occurrence, location of the hazard, speed of onset, including early warnings (if issued), and spatial extent.

CALAMITY DATA

In some countries, comprehensive databases and annual reports exist of declared disasters at the resolution of a province (or sub-province) and include for agricultural assets information such as (i) area affected by different degrees of damage extent or area affected in terms of total and partial losses, (ii) onset and duration of the disaster, with occasional descriptions of the temporal and spatial development of the disaster, (iii) mitigation measures taken, such as opening of dams to release flood water, emergency vaccination for livestock or mobilisation of additional firefighting resources, and (iv) affected industry sectors, including economic losses, insured losses and population affected. For certain types of disasters, countries report in a standardised format to international organisations such as the World Organisation for Animal Health (OIE) or the Centre for Research on the Epidemiology of Disasters (CRED), which maintains an Emergency Event Database (EM-Dat) for general disasters.

Improvements in crop genetics, irrigation systems and flood protection (e.g. dams) reduce the vulnerability to a disaster and influence the temporal development and spatial extent of a disaster. Meanwhile, the greater specialisation in production (monocultures) in recent years increases the exposure to a disaster. Therefore, historical disasters are often not directly comparable to current environments.

Crop Insurance Pricing Using Calamity Data in China

China has comprehensive and detailed agricultural disaster statistics which initially were used to determine crop insurance premium rates for the main crop types and perils. Insurance policies under the national crop insurance programme are peril-specific, with different franchises and deductibles applied per peril, and as such follow the convention of government-declared disaster areas, often referred to as area-affected data.

Area-Affected Data
Area-affected data are available for drought, flood, hail and wind, frost and typhoon at three damage extents, including areas slightly affected (sown areas with 10–30% of damaged area), areas affected (30–80% damage) and areas with total losses (over 80% damage). These data are consistently available at province level since 1949, with data after 1965 to be considered as more reliable. For some provinces, prefecture and county-level data are available but often only for the perils of drought and flood. The total loss area (*TLA*) in a given year i for a given peril p is defined as:

$$TLA_{i,p} = a_1\left(ASA_{i,p}\right) + a_2\left(AA_{i,p}\right) + a_3\left(ATL_{i,p}\right)$$

with *ASA* as areas slightly affected, *AA* as areas affected, *ATL* the area with total losses and a_1, a_2 and a_3 as constants representing the loss level for the three damage extents, e.g. 0.2 for damage extents of 10–30% in the case of *ASA*. The average annual crop loss (*AACL*) for a given peril *p* over *n* years consists of the risk rate and is defined through:

$$AACL_p = \sum_{i=1}^{n} \frac{TLA_{i,p}}{TAP_i}$$

with *TAP* as the total crop area planted in year *i* at the resolution of a province, prefecture or county.

Limitations of Area-Affected Data
While area-affected data provide valuable information about peril-specific hazard intensity at regional level, they include several limitations. The data represent the entire crop production and should be representative for the main crop types (e.g. rice, corn, soybean, wheat), but are less meaningful for secondary crop types (e.g. sunflower, rapeseed, cotton), which have different hazard vulnerabilities. Further, significant shifts in crop types over time (e.g. increased corn areas and reduced rice areas) modify the overall vulnerability of all crop types and can lead to either over- or underestimation of risk based on calamity data. Area-affected data are not crop specific, which is overcome by Chinese insurers for risk pricing by using crop yield data and relative variability compared to yields averaged over all crops, which de facto represents the area affected of all perils. An additional limitation is that area-affected data are reported on a calendar-year basis and in the case of winter crops that are planted in autumn and harvested in the summer of the following year (e.g. rapeseed in central China), areas affected are reported in two calendar years. Further, area-affected data do not reveal the establishment of irrigation systems and flood protection measures, which generally have decreased the area affected by droughts and floods. With more than 10 years of crop insurance loss history, insurance claims ratios have been used to validate and adjust the initial insurance terms or conditions that were derived from area-affected data.

4.6 LIVESTOCK AND AQUACULTURE DATA

Livestock and aquaculture risk transfer products rely essentially on production statistics (inventories) and past mortality ratios from individual producers or producer associations. As large-scale mortality events might not have occurred at a particular site, regional livestock and aquaculture production statistics from government surveys and industrialised producers are used to assess regional loss potentials and classify risks.

LIVESTOCK SURVEYS

In most countries, government agencies undertake frequent livestock surveys that are based on stratified sampling, including onsite interviews or phone calls with producers, web-based questionnaires, recoding carcass weights in abattoirs, aerial surveys for nomadic livestock and, on some occasions, recording animals through electronic tags. Livestock slaughter data are typically collected from slaughterhouses and processing plants, which are often under government supervision, but would not include all slaughter operations. In livestock production systems that show large spatial variability, samples are typically stratified according to vegetation type and ownership structures. Large commercial livestock producers are typically listed in government registers and form an integral part of the surveyed livestock population.

The frequency of surveys varies in function of the reproduction cycle of the animals and typically ranges from annual (cattle) or half-yearly (pork) to at least quarterly (poultry), with statistics published at the resolution of a province or a state. Budgetary and resource constraints oblige most countries, especially low-income countries, to narrow the collection of livestock data and indicators.

Livestock Indicators

Livestock surveys form the basis for deriving different indicators that reveal economic productivity and are mostly available for the main livestock types, including cattle, sheep, pigs, goats and poultry. Livestock indicators are derived from livestock surveys and typically include (i) current livestock inventory in terms of number of animals, annual births and number of slaughtered animals per livestock type and production system, (ii) quantity of produced animal products, including meat, milk and eggs, (iii) prices of livestock and livestock products, and (iv) number of affected and diseased animals per type of disease (Table 4.1).[59] As member countries must report particularly harmful epidemic diseases to OIE (Section 3.10), the disseminated information includes data on particular outbreaks, comprising affected and culled livestock.

Livestock Mortality

In some countries, livestock surveys provide the cause of livestock mortality data per main livestock species, including natural perils, predators, diseases, digestive and respiratory problems, and birth problems at national or provincial level. Statistics on indemnity payments from government compensation funds contain information on the number of culled livestock from notifiable diseases and amounts dispersed for direct losses (loss of animal values through culling) and indirect losses (costs for destruction of livestock, disposal of carcasses, disinfection of facilities). Additionally, industry-based disease funds that contain financial contributions of government agencies and livestock producers include data on epidemic disease outbreaks. For countries with endemic diseases, the overall cost of vaccines has been used to reconstruct the number of infected livestock from disease outbreaks.[60]

AQUACULTURE SURVEYS

Surveys of fisheries and aquaculture typically measure variables related to production, the environment (e.g. composition of stock and the health of the surrounding environment) and the socio-economic context (e.g. prices paid and received, number

---

[59] Moss, J., Morley, P., Baker, D. et al., 2016: Improving Methods for Estimating Livestock Production and Productivity – Literature Review. Technical Report Series GO-11-2016, 82p.

[60] Knight-Jones, T.J.D. and Rushton, J., 2013: The economic impacts of foot and mouth disease – What are they, how big are they and where do they occur? *Prev. Vet. Med.*, 112(3), 161–73.

TABLE 4.1   Overview of livestock indicators from surveys that are most relevant for risk transfer products.

Indicator	Sub-Indicator	Definition	Use for Risk Transfer
Animal production	Total animals	Total number of animals per species (overall population)	Indication of livestock population and herd dynamics over time per country or region (e.g. province or state)
	Total slaughtered animals	Number of animals slaughtered per species	
	Total meat	Number of slaughtered animals times average weight of slaughtered animal by species	
	Total milk	Number of lactating animals per species times average daily production times 30 times production months	
Animal health	Total cases	Total number of sick animals and dead animals per disease and species	Indication of disease frequency and severity of total cases relative to total animals over time per country or region (e.g. province or state)
	Cases per 10 000	Total number of sick and dead animals per disease and species relative to 10 000 animals in the overall population	Indication of disease-related mortality
	Total animals destroyed	Total number of animals killed for control of a disease under government order per disease and species	Indication of government slaughter order enforcement
	Vaccination coverage	Total number of animals vaccinated against a disease relative to the overall population	Indication of emergency response and preventative measures

Source: Adapted from Moss et al. (2016).

of individuals depending on the sector for livelihood).[61] In aquaculture surveys, production is represented as the weight or volume of biomass per species and reported according to categories of size and type of operation. Often aquaculture surveys are

---

[61] Berg E. and Kaiser, M., 2017: Gaps and Methodological Approach: A Critical Analysis of Methods for Surveys of Fisheries and Aquaculture. Technical Report 28, Global Strategy Technical Report, Rome, 44p.

based on multiple frame surveys where different sources of information are combined to increase coverage.

Aquaculture surveys are typically undertaken on-site (frame surveys) or by interviewing a statistically representative number of aquaculture operations. In industrialised production systems, production statistics are typically available from industry associations or individual large producers, which frequently determine inventory values. In smallholder aquaculture production systems, financial constraints often limit on-site surveys and favour household censuses and general agricultural surveys in which aquaculture might be included.

4.7 FORESTRY DATA

Forestry surveys provide regular information on productivity per main tree species and production systems at regional and national scale. In some markets, specific reports and databases provide information of damaged areas and severity for large-scale natural disasters such as wildfires and storms. While risk transfer products are based on inventories and past loss information of individual timber plantations, forestry surveys provide important data about the general productivity and damage from certain disasters, which might be reflected in individual plantation data.

FOREST SURVEYS

Forest surveys are periodically undertaken by government agencies and industrialised timber companies to assess the status of timber production that is estimated through field surveys and supported by remote sensing data. Field surveys are undertaken in selected forest stands by stratified sampling to derive a statistically representative sample of larger forest areas.[62] Field surveys provide volume and biomass estimates for individual trees in a sample area and these are aggregated for the sample area. The growing-stock density ($m^3\,ha^{-1}$) and biomass density ($tons\,ha^{-1}$) are calculated by dividing the total tree volume or biomass by the surface of the sample area. Remote sensing data from air-borne and satellite-based sensors allow classification of different land use covers and are increasingly used to support the extrapolation of stock density and biomass from field surveys to wider areas.

Based on field surveys and spatial extrapolation, the total volume and biomass are calculated and are often a coordinative effort between government agencies (natural woodlands) and industrialised timber companies (plantations). Depending on the forest composition, volume and biomass estimations are developed per type of forest and dominant tree species.

Natural Disaster Data

In some countries, government agencies collect statistics of damage to forest from wildfire and windstorms to assess overall losses and to indemnify private forest owners through government compensation schemes. These data typically include the area

---

[62] Scott, C.T. and Gove, J.H., 2002: Forest inventory. *Encyclopedia of Environmetrics*, 814–20.

damaged by severity extent (e.g. partial or total losses), the timber volume and biomass damaged as well as estimates of economic losses.

Historical Fire Data
Historical fire data are typically collected by fire and land management agencies and include timing, location and cause of wildfires. On some occasions, the area burnt is recorded additionally and special databases have been established for fires above a certain size threshold (mainly large and catastrophic-type fires) where more details are recorded. Forest management agencies and weather services provide fire weather indices and projections, using mechanistic and analytical models on the probable spread of active wildfires over space and time. Where forest occurrence reports are not available, satellite images may determine hotspots (i.e. active fires that show strong signals on infrared channels) and area burnt from changes in visual imagery before and after a fire event (Section 4.3).

Most historical forest fire occurrence data are likely to show a trend over time, which is difficult to determine and can be a function of (i) land use changes that affect the size of the forested area and the urban–wildland interface, (ii) changes in dominant tree species, which in turn show different vulnerabilities to fire events, and (iii) changes in the regulation on reporting and addressing forest fires, with the use of remote sensing being one of the main contributors towards earlier recognition of fires.

BIBLIOGRAPHY

Alexandridis, A.K. and Zapranis, A.D. (2013). *Weather Derivatives: Modelling and Pricing Weather-Related Risk*. Springer, 300p.

Dischel, R.S. (2002). *Climate Risk and the Weather Market: Financial Risk Management with Weather Hedges*. Risk Books, 300p.

Hartkamp, A.D., De Beurs, K., Stein, A. and White, J.W., 1999: *Interpolation Techniques for Climate Variables*, NRG-GIS Series 99–01, 26p.

Hennemuth, B., Bender, S., Bülow, K. et al., 2013: Statistical Methods for the Analysis of Simulated and Observed Climate Data, Applied in Projects and Institutions Dealing with Climate Change Impact and Adaptation. CSC Report 13, Climate Service Center, Germany, 135p.

Jewson, S., Brix, A., and Ziehmann, C. (2010). *Weather Derivative Valuation: The Meteorological, Statistical, Financial and Mathematical Foundations*. Cambridge: Cambridge University Press, 392p.

Kogan, F., Powell, A., and Fedorov, O. (2009). *Use of Satellite and In-Situ Data to Improve Sustainability*. Springer published in cooperation with NATO Public Diplomacy Division, 301p.

Lupo, A. and Kininmonth, W. (2013). Global climate models and their limitations. In: *Climate Change Reconsidered II*, 9–148. Physical Science.

Moss, J., Morley, P., Baker, D. et al., 2016: *Improving Methods for Estimating Livestock Production and Productivity – Literature Review*, Technical Report Series GO-11-2016: 82p.

Von Storch, H. and Zwiers, F.W. (2003). *Statistical Analysis in Climate Research*, 3e, 484. Cambridge: Cambridge University Press.

Wallach, D., Makowski, D., Jones, J., and Brun, F. (2013). *Working with Dynamic Crop Models: Methods, Tools and Examples for Agriculture and Environment*, 2e. Academic Press, 405p.

Wilks, D.S. (2011). *Statistical Methods in Atmospheric Sciences*, 3e. Academic Press, 704p.

World Bank, 2015: Increasing Agricultural Production and Resilience Through Improved Agro-Meteorological Services. Report 94 486-GLB, Washington DC, 64p.

CHAPTER 5

Agricultural Insurance

5.1 INTRODUCTION

Agricultural insurance covers agricultural production assets which are all biological systems and include crop, livestock, aquaculture, equine and bloodstock, forestry and greenhouses. Insurance is the main and often the only way to transfer production risks from individual producers, agribusinesses and government entities to (re)insurers or capital markets. Agricultural insurance is one of the fastest growing lines of insurance business, is a major contributor to rural development and stability, and is typically part of a national disaster risk management and financing framework, under which particularly crop and livestock insurance benefits from government premium subsidies. Risk management products including insurance have significantly contributed to the growth in agricultural production through the provision of safety nets for farming communities and collateral for lending.

Over time, most of the initial public sector insurance schemes have evolved into public–private partnerships with substantial government support, while commercial insurance has existed in parallel. Agricultural insurance has developed differently in markets with large farm structures with mainly indemnity-based products compared with smallholder systems where index insurance and calamity-based schemes have been implemented. The recognition of agricultural insurance as an allowed form of support of governments under World Trade Organization (WTO) rules and more integrated disaster risk financing strategies has led to significant growth in agricultural insurance, from a global premium of US$10.2 billion (2006) to US$30.7 billion (2017).

This chapter first provides an overview of the main agricultural insurance markets based on data collected for each country and agricultural insurance line of business (2006–2017). The main products are briefly introduced and benefits and challenges of indemnity- and index-based products elaborated thereafter. Further, an overview of the main agricultural insurance systems and some specific operational forms is provided. This chapter closely links to Chapter 2 (Concepts of Insurance), Chapter 3 (Agricultural Perils and Risk Modelling Concepts) and Chapter 4 (Agricultural Data and Proxies) and forms the basis for the subsequent chapters that are dedicated to crop, livestock, aquaculture and forestry insurance (Chapters 6–9).

5.2 GLOBAL AGRICULTURAL INSURANCE MARKETS

Agricultural insurance has developed from initially covering single perils to comprehensive insurance and has supported the structural changes in the sector. Over the past 30 years, some of the larger public sector insurance programmes have been transformed into public–private partnerships (PPPs), index-based insurance has emerged for smallholder production systems, and government risk transfer products and insurance for agribusinesses have been developed. Future trends in agricultural insurance will depend on the continued development of the agricultural sector, climate variability, possibly driven by climate change, further globalisation and greater agricultural finance and investments, which are necessary to increase food production to satisfy future demand.

DEVELOPMENT OF AGRICULTURAL INSURANCE

The agricultural insurance industry has gone through different development phases that are closely related to the industrialisation, specialisation and globalisation of the agricultural sectors. Agricultural finance and risk transfer (including insurance) have largely contributed to the industrialisation and verticalisation of the general growth of agricultural production.

The first agricultural insurance products emerged over 200 years ago in various European countries in the form of crop hail insurance and basic livestock covers that were offered by mutual insurers and cooperatives (Section 6.3). In the 1930s, multi-peril crop insurance (MPCI) products emerged to offer comprehensive protection and increasingly benefited from government support through premium subsidies and reinsurance protection, which is often necessary to cover systemic risks and increase insurance penetration to a level where adverse selection becomes manageable. With increasing commodity price volatility in globalising markets, MPCI was extended in some markets to provide revenue and income protection for most crop and certain livestock types. Forestry and aquaculture insurance have largely remained private sector insurance initiatives and have become more complex over time. Agricultural insurance in low-income countries, particularly those with smallholder structures, has evolved differently from that in high-income countries in that insurance products such as calamity-based and indices have been piloted and implemented.

From Public Sector Programmes to Private–Public Partnerships

Initially, most agricultural insurance programmes were either private sector initiatives that covered idiosyncratic risks (e.g. crop hail) or public sector programmes which portected against systemic perils (e.g. drought, flood). In the past 30 years, most public sector programmes have been transformed into PPPs, particularly for crop insurance (e.g. USA, India, Mexico), as the financial burden to the public sector increased significantly and private sector insurers offered additional distribution capabilities, underwriting experience, capital and access to reinsurance markets.

Under PPP-based programmes, governments typically provide some form of financial support, including catastrophe reinsurance and premium subsidies (Section 5.5), which led to increased insurance penetrations and large growth, particularly in the crop segment. Under PPP, agricultural insurance schemes became part of national disaster management and financing frameworks and complemented or largely substituted disaster assistance and relief programmes. In some markets, dedicated government agencies provide insurance terms (e.g. USA, China), while in other markets, co-insurance pools have formed (e.g. Spain, Turkey). In several countries where public sector insurance schemes still exist, a transition into PPP systems is being evaluated (e.g. Japan, the Philippines). Unlike crop insurance, forestry and aquaculture insurance are entirely private sector solutions, while livestock insurance has evolved as both PPPs or private sector initiatives. The acceptance of most agricultural insurance as green- or amber-box instruments under WTO regulation has provided legitimation for governments to support the agricultural sector through risk transfer products.

Mature Agricultural Markets

High-income countries show a large range of agricultural insurance products that are mostly indemnity-based, benefitting from substantial government support. Index-based products exist but are generally rare and cover (i) risks that are otherwise difficult to insure (e.g. grassland, apiculture), (ii) pure price risks and gross margins (e.g. livestock), or (iii) catastrophe risks (e.g. area-yield indices). Under the general securitisation of insurance risks for capital market risk transfer, agricultural insurance and reinsurance risks in the USA have been transacted under industry loss warranties and reinsurance sidecars (Section 11.3).

Developing Agricultural Markets

Agricultural insurance is relatively new in low-income and many middle-income countries, where numerous pilots have been undertaken but few larger programmes have been established. Agricultural insurance schemes have evolved through (i) public sector initiatives or transformations of government programmes into PPPs (e.g. India, Brazil), (ii) private sector initiatives that have been integrated into PPPs (e.g. China), (iii) integrating insurance into government disaster assistance programmes (e.g. Thailand, Pakistan), and (iv) international support from multilateral financing institutions to develop index-based products to cover rural cooperatives and lending institutions (mainly Africa and parts of Asia). In the past 15 years, more than 150 index-based pilot programmes have been supported by donors in over 50 countries. In several markets, smallholders are insured in different schemes than commercial or near-commercial farmers, where under PPP, different government premium subsidy levels are applied. As disaster assistance and relief programmes can be costly for smaller risk-prone low-income countries, macro-level risk transfer programmes have been established for agricultural assets (e.g. Mexico, Peru, China) to provide immediate funds after severe natural disasters. In Africa, risk pooling among countries has led to parametric drought insurance through the African Risk Capacity (Section 6.11).

Future Developments of Agricultural Insurance

Due to largely different production systems, farming methods, and average farm sizes and market access, the development of agricultural insurance will continue to take different approaches in developed compared with developing markets. Generally, agricultural insurance will continue to evolve alongside government policies, agricultural finance initiatives and continued structural changes in production systems that potentially lead to higher concentrations of risks. The continued availability of government support is fundamental for most programmes that are based on PPPs and their expansion. Some of the remaining public sector systems might see a transformation into PPPs.

Climate change adaptation and mitigation will become increasingly important in the most exposed markets and agricultural production systems where risk transfer of natural disaster risks can play an important role. More specialised and integrated production in increasingly global markets will require risk transfer solutions that cover food system shocks and failures at national and international levels. As a globalising supply chain is vulnerable to local supply constraints (e.g. seed, fertiliser, vaccination, equipment) that can have over-regional financial consequences, business interruption insurance is one area that could see increasing interest for insurance. With an increase in the traceability of agricultural products and food safety becoming more important for consumers, efficient liability insurance products are likely to be on demand. Similarly, requests for environmental liability insurance in the agricultural sector are likely to grow as more stringent environmental laws and regulations are being implemented. With greater production volatility, the increasing financial burden of small low- or middle-income countries with large disaster assistance programmes could lead to higher demand for regional or over-regional risk pooling and risk transfer.

Big data algorithms are likely to change the understanding and prevention of risks at different levels and will support the development of tailor-made insurance covers. As with other lines of insurance, agricultural insurance will benefit from new technologies that increase efficiency at lower cost and include general digitisation through digital platforms and blockchains, distribution of products through smart phones, and the use of drones for risk and loss assessments. Initiatives that target permanent crop monitoring at field level will provide large datasets, based on which more efficient indices can be developed with lower basis risk, which will be beneficial for smallholder structures.

5.2.1 AGRICULTURAL INSURANCE PRODUCTS

Agricultural risk transfer products have largely developed in function of specific market needs that include (i) the type and development level of the agricultural production system and average farm sizes, (ii) the main perils, which can be random and local (idiosyncratic) or widespread, affecting the entire agricultural sector (systemic), (iii) the government strategy for disaster risk financing and government support, including premium subsidies and reinsurance, (iv) distribution channels, (v) the availability of historical losses and proxies, and (vi) the familiarity of policyholders with risk transfer instruments and the affordability of insurance.

Broadly, agricultural insurance covers production assets (biological systems) under general concepts of insurance and includes classes such as crops, livestock, equine and bloodstock, pets, aquaculture and forests (Table 5.1) that are mainly covered for natural perils and biological perils (Section 3.2). Generally, agricultural insurance products can be categorised into (i) indemnity-based products that rely on dedicated specialists for on-site loss adjustment, (ii) index-based (or parametric) products that use indices derived from crop yield data, weather data, satellite data (e.g. vegetation indices), crop model outputs or other proxies that directly relate to loss extents, and (iii) hybrid products that use a combination of index-based triggers with indemnity insurance (Table 5.1).

TABLE 5.1 Overview of the main agricultural insurance lines, sub-classes, insured perils and products.

Type	Sub-Types	Exposure (Examples)	Insured Perils (Non-Exhaustive)	Main Insurance Products
Crop insurance *Chapter 6*	Annual field crops	Rice, corn, wheat, barley, soybean, oat, canola, cotton, lentils	Natural perils (mainly hail, frost, storm, drought, flood, snow), fire, some pests and diseases	Named perils, multi-peril, weather index, yield index, satellite index, model index, revenue insurance, income insurance
	Perennial field crops	Sugarcane		
	Vegetables (field)	Tomatoes, salad, cabbage, spices		Named perils, weather index
	Horticulture crops	Apple, pear, cherry, citrus, lychee, kiwi, f.g, pineapple, banana, berries		
	Horticulture (nuts)	Almond, walnut, macadamia		
	Industrial tree crops	Tea, coffee, rubber, coconut, cacao		
	Viticulture	Grapes, vines		
	Ornamental plants	Flowers		Named perils
	Medical plants	Hemp, opium		
	Pasture land	Grassland, rangeland	Drought	Satellite and weather index
Livestock insurance *Chapter 7*	General livestock	Cattle, pigs, sheep, goats (all in captivity or supervised)	Mortality from natural perils (mainly storm, flood), FLEXA, accidents, diseases and epidemic diseases (excl. government slaughter order), some aspects of business interruption, fertility of breeding animals, abortion risk	Named perils, satellite index (drought), mortality index, revenue insurance, income insurance
	Specialised livestock	Fur animals (mink), deer, free-ranging animals (yak)		Named perils
	Poultry	Chicken, duck, turkey, ostrich		Named perils
	Breeding animals	Cattle, pigs, poultry		Named perils
	Zoo/circus animals	Elephant, dolphin, tiger, lion, bear	Mortality from accidents, diseases with sometimes business interruption	Named perils

(Continued)

TABLE 5.1 (*Continued*)

Type	Sub-Types	Exposure (Examples)	Insured Perils (Non-Exhaustive)	Main Insurance Products
Equine insurance	Equine	Pleasure and show horses	Mortality from accidents, FLEXA, cholic, covering sometimes transport, quarantine and third-party liability	Named perils
Bloodstock insurance	Bloodstock	Racing horses	Mortality, transport, some aspects of third-party liability	Named perils
Pet insurance	Breeding horses	Stallions, mares, foals	Reduced fertility, mortality	Named perils
	Pets	Dogs and cats	Medical expenses and mortality	Named perils
Aquaculture insurance *Chapter 8*	General aquatic stock (on- and off-shore)	Tuna, salmon, tilapia, barramundi, carp, trout, oysters, shellfish, shrimps	Disappearance from natural perils (storm, flood), mortality from diseases, FLEXA, predators, collision, some aspects of business interruption	Named perils, weather index
	Special aquatic stock (on- and off-shore)	Seaweed, oysters (pearl), sea cucumber, crabs, shellfish	Mortality from natural perils, FLEXA, diseases	Named perils, weather index
	Ornamental fish	Koi, arowana	Mortality, loss of juvenile stock	Named perils
	Equipment and facilities	Nets, cages, equipment, buildings, facilities	Natural perils, FLEXA, collision	Named perils

Forestry insurance *Chapter 9*	Commercial timber (plantation)	Broadleaved and needle tree species	Natural perils (mainly storm, wildfire, flood, drought), sometimes pests and diseases, additional costs (re-establishment, claims preparation), carbon credits (in some markets only)	Named perils, some index products
	Specialised timber (plantation)	Bamboo, sandalwood, teak		
	Natural woodlands (public-owned)	Various native tree species		
	Garden trees, nurseries	Decorative trees and shrubs	Natural perils	Named perils
Greenhouse insurance	Plants (content)	Vegetables, flowers	Natural perils, FLEXA	Named perils
	Equipment and facilities	Structures (sometimes insured under property), electrical equipment (e.g. drip irrigation, sprinklers)	Natural perils, FLEXA, machinery breakdown, malicious damage, aspects of business interruption, third-party liability	Named perils

FLEXA: Fire, Lightning, Explosion and Aircraft impact.

5.2.2 AGRICULTURAL INSURANCE MARKETS

Agricultural insurance has seen large growth over the past 30 years, with a pronounced increase in the number of programmes and premium volume in the past 15 years (Figure 5.1). The global agricultural insurance premium tripled from US$10.2 billion in 2006 to US$30.7 billion in 2017. A large part of the growth has been contributed by emerging markets, which generated a premium of US$2.4 billion in 2006 (24% of the total) and increased to US$14 billion in 2017 (46%). In 2017, North America contributed 42% of the global premium (59% in 2006), 40% came from Asia-Pacific (16%), 13% from Europe, including Russia/Ukraine (20%), 4% from Latin America (3%) and 1% from Africa (2%). China and India alone now generate a premium volume of US$10.8 billion compared with US$250 million just 12 years ago (Table 5.2) and

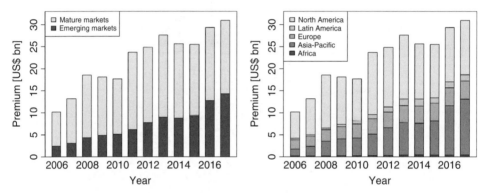

FIGURE 5.1   Left: Agricultural insurance premium in emerging and mature markets, 2006–2017. Right: Agricultural insurance premium per main geography (continents).
Data source: Industry reports and discussions with leading (re)insurance underwriters.

TABLE 5.2   Top 10 agricultural insurance markets ranked by premium in 2017 in comparison with 2006.

Country	Premium (2006, US$ Million)	Premium (2017, US$ Million)	Growth (%)
USA	4985	11098	123
China	100	7074	6974
India	150	3804	2436
Canada	980	1561	59
Spain	680	916	35
Japan	1028	760	–26
Brazil	350	642	83
France	80	610	663
Italy	262	480	83
Turkey	40	450	1025
Total	8655	27395	217
Share of global market	85%	89%	

Data source: Industry reports, AXCO and discussions with leading (re)insurance underwriters.

agricultural insurance has advanced to become the third largest line of insurance in India and China.

The large growth can be contributed to a number of factors, including (i) new programmes with substantial government support in emerging markets (e.g. India, China, Brazil), (ii) higher commodity prices that increased the exposure and premium volumes in markets with MPCI and revenue insurance (e.g. USA, Canada), and (iii) an increase in insurance penetrations in most programmes. However, most premium is generated by just a few markets. In 2017, the 10 largest agricultural insurance markets contributed 89% to the total agricultural insurance premium; they grew by 217% between 2006 and 2017 (Table 5.2). Over the past 12 years, China showed the largest growth, with a sevenfold increase of premium, followed by India and Turkey. The largest premium growth in monetary terms occurred in China (+US$6.9 billion), followed by the USA (+US$6.1 billion), India (+US$3.6 billion) and Canada (+US$581 million). Among the largest 10 markets in 2017, Japan was the only country that showed a reduction of US$268 million in premium volume between 2006 and 2017.

Crop insurance is by far the largest agricultural line of business, with a premium volume of US$27.65 billion (2017), contributing 89.9% of the total agricultural insurance premium. With a premium of US$2.27 billion, livestock insurance portfolios contribute 7.4% to the total premium, while forestry, with a premium volume of US$557.4 million, consisted of 1.8% of the total. Aquaculture schemes produced US$161 million (0.5% of the total) and other products, including equine/bloodstock, pets and greenhouses, generated US$112 million (0.4%) in 2017.

While index insurance is gaining in importance due to strong growth in emerging markets (particularly India) and consisted of 13.5% of the global agricultural premium in 2017, indemnity-based products (86.5%) are by far the largest type of products used for crop, livestock, aquaculture, forestry insurance, equine/bloodstock and greenhouse insurance.

For crop insurance, named-peril insurance produced US$11.8 billion in premium, MPCI-type products (including revenue and income insurance) generated US$11.6 billion premium, while index-based products reached close to US$4 billion in 2017 (Table 5.3). Similarly, for livestock, where indemnity-based products contributed US$2.1 billion in premium and index solutions, including price, gross margin and satellite-based drought covers, generated US$167 million. For forest and aquaculture, almost all products are indemnity-based while index covers are piloted in some countries, particularly in China.

NORTH AMERICA

North America is the largest agricultural insurance market with US$12.6 billion premium in 2017 – 42% of the global agricultural insurance premium volume. With a premium volume of US$11 billion, the USA remains the largest agricultural insurance market globally.

USA

US crop insurance started as an experiment to address the effects of the Great Depression and crop losses in the Dust Bowl in the 1930s.[1] The Federal Crop Insurance Corporation (FCIC) was created in 1938 to facilitate crop insurance and is

---

[1] Glauber, J.W., 2012: The growth of the federal crop insurance program, 1990–2011. *Amer. J. Agr. Econ.*, 95(2), 482–8.

TABLE 5.3 Insurance premium per main product and line of business in 2017, including key markets and size (in brackets).

Line of Business	Product	Types	Key Markets	Premium 2017 (US$ Million)	Ratio of Total Premium
Crop (*Chapter 6*)	Named-peril insurance	All named-peril crop insurance	NA, EU, LA, China (all large), South Africa, Australia/New Zealand (all small)	11 896	38.7%
	Calamity-based crop insurance	Named-peril crop insurance with calamity trigger	Thailand, Pakistan	79	0.2%
	Multi-peril crop insurance	MPCI, revenue crop insurance, income insurance	NA, Brazil (both large), Argentina, South Africa, Morocco (all small)	11 684	38.0%
	Area yield index insurance	Area-based crop insurance (area yield index, area-revenue insurance)	India (large), USA (large), Africa (all small)	3599	11.7%
	Weather index insurance	All weather, satellite and model driven indices	India (large), Africa, China (all small)	392	1.3%
Livestock (*Chapter 7*)	Named-peril insurance	All named-peril livestock insurance (including epidemic disease covers)	China, Japan, EU, South Korea (all large), Australia, Africa, LA (all small)	2105	7.0%
	Index insurance	Margin products, price indices, NDVI products	China, USA (all large), Mexico, Africa (small)	167	0.5%
Aquaculture (*Chapter 8*)	Named-peril insurance	All mortality and named-perils insurance	China, South Korea, Chile, EU (all large), other countries (small)	159	0.5%
	Index insurance	Weather indices	China (small)	2	0.01%
Forestry (*Chapter 9*)	Named-peril insurance	All named-peril forestry insurance	China (large), EU, LA, South Africa, Australia, SE Asia (all small)	555	1.8%
	Index insurance	Fire and windstorm covers, government fire cost insurance	China, USA, others (all small)	2	0.01%
Others	Various types of cover	Including bloodstock, equine, pet and greenhouses	Various countries	112	0.3%
	Total			30753	100%

NA, North America; EU, Europe (incl. Russia and Ukraine); LA, Latin America.

managed and operated by the Risk Management Agency (RMA), which is part of the US Department of Agriculture (USDA). For its first 40 years, crop insurance was available in limited areas; by 1980, only about half of the counties and 26 crops were covered. Farmers initially relied on the government disaster programme for compensation in case of prevented planting and yield reduction from natural disasters.[2]

With the 1980 Federal Crop Insurance Act, insurance expanded, and it grew further with premium subsidy levels increases in 1994 and in 2000. The FCIC subsidises most insurance products, contributes to administrative costs for insurers and provides catastrophe reinsurance protection at state level. The RMA provides product development and underwriting services for all subsidised products. Initially, crop insurance was limited to MPCI policies (Section 6.5), but revenue insurance rapidly became the main product (Section 6.6). Other crop insurance products include area-yield policies, area-yield revenue insurance and whole-farm income plans. Rainfall-based index contracts are available for forage and apiculture (Section 4.2). Additionally, subsidised livestock price insurance and gross margin products produced a US$34 million premium volume in 2017 (Section 7.6). Clam farmers benefit from subsidised aquaculture insurance in certain states (Section 8.4). The total premium of all FCIC-subsidised agricultural insurance products reached US$10.07 billion in 2017.

Crop hail insurance is offered purely as a commercial product and generated a premium volume of US$958 million in 2017 (Section 6.4). Forestry insurance is offered by private sector insurers and is marginal.

Canada

Crop insurance emerged in Western Canada in the 1930s but found more traction only in the 1980s when the current MPCI products were introduced. The government provides substantial premium subsidies and MPCI products are exclusively sold by province-based government insurers. Crop insurance forms an integral part of the government's risk management framework under AgInsure (Section 6.7) and operates in combination with AgriStability (margin-based whole-farm revenue programme) and AgriInvest (saving accounts). In 2017, the premium volume for the AgInsure MPCI programmes reached US$1.28 billion.

Crop hail insurance is offered as a standalone product by private sector insurers on a purely commercial basis and produced US$230 million in premium in 2017. Revenue livestock insurance such as the Western Livestock Price Insurance Program (WLPIP) is a private sector scheme but benefits from government support for research and development. The poultry sector has developed its own insurance programmes through reciprocal insurance exchanges (Section 7.3). Forestry and aquaculture insurance remain marginal as private sector programmes. The Agriculture Financial Services Corporation (AFSC) was one of the first insurers to develop satellite-based pasture insurance (Section 6.10) and transferring excessive cost for wildfire fighting in a parametric form to reinsurance markets (Section 9.6).

---

[2] Congressional Research Service, 2015: Federal Crop Insurance: Background. CRS Report R40532, Washington, DC, 23p.

EUROPE (INCLUDING RUSSIA AND UKRAINE)

Europe, including Russia and Ukraine, is the third largest agricultural insurance market with a premium volume of US$4.1 billion in 2017 and contributed overall 13% to the global premium. Crop hail and combined named-peril policies consist of most of the agricultural insurance premium.

Greece and Cyprus are the only countries where crop insurance is compulsory and is provided exclusively by the public sector. Crop hail insurance is mostly operated on a commercial basis, with only few countries providing subsidies (e.g. Austria, the Czech Republic, Italy, Baltic States, Portugal, Romania and Spain), while combined named-peril covers often benefit from government support, and all MPCI programmes receive premium subsidised at various levels.[3] Besides insurance, calamity funds, mutual funds and disaster assistance payments are the main risk management approaches for agricultural producers.

Crop Insurance

Crop hail insurance started in Central European countries more than 100 years ago and by the early 2000s almost all European countries had crop hail programmes, which in many cases evolved further into combined named-peril covers.

Combined named-peril crop insurance started with crop hail insurance, to which other main perils (e.g. fire, frost, flood, rainstorm, strong wind) were gradually added, with the exclusion of drought. For example, Italy initially had only crop hail insurance but modified the policy to include at least two natural perils, one being hail. Turkey has developed a combined named-peril crop cover that is offered under the Tarsim insurance pool (Section 5.6).

MPCI exists in Spain, which was the first country in Europe to introduce yield-based insurance where the government collaborates with farm unions and a PPP with five insurers and a national reinsurer (Agroseguro). In Russia and Ukraine, MPCI is the dominant form of crop insurance, with government premium subsidies in Russia and a commercial product in Ukraine.

Index-based crop insurance was launched in Spain in 2001 to cover pasture land through satellite-derived vegetation indices at coarse resolution. France introduced a similar product in 2016 (Section 6.10). An area-yield index insurance programme was introduced in the UK in 1998 but was discontinued due to small take-up rates. Austria introduced weather index insurance in 2007 to cover drought risk and to complement the crop hail and other named-peril products.

Livestock, Aquaculture and Forestry Insurance

Livestock insurance exists in Austria, Germany, Bulgaria, the Czech Republic, Finland, Greece, Poland, Spain, Sweden and the UK, covering livestock mortality and/or business interruption following government-ordered culling for epidemic diseases (Section 7.5). In countries where public assistance is absent for losses from epidemic diseases, private insurance schemes have been developed for some livestock classes (e.g. Germany, Netherlands, Sweden, Spain, the UK, Italy). The insurance of consequential losses from

---

[3] European Commission, 2006: Agriculture Insurance Schemes. Administrative Agreement AGRI-2005-0321, 241p.

epidemic livestock diseases has achieved high penetration ratios in some countries (Section 7.5). In Greece and Spain, PPP programs have been established where the government acts either as an insurer or as a reinsurer of a subsidised livestock mortality insurance.

Forestry insurance has been developed mainly as a request from private forest owners and larger cooperatives. Insurance for private forest owners exists in France and Spain, while mutual insurers and landowner associations provide plantation insurance in Scandinavia (Section 9.3). Industrialised aquaculture production is insured in Norway, the UK and the Mediterranean (Section 8.3). Insurance for greenhouses structures and contents is important in the Netherlands.

ASIA-PACIFIC

Agricultural insurance has developed rapidly and has become the second largest market, with a premium volume of US$12.3 billion in 2017 and a contribution of 40% to the global premium. In 2010, agricultural insurance was present either in a pilot form or as fully mature national-level programmes in 20 out of 44 countries.[4]

Japan

Agricultural insurance in Asia started in Japan in the 1930s as MPCI under what became later Nogyo Kyosai Seido (NOSAI), which is operated by a government cooperative network with compulsory insurance for some crop types (Section 5.5). Livestock mortality insurance is provided on the same basis. The premium volume of this public sector scheme was estimated at US$760 million in 2016. Due to high costs of NOSAI for premium subsidies and loss payments through different government levels, the development of a PPP-based revenue scheme is under discussion for rice.

China

Agricultural insurance in China dates to the 1950s. After several trials, the National Agricultural Insurance Program (NAIP) started in 2007, with government premium subsidies from the central government (40%), provincial government and in some cases prefecture governments (40%).[5] The initial challenge was to find an insurance product that could cover a large number of small crop and livestock farms in different production systems and climate zones.

The National Agricultural Insurance Program
In 2007, NAIP covered the main field crops as well as cattle and pigs in the provinces of Hunan, Jilin, Inner Mongolia, Xinjiang, Sichuan and Jiangsu and generated a premium volume of US$800 million. Some provinces and autonomous regions began their own programmes, including (i) Beijing province, where a disaster risk reserve fund was established to compensate insurers in case the annual loss ratio exceeds 160% (Section 1.3), and (ii) Zhejiang province, where the government entered into

---

[4] FAO, 2011: Agricultural Insurance in Asia and the Pacific Region. RAP Publication, Bangkok, 238p.
[5] Wang, M. et al., 2011: Agriculture insurance in China: history, experience and lessons learned. *Int. J. Disaster Risk Sci.*, 2(2), 10–22.

a loss-sharing partnership with insurers through a pool-like structure. In 2008, NAIP was expanded to 17 provinces and produced US$1.66 billion in premium covering 90 million farming households. In 2009, natural woodlands and timber plantations were included in the programme and in 2012, government-subsidised aquaculture insurance pilots started. All insurance under NAIP benefits from premium subsidies. In 2017, NAIP grew to become the second largest agricultural insurance market globally after the USA, with a premium of US$7.01 billion and 40% of the main crop area, 75% of breeding sows, 25% of the forest area being insured and with aquaculture insurance expanding. A total of 23 insurers, including both large multi-line and specialist agricultural insurers, are licensed to write agricultural insurance.

Crop Products
While the scope of insurance has been increasing, the concept of the crop insurance products under NAIP has not changed much since its implementation. Most crop insurance is based on named-peril policies and includes peril-specific franchises and deductibles (Table 5.4). In some provinces, systemic perils have a high franchise (e.g. 30% for drought) compared with localised perils such as hail (e.g. 10%). Premium rates are crop specific and uniform at province level, varying between 3% and 10%. The initial risk premium rates for crop insurance were derived from calamity-declaration data (area-affected data), which reveal the extent of physical damage by peril on agricultural land (Section 4.5). In some provinces (e.g. Liaoning until 2015), certain perils used to be offered through endorsements where a peril could be added at an additional premium. The sum insured is based on production costs and represents 40% of the commercial crop value. For larger state farms in the provinces of Heilongjiang and Xinjiang, insurers offer MPCI products.

Livestock insurance covers mortality due to accidents, natural disasters and diseases at agreed values and compensates for differences in government payments and agreed values in case of epidemic disease. The NAIP livestock scheme, with a premium of US$1.3 billion, is by far the largest livestock insurance programme globally (Section 7.3). Gross margin insurance is available for pig farmers based on a ratio of pig prices relative to feed costs (Section 7.6). Forestry insurance provides indemnity for natural disasters for reforestation costs of natural woodlands and plantations (Section 9.3). Aquaculture is a newer insurance and has expanded gradually in different provinces to provide indemnity- and index-based insurance against natural disasters and named diseases (Section 8.3).

Under NAIP, insurance terms are determined by province governments and the China Insurance Regulation Commission (CIRC) in discussion with admitted insurers. Province governments allocate counties to insurers to achieve balanced portfolios and township governments support the marketing and loss adjustment.

Reinsurance Protection
Most province governments provided reinsurance protection to insurers against large losses at province or prefecture level until 2015 when the China Agricultural Reinsurance Pool (CARP) was introduced. CARP is led by China Re with the participation of several insurers to provide more domestic reinsurance capacity, with a minimum compulsory cession of 50% of all reinsurance placements to CARP. International reinsurance provides additional capacity.

TABLE 5.4 Crop insurance terms for selected crop types and provinces (2008 and 2016) under the National Agricultural Insurance Program in China.

Province/Crop	2008					2016				
	Perils[a]	TIV[b]	Franchise (%)	Deductible (%)	Rate (%)	Perils[a]	TIV[b]	Franchise (%)	Deductible (%)	Rate (%)
Hebei/Corn	H	260	30	0	7.0	D, Fl, Fr, H	400	D:50 Others:10	0	6.0
Zhejiang/Rice	Fl, Fr, H, T	200 or 400	30	0	5.0	D, Fl, Fr, H, T	900	20	0	5.0
Shandong/Corn	D, Fl, Fr, H	300–500	20	0	2.0	Fl, H	350	20	0	4.3
Sichuan/Rice	D*, Fl, Fr, H *Optional cover	All:300 w/o D:100	30	0	All:10 w/o D:5.0	D, Fl, Fr, H	400	20	0	4.5
Xinjiang/Cotton	D, Fl, Fr, H	400 or 500	0	15	7.0	D, Fl, Fr, H	800	20	0	6.0
Heilongjiang/Rice	D, Fl, Fr, H, P&D	200	30	3 or 5	7.5	D, Fl, Fr, H	220	30	0	6.8

Perils: D, Drought; Fl, Flood; Fr, Frost; H, Hail and Wind; T, Typhoon; P&D, Pests and Diseases.
TIV: Total Insured Value in RMB/mu, with a mu equal to 1/15 of a hectare.
Data source: CIRC and personal discussion with leading insurance underwriters in China.

Future Developments
Different government entities have encouraged insurers to start index insurance pilots to experiment with less cost- and labour-intensive crop insurance products. Area-yield and weather index pilot schemes started in 2010 in different provinces, partly with government premium subsidies and a perspective to complement crop insurance products offered under the Agricultural Insurance Act, mainly for perils that were not covered or for non-insured crop types. A further initiative includes the evaluation of regional (e.g. province-based) disaster risk management and pooling structures for agricultural risks. In general, China aims to transform its agriculture sector from smallholdings to market-orientated larger farms, which increases the need for risk transfer.

India

India started with crop insurance in the form of area-yield index insurance in 1979 and this developed over several schemes into the current Pradhan Mantri Fasal Bima Yojana (PMFBY) programme in 2016 (Section 6.8). PMFBY provides area-based coverage for yield reduction and indemnity-based insurance for local calamities (hailstorm, landslide and inundation), prevented sowing and post-harvest losses. Insurers compete for PMFBY insurance business through seasonal or annual tenders issued by state governments where contracts are awarded on the basis of the most competitive pricing for requested coverage levels. With the introduction of PMFBY, the Weather-Based Crop Insurance Scheme (WBCIS) was modified to cover mainly horticultural crops for which yield-based insurance was not feasible (Section 6.9). Combined over the Kharif and Rabi seasons, PMFBY reached a premium of US$3.2 billion in 2016/17 and latest estimates projected a growth to US$3.8 billion for 2017/18. The government has been operating a livestock insurance programme that is compulsory for borrowing dairy farmers, with a premium volume of US$30 million.

Southeast Asia

In Southeast Asia, one of the first national crop insurance schemes was developed in the Philippines in 1978 through the Philippines Crop Insurance Company (PCIC), operating as a public sector programme in which agricultural insurance is tied to bank loans; it reached US$53 million in premium in 2016 (Section 3.8). Similarly, the national Thai rice insurance scheme, which generated a premium of US$72 million in 2016, is distributed by the Bank for Agriculture and Agricultural Cooperatives and losses are based on declared calamities and individual loss adjustment (Section 6.4). Vietnam developed a pilot crop, livestock and aquaculture insurance programme with government subsidies in 2012 and used government officials in rural areas to promote insurance and support loss adjustment. Indonesia, Laos, Cambodia, Sri Lanka, Bangladesh and most recently Myanmar have started with crop insurance pilots.

South Korea

In South Korea, the National Agricultural Cooperative Federation (NACF) handles all main aspects of the government-subsided crop and livestock insurance schemes which reached a premium volume of US$311 million in 2017. The government provides stop-loss protection for the insurer under the crop programme, which covers mainly horticulture crops and rice under a combined named-perils policy for losses from typhoon, hail and frost. Similar to the NACF, the National Federation of Fisheries Cooperatives

(NFFC) provides insurance to the aquaculture industry, with an estimated premium income of US$10 million in 2016.

Mongolia

Mongolia pioneered the first livestock mortality index insurance to cover semi-nomadic herders against high livestock mortality in severe winters and reached a premium volume of US$720 000 in 2016 (Section 7.6).

Australia and New Zealand

Australia and New Zealand both have pure private sector programmes that generated a premium of US$196 million (2017) with high penetration ratios, particularly for crop hail insurance (broadacre) in Australia. Forestry insurance is well developed for private owners in Australia, and New Zealand is one of the most advanced markets for forestry carbon credit insurance (Section 9.5).

LATIN AMERICA (INCLUDING THE CARIBBEAN)

Agricultural insurance in Latin America is estimated at US$1.2 billion (2017). A large variety of products exists, and Brazil, Mexico and Argentina are the largest markets.[6] By now, most countries in Latin America have developed agricultural insurance programmes or are piloting different schemes.

Brazil

In Brazil, agricultural insurance in 1954 was through the National Agricultural Insurance Company (CNSA) and the Rural Stability Fund (1966) to provide insurers with additional coverage for disasters and products developed by the Reinsurance Institute of Brazil (IRB).[7] CNSA operated until the mid-1990s when private insurers started offering crop hail insurance for fruits and later MPCI products at provincial level. The experience has not been satisfying, with an average loss ratio of 181% (1995–2005) and severe drought and flood losses in 2003 and 2004. Area-yield index insurance was introduced in Rio Grande do Sul in 2000 for corn producers. Besides, several states offered their own public sector subsidised MPCI programmes, which were subsequently discontinued due to high underwriting losses.

As a response to the losses, the government created the Brazilian Rural Insurance Premium Subsidy Program (PSR) in 2003 to provide a minimum of 40% premium subsidies. The MPCI products under PSR rapidly expanded to 12 million ha (over 10% of the arable land) with a premium volume of US$463 million in 2015, with grains contributing 75% of the premium, fruits 17.5%, vegetables 3.7%, and livestock and forestry 0.8%. A major contributor to growth occurred when the Bank of Brazil, as the main lender for agriculture, made crop insurance compulsory for its clients. However, late releases of government subsidies to insurers due to frequent budgetary shortfalls have been causing cash flow constraints. In 2016, during the financial crisis

---

[6] World Bank, 2010: Agricultural Insurance in Latin America: Developing the Market, World Bank Report 61963-LAC, 152p.

[7] Loyola, P. et al., 2016: Analysis of the Brazilian program of subsidies for rural insurance premium: evolution from 2005 to 2014. *Modern Appl. Sci.*, 10(7), 87–98.

in Brazil, the government could not pay the subsidies and the entire market was forced to adjust coverage levels during the crop season, which led to a decrease in the market premium to US$400 million. In 2017, the premium increased to US$642 million with non-subsidised business gaining in importance. Increasingly, cooperatives (e.g. Coamo) and agricultural investment funds buy area-yield index covers and revenue insurance to manage production volatility. Revenue insurance in Brazil is seen as a possible way to lower the government's annual average spending of US$1.7 billion to support grain prices and the US$1.3 billion to service defaulted farm debts.

PROAGRO was developed in 1974 as a government guarantee programme for small and medium-sized crop and livestock farmers to protect against loan defaults from natural disasters as well as from pests and diseases, and this continues to be operational. In 2017, PROAGRO achieved a premium income of US$132 million.

Mexico

Mexico started with crop insurance in 1926 and government-subsidised MPCI was linked to farm credits and made compulsory through the public insurance agency ANAGSA in 1961. Due to poor results, ANAGSA was discontinued in 1990 and replaced by a new government-owned specialist agricultural insurer (Agroasemex), which introduced an improved range of crop, livestock, forestry and aquaculture insurance products and strengthened underwriting and loss adjustment systems. The Agroasemex programmes obtained premium subsidies from the federal government. In the early 1990s, private-sector insurers were given incentives to start offering agricultural insurance products and services through provision of premium subsidies. Additionally, the government since 1988 has promoted the formation of mutual crop and livestock insurance schemes linked to group loans (Fondos de Asguramiento) and in 2016, 370 self-insurance funds provided agricultural insurance to their members for a premium volume of US$84 million (Section 5.6).

Government support in Mexico can be summarised according to the size of farmers as (i) premium subsidies for commercial farmers (<20 ha), (ii) for semi-commercial farmers (5–20 ha) the establishment of Fondos with premium subsidies, and (iii) subsistence farmers (<5 ha), who make up 73% of all farmers in Mexico, with 100% subsidised premiums for catastrophe protection through the Agricultural Fund for Natural Disasters (CADENA[8]) funded through the federal government (85%) and state governments (15%). Further, the government provides reinsurance protection through Agroasemex and training and education for Fondos. In 2016, the overall agriculture premium in Mexico reached US$410 million, with most premium contributed by the crop segment.

A large variety of insurance products exists in Mexico, which can broadly be grouped into (i) named-peril (mainly hail and frost) and MPCI for natural disasters and pests and diseases as well as livestock mortality insurance that includes epidemic diseases but excludes government slaughter order for the commercial and semi-commercial farming segment, and (ii) index crop insurance and satellite-based livestock insurance for mortalities related to drought for subsistence farmers who cannot access loans (Section 7.6).

To obtain budget stability, the government buys parametric catastrophe risk protection from reinsurers and capital markets (cat bonds) for the Natural Disaster Fund

---

[8] World Bank, 2013: Mexico Agriculture Insurance Market Report: CADENA Catastrophe Insurance. World Bank Publication, Washington, DC, 4p.

(FONDEN) that covers property and infrastructure. In the case of CADENA, each state buys individual insurance and reinsurance protection from the domestic as well as from international markets to protect agricultural assets.

Argentina

The Argentinian crop hail industry started in 1898 and has been operating as a private market product, with 25 insurers competing for market share. The total agricultural insurance premium reached US$249 million in 2016, of which 95% stemmed from crop hail insurance covering 45% of farms and 50% of the cultivated area. MPCI was introduced as fully commercial products in the 1990s to insure systemic perils including drought at coverage levels between 40% and 65%. MPCI is offered at farm level or at aggregated level, which is of interest to agribusinesses and investment funds. Federal government support is limited to providing technical assistance to insurers and to operating an emergency fund.

AFRICA (INCLUDING THE MIDDLE EAST)

Agricultural premium in Africa and the Middle East is estimated at 414 million (2017). Key markets include South Africa with a premium of US$150 million, Israel (US$80 million), Morocco (US$42 million), Algeria (US$31 million) and Zimbabwe (US$20 million). Agricultural insurance in Africa can be divided into established markets, where insurance has existed over several decades, and emerging insurance markets, where insurance is relatively new or is piloted through various index products and innovative distribution channels.

Established Markets

Established agricultural insurance markets exist in North Africa, parts of the Middle East (mainly Israel) and southern Africa, including South Africa, Zambia and Zimbabwe. Crop insurance in North Africa started through the establishment of agricultural mutual insurers and include the Caisse Nationale d'Assurances Mutuelles Agricoles (Tunisia, premium volume of US$3 million), the Mutuelle Agricole Marocaine d'Assurance (Morocco, US$42 million) and the Caisse Nationale de la Mutualité Agricole (Algeria, US$31 million). In Israel, Kanat was established as a government insurance fund for natural disasters for agriculture and offers MPCI products with a compulsory basic coverage and natural disaster insurance for perils not covered under MPCI (e.g. pests and diseases).

Crop insurance in South Africa has been focusing on large commercial farms through private sector named-peril insurance (mainly hail) and MPCI products.

Developing Markets

In developing markets, agricultural insurance is often not an integral part of government disaster risk management and financing strategies and new pilots are typically facilitated by development banks in collaboration with local insurers. In most markets, agricultural insurance programmes are small and have changed considerably over time, with several pilots starting each year at different levels, typically covering drought. Due to a general lack of data, operational challenges and smallholder structures, most agricultural insurance is index-based and includes (i) microinsurance with links to credit, (ii) macro-insurance where government entities benefit from fast payouts for disaster assistance following a natural disaster, and (iii) modified macro-insurance where smallholders obtain payouts through a risk aggregator such as an input supplier or a cooperative.

Microinsurance
Microinsurance is generally known as protection of low-income people against specific perils in exchange for regular premium payments proportionate to the likelihood and cost of the risk involved. Microinsurance differs from insurance in that it often involves community-based organisations as providers, uses microfinance institutions as distributors, and tends to have a limit on the sum insured per policy. Microinsurance works essentially like traditional insurance as it uses the same generally accepted practices, including actuarial pricing, underwriting, claims handling and reinsurance, but with the key difference that products are offered exclusively to poor households in low-income countries.

In Africa, microinsurance products for smallholder farmers were first introduced in Malawi (2005) and in Ethiopia (2006), which formed the basis of the development of further products in other countries. Assurance Récolte Sahel was launched by the World Bank in 2011 to provide index-based drought cover for Senegal (peanuts, corn), Mali (cotton, corn), Burkina Faso (cotton, corn) and Benin (corn). Through its Global Index Insurance Facility (GIIF), the International Finance Corporation (IFC) supports several pilot programmes, including cotton weather indices in Mozambique that were based on satellite-derived weather data (Section 4.2). The World Food Programme and Oxfam America launched the R4 Rural Resilience Initiative in Ethiopia, Senegal, Malawi, Zambia and Kenya to support risk management for vulnerable rural households, including weather index covers. In Kenya and Ethiopia, the Index-Based Livestock Insurance Pilot (IBLIP) provided payouts to Kenyan livestock smallholders based on satellite vegetation indices that relate to drought and increased mortality (Section 7.6). In 2014, the World Bank initiated the development of (i) the Kenya Livestock Insurance Program (KLIP), which compensates semi-nomadic herders for reduced fodder quality based on Normalised Difference Vegetation Index (NDVI) indices (Section 7.6), and (ii) the Kenya National Agriculture Program (KNAP), which uses area-yield indices.

Macro-insurance
One of the first macro-insurances that provides indemnity to government entities was established in Kenya in 2006 through rainfall indices.[9] In 2008, the World Bank developed a drought cover based on modelled Water Requirement Satisfaction Indices (WRSI) for national corn shortfalls in Malawi with risk transfer in derivative form to reinsurers and capital markets to provide fast payouts for the government to import corn.[10] More recently, the African Risk Capacity started to provide over-regional drought insurance that is based on WRSI and provides payouts to governments for immediate financial relief (Section 6.11).

---

[9] Bhushan, C. et al., 2016: Insuring Agriculture in Times of Climate Change. A Scoping Study on the Role of Agriculture Insurance in Protecting Farmers of Asia and Africa from Extreme Weather Events. Centre for Science and Environment, New Delhi, 80p.
[10] Syroka, J. and Nucifora, A., 2010: National Drought Insurance for Malawi. World Bank Policy Research Working Paper 5169, Washington, DC, 22p.

Innovative Distribution Channels

To overcome lacking insurance infrastructure in rural Africa, alternative distribution channels are used, including microfinance institutions (e.g. One Acre Fund that serves 180 000 farmers in East Africa), input suppliers (e.g. SeedCo in Zimbabwe), cooperatives (e.g. Coprocuma in Mali) and mobile phone companies (e.g. Safaricom in Kenya). Additionally, administration is facilitated in some markets by the use of e-vouchers, as in Zambia where smallholders obtain vouchers from the government to purchase input subsidies and weather index insurance to obtain a payout for dry spells and excessive rainfall events through the e-voucher platform. The scheme in Zambia covered over one million farmers in 2016 for a premium volume of US$10 million and as such is probably the largest smallholder insurance programme in Africa.

5.3 BENEFITS OF AGRICULTURAL INSURANCE

Agricultural insurance provides a number of direct benefits for policyholders, which are typically individual producers or farming groups, and indirect benefits for the agricultural supply chain, the government and the wider economy. Risk transfer directly supports the viability of producers, prevents farm failures and consolidation of distressed farms and production assets. A system without transfer of production risks to (re)insurance markets would generally lead to lower lending, higher financial costs for governments through disaster assistance and more frequent failures of supply chains, especially in the wake of extreme climate events and outbreaks of epidemic diseases.

PRODUCER BENEFITS

Foremost, agricultural insurance provides stability in financial returns for producers and supports fast financial recovery after a disaster, which fosters continued investment in production. With agricultural insurance, farmers have been able to plan on longer-term investments in higher-yielding but riskier assets, which leads to higher productivity. As insurance provides indemnities within a reasonable time after the occurrence of a disaster, producers are able to repay loans and creditors for input supplies and services, which overall increases the creditworthiness of the agricultural sector. In some markets, loans are linked to insurance and an insurance contract can lead to lower borrowing rates. Insurance further increases risk awareness, risk management standards and the adaptation of newer technologies, particularly as certain aspects are mandated in insurance contracts.

In markets that offer revenue and income insurance for crop and livestock operations, producers can transfer production as well as a portion of financial risks. Revenue insurance is an advantage for producers with forward contracts where production is sold before harvest, as revenue insurance provides for revenue shortfalls at harvest prices, which in case of a production shortfall allows the producer to pay for non-delivered production under the forward agreement.

For subsistence farmers in low-income countries without access to finance, agricultural insurance provides a safety net and prevents the selling of productive assets (e.g. livestock) in case of crop failure. The availability of insurance gives smallholders the opportunity to specialise and to invest in more profitable production assets, and it changes the common safety-first behaviours, thus minimising the likelihood that revenues fall below critical levels.

SUPPLY CHAIN BENEFITS

Through transfer of production risks, agricultural insurance provides financial stability for different supply chains in that producers remain liquid, with lower default risks in case of the occurrence of natural and biological hazards. Risk transfer further increases the creditworthiness of producers and entire sub-sectors as it acts as collateral for loans, which financial institutions would otherwise be reluctant to provide as agriculture is seen as a high-risk sector. In the same way, insurance provides producers with liquidity following the impact of a disaster, which allows repayments of input supplies and services. The purchase of crop insurance has been shown to increase land values through a certain degree of production specialisation and conversion of grassland into cropland.

GOVERNMENT BENEFITS

Depending on the way in which agricultural insurance is embedded into a government's disaster financing strategy, it can have several benefits, including (i) reduction of public expenditure to support commercial producers after disasters, (ii) social protection of smallholders and subsistence farmers, and (iii) government budget stability and immediate post-disaster indemnity payment to obtain increased liquidity for disaster relief. However, most national agricultural insurance programmes require substantial government subsidies to cover systemic perils, increase affordability and achieve insurance penetrations that adverse selection becomes manageable. As most agricultural insurance is a recognised instrument under WTO regulation (mostly green box instruments), it represents an attractive way for governments to support the agricultural sector.

LINKING INSURANCE TO CREDITS AND GUARANTEES

Limited access to credit has long been identified as an important constraint for farmers in low-income countries, and governments, international donors and development banks have made efforts to introduce programmes to increase lending to the agricultural sector, with insurance building the necessary safety nets for production risks. However, many smallholders remain without access to credit and the reluctance of financial services providers (FSPs) has been identified to be related to (i) information asymmetries, which leads to adverse selection and moral hazard of borrowers, (ii) high transaction costs to reach and evaluate the creditworthiness of large numbers of smallholders borrowing small amounts, (iii) enforcement constraints in distinguishing between the lack of willingness or ability to repay loans, (iv) the absence of limited availability of suitable collateral, and (iv) ambiguity aversion of FSPs in rather serving familiar clients with known risks than expanding into new areas and risks.[11] A further reason for limited lending is the presence of systemic risks, including price and production risks, which can affect a large number of borrowers at the same time and require the restructuring of loans to avoid default.

FSPs that engage in agricultural lending with smallholder typically try to limit loan default risk through (i) demanding high collaterals or collateral substitutes, such

---

[11] Clarke, D. and Dercon, S., 2009: Insurance, Credit and Safety Nets for the Poor in a World of Risk. UN/DESA Working Paper 81, New York, 18p.

as co-signers or joint-liability lending groups, (ii) requesting a certain degree of diversification in that farming income has to be complemented by non-farming revenues, and (iii) demanding that loan beneficiaries are to participate in government-sponsored loan guarantee programmes. Although an FSP can geographically diversify the lending portfolio from systemic risks, most microfinance institutions, credit unions and rural banks have a small number of branch offices and show a certain degree of geographical concentrations of borrowing farmers. In principle, FSPs prefer collateral and credit guarantees to insurance as they cover any reason for default while insurance indemnifies only losses from predefined perils. In order to improve lending in smallholder agricultural production systems, a combination of credit-linked insurance and credit guarantee programmes has been implemented.

Credit-Linked Insurance Programmes
Generally, agricultural insurance can be linked to credit in smallholder systems through (i) direct farmer insurance, where an insurer sells covers to farmers, collects premiums and pays indemnities, and where farmers voluntarily inform FSPs about purchased insurance that acts as a collateral to obtain higher lending or preferential interest rates, (ii) credit-linked insurance, where an FSP, and increasingly input suppliers, processors and cooperatives, acts as the distribution channel and aggregator for the insurer and where the insurance policy covers the loan amount or an additional cash position that provides farmers with liquidity, and (iii) meso-insurance, where an insurer covers the agricultural loan portfolio of an FSP against defaults from systemic production risks.[12] Credit-linked insurance requires a close collaboration between an insurer and a FSP and is often arranged in that it is compulsory for a certain farming segment (mainly smallholders) or agricultural sub-sectors and has the advantage that administration is simplified, risk diversification is increased and adverse selection is largely mitigated. Compulsory credit-linkd insurance schemes typically benefit from government premium subsidies. One of the largest credit-linked insurance programmes is operated in India through (i) Pradhan Mantri Fasal Bima Yojana (Section 6.8), which is an area-yield index programme, and (ii) the Restructured Weather-Based Crop Insurance Scheme (Section 6.9), which is based on weather indices.

It is commonly agreed that credit-linked insurance works best in environments with high covariate risks and with farmers that have limited collateral. While credit-linked insurance often provides the only means to reach large numbers of smallholders to create diversified risk pools, social insurance has been proposed as a more efficient approach to cover farmers in high-risk areas (e.g. flood plains, highly drought-prone areas without irrigation). A potential downside of credit-linked insurance is that uninsured losses, or losses that are insurable but do not qualify for indemnity (e.g. from index-based products with large basis risk), will impact an insured badly in that the insurance premium and the defaulted loan become payable.[13]

---

[12] Meyer, R.L. et al., 2017: Unlocking Smallholder Credit: Does Credit-Linked Agricultural Insurance Work? World Bank Publication, Washington, DC, 60p.

[13] Clarke, D., 2011: Theory of Rational Demand for Index Insurance. Economics Series Working Papers 572, University of Oxford, 40p.

Credit Guarantee Programmes

As an alternative or complementation to credit-linked insurance, credit guarantee programmes have been established to reduce borrowing risks of smallholders. Like insurance, credit guarantees cover individual or loan portfolios of FSPs, but unlike insurance, credit guarantees cover all reasons for loan default. Credit guarantees can be distinguished into (i) individual loan guarantees, which provide partial coverage for the underlying principal loan amount that is agreed between the borrower and the lender, (ii) investment facility guarantees, where a bond issue is guaranteed through a guarantee agency which is often used when a developing economy has functioning capital markets and medium- to long-term investment funds are required, (iii) portfolio guarantees, where partial guarantees are provided for a number of loans from one lender to several borrowers, and (iv) portable guarantees, where a borrower can compare competing loan terms and offers from various lenders.[14] While individual loan guarantees establish a direct relationship between the borrower and the lender, they incur high costs and are therefore mainly used for commercial farming systems. Portfolio guarantees are more cost efficient in reaching a large number of borrowers and are the predominate form of guarantees in smallholder production systems, particularly through microfinance institutional guarantees.

Credit guarantee systems (CGSs) are used to increase investment into the agricultural sector and to ensure that investments are directed towards target groups and industries that are considered too risky for adequate financing without such risk-sharing incentives. Most CGSs focus on portfolio risks of small and microfinance institutions that have limited access to guarantees. Initially, CGSs typically rely on government funds and contributions from donors for capitalisation and aim to operate sustainably and without the need for repeated capital infusions. However, due to systemic risks and resulting high loan default rates, a larger number of CGSs remain dependent on frequent third-party capital infusion and are highly funded by the public. Further, the lack of transparency in reporting financial results, misuses of funds and political interferences has led to financial losses of many CGSs. It has been shown that CGS default rates tend to increase with the degree of government involvement and the age of the credit guarantee system.[15]

5.4 CHALLENGES OF AGRICULTURAL INSURANCE

As with most types of insurance, agricultural insurance is challenged by covering systemic risks, minimising adverse selection, controlling moral hazard and accurately assessing the demand of insurance when new products are developed. Additionally, underwriting standards, pricing approaches and claims management processes need to fulfil the specific requirements of insuring biological systems such as crops, livestock, aquaculture and forestry risks. Particular challenges arise with agricultural production systems in low-income countries, which often include smallholder structures, limited insurance infrastructure and data, little government support and a general unawareness

---

[14] Zander, R. et al., 2013: Credit Guarantee Systems for Agriculture and Rural Enterprise Development. FAO Publication, Rome, 124p.
[15] Beck, T. et al., 2008: The Typology of Partial Credit Guarantee Funds around the World. World Bank Policy Research Working Paper 4771, Washington, DC, 38p.

of farmers with insurance concepts where a premium is paid upfront and an indemnity might be obtained.

SYSTEMIC RISKS

The insurance of systemic perils, which are highly correlated losses that are difficult to diversify, requires insurers to build reserves to pay unforeseeable losses, add catastrophe loadings into pricings and transfer risks to reinsurance markets to obtain financial protection for extreme loss events. Agricultural insurers have successfully covered systemic risks, largely through the availability of government premium subsidies, catastrophe protection, and the development of specific risk pricing and modelling approaches. Risk layering is one of the fundamental concepts in understanding and managing systemic risks within an agricultural production system (Section 1.3).

Insurability of Agricultural Risks

In accordance with the general theory of the insurability of risks (Section 2.3), agricultural insurers can cover systemic risks only if the following six conditions can be addressed:

- Losses must be uncorrelated for the insurer to achieve a balanced insurance portfolio (pooled risks) and charge affordable premium rates. With agricultural insurance, risks are correlated in the case of systemic perils and require geographical and product diversification as well as reinsurance protection.
- The insurer must be able to manage and control asymmetric information, including adverse selection, and fraud among the insurance buyers, which is typically addressed through risk classification and risk-adequate insurance terms as well as monitoring of the insured.
- Economically viable premium rates perceived by the policyholder for the value of insurance must be greater than or equal to the cost of retaining the risk. Farmers are often not willing or able to pay for insurance, but government premium subsidies help make agricultural insurance affordable and achieve a sustainable insurance penetration, which lowers adverse selection and market failure.
- Insurers must have limited liability in order to prevent market failure, which is addressed through the definition of maximum limits per insured risk and risk transfer. With the potential of most agricultural insurance products to experience catastrophe-type losses, insurers have the option to (i) set aside adequate reserves, which in practice is unlikely due to high opportunity costs for capital and tax disincentives, or (ii) obtain catastrophe risk protection from the government, reinsurers or capital markets.
- The insurer must be able to compute risk-adequate premium rates through loss distributions, including loss frequency and severity which is based on either historical or modelled data. Agricultural insurers have developed specific pricing and modelling approaches; however, the wealth and access of data from developed markets often limit application in less developed markets, where new approaches need to be developed according to data availability and the market context.
- The insurer must be able to price risks among different risk classes to avoid concentrations of high-risk insurance buyers that drive up the costs of insurance and can ultimately lead to market failure. Limited data and the difficulty in classifying risks have been a challenge in agricultural insurance, particularly in low-income countries.

ADVERSE SELECTION AND MORAL HAZARD

Adverse selection and moral hazard both relate to optimising policyholders' choices and have affected most agricultural insurance programmes and particularly those that are indemnity-based.

Adverse Selection

Adverse selection is based on a high degree of asymmetric information, where insurers do not obtain all data from policyholders to assess risks, which leads to a higher probability of indemnity payments that cannot be reflected in the premium structure.[16] Adverse selection in agricultural insurance can be differentiated as (i) intertemporal, which results from producers only insuring in periods when risk is above normal, and (ii) spatial, where only high-risk farmers buy insurance and low-risk producers (who are subsidising the high-risk farmers) perceive little value in insurance, which often occurs when insurers fail to classify risks and offer the same terms to all policyholders. A further form of spatial adverse selection occurs when policyholders insure only more exposed production sites.

Numerous studies have demonstrated a certain degree of adverse selection in the US MPCI programmes, with only farmers with above-average risk purchasing insurance.[17] Crop insurance products that cover systemic perils (e.g. drought under MPCI) tend to have higher adverse selection ratios than named-peril insurance (e.g. hail under crop hail policies) where losses are more random and localised. Livestock, forestry and aquaculture insurance tend to have less adverse selection as often an onsite risk assessment is undertaken before insurance incepts and allows better risk classification.

Statistical models have been developed to assess the level of adverse selection and moral hazard in crop insurance.[18] Crop insurers address intertemporal adverse selection by setting policy inception dates before planting times and introducing waiting periods before covers incept. Spatial adverse selection can be controlled through (i) classification of producers into risk classes to derive insurance terms for each risk group, (ii) mandating the insurance of all production assets, (iii) mandatory insurance programmes, and (iv) index products where indemnities are determined by independent indices which do not reflect the individual performance at farm level.

Moral Hazard

Moral hazard occurs as insured producers intentionally alter normal loss mitigation practices in the event of loss and thereby influence the loss amount that is assumed to be received as an insurance indemnity. Examples of moral hazard include crop farmers using less crop-protection and committing less labour when crops show signs of disease, or livestock operators switching ear tags of livestock with diseases.

---

[16] Just, R.E. et al., 1999: Adverse selection in crop insurance: actuarial and asymmetric information incentives. *Amer. J. Agr. Econ.*, 81(4), 834–49.

[17] Goodwin, B.K., 1993: An empirical analysis of the demand for multiple peril crop insurance. *Amer. J. Agr. Econ.*, 75(2), 425–34.

[18] Quiggin, J. et al., 1993: Crop insurance and crop production: An empirical study of moral hazard and adverse selection. *Aust. J. Agr. Econ.*, 37(2), 95–113.

Statistical models have been proposed to quantify and detect moral hazard in crop insurance.[19] Insurers try to minimise moral hazard by (i) collecting a maximum of information on the policyholder, (ii) monitoring the policyholders, which however leads to increased costs and is likely to be perceived as intrusive, (iii) introducing loss-sharing structures such as franchises and deductibles, (iv) applying multi-year insurance contracts, which statistically will detect moral hazard of an individual policyholder relative to other policyholders, and (v) obliging the policyholders to use appropriate cultivation and management techniques and to avoid unreasonable risks. Policy wordings mostly include a clause that insureds are to adopt all necessary practices and not to aggregate the loss or abandon the insured asset. When moral hazard is evident, the most common practice for insurers is to reject a claim or reduce the loss amount.

INSURANCE DEMAND AND AFFORDABILITY

Agricultural insurance is often driven by demand and supply and may depend on a large number of factors, including risk awareness, affordability, alternative risk management options and economic as well as market conditions. The value perceived by a potential policyholder in the way insurance increases income and stabilises earning variability and the affordability of an available cover are important factors that determine demand.

Value Attached to Insurance

In the economic theory, a producer's decision to buy crop insurance is a measure of insurance demand and affordability and has been shown to depend largely on the producer's (i) utility function of income in that insurance will increase the income and reduce the variance of future incomes, (ii) the current income, while the cost a producer attaches to risk typically declines with increasing profits, (iii) the subjective perception of the frequency distribution of future income, and (iv) the cost and coverage of the insurance contract.[20] The underlying assumption is that agricultural producers are to some degree risk averse in that a risk investment is undertaken only if there is a strictly positive return, which in insurance terms means that a potential policyholder buys insurance protection only if they perceive a benefit. The effectiveness of insurance as a function of benefits for the policyholder is mainly tested through the expected utility function, but also through the expected shortfall and the spectral risk measure.[21] The expected utility (*EU*) function of a producer's wealth is defined through:

$$EU(w_0 + w) = \frac{1}{1-\theta} \cdot (w + w_0)^{(1-\theta)}$$

with θ as a constant describing relative risk aversion, w_0 as a producer's initial wealth and w as a producer's net income (including cost of insurance and indemnities received).

---

[19] Chambers, R.G., 1989: Insurability and moral hazard in agricultural insurance markets. *Amer. J. Agr. Econ.*, 71(3), 604–16.
[20] Sherrick, B.J. et al., 2004: Factors influencing farmers' crop insurance decisions. *Am. J. Agric. Econ.*, 86(1), 103–14.
[21] Conradt, S. et al., 2015: Tailored to the extremes: Quantile regression for index-based insurance contract design. *Agric. Econ.*, 46, 537–47.

While widely used in academic studies to prove the value of an insurance solution, the effectiveness of risk reduction of insurance is hardly applied in practice by insurers to understand buying behaviours of potential policyholders.

Affordability of Premiums

Insurance premiums must be commercially attractive and affordable for a potential policyholder who is willing to pay for a given insurance cover. While affordability relates to having the financial means to buy insurance, willingness to pay refers to the price below which a consumer will definitely buy an available insurance product.

While affordability of agricultural insurance is not a concern in high-income countries but willingness to pay is the challenge, smallholders in low-income countries are often willing to pay for insurance but cannot afford it out of their own means. Insurers address the affordability through (i) applying for government premium subsidies support from international donors or development banks, and (ii) developing specific products such as microinsurance for low-income households.

Empirical Evidence

Several studies have revealed that insured crop farmers are more sensitive than non-insured producers to changes in the preceding season's yield volatility and that participation in crop insurance schemes is positively related to yield variability.[22] The degree of crop diversification and irrigation extent, which are effective risk management measures, can decrease the demand for crop insurance.[23] Farm size has been found to be a positive indicator of production risk and crop insurance adaptation ratios; however, for very large farms and increased risk management capabilities, the demand for insurance typically decreases. In the USA, the level of farm income and perceived risk of loss often determine the type of crop insurance programme: (i) high-risk farmers prefer revenue insurance compared with yield insurance and individual coverage rather than area-based insurance, (ii) high-risk farmers often choose high coverage levels, (iii) producers that obtained an insurance payment are more likely to buy insurance with higher coverage level in the next season, and (iv) farmers with higher expected yields than the county average, that are used to define insurance rates, are likely to purchase higher coverage levels.[24] Generally, the availability of premium subsidies from governments increases the demand for insurance, while direct support payments can decrease the need for insurance.

Compared with mature insurance markets, producers in emerging markets can show different behaviours towards insurance, including (i) little experience with financial instruments and lack of awareness of the concept of risk transfer, (ii) lower exposure to fluctuations of commodity prices, particularly in the presence of minimum support prices and procurement schemes offered by the government, (iii) lower income levels, with the cost of insurance being a main constraint for insurance adaptation, and (iv) income from non-agricultural sources act as a risk diversifier and generally

---

[22] Cabas, J.H. et al., 2008: Modeling exit and entry of farmers in a crop insurance program. *Agr. Resour. Econ. Rev.*, 37, 92–105.

[23] Santeramo, F.G. et al., 2016: Farmer participation, entry and exit decisions in the Italian crop insurance programme. *J. Agric. Econ.*, 67(3), 639–57.

[24] Makki, S.S. and Somwaru, A., 2001: Evidence of adverse selection in crop insurance markets. *J. Risk Ins.*, 68(4), 685–708.

decreasing the interest in insurance.[25] Further, producers in low-income countries typically have underdeveloped risk mitigation infrastructure (e.g. irrigation) and restricted access to supply chains, and show high covariance in returns among portfolio assets as returns on most assets are dependent on agricultural outcomes in the community.[26] In India, the low voluntary demand for index-based crop insurance is driven by factors including affordability, the availability of alternative risk-sharing agreements, the perceived value of the product, the understandability of the product, trust in the product and insurer, and basis risk.[27]

OPERATIONS, ADMINISTRATION AND DISTRIBUTION

Efficient insurance operations including distribution, administration, risk-adequate underwriting and cost-efficient and timely loss adjustment are important requirements for successful programmes. However, running efficient operations is challenging and depends on the level of heterogeneity of policyholders, the type of insurance product, and the level of technology used for distribution, administration and loss adjustment.

Underwriting and Pricing

Agricultural insurance relies on most of the basic principles of insurance but at the same time requires specific underwriting, modelling and pricing approaches that fundamentally differ among crop, livestock, aquaculture and forestry risks (Chapters 6–9). Underwriting and pricing are key challenges as often (i) production and weather data are difficult to access, show inconsistencies and significant trends that need to be removed, (ii) most production systems show a high degree of heterogeneity in production methods and productivity levels, (iii) historical claims data need to be standardised as insurance products have evolved over time, (iv) catastrophe losses might not have occurred in historical claims data but have large loss potentials and need to be modelled, and (v) adequate reserves and reinsurance are essential to achieve risk-adequate solvency levels. However, agricultural insurance is in many markets not as strictly regulated as more general insurance business.

Pricing of agricultural risks follows the concepts of general insurance pricing, using schedule rating, experience and exposure rating (Section 2.4); it varies, however, with the underlying data representing biological systems and requires actuarial as well as catastrophe modelling skills. As agricultural risk management is highly specialised, adequate training courses for insurance underwriting and pricing are rare while certification courses have yet to be developed.

Loss Adjustment

The timely and accurate adjustment and payment of losses to affected policyholders is a cornerstone of agricultural insurance. Loss adjustment requires numerous experts

---

[25] Wang, M. et al., 2016: Factors affecting farmers' crop insurance participation in China. *Can. J. Agric. Econ.*, 64, 479–92.

[26] Collier, B. et al., 2009: Weather index insurance and climate change: Opportunities and challenges in lower income countries. *Geneva Papers on Risk and Insurance*, 34, 401–24.

[27] Cole, S. et al., 2013: Barriers to household risk management: evidence from India. *Amer. Econ. J.*, 5(1), 104–35.

and data systems that allow simultaneous processing of a large number of claims, which can cause significant costs and requires special expertise. The use of technology to support and increase the efficiency of loss adjustment (e.g. drones, satellite imagery) needs substantial investments to integrate these technologies into existing loss assessment processes. Loss adjustment manuals define the adjustment approach through sampling to determine loss of quantity, quality and biomass, which are translated into monetary terms relative to values of the insured assets before a loss event occurred (Chapters 6–9). Disease-related claims in livestock and aquaculture insurance require diagnostic laboratories where the cause of mortality can be established. As loss adjustment is specific per asset class, expertise is required for each domain, i.e. a crop loss adjustor will struggle to investigate livestock or aquaculture damage and vice versa. Defined through the type of insurance product, loss adjustment is (i) based on individual farms in systems with large farming units, or (ii) largely assisted by government agencies through calamity-based insurance (e.g. Thailand) or combined named-peril covers (e.g. China), or is largely replaced through indices (e.g. India) in production systems with smallholder structures.

Insurance Distribution

As agricultural insurance is often the first insurance in rural areas, investments into efficient distribution channels are necessary to reach a critical mass of potential policyholders with a proven interest in and demand for risk transfer. While mature agricultural markets contain a developed farm service industry in rural areas, smallholder systems in low-income countries lack insurance infrastructure and often rely on risk aggregators to distribute insurance products.

Agricultural insurance uses conventional and alternative distribution channels according to the level of rural infrastructure. The most common include (i) insurance agents and direct brokers, (ii) mutual insurers and cooperatives in providing insurance besides other benefits (e.g. credit, input supply, machinery) to members, (iii) agricultural lenders and microfinance institutions through bundling insurance with loans (bancassurance), (iv) input suppliers such as seed producers (e.g. Pioneer and Monsanto in India) and machinery/equipment manufacturers (e.g. John Deere in the USA) that offer insurance as part of the value proposition, (v) processors such as crushers, millers and ginners, (vi) government administrative structures such as village representatives, and (vii) internet platforms, internet kiosks, smart phones and social media that are linked to payment systems.

The cost for distributions are highly variable depending on the distribution channel and range from 3% to 5% for bancassurance, 15% using government infrastructure, and 20% to 40% in the case of agent networks.

5.5 AGRICULTURAL INSURANCE SYSTEMS

While agricultural insurance started through cooperatives and mutual associations, different forms have evolved. From the level of government involvement in agricultural insurance, three systems can be distinguished: private sector systems, public sector programmes and PPP. As most agricultural insurance is linked to government risk management and disaster financing strategies, several markets have seen changes between insurance systems, particularly the transformation of public sector programmes into partnerships with the insurance industry (PPP).

PRIVATE SECTOR SYSTEM

Under the private sector system, commercial insurers, or mutual insurers, exclusively manage all aspects of agricultural insurance under pure market-based insurance systems that do not benefit from government support. Commercial insurance products are tailored to the need of policyholders under flexible products and cover perils and risks that are typically not addressed by government compensation schemes (e.g. hail, frost, wildfire, certain diseases) or provide indemnity in addition to government payments (e.g. epidemic livestock diseases). Most crop hail insurance programmes, livestock, aquaculture and forestry products are based on private sector insurance systems. Due to high-risk concentrations and fragmented markets, some commercial insurance programmes suffer from adverse selection and moral hazards, with low insurance penetration, low risk diversification and high premium rates. The presence of systemic perils requires substantial reinsurance protection.

Examples of Private Sector Systems

Private sector systems exist in North America and include crop hail insurance (Section 6.4), forestry and aquaculture covers, and livestock base mortality insurance. In Europe, most crop hail, livestock, forestry and aquaculture insurance operates under commercial programmes. In Latin America, crop hail and MPCI insurance in Argentina is the best-known example of a pure private sector system. Similarly, all agricultural insurance in Australia, New Zealand and South Africa are private sector systems and products are mainly offered to large commercial farms. Except in some pilot programmes, commercial insurance is rare in markets with smallholder and subsistence farming structures in Asia, Africa and parts of Latin America.

PUBLIC SECTOR SYSTEM

Under the public sector system, agricultural insurance is entirely controlled and administrated by the government and often includes one unified product with standardised insurance conditions that is distributed by a monopolistic government-owned insurer. Government insurance programmes often target smallholders and operate under social welfare aspects as one of several programmes that support the financial viability of subsistence farmers. Often, smallholders benefit from 100% premium subsidies, while larger farmers are typically required to contribute to some extent towards the cost of insurance and administration. These programmes often include high insurance penetrations and risk diversification, particularly where insurance is compulsory (e.g. for borrowing farmers). Public sector insurance schemes are considered inefficient as uniform insurance terms are applied and policyholders are often not classified according to risk.

Performance of Public Sector Programmes

Most public schemes have created large fiscal liabilities on government budgets, and most programmes are characterised by high administrative costs and claims ratios, e.g. the FCIC programmes (USA) incurred a cost ratio of 55% and a loss ratio of 187% relative to premium contributed by producers (1980–1989), the ANAGSA schemes (Mexico) produced a cost ratio of 47% and a loss ratio of 318% (1980–1989), the Pro-Agro programme (Brazil) showed a cost ratio of 28% with a loss ratio of 429% (1975–1981), the programme of the Philippine Crop Insurance Corporation (Section 3.8) showed cost ratios of 180% and 395% as an average loss ratio (1981–1989).[28]

Most of the initial public sector programmes were discontinued or have been transformed into PPPs, including for example the FCIC programmes in the USA in 1980 and the social welfare agriculture scheme National Agricultural Insurance Scheme (NAIS) in India in 2010 (Section 6.8). However, some programmes have continued, including ProAgro in Brazil, NOSAI in Japan and the Philippine Crop Insurance Corporation (Section 3.8). Canada has a large public sector MPCI programme that is under AgInsure, a fundamental part of support for the agricultural sector, and is administrated by province-owned insurers that operate at standards that are comparable to private sector insurers.

Government Agricultural Insurance in Japan

Japan's agriculture sector contributes only 1% to the country's GDP, with only 22% of Japan's land mass suitable for agricultural production. Japan has a farming population of 2.16 million and 1.5 million farms, most of which are small (average of 1.9 ha). Only 11% of all farms operate on a full-time basis – the vast majority are part-time farms. Additionally, the average age of farmers is high at 65 years. Under agricultural policies in Japan, most agricultural sectors have been heavily protected through high import tariffs. Income subsidies for small farms are thought to prevent the necessary consolidation of farmers into larger production units. A decline in the farming population as well as exposure to more severe natural disasters under climate change conditions have provoked concerns about future food security in Japan.

Agricultural Risk Management in Japan

Japan has a long tradition in the management of weather shocks and agricultural income. The Livestock Insurance Act was enforced in 1929 and the National Forest Insurance Law was enacted in 1937, followed by the Crop Insurance Act in 1938. Following a reorganisation of agricultural organisations, the Agricultural Disaster Compensation Act was introduced in 1947 based on the principle of solidarity to provide stability to farmers. Based on mutual aid, the Agricultural Mutual Relief (AMR) programme has been operated by the Agricultural Mutual Relief Associations (AMRAs) for each region or municipal governments. The agricultural insurance scheme, known as NOSAI, is part of the AMR programme.[29]

---

[28] Hazell, P.B.R., 1992: The appropriate role of agricultural insurance in developing countries. *J. Int. Dev.*, 4, 567–81.

[29] Nakamura, N. et al., 2016: Agricultural insurance in Japan: Stakeholders' opinions on its effectiveness and ways forward. In Prabhaker, S.V.R.K. (ed): Case Studies in Insurance Effectiveness: Some Insights into Costs and Benefits. Southeast Asia Disaster Prevention Research Institute (SEADPRI), 138p.

Nogyo Kyosai Seido (NOSAI)

NOSAI includes over 300 cooperatives at the local, regional and national levels. The need for the government to intervene and provide better conditions for the agriculture sector was reinforced through the Food, Agriculture and Rural Areas Basis Act of 1999. Under NOSAI, the Japanese government provides subsidies for insurance premiums and operating costs while acting as a reinsurer of last resort. Agricultural insurance as a safety net for farmers following natural disasters is seen as a key contributor to food security and to stabilising rural areas that are less developed than urban centres. Under NOSAI, farmers make contributions to a joint reserve fund in advance that is managed by a cooperative and based on the concept of mutual voluntary relief of farmers in that mutual aid insurance money will be paid from the joint reserve fund if damage has occurred. NOSAI provides mandatory crop and livestock insurance (rice, wheat, barley, cattle, pigs) and voluntary insurance for crops (sugarcane, certain field crops, fruit/fruit trees), greenhouses, farm property and agricultural machinery.

Under NOSAI, premium rates are set when the cooperatives/federations pay reinsurance premiums to the government, and management fees for cooperatives to run the insurance scheme are included in the national budget. Premium rates are set as flat rates on a no-loss no-profit basis and are determined from disaster statistics, agricultural production data and information from farmers. Through flat rates, farmers in high-risk areas benefit over-proportionally more from premium subsidies and resulting indemnity compared with producers in low-risk regions. Indemnities are triggered directly through a disaster declaration act or producers filing a claim which is adjusted by competent NOSAI personnel. Rice, wheat and barley, which are the main crops insured, are covered under yield-based MPCI policies, with coverage levels varying according to the unit of insurance, e.g. for paddy rice 70% coverage for an entire farm, 80% for a damaged field (part of the entire farm). The 300 cooperatives are the exclusive delivery channel for agricultural insurance.

As local cooperatives (even at prefecture level) will not be able to financially absorb losses from severe overregional disasters, liabilities are reinsured by AMR agencies, including municipal governments, prefecture federations and the government as the last resort.

Performance of NOSAI

Overall, NOSAI insures over two million policies for crop insurance and 6.7 million policies for livestock. In 2011, crop insurance premiums reached around US$220 million and livestock was US$527 million. Over the period 2001–2011, crop insurance performed at an average loss ratio of 81%, with 22% (2001) as the lowest and 343% as the highest loss ratio (2003).

For crop insurance, NOSAI indemnifies only for reductions of yield from natural disasters (MPCI), while fluctuations in crop prices have been compensated through the Income Security Program for Farmers since 2009. In 2013, the scheme was discontinued and the Program for Stabilisation of Management Income was introduced to cover producers' income deficits. NOSAI has been criticised for causing large financial burdens to the government budget through subsidies and reinsurance protection. A change of the current agricultural insurance systems into private-public sector system has been under discussion since 2014, with potentially a revenue insurance pilot starting for rice producers.

PRIVATE–PUBLIC SECTOR SYSTEM

Under the private–public sector system, the private and public sectors collaborate under a PPP to administrate and underwrite agricultural insurance programmes. Today, most larger agricultural insurance programmes are operating as PPPs where insurance risk transfer is an integral part of government risk management and complements disaster assistance programmes. These systems typically reveal well-diversified portfolios, reduced adverse selection due to high penetration ratios, are managed under reasonable costs for administration and produce sustainable underwriting results as technical and commercial underwriting criteria are applied. However, PPPs require substantial government support in the form or subsidies and reinsurance protection.

Forms of Private–Public Sector Systems

Different forms can be distinguished, including (i) commercial competition with a low level of control where private insurers select risks and determine insurance conditions independently and where the public sector provides premium subsidies, e.g. Brazil (MPCI), Europe (combined named-peril insurance), (ii) commercial competition where private insurers underwrite agricultural risks but the public sector determines the framework and terms and provides subsidies while obliging in some cases (e.g. USA) to cover all types of farmers, (iii) monopolistic private coinsurance pools where private insurers act as agents and implement subsidised programmes, with strong involvement from the public sector in terms of policy design and insurance terms (e.g. Tarsim in Turkey) and the additional benefit of government reinsurance (e.g. Agroseguro in Spain), and (iv) monopolistic private insurers or cooperatives operating under the instruction of the public sector to underwrite subsidised schemes exclusively (e.g. NACF in South Korea).

Government Intervention

Governments typically focus on supporting the agriculture sector through direct payments and policy measures on agricultural inputs and outputs, production quotas, price support mechanisms, logistics (warehousing), low-interest loans, tax reliefs and disaster assistance programmes. For a government, agricultural insurance and risk transfer is often a strategy to complement or ultimately replace other support schemes while covering production risk and in some cases revenue risk (production and price risks).

Government involvement in an agricultural insurance scheme is often justified through (i) underdeveloped insurance infrastructure and services, (ii) inability and/or willingness of private insurers to implement agricultural insurance schemes due to high initial investments, the presence of systemic risks that prevents diversification and lack of expertise, and (iii) the need for catastrophe risk protection due to the insurance of systemic risks. Government support for agricultural insurance generally includes the provision of (i) legal frameworks and regulatory supervision, (ii) data and information systems, including weather data from meteorological services and production statistics from agricultural surveys, (iii) modelling services, including early warning systems and product design, (iv) education, training and development of awareness of insurance solutions, (v) distribution of insurance products (in some markets) and support for loss adjustment (in some markets), (vi) premium subsidies and cost subsidies for administration (in some markets), and (vii) risk financing through reinsurance.

Criticism of government intervention in agricultural insurance include (i) reinsurance and capital markets are deep enough to absorb losses from systemic perils, (ii) highly subsidised crop insurance premiums change production management in that farmers apply less crop protection and fertiliser, grow riskier crops and bring riskier land into production, and (iii) substantial subsidies that are financed through tax payers or deficit borrowing to guarantee producers' incomes generate large distortions in other segments of the economy.[30] It has been suggested that a government should prioritise intervention in agricultural insurance in (i) addressing large systemic risks that affect agricultural production through disaster financing, including risk transfer and allowing the private sector to develop insurance products for individual, independent farm risks, (ii) developing databases and risk maps that improve identifying, analysing and pricing risks, and (iii) creating strong regulatory frameworks and effective financial systems.[31]

Government Subsidies

Government subsidies are a key component of private–public sector systems to make insurance more accessible and affordable and to increase insurance penetration and manage systemic risks in diversified portfolios with limited adverse selection. Market-enhancing insurance subsidies promote the development of risk market infrastructure and competitive (re)insurance markets while preventing market failure.[32] Overall, upfront costs to a government of providing premium subsidies are estimated to be 44% of the original gross premium; 68% in the case where operational and other costs are additionally subsidised.[33] Meanwhile, subsidies for social safety nets and wealth transfer to rural communities can distort markets and create significant reliance on indemnities as a risk management strategy.

WTO Rules for Agricultural Insurance Subsidies
Under the WTO agreements, public aid and support for the agricultural sector has to comply with the specific rules.[34] The WTO differentiates government aid and support according to *boxes* with different colours into (i) green subsidies that are permitted and have a minimal impact on trade (e.g. most general government services including research, disease control, infrastructure and food security), (ii) amber subsidies that are to be reduced or gradually discontinued, and (iii) red subsidies that are forbidden. Additionally, the blue box contains aids and subsidies for goods that have a production limitation (e.g. milk in the EU).

Eligibility for financial support to agricultural disaster relief schemes and financing of agricultural insurance premium subsidies against impacts of natural disasters

---

[30] Goodwin, B.K. and Smith, V.H., 2013: What harm is done by subsidizing crop insurance? *Am. J. Agric. Econ.*, 95(2), 489–97.

[31] World Bank, 2005: Module 10: Managing Agricultural Risk, Vulnerability and Disaster. World Bank Publication 34392, Washington, DC, 536p.

[32] Cummins, J.D. and Mahul, O., 2009: Catastrophe Risk Financing in Developing Countries: Principles for Public Intervention. World Bank Publication, Washington, DC, 299p.

[33] Mahul, O. and Stutley, C.J., 2010: Government Support to Agricultural Insurance: Challenges and Options for Developing Countries. World Bank Publication 53881, Washington, DC, 250p.

[34] http://www.wto.org/english/docs_e/legal_e/14-ag_01_e.htm (accessed January 2018).

is determined as a loss of income from agricultural activities, which (i) exceeds 30% of average gross income, or (ii) is equivalent in net income terms in the preceding three-year period, or a three-year average based on the preceding five-year period, excluding the highest and lowest entries. Further, the amount of payments cannot exceed 70% of a producer's loss in that year and any payment in combination with other payments (especially received from losses due to natural disasters) cannot exceed 100% of the loss in that year. A disaster must be officially recognised by a government, with production losses above 30% of the actual production over three-year equivalent periods.

As most agricultural insurance schemes provide coverage above 70% and/or establish losses from disasters based on average production levels relative to a three-year or five-year period and do not rely on (or wait for) government disaster declarations before indemnity payments, premium subsidies of agricultural insurance schemes are considered amber box instruments. Most countries report the support of agricultural insurance as non-product specific amber box support and support for product delivery (e.g. subsidies for administration and distribution of insurance) as green box support.

5.6 FORMS OF AGRICULTURAL INSURANCE OPERATIONS

Based on the agricultural insurance system and the regulatory environment, agricultural insurance operations have developed mainly as government insurers (public sector system), private insurers (private system) and a mixture of different forms, including cooperative and mutual insurers as well as co-insurance pools (private, public and private–public sector system).

COOPERATIVE AND MUTUAL INSURERS

Cooperative insurers are often (at least initially) owned by members and operate for the benefit of their policyholders who follow the principles of the cooperative. Cooperative insurers can be formed as stock companies, mutual insurers or any other form that is allowed by regulators. Often agricultural cooperatives provide members joint access at lower costs to input supplies (e.g. fertiliser, credit, fuel, irrigation, crop protection), credit and loans as well as education and retirement benefits and offer agricultural insurance as an additional service.

Mutual insurers operate typically on a non-profit basis and are owned by the members, which are also the policyholders, and operate under (i) an advance premium system, where the member pays the insurance premium at the beginning of the insurance period and can obtain a return premium in case of good operational performance of the mutual, or (ii) an assessment system, where members might pay some insurance premium but are liable for a share of the mutual's expenses and losses.

Self-insurance systems (SISs) include self-insurance funds, which use internal means to finance losses and involve the establishment of a fund for risk management of unexpected losses by a group of businesses with similar interests and exposure to risks. In agriculture, the development of SISs is often driven by farmers to improve access to credit where the fund is pledged as collateral that is accepted by formal banking standards for joint loans and credits.

Examples in Agriculture

Examples of cooperative and mutual insurers in agriculture include the Co-operative Hail Insurance Company (Canada), the Swiss Hail Insurance Company (Switzerland), Sunlight Agricultural Mutual Insurance in Heilongjiang province (China), the Caisse Nationale d'Assurances Mutuelles Agricoles (Tunisia), Sancor Seguros and La Segunda (Argentina) and the National Mutual Insurance Federation of Agricultural Cooperatives (Japan). While some agricultural mutual insurers are specialised and cover only members of the same industry sector against selected loss events (e.g. Co-operative Hail Insurance Company), others have expanded to operate in several countries (e.g. Swiss Hail Insurance Company, Sancor Seguros) and others have expanded from agricultural insurance into general insurance (e.g. Mutual Insurance Federation of Agricultural Cooperatives).

The Fondos de Aseguramiento (Fondos) in Mexico is an example of a SIS where over 370 fondos provide agricultural insurance, with a premium volume of US$84 million, which is around 20% of the total agricultural premium. The development of SISs in Mexico emerged out of smaller and subsistence farmers' need to obtain agricultural insurance in order to access credits.[35] Fondos require government approval, operate in limited regions and require no capital, but to guarantee solvency, they must purchase adequate reinsurance.

CO-INSURANCE POOLS

Co-insurance pools consist of insurers which provide capacity, that typically defines the share in the pool and the allocation of premium and loss amounts. Co-insurance pools are (i) established on the initiative of the insurers to reduce costs for underwriting, claims management and reinsurance and to develop central expertise, or (ii) mandated by the government to increase the insurance penetration and maintain comparable insurance terms and conditions. Pooling risks from insurers is usually more efficient than holding capital on each insurer's balance sheet or in government budgets, and through regional diversification, reduced premium rates can be offered to policyholders. Difficulties in a pooling arrangement include the agreement on a methodology to (i) allocate shares to members in function of the size and performance of the underlying business, (ii) set retentions per member, and (iii) split the cost for joint catastrophe reinsurance. A pool can therefore function only through close cooperation between the members or through a management entity that acts on behalf of the pool.

In agriculture, co-insurance pools are predominately formed as an initiative of the government – examples include Agroseguro (Spain) and TARSIM (Turkey). In order to increase reinsurance capacity, reinsurance pools have been formed for agricultural exposure and include the China Agricultural Reinsurance Pool (CARP) and the Southeast Asian Agriculture Risk Pool.[36]

---

[35] Ibarra, H., 2004: Self-insurance Funds in Mexico. Catastrophe Risk and Reinsurance. Risk Books, 287–304.
[36] Corona, S., 2013: The Case for a Southeast Asian Agriculture Risk Pool. Geneva Association Risk Management Newsletter 53, Geneva, 5p.

Agricultural Insurance Pool in Turkey

In Turkey, agriculture contributes 8.8% to GDP and the country is the seventh largest agricultural producer at global scale, with 2.2 million farmers. Agricultural insurance started in 1957 and developed slowly as a private sector initiative through named-peril insurance (mainly hail and frost) for field and horticulture crops and some livestock classes and greenhouses. Underwriting was based on limited data, inadequate actuarial expertise, difficulties with loss adjustment and high loss ratios in some years due to systemic frost events. In 2002, the insurance penetration reached 0.6% of the total agricultural land, with Basak Sigorta as the leading insurer with a premium volume of agricultural business of US$3.8 million.

Development of TARSIM

In 2005, the Turkish Agricultural Insurance Act was accepted and the Turkish Agricultural Insurance Pool (TARSIM) was founded upon the initiative of insurers as a government-supported insurance pool for agricultural risks.[37] TARSIM operates as a monopolistic private coinsurance pool and is managed by a board composed of the Ministry of Food, Agriculture and Livestock, the Treasury Department, the Insurance Association of Turkey and the Union of the Agricultural Chambers. For agricultural policies underwritten by 24 private insurers that are part of TARSIM, the government provides premium subsidies, public co-financing of catastrophe losses, uniform insurance terms and centralised loss adjustment. Private insurers distribute the insurance products under their franchise through agent networks in exchange for a commission from TARSIM and cede 100% of the risks and premiums to TARSIM. Through retrocessions, the individual insurers can voluntarily participate in TARSIM.

TARSIM covers a wide range of agricultural risks, including (i) crops (75% of premium volume) such as field crops, fruits, vegetables and flowers covered for natural perils including hail, storm flood, earthquake, landslide as well as frost (fruit only) but excluding drought, (ii) livestock (20.9%) such as cattle, sheep, goats and poultry insured against mortality due to diseases (excluding epidemic diseases and theft), (iii) greenhouses (3.7%) covered for most natural perils, equipment failure and structural damage, and (iv) aquaculture (0.4%) such as tuna, sea bass, sea bream and trout with insurance for mortality due to natural perils and diseases (excluding epidemic diseases) as well as damage to equipment (cages and nets).

Performance of TARSIM

Since its inception in 2005, the insurance penetration has increased to 14% of the total agricultural land, with a premium volume of US$450 million (2017) for 1.4 million policies. Between 2007 and 2016, the average loss ratio reached 68%, with a minimum of 45% (2008) and a maximum of 88% (2007). TARSIM buys proportional reinsurance from international markets and the retained business benefits from government reinsurance.

---

[37]Tekin, A. et al., 2017: Development of implementation of agricultural insurance in Turkey. *Econ. Eng. Agric. Rural Dev.,* 17(2), 355–64.

BIBLIOGRAPHY

ADB 2017: Agriculture Insurance. ADB Brief 77, Manila, 8p.

Churchill, C. and Matul, M. (2012). *Protecting the Poor: A Microinsurance Compendium*, vol. II. Geneva: International Labour Organization, 666p.

Cummins, J.D. and Mahul, O. (2009). *Catastrophe Risk Financing in Developing Countries: Principles for Public Intervention*. Washington, DC: World Bank Publication, 299p.

GIZ (2016). *Innovations and Emerging Trends in Agricultural Insurance*. Eschborn: GIZ Publication, 56p.

Gonulal, S.P., Goulder, N. and Lester, R., 2012: Bancassurance A Valuable Tool for Developing Insurance in Emerging Markets. World Bank Policy Research Paper 6196, Washington, DC, 69p.

IFC (2014a). *Introduction to Agricultural Insurance and Risk Management. Manual 1.* Washington, DC: IFC Publication, 50p.

IFC (2014b). *Actuarial Basics. Manual 2.* Washington, DC: IFC Publication, 59p.

IFC (2014c). *Data and Information Management. Manual 3.* Washington, DC: IFC Publication, 39p.

IFC (2014d). *Credit and Insurance. Manual 4.* Washington, DC: IFC Publication, 34p.

IFC (2014e). *Risk Transfer and Capital Adequacy. Manual 5.* Washington, DC: IFC Publication, 58p.

Kang, M.G., 2007: Innovative agricultural insurance products and schemes. FAO, Agricultural Management, Marketing and Finance Occasional Paper 12, Rome, 54p.

Mahul, O. and Stutley, C.J. (2010). *Government Support to Agricultural Insurance: Challenges and Options for Developing Countries*. Washington, DC: World Bank Publication 53881, 250p.

Ray, P.K. (1981). *Agricultural Insurance: Theory and Practice and Application to Developing Countries*, 2e. New York: Pergamon Press, 419p.

Rosema, A., de Weirdt, M., Foppes, S., and Wilczok, C. (2010). *FESA Micro-Insurance: Methodology, Validation, Contract Design*. Delft: EARS Earth Environment Monitoring BV, 96p.

Sandmark, T., Debar, J.-C. and Tatin-Jaleran, C., 2013: The Emergence and Development of Agriculture Microinsurance. Microinsurance Network Discussion Paper, 43p.

Schaefer, L., Waters, E., Kreft, S. et al. (2016). *Making Climate Risk Insurance Work for the Most Vulnerable: Seven Guiding Principles*. Bonn: Munich Climate Insurance Initiative, UNU-EHS Publication Series Policy Report 1, 35p.

World Bank (2005). *Managing Agricultural Production Risk Innovations in Developing Countries*. Washington, DC: Agriculture and Rural Development Department, 129p.

CHAPTER 6

Crop Insurance

6.1 INTRODUCTION

Crop production is one of the key sectors of agriculture and provides food staples, feed for livestock and agricultural raw materials for many other industries, including biofuel production. Crop production has grown significantly, while at the same time production volatility has increased as the industry has specialised (monocultures) and is therefore more exposed to adverse weather conditions and market forces in a globalised grain and oilseed industry. Risk management, including risk transfer in the form of insurance, has been supporting production of the *green revolution* and developed different products tailored to the needs of individual markets.

This chapter gives an overview of trends in the crop sector and describes the main indemnity- and index-based crop insurance products. Named-peril crop insurance (NPCI) is discussed in the form of crop hail insurance and frost insurance, with calamity-based insurance as a special case. The following sections focus on multi-peril crop insurance (MPCI), which forms the basis for revenue insurance (RI) and income insurance. Index-based crop insurance is discussed for area-yield indices, weather indices and satellite- as well as model-based indices. The main crop insurance markets are discussed from a product point of view in the corresponding sections. The pricing and underwriting of some of the main insurance products are demonstrated through the example of corn production in Adams County (Illinois, USA).

6.2 SECTOR TRENDS

Between 1961 and 2015, global agricultural output more than tripled and arable land increased overall but particularly for main crops such as corn, wheat, rice and soybeans. While large farming operations have been established in most high-income countries, 90% of the estimated 570 million farms worldwide are still family farms in low-income countries, with typical farm sizes below 5 ha.

For key staple crops, yields increased by more than 200% between 1960 and 2016 (Figure 6.1), but annual average increases have slowed to 1% since the 1990s. Yield gaps, which reveal the difference between actual and potential yields in a given

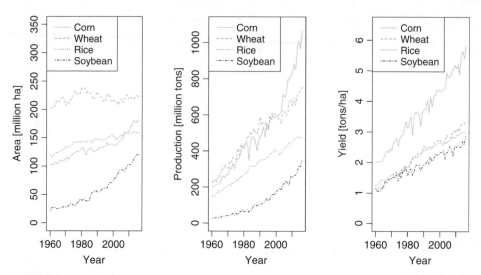

FIGURE 6.1   Development of global area planted (left), global production (middle) and global yield (right) of corn, wheat, rice and soybeans, 1960–2016.
Data source: FAOSTAT and USDA/FAS.

production environment, are larger than 50% in most low-income countries and are the result of limited access to more productive technologies and low market integration of smallholders.[1] Increases in area planted and yield led to production growth of 534% for corn (1961–2016), 323% for wheat and 319% for rice; it was most pronounced for soybeans at 1400% (Figure 6.1).

However, production of key crops is concentrated in a few countries, with a large amount of overlap across different crop types. Nearly 60% of corn is produced in the USA and China and the top 10 producing countries generate around 80% of global production. Similarly, half of the rice comes from China and India and the largest 10 producing countries provide 86% of the global rice, with Southeast Asia producing 30%. Soybean production is even more concentrated, with the USA, Brazil and Argentina alone generating 80% of global soybean supplies, which are mostly used for livestock feed. The high concentration of production makes global supply highly sensitive to large-scale climate disasters in these markets.

The agriculture sector needs to produce almost 50% more food, feed and biofuel by 2050 relative to 2012 to satisfy demand from a growing population and changes in diets as a function of increased wealth in low- and middle-income countries.[2]

---

[1] Yield-gap analyses for the main crop types are shown in the *Global Yield Gap Atlas*, available at www.yieldgap.org (accessed November 2017).
[2] FAO, 2017: The future of food and agriculture – Trends and challenges. FAO Publication, Rome, 180p.

6.3 OVERVIEW OF MAIN CROP INSURANCE PRODUCTS

Crop insurance is the most important type of agricultural insurance and contributed with US$27.65 billion around 89.9% of the total agricultural premium in 2017. The USA remains the largest crop insurance market while Asian countries, particularly China and India, have shown large growth in recent years (Section 5.2).

Crop insurance initially covered only named perils such as hail, but it gradually developed under MPCI in the 1960s to include systemic perils such as droughts, flood and cyclones. To cover revenue volatility from yield and price fluctuations, RI developed in the 1990s as part of national agriculture risk management strategies in mature agriculture economies such as the USA. Income insurance followed in the late 1990s, covering income volatility based on fiscal data from a variety of commodities. As developing agricultural systems, particularly with smallholder structures, pose challenges to implementing crop insurance products from developed markets with large farm units, products have either been modified or new products have been created, including (i) calamity-based crop insurance (CBCI) (e.g. Thailand, Pakistan), which acts mainly as add-on coverage to existing disaster compensation schemes from governments, (ii) comprehensive named-peril insurance (e.g. China), and (iii) area-yield index insurance and weather indices (e.g. India, parts of Africa). For grasslands, satellite-based vegetation indices have been used as the basis of individual insurance (e.g. USA, Canada, France) or as macro-level risk transfer schemes in emerging markets related to livestock (e.g. Mexico, Kenya). With the expansion of crop insurance products, the insurable crop types and perils have increased, now covering most types of field crops, horticulture products, viticulture and ornamental as well as medical plants.

CROP INSURANCE PRODUCTS

Crop insurance products can be classified into indemnity-based and index-based insurance. The two types of crop insurance products have co-existed in some markets (e.g. Europe, North America) where crop hail insurance is indemnity based and all other perils are covered under MPCI or RI products. Area-yield and weather index insurance (WII) exists in countries with developed and developing agricultural systems.

Both product types have advantages and challenges, which essentially depend on (i) the diversity and sophistication level of the agricultural production system, (ii) the size of farms and the level of farmers' risk management capabilities, (iii) the main perils that drive the need for risk transfer, (iv) the level of existing insurance infrastructure that allows efficient distribution and claims handling, (v) the availability and quality of historical data that permits risk-adequate pricing and underwriting, (vi) the level of government support in terms of premium and cost subsidies, reinsurance protection and distribution of products, and (vii) the legislative frameworks in which the role of crop insurance is anchored.

Indemnity-Based Crop Insurance
Indemnity-based crop insurance products require dedicated resources for distribution, tailor-made (farm-based) coverage and insurance terms as well as substantial manpower to undertake loss adjustment (Table 6.1). For MPCI, revenue and income insurance, government subsidies are often required to make products affordable and to

TABLE 6.1 Overview of the main types of crop insurance products.

Type of Product	Characteristics	Perils Covered	Advantages	Disadvantages	Most Suitable Application
Named-peril crop insurance (NPCI) Section 6.4	■ Farm-based insurance ■ Specific named perils insured ■ Loss assessment at farm level ■ Often operated on commercial basis (i.e. without government subsidies) ■ Widely used in mature markets	■ Hail and/or frost, often with extension for FLEXA[a], wind and localised natural perils (e.g. earthquake, mudflows)	■ Insurance of localised perils at farm level ■ Insurance of losses during different phenological stages ■ Tailor-made covers with numerous options for policyholder (deductibles, franchises, adjustment of sum insured, premium discounts in function of loss mitigation measures)	■ Adverse selection and moral hazard ■ Systemic perils (e.g. drought, flood, hurricane/typhoon) are not insured ■ High costs for administration, distribution and loss adjustment	■ Individual large farms (>20 ha) and specialised farms in well-developed agricultural production systems (e.g. North America, Europe, Latin America, parts of Africa) ■ Individual small farms with policies issued at aggregated level (e.g. China)
Calamity-based crop insurance (CBCI) Section 6.4.3	■ Farm-based insurance ■ Specific named perils insured ■ Loss assessment at farm level but only following an officially declared calamity of regional scale ■ Often acts as a top-up cover for government disaster compensation schemes and benefits from government subsidies	■ Drought, flood, strong wind (including hurricane/typhoon) and some named pests and diseases	■ Insurance of systemic perils ■ Use of existing calamity declaration procedures of government as first loss trigger with losses adjusted at farm level ■ Low administrative costs since loss adjustment is often undertaken in collaboration with government for disaster-declared areas	■ Adverse selection ■ Only perils that lead to disasters are insured and only calamity-declared areas qualify for indemnity ■ Disaster declarations contain a high degree of subjectivity and can be politically motivated ■ Often only total losses are compensated	■ Individual farms of various sizes as top-up insurance within government ad-hoc disaster frameworks (e.g. Pakistan, Thailand)

| Multi-peril crop insurance (MPCI) Section 6.5 | ■ Farm-based insurance
 ■ Yield-based all-peril insurance
 ■ Often requires government subsidies and in some markets government reinsurance protection | ■ All natural perils (e.g. drought, flood, hurricane/typhoon, frost) with named pests and diseases (in some markets) | ■ Insurance of systemic perils at farm level, which corresponds to requests from most growers
 ■ Forms the basis for extensions such as revenue insurance | ■ Adverse selection and moral hazard
 ■ High costs for administration, distribution and loss adjustment (yield)
 ■ Localised perils (e.g. hail) hardly lead to low yields that trigger a payout
 ■ Pricing needs to rely on area-based yields (e.g. per county), with adjustments to reflect farm-level yield volatility
 ■ Needs often government subsidies to make policy affordable and to achieve acceptable penetration to limit adverse selection | ■ Individual and large farms (>20 ha) in well-developed agricultural production systems with government support |

(Continued)

TABLE 6-1 (*Continued*)

Type of Product	Characteristics	Perils Covered	Advantages	Disadvantages	Most Suitable Application
Revenue insurance Section 6.6	▪ Farm-based insurance based on revenues (gross sales) as a function of yield and price volatility ▪ Often requires government subsidies and in some markets government reinsurance protection	▪ All natural perils (e.g. drought, flood, hurricane/ typhoon, frost) with named pests and diseases (in some markets) ▪ Commodity price volatility from spot markets or futures/ option markets	▪ Insurance of systemic perils and price risks at farm level	▪ High costs for administration, distribution and loss adjustment (yield) ▪ Pricing needs to rely on area-based yields (e.g. per county) with adjustments to reflect farm-level yield volatility and price volatility at national or sub-national level ▪ Needs often government subsidies to make policy affordable and to achieve acceptable penetration to limit adverse selection	▪ Individual and large farms (>20 ha) in well-developed agricultural production systems with liquid commodity exchanges and government support (e.g. USA)
Income insurance Section 6.7	▪ Farm-based insurance based on income (gross sales net of expenses) for all main farm activities (crops, livestock and sometimes forestry) ▪ Often requires government subsidies and in some markets government reinsurance protection	▪ All natural perils, price risk and any other factors that result in low farm income	▪ Insurance of systemic perils, price risks and any other factor that produces low farm income	▪ High costs for administration and distribution ▪ Product relies on past tax filings of grower with numerous adjustments to reflect current operational conditions ▪ Often operated as a pure public (insurance) scheme ▪ High complexity for underwriting and pricing	▪ Individual and large farms (>20 ha) in well-developed agricultural production systems with established tax filing systems and government support (e.g. Canada)

| Area-yield index insurance (AYII) Section 6.8 | ▪ Individual area-based yield insurance (e.g. county or sub-district) for individual farms with indemnities to all policyholders that are affected by low area-yield independently of losses at farm level
▪ Aggregated area-based yield insurance (e.g. several counties or sub-districts or countries) for agribusinesses (e.g. processors) with indemnity if the overall agreed production is below a predefined level | ▪ All natural perils (e.g. drought, flood, hurricane/typhoon, frost) with named pests and diseases (in some markets) | ▪ Insurance of systemic perils on area-basis
▪ Limited adverse selection and moral hazard as losses are determined on an area-basis
▪ Low costs for loss adjustment as actual yields are measured by government agencies (stratified sampling frameworks)
▪ Forms the basis for extensions such as area-based revenue insurance | ▪ Basis risk due to different yield volatility at farm level compared to the area on which index is based
▪ Localised perils (e.g. hail) hardly trigger a payout on an area-basis | ▪ Individual farms in relatively homogeneous areas in developing agricultural production systems (e.g. India)
▪ Individual farms in well-developed production systems as catastrophe protection (e.g. USA)
▪ Agribusinesses to manage production volatility (aggregate yield index cover)
▪ Macro-level risk transfer |

(Continued)

TABLE 6-1 (*Continued*)

Type of Product	Characteristics	Perils Covered	Advantages	Disadvantages	Most Suitable Application
Weather index insurance (WII) Section 6.9	▪ Insurance based on weather data from weather stations over pheneological stages or the entire growth cycle ▪ Needs specialist expertise to structure indices	▪ Perils recorded by weather stations (e.g. rainfall, temperature, humidity, wind, snow) ▪ Combinations of weather parameters can cover some pests and diseases	▪ Individual events and systemic perils can be covered ▪ Individual crop growth phases can be insured with in-season pay-outs ▪ Limited adverse selection and moral hazard as losses are determined from weather station data ▪ Low costs for loss adjustment as losses are derived from weather parameters	▪ Basis risk due to weather variables alone not entirely relating to losses and weather conditions at a farm being different from the location of the weather station ▪ Concept and indices difficult to understand for producers in developing markets and smallholders ▪ Perils that are not recorded at weather stations (e.g. riverine flooding, hail), are not insurable ▪ Requirement for fall-back methodology and/or data in case data used for the indices are not available ▪ High cost for weather data acquisition (in some markets)	▪ Individual farms within 25 km distance from weather stations and relatively homogenous production systems ▪ Agribusinesses to manage production volatility (meso-level risk transfer) ▪ Government entities (macro-level risk transfer)

Satellite-based index insurance (SBII) Section 6.10	■ Insurance based on vegetation indices (e.g. NDVI) from satellites ■ Data available for 20 years at high resolutions (1 x 1 km or smaller) ■ Often combined with ground observations of loss adjustors ■ Mainly used for pasture/grass-land insurance	■ Deteriorating vegetation conditions (mainly due to drought)	■ Limited adverse selection and moral hazard as losses are determined from satellite data ■ High resolution ■ Low costs for loss adjustment (mainly data acquisition and costs for processing data)	■ Basis risk due to vegetation health indices only measuring greenness of vegetation which can differ from actual losses ■ Satellite data can include biases and vegetation indices need calibration with crop cycles ■ High investment in index development and collaboration through experts ■ Short historical time series of satellite data (maximum 20 years)	■ Pasture and grass-land insurance for larger areas ■ Agribusinesses to manage production volatility (meso-level risk transfer) ■ Government enti-ties (macro-level risk transfer)
Model-based index insurance (MBII) Section 6.11	■ Insurance based on water balance indices (e.g. WRSI) of various complexities ■ Insurance based on yield output from mechanistic crop models with complex input parameters (e.g. soil types/profiles and cultivar information/coefficients) and cali-bration efforts	■ Mainly water deficit/lack of soil moisture and plant-specific drought stress/losses	■ Relates better to drought-related yield reduction than weather parameters alone ■ Low costs for loss adjustment but with costs for data processing/modelling	■ Basis risk in that indices do not relate to actual losses (e.g. crop coef-ficients do not reflect cultivar planted, losses from pests and diseases which are not modelled) ■ High sensitivity to cultivar-specific coefficients ■ High investment in index development and reliance on experts for computation	■ Agribusinesses to manage production volatility (meso-level risk transfer) ■ Government enti-ties (macro-level risk transfer)

a FLEXA stands for Fire, Lightning, Explosion and Aircraft impact.

achieve a sustainable insurance penetration that minimises adverse selection. Challenges of indemnity-based crop insurance include moral hazard, adverse selection and, in some markets, high costs for administration and loss adjustment, limited historical data that makes risk pooling difficult and the requirement of substantial reinsurance protection to insure systemic perils (Section 5.5).

Index-Based Crop Insurance

To overcome the main issues of indemnity-based crop insurance, index-based crop insurance (also called parametric insurance) uses weather, yield, satellite and model data to determine indemnities (Table 6.1). However, indices induce inherent basis risk in that the indices do not perfectly correlate to loss experiences of an individual policyholder. While used in mature agricultural markets for special crops (e.g. pasture) and to cover catastrophe-type losses that affect larger regions, index-based crop insurance has been promoted in developing agricultural markets with smallholder structures as a key risk management instrument. Unlike indemnity-based crop insurance, indices need regulatory approval to assure an insurable interest.

6.4 NAMED-PERIL CROP INSURANCE

NPCI is the oldest form of crop insurance. It started as crop hail insurance to which other random and localised perils have been added gradually, including frost, landslide, wind and, in some cases, pests and diseases. Crop hail insurance remains the main NPCI product in North America, Europe, Australia/New Zealand, Latin America (especially Argentina) and South Africa. Frost insurance is selectively offered in some markets as a stand-alone insurance cover or as part of an NPCI policy. For high-value crops (e.g. horticulture), NPCI covers perils such as hail, frost, windstorm, volcanic eruption, flood and some named pests and diseases. CBCI is a special form of NPCI where indemnity is triggered first through a declared calamity by a competent government authority and individual losses are adjusted thereafter.

NPCI is most suitable to cover random and localised perils that have a large loss potential for an individual or a smaller group of insureds; however, NPCI is not the preferred form of insurance for systemic perils (e.g. drought, flood, cyclones) and smallholder agricultural structures.

6.4.1 HAIL INSURANCE

Crop hail insurance has existed in Europe for over 150 years and has evolved into a combined NPCI policy that covers other named perils. In markets with large production units (e.g. USA, Canada), crop hail insurance is offered as a separate product besides yield-based MPCI as hailfall alone would hardly reduce crop yield levels below the triggers under MPCI.[3] The economic benefits for a grower to buy crop hail insurance in combination with other crop insurance products (e.g. revenue covers) have

---

[3] Mare, F., et al., 2015: Estimating the maximum value of crop hail insurance under stochastic yield and price risk. *Agrekon*, 54(4), 28–44.

theoretically been examined.[4] In markets with small production units, hail and frost risks are included in a combined NPCI policy (e.g. China, Section 5.2) or are part of the perils covered under area-yield index insurance (AYII) (e.g. frost in India), or consist of a separate endorsement to AYII (e.g. hail in India, Section 6.8).

Hail damage shows very high spatial and temporal variability and hail occurrence can be predicted only through weather radar images 30 minutes before occurrence (Section 3.5). Crops typically show damage with hailstones of diameters above 10 mm, while severe wind gusts and strong convective precipitation cause additional damage. The damage extent depends on the hailfall intensity and duration and the phenological stage of the crop when losses occur. For field crops, hail damage results in stand reduction, stem breakage, crippled plants, defoliation and grain losses that can lead to severe yield reduction (Section 3.5). Field crops are typically insured against reduced quantity while horticulture crops are covered for loss of quality and resulting downgrades.

Crop Hail Insurance in the USA

US crop hail insurance is offered by private insurers as commercial, non-government subsidised products known as private crop insurance policies. Most farmers buy yield-based MPCI insurance and as local hailfalls hardly trigger the standard 85% MPCI coverage level, crop hail insurance complements MPCI for spot hail losses at the level of individual fields. Private insurers, which also offer government-subsidised MPCI, made large efforts to tie crop hail covers to MPCI as a packaged product. It gradually became a market practice to offer crop hail insurance at below average loss cost to obtain access to the better-priced MPCI policies from the same farmer and to develop large and well-diversified portfolios. In 1998, the insurers introduced Crop Production Plans (CPPs) as a companion to the MPCI policy to cover hail losses that fall below the coverage level of the yield-based MPCI policies. Policy provisions of the CPPs followed features captured under MPCI, such as guaranteed yield and price on which crop hail insurance was newly based.

In the relatively average 2011 hail season, the US crop hail industry portfolio incurred a loss ratio of 115.6%, which was primarily due to inadequate rates and competition among insurers to win farmers with underrated crop hail covers for MPCI products. The losses under the crop hail policies severely impacted the profitability of the MPCI portfolios and therefore forced some insurers to increase crop hail rates in 2012, while losing market shares to competitors which did not increase terms. In 2014, a very active year for hail, there was a loss ratio of 122%, which was only the third time since 1948 that loss ratios exceeded 100%. Among the different hail insurance products, the CPPs incurred a 178% loss ratio.

In 2013, the Risk Management Agency (RMA), which oversees government-supported crop insurance products and pricing in the USA, introduced a new regulation stipulating that an approved insurer cannot request a farmer to purchase an MPCI policy in order to be eligible to purchase a private crop insurance policy or endorsement offered by that insurer. De-linking crop hail insurance from MPCI has led

---

[4]Vercammen, J. and Pannell, D.J., 2000: The economics of crop hail insurance. *Can. J. Agr. Econ.*, 48, 87–98.

to improvements in insurance premium rates. In 2017, crop hail insurance produced US$958 million of premium and showed an average loss ratio of 81% (2004–2017).

Crop Hail Insurance in Switzerland

Crop hail insurance started in Switzerland through mutuals in 1818, but several initiatives to expand coverage failed due to the lack of geographical diversification. In 1880, the Swiss Hail Insurance Company (SHIC) was founded as a cooperative to insure crop farmers. In the first year SHIC incurred a high loss ratio of 140% and farmers were retroactively requested to pay more premium. Following further losses, hail risk was re-evaluated, administrative costs were loaded to risk rates and the government provided 50% premium subsidies in 1898. SHIC's portfolio experienced significant growth during the Second World War as the government ordered all available arable land to be planted to assure food security, and prices for agriculture goods generally increased. While initially only hail damage was insured, coverage expanded in the 1960s to include storm, flood, erosion, landslide, fire, lightning and earthquake. In 1967, the government abandoned premium subsidies for crop hail insurance to support farmers through guaranteed prices and direct payments.

Over time, SHIC's premium volume developed from US$3 million in the 1920s to US$50 million in 2016 with 35 000 policies. On average, 90% of SHIC's annual loss burden stems from hail, with the remaining loss from other insured perils such as windstorm, flooding, landslide and fire. The worst year was 2009, with a loss ratio of 215%, and the most expensive single hail event occurred on 2 June 1994 when a massive cold front produced several hailstorms of unusual length and a loss ratio of 170%.

Crop Hail Insurance Products

Today, SHIC insures over 80 crop types, with a penetration ratio in terms of arable land of 75% for field crops and vineyards, 50% for vegetables, flowers and fruits, and nearly 100% for tobacco. SHIC provides the following two main products:

- Individual Crop Hail Insurance (ICHI) is mainly used for specialised crops (e.g. orchards and vineyards) and covers hail (main risk), storm, flood, erosion, landslide, fire, lightning and earthquake. Certain exposures, including vineyards, berries and tobacco, are only insurable under ICHI. Areas to be insured are submitted by producers through a planting schedule that is verified by SHIC. The sum insured is defined as production costs representing about 60% of the commercial value.
- Comprehensive Crop Hail Insurance (CCHI) is the main product for field crops and grassland and covers the same perils as ICHI but with the difference that planting schedules are not verified. SHIC provides a standardised sum insured based on the commercial value per crop type as a function of average historical yields and projected commodity prices. Policyholders can increase or decrease the sum insured up to 25% to reflect farm-based production relative to the standard.

ICHI and CCHI require all fields of a farm that produce a given crop type to be insured. Deductibles and franchises are applied at field level as listed in the planting schedule. For most crop types, a 10% franchise based on sum insured applies with a deductible of (i) 5% of the loss, with an increase to 10% in the case of severe losses to field crops, and (ii) 20% of the loss, which decreases with increasing losses for horticulture crops. For two years of claims-free experience, a no-claims bonus of 10% of the premium, with the maximum discount being 40%, is granted. In case of losses, the premium will increase by 10% at renewal.

Pricing of Hail Risk
SHIC has developed a database with historical claims from farmers dating back to the 1880s. Insurance data including claims are first averaged per municipality and crop type. Claims are standardised for franchise and deductible levels and moving averages are used to compute risk premium rates based on (i) the last 20 years in case no large loss events are included, or (ii) the last 40 years when large losses occurred in the last 20 years. When risk premium rates for a specific crop type show significant differences among neighbouring municipalities, a special analysis is undertaken to identify the cause, after which a geographical smoothing is applied. Given the high insurance penetration and the availability of at least 40 years of detailed claims information, SHIC does not apply a catastrophe loading on the risk premiums but uses over 100 years of claims records to reveal trends in hail frequency and severity on a portfolio level.

Insurance Terms
The unit of crop hail insurance is either the entire farm or individual fields for larger farms, with policies offered as annual policies covering one hail season or term policies that span several crop seasons and include endorsements to account for exposure changes and a discount as a result of lower administrative costs. Against additional premium, some insurers grant extension of coverage, e.g. in the case of delayed harvests. Insurance usually incepts within 24 hours of application provided that the crop has emerged from the ground and coverage can be bought until the crop has reached a normal stand. In some markets, insurance can be purchased at any time in the crop growth cycle as hailfalls are both random and difficult to predict. For horticulture crops, fruit trees must have a minimum age to be insurable or must have produced a certain quantity of fruits during past years.

Definition of Sum Insured
Insurance covers the expected value of the crop defined as (i) the commercial value of the crop, which is calculated from expected yield and commodity prices, or (ii) the production costs that represent the replacement value and are derived as a portion of the commercial value or are based on actual input supply and labour cost. The sum insured for high-value crops (e.g. horticulture and viticulture) is usually based on commercial values and for field crops on either commercial values or production costs. Insurers typically provide options for deductibles and franchises to make insurance affordable and to reduce moral hazard.

Some crop hail policies have escalator or stepladder endorsement where the sum insured increases progressively over time from the date of application. For example, a 5% Stand-Date Escalator Clause provides that insurance becomes effective when the crop shows a stand and 25% of the sum insured is recognised until the fifteenth day after the crop shows a stand, after which the sum insured increases 5% each day until the full sum insured is realised.

Some crop hail policies include a replanting provision, where losses are compensated for total damage in early vegetative stages with (i) an immediate payout when replanting is not an option, or (ii) a provision over a pre-agreed value or a percentage of the sum insured while the replanted crop continues to be insured, with a final claims payment at harvest with the yield of the replanted crop considered. In case the replanted crop incurs subsequent hail damage, the loss is determined by multiplying the percentage of loss by the coverage remaining after accounting for the percentage of loss due to replanting.

Franchises and Deductibles

To better manage moral hazard, insurers typically introduce loss-sharing features such as deductibles and loss thresholds such as franchises, which as shown in the example of crop hail insurance in Canada can take the following formats:

- 10% Straight Deductible (10S) with the provision that indemnities occur if the loss is above the 10% threshold above which the policyholder always retains 10% of the loss amount, e.g. at a damage of 5%, the insured retains the loss, and at a damage of 40%, the insurer covers 30% of the loss.
- 10% Deductible Disappearing at 40% (10D) applies a 10% deductible on all losses above 10% up to 30% damage, a linearly decreasing deductible between losses of 30–40% and no deductible for losses above 40%, e.g. at damage of 25%, the insurer indemnifies 15%, while at a damage of 35%, indemnity reaches 30% with a 5% deductible, and at 40% damage extent, the insurer compensates 40% of the loss.
- 10% Deductible with Increasing Payment Factor (10IP) applies a 10% deductible to all losses above 10%, and above a damage of 70%, insurance payouts increase linearly by 1% for each 1% damage, e.g. at 50% damage, the insurer compensates 40%, at 75% damage, the insurer pays 70% of the loss.
- Excess Over 5% Loss Disappearing at 25% (5XS) includes a 5% deductible for all losses with the provision that for losses above 5% up to 25%, the indemnity of the insurer increases by 25% and provides full coverage for losses above 25%, e.g. at a damage of 5%, the insured retains the full loss, while at a damage of 20%, the insurer pays 18.75% (increased by 25% from the indemnity of 15% at a loss of 20% and with a 5% deductible).

Pricing

Pricing crop hail insurance mostly relies on standardised historical claims data, while proxies such as hail days and hail tracks from satellite and radar data support risk analysis (Section 3.5).

Standardising Insurance Claims

As insurance terms have changed for a given crop type over time, claims data are standardised in (i) removing deductibles, franchises and other features that influenced losses (e.g. changes in loss adjustment regulation, presence of hail nets), and (ii) adjusting the sum insured to a common basis. Historical claims can reveal trends that can be driven by changes in hail intensity and frequency, insurance penetration and/or planted area of an insured crop. The use of time series analyses to identify periodicities has been suggested to detrend and predict short-term trends (one to five years) in annual hail claims.[5] As particularly large losses distort average expected losses, such losses

---

[5] Neill, J.C., 1981: An approach to crop-hail insurance rate revision. J. *Appl. Meteorol.*, 20, 1391–99.

are typically removed from the claims data and used to compute a separate regional catastrophe loading.

Some crop hail insurance markets have long time series of historical insurance claims.[6] Credibility studies of crop hail claims series in the USA have shown that for a given township, considerably longer times series than the historical loss series are required to achieve 95% confidence that a base rate is within the risk adequate mean.[7] Time series of hail days from weather observers (Section 3.5) have been suggested to prolong hail insurance claims data and have shown good correspondence with annual and monthly hail loss costs from crop insurers in the USA.[8] When hail days, weather stations data and historical crop hail claims are available, hail intensity indices can be derived and form a valid basis for hail risk pricing in uninsured periods and regions.[9]

Pricing Based on Insurance Claims
Based on aggregated and standardised historical claims data, the average loss cost ratio (LCR) for a given year t and an insurance policy i can be determined as:

$$LCR_t = \frac{\sum_i I_{t,i}/SI_{t,i}}{N}$$

where SI is the sum insured, I is the indemnity and N is the total number of insurance policies. The base rate (BR), which is also called risk premium rate, is obtained for the total number of years (T) through:

$$BR = \frac{\sum_t LCR_t}{T}$$

Base rates are typically developed first for the main crop types, from which base rates for other crop types are derived in applying rate weights that reflect hail vulnerability grades and are reasonably comparable among different countries (Table 6.2). For example, tobacco is one of the crops most vulnerable to hailfall, with a base rate that is up to seven times higher than for less vulnerable crops such as wheat. Base rates can show high spatial discontinuities that reflect the random nature of hailfalls and to avoid inhomogeneities and outliers, minimum and maximum base rates are determined at regional level and geographical smoothing is applied.

---

[6] For example, hail claims data date back in Europe to the 1880s and are available in the USA since 1924 at the resolution of a township.
[7] Roth, R.J., 1960: The rating of crop hail insurance. Proceedings of the Casualty Actuarial Society, 108–46.
[8] Changnon, D. and Changnon, S.A., 1997: Surrogate data to estimate crop-hail loss. *J. Appl. Meteorol.*, 36(9), 1202–10.
[9] Changnon, D. et al., 2000: A method for estimating crop losses from hail in uninsured periods and regions. *J. Appl. Meteorol.*, 40, 84–91.

TABLE 6.2 Crop classification according to general hail vulnerability, with weights relative to the base rate of vulnerability class 1.

Hail Vulnerability	Crop Types (examples)	Base Rate Weights (%)
1	Wheat, fall rye, triticale barley, oats, mixed grain, flax, sunflowers, canary seed, silage, corn, grain corn, potatoes	100
2	Soybeans, canola, rapeseed, lentils	150
3	Mustard beans, millet seed	175
4	Field peas, hemp, ryegrass seed, alfalfa seed, onions, carrots, parsnips, broccoli, cabbage, cauliflower, leeks, peppers, pumpkins, sweet corn, strawberries, winter squash	200
5	Buckwheat	250
6	Green feed, hay types	75
7	Table grapes, cherries, salad, spinach, tomatoes, cucumber, melons, tobacco (air drying)	500
8	tobacco (tube drying)	700

Source: Classes 1–6 from MASC (2015), classes 7–8 based on personal communication with the Swiss Hail Insurance Company.

The commercial premium rate (*CPR*) is derived from the base rate in adding catastrophe and administrative loadings and is obtained as:

$$CPR = (BR + CL) \times AL$$

with *CL* is the catastrophe loading that has been determined over-regionally before base rates were calculated and *AL* as the administrative loading including costs for marketing and distribution, data acquisition, loss adjustment and capital, which in combination can easily reach 20–30% of the CPR.

Loss Mitigation Measures
In areas that are prone to hail damage, high-value horticulture crops are increasingly protected through nets and insurers typically grant a premium discount of up to 80% relative to base rates. Premium rates of hail nets, plastic rain roofs and supporting structures are comparable to property rates and are in the range of 0.2–0.8% of sum insured.

In some countries, hail-suppression equipment including rockets and aeroplanes is used to modify characteristics of hail-bearing thunderstorms through seeding additional condensation nuclei (typically silver iodide). The additional condensation nuclei are thought to reduce the amount of supercooled water and lead to more numerous and smaller hailstones on the ground. Scientific experiments where hailstone distributions of seeded and non-seeded hailstorms have been analysed have not provided clear evidence that hail suppression is effective.[10] In some cases, farmers that belong to hail suppression groups request crop hail insurance premium discounts due to reduced hail

---

[10] Federer, B. et al., 1986: Main results of Grossversuch IV. *J. Appl. Meteorol. Climatol.*, 25(7), 917–57.

risk, but this typically is declined by insurers due to the lack of scientific evidence on the efficiency of hail suppression.

Pricing Without Insurance Claims

Developing base rates for new hail insurance programmes is challenging as hail frequency and severity are not measured consistently (Section 3.5) and the vulnerability of crops to hail depends on the time of hailfall in a crop's growth cycle. Often, experience from crop hail insurance in other countries with similar crop types is used to derive a first set of base rates. Additionally, proxies that reflect regional hail frequency and severity are used, including (i) property hail damage claims to derive regional hail risk maps and factors of the relative variance of base rates over rating areas, (ii) hailpad networks, which derive hail stone spectra as a function on impacts on Styrofoam plates, or (iii) hail days, satellite imagery (cloud top temperatures), data from lightning detection networks and weather radars (Section 3.5). New crop hail insurance schemes typically start on an experimental basis where the main crop types are insured in different pilot regions and with basic insurance coverage and gradually expanded in terms of area insured, crop types, coverage options and perils.

Loss Adjustment

Loss adjustment of hail damage is undertaken by qualified personnel in on-site inspections at the time of loss to estimate the potential loss at harvest and to assess replanting options at early vegetative stages. Loss adjustors use comprehensive manuals that include images of typical hail damages over different crop growth phases and stand reduction and defoliation curves that are based on field data and laboratory experiments where crops are artificially damaged at different growth stages. The experience from crop hail insurers has shown that assessed losses by different trained adjustors are within 10% of each other. Hail damage assessments carried out by insurance adjusters are time consuming and costly, and they involve a certain degree of subjectivity.

Remote-sensing technology and unmanned aerial vehicles are increasingly supporting on-ground loss adjustment at high resolution and at low cost, with several field experiments being carried out in different markets. Satellite-based vegetation indices such as the Normalized Difference Vegetation Index (NDVI) (Section 4.3) can identify hail damage based on characteristic changes in the spectral signatures after hail damage and require at least 30 images for post-storm hail damage assessment and 5 m resolution images to confirm hail damage.[11] Unmanned aerial vehicles such as drones provide high-resolution imagery that allows the development of vegetation indices, which in a study of potatoes showed that hail damage extents were accurately detected and related well to yield losses, particularly in early growth phases.[12] Airborne Light Detection and Ranging (LiDAR) accessed corn canopy heights and defoliation extents from hail damage in 60% of the cases in a testing area in Austria.[13]

---

[11] Bell, J.R. and Molthan, A.L., 2016: Evaluation of approaches to identifying hail damage to crop vegetation using satellite imagery. *J. Operational Meteor.*, 4(11), 142–59.

[12] Zhou, J. et al., 2016: Aerial multispectral imaging for crop hail damage assessment in potato. *Comput. Electron Agric.*, 127, 406–12.

[13] Vescovo, L. et al., 2016: Hail defoliation assessment in corn (*Zea mays* L.) using airborne LiDAR. *Field Crops Res.*, 196, 426–37.

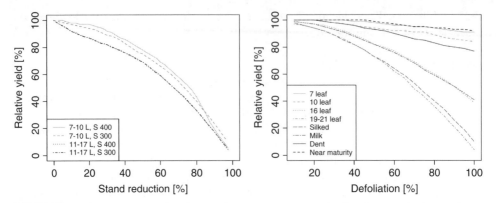

FIGURE 6.2   Left: Relative yield reduction for corn at the 7–10 leaf and 11–17 leaf growth stage from stand reduction due to hail, with each a plant density of the original stand (S) of 300/ acre and 400/acre. Right: Relative corn yield in function of defoliation extents at different corn growth stages.
Data source: NCIS.

Loss Adjustment of Field Crops

Loss adjustment of field crops involves the assessment of (i) direct damages, which result from stand reduction, crippled plants and damage to ears and stalks, and (ii) indirect damages caused by defoliation. Areas to be sampled are identified within fields and are based on (i) areas of 1/100 acre as used in the USA for corn, or (ii) rows within fields as used in Europe where 100 plants and/or 100 leaves and/or 100 ears are inspected on small fields (<1 ha) with a homogenous loss pattern while for larger fields with nonhomogeneous loss patterns, several rows are sampled. Loss adjustment is based on the type of damage and includes the following approaches for corn:[14]

- Stand reduction occurs mainly in the early growth stages and loss adjustment is undertaken within 7–10 days so that living and dead (discoloured) plant tissues can be distinguished. In comparing the yield potential at its original population and plant density with the yield potential of the reduced population, the percentage of yield loss is determined using crop-specific stand reduction curves (Figure 6.2). The extent of stand reduction forms the basis for replanting.
- Ear damage occurs from hail damage at final crop growth stages and is determined through a ratio of the damaged kernels relative to all kernels in a representative sample. In case stand reduction occurs at the same time as ear damage, the percentage of ear damage is adjusted to account for plants lost through stand reduction.
- Stalk damage leaves bruises on stalks and losses are adjusted in calculating the number of destroyed plants relative to all plantings in a representative sample.
- Defoliation is the loss of leaf area which results in lower yield and is determined through defoliation curves at different growth stages (Figure 6.2).

---

[14] Vorst, J.V., 1990: Assessing Hail Damage to Corn. National Corn Handbook NCH, 4p.

TABLE 6.3 Quality downgrading of apples following hail damage.

Downgrading	Grades	Downgrading Factor	Description and Use
Class I reduced to	Class I	0%	Fresh apple for human consumption: clean, well-formed and free from decay, injuries, scars, discoloration and russeting.
	Class II	25–35%	Fresh apple for human consumption: meets criteria of Class I except for the presence of hail marks (healed broken skin), colour, russeting and invisible water core.
	Utility apple	65–75%	Apple for industrial usage (e.g. juice or dried fruit).
	Total loss	100%	Total loss with serious injuries, brown decay or mould that does not allow industrial usage.

Source: Adapted from USDA (2002).

Loss Adjustment of Horticulture Crops

Most hail insurance policies for horticulture crops cover fruit quality at harvest, relative to standard grade requirements per purpose of use (e.g. fresh apple, processing apple). In some markets, quantity losses are additionally insurable under crop hail policies. Packing houses and retailers have stringent quality requirements in terms of shape, diameter and appearance of the fruit surface, which is commonly defined by fruit marketing boards in collaboration with government agencies.

Insurance loss adjustment for horticulture crops first determines a representative sample of fruit trees within a hail-damaged plot. In the USA, the lesser of five trees or 5% of the number of trees and 30 apples is assessed, with increasing sample density with inhomogeneous damage extents.[15] In Europe, three trees in a row and at least 100 fruits are sampled, with more samples taken in case of large orchards and a high variability in damage extents. Crop hail policy wording usually includes a clause on loss adjustment criteria and procedures for quality downgrades.

For hail loss adjustment in orchards, the gross production is determined for harvested or to be harvested areas and unharvested areas, which typically have experienced hail damage at the early growth phase. The damage extent is derived in calculating the damaged and undamaged production through quality reduction factors that include several downgrades across fruit classes (Table 6.3). Loss adjustment occurs prior to harvest but as harvest time varies, fruit quality is also assessed from harvested apples that are to be kept at the orchard. Under fruit tree insurance, only total losses are compensated if the fruit tree is damaged to such an extent that it is uneconomical to maintain the tree.

---

[15] USDA, 2016: Apple loss adjustment standard handbook, FCIC-25030, 52p.

6.4.2 FROST INSURANCE

In markets where yield-based crop insurance products (e.g. MPCI) are the main form of insurance, frost is typically covered as one of the perils that lead to insured yield reduction. In countries with NPCI products, frost is usually offered as an additional peril under crop hail insurance policies. For large horticulture farms, special frost covers are offered under both indemnity- and index-based products.

Although summer crops are planted after and before typical frost risk periods, unusually late or early frost and low temperature events can cause severe damage. Winter crops which are planted in late autumn and harvested in summer of the following year in the northern hemisphere harden during frost conditions in the early vegetative growth phases; however, alternative periods of freezing and thawing and the lack of insulating snow cover can lead to winterkill (Section 3.6). Horticulture crops are exposed to frost from bud formation to flowering (spring frosts) and during ripening (autumn frosts), which can impact both quantity and quality of fruits produced. The extent of frost damage generally depends on the crop variety, the sensitivity to frost, the time and duration of the frost event and environmental conditions before and after the frost event (Section 3.6).

Insurance Terms

Frost insurance covers different occurrences of frosts, which can include spring frost, autumn frost and winter frost (winterkill). Frost insurance coverage for spring frost starts typically seven days after the end of the usual spring frost season and ends seven days before the usual first autumn frosts. A frost event is typically defined through air temperature of $-2°C$ measured at a weather station. Spring frost is defined as a drop in air temperature to $0°C$ and below at times when the mean temperature for 24 hours remains above $0°C$. Insurers typically require all fields and orchards to be insured and impose a 168-hour waiting period before inception of the cover to avoid adverse selection. As with crop hail insurance, the sum insured for a frost cover is either the commercial value or production costs, and franchises typically range between 10–30% of sum insured with scaled deductibles. For large horticulture risks, policies include per event deductibles as well as annual aggregate deductibles and minimum monetary loss amounts or area damaged to avoid costly loss assessment for small claims.

For high-value horticulture crops, frost mitigation measures have been shown to reduce frost damage and include (i) active measures during the frost event, such as organic insulation covers, heaters, sprinklers that create an insulating water layer, wind machines and helicopters to mix air layers, and (ii) passive measures such as plant genetics for higher frost hardiness and landscape modification to create microclimates. Insurers typically grant premium discounts if properly maintained frost mitigation measures are in place.

Pricing

As for crop hail insurance, the calculation of risk premium rates (base rates) for frost covers follows the concept of LCR ratemaking and is based on standardised historical frost claims data. However, frost events are rarer than hail occurrences and claims data are often not sufficient to directly derive base rates. In such cases and for new frost covers, frost vulnerability is determined from temperature data in

TABLE 6.4   Corn yield loss from frost in function of leaf area damage and resulting yield losses in the USA.

Development Stage	Leaf Area Destroyed (%)				
	20	40	60	80	100
	Yield Loss (%)				
Tassel	7	21	42	68	100
Silk	7	10	39	65	97
Blister	5	16	30	50	73
Milk	3	12	24	41	59
Dough	2	8	17	29	41
Dent	0	4	10	17	23
Black Layer	0	0	0	0	0

Source: Adapted from University of Wisconsin (2014).

assessing (i) hardening capabilities of winter crops in terms of soil and air temperature, (ii) sensitivities to frost during different growing stages for spring and summer crops, and (iii) the mechanism that leads to frost development, i.e. advective or radiative frost (Section 3.6). One method used to determine frost risk is the computation of frost days, based on historical records of minimum air temperatures below a threshold level of 0°C or below the lethal minimum temperature (Section 3.6). Mapping the number of frost days within the growing period and area provides an overview of frost frequencies and allows categorising of frost risk zones. Most frost insurance products are priced on frost days with minimum air temperature records of at least 30 years and a knowledge of the relevant threshold temperatures. However, this methodology does not account for the duration of a frost event, which can last from minutes to several hours and largely determines the extent of damage. More advanced methods either develop frost vulnerability in function of frost duration or use outputs of mechanistic crop models (Section 4.4).

Loss Adjustment

Frost losses are assessed in the same way as hail damage, including (i) counts of plant survival ratios (stand reduction) and impacts on yield, and (ii) leaf area destruction of different extents that leads to yield losses (Table 6.4).[16] Yield losses from frost damage tend to be directly proportional to the stage of maturity of the crop and the amount of plant tissue damaged. Yield reduction curves rely on scientific experiments where frost impact to a variety of crop types at different phenological stages is derived from field and laboratory experiments where crops are artificially frosted to assess damage extents. An alternative method in the visual inspection of frost damaged field crops is the measurement of the electrical resistance of plant tissue, the analysis of chlorophyll

---

[16] Bremer, J.E. et al., 1995: Assessing Hail and Freeze Damage to Field Corn and Sorghum. Texas Agricultural Extension Service, 8p.

fluorescence and enzyme activity measurements, which requires special equipment and is costly. Digital colour photographs have been found to be reliable identifiers of frost damage during critical plant growth stages through characteristic spectral signatures.[17]

6.4.3 CALAMITY-BASED CROP INSURANCE

CBCI is a newer form of NPCI and is closely tied to government disaster compensation schemes where producers receive ad-hoc payments in cases where a competent government agency has declared a disaster in a certain area. CBCI programmes contain a two-stage trigger mechanism in that first a calamity or disaster needs to be declared, after which losses are assessed by loss adjustors at farm or field level.

CBCI covers natural perils including drought, flood, hail, cyclone and frost as well as systemic plant pest and diseases (e.g. grasshopper infestations). Under CBCI, farmers are covered for all insured perils and can therefore not select individual perils and cover options. Some perils (e.g. pests and diseases) can be sub-limited to avoid large-scale moral hazard. CBCI typically covers main crop types for total losses and does not contain loss reducing features such as franchises or deductibles.

Loss adjustment for CBCI follows essentially the same processes as for other NPCI products and when CBCI is tied to government disaster compensation schemes, government agencies support loss evaluations since the disaster-declared areas are regularly surveyed by the same authorities.

CBCI schemes are currently operated in Pakistan and Thailand. In China, calamity declared areas were used to develop the initial crop insurance risk rates under the National Agricultural Insurance Program (Section 4.5).

Calamity-Based Rice Insurance in Thailand

Thailand produces close to 27 million tons of rice (2016) in two distinct seasons on 10 million ha of land. The main season rice provides on average 21 million tons, with key growing areas in the north-east and along fertile and flood-prone areas of the Chao Phraya river, while the second season contributes an additional two million tons from irrigated areas in central Thailand. Overall, 25% of the rice area is irrigated and access to higher-quality input supplies has increased rice yields over time. In 2011, Thailand was the largest rice exporter, with a 30% global market share. Most rice is produced by subsistence farmers that operate on small plots and sell surplus production to government agencies or traders depending on price levels offered.

To further support rice farmers, the newly elected government introduced a rice price protection scheme (RPPS) in 2011 that paid rice farmers 50% more than current world market prices to alleviate rural poverty. As global rice prices decreased over time and more rice was exported by other countries, Thailand ended up with large rice quantities (17–18 million tons) and an overall loss under RPPS of at least US$8 billion. With a change in government, RPPS was abandoned in 2014 and Thailand returned to being the second largest rice exporter after India. Rice farmers in Thailand obtain disaster payments from the government under the Disaster Relief Scheme of THB 1113/rai

---

[17] Cruz, A.M. et al., 2011: Digital Image Sensor-Based Assessment of the Status of Oat (*Avena sativa* L.) Crops after Frost Damage. *Sensors*, 11(6), 6015–36.

(US$195/ha) in case of total losses in disaster-declared areas. Although production costs are THB 4500 per rai (US$787/ha), the disaster payments help farmers to recover some of the costs and prepare for the next season.

Rice Insurance Programme

To provide additional protection for rice farmers against natural disasters, the government implemented a new rice insurance programme in 2011 with 50% premium subsidies. The programme operates as CBCI and is closely tied to the Disaster Relief Scheme. In its initial form, the scheme compensated rice farmers for THB 606/rai for losses in early growth stages and THB 1400/rai for mature rice crops based on government disaster declarations and onsite loss adjustment. Rice farmers in a disaster-declared area can obtain a payout from the Disaster Relief Scheme and an indemnity from the insurance programmes. Loss adjustment is undertaken by agriculture extension officers. The Bank of Agriculture and Agriculture Cooperatives (BAAC) as the main lender to the agricultural sector is responsible for (i) the distribution of the insurance policies as part of its wider services to the farming community, and (ii) the collection of farmers' premium payments and paying claims payments to farmers' bank accounts.

The initial pricing of the rice insurance scheme relied on historical data, including (i) national-level disaster declaration areas, with total losses to rice production for flood, drought, pest, frost, wind storm, hail and damage from roaming elephants (1993–2010), with missing values for some perils in some years, and (ii) national rice area planted and harvested for the main season rice (1993–2010), which resulted in a national-level loss cost of 12%.

Performance of the Rice Insurance Scheme

In the first year (2011), 160 000 ha (one million rai) of main-season rice were covered for a premium volume of US$3.5 million, of which 90% was ceded as proportional reinsurance to international markets. In 2011, one of the most severe periods of flooding occurred in Thailand and caused significant damage to rice production, which resulted in a loss ratio of 550% for the new rice insurance scheme. Post-event analyses revealed a high degree of adverse selection in that mainly farmers in flood-prone areas had enrolled for insurance. Considerable efforts were undertaken to (i) obtain historical disaster statistics at provincial level and data on the duration of disaster events, (ii) recalculate risk rates at provincial level, (iii) introduce pest and disease coverage (mainly plant hoppers) with a loss limit as an additional peril to reduce adverse selection as, unlike flood, pest and diseases can impact farmers in all regions, and (iv) tie the insurance scheme to loans from BAAC. Only some of these measures were implemented for 2012, with 112 000 ha insured and a loss ratio of 295% due to drought. In 2013, the scheme was put on hold, but it continued in 2014 with increased premium rates for newly developed risk zones ranging from 10% to 40% and 100 000 ha insured at profitable underwriting results due to the absence of major disasters. With the discontinuation of the RPPS in 2014 and an outlook for drought for 2015, the rice insurance scheme gained importance. In 2015, the scheme covered 240 000 ha with a premium volume of US$16 million. In 2016, the scheme became 100% subsidised by the government for farmers with loans from BAAC and included second-season rice. The sum insured was redefined at THB 1111/rai (US$194/ha) for all perils except for pests and diseases where only 50% of the sum insured is covered. As a result, the 2016 rice scheme grew to 4.6 million hectares and a premium volume of close to US$72 million and the involvement of 16 insurers, making it the largest agricultural insurance programme in Southeast Asia.

Despite the larger acceptance of the rice insurance scheme, concerns remain about the objectivity of the way in which local governments declare disasters. Suggestions by insurers to overcome such concerns include a proposal to develop an area-yield index programme.

Calamity Data

Most governments record natural disasters and publish data including (i) total area affected by peril and/or area affected by peril at different degrees of damage extent, (ii) total and partial losses in terms of area, (iii) onset and duration of the disaster, with descriptions of the temporal and spatial development, (iv) mitigation measures taken, and (v) industry sectors affected, including economic losses, insured losses and population affected (Section 4.5). National disaster declaration processes and response plans require the recording of the temporal and spatial disaster extent and reporting to international organisations such as CRED or OIE, which is essential to obtain international support following disasters (Section 4.5).

While calamity-declared areas provide valuable proxies, they contain limitations which are driven by changes in (i) land use and planted crop types, (ii) flood management and irrigation schemes, (iii) crop varieties that show higher tolerance to drought and/ or flood conditions, and (iv) government disaster declaration and reporting standards and procedures. Additionally, disaster declarations are often not based on quantitative criteria such as a minimum area being affected by a certain intensity and duration. Further, calamity declarations can be politically motivated and if processes are not properly implemented in the national disaster management plans, over-declarations can occur.

Pricing With Calamity Data

Per definition, pricing of CBCI relies on historical peril-specific disaster declared areas for an administrative area (e.g. a district or province). Based on historical disaster-declared areas, the total loss area (TLA) for a peril p and damage degree a in a given year i is obtained through:

$$TLA_{i,p} = a_1\left(LDE_{i,p}\right) + a_2\left(MDE_{i,p}\right) + a_3\left(HDE_{i,p}\right)$$

with LDE_i as the area of low damage extent (e.g. damages between 10% and 30%), MDE_i as the area of medium damage extent (e.g. 31–65%) and HDE_i as the area with a high damage extent (e.g. 66–100%), with a_1, a_2 and a_3 as constants representing the loss level for the three damage extents, (e.g. $a_1 = 0.2$ for LDE_i). The average annual crop loss (CL_p) for a given peril p is subsequently obtained through:

$$CL_p = \sum_{i=1}^{n} \frac{TLA_{i,p}}{TAP_i}$$

with TAP_i as the total crop area planted in year i. CL_p is often taken directly as the risk premium rate, which however can lead to severe underestimation of risk as indemnity occurs typically at farm level while aggregated data are used for pricing.

6.5 MULTI-PERIL CROP INSURANCE

MPCI is an indemnity-based product that covers yield reductions from both idiosyncratic (random) and systemic natural perils at farm level. In North America the term MPCI was originally applied to yield-based insurance and strictly speaking includes revenue and income insurance products, since these are also based on crop yield and cover multiple perils.

With the insurance of systemic perils such as drought and flood and often benefitting from government premium subsidies, MPCI programmes typically complement or replace government disaster assistance schemes that are considered (i) unfair in that producers in riskier areas and with riskier crops benefit disproportionately more, and (ii) inefficient in that it distorts market signals of risk exposure and encourages producers to assume more risk, gradually creating a cycle of larger losses. MPCI is most used in markets with large farms and field crops and is less suited for agricultural systems dominated by smallholders. MPCI is not the best risk transfer product for horticulture crops where yield is a complex function of the age of the cultivar (e.g. fruit trees or wines), the variety and climatic conditions of previous seasons, e.g. drought results to lower fruit production for at least one and up to three following seasons.

MPCI MARKETS

MPCI has been implemented in North America, parts of Europe (mainly Spain), parts of Latin America and in South Africa.

USA

The Federal Crop Insurance Corporation (FCIC) was founded in 1938 to provide yield-based crop insurance for the major crop types and the main producing regions.[18] The programme was offered on a pilot basis and initially covered only wheat for 165 000 policies. As participation rates were low and losses high, the MPCI scheme was briefly discontinued in 1944, but it was reintroduced in 1945 due to political pressure and with improved underwriting and loss adjustment controls.

Actual Production History and CAT Plans
Under the Federal Crop Insurance Act of 1980, the MPCI scheme started to operate under a private–public partnership, with increased government support in the form of premium subsidies, distribution costs and loss adjustment expenses. Individualised premium rates based on historical farm yield, called actual production history (APH), were introduced and private sector insurers were encouraged to deliver crop insurance to increase sales. The loss ratio of MPCI programmes from 1981 to 1983 averaged at 150%, which was the result of rapid expansion into new areas without adequate data and the presence of adverse selection and moral hazard of policyholders. In 1994, a restructuring occurred, with increased subsidy levels and the introduction of catastrophe insurance (CAT) with fully subsidised premiums for a coverage of losses exceeding

---

[18] Glauber, J.W., 2012: The growth of the Federal Crop Insurance Program, 1990–2011. *Amer. J. Agr. Econ.*, 95(2), 482–88.

50% of average yield at 60% of the commodity price. In 1996, more subsidies were introduced to support premium rates, with the rule that farmers without crop insurance were not eligible for disaster benefits. Also, in 1996, the RMA was founded to administrate the FCIC programmes and the development of actuarially sound rates.

Today, MPCI products in the stricter sense of the term are available as (i) APH, which protects against loss in yield from most natural disasters and pests and diseases and guarantees a yield based on a producer's APH and with pre-set prices used to determine the guarantee and premium, and (ii) yield protection (YP), which provides insurance for the same perils as APH but with projected prices from futures contracts at planting time. MPCI products pay indemnities if losses are caused by specific perils which include adverse weather conditions, fire, insects and plant diseases (excluding damage to insufficient pest and disease control), wildfire, earthquake, volcanic eruption and failure of irrigation water supplies. Producers can then select from given parameters the level of the farm-based normal yield (ranging from 50% to 85%), the projected price level used to establish the sum insured (55–100%) and the coverage level (50–85%).

RI that covers shortfalls in the product of yield and price started in 1997 as a pilot and rapidly became the main crop insurance policy (Section 6.6). Gradually, crop insurance became the primary form of catastrophic protection and led to the discontinuation of the disaster programme and showed an average loss ratio of 98% (1994–2003).

For FCIC approved products, insurers are required to buy a reinsurance protection from RMA under a standard reinsurance agreement (SRA). SRA caps the insurer's profit and loss from MPCI policies and each insurance policy is allocated to a fund according to risk levels.

RMA Pricing Approach

The RMA MPCI pricing methodology relies on historical claims data for a county/crop combination and standardises these data by separating replanting losses from production losses and from optional covers, excluding losses from high-risk land (e.g. flood plains), removing effects where several crop types are jointly insured and removing impacts of different coverage options to a standard coverage level of 65%.[19] Difficulties in standardising historical claims include different commodity prices and variable units of insurance such as farm insurance and enterprise-level insurance. Standardised claims data exist for most crops at aggregated levels since 1975 in the *Statplan* database. Catastrophe losses are removed for losses at the 80th percentile of historical claims at county level and redistributed in form of a catastrophe loading at state level.

Based on the standardised claims, a risk rate is established for each county. Credibility weighting in function of area insured is applied to smooth risk rates among adjoining counties and was initially weighted with 60% for the target county and 40% for the neighbouring counties. Adjustments relative to the county risk rate are undertaken for individual producers through a yield ratio that is based on the last 4–10 years of actual yield history at a farm relative to a reference yield at county level. Additionally, a practice factor is introduced to reflect the agricultural production method (e.g. irrigation extent) of a producer relative to the practices at county level. A unit division factor accounts for aggregation (e.g. enterprise policies) and provides a discount to the

---

[19] RMA, 2008: Rate Methodology Handbook: Actual Production History. FCIC-11010 (RMH-APH), 100p.

county risk rate according to the aggregation level of the insurance policy. These different adjustment factors are used to derive a risk rate for an individual producer relative to the county risk rate, based on which rate relativity factors are applied to obtain rates for individual coverage options. Specific loadings are added for coverage of prevented planting, replanting covering the additional costs of re-sowing and quality adjustment which provides indemnities in case of low crop quality.

Performance of MPCI
In 2017, MPCI products that covered yield only included (i) APH with a premium volume of US$865 million and an average loss ratio of 91% (1989–2017) and (ii) YP products, which generated a premium of US$472 million with an average loss ratio of 97% (2011–2017). As a comparison, all FCIC crop insurance programmes produced a premium volume of US$10.07 billion in 2017 and incurred an average loss ratio of 84% (1989–2017). The government subsidised an average of 62% of the costs of crop insurance, with premium subsidies depending on the coverage level.

Canada
In Canada, MPCI started in 1950 and evolved to cover like in the USA, yield reductions from natural disasters and pests and diseases with guarantees determined based on projected prices. Crown companies, which are insurers owned by province governments, manage the MPCI programme. In 2017, the premium volume of MPCI products reached US$1.285 billion.

Europe
In Europe, Spain was the first country to implement MPCI-type policies in 1978 and saw a significant growth from US$200 million premium (1996) to US$700 million (2008). In France, MPCI was introduced in 2005 to cover systemic perils besides the traditional and very common crop hail insurance policies. European MPCI policies differ from US products in that (i) fewer perils are insured and a larger area has to be affected by a peril, and (ii) insured yields can be modified according to the productive conditions of the insured farm. As a result, European MPCI programmes have higher loss adjustment costs but contain lower moral hazard, which is one of the key issues with the US-type MPCI products.

Latin America
Following a series of droughts between 2002 and 2003, Brazil expanded and subsidised MPCI products, which led to large growth, particularly with farmers that obtained loans from Banco do Brasil, for which crop insurance was made mandatory. In Argentina, MPCI targets corporate farms and complements the much larger NPCI schemes, which predominately cover crop hail damage.

South Africa
In South Africa, the only market where MPCI policies are not subsidised by the government, MPCI products were developed by the private sector for large commercial farms to provide cover besides the conventional crop hail insurance policies. Due to significant competition among private insurers in South Africa, producers benefited from low premium rates, which in turn resulted in large losses from droughts (e.g. 2006/7 and flood events in 2009–2011) at loss ratios over 400%.

Asia-Pacific

Japan started with MPCI policies in 1939; it operates a public-sector insurance scheme for all rice and wheat growers (Section 5.6). In a certain sense, the crop insurance programme in the Philippines could be seen as MPCI products as it covers individual smallholders for farm-based yield reductions (Section 3.8). More recently, the introduction of MPCI-type policies is under consideration in Australia to cover the systemic perils of drought and flood besides the existing NPCI insurance covers.

Challenges With MPCI Products

Challenges with MPCI schemes, as evidence from the USA demonstrates, include (i) moral hazard when insureds increase the likelihood and/or magnitude of receiving an indemnity, (ii) adverse selection when the insurer is unable to classify policyholders according to risk profiles and fails to charge appropriate premium rates, so portfolios include increasing numbers of high-risk farmers with low premium rates, and (iii) need for substantial government subsidies to increase insurance penetrations to a level where adverse selection becomes manageable. In many developed countries, tightening government budgets are likely to create challenges for the future financial sustainability of MPCI programmes and research is focusing on ways in which existing programmes can be modified to reduce government costs while maintaining a viable safety net for crop producers.[20]

INSURANCE TERMS

MPCI requires the definition of an expected yield, a coverage level relative to the expected yield within which indemnity becomes payable and a sum insured (guarantee). The expected yield is typically determined as the average from the historical farm records over a certain time (usually 5–10 years), which is to be updated through moving averages each year. Yield of the surrounding farms or for an administrative area (e.g. county or sub-district) is used to fill missing farm yield records. Coverage levels typically range from 50% to 85% of expected yield and depend on the crop type and risk zone.

The sum insured per surface unit for a given crop type is defined by multiplying the expected yield by a commodity price, which in turn is established as (i) the average of historical commodity prices at harvest time (e.g. the last three years) and is pre-agreed in the policy wording, or (ii) a projected price determined from averaging closing prices of futures contracts before planting. Most MPCI products use averaged historical commodity prices.

Premium Rates

Premium rates of MPCI products are based on the sum insured (guarantee) and relativity factors are used to derive rates for different coverage levels relative to a standard per crop and region. For example, under US MPCI, a premium rate for 55% coverage can be nearly half of the rate at a 75% coverage level (Table 6.5). Conceptually, differences in rate relativity factors reflect differences in the higher moments of the loss domain of the presumed underlying yield distribution.

---

[20] Barnett, B., 2014: Multiple-peril crop insurance: Successes and challenges. *Agr. Finance Rev.*, 74(2), 200–16.

TABLE 6.5   Example of rate relativity factors for different coverage levels in the USA.

Coverage Level	Rate Relativity Factor
85%	1.60
80%	1.22
75%	1.00
70%	0.79
65%	0.65
60%	0.51
55%	0.47

Source: After Coble et al. (2010)

PRICING

Pricing of MPCI programmes relies on standardised historical claims data in markets with long insurance track records and uses observed farm-level and area-yield data to derive risk premium rates.

Pricing With Historical Claims Data

In markets with long histories of claims data like in the USA, pricing is based on stand-ardised and aggregated claims data. Ideally, historical claims would be categorised in function of the main production practices that have a large impact on risk profiles (e.g. irrigation extent); however, such information is hardly available through insurance data. Further, consistent farm-level yield data histories are rare and even if they are available, changes in production methods and input supplies would make earlier yield records hardly comparable to today's production environment. Therefore, MPCI pricing relies on area-based historical claims data, area crop yield and farm-based yield time series.

To reduce the influence of outliers from low-frequency and high-severity events from historical claims data, a catastrophe loading is determined in removing catastrophe losses and redistributing these losses at a higher geographical entity. As crop insurance programmes typically expand over time, the more recent years in insurance claims obtain relatively more weight compared with earlier years when insurance penetration was low and coverage options limited. One way to address this is to weight historical loss costs with weather parameters in assigning a probability to the historical loss as weather distributions tend to be more stable than yield distributions.

Based on standardised claims, the liability ($L_{t,i}$) for a given year t for a policy i and a given crop type is calculated in units of production per unit of land as:

$$L_{t,i} = E(y_{t,i}) \times Cover$$

with $E(y_{t,i})$ as the expected yield and the *Cover* set at a standard level (e.g. 65%). The indemnity ($I_{t,i}$) is subsequently obtained in terms of production per unit of land as:

$$I_{t,i} = \max(0, L_{t,i} - y_{t,i})$$

with $y_{t,i}$ as the realised yield at policy level. Based on the indemnity and liability, a loss cost ratio (LCR) per crop type is calculated as:

$$LCR_{t,i} = I_{t,i} / L_{t,i}$$

This approach works well if liabilities and expected indemnities are constant over time; however, liabilities are often found to be trending as expected yields often increase with time driven by improved technology. In the case where liability growth rates are larger than growth rates in expected indemnity, LCR will be upward-biased and will trend downwards over time, which needs correction through a multiplicative adjustment factor.[21]

Pricing MPCI with Yield Time Series
As historical claims data are not available for new MPCI schemes or reveal significant gaps, historical yield data at farm level and for administrative areas, as available from government production surveys, are used for pricing.

Yield time series require a trend analysis as yields often increase over time due to improved crop management practices (Section 4.4). Empirical evidence has shown that the choice of the detrending method of crop yields has a large impact on risk premium rates of MPCI products.[22] In short yield time series, low-frequency but high-severity loss events (e.g. major droughts) might not be accurately reflected in the observations and may lead to an underestimation of risk.[23] Alternatively, the presence of a catastrophic loss event in historical yield data can result in overestimation of risk in case the return period of the event is higher than the length of the yield time series. To increase the range of possible yield outcomes based on historical yield observations, PDFs are used through parametric, non-parametric or semi-parametric methods (Section 4.3). The expected loss (EL) becomes a function of the yield $f(x)$ and is calculated as:

$$EL(x) = \int_{-\infty}^{\infty} f(x)dx \left(\gamma \mu - \int_{-\infty}^{\infty} yx(x)dx / \int_{-\infty}^{\infty} f(x)dx \right) with \, \mu = \int_{-\infty}^{\infty} xf(x)dx$$

with γ as the coverage level and $\propto$ as the expected yield. The choice of the most suited PDF for crop yields can considerably impact risk premiums levels. Pricing of MPCI products with aggregated yield data requires adjustment for (i) yield history and yield expectations at farm level, which is undertaken through a regression analysis to establish a statistical relationship between farm yields and area-yields, and (ii) loss expectations for policy options such as cover for quality while loss expectations for replanting covers need to be estimated from other than yield data.

It must be noted that aggregated yield data can severely reduce both random and systematic variation of crop yields.[24] Several studies have shown that while the mean

[21] Woodward, J.D. et al., 2011: Actuarial impacts of loss cost ratio ratemaking in U.S. crop insurance programs. *J. Agr. Resource Econ.*, 36(1), 211–28.
[22] Atwood, J. et al., 2003: Are crop yields normally distributed? A reexamination. *Amer. J. Agr. Econ.* 85(4), 888–901.
[23] Glauber, J.W., 2004: Crop insurance reconsidered. *Amer. J. Agr. Econ.*, 86(5), 1179–95.
[24] Claassen, R. and Just, R.E., 2011: Heterogeneity and distributional form of farm-level yields. *Amer. J. Agr. Econ.*, 93(1), 144–60.

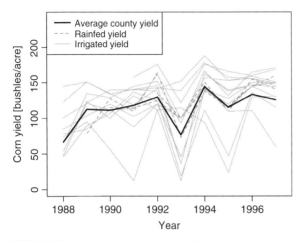

		Rate at 80% coverage	
Farm/field	Years	Observations	Beta
1	9	5.2%	4.1%
2	8	0.1%	0.8%
3	6	0.8%	1.2%
4	10	1.0%	1.9%
5	10	6.6%	4.7%
6	10	12.3%	11.7%
7	10	6.6%	4.7%
8	10	5.4%	3.7%
9	10	2.9%	3.6%
10	10	15.0%	11.9%
11	7	0.8%	0.2%
12	10	5.6%	4.0%
13	10	16.4%	15.0%
14	10	5.7%	4.9%
15	10	0.1%	0.5%
County	**10**	**6.0%**	**5.3%**

FIGURE 6.3 Left: Corn yield of 15 fields of different farms in Lyon County (Iowa, USA) that are irrigated or rainfed and average county corn yield (1988–1997). Right: Number of years of available yields of the 15 fields and risk premium rates at 80% coverage based on historical yields (observations) and modelled through a beta distribution based on observed yields. *Data source*: NASS and RMA.

crop yield remains comparable at aggregated geographical level (e.g. county) compared with farm level, the standard deviation and coefficient of variance can decrease up to five times with a usual aggregation bias of factor two.[25] Results from the US MPCI scheme suggest that reference yields calculated from county yields do not necessarily represent actual yield levels of pools of policyholders in the same county.[26] Therefore, MPCI pricing often relies on a combination of historical claims data, observed yield at farm and aggregated levels, and weather data.

Example of MPCI Pricing

The example of corn in Lyon County (Iowa, USA) is used to demonstrate the level of difference in risk premium rates at a coverage level of 80% based on yields of 15 different fields and county-level yield data. Corn yield data for Lyon County are available from the National Agricultural Statistics Service (1968–2015) and from RMA for individual fields (various time lengths up to 1997).

Although 10 years is too short to identify a yield trend, a slightly positive trend in yields at field level and in the county yield can be observed (Figure 6.3). Yields at county and on most fields show a reduction in 1993 due to excessive rainfall and flooding. The standard deviation as a ratio of the mean ranges for field-level yields from 12% (stable) to 50% (volatile) while the same measure is 22% for the county yield. Risk rates at a coverage level of 80% vary based on the observed yield from 0.1% to 16.4%, while it is 6.0% at county level. Using a beta distribution on the observed yields, risk rates

---

[25] Finger, R., 2012: Biases in farm-level yield risk analysis due to data aggregation. *Ger. J. Agr. Econ.*, 61 (1), 30–43.
[26] Rejesus, R.M. et al., 2010: Evaluation of the reference yield calculation method in crop insurance. *Agr. Finance Rev.*, 70(3), 427–45.

at 80% coverage range between 0.2% and 15.0%, with the county risk rate at 5.3% (Figure 6.3). This example shows the variability of field-level yields relative to county yield and as a result, large differences in risk rates.

LOSS ADJUSTMENT

Loss adjustment for MPCI determines actual yield per policyholder and is undertaken by trained professionals with loss adjustment manuals and a clearly defined methodology as to how yield is derived through sampling. To estimate actual yield at harvest, the minimum number of samples per field is determined in function of the average stage of growth and visible damage extent and the row distance established through measurement – for example, in the USA at least three samples are taken for fields ranging from 0.1 to 10 acres.

The determination of yield reduction as a function of plant density (row distances) and growth stages, shown in the example of corn in the USA, includes (i) stand reduction through relevant reduction curves, with an assessment of replanting from damage at early vegetative stages, (ii) maturity line weight for vegetation stages close to harvest, with weighing ear samples according to maturity and deriving yield, and (iii) weight method when kernels are fully developed at maturity in taking the weight of the sampled ears and deriving yield.[27]

6.6 REVENUE INSURANCE

RI covers producers against volatility in revenues, which are based on gross sales, i.e. the proceeds received by selling the harvested crop production at a certain price. RI is often an extension of existing MPCI-type products where shortfalls in the product of yield and price are insured. The basic version of RI indemnifies producers when actual revenue, as a combination of yield and commodity prices at harvest, is below planting price levels, which results in low revenue relative to the pre-agreed revenue guarantee. RI covers have been developed based on individual grower revenue histories and as products that use area-based revenues that are a function of area-yield and prices. In the USA, a special version of the basic form of RI, called revenue protection (RP), is used in that producers obtain a payout for revenues that result from any combination of low yields and/or the difference between harvest and planting prices, including the possibility that harvest prices are above prices at planting level.

REVENUE INSURANCE MARKETS

RI products are implemented in Canada, the USA, Europe (Spain) and Brazil and are under discussion in several Asian countries.

Canada

RI was first implemented in several Canadian provinces as the Gross Revenue Insurance Program (GRIP) in 1991 and benefited from government premium subsidies to

---

[27] USDA, 2013: Corn Loss Adjustment Standards Handbook – 2014 and Succeeding Crop Years. FCIC Publication 25080, 104p.

guarantee a gross revenue target for grain and oilseed growers. For example, in Saskatchewan (Central Canada), GRIP offered a 70% guarantee of gross revenues that were based on observed yields and a 15-year indexed moving average of commodity prices. GRIP was discontinued in 1995 due to budget pressures.[28]

USA

In the USA, numerous studies have tried to demonstrate that farm incomes could be stabilised and payments to growers could be substantially lower under RI than under price support policies.

Revenue Protection
In 1997, RI started in the USA in the form of crop revenue coverage (CRC) and revenue assurance (RA) as an initiative of the private sector and government approval and support. The RI products grew rapidly due to (i) a wider coverage compared with MPCI-type policies, (ii) the availability of substantial premium subsidies, and (iii) the 1996 Federal Agriculture Improvement and Reform Act, which cancelled the existing deficiency payments to compensate producers for commodity price variability.

In 2011, CRC and RA were revamped into (i) RP, which provides a grower with protection against revenue losses as a result of yield volatility from natural causes as well as pests and diseases and changes in the harvest price relative to a projected price from futures prices, and (ii) revenue protection with harvest price exclusion (RP-HPE), which operates like RP with the difference that the guaranteed revenue is based on projected prices, i.e. the guarantee is not increased in case the harvest price is greater than the projected price.[29] The periods during which the projected and harvest prices are determined vary by region. In 2017, 1.5 million RP policies were sold with a premium volume of US$7.6 billion and 9111 RP-HPE policies generated a premium income of US$32.2 million.

Whole-Farm Revenue Protection (WFRP)
WFRP was introduced in 2015 as a pilot programme in 45 US states, replacing adjusted gross revenue (AGR) and adjusted gross revenue lite (AGR-Lite).[30] WFRP was developed to cover specialty crop farmers who often produce many different fruit or vegetable commodities as it was not feasible to develop separate insurance products for each of these specialty commodities. WFRP provides a holistic safety net for low revenues from an unavoidable natural cause for (i) commodities that are produced during the insurance period, (ii) commodities that are bought for resale during the insurance

---

[28] Gray, A. et al., 1995: Farm level impacts of revenue assurance. *Rev. Agr. Econ.*, 17, 171–83.

[29] In the USA, options on futures contracts began trading in October 1984 for soybeans, in March 1985 for corn and in November 1986 for wheat on the Chicago Board of Trade (CBOT), which merged later with the CME Group. The *base price* for corn (soybeans) is the average of the December (November) CME Group daily futures contract prices during February (February). The *harvest price* for corn (soybeans) is the average of the December (November) CME Group daily futures contract prices during October (October), reflecting market conditions during harvest time.

[30] Risk Management Agency (RMS), 2015: Whole-Farm Revenue Protection Pilot Handbook. USDA/RMA Report FCIC-18160, 174p.

period, and (iii) all commodities on the farm except for timber, forest products, pets and sport/show animals. WFRP provides additional protection for replanting costs for up to a maximum of 20% of the expected revenue when at least 20% or 20 acres of the crop needs replanting.

The approved revenue is determined from the farm operation report and is the lower of the expected revenue or the whole-farm five-year historic average revenue from tax filings. In cases when farm operations have been growing, an indexation is used to account for growth in the approved revenue. The insured revenue is calculated by multiplying the approved revenue by the coverage level. The maximum insured revenue is set at US$8.5 million at a farm, out of which a maximum US$1 million can be generated from animals and animal products, a maximum of US$1 million from greenhouse and nursery products, and less than 50% of the total revenue from commodities purchased for resale. Special attention is given to expenses (as filed in the tax forms) and in cases where expenses are below 70% of the five-year average expenses, a downward adjustment of the insured revenue is undertaken based on the assumption that a change in the operation has led to lower expenses. Coverage levels range from 50% to 85% in 5% increments and are a function of the number of commodities produced at a farm, i.e. only highly diversified farms that produce at least three commodities qualify for 80% and 85% coverage.

Farm diversification, which reduces revenue risk, determines the level of government premium subsidies, with a maximum of 80% for farms that produce at least three commodities. The farm-level premium rate depends on (i) the location (county) of the farm, (ii) the types and total number of commodities produced, and (iii) the amount of farm revenue of each commodity produced. For farms that have a commodity that is insured under other approved insurance plans (e.g. RP), at least two further commodities must be grown on the farm to be eligible for WRFP while the WFRP premium rate is reduced due to the coverage provided by other policies.

A claim can be filed only once taxes have been filed for the period of insurance. An indemnity occurs when the gross adjusted revenue falls below the insured revenue. The gross revenue is established from the revenue filed for taxes and adjusted by (i) excluding inventory from commodities sold that were produced in previous years, and (ii) including the value of commodities produced that have not yet been harvested or sold. Losses for replanting are paid during the insurance period based on an assessment of the insurer.

WFRP allows a producer to insure a wide variety of crops and livestock products and includes coverage for higher-value specialty products (e.g. unique varieties, organic products, seeds, humanely produced livestock) that have not been insurable before. The experience with WFRP has shown implementation challenges, particularly for specialty crop growers, including (i) the need for extensive recordkeeping with at least five years of tax filing records, (ii) increased costs to transform cash-based farm accounting to accrual accounting, which is required for insurance, (iii) dramatic changes in farmed commodities in function of prices offered by processors, (iv) the need for farm-level yield or revenue distributions of each produced commodity to develop joint probability distributions, which is hardly feasible and led to the development of more pragmatic pricing approaches with the risk of inadequate premium rates, and (v) multiple harvest of certain specialty crops (e.g. vegetables), which can cause moral hazard. In 2017, 2845 WFRP policies were sold for a premium volume of US$145 million, with an average loss ratio of 86% (2015–2017).

Europe

In Europe, RI was first proposed in the UK in 1999 but failed as a private sector initiative. Similarly, a pilot RI programme of potatoes and strawberries in Spain in 2000 was not successful and was discontinued, although it has been reconsidered for implementation since 2014.[31]

Brazil

In Brazil, RI was developed by the private sector for agribusinesses as standard crop insurance products could not fulfil the needs of grain aggregators, processors and investment funds. As most Brazilian farmers use prices for CBOT, RI covers that use CBOT prices include a pre-agreed currency exchange rate of the Brazilian real against the US dollar to limit adverse currency rate developments.

Asia-Pacific

RI was recently under discussion in India, but the concept was dropped, with a focus on increasing insurance penetration of area-yield index products. Similar discussions were held in China, where liquid commodity exchanges exist and where the ultimate goal seems to be to introduce RI once the current named-peril insurance products are changed to more MPCI-type yield insurance policies.[32] As Japan seeks to transform its government-run rice insurance scheme into a private–public partnership (Section 5.5), RI seems to be one of the most attractive propositions for rice farmers.

Challenges of Revenue Insurance

As with MPCI, RI is most suited for large production units and main crop types (e.g. rice, wheat, corn, soybean, cotton) where reliable and longer time series of commodity prices exist, e.g. from future markets.

Pricing and underwriting of RI products is demanding in that farm or area-yields need to be simulated and price volatility modelled while performing joint yield-price simulations and preserving the correlations. Rating errors may reflect incorrect assumptions on yield and/or price distributions, data inconsistencies and the length of the combined yield-price time series as well as more fundamental issues with the rating methodology as such.

The implication of severe rating errors for RI products is inefficient insurance products that do not find support in the market. Difficulties in pricing yield and price volatility due to lack of reliable data and liquid markets and the relatively high premium rates often prevent the wider development of RI outside the USA.

In countries with government schemes that provide minimum commodity prices, RI will be an additional and relatively costly risk management measure and makes economic sense only if it can complement or replace existing government-supported price schemes. Depending on the size of an RI scheme and the number of crop types covered, the systemic exposure from yield volatility and even more so from price fluctuations creates large liabilities, which will require government-backed catastrophe protection.

---

[31] Ahmed, O. and Serra, T., 2015: Economic analysis of the introduction of agricultural revenue insurance contracts in Spain using statistical copulas. *Agr. Econ.*, 46(1), 69–79.

[32] Cole, J.B. and Gibson, R., 2010: Analysis and feasibility of crop revenue insurance in China. *Agric. Agric. Sci. Procedia*, 1, 136–45.

INSURANCE TERMS

RI which uses farm-based yields establishes the expected revenue before planting in multiplying an expected or average historical farm yield with an expected harvest price as the average of spot markets or futures contract prices. Area-based RI uses the same approach but with the difference that average or expected area-based yields are used.

Producers are usually allowed to select a coverage level, which is typically between 65% and 75% of the average historical farm yield when individual fields are insured and increases to 80–85% in the case of all fields being covered due to a diversification effect. Based on the expected revenue and a selected coverage level, the guaranteed revenue is calculated by multiplying the guaranteed yield with the expected harvest prices and the area insured, based on which premium amounts are determined. At harvest time, the final guaranteed revenue is established in function of the guaranteed yield and the actual harvest price, which is averaged over a pre-agreed time (e.g. 10 days spot market prices or 30 days futures contract prices) and multiplied by the area insured. At the same time, the actual revenue is calculated by multiplying the actual yield with the actual harvest price (or the difference of the base and harvest prices as under RP products in the USA) and the area insured. Actual yields are determined through on-site loss adjustments in same way us under MPCI-type policies. An indemnity is received in case the actual revenue is below the final guaranteed revenue.

However, as harvest prices are taken from regional or national commodity exchanges (spot markets and/or future contracts), these prices can differ greatly from local prices such as prices paid by grain elevators. These differences are known as basis and the variability of this basis over time is called basis risk. Basis risk results from the imperfect correlation of price indices with actual prices.

PRICING

The pricing of RI products requires accurate crop yields at different geographical resolutions as well as historical and forward-looking commodity prices to establish expected and guaranteed revenues. The main challenge is to relate the distribution of crop yields to the distribution of prices while performing joint simulations so that correlations are preserved. An additional complexity arises when farm yields need to be related to area-based yields (e.g. a county) where longer times series are available, which in turn needs to be correlated to yields of areas for which commodity price information is available (e.g. a province or state).

The common pricing approach for RI involves four steps in (i) establishment of yield and price PDFs, (ii) estimation of correlations between yield and price distributions, (iii) joint simulation of correlated yield and price events, and (iv) computation of estimated losses at different geographical resolutions and coverage levels, through geographical downward adjustments.[33]

---

[33] Coble, K.H. et al., 2010: A comprehensive review of the RMA APH and combo rating methodology. Final report. Prepared by sumaria systems for the Risk Management Agency (RMA), 157p.

Sources of Commodity Prices

RI mostly relies on forward-looking prices from futures markets; however, for crops that are not traded at futures markets, expected prices over the period of insurance have been derived from historical data. Historical price data are imperfect estimators of future expected price or price volatility, particularly in the presence of significant structural market changes (e.g. new trade agreements). Futures, options and spot-market prices are available from financial market platforms and terminals (e.g. Reuters, Bloomberg) but require a subscription. Some open source platforms provide access to agriculture commodity data from several exchanges and barchart markets.[34]

Price Volatility Indices
A reliable price volatility index needs to fulfil the following criteria: (i) standardisation, which refers to the need of the market participant to know that the underlying commodity, futures or products are consistent and to a large extent deliverable, (ii) verifiable pricing, where parties of the same trade are able to replicate and reasonably forecast price index values, (iii) frequent price dissemination to assure wide access, e.g. through the internet or bulletins, (iv) competitive price determination without manipulation of trading, delivery or input data that are used to compute the price index under free market conditions, and (v) value representation in the price index that largely reflects the underlying risk and general valuation while market participants accept that some inaccuracies exist.[35]

A key concern with agricultural commodities is that farmers sell production in function of expected prices and can store commodities to be sold later at optimal prices, which can lead to distortions in price volatility measures. Corn, soybean and spring wheat prices in the USA show that for periods early in the growing season, price distributions from options trades offer higher reliability than distributions based on historical futures trades.[36] Further, volatility in commodity prices of main crops has been shown to be higher than volatility in crop yield, e.g. for US corn, yield varies between 12% (state level) and 25% (farm level) and prices between 17% (state level) and 28% (farm level).[37] Generally, spatial disaggregation increases price and yield variability, while yield variability increases typically faster than price and revenue variability.

Calculation of Yield Volatility

Crop yield data are examined for inconsistencies and outliers, after which the data are, if justified, detrended and deviations in percentages from the trend (residuals) computed, to which a suitable parametric or non-parametric PDF is fitted (Section 4.4). While parametric (e.g. beta) and non-parametric (e.g. kernel) functions are often used to establish yield densities, the most suitable distribution depends on the length of the data records

---

[34] For example, www.quandl.com, which is a source of open, commercial and alternative data for investment professionals and includes soft commodity prices.

[35] Cole, J., 2002: Designing and pricing new instruments for insurance and weather risks, in *Risk Management: The State of the Art*, S. Figlewski and R. Levich (eds.), Kluwer Academic Publishers, 79–85.

[36] Buschena, D. and Ziegler, L., 1999: Reliability of options markets for crop revenue insurance rating. *J. Agr. Resource Econ.*, 24(2), 398–423.

[37] Coble, K.H. et al., 2007: Policy implications of crop yield and revenue variability at differing levels of disaggregation. In annual meeting of the American Agricultural Economics Association, Portland, USA, 29p.

and the presence of outliers. To avoid computational difficulty and complexity when yield PDFs are to be combined with price PDFs, yield PDFs in earlier RI products have been chosen to follow a censored normal distribution, which however violates some of the common characteristics of crop yield distributions such as heteroscedasticity and negative skewness (Section 4.4). Flexible multivariate models that can describe major data properties, higher-order moments, fat tails, co-extreme movement and tail dependence can combine any type of parametric or non-parametric PDFs of yields and prices.

Calculation of Price Volatility

To establish price volatility, percentage change from base prices at planting time to prices at harvest time are calculated. The measurement of price risk heavily depends on assumptions relative to the distribution of the underlying price movements. The main approaches to model price volatility include the Present Value Method (PVM), the Black–Scholes Option Pricing Method (BSOPM) and the Geometric Brownian Motion (GBM).

Present Value Method

The PVM is the most used method to value insurance contracts including price volatilities. PVM prices insurance contracts at present value of the expected indemnity and is straightforward in computation; however, it requires arbitrary assumption of discount rates. Under PVM, the price value at planting time of an RI contract based on a crop revenue index Y_t that is realised and observed at harvest period t when revenues are realised, and any insurance indemnities are paid, is written for a guarantee level (G_t) as:[38]

$$P_{t-1}(G_t) = (1+\gamma_t)\beta_t E_{t-1}[\max(G_t - Y_t, 0] = (1+\gamma_t)\beta_t \int_0^{G_t}(G_t - Y_t)h(Y_t)dY_t$$

with γ_t as a loading factor that reflects costs of risk premium and the insurance transaction for the time period of $t-1$ to t; γ_t is usually positive and a negative value signifies that the premium does not cover the present value of expected indemnities and a value of zero is equivalent to the actuarially fair premium rate, β_t is a discount for the expected indemnity back to the planting time at a risk-free rate, E_t is the expectation that is conditional on information available at a given time and $h(Y_t)$ is the PDF for Y_t conditional on information available at $t-1$.

The RI contract is based on a contingent claim with a payout at harvest time t over the difference between a guaranteed level of the revenue index, the level of guarantee (G_t) and the realised harvest value of the revenue index Y_t when $Y_t < G_t$. The insurance indemnity is written as $\max(G_t - Y_t, 0)$ with a premium value of $P_{t-1}(G_t)$.

A key advantage of PVM is that it is highly flexible and can include any underlying PDF $h(Y_t)$ but it has the disadvantage that the loading factor γ_t must be predetermined and can have a large impact on the premium value $P_{t-1}(G_t)$. Setting the loading factor at 0 is unrealistic because agricultural contracts typically involve non-diversifiable risk that must be priced. A simplified formula for the premium value has been developed in case $h(Y_t)$ is lognormal. Often, sensitivity analyses are undertaken to evaluate how the premium value changes with different loading factors.

---

[38] Myers, R.J. et al., 2005: How should we value agricultural insurance contracts. Paper prepared at the American Agricultural Economics Association Annual Meeting, Providence, Rhode Island, 24–27.

Black–Scholes Method
The BSOPM is the most used method to valuate financial derivatives using the contingent claim method. Under the BSOPM terminology, an RI contract provides a producer the right, but not the obligation, to claim a fixed amount in the event of an indemnifiable loss, while the probability of a loss is known only up to the observed distribution of both crop yield and commodity prices. RI products are similar to a European put option, which is a financial derivative and is mostly valuated through BSOPM assuming that prices are lognormally distributed.[39] BSOPM has been used to value crop RI insurance contracts[40] and assumes that prices are lognormally distributed, which was the case for the earlier RI products in the USA. Based on BSOPM, price changes from planting to harvest can be established based on a futures prices at planting time (P_p) and harvest prices of the same futures contracts (P_h) as:[41]

$$F(P_h) = \left(\sqrt{\pi\sigma}\right)^{-1} \exp\left[\frac{-0.5\left(\log\left(P_h - \mu\right)\right)}{\sigma^2}\right]$$

with μ as the mean and σ as the standard deviation from the lognormal distribution estimated from option trades. The BSOPM contains several main assumptions that can cause potential problems for agricultural revenues in that (i) crop prices are not always lognormally distributed and lognormality suggests a proportional relationship between the variance and the mean of the observed data, which might not be the case for crops, (ii) stochastic processes[42] underlying revenues from agricultural commodities may not be completely continuous (as is often assumed) but rather show continuous as well as discrete components in the form of sudden jumps, (iii) farm revenues are not tradable and are not influenced by constant updating of buying and selling positions in the options market under non-arbitrage conditions, and (iv) a producer's revenue is often derived from more than one commodity. The evidence that agricultural commodity prices include sudden jumps due to shocks that are often driven by low yields has led to the use of pricing approaches that allow both continuous and discrete jumps.[43]

Geometric Brownian Motion
The GBM allows prices to be continuous and concrete through a continuous-time stochastic process where the logarithm of a randomly varying quantity follows the Brownian motion. The GBM is used in mathematical finance to model stock prices and incorporates components of the BSOPM to describe the movement of time series of asset prices. The GBM has two components in (i) a certain component, which represents

---

[39] Stokes, J.R. et al., 1997: The pricing of revenue assurance. *Amer. J. Agr. Econ.*, 79, 439–51.
[40] Turvey, C., 1992: Contingent claim pricing models implied by agricultural stabilization and insurance policies. *Can. J. Agr. Econ.*, 40, 183–98.
[41] Buschena, D. and Ziegler, L., 1999: Reliability of options markets for crop revenue insurance rating *J. Agr. Resource Econ.*, 24(2), 398–423.
[42] Any variable that shows a change in value over time in an uncertain way is said to follow a stochastic process. Stochastic processes can be discrete (value of the variable can change only at certain fixed points in time) or continuous (value of the variable changes at any time) with respect to time.
[43] Richards, T.J. and Manfredo, M.R., 2003: Infrequent shocks and rating revenue insurance: A contingent claims approach. *J. Agr. Resource Econ.*, 28(2), 233–51.

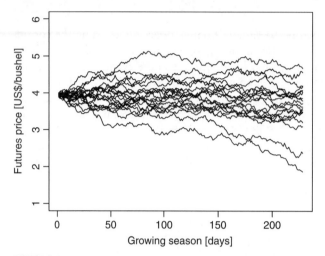

FIGURE 6.4 Example of 20 realisations of futures prices using the Geometric Brownian Motion for corn futures prices in Illinois (USA), with a starting point of US$3.96/bushel and an implied volatility of 17.23% for 1 March to 15 October (228 days).
Data source: CBOT.

the return that a stock will earn over time, which is called drift of the stock, and (ii) an uncertain component, which is a stochastic process that includes stock volatility and an element of random volatility, called implied volatility.

The GBM has been used to model agricultural commodity prices[44] and to price crop RI products.[45] For the use of the GBM to price RI products, the drift is the expected return on capital over the period of insurance (i.e. the crop season) and the implied volatility is determined from capital markets or computed from the data (Figure 6.4).

Calculation of Yield-Price Correlations

In major production regions for commodities where production is a main part of the global market, or in markets that are protected from global markets, yield and prices tend to be negatively correlated in that with high production, prices decline and vice versa. In markets with production that is of lower importance at the domestic and global scale, yield and prices are typically unrelated. For example, negative yield-price correlations exist for corn and soybeans in the US Midwest, which is the dominant production region and of global importance; however, yield and prices are non-related for the same commodities in southern US states, which produce lower quantities.

Studies of yield-price correlations of US RI products have shown that strong correlations exist for certain crop types at farm as well as at national level.[46] As in many markets and main crop types, yields and prices can be related, joint yield-price simulations for RI products evolved from the initial additive approach to the use of copula functions (Table 6.6).

[44] Hennessy, D.A. and Wahl, T.I., 1996: The effects of decision making on futures price volatility. *Amer. J. Agr. Econ.*, 78(3), 591–603.

[45] Richards, T.J. and Manfredo, M.R., 2003: Infrequent shocks and rating revenue insurance: A contingent claims approach. *J. Agr. Resource Econ.*, 28(2), 233–51.

[46] Coble, K. et al., 2000: Implications of crop yield and revenue insurance for producer hedging. *J. Agr. Resource Econ.*, 25(2), 432–52.

TABLE 6.6 Overview of the main methods for pricing revenue insurance products.

Method	Complexity	Yield Data	Price Data	Joint Simulation	Comments
Additive method	Low	Detrended observed or modelled yield (any PDF)	Observed or simulated price differentials (usually lognormal)	Adding price volatility to risk rates determined from yield volatility	Conservative approach as negative yield-price correlations are ignored
Simple simulation	Low	Detrended and modelled yield (censured normal or lognormal)	Modelled price differentials (lognormal)	Simulation that easily allows the combination of modelled yield (e.g. lognormal or censured normal) with modelled prices (lognormal)	Crop yields are rarely lognormal or normal distributed
Black–Scholes with copula functions	High	Detrended and modelled yield (any PDF)	Black–Scholes Option Pricing Model (BSOPM) with lognormally distributed price differentials	Copula functions to combine modelled yield (any PDF) with modelled price (lognormal)	BSOPM assumes continuous prices but soft commodity prices often show sudden jumps and farm revenues are not tradable
Geometric Brownian Motion with copula functions	High	Detrended and modelled yield (any PDF)	Geometric Brownian Motion (GBM) with simulations (random walks) of prices	Copula functions to combine modelled yield (any PDF) with modelled price (lognormal)	GBM allows continuous and discrete (jumps) price movements but requires determination of shift and implied volatility

Additive Methods and Simple Simulations
The additive method simply assumes that yields and prices are independent, and RI covers are priced in adding the price volatility to the risk rates determined from yield volatility. This approach was initially used for the earlier US CRC products.[47] However, ignoring negative correlations between yield and price distributions implies that the risk from revenue shortfall is lower than the risk from price and yield shortfalls considered in isolation, which leads to conservatively priced RI products. An approach that respects yield-price correlations is to choose the PDFs of yield and prices in a way that allows simple simulations where price distributions are assumed to be lognormally distributed following the BSOPM approach and yield distributions are selected to follow a censored normal distribution.

Copula Functions
A more complex approach to develop joint yield-price series that allows joint simulations of any type of PDF for yields and prices are copula functions. Under copula functions, marginal distributions are linked to form a joint distribution. Copula functions are widely used by insurance actuaries to model multiple sources of risk at various degrees of correlation. One of the advantages of the copula approach is that the estimation and inference are based on standard maximum likelihood procedures, which allows efficient estimation of the assumed copula model. While mathematically complex, the copula methodology allows the development of joint distributions of a variety of underlying parametric and non-parametric PDFs. Copula functions facilitate the joint simulation of yield and prices under the BSOPM and the GBM and have been used to price RI products[48] as well as farm-income insurance policies.[49]

Geographical Downward Adjustments
As consistent yield data and commodity prices are typically available only at geographically aggregated levels (e.g. county for yield and province for prices), risk premium rates established at these resolutions need to be downward adjusted to farm level in relating farm-level yields to yields at aggregated levels. Often, a Monte Carlo simulation is used to compute RI losses over a range of different coverage levels, which is assumed to be constant for all producers in the administrative area (e.g. county).

Example of Revenue Insurance Pricing
As with the example of corn in Adams County (Illinois, USA), the following shows a step-by-step approach to pricing two types of revenue cover: (i) a payout in case the harvest price is lower than the base price at planting, called RP-HPE in the USA, and (ii) a payout of the higher of the base price and the harvest price, called revenue protection (RP) in the USA.

---

[47] Goodwin, B.K. et al., 2000: Measurement of price risk in revenue insurance: implications of distributional assumptions. *J. Agr. Resource Econ.*, 25(1), 195–214.

[48] Goodwin, B.K. and Hungerford, A., 2014: Copula-based models of systemic risk in US agriculture: implications for crop insurance and reinsurance contracts. *Amer. J. Agr. Econ.*, 97(3), 879–96.

[49] Zhu, Y. et al. 2008: Modeling dependence in the design of whole farm insurance contract – a Copula-based model approach. In Selected Paper prepared for presentation at the American Agricultural Economics Association Annual Meeting, Orlando, USA, 27–29.

Pricing Yield Volatility

First, county-level corn yields are linearly detrended for the period for which both yield and commodity price data are consistently available (1990–2015). Testing different PDFs, the logistic function produces the best fit for the detrended corn yield data and additionally, a normal distribution function is used to demonstrate the difference. The guaranteed yield is taken from the online *iFarm* Crop Insurance Premium Calculator for corn in Illinois at 154.89 bushels/acre, which compares to 139.17 bushels/acre as the historical average (1990–2015) and 156.74 bushels/acre from detrended yield data (1990–2015).

Pricing Price Volatility

For the RP cover, the base price (average of February prices) and harvest prices (average of October prices) from the December futures contracts (contract CZ17) of CBOT is established for the period of available data (1990–2015). In about one third of the years, harvest prices were above base prices, while in two thirds of the years, the opposite occurred (Figure 6.5). Price differentials show phases of continuity but include several discrete phases (jumps) in 2008 and in 2013 (Figure 6.5). For the RP-HPE cover, spot market prices for corn are used from CBOT at planting and harvest time. Price differentials for the RP and RP-HPE covers are simulated using a GBM with a shift factor of 0 and an implied volatility of 17.23% as calculated from the price data.

Joint Yield-Price Simulations

The analysis between the detrended corn yields and the corn price differentials reveals a strong negative correlation (–0.75) and implies that high yields result in most cases in lower prices and vice versa (Figure 6.5). This is not surprising given that Adams County is in the Corn Belt in the US Midwest, which is a major global corn-producing region. For pricing, a yield-price correlation coefficient of –0.75 is taken and to test the sensitivity, a coefficient of –0.3 is used additionally, assuming a more elastic market.

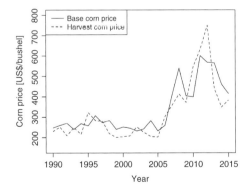
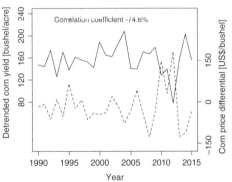

FIGURE 6.5   Left: Base corn prices (averages of February) and harvest corn prices (averages of October) from the December futures contracts (CBOT contract CZ17), 1990–2015. Right: Detrended corn yield for Adams County (Illinois, USA, solid line) and corn price differentials from harvest and base prices (dotted line), 1990–2015.
Data source: NASS and CBOT.

TABLE 6.7 Risk premium rates for the revenue protection (RP) and the revenue protection with harvest price exclusion (RP-HPE) products, with yield distributions following a logistic and a normal function and yield-price correlation coefficients of –0.75 (as observed) and –0.30.

Product	Yield Distribution	Correlation	Risk Premium Rates Per Coverage Level		
			70%	80%	85%
RP	Normal	–0.75	3.8%	12.9%	21.9%
RP	Logistic	–0.75	4.3%	12.4%	20.6%
RP	Normal	–0.30	5.6%	16.2%	26.1%
RP	Logistic	–0.30	5.7%	14.4%	24.7%
RP-HPE	Normal	–0.75	1.0%	3.9%	7.9%
RP-HPE	Logistic	–0.75	1.4%	4.5%	8.2%
RP-HPE	Normal	–0.30	3.7%	10.6%	17.5%
RP-HPE	Logistic	–0.30	4.0%	10.7%	17.3%

For the combination of the yield distribution (logistic function) and the price differential distribution (simulated with GBM to be lognormal), a copula function is used to obtain the joint yield-price distribution. This joint distribution forms the basis for deriving risk premium rates for different coverage levels set at 70%, 80% and 85% (Table 6.7).

Risk Premium Rates
As expected, risk premium rates for the RP-HPE cover are lower than for the RP product as RP-HPE compensates for low revenues only in cases when harvest prices are below (and not below or above) base prices at planting. Risk premium rates that are based on normally distributed yields are considerably lower compared with the logistic function as the normal distribution assumes equal probabilities of low and high yields realtive to the mean yield (i.e. no skewness), which is not suitable for crop yields. Increasing coverage level (e.g. from 70% to 85%) largely increases the risk premium rates, which is necessary to compensate against more frequent shortfalls in revenues. The use of a lower yield-price negative correlation (–0.30) compared with the correlation of the observations (–0.75) results in higher risk premium rates. This example shows that risk premium rates of RI products are highly sensitive to the yield density distribution and the extent of the yield-price correlation.

6.7 INCOME INSURANCE

Income insurance provides coverage for volatility of farm income, which is determined by deducting expenses (e.g. for input supplies) from revenues and therefore differs from RI (Section 6.6) where low revenues are compensated. Income insurance covers covariate risks that cause low income from different farming activities that can include crop farming, livestock rearing and on some occasions timber and aquaculture production. As such, income insurance has the widest coverage of all agricultural insurance products and is based on the concept that pooling risks over different farm activities diversifies risks and leads to lower costs compared with individual insurance for each commodity. Whole-farm insurance developed in the form of (i) farm income insurance, which protects against margin losses at farm level as determined through cost and revenue accounting rules, and (ii) combined RI, which covers revenues from different crop types and other agricultural activities including livestock, forestry and/or aquaculture farming.[50]

Due to its wide coverage and the reliance of tax filing information, income insurance is most effective if it is embedded in government risk management frameworks. As income insurance comes with substantial administration, only larger and well-developed farm operations are targeted for insurance. The benefits of insurance of farm-based income risk compared with financial instruments have been widely explored in an international context.[51]

INCOME INSURANCE MARKETS

Income insurance has only been implemented over longer time frames in Canada under the Canadian Farm Income Program (CFIP) and modified versions under the Canadian Agricultural Income Stabilization (CAIS) and AgriStability. In India, a Farm Income Insurance Scheme (FIIS) was briefly implemented from 2003 to 2004 with coverage of average yield and minimum support prices for wheat and rice farmers. In the USA, farm income insurance in its stricter sense is not available; however, WFRP (Section 6.6) covers revenues of certain agricultural activities at farm level.

Europe

In Europe, income insurance has not been implemented, but farming income has been guaranteed through price intervention under the Common Agricultural Policy (CAP), input subsidies, subsidised crop and livestock insurance (focusing on production volatility), public works and emergency responses. However, these policies have been shown to be insufficient in coping with future challenges, which include environmental deterioration, climate change, trade distortions and budgetary constraints. The CAP 2014–2020 has promoted the adoption of income insurance as a comprehensive scheme to cover both production and market risks in a holistic way.[52]

Canada

In 1992, net income stabilisation accounts (NISAs) were implemented to provide farmers with incentives to accrue funds through deposits in high-income years to benefit them in low-income years.[53] The government provided matching contributions and a 3% interest rate bonus on the account balances while farmers contributed to administrative costs and paid taxes to withdraw funds. However, with potential tax liabilities

---

[50] Bielza, M. and Garrido, A., 2009: Evaluating the potential of whole-farm insurance over crop-specific insurance policies. *Span. J. Agr. Res.*, 7(1), 3–11.

[51] OECD, 2000: Income risk management. OECD Agriculture and Food Report, Paris, 147p.

[52] Pérez-Blancoa, C.D. et al., 2016: Revealing the willingness to pay for income insurance in agriculture. *J. Risk Res.*, 19(7), 873–93.

[53] Dismukes, R. and Durst, R., 2006: Whole-farm approaches to a safety net. USDA-ERS Economic Information Bulletin No. 15, 25p.

upon withdrawal, low interest rates in the borrowing market and the availability of other ways to cover income shortfalls, NISAs attracted low participation. In 1998, the NISA was supplemented by the Agriculture Income Disaster Assistance (AIDA) and the CFIP in 2000. In 2004, the NISA and the CFIP were replaced by the CAIS programme,[54] which combines income stabilisation and disaster assistance as part of the overall agricultural policy framework.

Canadian Farm Income Program

CAIS does not depend on account balance accumulation and provides immediate coverage in the case of income reduction. CAIS resembles a fully subsidised whole-farm income insurance programme in that farmers transfer risk to the government and contribute a premium as a flat fee of CA$1000 per margin insured. The covered amount of income is based on a producer's margin as reported through tax filings. A margin is defined as the accrued income (net of adjustments for inventory, receivables and payables) that arises from sales of agricultural commodities net of expenses from the primary production of different commodities on the farm but excluding cost of capital, depreciation, wages and salaries and net of any government payments and insurance indemnities.

The reference margin is determined as the Olympic average (omits the highest and lowest values) of farm income of the last five years. Indemnities occur when the margin is below the reference margin and is based on a three-tier system where government loss participation increases with the loss extent in that (i) margin is within 85% of the selected margin, the producer receives 50% of the shortfall, (ii) the margin is below 85% but above 70%, with 70% of the shortfall compensated, and (iii) the margin is below 70%, when 80% of the shortfall is indemnified. The final indemnity is the sum of the three-tier payouts while the total indemnity is limited to 70% of the total shortfall below the margin. In case the margin is negative (financial loss), the government compensates 60% of the negative portion of the programme year margin decline. Premium rates (PR) are considered as not actuarially sound since they are tied to the targeted income rather than the risk and computed as:

$$PR = 0.85 \times \frac{z}{1,000} + CA\$55$$

with z being the margin and the CA$55 covering the administrative costs.

AgriInvest, AgriStability and AgInsure

In 2007, CAIS was replaced by three new programmes, AgriInvest, AgriStability and AgInsure, which jointly provide holistic coverage in combining savings accounts for smaller income variability, margin-based insurance for larger volatilities in income and insurance against low yield.[55] All three programmes are government-administered and benefit from substantial subsidies.

---

[54] AgriCorp, 2007: Canadian Agricultural Income Stabilization (CAIS) Program. 23p.
[55] Canada Revenue Agency, 2016: Farming Income and the AgriStability and AgriInvest Programs Harmonized Guide, 117p.

AgriInvest provides savings accounts for producers to protect against small declines in income and supports investments that assist in the mitigation of risks. Farmers can set aside 1.5% of eligible sales into a savings account which is matched by a government contribution.

AgriStability is similar to CAIS and is a margin-based programme that provides income support for larger income losses. In comparison with CAIS, AgriStability does not provide protection for reduced margins above 85%, while government indemnity is set at 70% for margins between 85% and 60%, with any negative margin being compensated to 60%. The programme also accounts for livestock and crop inventories under a hybrid valuation method where start-of-year and end-of-year prices are estimated to establish changes in the values of the inventories over the fiscal period. The producer contributes a flat fee of CA$3.15 for every CA$1000 of reference margin protected, with a minimum fee per policy of CA$45 and an additional fee of CA$55 to cover administrative expenses.

AgInsure includes government-subsidised MPCI policies that provide payouts for yield reduction so that insurance indemnity is obtained.

INSURANCE TERMS

For farm income insurance, the most reliable and time-consistent sources of farm income are tax filings of agricultural producers with fiscal authorities that follow clear accounting rules. Income insurance is certainly the most complex agricultural insurance product to implement and administrate.

Accounting Rules and Adjustments

Generally, two accounting methods are used to record farm revenues: (i) the cash method, where income is reported in the fiscal period as it is received and expenses are considered as paid, and (ii) the accrual method, with income is reported as it is earned (and not received) and expenses are deducted when they are incurred (independent of the payment date) and with the value of all inventories (e.g. livestock, crops, feed, fertiliser) being part of the calculation. Inventories can be valued at cost through replacement values or at fair market value with proceeds to be received in case of sales. A change in tax reporting standards and accounting method can lead to inconsistencies and increased volatility in farm revenues and needs to be addressed in historical data. Additionally, farmers, like other tax payers, tend to optimise taxable income through acceleration or deferring income or expenses to smooth income to avoid higher tax brackets, which can result in lower apparent farm income variability.

In most cases, fiscal revenues and costs need adjustments, including income from previous production cycles (e.g. processed crops from the previous season) and larger structural changes (e.g. increased investments, changes in farmed area). The use of tax information for income insurance can have a significant impact on both the potential number of eligible farmers and the measured level and variability of farm income. Income insurance programmes typically include a minimum monetary amount of revenues from agricultural activities relative to other non-agricultural revenues.

Calculating Programme Margins

For income insurance, the programme margin is determined in function of the reported income net of expenses over the period of insurance, adjusted for changes in purchased inputs, receivables, payables, inventory and structural changes. The programme margin uses an assessment of the productive capacity of a farm operation and includes (i) productive capacity as measured according to the type of livestock, e.g. number of animals fed on a cattle feeder operation, and (ii) productive areas for crops, e.g. those already producing a crop, or that will be productive in the first year. Income insurance provides indemnity when the programme margin is below the coverage level of the reference margin, which is determined using a given number of historical farm records filed under tax declarations.

PRICING

Detailed pricing of income insurance products is highly complex as incomes need to be adjusted from historical farm records or tax filing statements for each agricultural commodity and subsequently correlated and simulated using volatility in production, price and expenses, including numerous random variables. While one could obtain the necessary data, the costs to undertake detailed statistical simulation for each commodity at farm level are likely to make income insurance highly expensive. For joint simulations, copula functions have been suggested to solve the problem of mathematically combining different probability distributions of the underlying farming assets while preserving joint correlations.[56] An alternative is the use of discrete-state stochastic programming, which is part of the more general family of compact factorisation and is used to solve large state-contingent portfolio problems using piece-wise linear constraints in representing the correlated risks by multiple discrete states of nature rather than a continuous probability distribution.[57] Due to the high complexity in reliably pricing farm income, larger programmes such as AgriStability in Canada apply nonactuarial flat rates, with the margin being the only variable.

6.8 AREA-YIELD INDEX INSURANCE

AYII is essentially based on the concept of MPCI but with the difference that indemnity occurs at a geographically larger area than a farm. AYII is designed to cover high-severity and low-frequency loss events from systemic perils (e.g. drought, flood, cyclone) where most famers can be affected at the same time over larger areas. In financial terms, AYII can be seen as a put option on the average yield for the area of insurance.

Based on advantages of index-based insurance over indemnity-based schemes (including lower adverse selection, less moral hazard and lower costs), AYII schemes have been developed in several countries (i) that predominantly have a number of small farms and a lack of insurance infrastructure in rural areas that prevent farm-based crop insurance such as MPCI (e.g. India), or (ii) where insurance indemnity of systemic perils through farm-based insurance (such as MPCI) is limited, costly and inefficient, therefore acting as catastrophe protection (e.g. USA). AYII forms the basis of area-based revenue protection in the USA.

[56] Zhu, Y. et al., 2008: Modeling dependence in the design of whole farm insurance contract – a Copula-based model approach. In Selected Paper prepared for presentation at the American Agricultural Economics Association Annual Meeting, Orlando, USA, 27–29.
[57] Turvey, C.G., 2012: Whole farm income insurance. *J. Risk Ins.*, 79(2), 515–40.

Most AYII programmes benefit from government support in the form of premium subsidies and/or government reinsurance protection for catastrophe-type losses. AYII is increasingly used by grain aggregators, processors and logistics companies to manage production risk from weather-related fluctuations in revenues and fixed costs.

AREA-YIELD INDEX INSURANCE MARKETS

The largest AYII programmes are operated in India to cover smallholder farmers and in the USA to provide catastrophe risk protection. AYII has been implemented in several other countries or is being piloted, including in Latin America (e.g. Brazil, Peru), Asia (Vietnam) and Africa. In China, the potential use of AYII compared with the current indemnity-based crop insurance programmes has been investigated, with the conclusion that despite basis risk, AYII is a viable alternative.[58]

India

AYII was implemented in India in 1979 as a mechanism to mitigate risks of natural disasters on farm production. The initial challenge was to find an insurance product that could cover large numbers of smallholders, a multitude of crop types in different micro climates and systemic perils such as droughts, cyclones and floods. In 1985, the government introduced the Comprehensive Crop Insurance Scheme (CCIS) for borrowing (loanee) farmers, with government-owned General Insurance Corporation of India (GIC) as the only insurer. Based on CCIS (1985–1998), AYII transitioned to the National Agricultural Insurance Scheme (NAIS), which co-existed with a modified National Agricultural Insurance Scheme (mNAIS) until it was redefined and significantly expanded into Pradhan Mantri Fasal Bima Yojana (PMFBY).

National Agricultural Insurance Scheme (1999–2015)
NAIS began in the 1999 winter (Rabi) crop season with GIC as the only insurer until the Agriculture Insurance Company of India (AICI) as a specialist agricultural insurer was established in 2002. As with CCIS, insurance under NAIS was compulsory for loanee farmers.

The sum insured was determined through average yield and the minimum government support price. Coverage levels were derived in functions of coefficients of variations of observed yield as 60%, 80% or 90%. Guaranteed yields were based on the moving average of the past three years (rice and wheat) and five years (other crops) at district level. Premium rates for food and oilseed crops differed only according to the crop classifications, ranging from 1.5% (wheat) to 3.5% (oilseeds), and were uniform across India. Annual commercial and horticulture crops were insured at actuarial premium rates. Premium costs were only subsidised by the government at 10% for smallholders.

While yield reduction risk was insured at sub-district level for major crop types, localised perils such as hailstorm, landslide, cyclone and flood were covered at farm level through indemnity-based products. At the beginning of a crop season, the state

---

[58] Zhang, Q., Wang, K. and Boyd, M., 2011: The effectiveness of area based yield crop risk insurance in China. *Hum. Ecol. Risk. Assess.*, 17(3), 566–79.

government notified which crops and districts were to be insured in function of available historical yield data, planted area and the government's ability to measure actual yields through crop cutting experiments (CCEs).[59]

Over the time of Rabi 1999 to Kharif 2014 (30 seasons), NAIS incurred a loss cost of 9.5% and a loss ratio of 314%, with an average original premium rate of 3.5%; overall, only 5 out of the 26 states produced loss ratios below 100%. NAIS covered 30 crops for the Rabi season and 35 crops for the Kharif season. The complex procedure of CCEs and the large number of different crop types led to significant delays until the CEE results were available to settle insurance claims. With the need to cover more farmers under NAIS and with India's predominantly rainfed agriculture being exposed to systemic droughts, flooding and cyclones, the financial burden on the government's budget to absorb large losses under NAIS increased significantly. As a response, a modified version of NAIS (mNAIS)[60] was introduced as a pilot during the 2010 Rabi season.

Modified National Agriculture Insurance Scheme (2010–2015)
mNAIS, compared with NAIS, was based on actuarial premium rates which varied by crop and district but were capped at 8–10% (food crops and oilseeds) and at 12% (commercial crops), with coverage levels of 70%, 80% and 90% at district level. Guaranteed yields were calculated at sub-district level as the moving average of the last seven years of yield observations, omitting government-declared calamity years. mNAIS covered yield reductions on standing crops as well as prevented sowing/planting, local calamities (landslides and hail) and post-harvest loss due to cyclones and torrential rainfall. In the case of adverse seasonal conditions during the crop season (e.g. from floods, dry spells, droughts) and yields at 50% of normal, an on-account payment of up to 25% of sum insured became payable to affected farmers based on meteorological data and satellite imagery. Pricing relied on averages of the last 10 years of historical yields from CCEs.

Most insured farmers under mNAIS were loanee farmers (mandatory insurance), with non-loanee farmers buying insurance on an ad-hoc basis depending on seasonal production outlooks. Compared with NAIS, private insurers were allowed under mNAIS, premium costs were consistently subsidised and government reinsurance protection was removed. The experience with mNAIS was that claims payouts took up to 12 months following harvest until CCEs were available for loss settlement. The CCE process has been criticised for lack of reliability, accuracy and very long reporting times, which all lead to issues in basis risk and delays in claims settlement. Between 2010 and 2014, AICI as the main insurer of mNAIS incurred a loss cost of 10% and a loss ratio of 92%, with an average original premium rate of 11%. This was a clear

---

[59] In India, CCEs are conducted through multistage stratified sampling in each of the sub-districts known as Tehsils/Taluks. Based on normal crop acreage, adequate numbers of villages are randomly selected for each Tehsil/Taluk and in each selected village two fields are randomly sampled and within the selected field a plot size of 0.0025 to 0.01 ha is randomly selected for a given crop type. The yield measurements are first aggregated at the Tehsil/Taluk sub-district and then at district and state level.

[60] Clarke, D.J., 2012: Index Based Crop Insurance Product Design and Ratemaking: The Case of Modified NAIS in India. World Bank Policy Research Working Paper 5986, Washington DC, 32p.

improvement compared with NAIS and mNAIS allowed India to shift to a private–public system that included the involvement of private insurers and with the benefit of international reinsurance protection.

Pradhan Mantri Fasal Bima Yojana (Since 2016)

To overcome the shortcomings of mNAIS, PMFBY,[61] which translates as Prime Minister's Crop Insurance Scheme, was introduced in 2016 to (i) provide financial support to farmers with crop losses from unforeseeable events, (ii) stabilise farmers' incomes to ensure continuance in farming, (iii) encourage farmers to adopt modern agriculture practices, and (iv) enhance agriculture credits, which in turn should contribute to food security, crop diversification and growth.

As under the previous schemes, PMFBY covers a larger number of crop types against losses from (i) non-preventable perils including drought, dry spells, flood, pests and diseases, landslides, fire, lightning, storm, hail and cyclones that cause yield reductions to standing crops, (ii) local calamities such as hailstorm, landslide and inundation for standing crops, with indemnity limited to the cost of input supplies and losses to be adjusted by assessors, (iii) adverse conditions that lead to prevented sowing/planting, with at least 75% of the insured area being affected and indemnity limited to 25% of sum insured, (iv) unseasonal rainfall (including cyclones) causing post-harvest losses for drying crops within 14 days of harvest with onsite loss adjustment. Depending on the granularity of the historical yield data from CCEs, the unit of insurance is a village or village panchayat or a sub-district. PMFBY provides on-account payments for immediate financial relief during the growing season in areas where adverse weather conditions such as flood, prolonged dry spells and droughts cause a likely yield reduction of at least 50% as estimated from weather records and satellite data. Under PMFBY, farmers pay a flat premium rate or an absolute portion of the actuarial rate, whichever is the lower, fixed at 2.0% (1.5%) for all food grains and oilseeds in the Kharif (Rabi) season and 5% for annual commercial and horticulture crops. The difference in premium from farmers' contributions to the actuarial premium rate is subsidised by the government. As under NAIS, the government provides insurers with stop-loss reinsurance for loss costs above 35% or when loss ratios exceed 350% in a given season to facilitate the large growth of PMFBY and potentially limited international reinsurance capacity. Under PMFBY, the panel of insurers was expanded compared with under mNAIS.

State governments issue open tenders for insurers to bid for districts and crops grouped in clusters, which include different crop types in 3–15 districts that show various degrees of risks. For the bids, insurers provide the state government with actuarial premium rates for each crop and district within a cluster based on an average 10 years of historical yields from CCEs. The bidding process is mainly undertaken for a single crop season and the main criterion for an insurer to win the cluster is often the lowest premium quoted. Government agencies and approved private organisations conduct CCEs at harvest time and provide the recorded yield information within a month to insurers and other stakeholders. CCEs are increasingly supported by satellite imagery and drones and through the presence of insurers.

---

[61] Bhushan, C. and Kumar, V., 2017: Pradhan Mantri Fasal Bima Yojana: An Assessment. Centre for Science and Environment, New Delhi, 40p.

The introduction of PMFBY has led to significant growth, with a premium volume of US$3.2 billion achieved in the 2016/2017 season, making India the third largest agricultural insurance market on a global scale and the largest market for AYII. PMFBY is clearly an improvement compared with the earlier NAIS and mNAIS, but challenges remain in (i) pricing AYII on 10 years of yield data, which can lead to over- or underestimation of risk, (ii) delays in CCEs causing late insurance payments, and (iii) reinsurance incepting before risk clusters are tendered with insurers, with reinsurance terms priced on unknown portfolio compositions.

USA

AYII was introduced as a pilot scheme for selected crops and regions in 1993 under the Group Risk Plan (GRP), where catastrophe risk protection for low yields at the level of a county was provided. GRP was subsequently modified into the current area-yield production (AYP). Empirical evidence has shown that a farmer's choice between AYII and farm-level yield insurance such as MPCI and revenue covers typically depends on a trade-off between higher basis risk under AYII and higher premium costs for MPCI products.[62] The importance of AYP has been decreasing, from 12 188 policies sold under GRP in 2011 to 4383 policies sold under AYP in 2017, with a premium volume of US$9.4 million.

Based on GRP, Group Risk Income Protection (GRIP) was implemented as an area-based RI product at a resolution of a county and subsequently transformed into (i) area revenue protection (ARP) with increasing guarantees in case harvest prices are above base (planting) prices, and (ii) area revenue with harvest price exclusion (ARPwHPE) with a guarantee only if harvest prices are below base prices. In 2017, 11 828 ARP policies were issued for a premium volume of US$133 million while ARPwHPE generated a premium volume of US$809 000 through 189 policies. The average weighted loss ratio of ARP and ARPwHPE reached 88% (2011–2017).

Challenges of Area-Yield Index Insurance

While limited adverse selection and moral hazard and lower administrative costs are key advantages of AYII compared with farm-yield based insurance products, AYII induces inherent basis risk. Basis risk arises as area-yields do not entirely reflect the volatility of farm yield, which can be highly variable, driven by factors such as elevation, soil type, drainage and irrigation extent, weather patterns, input supplies and management practices (Section 4.4). Generally, basis risk under AYII programmes increases with heterogeneity in production conditions. Several studies have shown that the standard deviation of crop yields at farm level compared with more aggregated levels (e.g. county or sub-district) can decrease up to five times, with a usual aggregation bias of factor two.[63] Using highly aggregated yield data (e.g. at resolutions of a province or state) is not suitable for AYII products that indemnify individual farmers and results in inefficient products.

---

[62] Deng, X. et al., 2007: Is there a viable market for area-based crop insurance? *Amer. J. Agr. Econ.*, 89(2), 508–19.

[63] Claassen, R. and Just, R.E., 2011: Heterogeneity and distributional form of farm-level yields. *Amer. J. Agr. Econ.*, 93 (1), 144–60.

INSURANCE TERMS

As with MPCI, AYII relies on observed area-based yield that is typically available from sampling surveys of government entities (Section 4.4). Area-yield insurance schemes generally follow administrative boundaries, although the use of agro-climatological zones would be more appropriate. One exception is the AYII scheme in Quebec (Canada), where indexes are based on contiguous and not administrative zones. The investigation of an optimal AYII contract where the policyholder can vary the insured yield and select a coverage level shows that while the optimum yield depends on the policyholder's degree of risk aversion and the level of premium costs, the selection of coverage level does not depend on these factors under the framework of the policyholder's utility function.[64]

Guaranteed Yields

Guaranteed yields, which are also called insured yields or trigger yields, are determined as the straight average or the Olympic average (omits the highest and lowest yield value) from the most recent historical observations, with the guaranteed yield (GY) calculated as:

$$GY = y_{Average} \times coverage$$

In some markets (e.g. India), yields in years with severe disasters as declared by government agencies are removed from the yield observations that are used to calculate guaranteed yields for AYII, the rationale being that very low yields should not be considered for the calculation of the expected yield. In most markets, producers can select the coverage level between 70% and 85% in 5% increments; however, there are AYII programmes where coverage levels are determined by the insurer in function of the risk in a given area and for a given crop type.

As an alternative to average historical yields, the projected guaranteed yield (GY_p) includes the expectation of yield for the next insurance period based on trends in historical yields and is calculated as:

$$GY_p = y_{Forecast} \times coverage$$

Using $y_{Forecast}$ has the advantage that trends in observed yields are respected while using $y_{Average}$ can underestimate (overestimate) expected yields in case of strong positive (negative) trends in the observed yields and therefore add to basis risk.

Sum Insured and Indemnity

The sum insured (SI) per surface unit under an AYII policy is defined through:

$$SI = GY \times Price$$

with GY as the guaranteed yield either as the average of the most recent historical years or based on trend projections and with *Price* determined from (i) average historical spot

[64] Mahul, O., 1999: Optimum area-yield crop insurance. *Amer. J. Agr. Econ.*, 81(1), 75–82.

market or government minimum support prices or (ii) futures market prices. Prices are often set by the insurer, but in some markets (e.g. the USA), the farmer can choose the price level within a range of 60–100% of the price notified by the insurer and additionally select a scale factor (ranging from 90% to 150%) relative to the sum insured. The indemnity (I) is typically linear relative to the sum insured and is defined through:

$$I = AP \times Price \times \max[GY - AY, 0]$$

with AY as the actual yield from competent government resources based on agricultural surveys and stratified sampling (Section 4.4) and AP as the area planted of an individual policyholder expressed in surface units.

AGGREGATE-YIELD INDEX INSURANCE

Aggregate yield index covers (AYICs) are an extension of AYII in that coverage is defined not only over one area but often over several areas, e.g. counties or provinces. AYICs are gaining interest from agribusinesses to manage costs and earnings through volume volatility driven by volatility in yield and/or area harvested that results in lower than expected crop volume. Insurance contracts typically contain a provision to adjust volume-based triggers when area planted and/or area harvested falls below a predefined threshold, e.g. 90% of the average area planted of the last five years. AYICs also contain a clause that allows for adjustments of market shares of sourced commodities. The payout function of AYICs is typically linear in that a production shortfall below the trigger is compensated through a pre-agreed amount which is independent of the amount of shortfall and is defined in function of gross margin or certain fix costs (e.g. for infrastructure or commissioned transportation). United Grain Growers (UGG) was probably the first grain handling company to purchase AYICs to hedge against weather-related grain volume volatility over several Canadian provinces and grain types.

AYICs are suitable for crops only where the volatility of yields (i.e. biomass) has a direct financial impact on costs or earnings of an agribusiness. While most field crops qualify for AYIC structures, sugarcane for example is an exception, as the sucrose content is not a direct function of yield (biomass) and excessive rainfall during the growing season and particularly during harvest time lowers sucrose levels but not yields. In such cases, risk transfer through WII or weather derivatives is more appropriate than yield-based structures. Similarly, for horticulture and plantation crops, where yield is a function of the age of the plant and adverse weather conditions in the previous season (e.g. drought or frost) can impact yield in following season, AYICs are highly challenging to develop.

Sources of Crop Production Volumes

AYICs require crop production as a function of yield and area harvested of the underlying areas (e.g. counties or sub-districts) and the share of the market production of an agribusiness for processing, storage or transportation. Usually, crop production data are available from (i) government production surveys, which provide an assessment of the production and area harvested (or planted) in an area, (ii) grain elevators and terminals, which measure the delivered production of an individual producer, which, aggregated over a given area, is equal to or lower than government production records, and (iii) own yield records of an agribusiness, which is common under contract-farming arrangements. Often agribusinesses' trust in government yield records is limited and delays in yield reporting are common issues.

Agribusinesses with own production or contracted production (contract farming) often show higher crop yields relative to the area-based yield of government surveys, which can be a function of usage of (i) higher-quality input supplies (e.g. seed, fertiliser, crop protection) and more productive soil, and (ii) more advanced crop management (e.g. irrigation, precision farming, soil treatment, weather forecasts). In such cases, AYICs can be based on an uplift factor of the expected yield of an agribusiness relative to government area yield expectation as long as years with low yields (which will trigger an indemnity) for the area are in proportion with shortfalls experienced by the agribusiness.

Alternatively, AYICs can be defined on site-specific production surveys by third parties, which however adds to the overall cost, particularly if surveys are conducted over wider areas. Outputs from mechanistic crop models (Section 4.4) or yield forecast models can be used as long as the agribusiness accepts model outputs and the insurer has access to historical data. When an agribusiness owns or contracts most of an area's production and therefore determines the official production records, AYICs usually require that production is to be verified by an independent third party.

Aggregate Crop Shortfall Insurance in Canada

Grain handling companies are exposed to a variety of risks, including reduced revenues due to low grain production and high fixed costs in drought years. UGG in Canada was probably the first grain-processing corporation to use AYIC to hedge against weather-related grain volume volatility across several Canadian provinces and grain types. Through several mergers in the Canadian grain handling industry, the original grain volatility insurance product was maintained at least until Glencore, a large commodity company, bought the business in 2012.

United Grain Growers

UGG was founded in 1906 as a farmers' cooperative and became a public company in 1993, having a market share of 15% in grain handling in Canada in 1999. UGG operated four main business segments: (i) grain handling services to identify sources of grains and oilseeds for delivery to exporters and domestic processors and operation of 105 grain elevators in 2000, (ii) crop production services to provide inputs to farmers, (iii) livestock services to deliver inputs to cattle, hog and poultry farms, and (iv) business communications. Services for grain handling and crop production contributed over 80% to UGG's CA$209 million income in 1999.

The process of being listed on the Toronto Stock Exchange in 1993 and requirements to disclose risk exposures led UGG to implement enterprise risk management. A risk assessment in 1997 revealed that UGG was exposed to 47 types of risks and that six of those had potentially large impacts on earnings: environmental liability, impacts of weather events on grain volume, counterparty risk, credit risk, commodity price risk and inventory risks.[65] Adverse weather conditions and lower available grain volumes from different provinces and grain types were considered as one of the main non-managed risks.

---

[65] Harrington, S.E. et al., 2002: Enterprise risk management: the case of United Grain Growers. *J. Appl. Corp. Finance*, 14(4), 71–81.

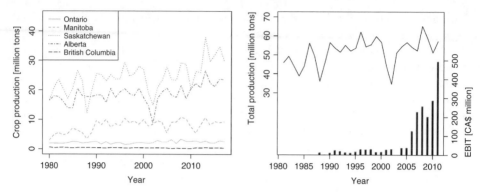

FIGURE 6.6   Left: Production of barley, canola, oats, wheat and flaxseed in five Canadian provinces, 1980–2017. Right: Production of the same main crops as Left (solid line) and EBIT for the grain handling divisions of United Grain Growers, 1988–2000, Agricore United, 2001–2006 and Viterra, 2007–2011 (columns).
Data source: Statistics Canada and Annual Reports of United Grain Growers, Agricore United and Viterra.

Grain handling is a high-volume and low-margin business where fixed costs for grain elevators are 80–85% of the total costs. Large shortfalls in available grain volume can severely impact revenues when total costs cannot be covered and additional funds are required from capital markets. Following the 1988 drought, UGG incurred a reduction in earnings before interest and tax (EBIT) in grain handling from CA\$12 million (1988) to CA\$1 million (1989) when grain volumes decreased significantly in Saskatchewan (Figure 6.6). A regression analysis revealed that June temperatures and July rainfall explained 60–70% of the annual variation in crop yields in most provinces.[66]

To manage grain volume volatility, UGG initially explored weather derivatives, but financial institutions were not able and willing to hedge the risk. UGG then purchased an AYIC for a three-year term (2000–2002), with an annual limit of CA\$35 million above its retention and a maximum limit of CA\$80 million over the three-year period. The grain volume insurance worked as a put option on grain volume where UGG obtained a payout for its 15% share of the grain volume produced over different provinces if the industry grain volume, as measured by the Canadian Grain Commission, was below the average of the last five years. The contract contained a provision to adjust for changes in UGG's market share over time and grain products which included barley, canola, oats, wheat, flaxseeds and certain types of peas. Each tonnage of shortfall was indemnified using UGG's gross margin per tonne of grain shipment.

During the three-year period, Saskatchewan and Alberta experienced a drought in the summer of 2001 and a severe drought in the summer of 2002. As a result, industry-wide exports of grains and oilseeds reduced by 17% and shipments declined by 27%. The grain handling industry, including UGG, experienced earnings that were significantly lower than fixed costs related to infrastructure. As a result, UGG's EBIT from grain handling for 2001/2002 reduced by CA\$35 million and dropped by CA\$43.5 million in 2002/2003.

---

[66] Harrington, S. and Niehaus, G., 2003: United Grain Growers: enterprise risk management and weather risk. *Risk Management and Insurance Review*, 6(2), 193–217.

The AYIC paid CA$7.5 million (equivalent to 21% of the CA$35 million cover) in 2001 and an additional CA$4.6 million in 2002, helping UGG to maintain its earnings and cash flows.

From Agricore United to Viterra
In 2001, Agricore, a large Canadian grain handling company, bought UGG and became Agricore United. Agricore United bought a three-year AYIC protecting market share and profit margin per ton of grain handled with a CA$25 million annual limit and an overall limit of CA$52.8 million over the three-year term. In 2007, when the Saskatchewan Wheat Pool bought Agricore United and formed a listed company called Viterra, an AYIC was bought in 2008 and was reinsured by international markets as an aggregate excess of loss (AXOL) contract. The cover included production-related losses from (i) climatic perils including drought, excess rainfall, flood, wind, hail, frost and excess temperature, (ii) biological perils including insects, pests and wildlife damage, and (iii) natural perils including fire, lightning, earthquake and volcanic eruption. The agreement covered oats, barley, peas, flaxseeds and canola in the provinces of Alberta, Saskatchewan, Manitoba and British Columbia. The AXOL provided for a limit of CA$60 million, with a portion of the capacity committed for a three-year term.

From Viterra to Glencore
In 2009, Viterra bought the Australian Barley Board to expand its global footprint, to lower transport costs by shipping grain from Australia (rather than from Canada) to the growing Asian markets and to hedge against weather risks with grain production in two hemispheres. To manage grain production volatility and impacts on revenues for the joint operation in Canada and Australia, Viterra bought an AYIC over CA$75 million capacity in 2011. In 2012, Glencore, one of the largest global commodity companies, bought Viterra and based on the best knowledge, Glencore was retaining grain volume volatility under its globally diversified balance sheet.

PRICING

The pricing approach for AYII contracts follows the same methodology used for MPCI covers (Section 6.5) but with the difference that standardised historical insurance claims (where available) and mostly area-based yields are required with no subsequent adjustment to reflect farm-based yields. As consistent and standardised historical claims data are often limited, and AYII directly relies on area-yield data, most pricings directly use historical yield data at a given resolution.

Pricing with Yield Time Series
Historical area-yield data are first examined for outliers and inconsistencies and if statistically significant, yields are detrended using various statistical methods (Section 4.4). Special attention needs to be given to the level of inhomogeneity of production in function of soil types, climate and management approaches to understand potential variability of yields and trends. Linear detrending is the most common approach, particularly for shorter-yield time series and in the presence of strong trends, an investigation into factors that drive the trend (e.g. increased irrigation, new crop cultivars or better input supplies) is essential, particularly if surrounding areas show a similar

trend. For AYII in the USA, trends in observed yields are addressed through a piece-wise linear approach (Section 4.4) in that spline regression techniques are applied to estimate three linear segments with different slopes.

The decision to detrend yields and to base guaranteed yields on the trend (fore-casted yield) or on past averages can have a significant impact on average yields and risk premium rates. Further, ignoring trends in area-yields and using past average yields can lead to the under- or overestimation of guaranteed yields, high basis risk and low acceptability of the products in the market. Equally, wrong representations of yield densities can lead to rates that are not risk adequate and to increased basis risk in general.

With longer-yield time series that are judged to include a reasonable spectrum of yield realisations (particularly low yields which will trigger an indemnity under AYII), the expected loss (*EL*) can be determined through a historical burning cost (HBR) method as:

$$EL(x) = Emax[\gamma\mu - x, 0] = Prob[x < \gamma\mu][\gamma\mu - E(x \mid x < \gamma\mu)]$$

where γ is the coverage level and μ is the expected yield.

With shorter-yield time series and series that are judged not to represent ade-quate yield volatility on the observations, a parametric or non-parametric PDF is used to obtain a wider range of possible yield realisations $f(x)$ (Section 4.4). The EL is defined through:

$$EL(x) = \int_{-\infty}^{\infty} f(x)dx\left(\gamma\mu - \int_{-\infty}^{\infty} yx(x)dx / \int_{-\infty}^{\infty} f(x)dx\right) with \mu = \int_{-\infty}^{\infty} xf(x)dx$$

The choice of $f(x)$ determines the EL and the resulting base rate or pure risk rates. In markets where producers can choose a scale factor under AYII (e.g. the USA), this needs to be included in the pricing.[67] The EL is subsequently transformed and expressed in the form of a risk rate or base rate. With highly stable yields as often experienced in production systems with high irrigation extents, base rates can be low or even zero (i.e. no historical yield or modelled yield has triggered the cover), even though a certain prob-ability of loss exists. Insurers address base rates that are low or zero in smoothing base rates using neighbouring areas and introducing minimum rates to obtain spatially con-sistent rates. For some AYII schemes, a catastrophe loading is added, which for example in the USA is based on state levels, with two standard deviations lower than the average of yields of the last four normal (non-catastrophic) years.[68]

Example of Area-Yield Index Insurance Pricing

The example of corn in Adams County (Illinois, USA) is used to demonstrate the level of difference in risk premium rates at coverage levels of 75% and 85% depending on

---

[67] Deng, X. et al., 2007: Is there a viable market for area-based crop insurance? *Amer. J. Agr. Econ.*, 89(2), 508–19.

[68] Goodwin, B.K. and Ker, A.P., 1998: Nonparametric estimation of crop yield distributions: Implications for rating group-risk crop insurance contracts. *Amer. J. Agr. Econ.*, 80(1), 139–53.

the number of years of data used, detrended yields and observed yields, and using different PDFs on detrended yield residuals.

Risk Rates Based on Observed Yield
First, a trend analysis is undertaken through linear detrending, which reveals a statistically significant positive trend for the period of 1968–2015 (Figure 6.7). Using the observed yields and therefore ignoring the positive yield trend leads to significantly higher risk premium rates (4.22–12.13%) compared with detrended yields (0.26–1.10%) at a coverage of 75% and 85% (Figure 6.7). This is an expected outcome as with positive yield trends, the use of the observations for pricing leads to an overestimation of risk as historical yields were significantly lower compared with the more recent yields (on which guaranteed yields are defined) and trigger high payouts, which require a high-risk rate. The approach to defining the guaranteed yield influences the risk premium rates, with all available years producing the lowest risk rates and with projected yields resulting in the highest rates for both the 75% and 85% coverage levels. Given the positive trend, the use of detrended data for all available years and a guaranteed yield based on projections from the trend is the most suitable approach to pricing an AYII for corn in Adams County and produces risk rates of 1.10% at 75% and 2.23% at 85% coverage (Figure 6.7).

Risk Rates Based on Modelled Yield
With 48 years of observed yields available and the presence of both high and low yield realisation, using the detrended observations would be adequate to derive risk rates. This was tested in using PDFs to increase the range of possible yield variability in applying two parametric distributions (normal and beta) and a non-parametric kernel method to derive risk rates at coverage of 75% and 85% (Figure 6.8). The results show

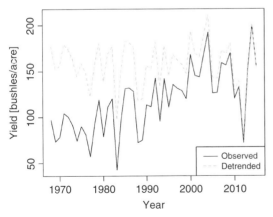

Detrending	Guaranteed yield	Coverage	Rate
Yes	Last 5 years	75%	0.76%
Yes	All years	75%	0.26%
Yes	**From trend**	**75%**	**1.10%**
No	Last 5 years	75%	8.73%
No	All years	75%	4.22%
No	From trend	75%	12.13%
Yes	Last 5 years	85%	1.22%
Yes	All years	85%	0.54%
Yes	**From trend**	**85%**	**2.23%**
No	Last 5 years	85%	12.83%
No	All years	85%	6.97%
No	From trend	85%	7.64%

FIGURE 6.7 Left: Observed and linearly detrended corn yields in Adams County (Illinois, USA), 1968–2015. Right: Risk premium rates for corn in Adams County (Illinois, USA) based on detrended and observed yield data for coverage levels of 75% and 85% and guaranteed yield based on the last five years, all years and projected yields, from the linear trend with the most suitable approach (in bold).
Data source: NASS.

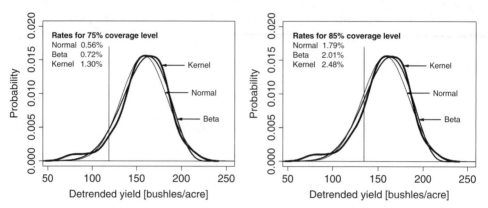

FIGURE 6.8 Risk premium rates derived for linearly detrended corn yields in Adams County (Illinois, USA), 1968–2015, using a normal probability density function (Normal), a beta probability density function (Beta) and a non-parametric kernel function (Kernel) for Left: coverage level 75% and Right: coverage level 85%.
Data source: NASS.

that risk rates with the normal distribution are 0.56% (75% coverage) and 1.79% (85%), which are well below the 1.10% and 2.23% obtained from the detrended yield observations alone. It is well known that the normal distribution is symmetrical (i.e. equal weights are given to low and high yield realisations) and does not adequately describe the nature of crop yields (Section 4.4).

Risk rates derived from the beta distribution reach 0.72% (75% coverage) and 2.01% (85%) and are more comparable to the rates obtained from the detrended observed yields. The non-parametric kernel distribution produces slightly more conservative risk rates of 1.3% (75% coverage) and 2.48% (85%).

6.9 WEATHER INDEX INSURANCE

WII uses indices that are defined through weather parameters to indemnify losses which are closely related to actual losses in crop production. WII is based on the concept of weather derivatives and has been used in agriculture in the form of insurance since the early 2000s. In agricultural markets with predominately small farms, index-based crop insurance products (including WII) are considered viable and efficient alternatives to indemnity-based insurance and are often the only feasible option to facilitate risk transfer. The United Nations promotes the use of WII as a soft climate change adaptation measure for low- and middle-income countries and multilateral finance institutions have been supporting the development of a WII programme for ex-ante financing.

Key advantages of WII compared with indemnity-based products include (i) limited or eliminated information asymmetries and moral hazard as premiums are independent of participation rates and risk levels of individual insureds,[69] (ii) lower costs as

---

[69] Berg, E. and Schmitz, B. 2008: Weather-based instruments in the context of whole-farm risk management. *Agr. Finance Rev.*, 68(1), 119–33.

payouts are settled through weather station data and analysed and classified into risk groups,[70] and (iii) faster payouts as weather data are generally available within days. Compared with yield-based insurance, WII can cover individual weather events rather than the cumulative consequence of low yields and is generally more easily available than yield data. However, the overall uptake of index-based crop insurance in small-holder structures and with agribusinesses has been slower than expected. The effectiveness of newly developed WII covers for potential policyholders in terms of financial costs and benefits (hedging efficiency) has been analysed using expected utility functions, expected shortfall and spectral risk measures.[71] In practice, the hedging efficiency of weather indices is hardly assessed by insurers and is assumed to be acceptable for predominately risk-averse potential insurance buyers.

WEATHER INDEX INSURANCE MARKETS

WII has been implemented in different markets, with the largest programme run in India under the Weather-Based Crop Insurance Scheme (WBCIS), providing complex covers for horticulture and field crops. In Asia, WII pilots are in operation in China, Bangladesh and Sri Lanka. Africa has seen a larger number of WII programmes to cover various crop types using both weather station data and satellite-based weather parameters.[72] In Latin America, Mexico was the first country to introduce WII, in 2003, as a macro-level rainfall deficit cover for state governments which are responsible for distributing the indemnity to smallholders. In some markets, weather indices are used in conjunction with indemnity-based crop insurance, with double triggers where first weather indices need to be triggered before losses are adjusted onsite. Increasingly, agribusinesses enquire about WII as hedges against production volatility and related fluctuations in revenues, earnings or fixed costs.

India

WII was introduced by ICICI Lombard, a leading Indian insurer, with support of the World Bank in 2003 and was linked to agricultural loans. The pilot scheme included groundnut and castor farmers in one district in Andhra Pradesh and was gradually expanded for other crop types in eight states. In 2004, IFFCO Tokio General Insurance developed a rainfall index scheme for Andhra Pradesh, Karnataka and Gujarat and the AICI implemented rainfall insurance (Varsha Bima) in 10 states to cover deficit rainfall over different crop phases including sowing failure. In 2005, the first weather insurance contracts were implemented for horticulture crops, including mangoes (excess rainfall, frost, temperature volatility, wind) and apples (frost chilling units, temperature, rainfall).

---

[70] Barnett, B.J. and Mahul, O., 2007: Weather index insurance for agriculture and rural areas in lower-income countries. *Amer. J. Agr. Econ.*, 89 (5), 1241–47.

[71] Conradt, S. et al., 2015: Tailored to the extremes: Quantile regression for index-based insurance contract design. *Agr. Econ.*, 46, 537–47.

[72] Tadesse, M.A. et al., 2015: Weather index insurance for managing drought risk in smallholder agriculture: Lessons and policy implications for sub-Saharan Africa. *Agr. Food Econ.*, 3(26), 1–21.

Weather-Based Crop Insurance Scheme (2007–2015)
Commissioned by the government, AICI developed the WBCIS and started a pilot for 20 crop types in the 2007 Kharif season.[73] WBCIS benefited from government premium subsidies between 25% and 80% depending on the region and crop type, with an average subsidy of 63%. Subsequently, private insurers participated in WBCIS, which led to a considerable growth through agricultural cooperatives and insurance agents that are part of the network of large multi-line insurers. WBCIS premium rates were actuarially determined but with a cap of 8–10% for food crops and oilseeds and 12% for commercial crops. WBCIS was compulsory for loanee farmers but insurance penetration with non-loanee farmers remained low.

Between 2007 and 2014, AICI, the main provider of WBCIS, incurred a loss cost of 6.5% and a loss ratio of 68.5%, with an average original premium rate of 9.5%. In 2015, WBCIS used over 50 different types of weather indices, with most covers being multicover and multiphase indices. Key constraints that limited further growth included (i) the low density of weather stations in some areas, which insurers tried to overcome by renting weather stations during the crop insurance season, and (ii) time periods of 30–75 days until weather data were received from government agencies, causing delays in claims settlements.

Restructured Weather-Based Crop Insurance Scheme (Since 2016)
In 2016, when crop insurance programmes were redefined in India (Section 6.8), WBCIS was transformed into the Restructured Weather-Based Crop Insurance Scheme (RWBCIS).[74] As with WBCIS, RWBCIS covers food crops (cereals, millets and pulses), oilseeds and commercial/horticultural crops against adverse weather conditions including (i) rainfall through deficit rainfall, excess rainfall, unseasonal rainfall, rainy days, dry spells and dry days, (ii) temperature, particularly high temperature (heat) and low temperature, (iii) relative humidity, and (iv) wind speed. Under RWBCIS, hailstorm and cloud burst are covered as an endorsement with onsite loss adjustment. RWBCIS premium rates for farmers are determined as flat rates following the convention of the new area-yield index programme called *PMFBY* (Section 6.8), with the government compensating the difference between the flat rate and the actuarial premiums in the form of subsidies.

As under all government crop insurance schemes, insurers obtain RWBCIS business through tenders with state governments, in quoting premium rates for given weather index structures. The State Level Coordination Committee on Crop Insurance provides the insurer with the structure of weather indices and facilitates meetings between insurers and agronomists to determine (i) correlations between weather parameters and yield data, (ii) key features of term sheets, including triggers and indemnity functions, (iii) sum insured per reference unit of insurance, and (iv) automatic weather and rain gauge stations to be used for insurance purposes.

The premium volume for RWBCIS for 2016/2017 reached close to US$250 million, with the Kharif season contributing US$143 million. As such, RWBCIS is by far the largest WII programme at a global scale and has been a role model for pilots in other parts of the world.

---

[73] Clarke, D.J. et al., 2012: Weather Based Crop Insurance in India. Policy Research Working Paper 5985, World Bank, Washington DC, 310p.
[74] Department of Agriculture, 2016: Operational Guidelines – Restructured Weather-based crop insurance scheme. Department of Agriculture, Cooperation and Farmers Welfare, New Delhi, 11p.

Challenges of Weather Index Insurance

Key reasons for the slow adaptation with smallholders include (i) basis risk, which is inherent to all index-based products and occurs through the imperfect correlation between the index and actual crop production losses, (ii) coverage, which is limited to perils directly measurable at weather stations, e.g. flood and hail are difficult to insure with WII alone, (iii) affordability of premiums for policyholders, (iv) lack of weather and yield data or unreliable data, (v) lack of understanding of WII concepts by policies and insurers, and (vi) mistrust of policyholders towards WII indemnity structures and insurance companies.[75] Insurers are often reluctant to invest in WII due to high initial costs for weather data and they see WII as easy for potential competitors to replicate. Specialised producers (e.g. horticulture, viticulture) and the agribusiness industry often perceive WII as complex and costly, with the additional challenges of relating revenues to a particular weather event that is parameterised through weather variables alone.

Basis Risk

Basis risk is one of the key limitations in the widespread use of WII. It has been intensively analysed and classified into (i) spatial basis risk, which occurs through the variability of weather patterns at the insured location relative to the location of the weather station; despite the common practice to only insure locations in relatively homogeneous terrain within a circle of 15–20 km of the next weather station, local microclimates are difficult to parameterise, (ii) temporal basis risk, which arises when periods/phases of indices are not aligned with the actual crop growth phases; crop growth phases vary each season according to the cultivar and planting dates are often determined as a function of soil conditions and weather forecasts, and (iii) product basis risk, which occurs when the index fails to quantify the meteorological perils intended to be insured.

Spatial basis risk can be reduced through (i) insurance of areas susceptible to highly covariate weather variables (e.g. drought or frost), (ii) gridding weather station data to more accurately determine local weather risk, and (iii) offering WII on a portfolio basis with multiple weather stations as triggers.[76] Measures to reduce temporal basis risk include the use of phenological observations and growing degree days (GDDs) to define growth phases rather than applying static calendrical definitions.[77] Local agronomic experts and outputs of crop models have been used to limit product basis risk and the use of water-capacity indices (rather than pure precipitation indices) has been suggested for drought.[78]

---

[75] Patt A. et al., 2010: How much do smallholder farmers understand and want insurance? Evidence from Africa. *Global Environ. Change,* 20, 153–61.

[76] Norton, M.T. et al., 2013: Quantifying spatial basis risk for weather index insurance. *Journal of Risk Finance,* 14(1), 20–34.

[77] Dalhaus, T. and Finger, R., 2016: Can gridded precipitation data and phenological observations reduce basis risk of weather index–based insurance? *Weather Clim. Soc.,* 8, 409–19.

[78] Kellner, U. and Musshoff, O., 2011: Precipitation or water capacity indices? An analysis of the benefits of alternative underlyings for index insurance. *Agric. Sys.,* 104(8), 645–53.

WEATHER INDICES IN AGRICULTURE

In most agricultural production systems, crop growth is driven by rainfall and temperature, which often explains a major part of yield volatility, particularly in rainfed systems. Therefore, WII has been developed for adverse rainfall (cumulative anomalies, deficit and excess rainfall, dry days) and/or temperature conditions (heat and frost days) in predominately rainfed agricultural systems (Table 6.8). While there is demand for WII to cover plant pests and diseases, structuring such indices is highly complex as weather conditions must reflect the onset of the diseases as well as the severity over different growth phases.[79] For example, conductive conditions for potato blight for severity level 1 include (i) relative humidity ≥90% between the time of 16:00 and 18:00 and an average temperature of 7.2–11.6°C, or (ii) relative humidity ≥90% between 13:00 and 15:00 with 11.7–15°C, or (iii) relative humidity ≥90% for 10–12 hours with 15.1–26.6°C.[80] Thresholds of conductive conditions are based on field and laboratory experiments or epidemic plant disease models.[81]

Index Structures

The structure of WII cover must reflect the relevance of meteorological variables in terms of actual losses (e.g. crop yield reduction) and contain a minimalised level of basis risk. Weather indices used in agriculture can be classified as cumulative indices, multiphase indices and multicover indices, which are often combined into one WII structure. Whether a cumulative, a multiphase or a multicover index is best suited for a particular risk largely depends on the underlying data, the loss-driving peril and the availability of weather and agricultural data.

Cumulative Indices
Cumulative indices cover the entire crop growth phase through a single parameter (e.g. cumulative rainfall) or multiple parameters (e.g. cumulative rainfall, consecutive number of dry days and heat days), with a payout for deviations against average values.

Multiphase Indices
Multiphase indices contain payout functions per crop growth phase (i.e. per phenological stage) based on the perception that meteorological variables are more critical for a certain crop growth phase (e.g. rainfall during the flowering phase) than the entire growth cycle. Multiphase indices can consit of single or multiple weather variables.

Multicover Indices
Multicover indices are based on combinations of indices that include (i) indices that reflect intensities (e.g. rainfall amounts) with frequency (e.g. number of dry days), or

---

[79] Norton, M., 2016: Applying weather index insurance to agricultural pest and disease risks. *Int. J. Pest Manage.*, 62(3), 195–204.
[80] Raposo, R. et al., 1993: Evaluation of potato blight forecasts modified to include weather forecasts: A simulation analysis. *Phytopathol.*, 83, 103–8.
[81] Maanen, A. and Xu, X.M., 2003: Modelling plant disease epidemics. *Eur. J. Plant Pathol.*, 109, 669–82.

TABLE 6.8 Overview of the most common weather indices used for agricultural crops.

Variable	Cover Type	Index	Description
Rainfall	Cumulative rainfall (CR)	$CR = \sum_{t=1}^{n} R_t$	Measures the total rainfall over a time period n that reflects the entire crop growth cycle or individual growth phases.
	Deficit rainfall (DR)	$DR = \sum_{t=1}^{n} \min(0, R_{min} - R_t)$ R_{min} represents the tolerance to water constraints of a crop and time period and is generally available from agricultural extension offices, literature or crop models. A more pragmatic way is to determine R_{min} from the rainfall data.	Measures the shortfall of total rainfall over a time period n that reflects the entire crop growth cycle or individual growth phases below a reference rainfall level of R_{min}.
	Excess rainfall (ER)	$ER = \sum_{t=1}^{n} \max(0, R_t - R_{max})$ R_{max} represents the excess water tolerance of a crop and time period and is generally available from agricultural extension offices, literature or crop models. A more pragmatic way is to determine R_{max} from the rainfall data.	Measures the excess of total rainfall over a time period n that reflects the entire crop growth cycle or individual growth phases above a reference rainfall level of R_{max}.
	Number of dry days (NDD)	$NDD = \max(0, R_{Threshold} - R_t)$ $R_{Threshold}$ reveals the minimum daily rainfall required for a crop and is available from agricultural extension offices or can be determined from the rainfall data. Often $R_{Threshold}$ is set at 0 mm or 2.5 mm per day. An alternative to NDD is the *number of consecutive dry days* (NCDD) where dry days are measured only in a sequence of a certain number of days with rainfall below $R_{Threshold}$.	Measures the number of dry days over a time period that reflects the entire crop growth cycle or individual growth phases with a dry day defined through rainfall below $R_{Threshold}$.
	Number of wet days (NWD)	$NWD = \max(0, R_t - R_{Threshold})$ $R_{Threshold}$ reveals the maximum daily rainfall that a crop can tolerate and is available from agricultural extension offices or can be determined from the rainfall data. Often $R_{Threshold}$ is set at 10 mm per day. An alternative to NWD is the *number of consecutive wet days* (NCWD) where wet days are measured only in a sequence of a certain number with rainfall above $R_{Threshold}$.	Measures the number of wet days over a time period that reflects the entire crop growth cycle or individual growth phases with a wet day defined through rainfall above a threshold rainfall $R_{Threshold}$.

(Continued)

TABLE 6-8 (Continued)

Variable	Cover Type	Index	Description
Temperature	Number of frost days (NFD)	$NFD = \sum_{t=1}^{n} T_{actual} < T_{Threshold}$ $T_{Threshold}$ is the temperature below which a crop suffers freeze and frost damage, set as the lethal minimum temperature (Section 3.6) as available from agricultural extension offices or literature. Often $T_{Threshold}$ is set at 0°C. An alternative to NFD is the *number of consecutive frost days (NCFD)* where frost days are measured only in a sequence of a certain number of days.	Measures the number of days over a time period n with actual temperatures below $T_{Threshold}$.
	Chilling degree hours (CDH)	$CDH = \sum_{t=1}^{n} \max(0, T_{Threshold} - T_t)$ For mid latitudes $T_{Threshold}$ is often set at 7.2°C during the winter months.	The number of hours over winter days when the temperature is below a threshold temperature $T_{Threshold}$ that is necessary for stone fruit trees to prepare buds to enter dormancy and harden (develop freeze resistance) over winter and to develop normal flowers and leaves with warming temperatures.
	Disease conductive days (DCD)	Complex computation including relative humidity (RH) and temperature during certain time periods of a day and plant growth phase, e.g. number of potato blight conducive events: RH >85% for two continuous days and the maximum and minimum temperature on the day to be between 7 and 26°C for four consecutive days.	Measures the temperature above a threshold during days with high relative humidity above a certain level that is conductive to the development of certain plant diseases.
Wind	Highest monthly average daily wind speed (HMADWS)	$HMADW = \max\left\{\dfrac{1}{n}\sum_{t=1}^{n} W\max(t,m)\right\}$	Measures the highest monthly average maximum wind speed, set to reflect occurrence of convective storms.
	Wind speed (WS)	$WS = \sum_{t=1}^{n} \max(0, W_t - W_{\min})$	Measures the upward deviation of wind speed compared to fortnightly average highest monthly average, set to reflect occurrence of severe convective storms.

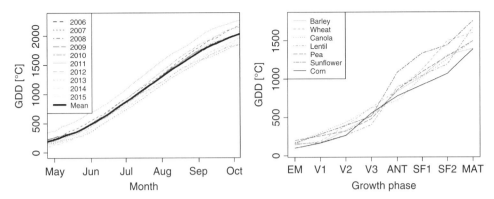

FIGURE 6.9 Left: Cumulative GDDs for corn in Adams County (Illinois, USA), 2006–2015 (1 May–30 September) and the mean cumulative GDDs. Right: Cumulative GDDs for different crop types and growth phases summarised in emergence (EM), vegetative phases (V1, V2, V3), anthesis (ANT), seed filling phases (SF1, SF2) and maturity (MAT) in the Midwest of the USA. *Data source*: NCDC (left plot) and Miller et al. (2001) (right plot).

(ii) cumulative indices (e.g. rainfall amounts over the entire growth phase) that are combined with multiphase indices (e.g. number of dry days per growth phase). Multicover indices are complex but, in some instances, necessary to best describe yield volatility through weather parameters. Multicover indices are often a trade-off between reduced basis risk and the understandability and acceptability of the index structure by policyholders.

Crop Growth Phases
The definition of a WII structure requires the determination of planting and harvest times and in the case of multiphase indices, the division of the crop growth period into different phenological stages. While field crops include up to 10 distinctive phenological growth stages, the main growth phases can be divided into vegetative (sowing to development of plant tissues) and productive (tassel initiation to maturing) phases. Planting and harvest dates as well as individual growth phases are typically determined through crop calendars or derived from growing degree days (GDDs).

Crop Calendars and Phenological Observations
Crop calendars are available from agronomy resources and include typical planting and harvest dates defined through a date or dates within a range of days. However, as planting and harvest dates vary in each season in function of growing conditions (Figure 6.9), using static dates for WII increases basis risk in that variable planting and harvest dates of past seasons are ignored. Besides crop calendars, phenological observations from public networks are available in some countries and reflect past dates of key growth stages, including planting and harvest times, and were found to considerably reduce basis risk through more accurate WII structures.[82]

---

[82] Dalhaus, T. and Finger, R., 2016: Can gridded precipitation data and phenological observations reduce basis risk of weather index–based insurance? *Weather Clim. Soc.*, 8, 409–19.

Growing Degree Days

An alternative to crop calendars and phenological observations is to determine the main phenological stages through GDDs, which has the advantage that planting dates and the main growth stages are kept flexible over historical years, which should result in more accurate WII products. A GDD is a daily measure of heat units over the crop growth cycle and is computed as:[83]

$$GDD = \sum_{t=1}^{n} \max(0, (T_{Average} - T_{Base}))$$

with $T_{Average} = (T_{max} + T_{min})/2$ and with T_{Base} as the temperature above which a crop grows through accumulated heat units. Often, a cut-off method is used to (i) cap the daily maximum temperature at a certain level, above which crop growth does not further increase ($T_{max\,cutoff}$), and (ii) limit the daily minimum temperature below a certain level ($T_{min\,cutoff}$), which often corresponds to T_{Base}. For corn in mid latitudes, $T_{max\,cutoff}$ is typically set at 30°C and $T_{min\,cut\,off}$ as well as T_{Base} at 10°C.

Cumulative GDDs provide a thermal calendar and indicate through accumulated heat units when a certain growth stage occurs, which varies among crop types (Figure 6.9). Based on GDD requirements, individual phenological phases can be predicted from actual or historical temperature observations and provide more accurate physiological estimates than counting calendar days of individual growth phases.[84] GDD-based planting and harvest times, as well as phenological phases that are applied individually to historical crop seasons, can considerably improve the quality of multiphase WII products.[85]

INSURANCE TERMS

A WII contract follows the concept of a put option and is fully defined through the sum insured, the trigger (also called strike), the limit and the modality of the indemnity function. The sum insured is typically determined as (i) the product of average or projected yield and commodity prices, or (ii) the cost of production, including input supplies, labour and machinery/equipment.

Indemnity and Indemnity Function

The indemnity (I) as a monetary value per surface unit (e.g. 1 US$/ha) that is received through the indemnity function for insufficient realisations (deficit) of an underlying weather variable is defined as:[86]

---

[83] McMaster, G.S. and Wilhelm, W.W., 1997: Growing degree-days: one equation, two interpretations. *Agr. Forest Meteorol.*, 87, 291–300.

[84] Miller, P. et al., 2001: Using Growing Degree Days to Predict Plant Stages. Montana State University, 8p.

[85] Conradt, S. et al., 2015: Flexible weather index-based insurance design. *Clim. Risk Manag.*, 10, 106–17.

[86] Vedenov, D.V. and Barnett, B.J., 2004: Efficiency of weather derivatives as primary crop insurance instruments. *J. Agr. Resource Econ.*, 29, 387–403.

$$I = f(i \mid x, Tr, Ex) = x \times f(x) = \begin{cases} 0, if\ i > Tr \\ \dfrac{Tr - i}{Tr - Ex}, if\ Ex < i \leq Tr \\ 1, if\ i \leq Tr \end{cases}$$

with i as the realised value of the underlying weather parameter, x as the sum insured, Tr as the trigger and Ex as the exit below which indemnity seizes. Correspondingly, the indemnity for a if contract that protects against excessive realisations of an underling weather variable i uses $\dfrac{i - Tr}{Ex - Tr}$ if $Tr \leq i < Ex$ and with a payout of 0 *if* $i \geq Ex$ or a payout of 1 *if* $i < Tr$.

In practice, exits aim to reduce exposure and obtain affordable premium rates. Based on the trigger and exit, the limit (L) is defined as $L = Tr - Ex$. The tick size (also called the notional) is the monetary payout for each realisation of the index in function of an underlying weather parameter (e.g. US\$/mm rainfall). The indemnity function defines the modality of payouts and can be (i) linear with proportional payout, (ii) binary with a full payout once the trigger has been reached, or (iii) step-wise in that the payout increases with increasing realisations of the index.

Triggers

Triggers are set to cover past production losses that are reproducible through weather parameters. Standard techniques to establish triggers for WII include (i) realisations of a weather parameter at a certain quantile (e.g. 70%) from the weather observations alone or through modelled distributions,[87] (ii) a given standard deviation (e.g. 50%) above/below the mean weather variable from historical observations, or (iii) determination through polynomial regressions in function of crop yield.[88] In practice, several iterations take place from the first setting of the trigger to the final definition in function of the level of the resulting risk premium rates and market expectations in terms of affordability.

Term Sheets

The specific terms and conditions for WII contracts are stated in term sheets and include the following key components: (i) location of the risk and reference weather station or grid cell identity number in case gridded data or satellite-based climate data are used, (ii) crop season or contract year, crop type and area insured, (iii) type of weather index and for each phase: period (start and end date), trigger(s), exit(s), tick size(s) and limit(s), (iv) premium rate, premium amount and sum insured (per phase and overall total), and (v) any special features such as e.g. rolling limits (Figure 6.10). The term sheet is attached to the general insurance conditions in the policy wording.

---

[87] El Benni, N. et al., 2016: Potential effects of the Income Stabilization Tool (IST) in Swiss agriculture. *Eur. Rev. Agric. Econ.*, 43, 475–502.

[88] Chen, W. et al., 2017: Rainfall index insurance for corn farmers in Shandong based on high-resolution weather and yield data. *Agr. Finance Rev.*, 77(2), 337–54.

TERM SHEET			
STATE	**Rajasthan**	SEASON	**Kharif 2012**
CROP	**Maize**	DISTRICT	**Banswara**
REFERENCE WEATHER STATION	**Notification**	TEHSIL	**All**

DEFICT RAINFALL		PHASE I	PHASE II	PHASE III
RAINFALL	PERIOD from	25 June 2013	16 July 2013	16 Aug 2013
VOLUME	PERIOD to	15 July 2013	15 Aug 2013	30 Sept 2013
	INDEX	Aggregate of rainfall over respective Phases		
	Strike I (<)	100	240	140
	Strike II (<)	53	124	75
	Exit	5	8	10
	Rate I (RS/mm)	10.95	7.59	10.46
	Rate II (RS/mm)	16.42	11.38	15.69
	Maximum Payout (RS)	1300	2200	1700
	TOTAL PAYOUT	5200		

RAINFALL	PERIOD from	1 July 2013
DISTRIBUTION (Single Payout)	PERIOD to	10 Sept 2013
	INDEX	Number of the days in a spell of Consecutive Dry Days
	Strike (≥)	15
	Exit	72
	Payout per Day (RS)	43.86
	TOTAL PAYOUT	2500

EXCESS RAINFALL (Single Payout)		PHASE I	PHASE II	PHASE III
	PERIOD from	25 June 2013	16 July 2013	16 Aug 2013
	PERIOD to	15 July 2013	15 Aug 2013	30 Sept 2013

	INDEX	Maximum of 3 consecutive days' cumulative of rainfall in respective Phases		
	Strike I (<)	120	150	100
	Strike II (<)	285	350	300
	Exit	450	550	500
	Rate I (RS/mm)	3.15	4.40	3.40
	Rate II (RS/mm)	4.73	6.60	5.10
	Maximum Payout (RS)	1300	2200	1700
	TOTAL PAYOUT		5200	

SUM INSURED	7700
Premium (RS)	770
Premium (%)	10.00

FIGURE 6.10 Example of a term sheet as used in Rajasthan (India) for corn in the Kharif 2012 season. The WII protects against severity of deficit rainfall (deficit rainfall cover with three phases), the frequency of deficit rainfall events over the growing season (number of consecutive dry days, one phase) and the frequency of excessive rainfall events (number of consecutive days of cumulative rainfall with three phases), with an *either or* payment for deficit rainfall and excessive rainfall as experiencing both deficit and excessive rainfall over the same growth period was judged to be extremely rare. The sum insured reveals the total maximum payout for the three covers. The reference weather station and the area insured are specified in individualised agreements between the insurer and the policyholder and in case of loanee farmers attaches automatically to the agricultural loan. A Thesil is a sub-unit of a district.
Source: Adapted from State Government of Rajasthan.

PRICING

As weather data can include discontinuities, errors and missing values, statistical methods are used to analyse the weather variables (Section 4.2). The investigation of trends in the weather data is essential as ignoring trends can lead to inefficient WII products and inadequate risk rates. Both parametric (e.g. linear, piece-wise and exponential functions) and non-parametric methods (e.g. moving averages, kernel or ARIMA) can be used to detrend weather data (Section 4.2).

WII is typically priced through (i) the expected loss calculation (ELC) where a PDF is applied to the detrended residuals of the underlying weather variables, which forms the basis of risk rates, or (ii) the HBR method where risk rates are directly calculated from the historical detrended weather variables. The HBR method is more commonly used as a large number of contracts can be efficiently priced and is well suited if weather data are available for at least 15 years.

A correlation analysis between the weather indices and loss proxies, which are commonly yields or damaged area, is of fundamental importance to minimise basis risk. While the overall correlation coefficient provides an indication as to what extent crop yield volatility can be explained by one or several weather parameters, the tail dependency correlation, that describes how well negative (e.g. rainfall deficit) and/or positive (e.g. excessive rainfall) realisations are described by the weather parameter(s), is equally important. Satellite-based weather data, gridded climate data and reanalysis data increasingly support the development and pricing of WII covers (Section 4.2).

Expected Loss Calculation

With the ELC method, the risk premium rate (*RPR*) as expressed in indemnity per currency unit for a WII contract that protects against insufficient relations (deficit) of the underling variable is obtained through:

$$RPR = \int_0^{Ex} h(i)\,di + \int_{Ex}^{Tr} \frac{Tr-i}{Tr-Ex} h(i)\,di$$

with $h(i)$ as the PDF (e.g. Weibull or gamma) of the underlying weather variable i, Tr as the trigger and Ex as the exit. Correspondingly, RPR for a contract that protects against excessive realisations of the underlying weather variable uses:

$$RPR = \int_{Tr}^{Ex} \frac{i-Tr}{Ex-Tr} h(i)\,di + \int_{Ex}^{\infty} h(i)\,di$$

Historical Burn Rate Calculation

Under the HBR method, the observed weather parameters are directly used to define the probability of occurrence under the assumption that (i) payouts based on observed weather variables provide an accurate distribution of potential indemnities, and (ii) weather parameters are stationary, i.e. independent and identically distributed over time. The risk premium rate is calculated by using the average of the indemnity obtained from the underlying data and the sum insured for each contract period over the same time frame.

However, rare occurrences in realisation of the weather parameter, particularly catastrophe-type events, might not have been experienced within the time frame of the observation. This can be addressed through the introduction of a catastrophe loading (*CL*), defined as:[89]

$$CL = \alpha \times \left(\max_t \left[\frac{BC_t}{SI} \right] - RPR_{HBR} + DUF \right)$$

[89] Clarke, D.J. et al., 2012: Weather Based Crop Insurance in India. Policy Research Working Paper 5985, World Bank, Washington DC, 29p.

with α as the insurer's cost of capital, which reflects the return required of capital hold relative to the risk, BC_t as the burning cost in year t, SI as the sum insured, RPR_{HBR} as the risk premium rate obtained through the HBR method and DUF as a data uncertainty factor, which is a loading for missing, incomplete data and the pricing methodology chosen and is often calculated as a function of the standard deviation or the standard errors.

Commercial Premium Rate

Based on the risk premium rate obtained, loadings that include administrative costs and in some cases data uncertainty factors are added to obtain the CPR. Depending on the size of the WII programme and costs for administration, distribution and acquisition of weather data, loadings can be 30–50% of the CPR.

Example of Weather Index Insurance Pricing

The example of corn in Adams County (Illinois, USA) demonstrates the development of a drought index that uses cumulative rainfall and heat days for each historical crop season that is determined through GDDs. The development requires daily weather data, corn yield and an understanding of the production environment.

Production Environment and Drought Occurrence

In Adams county only 0.5% of the corn area is irrigated and a hybrid corn cultivar is typically used. Corn yield data (1968–2015) show production shortfalls in several years (Figure 6.11) and Illinois corn production reports confirm low yields in 1983 (drought), 1988 (drought), 1983 (insect infestations), 1993 (excessive rainfall and lack of heat), 2005 (drought), 2010 (excessive rainfall) and 2012 (drought), which also occurred in surrounding counties. As corn yields show a statistically significant positive trend, the data are linearly detrended (Figure 6.11).

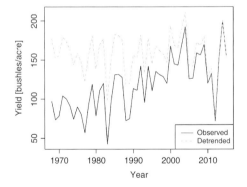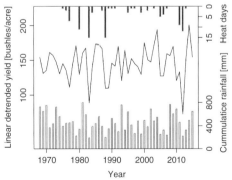

FIGURE 6.11   Left: Observed and linearly detrended corn yields in Adams County (Illinois, USA), 1968–2015. Right: Linear detrended corn yield (left axis, solid line) in Adams County (Illinois, USA), with cumulative rainfall (right axis, columns) and cumulative number of heat days (right axis, columns) for growth periods defined in each year through GDDs.
Data source: NASS and NCDC.

Corn Growth Phases and Weather Parameters
Corn growth phases are calculated using GDDs, with (i) planting dates defined when daily temperatures are above 15°C and cumulative rainfall is of at least 14 mm, and (ii) harvest dates set when 13–15°C GDDs are reached and with a cut-off date for harvest at 30 October. The shortest GDD-based growth phase lasted 126 days (1983) and the longest 173 days (1992).

Daily precipitation and temperature data are available since 1 June 1948 from the weather station at Quincy airport and were aggregated for each GDD-derived corn growth phase (1968–2015). Often rainfall and temperature determine yield in combination, with yield reductions stemming from low rainfall and high temperatures in the form of heat days. Therefore, cumulative seasonal rainfall and cumulative numbers of heat days (days with average temperature > 30°C) are calculated, which both did not show a statistically significant trend.

Correlation Analysis
Cumulative rainfall correlates with +0.23 to detrended corn yields and cannot sufficiently explain yield volatility. Cumulative heat days correlate with −0.68 to detrended yields and with −0.50 to cumulative rainfall, revealing that a WII product for drought needs to include cumulative rainfall and heat days with triggers that can be established through multilinear regression (Figure 6.11).

6.10 SATELLITE-BASED INDEX INSURANCE

Satellite data and imagery have been used to develop a large range of vegetation and biophysical indices that support the monitoring of vegetation at high spatial and temporal resolutions (Section 4.3). Insurance applications use vegetation and biophysical indices to cover drought damage to pasture land and livestock mortality. Satellite-based indices offer valuable alternatives where indemnity-based crop insurance is not feasible or is costly and crop yield and weather data do not allow the development of efficient products.

One of the first satellite-based pasture indices applied for insurance, was developed in Alberta, Canada in 2001. In the USA, pastures and rangeland can be insured for declining productivity through vegetation indices (NDVI) at a resolution of 8 km. In Mexico, the federal and state governments fully subsidise macro-level NDVI covers for payouts to small livestock farmers in case of drought impact on pastures and grazing land that causes high livestock mortality on a grid of 1 km. The NDVI programme in Mexico has rapidly expanded since its implementation in 2007, with 13 million hectares of pasture in six states to 55 million hectares in 20 states in 2010 and a premium volume of US$8.5 million. The use of NDVI for pasture insurance has been investigated in Argentina[90] and has been implemented as a pilot programme in Uruguay.

In Spain, satellite-based insurance for pasture land started in 2001 and is based on 10-day 250 m resolution Moderate Resolution Imaging Spectroradiometer (MODIS)

---

[90] Bacchini, R.D. and Miguez, D.F., 2015: Agricultural risk management using NDVI pasture index-based insurance for livestock producers in south west Buenos Aires province. *Agr. Finance Rev.*, 75(1), 77–91.

to supplement livestock feed in case of drought conditions and produced a premium volume of EUR9.8 million (2011). In India, NDVI in combination with temperature measurements was used for wheat insurance under multiphase weather indices.

Satellite-based vegetation indices have been shown to be able to quantify drought over large spaces and reveal promising applications for semi-arid climates in Africa.[91] Several pilots use NDVI as a measure of drought in semi-arid climates of Senegal, Mali, Ethiopia, Nigeria and Kenya, and resulting crop yield reductions at various geographical resolutions. In Zimbabwe, district-based NDVI insurance is offered for cotton and maize farmers and provides better protection than rainfall-based indices.[92] In Kenya, the Kenya Livestock Insurance Program (KLIP) covers pastoralists against drought-related livestock mortality (Section 7.6).

While remote sensing data are available for over 20 years and are continuously increasing in resolution while becoming at the same time more affordable and more available, several technical factors still limit the wider use of satellite-based insurance.[93] As satellites are replaced and research missions are discontinued, remote sensing data are no longer available and new data from different satellites require a recalibration of insurance indices, e.g. the widely used Advanced Very High Resolution Radiometer (AVHRR) time series was discontinued in January 2010. Further, data from large-swath optical sensors are known for statistical instability due to large background noises, which leads to undetected and misclassified pixel as well as data gaps. Depending on the production environment, basis risk can be significant and requires ground assessment for insurance products (e.g. as in Canada) and recalibration in cases of delayed planting and major changes in crop types and crop rotations.

VEGETATION INDICES

One of the most commonly used vegetation indexes is the NDVI, which is a reasonably good indicator for drought and resulting yield volatility, however with a large variability in correlation to actual yields at field level.[94] NDVI is calculated from the visible and near-infrared satellite imagery and compares crop growth at a given time (e.g. a week) relative to normal conditions, determined from historical imagines over the same time (Section 4.3).

NDVI is considered a valuable insurance approach for range- and grasslands and macro-level risk transfer products in areas with high drought risk with a payout at aggregated level, e.g. to a government entity. However, NDVI as a proxy for field-based crop insurance is considered not suitable as (i) the relationship between yield and NDVI is highly volatile,

[91] Rojas, O. et al., 2011: Assessing drought probability for agricultural areas in Africa with coarse resolution remote sensing imagery. *Remote Sens. Environ.*, 115, 343–52.

[92] Makaudze, E.M. and Miranda, M.J., 2010. Catastrophic drought insurance based on the remotely sensed normalised difference vegetation index for smallholder farmers in Zimbabwe. *Agrekon*, 49(4), 418–32.

[93] De Leeuw, J. et al., 2014. The potential and uptake of remote sensing in insurance: A review. *Remote Sens.*, 6(11), 10888–912.

[94] Turvey, C. and McLaurin, M.K., 2012: Applicability of the Normalized Difference Vegetation Index (NDVI) in index-based crop insurance design. *Weather Clim. Soc.*, 4, 271–84.

(ii) crop rotations would require permanent recalibration of NDVI, and (iii) planting and harvest times are variable and often cannot be reflected in vegetation indices.[95]

Satellite-Based Pasture Insurance in Alberta

The Agriculture Financial Services Corporation (AFSC) in 2001 was one of the first insurers to develop a pasture insurance product that is based on NDVI. As pasture growth conditions are difficult to measure on the ground due to continuous livestock grazing and different grazing management strategies, a satellite-based index insurance product proved to be an efficient approach. The initial version of the index product covered only areas (pixels) with at least 80% native pasture. Based on comparisons of NDVI with actual pasture production from cage clipping systems and correlations between seasonal precipitation and NDVI of 0.65, NDVI was judged as an adequate indicator. However, in some instances, increased weed growth on pasture land in dry seasons led to high basis risk, which resulted in a modification of the product into satellite yield insurance (SYI).

Satellite Yield Insurance
SYI uses pasture yield information that is collected by AFSC during the season to supplement NDVI measurements in years where the correlation between NDVI and production is low. AFSC established risk areas for which the normal expected yield for each pasture type is determined based on recommended cattle carrying capacity. The base yield is set at 80% of the normal expected yield on which insurance coverage is based for every farm in a given risk area. The sum insured (or dollar coverage) is obtained by multiplying the base yield with a uniform price for all pasture types in a risk area. Policyholders can individualise coverage by (i) defining the length of the season as either short (mid-May to end of July) or long (mid-May to end of August), (ii) splitting the short or long season into two sub-seasons, and (iii) allocating insurance coverage ratios for the sub-seasons. SYI is based on a pasture vegetation index (PVI_i) that for a given year i is based on re-scaled NDVI values and the normal $NDVI_N$ and is defined as:

$$PVI_i = NDVI_i - \left(0.8 \times NDVI_N\right)$$

The NDVI measurements are provided from the NOAA satellite network at a 1 km resolution, with data available since 1987. During the pasture season, PVI is calculated for each grid that is identified by a pasture land use mask and is integrated per township over a week. An insurance payment occurs (i) for the full season if the actual PVI is <90% of the average PVI, with a linear payout structure of 2.5% of sum insured for each PVI value of 1, and the full sum insured is compensated at a PVI ≤ 50%, and (ii) for the split seasons if the actual PVI is <85% of the normal PVI, with a linear payout structure of 2.5% of sum insured for each PVI reduction of 1 unit with a full payment for a PVI ≤ 45%.

Performance of Satellite Yield Insurance
In 2016, SYI covered 699 727 ha of pasture land in Alberta and generated a premium volume of US$3 million for an overall liability of US$12 million and with an average loss ratio of 92% (2001–2016).

---

[95] Bokusheva, R. et al., 2016: Satellite-based vegetation health indices as a criteria for insuring against drought-related losses. *Agric. For. Meteorol.*, 220, 200–6.

BIOPHYSICAL INDICES

While NDVI is clearly the most used vegetation index for agricultural risk transfer, newer developments have suggested the use of satellite-based biophysical variables such as the Vegetation Cover Fraction (fCover, Section 4.3) that provide more robust measurements of vegetation properties. The only known satellite-based insurance application that uses fCover is used for pasture in France.

Satellite-Based Pasture Insurance in France

Droughts can significantly reduce quantity and quality of pasture production and based on large losses in the past and a general government initiative to increase risk transfer in agriculture, a pasture insurance pilot was developed in 2010. Traditional crop insurance products are not suitable for grassland and pasture as (i) grassland management systems are highly variable among producers and therefore quantity as well quality is difficult to compare, (ii) pasture lands are harvested several times during the season or are grazed by livestock, which will need permanent monitoring, and (iii) losses in forage production do not appear directly in farm accounts.

Forage Production Indices
In 2016, a forage production index (FPI) based on satellite-derived fCover was piloted and was commercially implemented in 2017. FPI for a given year n (FPI_n) is computed daily as:[96]

$$FPI_n = \sum_i^j \left(fCover_i - NPV \right)$$

with i chosen as 1 February and j as 31 October representing the pasture growth period. *NPV* is the net primary vegetation, which is the biomass that could be harvested, and is subtracted from the fCover. NPV is an empirical value and is based on grassland yield data. The process to compute fCover values is complex and involves the following main steps: (i) daily satellite imagery of 200 m and 250 m resolution is analysed by a vegetation model, an atmospheric model and a soil model to generate daily high-resolution fCover grids, (ii) daily fCover data are aggregated over 10-day periods, (iii) fCover values per land use class (including grassland) and spatial aggregation to 6 km grids are calculated, and (iv) fCover values to daily values, which are used to compute the FPI, are interpolated.

A direct comparison between grassland biomass measurements using a motorised mower and FPI indicates that fCover is an appropriate proxy for grassland biomass production. For the insurance solution, triggers are set as the five-year Olympic average of FPI values (omits the highest and lowest value) and risk rates are determined from the FPI values that are computed for the duration of available satellite data (2000–2015).

---

[96] Roumiguié, A. et al., 2015: Validation of a Forage Production Index (FPI) derived from MODIS fCover time-series using high-resolution satellite imagery: Methodology, results and opportunities. *Remote Sens.*, 7, 11525–50.

6.11 MODEL-BASED INDEX INSURANCE

Model-based indices use meteorological variables and site-specific parameters (mainly soil type, soil profile) to compute (i) water requirement levels through water balance equations, or (ii) crop growth conditions over different time steps during the growing season through crop models (Section 4.4). The use of model-driven indices for crop insurance has been limited so far, which is related to (i) the complexity of the indices and data requirements, (ii) difficulties for policyholders to understand and relate to the indices, and (iii) basis risk in that modelled indices do not accurately reflect yield losses at farm level or within a model grid. Model-based indices have a promising potential for macro-level risk transfer products. The only documented use of modelled indices for crop insurance is with the African Risk Capacity (ARC), where drought risks are covered in different countries through a Water Requirements Satisfaction Index (WRSI). The use of yield outputs from mechanistic crop models for crop insurance has been investigated through academic studies.

WATER-BALANCE EQUATION INDICES (WRSI)

Developed as an agricultural drought index, WRSI is a fundamental part of drought condition monitoring in Africa and Central Asia. WRSI has been shown to be a good indicator of crop performance as it is based on water availability during the growing period and is computed through a water-balance model and a crop-specific linear yield-reduction function.[97] WRSI is used for the monitoring of water deficit during the growing season and reveals the ratio of seasonal actual evapotranspiration of a crop relative to normal seasonal water requirement (Section 3.3).

While initially configured to be used with weather station data, WRSI is increasingly computed from gridded weather and satellite-derived weather data, which have the advantage of generating high-resolution water deficit maps. In an operational context, the Famine Early Warning Systems Network (FEWS-NET) uses satellite- and ground-based rainfall data to compute WRSI values (Geo-WRSI) to monitor agricultural areas for signs of drought.[98]

WRSI Drought Indices used by the African Risk Capacity

African countries are among those most severely affected by droughts and the agricultural sector, as a large contributor to GDP, is particularly exposed. Due to generally low resilience and adaptation, and rainfed agricultural production systems, African countries are feeling the potential impacts of climate change more severely.

Droughts in Africa
Droughts in Malawi cause high losses to the agricultural sector, ranging from a 1.1% reduction in GDP for a five-year drought to a 21.5% reduction for a 25-year event.[99]

---

[97] Frère, M. and Popov, G.F., 1986: Early agrometeorological crop yield forecasting. FAO Plant Production and Protection Paper 73, Rome, 150p.
[98] https://earlywarning.usgs.gov/fews/software-tools/4 (accessed September 2017).
[99] Pauw, K. et al., 2010: Droughts and Floods in Malawi: Assessing the Economy-wide Effects. International Food Policy Research Institute, Washington, 44p.

Lower economic growth causes large budget dislocation, erodes development gains and resilience, requires emergency grain imports at international prices to maintain food security and often needs emergency aid from the international community. Most of the typical ex-post disaster responses force governments to reallocate funds on an ad-hoc basis while appeals for international assistance often arrive late. Today, close to 50% of all emergency multilateral food assistance to Africa is due to natural disasters. Contingent funds that are linked to reliable early warning systems are thought to offer the best solution for providing earlier and more efficient responses to slowly developing weather disasters such as droughts.

Insurance Through African Risk Capacity
The ARC was founded in 2012 to provide members of the African Union fast-disbursing funds in the aftermath of severe droughts. A cost-benefit analysis of ARC for African countries shows that (i) early intervention in developing droughts reduces negative coping actions at household level, (ii) an insurance solution would provide a faster payout compared with traditional emergency appeals for assistance, and (iii) large-scale risk pooling over several countries could save individual countries up to 50% of cost related to emergency funding.[100] For a country to participate in ARC, several requirements need to be fulfilled, including (i) customising the Africa Risk View Software (ARVS) to quantify drought risk and define payout functions for over 20 crop types supported by ARVS, (ii) defining drought exposure and the risk transfer parameters, (iii) formulating a contingency plan of how indemnities are used, and (iv) committing to capacity building.

Africa Risk View Software
ARVS quantifies drought risk and population affected and determines payouts. ARVS uses RFE 2.0 10-day rainfall data at a 0.1° resolution (about 10 km) that are available since 2001 and include ground weather station data and satellite-based weather data (Section 4.2). Alternatively, ARVS can use data from the African Rainfall Estimate Climatology and TAMSAT, which are available for larger parts of Africa since 1983. Rainfall data form an integral part to compute 10-day WRSI, which indicates water deficit during the growing season and expected reductions in crop yield. In ARVS, drought is defined as the negative deviation of the seasonal WRSI compared with normal conditions, which are computed from the previous five seasons. A mild drought is considered at WRSI values between 80% and 90%, a medium drought with values of 70–80% and a severe drought with values below 70% of normal. The vulnerability of the population to mild, medium and severe drought is defined per vulnerability zones, which are regularly updated based on household surveys.

The exposure is defined as the response cost per number of population affected by mild, medium and severe droughts in accordance with a country's contingency plans. Default settings use a response cost of US$100 per person in countries with one rainfall season and US$50 per person and season in countries with two rainfall seasons. Currently, response costs are assumed to be uniform within a country and to represent the average cost over mild, medium and severe droughts. Simulations of ARVS suggest

[100] Clarke, D.J. and Vargas Hill, R., 2013: Cost-Benefit Analysis of the African Risk Capacity Facility. International Food Policy Research Institute (IFPRI) Discussion Paper 01292, 63p.

that a widespread catastrophic drought in sub-Saharan Africa could trigger response costs of US$3 billion today, which would put an unprecedented financial strain on several countries.

Performance of the Risk Pools
Drought exposure of several countries is combined in a risk pool managed by ARC. ARC buys a multilayer aggregated excess of loss reinsurance from international markets to protect against large to severe droughts that can affect different countries at the same time. Since 2014, ARC has managed three risk pools and aims to reach US$1.5 billion of exposure by 2020, covering 30 countries and a population of 150 million. ARC further plans to offer insurance against flood and has implemented a cyclone model.

The first risk pool (2014/15) included Kenya, Mauritania, Niger, Senegal and Mozambique, with a maximum limit of US$30 million per country and a reinsurance protection of US$55 million above ARC's US$15 million retention. Drought events in 2015 triggered a payout of US$26 million in Mauritania, Niger and Senegal. The second risk pool (2015/16) consisted of Kenya, Mauritania, Niger, Senegal, the Gambia, Mali and Malawi, a reinsurance protection of US$72 million above US$20 million and an enlarged reinsurance panel including Nephila as an investment fund. Only Malawi incurred drought conditions, but ARVS did not compute a drought as farmers switched to a shorter maturing corn variety (90 days) compared with a longer maturing variety (160 days) used in ARVS. After recalibration of ARVS and a retroactively amended insurance policy, the Malawi government received an indemnity of US$8 million. The experience in Malawi has shown the necessity to validate in-season input data for ARVS, which was addressed through additional resources monitoring and reporting crop growth conditions. The third risk pool (2016/2017) included Burkina Faso, Niger, Senegal, the Gambia, Mali and Mauritania. Kenya left the risk pool due to elections and Malawi run out of time to re-enter the pool.

MECHANISTIC CROP MODELS

Seasonal averages of single weather parameters such as rainfall and temperature often correlate poorly with yield, particularly in areas with different irrigation extents and changes in crop management practices over time. Ideally, the pricing of yield-based risk transfer products (e.g. area-yield indices and MPCI) would be based on today's production environment, with weather parameters being the only main variable that is flexible over time. Mechanistic crop models are capable of incorporating several meteorological variables and dynamically model yield as a function of weather, soil and crop management decisions (Section 4.4). The use of yields computed from mechanistic crop models should generate lower basis risk, particularly compared with WII with single weather variables. However, crop models require many input parameters, which can be difficult to obtain, and estimations of variables can lead to inaccuracies in insurance products.[101] So far, only a few studies have explored the use of mechanistic crop models in agricultural insurance.

---

[101] Leblois, A. and Quirion, P., 2013: Agricultural insurances based on meteorological indices: realizations, methods and research challenges. *Meteorol. Appl.*, 20(1), 1–9.

The Use of Mechanistic Crop Models for Insurance

A study in Georgia (USA) used a daily corn growth simulation model (CERES) to generate corn yield in four counties (1971–2004) through different combinations of planting dates, soil types, irrigation extents and technology levels with daily rainfall, temperature and solar radiation being flexible parameters in the growing season.[102] County yields were obtained through irrigation extents as weights to obtain soil-specific yields and to compute the county yield as a function of area planted. The study shows that area-yield indices based on CERES-simulated corn yields perform well and while producers prefer indices based on observed yields, simulated yields can be used to generate yields in counties with missing data.

A study in Spain compared winter wheat yields from four mechanistic crop models to observed yield and concluded that modelled yields support the understanding of complex agronomic systems; however, they require calibration and include uncertainties, which need to be addressed before applications in crop insurance.[103]

BIBLIOGRAPHY

Alexandridis, A.K. and Zapranis, A.D. (2013). *Weather Derivatives: Modeling and Pricing Weather-Related Risk*. Springer, 300p.

Bielza, M. et al., 2007: Agricultural Risk Management in Europe. Proceedings of 101st EAAE Seminar on Management of Climate Risks in Agriculture, Berlin, July 5–6, 22p.

Coble, K.H. et al. (2010). *A Comprehensive Review of the RMA APH and COMBO Rating Methodology*. Washington DC: RMA/USDA Publication, 153p.

Collier, B. et al. (2010). *State of Knowledge Report–Data Requirements for the Design of Weather Index Insurance*. Lexington: Global AgRisk Publication, 153p.

European Commission (2006). *Agriculture Insurance Schemes*. Ispra: European Commission, 327p.

European Commission, 2013: The Challenges of Index-based Insurance for Food Security in Developing Countries. Proceedings of a technical workshop organised by the EC Joint Research Centre, Ispra, 284p.

Hull, J.C. (2015). *Option, Futures and other Derivatives*, 9e. Boston: Pearson Publishing, 892p.

IFAD (2010). *Potential for Scale and Sustainability in Weather Index Insurance for Agriculture and Rural Livelihoods*. Rome: IFAD, 153p.

IFAD (2011). *Weather Index-based Insurance for Agricultural Development. A Technical Guide*. Rome: International Funds for Agricultural Development (IFAD), 66p.

Jewson, S. et al. (2010). *Weather Derivative Valuation: The Meteorological, Statistical*. Financial and Mathematical Foundations: Cambridge University Press, 392p.

Josephson, G.R. et al. (1993). Crop-hail insurance ratemaking. In: *CAS Forum*, 155–201.

MASC (2015): *Hail Insurance Factsheet*. Manitoba Agricultural Services Corporation, 2p.

Miller, P. et al. (2001). *Using Growing Degree Days to Predict Plant Stages*. Montana State University, 8p.

Muhr, L., 2011: Crop Insurance for the Wealthy? Why Revenue Insurance Comes at a Price. Munich Re Report 302-07153, Munich, 12p.

Murphy, A.G. et al. (2011). *State of Knowledge Report: Market Development for Weather Index Insurance – Key Considerations for Sustainability and Scale Up*. Lexington: Global AgRisk Publication, 99p.

---

[102] Deng, X. et al., 2008: Alternative Crop Insurance Indexes. *J. Agr. Appl. Econ.*, 40(1), 223–37.

[103] Castaneda-Vera, A. et al., 2015: Selecting crop models for decision making in wheat insurance. *Eur. J. Agron.*, 68, 97–116.

Ray, P.K. (1981). *Agricultural Insurance – Theory and Practice and Application to Developing Countries*, 2nde. New York: Pergamon Press, 419p.

Roth, R.J., 1960: The Rating of Crop-Hail Insurance. Proceedings of the Casualty Actuarial Society, Volume XLVII, 108–46.

USAID, 2006: Index Insurance for Weather Risk in Low Income Countries. USAID Rural Finance Market Development Report, Washington DC, 51p.

USDA (2002). *United States Standards for Grades of Apples*. USDA Publication, 14p.

University of Wisconsin (2014): *Frost Effects on Corn*. Corn Agronomy, 7p.

Vinet, F. (2000). *Le risque-grêle en agriculture*. Paris: Editions Tec & Doc, 237p (in French).

World Bank, 2011: Weather Index Insurance for Agriculture: Guidance for Development Practitioners. Agriculture and Rural Development Discussion Paper 50, Washington DC, 102p.

World Bank (2017). *Risk Modeling for Appraising Named Peril Index Insurance Products – A Guide for Practitioners*. Washington DC, 315p.

CHAPTER 7

Livestock Insurance

7.1 INTRODUCTION

Livestock is an important agricultural sector as it contributes 30–40% of the global agricultural GDP and over 1.3 billion people directly depend on livestock for their livelihoods, including some 600 million poor farmers. While industrialised operations produce to satisfy the increasing demand for meat and dairy products, traditional livestock systems contribute to the livelihoods of 70% of the world's rural poor. Although impressive growth rates in production have been achieved in the past decades through specialisation, verticalisation and global trade, the sector is becoming increasingly vulnerable to unexpected production shocks (e.g. through outbreaks of epidemic diseases) and climate change. Insurance remains the main risk management approach for production risks and has been supporting the growth of livestock production in many markets through indemnity- and index-based products.

This chapter first provides an overview of livestock production systems and discusses trends in supply and demand of livestock products. It then gives an overview of the main risk transfer solutions, with a discussion of standard livestock insurance (SLI), extended livestock insurance, including epidemic disease insurance and consequential loss covers, index-based covers and revenue insurance.

7.2 SECTOR TRENDS

In the past two decades, increasing demand for livestock products has been met through a shift from extensive, small-scale, subsistence, mixed crop and livestock production systems towards more intensive and specialised, geographically concentrated and commercially oriented production.[1] Through high feed conversion ratios and short reproductive cycles, monogastric species (those with one stomach) such as pigs and poultry

---

[1] HLPE, 2016: Sustainable Agricultural Development for Food Security and Nutrition: What Roles for Livestock? Report by High Level Panel of Experts (HLPE) on Food Security and Nutrition of the Committee on World Food Security, Rome, 140p.

have seen some of the fastest production intensification. Highly verticalised production has led to a few aggregators owning the majority of national livestock inventories, with animal rearing being contracted to individual operators.

The livestock sector uses 80% of the agricultural land, which includes arable land, permanent meadows, pastures and land of permanent crops that are used for grazing and feed production. Livestock production has profound effects on the environment through land use changes that facilitate livestock rearing and feed production, degrading pastures through overgrazing and pollution of waterbodies. Livestock produces significant amounts of methane, which is a particularly potent greenhouse gas. Including all direct and indirect emissions along the production chain and counting for land use change, feed production and transport, livestock contributes an estimated 14.5% of global greenhouse gas emissions.

LIVESTOCK PRODUCTION SYSTEMS

Livestock production systems show a large diversity for which different classification schemes have been developed for monitoring of production and the development of economic indicators.

A classification that is based on the intensity of livestock production differentiates between (i) extensive production, which is the most traditional form and includes grazing and foraging, (ii) intensive production with large numbers of animals in confined facilities with feed ratios that support optimum growth (meat) or production (milk, eggs), and (iii) productions in many intermediate systems between extensive and intensive production. A classification that uses subsets of farming systems that relate to production intensities includes (i) landless livestock systems, which can be monogastric or ruminant, (ii) grassland systems in which crop-based agriculture is minimal, (iii) mixed rainfed systems, which include mostly rainfed cropping combined with livestock, and (iv) mixed irrigated systems where a significant proportion of cropping uses irrigation and is interspersed with livestock.[2]

Livestock production systems can be distinguished according to the production environment, reflecting production intensity, into (i) smallholder mixed farming systems, which are most common in Asia and Africa (600 million farmers) but also exist in high-income countries (30 million farmers), where livestock (mainly pigs, chicken and dairy) is reared besides crop production at low productivity levels, (ii) pastoral systems, which are most prevalent in Africa, Asia and Latin America, where 200 million nomadic and semi-nomadic pastoralists produce livestock products (mainly cattle, sheep, goats and camels) at low productivity levels, (iii) commercial grazing systems that produce beef, dairy and sheep in grasslands and pasture under commercial approaches, and (iv) intensive livestock systems for the commercial and large-scale production of dairy (two million farms), pigs (several million farms), poultry and beef (feedlots) in high- and middle-income countries.[3]

---

[2] FAO, 1996: World Livestock Production Systems: Current Status, Issues and Trends. Animal Production and Health Paper 127. Rome, 58p.
[3] HLPE, 2016: Sustainable Agricultural Development for Food Security and Nutrition: What Roles for Livestock? Report by High Level Panel of Experts (HLPE) on Food Security and Nutrition of the Committee on World Food Security, Rome, 140p.

Challenges Per Production System

Smallholder mixed farming systems, which provide most livestock products in low-income countries, face increasing challenges to access resources (land, water, input supplies), continued farm fragmentation among families, lack of entitlements/tenure, limited access to services (input supplies, finance) and markets, and exposure to endemic livestock diseases. Key challenges for pastoralist systems include conflicts for land and water, increased livestock mortality through extreme weather conditions (mainly drought and severe winter conditions), limited access to markets and services, and exposure to zoonotic diseases (livestock diseases that can spread to humans). Commercial grazing systems faces challenge through degradation of natural grassland, and conflict over land and forests areas for crop production and forestry. Intensive systems cause pollution, particularly near urban centres, losing genetic diversity, exposure to epidemic livestock diseases and foodborne diseases, overuse of antibiotics and antimicrobial resistance, and significant exposure to demand and global price volatility.

TRENDS IN LIVESTOCK PRODUCTION AND CONSUMPTION

The livestock industry has gone through significant structural changes and has set the speed of change in the overall agricultural sector given it is a large user of land and feed from grains and oilseeds that are increasingly transported over long distances.

Development of Livestock Production

Over the past 50 years, the global livestock population rapidly increased to reach close to 1.5 billion cattle, 200 million buffaloes, 1.2 billion sheep, 1 billion goats, 981 million pigs and 23 billion chickens in 2016 (Figure 7.1). The size of the 2016 livestock population had mostly doubled for all important species relative to 1961 and was most pronounced for the global chicken population, which grew nearly sixfold. While traditional livestock farming remains important, the industry has seen increased intensification, industrialisation and verticalisation in high- and middle-income countries. It is estimated that still 45% of the global pig population and 18% of the global chicken population are kept in traditional systems.[4]

Production of the main livestock products has significantly increased, e.g. the production of eggs from chickens grew by over 500% from 1961 to reach nearly 1.4 trillion in 2016, meat from cattle increased by 238% to 66 million tons, meat from pigs by 477% to 118 million tons, and milk production reached 659 tons in 2016 – doubled since 1961 (Figure 7.1). Future increases in livestock production are projected to come from greater numbers of animals rather than from higher per-animal productivity, requiring large quantities of grains and oilseeds for feed. To manage the increasing demand for livestock products, resource efficiency while reducing greenhouse gas emissions, strengthened resilience from environmental, economic and financial causes, increased investments and improved social equity and cultural integrity, including land tenure rights, are necessary.

---

[4] Robinson, T.P. et al., 2011: Global Livestock Production Systems. International Livestock Research Institute (ILRI), Nairobi, 152 p.

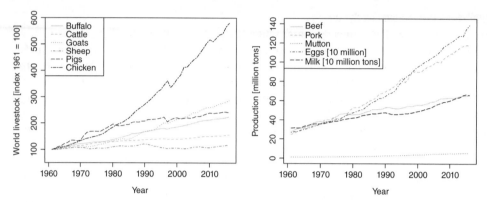

FIGURE 7.1 Left: Indexed (1961) global number of livestock for the main livestock types, 1961–2016. Right: Global meat, egg and milk production, 1961–2016.
Data source: FAOSTAT.

Development of Livestock Feed Requirements

Over 1961–2013, arable land, permanent meadows and pastures to produce livestock feed and grasslands for cattle-raising increased by 9%. As grains and oilseeds form a major component of livestock feeds, a larger part of the 1400% increase in global soybean production (1961–2016) is driven by the livestock sector. Brazil and Argentina are large soybean producers for livestock feed and the soybean area increased from only 0.3 million ha in 1961 to 53 million ha in 2013 on the back of forest areas which decreased in return. The European Union and China rely heavily on imported livestock feed. For example, China imported 61% of the global soybean export (mainly from Brazil, the USA and Argentina) in 2012 to feed its 472 million pigs, which makes up 48% of the global pig population.

Projections of Livestock Demand

Since the 1970s, the per capita consumption of dairy products has doubled, and tripled in the case of meat. Most consumption increase stems from expanding economies in low- and middle-income countries (particularly in Asia), while consumption has stagnated at high levels in high-income countries. Large-scale export of livestock products is dominated by a few markets, including Australia and New Zealand (dairy and sheep), the European Union (dairy and pork), the USA (beef, poultry, pork and dairy) and Brazil (beef and poultry). In 2010, animal products such as meat, milk and eggs provided 16% of total calories and 31% of dietary protein. Global demand for livestock products is projected to increase by 70% by 2050 relative to 2010, with the demand for red meat driven by low-income countries growing by 76%.[5]

---

[5] FAO, 2012: World Agriculture Towards 2030/2050: The 2012 Revision. ESA Working Paper 12-03, Rome, 154p.

7.3 OVERVIEW OF RISK TRANSFER SOLUTIONS

Globally, livestock insurance has developed as a function of livestock operations and the compensation framework for epidemic diseases under government biosecurity plans. The availability of government support for insurance (mainly premium subsidies) has led to considerable growth in many markets. The global livestock insurance premium reached US$2.27 billion in 2017, 7.4% of the total agricultural premium of US$30.7 billion. Livestock insurance is the second most important line of agricultural insurance after crop insurance.

LIVESTOCK INSURANCE PRODUCT TYPES

Compared with crop insurance, the development of livestock covers has been slower, with lower penetration ratios, and is consistently implemented in only a few markets.[6] Livestock insurance products have evolved over time and include (i) SLI, which provides basic coverage for accidents and non-contagious diseases, (ii) extended livestock insurance, which protects against losses from business interruption, transport and mortality from epidemic diseases, and is offered as endorsement to SLI or as a standalone cover, (iii) index-based livestock insurance, which includes area-based mortality ratios and satellite vegetation indices that relate to reduced pasture quality and quantity, and (iv) revenue livestock insurance, which protects against volatilities in livestock prices or gross margins (Table 7.1). In some markets, basic livestock mortality is covered as part of farm revenue insurance or under farm-package policies together with farm property and equipment.

Livestock of smallholders and smaller operators is typically insured through standard conditions, with limited options of franchises and deductibles, and risks are pooled through larger portfolios. Covers for large and industrialised operators are mainly insured as single risks, with tailor-made coverage based on comprehensive risk surveys.

LIVESTOCK INSURANCE MARKETS

While Europe has a long tradition of comprehensive livestock insurance, revenue covers are the dominant product in North America and basic covers prevail in most Asian countries. Latin America and Africa are least developed in terms of livestock insurance but reveal significant growth potential as biosecurity plans are evolving and livestock traceability systems are considered for implementation.

Europe
In Europe, livestock insurance has a long tradition. It started as mutual insurance in Germany in the 1830s and was implemented in Sweden and Switzerland in 1900. As all Western European countries are disease-free zones and livestock production has been commercialised early, SLI covers mortality from accidents and non-epidemic diseases. For outbreaks of epidemic diseases, the European Union provides compensation for

---

[6] Boyd, M., 2013: Livestock mortality insurance: development and challenges. *Agr. Finance Rev.*, 73(2), 233–44.

TABLE 7.1 Overview of the main types of livestock insurance products.

Type of Product	Characteristics	Perils Covered	Advantages	Disadvantages	Most Suitable Application
Standard livestock insurance (Section 7.4)	▪ Farm-based insurance covering individual animals (small operators) or herds (medium and large operators) ▪ Standard coverage ▪ Loss assessment at farm level	Livestock mortality from ▪ non-contagious diseases ▪ accidents and mortality from FLEXA[a], electrocution and injuries ▪ natural perils (mainly flood, storm)	Small operators ▪ Standard insurance conditions with some options (franchises, deductibles) Medium and large operators ▪ Tailor-made covers based on risk surveys and numerous options (franchises, deductibles, rebates in function of production system and loss mitigation)	▪ Adverse selection and moral hazard ▪ High costs for administration, distribution, and loss adjustment ▪ Standard insurance conditions for individual small farms in programs can be limited ▪ Losses from epidemic livestock diseases might be covered by government compensation schemes but consequential losses are typically not insurable	▪ Individual small farms (individual animal insurance) and individual large farms (herd insurance) in well-developed agricultural production systems (e.g. North America, Europe, Latin America, Asia-Pacific and parts of Africa) ▪ Individual small farms with policies issued at aggregated level (e.g. China)
Extended livestock insurance (Section 7.5)	▪ Farm-based insurance that extends to Standard Livestock Insurance or is available as a standalone product ▪ Often standardised coverage for small operators and	Livestock mortality from and/or during ▪ equipment failure (ventilation) ▪ transport and exhibitions/auctions (mainly breeding animals) ▪ birth complications	▪ Additional coverage as an extension of Standard Livestock Insurance ▪ Insurance of consequential losses including aspects of business interruption with	▪ Adverse selection and moral hazard ▪ High costs for administration, distribution, and loss adjustment ▪ Business interruption and related costs from epidemic disease outbreaks are difficult to estimate	▪ Individual operators with compliance to biosecurity plans and well managed operations covering additional perils in accordance with government compensation plans for values of culled livestock

additional benefits compared to government compensation plans for values of culled livestock

- tailor-made coverage for medium- and large operations
- Loss adjustment at farm level

- epidemic livestock diseases compensated at agreed values or as the difference of market value and government compensation (depending on biosecurity plan)

Additional coverage for
- reduced fertility
- consequential losses from epidemic diseases including business interruption and contingent business interruption, costs for repopulation, carcass removal, disinfection, vaccinations and additional veterinary costs, restricted access to markets and/or feed costs for livestock waiting for depopulation

(Continued)

TABLE 7.1 *(Continued)*

Type of Product	Characteristics	Perils Covered	Advantages	Disadvantages	Most Suitable Application
Area-based mortality index insurance (Section 7.6.1)	▪ Mortality indices based on livestock censuses before and after an event that causes catastrophic losses at regional scale ▪ Mortality is linked to clearly identifiable environmental conditions (e.g. drought, severe winter) ▪ Mortality indices for specific livestock types ▪ Production environment and risk mitigation strategies need to be similar over wider areas ▪ Needs considerable expertise to identify key perils and to structure indices	▪ All perils that lead to mortality	▪ Insurance of nomadic and semi-nomadic livestock in remote areas with lacking insurance infrastructure ▪ Limited moral hazard and adverse selection as payout is based on area-based mortality ▪ Low costs for loss adjustment as mortality is measured by government agencies during livestock censuses	▪ Increased costs to introduce additional livestock census to establish mortality of livestock population after risk period from a specific peril (e.g. drought, severe winter conditions) before reproduction of herds ▪ Basis risk due to different mortality ratios at farm level compared to the area on which the index is based ▪ Different causes of mortality cannot be distinguished	▪ Seminomadic and nomadic herders where livestock mortality can be linked to environmental conditions (e.g. severe winter, drought) that can otherwise not be parameterised through weather data or other proxies

| Satellite-based livestock mortality index insurance (Section 7.6.2) | ■ Indices that are based to natural perils (mainly drought) and relate directly to livestock mortality (mainly reduced quantity and quantify of fodder on grasslands)
■ Indices are based on model grids
■ Production environment and risk mitigation strategies need to be similar over wider areas
■ Needs considerable expertise to structure indices | ■ Perils reflected through weather data and/or satellite imagery (mainly vegetation indices for drought)
■ Index can directly be related to livestock mortality or used as input to livestock models that derive mortality | ■ Limited moral hazard and adverse selection as payout is based on model grids
■ Low costs for loss adjustment as mortality is measured through indices | ■ Basis risk due to indices not entirely relating to mortality at farm level relative to a model grid
■ Concept and indices difficult to understand for most stakeholders
■ Requirement for a fall-back methodology in case input data to compute the indices are not available | ■ Individual livestock operators in similar production environments
■ Agricultural supply chain to manage production volatility (meso-level risk transfer)
■ Government entities (macro-level risk transfer) |

(*Continued*)

TABLE 7.1 (Continued)

Type of Product	Characteristics	Perils Covered	Advantages	Disadvantages	Most Suitable Application
Livestock revenue insurance (Section 7.6.3)	• Index-based insurance covering • Price volatility of livestock types (mainly cattle, pigs, lambs) or products based on commodity prices • Gross margins based on livestock (mainly cattle, pigs) or livestock product (mainly milk) prices and costs of main grains/oilseeds used for feed • Products tailored to livestock production cycle of producer with durations from 1 to 12 months (USA) or up to three years (China)	• Volatility of livestock or livestock product prices • Gross margins of livestock and livestock products	• Products cover price volatilities or gross margins for different livestock types and products • Limited moral hazard and adverse selection as payout is based on indices • No cost for loss adjustment	• Products only available for livestock types and products that are traded at commodity exchanges • Feed costs are para-metrised through traded main commodities (e.g. corn, soybean meal) and needs conversion tables to accommodate other feed ingredients • Feed costs need to be translated into livestock weight through conversion factors • Basis risk as prices for livestock, livestock products, and feed costs at farm-level do not perfectly match prices at exchanges	• Individual livestock operators with main livestock types and a high familiarity of commodity prices • Agricultural supply chain to manage production volatility (meso-level risk transfer) • Government entities (macro-level risk transfer)

FLEXA stands for fire, lightning, explosion, and aircraft impact.

up to 50% of values from animals culled under government order, 70% of the costs of welfare slaughter and 50% of the organisational costs. In some countries, the government compensates losses that are above the level provided by the EU to fair market value through public funds or funds that are alimented by tax payments of farmers or levy fees.

Private sector insurance is offered for certain consequential losses following epidemic disease outbreaks and exist in Germany (Section 7.5), the Netherlands, Sweden, the UK and, to some extent, in Italy. Insurance penetration ratios for consequential loss insurance have reached close to 60% in Germany, 70% for cattle in Finland and 55% for cattle in Sweden.[7] Consequential losses are covered for several notifiable epidemic diseases and compensation is based on actual losses incurred, losses estimated for a predefined period of business interruption or through fixed amounts. In 2017, the total livestock insurance premium in Europe, including Russia and Ukraine, was estimated at US$305 million.

North America

The main form of livestock insurance in North America is revenue protection in the form of prices and gross margins with limited goverment support. In 2017, the total livestock insurance premium in the USA and Canada was estimated at US$64 million.

USA

Government-supported livestock insurance started in 2002 in the form of revenue covers to provide protection against (i) declining market prices through Livestock Risk Protection (LRP) for fed cattle, feeder cattle, swine and lambs, and (ii) lower than expected margins through Livestock Gross Margin (LGM) for cattle, swine and dairy cattle relative to feed prices such as corn and soybean meal (SM) (Section 7.6). After a withdrawal of LRP and LGM in 2003 following the detection of bovine spongiform encephalopathy (BSE), the products were reintroduced in 2004 but with substantial modifications. In 2017, the premium under LRP reached US$9.8 million and for LGM it amounted to US$8.3 million. Only 1% of the national cattle and pig inventory is insured, which is thought to be the result of risk-neutral behaviours of livestock farmers and the budget for government premium subsidies being limited to US$20 million per year.

Besides revenue insurance, some livestock operators can benefit from the Whole Farm Revenue Projection (WFRP) plan but only to the extent that livestock production revenues contribute less than 35% of the total farm revenues (Section 6.6). As the US livestock industry has a high degree of vertical integration, only a limited number of operators qualify to insure under WFRP, which was originally developed to cover speciality crops. Highly specialised livestock producers (e.g. feedlots) have arranged for tailor-made covers from private insurers.

The Livestock Indemnity Program (LIP) is a government disaster assistance scheme that covers livestock deaths above normal mortality from eligible loss conditions, including adverse weather conditions (e.g. hail, tornado, hurricane, heavy snowfall, blizzards,

---

[7] OIE, 2007: Pre-Feasibility Study Supporting Insurance of Disease Losses. OIE Publication, Paris, 133p.

extreme temperature), wildfires, earthquake and volcanic eruption, certain diseases and attacks by predators.[8] LIP pays 75% of the livestock market values as determined on the day before the loss. As the meat industry (particularly pigs and poultry) is highly verticalised and animals are owned by large integrators that benefit from LIP, farmers that are contracted to raise livestock to marketable values incur high business interruption risks from large mortality events. The high verticalisation of hog production led in 2012 to 145 producers owning 60% of the country's inventory, 685 producers possessing over 10 000 hogs and over 70% of hogs being produced by integrators under contract agreements where livestock farmers do not own the livestock.[9] Similarly, contract farming agreements dominate the poultry sector, with only 0.4% of birds produced by independent poultry operators and 0.3% produced on integrator-operated farms.[10] As a precondition of insurance is ownership of the livestock, contract farmers lack an insurable interest under the current regulation and are therefore not insurable.

Canada
Since 2012, hog and cattle producers in British Columbia, Alberta, Saskatchewan and Manitoba can benefit from the Western Livestock Price Insurance Program (WLPIP), which covers price declines relative to futures prices. The annual premium volumes generated by WLPIP have been fluctuating between US$5 million and US$50 million. WLPIP operates on a fully commercial basis, with the federal and province governments funding only the development and administration and offering deficit financing. Most provinces have implemented some SLI under AgriInsure (Section 6.7), including coverage for reduced milk production and mortality of dairy cattle and poultry from certain diseases.

Due to the limited supply of coverage from insurers, the poultry industry has developed insurance solutions through (i) the Poultry Insurance Exchange (PIE), which provides members with an egg-producer licence in Ontario, Saskatchewan and Alberta, services and insurance coverage for business interruption losses from salmonella and mycoplasma, and an extension planned for avian influenza, and (ii) the Canadian Egg Industry Reciprocal Alliance (CEIRA), which covers losses against salmonella in the egg production supply chain in all provinces. PIE and CEIRA operate as a reciprocal insurance exchanges through an unincorporated group of members that includes individuals and corporations which exchange insurance contracts to spread risks. The premium volume underwritten by PIE and CEIRA in 2017 reached US$10 million.

Asia-Pacific
The largest livestock insurance programmes in Asia are in China (US$1.3 billion premium in 2017), Japan (US$471 million), South Korea (US$30 million) and India (US$30 million). With a total premium volume of US$1.84 billion in 2017, Asia-Pacific is the main market for livestock insurance. Livestock insurance exists in other countries but at lower scale and is operated as pilots or considered for implementation. In most countries, governments provide premium subsidies, except in Australia and

---

[8] USDA, 2018: Livestock Indeminty Program. Factsheet, Farm Service Agency, 8p.
[9] RMA, 2015: Study on Swine Catastrophic Disease. RMA/Agralytica Publication, Alexandria, 84p.
[10] RMA, 2015: Final Study on Poultry Catastrophic Disease. RMA Publication, Kansas City, 163p.

New Zealand where limited livestock insurance operates on a commercial basis. In Mongolia, area-mortality indices cover livestock mortality following severe winter conditions since 2006 (Section 7.6).

China

China has some of the largest production in many livestock segments. Livestock insurance was piloted besides crop insurance and became sizable, with government premium support in 2007 under the National Agricultural Insurance Scheme (Section 5.2) on the back of a large-scale outbreak of blue ear disease (PRRS), which resulted in over 50 million dead pigs and caused a 50% increase in domestic pork prices. As several epidemic diseases are endemic, the government's biosecurity programme relies heavily on compulsory vaccination and financial compensation of destroyed animals. The 2015 amendment to the Animal Epidemic Prevention Law brought more transparency over how different provinces enact biosecurity plans and more strict enforcement of carcass removal and destruction.

The livestock policy provides standard coverage for mortality from accidents, natural disasters and diseases at agreed values and benefits from government premium subsidies. Epidemic diseases are covered for the difference between government payments from ordered culling and the agreed values under the insurance policy. Pilot schemes exist for poultry and a gross margin product for pig farmers as a function of pork prices and feed costs (Section 7.6). Premium rates vary by province and range typically between 5% and 6% for pigs at zero deductible and 8–10% for cattle at a 10% deductible. Corporate livestock producers (e.g. the dairy industry in Inner Mongolia) buy tailor-made mortality insurance and partly benefit from government premium subsidies.

India

Livestock insurance started in 1971 with public insurers offering compulsory insurance of small dairy farmers bundled with bank loans and government premium subsidies. In 2001, private sector insurers were allowed to offer livestock insurance, however with limited success. In 2006 the State Livestock Development Boards implemented an additional insurance programme for high-value cattle and buffaloes, with government premium subsidies but with a limitation of a maximum of two animals per beneficiary and the contingency that premium rates were not to exceed 4.5% for annual policies and 12% for three-year terms.[11] Under this scheme, veterinarians are used to establish market prices, to tag insured animals for identification and to issue certificates for validated claims. Government-imposed maximum premium rates that are considered low for the risks insured, moral hazard and fraud as well as lacking insurance infrastructure and veterinarians, are some of the reasons that livestock insurance is limited.

Latin America (Including the Caribbean)

Livestock production is an important industry in Latin America, where Brazil is the largest exporter of poultry and cattle, and four Latin American countries ranked among the top ten beef exporters in 2016. However, livestock insurance remains at low penetration and in 2017, the total livestock insurance premium reached only US$52 million.

---

[11] Sharma, A. et al., 2010: Livestock Insurance: Lessons from the Indian Experience. Report of Institute for Financial Management and Research (IFMR), 42p.

SLI is offered by private insurers for named perils covering mortality related to accidents for cattle and to a much lesser extent for pigs and poultry. In some countries, extended policies include specific non-epidemic diseases, theft, inland transportation and acts of terrorism on a very limited basis. Some epidemic livestock insurance exists in Mexico and Argentina, with compensation of values that are above government compensation programmes. Mexico, Brazil and Peru are among the countries that provide some level of premium subsidies for livestock insurance. Satellite-based drought indices have been used to cover resulting livestock mortality in Mexico for government entities (Section 7.6), with feasibility studies of similar products undertaken in other countries.

The demand for livestock insurance is likely to increase as Latin American countries are implementing compliance required for exporting markets, including increased traceability of animals through the supply chain, improved animal health monitoring and biosecurity plans.

Mexico

Mexico is the largest livestock insurance market in Latin America with a premium volume of US$46 million in 2017. Livestock insurance obtains government premium subsidies and is offered as (i) individual or collective SLI distributed by private insurers, fondos and mutuals for accident and mortality insurance as well as for epidemic disease covers for all main livestock types, and (ii) macro-level parametric insurance based on satellite-derived drought indices that relate to cattle mortality through reduced fodder, with a payout to regional government entities and for the benefit of smallholders (Section 7.6).

Africa (Including Middle East)

Livestock insurance in Africa is hardly developed – it reached a premium volume of US$5 million in 2017. The lack of livestock identification and traceability systems, limited access to markets, lose biosecurity plans and regulations as well as smallholder structures have prevented the implementation of livestock insurance in most markets. Several countries, including Kenya, have been experimenting with satellite-based drought covers that relate to livestock mortality through reduced fodder in grassland areas (Section 7.6). While large livestock operators exist (e.g. in South Africa), these are mainly retaining all production-related risks.

Challenges of Livestock Insurance

As a result of costly input supplies, stringent regulations (environmental protection, animal welfare and biosafety), requirements for traceability of products through the supply chain, international trade and dominance of a few very large producers, the livestock sector operates with thin margins that often limits the affordability of insurance. The risk of an epidemic disease outbreak is often perceived as minimal and producers rely on government agencies to provide compensation for lost livestock. However, due to an increasing reliance on financing of larger-scale operations, livestock insurance acts as a collateral and is imposed by capital providers to protect against production risks.

Difficulties in underwriting livestock risks include (i) presence of systemic losses from epidemic livestock diseases, with limited loss data and experience, (ii) exposure to changing regulations under biosecurity plans, (iii) moral hazard of policyholders, including changing ear tags and reducing feed ratios (starving) of disease-prone animals, and (iv) adverse selection where inadequate insurance terms lead to a concentration of high-risk policyholders in insurance portfolios. Additionally, the production of livestock includes different cycles (e.g. from a piglet to a hog) with specific risks and increasing values of each stage, where premium rates and coverage need to differ accordingly. Losses from diseases can reoccur in the following livestock cycle when facilities have not been properly disinfected. The unknown effectiveness of vaccines for newer types of epidemic diseases often makes insurers uncomfortable.

7.4 STANDARD LIVESTOCK INSURANCE

SLI is the main product used and provides indemnity-based named-peril coverage for several key production risks. SLI provides coverage for smaller operators that are typically covered in an insurance portfolio with predefined terms and conditions and large operators where insurance structures are tailor-made to specific needs and risks.

INSURANCE TERMS

SLI covers on-site livestock mortality from non-contagious diseases, accidents (mainly fire, lighting, electrocution, suffocation) and injuries that lead to culling and natural perils (mainly flood, windstorm and drought). Typical exclusions include natural mortality, slaughtering of animals for economic reasons, theft, losses from wildlife predators, mortality from epidemic diseases including government-ordered culling and quarantine orders, equipment failure (e.g. ventilation), feed and/or water contamination, negligence and poor management practices and losses related to confiscations, nuclear accidents, malicious damage, terrorism and strikes, riots and civil commotions. Coverage and exclusions vary per market and livestock type, while some of the exclusions such as mortality from epidemic diseases and related business interruption are insurable under extended livestock covers (Section 7.5).

Depending on the number of livestock of an operation, SLI covers (i) individual animals of smaller operators with standard insurance conditions, including deductibles for each animal, and (ii) herd insurance of larger producers where all animals are covered under one policy, with a deductible defined in terms of animals affected and/or a monetary loss amount. Individual animal insurance requires large administrative efforts as mortality of each animal needs to be reported and inspected. For herd insurance, insurers typically request all sub-units (e.g. barns) to be insured to minimise adverse selection since mortality rates can be different across a farm.

Identification of Livestock
A key condition for insurability of large livestock (e.g. cattle, pigs) is the identification of individual animals and consistent recording of present livestock by the operator. Identification methods depend on the livestock type and include (i) ear notching, where V-shape portions of the ears are removed, e.g. according to the litter number for pigs, (ii) ear tags such as pre-numbered plastic tags that are pierced through the ear, (iii) electronic collars that include an electronically readable tag, (iv) microchips with a radio transponder and antenna that is placed under the skin, (v) hot-iron or freeze branding

on the rump, (vi) nose printing, where patterns from a nose print unique to each animal (like a fingerprint for humans) are marked with ink, and (vii) tattoos with number and letter combinations. Insurers prefer implanted microchips to ear tags and collars, which can be exchanged easily and lead to moral hazard.

Valuation of Livestock for Inventories

Livestock producers regularly undertake livestock valuation in inventories for tax declaration and to apply for credits and loans with lending institutions. Depending on the livestock type and the length of farm records, different valuation methods are used to determine the overall livestock production or individual higher-value animals. Re-evaluations of livestock values can be necessary if a larger number of breeding animals are shifted into market animal classification (i.e. repurposing), e.g. nursing heifer calves are used as feed heifers rather than future replacement heifers, which reduces projected values.

Overall Valuation Methods

Actual cost valuation is based on costs of actual receipts that are directly attributable to producing or rearing livestock, including purchase costs, insemination expenses, maternal feed costs, and costs related to feed, veterinary expenses and employees. In some markets, standardised national average livestock rearing costs are available to facilitate valuations. Sometimes, cattle are valued under a herd scheme where the entire herd, as a function of species and age, is valuated at the beginning and at the end of a fiscal year through national average market values. Deemed cost valuations are used where a certain percentage of the open-market value is applied, e.g. 60% for cattle and 75% for sheep and goats. Net-realised valuations use sales proceeds less costs incurred to purchase and produce the stock to marketable condition. This method is used for production animals (e.g. laying hens, breeding sows), which are sold for slaughter only at the end of their productive lives, where costs are deducted from the anticipated cull value.

Individual Animal Valuation Methods

For higher-value animals (e.g. cattle), animals are valued individually in function of growth potential and expected finishing weights, which translates into market value and anticipated revenues. Often, frame scores are used which relate livestock hip height through scores to finishing weight (Figure 7.2). Alternatively, weight gain charts form the basis of individual animal valuation (Figure 7.2). Additionally, models have been developed to simulate life-cycle production of beef and dairy cow herds, including growth performance of offspring in rearing and fattening and economic weights.[12]

Requirements for Insurance

To qualify for insurance, livestock farmers need to demonstrate full legal ownership or a share of interest in the livestock, adherence to standard management practices,

---

[12] Wolf, J. et al., 2008: ECOWEIGHT 2.0 – C programs for modelling the economic efficiency of production systems in beef and dairy cattle. *Archives Animal Breeding,* 51(4), 397–401.

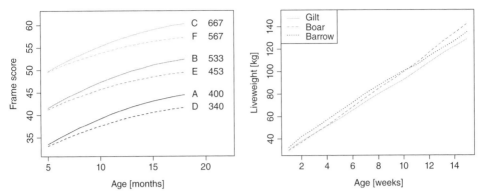

FIGURE 7.2 Left: Frame scores for steers (solid line) for score of 1 (A = low), 5 (B = medium) and 9 (C = high) and frame scores for heifers (dotted line) for a score of 1 (D = low), 5 (E = medium) and 9 (F = high), with the expected finish weight [kg], e.g. a steer with a frame score of 1 (A) is expected to reach 400 kg and a steer with a frame score of 9 (C) 667 kg. Right: Typical weekly weight gain for a guilt (young female pig), a barrow (castrated male pig) and a boar (intact male pig).
Data source: Wahlberg (2004) (left plot) and Pieterse et al. (2009) (right plot).

records of animal movements and expertise of key resources employed. Additionally, records of past mortalities including vaccinations and other loss mitigation measures taken must be kept and be accessible for the insurer. The livestock operator further warrants that livestock facilities including electrical circuits are regularly controlled, fire extinguishing devices are operational, and all livestock is free of injuries, lameness, disabilities and diseases. For larger livestock operations, insurers typically require a questionnaire or a risk survey to understand management standards, livestock rearing conditions and the main production risks.

Sum Insured

With the insurance application, the livestock operator submits a projected livestock inventory that for each unit of insurance (e.g. a barn) includes animal numbers per species (e.g. cattle) and type (e.g. dairy cattle) and age class reflecting the normal rearing cycle by production method. The sum insured is based on the declarations of the inventory and reflects market values; however, the sum insured can be below market value, particularly for policies without deductibles. The determination of the sum insured and market values and indemnity for herd insurance follows the concept of individual animal insurance but with the difference that the entire herd is considered as one unit of insurance. Insurers have developed databases that allow the verification of sum insured declared by operators in function of prevailing market values, livestock species, age class, region and production method. The policyholder is typically allowed to update market values during the insurance term and while upward adjustments require additional premium payments, downward adjustments result in a pro-rated return premium relative to the remaining term under the policy.

Indemnity

The indemnity under individual animal insurance is based on market values that are typically determined as (i) average published values (e.g. from auctions) for a given period before the death of an animal (e.g. 30 days) for breeding animals and meat producing livestock near the finishing stage, (ii) pro-rated market value for unfinished meat producing livestock, and (iii) prices at which animals could be sold to another owner for livestock where published prices do not exist. The indemnity is defined as the lower of the market value at the time of the loss or the sum insured stated in the policy schedule.

Livestock policies mainly compensate net of salvage. Salvage refers to the residual value of animals that have incurred injuries, disabilities or death. Due to stringent biosecurity and food safety regulations and traceability requirements of livestock products through the supply chain, diseased animals are destroyed, although some products (e.g. milk) would have a certain salvage value and could be marketed after appropriate treatment (e.g. pasteurisation of milk).

Premium Rates

SLI premium rates are based on the sum insured of an individual animal or an entire herd, depending on the policy wording and size of the operation. Typically, rates for individual animal insurance range for coverage of accidents and disease between 3% and 10% of the sum insured, with a deductible of 10–20%. Premium rates for herd insurance vary between 1% and 5% and typically include a 10–30% franchise of sum insured. As with other insurance products, no-claims bonuses are offered to the policyholder for loss-free years.

PRICING

Livestock insurance pricing relies on base rates of different perils that are covered and are specific per livestock type, age class, region and production environment (particularly size of the operation). Often, the initial base rate is determined for livestock mortality from non-contagious diseases and accidents, to which base rates for additional insured perils are added.

Livestock Mortality Ratios

Mortality ratios vary according to the age of livestock and the size of the operation and typically decrease with increasing age and increasing size of the operation. In the USA, average mortality is derived from large-scale surveys and varies for beef cattle between 1.7% (small operation) and 1.1% (large) and for dairy cattle from 5.7% (small operation) to 4.8% (large) and with mortality between 1.0% and 1.5% for feedlots (Table 7.2). For US pigs, average mortality decreases from nursery stage (3.6%) to weaning-finisher stage (1.4%) but increases in the finisher stage (3.5%), with generally higher mortality rates for larger operators (Table 7.2). Poultry typically shows rapidly increasing average mortality ratios from placement to processing but varies in function of the bird strain, management and housing conditions (Table 7.2).

The challenge in pricing livestock risks is to determine natural mortality (base mortality) from the overall mortality ratios as natural mortality is excluded from coverage.

TABLE 7.2 Mortality ratios as a function of animal age and herd size for calves and beef cattle, dairy cattle, pigs and poultry in the USA.

		Small	Medium		Large	
CATTLE	Death	<50 animals	50–99 animals	100–199 animals	>200 animals	All
Calves	At birth	2.9%	3.0%	3.2%	2.5%	2.9%
	Until weaning stage	4.0%	4.0%	3.5%	3.0%	3.5%
Beef cattle	After weaning stage	1.7%	2.0%	1.5%	1.1%	1.5%
Feedlot cattle						1–1.5%
DAIRY	Death	<30 animals	30–99 animals	100–499 animals	>500 animals	All
Dairy cattle	Adult stage	5.7%	4.9%	4.7%	4.8%	4.8%
PIG	Death	<2000 animals	2000–4999 animals		>5000 animals	All
Pig	Nursery stage	2.7%	3.4%		3.9%	3.6%
	Weaning to finisher stage	1.7%	1.4%		1.3%	1.4%
	Finisher stage	3.5%	4.4%		4.1%	4.1%
POULTRY	Broiler (meat)	Mortality of 1% (week 1, placement), 0.5% (week 2), 2–4% (week 6) when ready for processing with average mortality from placement to processing of 3.6%				
	Layer (eggs)	Mortality of 0.05% per week (young layers) to 0.18% per week (older layers)				

Source: Adapted from APHIS/USDA reports and livestock manuals.

For this, livestock insurers have developed standard mortality tables for the main livestock species in function of production systems, livestock density, age and region.

Pricing Livestock Mortality

Larger livestock operations, particularly in well-regulated markets, have detailed loss records, which allows the calculation of mortality ratios as the base rate. Insurers use regional mortality ratios as available from government livestock censuses to assess mortalities that might not have been experienced on a particular farm and to apply loadings to farm-based mortality. For new farms or operators with short track records, mortality ratios from neighbouring farms that are insured or where comprehensive records are available are applied and adjusted for site-specific conditions, including livestock density and management standards. Livestock insurers have developed comprehensive databases of historical mortality ratios by cause and apply schedule rates to standard livestock risks in function of the species and peril to be insured.

Small-scale farms often do not have consistent recordings of livestock mortality and causes of losses, particularly in poorly regulated markets. Base rates are developed from regional production and mortality statistics, and using the expertise of livestock extension officers, while experience is taken from other markets that have comparable production environments.

While base rates are typically determined from historical data through burning cost analyses (Chapter 2), the use of Bayesian credibility analysis has been suggested for livestock insurance pricing.[13] Base rates are loaded for uncertainty, unforeseeable events and administrative expenses, which can range from 30% to 50%, depending on the market.

LOSS ADJUSTMENT

Loss adjustment for SLI is undertaken on-site by specialised adjustors, which are often commissioned by insurers from third parties and include veterinaries. Establishing the cause of animal mortality can be complex and expensive, particularly for diseases where analyses from veterinary laboratories are required. Loss adjustors inspect statistically representative samples of affected or diseased animals, establish the market value at the time of the loss and extrapolate the overall loss extent from the sample to the number of insured livestock.

7.5 EXTENDED LIVESTOCK INSURANCE

Extended coverage is provided for mortality related to accidents and/or named epidemic livestock diseases that are not covered under SLI and is either an endorsement to SLI policies or offered as a standalone product.

ACCIDENT AND INFERTILITY INSURANCE

Accidents that lead to livestock mortality or loss of use that are typically not covered under SLI include (i) equipment failure (e.g. ventilation) through electricity shortcuts and non-performance of electricity generators as a backup in larger farms, (ii) transport risks and for livestock at auctions, and (iii) permanent infertility of breeding animals and birth complications. Typically, all losses under accident and infertility insurance are limited to a monetary amount per loss occurrence.

EPIDEMIC DISEASE INSURANCE

The outbreak of highly contagious livestock diseases (epidemics) can cause significant losses to producers, the industry and the wider economy (Section 3.10). The continuing industrialisation of livestock production, with more frequent movements of livestock in a globalised industry, has increased exposure to the spread of epidemic diseases.

---

[13] Pai, J. et al., 2014: Insurance premium calculation using credibility analysis: an example from livestock mortality insurance. *J. Risk Ins.*, 82(2), 341–57.

While some epidemic diseases are present in the livestock population (endemic) in low- and middle-income countries and do not necessarily lead to livestock mortality (e.g. foot and mouth disease), it is the reduced production and import bans of affected live-stock that lead to emergency slaughter of animals in most high-income countries. Classical swine fever (pig), avian influenza (poultry) and foot and mouth disease (multiple livestock species) are among the epidemic diseases that cause highest losses at a global scale (Section 3.10). Losses are greatest in countries that are declared disease-free and where no vaccination is used, which are typically high-income countries.

In most countries, government compensation schemes cover losses from ordered culling at market values while insurance indemnifies consequential losses and/or the difference of market values compensated by government and actual values. Options and futures have been suggested as risk management tools for some livestock species to protect against price shocks caused by disease outbreaks.[14]

Government Compensation Schemes

In most countries, government compensation schemes provide affected livestock operators with payouts for lost values of animals from notifiable epidemic diseases and government-ordered culling. Indemnity for culled livestock is based on market values, or a certain percentage of market value or is limited to a predefined maximum amount per livestock head. Often, compensation includes costs for animal destruction and disposal and in some cases, the destruction of animal-related products (e.g. milk, feed) is indemnified. In some countries, compensation is additionally available for costs arising from emergency control measures (e.g. vaccinations), laboratory analytics, animal transportation and/or disinfection. Government compensation schemes mostly exclude consequential losses from business interruption, movement restrictions and repopulation expenses.

From a government perspective, compensation schemes encourage early reporting of epidemics, cooperation for national disease treatment and best practice risk management standards, while they provide safety nets to mitigate catastrophic losses. However, compensation schemes require dedicated resources, involve moral hazard and risk-taking behaviours, can cause market distortions and might not provide payouts that affected livestock producers are expecting. To limit moral hazard, government compensation programmes typically involve all livestock producers, require a contribution of livestock operators in the form of an administrative fee and make indemnification a condition that the outbreak has been reported by an affected operator.

Compensation systems exist in different forms and include (i) public schemes that are fully government funded (e.g. Canada), (ii) public schemes that are partly funded by livestock producers (e.g. Germany, the Netherlands, Australia), (iii) private–public insurance schemes that can be mandatory or voluntary and obtain government premium subsidies (e.g. Spain), and (iv) private insurance schemes that complement government compensation programmes (e.g. the UK, the Netherlands, France).[15] In some

---

[14] Garming, B. et al., 2006: Incentive compatibility in risk management of contagious livestock diseases. In Koontz, S.R. et al. (eds), The Economics of Livestock Disease Insurance. CABI Publishing, Wallingford, 272p.

[15] OECD, 2012: Livestock Diseases: Prevention, Control and Compensation Schemes. OECD Publishing, Paris, 204p.

markets and for some epidemic diseases, livestock industry associations manage funds that are based on levies contributed by members to provide indemnification in case of losses from epidemic diseases.

Consequential Livestock Loss Insurance

Following the outbreak of an epidemic disease, direct consequential losses include business interruption, restricted movements of livestock, sales bans and increased expenses for repopulation, increased surveillance, vaccinations, feed of animals waiting for depopulation, carcass destruction, disinfection of livestock facilities and lost genetic stock. Indirect consequential losses include changes in consumer behaviour, livestock prices, import bans, and restricted access to domestic and international markets. Consequential losses often exceed direct losses for lost or culled animals. Generally, the probability of a farm being in a government-imposed quarantine zone with restricted movements and sales bans is multiple times higher than the same farm experiencing an actual outbreak of an epidemic disease.

In accordance with government compensation schemes, consequential livestock loss insurance (CLLI) covers (i) differences in livestock values recognised under a government scheme and actual market values, and/or (ii) business interruption and contingent business interruption. CLLI requires transparent legal frameworks, well-established government biosecurity plans and a clear distinction of losses indemnified through government compensation schemes following culling orders and losses covered through insurance.

To qualify for CLLI, producers need to demonstrate adherence to biosecurity regulation and warrant that the risk of farm workers spreading a disease within a farm and to other farms is minimal (e.g. by restricting workers to certain production units and disinfecting equipment and vehicles) and that contact between hobby animals and commercial livestock is limited. CLLI typically includes a waiting period (e.g. 30–90 days) after inception to exclude losses from infected livestock without clinical signs of a disease.

Business Interruption Insurance

Business interruption relates to reduced production from the outbreak of an epidemic disease and resulting costs for repopulation, laboratory and veterinary examinations and additional expenses for livestock destruction, carcass removal, disinfection and reestablishment. The indemnity for CLLI is based on the actual loss based on accounting records or a pre-agreed payment for each day of business interruption covering fix costs. For actual loss insurance, payouts can be limited to a percentage of the livestock value, and insurance based on pre-agreed values contains a limitation in number of days for an event.

Contingent Business Interruption Insurance

CLLI often includes coverage for contingent business interruption which arises through restricted movement orders of livestock and denied access, which is a major risk for highly verticalised producers where production is optimised to deliver products at the time they are needed. Equally, suppliers of livestock feed, specialised breeders of livestock and hatchery operators incur reduced sales that are contingent on government orders of denied access and restricted movements of livestock and related products.

Pricing of Epidemic Livestock Disease Insurance

The pricing of CLLI products that cover epidemic disease losses relies on the establishment of frequency, duration and severity of epidemic disease outbreaks. While the frequency describes the likelihood of disease occurrence in a given period in a given herd, the duration relates to the time a pathogen causes infections in a herd. The severity of an outbreak is a function of the duration of the outbreak and describes the degree by which the herd is affected. The loss function can be defined as:[16]

$$V(f,\lambda,\beta) = I \cdot f(t) \cdot \int \lambda^{-\beta} g(\lambda) d\lambda$$

with I as the indemnity amount in monetary terms, $f(t)$ as the probability of occurrence (frequency), λ as the duration with a probability distribution $g(\lambda)$ which is often gamma- or negative exponential-distributed and $\lambda^{-\beta}$ representing the severity. In general, the more frequently a disease occurs and the longer the duration of the outbreak, the higher the loss severity and the higher the risk premium rates. Government biosecurity plans that include culling and vaccination provisions have a large impact on frequency, duration and resulting severity of an outbreak and need to be included in the assumptions of the loss function. The representation of frequency, duration and severity is essential to obtain risk-adequate premium rates and often relies on mortality ratios and infection rates of past outbreaks in a given region or on experience from other markets.

However, epidemic outbreaks are rare events, while livestock production systems and government biosecurity and emergency response plans are constantly evolving. Therefore, actuarial extrapolations of loss experience from past outbreaks are likely unreliable predictors of future loss extents.

Pricing of epidemic disease insurance relies on scenarios or outputs of epidemic disease models. Epidemic disease models are state-transition models where disease spread occurs between animal units at specified locations and is influenced by the relative locations and distances between these units, disease control measures and infection rates (Section 3.10). Scenarios are based at regional or national level and consider key parameters such as numbers of susceptible animals, livestock density and the number of livestock species that can get infected by the same disease considering livestock transport vectors. A pragmatic approach includes the development of scenarios based on livestock density as a driving factor of disease spread, with assumptions on infection spreading and regional infection probabilities.[17]

Challenges with Epidemic Livestock Disease Insurance

Key changes in epidemic disease insurance include the establishment of determinable and measurable losses, unintentional losses, systemic losses that prevent efficient pooling of risks, moral hazard, lacking data for risk classification that leads to inadequate

---

[16] Turvey, C., 2006: Conceptual issues with livestock insurance. In Koontz, S.R. et al. (eds), The Economics of Livestock Disease Insurance. CABI Publishing, Wallingford, 272p.

[17] Jansson, T., 2006: Modelling the impact of compulsory foot and mouth disease insurance in the European Union. In Koontz, S.R. et al. (eds), The Economics of Livestock Disease Insurance. CABI Publishing, Wallingford, 272p.

premium rates, and adverse selection and uneconomically high premium rates.[18] Insurers are exposed to the effectiveness of government biosecurity plans and disease response, including slaughter efficiency during and after an outbreak. Non-compliance to biosecurity plans and phytosanitary laws by a few producers increases the risk of disease outbreaks and can cause large losses to compliant producers which are targeted for insurance. Further, limited data of past disease outbreaks and the dynamic growth of the livestock population and the general industrialisation of production often make historical losses hardly comparable to current exposure. Additionally, the duration of an epidemic disease outbreak is variable, ranging from several weeks to several months, and government orders for additional surveillance and loss mitigation measures at an infected farm can increase insured consequential losses above anticipated levels. To better manage moral hazard and adverse selection in the insurance of epidemic livestock diseases, in function of information asymmetry, theoretical frameworks have been developed to optimise indemnities.[19]

US insurers named key limitations as (i) potential for catastrophic losses due to the systemic nature of epidemic disease outbreaks, (ii) the lack of either private or governmental reinsurance, and (iii) associated catastrophic losses related to the market value of unaffected animals driven by demand and market prices decline in the event of an outbreak.[20]

Consequential Livestock Loss Insurance in Germany

Germany ranks as the largest pork and second largest cattle producer in Europe with some of the highest livestock densities, with over 180 000 cattle operations, 65 000 pig sites and 75 000 chicken producers. In recent years, several epidemic disease outbreaks were reported to the OIE, including highly pathogenic avian influenza (2006, 2017) and enzootic bovine leucosis (2010). It is estimated that medium-sized farms are 70 times more likely to be affected by restricted movement and sales orders than by government-ordered culling. Lost values of culled animals are compensated through a government programme and some consequential losses are covered by insurance products.

Government Compensation Scheme
Animal disease funds (Tierseuchenkassen) are the main institutional system for compensating producers against direct losses from epidemic diseases. These funds are publicly administered and include funding from the state governments and the European Union as well as mandatory levies from livestock producers (at least 25%), which assures adequate risk management standards and timely reporting of disease outbreaks. Levies are lower for producers with specific sanitary standards and for farms that did not record certain diseases in the past.

---

[18] Garming, B. et al., 2006: Incentive compatibility in risk management of contagious livestock diseases. In Koontz, S.R. et al., (ed), The Economics of Livestock Disease Insurance. CABI Publishing, Wallingford, 272p.
[19] Gramig, B. et al., 2009: Livestock disease indemnity design: when moral hazard is followed by adverse selection. *Am. J. Agric. Econ.*, 91(3), 627–41.
[20] OIE, 2007: Pre-feasibility study – supporting insurance of disease losses. OECD Publishing, Paris, 133p.

The animal disease funds pay for losses from official culling orders of a notifiable disease and costs incurred for culling and disposing of carcasses. Notifiable diseases include classical swine fever, BSE, avian influenza, bovine tuberculosis, African horse flu, foot-and-mouth disease, Aujeszky's disease, scrapie and anthrax. Loss payments are shared among the disease funds (25%), the state governments (25%) and the European Union (50%).

Business Interruption Insurance
Around 10 private insurers offer products that complement the payments of culled livestock under government order through the disease funds. Production insurance (Ertragsschadenversicherung) is available for cattle, pig and poultry operators and covers reduced production of livestock, business interruption and sales restrictions that result from accidents (e.g. ventilation breakdowns, feed contamination) and 19 epidemic livestock diseases (including foot and mouth disease, rinderpest, avian influenza, BSE and swine fever).[21] Additionally, insurance compensates for increased expenses related to veterinary examinations, repopulation, disinfection of farm property, disposal of diseased animals and destruction of contaminated products (e.g. milk). For business interruption in quarantine zones, insurance covers periods of 12 months from the onset of the epidemic disease, with the option to prolong coverage for 18 or 24 months. The indemnity is defined through pre-agreed values at inception of the policy or through on-farm assessment of production damage through accounting records, production data and actual market prices. To limit adverse selection and moral hazards, insurers impose a three-month period after issuing the insurance policy until coverage incept.

Livestock insurance produced US$160 million in premium in 2017 and achieved penetration ratios of 70% for broilers and 50% for dairy cattle. Vereinigte Tierversicherung is a specialised and the leading livestock insurer in Germany with over 40 000 contracts for a premium volume of US$56 million in 2017.

7.6 LIVESTOCK INDEX INSURANCE

Livestock index insurance uses indices to quantify livestock mortality ratios or volatility in livestock prices or gross margins. Broadly, three types of livestock indices are used in the industry: (i) area-based mortality index insurance (AMII), where livestock numbers over two consecutive censuses are used to determine mortality ratios, (ii) satellite-based mortality index insurance (SMII) for droughts, where satellite-based vegetation indices (mainly NDVI) are related to reduced pasture quality and quantity and resulting livestock mortality, and (iii) livestock revenue insurance that protects against livestock price volatility or gross margins parameterized through prices of livestock, livestock products and main feed components.

Livestock index insurance has the advantage over indemnity-based insurance in that it contains limited adverse selection and moral hazard as payouts are directly

---

[21] VTV, 2008: Allgemeine Bedingungen für die Ertragsschadenversicherung für die landwirtschaftliche und gewerbliche Tierproduktion (in German). Vereinigte Tierversicherung (VTV), 10p.

related to indices instead of to individual losses. Livestock index insurance should also incur lower costs as site-specific loss adjustment is not necessary. Like all index insurance products, livestock indices induce basis risk in that the indices do not perfectly correlate to losses at individual farms.

7.6.1 AREA-BASED MORTALITY INDEX INSURANCE

AMII uses regional livestock death ratios as indices for indemnity payment and works along the same concept as area-yield index insurance for crops (Section 6.8). In its most basic form, AMII relies on differences in livestock numbers established from various censuses over a given area. In most countries, government agencies undertake regular livestock censuses and surveys using stratified sampling frameworks to obtain a statistically representative sample, based on which economical metrics can be extrapolated on the entire population (Section 4.6). Livestock censuses typically include the number of animals per species and geographical area (e.g. a county or district), total livestock production for meat or milk, and data on livestock health, e.g. sick and dead animals (Section 4.6). The difference in livestock numbers between two census provides an overview of the herd dynamics as a sum of different factors, including (i) animal mortality through different causes, (ii) animals that have been culled as part of the normal production cycle, (iii) newborn livestock within the herd, and (iv) new animals that have been brought into the herd from outside.

AMII performs best in production systems with comparable livestock production methods and cycles, as well as sizes of production for a given livestock species. AMII is a valuable risk transfer solution for nomadic and semi-nomadic herders which are exposed to severe mortality from environmental conditions (e.g. severe winter conditions following drought), particularly if such events cannot reliably be quantified through weather data or other proxies alone. While AMII incurs low adverse selection and moral hazard as the regional livestock mortality index determines payouts, it induces inherent basis risk as livestock mortality varies over space. The only publicly known AMII programme operates in Mongolia (see below), where herders are protected against high livestock mortalities following severe winter conditions.

Requirement for Additional Livestock Censuses

As AMII realtes to mortalities from specific events with large loss potential (e.g. droughts, blizzards), the introduction of an additional census is often necessary to capture mortality after the impact of such an event during the natural livestock production cycle, i.e. before animals are culled for production and new livestock (including newborns) is integrated into the herds. Additional surveys need to follow the same methodology as the regular censuses to obtain comparable livestock numbers per species and region before and after the occurrence of a high mortality event. Although the implementation of additional surveys brings extra costs, the surveys also provide important data that improve the monitoring of livestock herds and production forecasts.

Index-Based Livestock Insurance Program (IBLIP) in Mongolia

Livestock herding consists of 80% of the agricultural activity in Mongolia and contributes 13% of GDP while employing 27% of the labour force. The collapse of the Soviet Union, a close ally of Mongolia, in the 1990s resulted in the privatisation of livestock

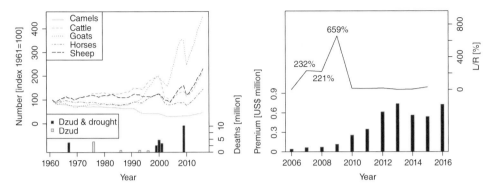

FIGURE 7.3 Left: Indexed (1961) numbers of main livestock types in Mongolia (left axis, lines), total livestock deaths (right axis, columns) due to dzud and drought and dzud in Mongolia, 1961–2016. Right: Premium volume (left axis, columns) and loss ratios (right axis, line) of the IBLIP in Mongolia, 2006–2016. Note that the year (e.g. 2009) designates the winter period (2009–2010).
Data source: FAOSTAT and Sternberg (2010) (left plot) and Yadamsuren et al. (2015) (right plot).

herds and the abandoning of restrictions on livestock numbers and certain government support (e.g. fodder storage and certain veterinary services). After privatisation, livestock numbers increased by 17.5% in 2000 and, driven by high demand for cashmere wool, livestock numbers grew by 85% between 2002 and 2008 (Figure 7.3). Around 70% of households with livestock are classified as herders, which operate under semi-nomadic and nomadic production environments, with most herders (47.6%) owning less than 200 livestock. With larger herds, grazing intensified and resulted in 70% of Mongolia's pasture land being degraded in 2012.

Dzuds and Extreme Livestock Mortality
Severe winters known as *dzuds* cause high livestock mortalities, particularly for smaller grazing animals such as goats and sheep, which make up most of the livestock population. Dzuds occur every three to seven years in the northern Asia drylands and are considered environmental disasters, with high economic losses, and they trigger the migration of large numbers of affected herders to urban centres to end up as urban poor without any income to rebuild the herds.

White dzuds are characterised through deep snow layers (>3.5 m) and cold average temperatures (≤40°C at night) and lead to the highest livestock mortalities, particularly if drought conditions prevailed in the summer before.[22] Livestock mortality results from starvation due to the inability to graze through the presence of heavy snow, extremely low temperatures and storms.

The worst recorded single-year dzud occurred in 1945 with a 33% mortality, followed by 2010 (20%) and 2001 (17%) respectively (Figure 7.3). In the 2010 dzud, 217 000 households (representing 28% of the population) were affected and 43 555 households lost the entire herd, with an additional 163 780 households losing at least

---

[22] Rao, M.P. et al., 2015: Dzuds, droughts, and livestock mortality in Mongolia. *Environ. Res. Let.*, 10, 1–12.

half of their animals. During 1999–2002, multiple dzuds reduced the national herd by 11.2 million livestock (30% mortality ratio), caused a loss of over US$500 million and increased the poverty rate to 40%.[23]

IBLIP

As part of the risk reduction and mitigation efforts, the government, with support from the World Bank, developed the Index-Based Livestock Insurance Program (IBLIP) in 2005 to provide payouts to enable livestock herders affected by high mortalities from dzuds to rebuild herds. The key challenge was to develop an effective and affordable livestock insurance product for semi-nomadic herders in vast grassland areas and with the potential for extreme losses.

Indemnity-based livestock insurance was not suitable due to the mobility of livestock, high moral hazard and adverse selection, limited data of mortality per household, and potentially high costs for monitoring and loss adjustment of individual herds. Weather indices as a proxy for livestock mortality were not feasible as weather station density is slow, dzuds are the result of different weather parameters (winter temperature, snow height, summer precipitation) and analyses revealed low correlations between mortality rates and weather. AMII was the only viable alternative and analyses of historical livestock data from censuses proved that a regional livestock mortality index captured past loss events to an acceptable level.

Development of an Additional Livestock Census

Through a census undertaken each December, the National Statistical Office of Mongolia has been recording adult livestock numbers since 1918 and livestock mortalities per soum (district) for sheep, goats, cattle, horses and camels since 1969. Although herds move across soums for grazing, most herder families choose winter camp in the same soum, which is considered in the census. As herders lose most animals during winter, and to assure indemnity payouts under IBLIP in the following summer, an additional mid-year (June) livestock census was implemented in 2006.

Main IBLIP Terms

IBLIP is a voluntary programme without government premium subsidies but with public reinsurance protection. Insurance is sold from April to June and the coverage period lasts from January to May of the following year to avoid adverse selection and information asymmetries. The triggers are based on livestock mortality per species and soum for adult livestock in comparing the June to the December census of the previous year. Premium rates are applied per livestock species and soum and herders can choose the sum insured as a percentage of the commercial value per animal, ranging from 25% to 100% – most select 30%. The commercial value per livestock species is based on monthly data of the previous year. Premium rates at soum levels average at 9.1% for cattle, 6.2% for sheep, 6.5% for goats, 5.6% for camels and 3.2% for horses.[24]

---

[23] Sternberg, T., 2010: Unravelling Mongolia's extreme winter disasters of 2010. *Nomad. People*, 14(1), 72–86.

[24] Mahul, O. and Skees, J., 2007: Managing Agricultural Risk at the Country Level: The Case of Index-Based Livestock Insurance in Mongolia. World Bank Research Paper 4325, Washington DC, 35p.

Risk Layering and Risk Transfer

IBLIP contains different layers of indemnity that are defined through separate triggers. For the low-risk layer with soum mortality below 6% per species, herders bear the full losses. In the mid-risk layer for mortalities between 6% and 30%, insurers enrolled in IBLIP provide indemnity to affected herders out of a mutual risk fund that draws on premiums collected from the insureds and reserves accumulated over past years. To regulate and administrate the mid-risk layer, a Livestock Insurance Indemnity Pool was established among the insurers, where insurers allocate annual collective reserves into the mutual risk fund when policies are sold. In the case of losses exceeding the capacity of the mutual risk fund, a government reserve account and reinsurance agreements with international markets provide indemnity. For the high-risk layer with mortalities per soum exceeding 30%, the Agricultural Reinsurance Company of Mongolia, with stop-loss protection from international markets and the state budget, provides indemnity. A recent analysis has shown that the probability of exceedance of 6% mortality in any given year in Mongolia is 26% (i.e. one in 3.8 years) and 8.7% (one in 11 years) for a mortality of 10%.[25]

Performance of IBLIP

IBLIP was implemented as a pilot in four aimags and 56 soums (2005–2009) and was gradually expanded to all 21 aimags and 330 soums (2010–2014). Between 2006 and 2015, IBLIP produced a loss ratio of 44.5%, with a maximum of 659% during the 2009/2010 dzud (Figure 7.3). The number of insured herders increased nearly eightfold, from 2422 (2006) to 18738 (2016), with 85% of all herders now being aware of the insurance programme. In 2016, the premium reached US$727 000 and seven insurers were authorised for IBLIP.

A survey showed that (i) herders buy livestock mortality insurance despite declines in cashmere prices, (ii) IBLIP contributed to poverty alleviation among smallholder herders, (iii) IBLIP acts as collateral for loans as banks offer lower interest rates to insured herders, (vi) wealthier herders with larger herds (above 350 livestock) bought insurance more frequently than small herders, (v) herders in areas with strong government links and herder organisations bought insurance more often, (vi) insured herders tend to pay more attention to the quality than to the quantity of livestock, and (vii) insured herders are more likely to invest in infrastructure with easier access to loans.[26]

7.6.2 SATELLITE-BASED LIVESTOCK MORTALITY INDEX INSURANCE

Pasture growth conditions are difficult to measure due to continuous livestock grazing and different grazing management strategies. Even more challenging is the determination of the level of distressed livestock and livestock mortality on drought-impacted pasture land over large areas with spare population and lacking infrastructure. Following the concept of satellite-based index insurance used to insure pasture land productivity (Section 6.10), satellite-based livestock mortality insurance (SMII) uses the same vegetation indices (mainly NDVI) to (i) directly quantify drought-related livestock

---

[25] Rao, M.P. et al., 2015: Dzuds, droughts, and livestock mortality in Mongolia. *Environ. Res. Let.*, 10, 1–12.
[26] Yadamsuren, U. et al., 2015: Index-Based Livestock Insurance Project: Implementation report 2005–2015. Munkhiin useg, 54p.

mortality ratios, or (ii) serve as inputs into econometric models that compute mortality through necessary fodder requirements. The development of the NDVI indices for SMII follows the same concept as used for pasture insurance (Section 6.10), with low NDVI values over a given time period relative to normal over the same period indicating drought stress for vegetation. As with other index-based products, SMII contains basis risk which arises from differences in index realisations (NDVI indicating drought and lower pasture quality and quantity) and the actual losses (livestock mortality related to reduced fodder from pasture land).

The first NDVI-based SMII started in Mexico in 2007 (see below). A similar product was implemented as a pilot in Uruguay in 2015 to protect small-scale cattle farmers. In the province of Buenos Aires (Argentina), an NDVI-based SMII product has been investigated for livestock producers.[27] Several African have been operating or testing such products including Kenya (see below) and Ethiopia.

Challenges with NDVI for Insurance Applications

While satellite-based NDVI indices are valuable proxies for livestock mortality in fragmented pastural livestock systems and facilitate insurance, several challenges arise. NDVI sensors are sensitive to cloud covers that block a satellite's view of the earth surface, while glare from the sun saturates pixels and soil background colours influence absorption and reflection at certain wavelengths (Section 4.3). Further, changes in the sensor's view angle as well as temporary malfunctions in satellite instruments can distort images. Significant changes in vegetation covers (e.g. shift towards mixed crop and pasture production) can create biases over time and require recalibration of NDVI mean values to reflect current land use covers.

NDVI-based insurance products require long time and spatially coherent time series and the low spatial resolutions in the 1980s (e.g. LANDSAT at 5 km spatial resolution) relative to current resolutions (e.g. MODIS at 250 m) hardly allow the development of 30-year time series at constant resolution, which is necessary to price and structure NDVI-based indices.

Index-Based Livestock Insurance in Mexico

In 2007, Agroasemex, a government-owned agricultural reinsurer, developed a SMII product that reflects drought-related livestock morality at a regional scale. The cover is purchased by federal and state governments which finance payouts for catastrophe livestock mortality to smallholders, which often stems from severe droughts and reduced livestock fodder from pasture land. Smallholders are defined as households owning fewer than 60 livestock units and are registered to receive automatic payouts. The federal and state governments fund 100% of the cost of premium following the decision that it is more cost effective than providing ex-post disaster compensation. The insured unit is defined as a homogeneous pasture zone that is aggregated at the level of an individual municipality.

The index is based on NOAA AVHRR daily NDVI data at a resolution of 1.1 km. Negative NDVI anomalies are computed for 10-day periods compared to average

---

[27] Bacchini, R.D. and Miguez, D.F., 2015: Agricultural risk management using NDVI pasture index-based insurance for livestock producers in south west Buenos Aires province. *Agr. Finance Rev.*, 75(1), 77–91.

NDVI values of the same time period. The declared value is defined as MEX450 per animal and the sum insured varies in function of feed supplement costs and livestock numbers for three phases ranging between 20% (Phase 1), 50% (Phase 2) and 20% (Phase 3) over the time of coverage (1 May–30 November).[28] An indemnity occurs in case of a negative NDVI anomaly for a 10-day period in each of the three phases of the coverage period.

From its implementation in 2007, the programme grew from 13 million ha of pasture in six states to 55 million ha in 20 states by 2010, equivalent to over 60% of all eligible small and marginal cattle producers. In 2011, the programme produced a premium volume of US$9.1 million at an average premium rate of 9.5% and an average loss ratio of 194% (2007–2011).

Index-Based Livestock Insurance in Kenya

In Kenya, livestock production contributes to 13% of GDP and the arid and semi-arid lands (ASALs) hold over 60% of the national livestock in nomadic and semi-nomadic environments. Many pastoralist households in ASALs rely largely on livestock for the main household income and incur high livestock mortalities in drought years, with average drought-related livestock mortality from 9% to 18% (1999–2013). Devastating droughts between 2008 and 2011 caused a decline of the national cattle herd by 9%, with losses over US$3.3 billion, which led to the government developing a fund to support a national livestock insurance scheme.[29]

Index-Based Livestock Insurance (IBLI)
In 2008, the International Livestock Research Institute (ILRI) together with Kenyan insurers started to investigate possible risk transfer products for drought-related livestock mortality in ASALs. Logistical challenges of issuing livestock mortality insurance to semi-nomadic pastoralists led to the decision to implement satellite-derived drought indices that relate to livestock mortality in drought years. The indices are based on NDVI, which is a strong indicator of vegetation conditions and the availability of forage under drought conditions in ASALs. The indices are based on NDVI data from NASA-AVHRR at an 8 km spatial and a 10-day temporal resolution that are generally available for Africa since 1981. NDVI was related through a statistical model to past livestock mortality data (2000–2007) for the long- and the short-dry season to predict livestock mortality to produce a response function. A payout occurs if evolving drought conditions predict livestock mortality ratios above 15% in a given area, reflecting forage scarcity and related livestock mortality at the end of the long- (March) and the short-dry season (October). The maximum payout covers full values of cattle, camels, sheep and goats and provides pastoralists with the financial means to restock the herds following drought seasons. Policies could be bought during a two-month window before the start of each dry season.

IBLI was launched in northern Kenya (Marsabit County) in 2010 with voluntary participation and premium rates for the 15% excess mortality cover of 3.25% in

---

[28] World Bank, 2013: NDVI Pasture Index-Based Insurance for Livestock Producers in Uruguay. Feasibility Study. Washington DC, 161p.

[29] World Bank, 2015: Kenya – Toward a National Crop and Livestock Insurance Program. World Bank Publication, Washington DC, 104p.

the lower and 5.5% in the upper areas of Marsabit. The standard herd was defined through tropical livestock units per species, including one cow, 0.7 camel, 10 goats or 10 sheep, with a standard set price per unit. Subsequently the pilot was expanded to other areas, including one implemented as a sharia-compliant structure under Takaful insurance.[30] The 2011 drought triggered payments for all insureds in October and to some extent in March 2012.

Different surveys showed that IBLI led to a decrease of 36% of distressed livestock sales to obtain income in times of hardship and a 33% reduction in necessary food aid in case of severe droughts.[31] Further, households with insurance have generally increased investments in maintaining livestock productivity through higher veterinary expenditures. However, the indices induce basis risk, which results in differences between predicted and area-average livestock mortality rates and variations of mortality among different households.[32] IBLI co-existed and complemented the Hunger Safety Net Program run by the government with cash transfer to the 100 000 poorest households.

Kenya Livestock Insurance Program
In 2014, the Kenya Livestock Insurance Program (KLIP) was introduced with 100% premium subsidy for the most vulnerable pastoralist households in ASALs that are pre-selected by the government, and for a household to (i) be active in pastoralism and own a minimum of five and a maximum of 20 tropical livestock units, (ii) not benefit from other programmes under the Kenya National Safety Net Program, and (iii) have access to a formal money transfer system (e.g. bank account, mobile money service) or commit to register after being selected for KLIP. The same cover is available for households that are not eligible for KLIP but without the benefit of premium subsidies. The livestock mortality index follows the indices of IBLI with the difference that eMODIS NDVI data are used and payouts are directly related to NDVI measurements.

A consortium of seven insurers issued the policies to 5012 households in two counties (Wajir and Turkana) in 2015 and expanded coverage to further counties to insure over 14 000 households in 2016. In 2016, a severe drought caused payouts of US$2.1 million in February to 12 000 households and US$3.1 million to 11 500 insureds in August against a premium volume of US$1.6 million. The plan is for households gradually to contribute to the cost of insurance under KLIP and to cover 65 000 households by 2020.

7.6.3 LIVESTOCK REVENUE INSURANCE

Livestock revenue insurance (LRI) uses indices developed from commodity prices (mainly futures market prices) and aims to reduce revenue risk from (i) volatility in livestock and livestock product prices under livestock price insurance, and (ii) volatility in gross margins

---

[30] Mude, A. et al., 2010: Index Based Livestock Insurance for Northern Kenya's Arid and Semi-Arid Lands: The Marsabit Pilot. ILRI report, 12p.
[31] ILRI, 2014: East African Herders Insure Against Drought: An Impact Narrative from Kenya and Ethiopia. ILRI Research Brief 23, 4p.
[32] Jensen, N. et al., 2015: The Favourable Impacts of Index-Based Livestock Insurance: Evaluation Results from Ethiopia and Kenya. ILRI Research Brief 52, 4p.

defined through prices of livestock or livestock products (e.g. milk) relative to prices of main feed ingredients (mainly corn and soybean meal) under gross margin insurance.

For efficient coverage, LRI requires the availability of transparent livestock and livestock product prices, ideally from liquid exchanges with historical prices and forward-looking prices such as futures. For gross margin products, historical and forward-looking price data for feed are additionally necessary. The specific requirements of LRI closely follow those for crop revenue insurance products (Section 6.6).

As LRI is based on indices, it reduces moral hazard and adverse selection, and incurs lower cost than indemnity-based insurance. LRI allows risk transfer for smaller livestock producers in developed markets who are not experienced in price hedging through livestock futures and options contracts. LRI through gross margin products provides large operators with a cost-efficient way to link livestock prices to feed prices at typically lower costs compared with purchasing separate options for livestock prices and feed through exchanges. As with all index-based insurance, LRI induces basis risk in that guaranteed livestock prices or margins do not correspond to local prices while feed compositions can vary and are not always reflected by commodities for which prices are publicly available.

In markets where governments provide minimum livestock and livestock product support prices or offer production agreements (e.g. quotas), LRI is difficult to implement as it covers similar risks. LRI therefore is typically part of government policy in addressing livestock price and margin volatility.

LIVESTOCK PRICE INSURANCE

Livestock price insurance (LPI) protects a livestock producer from declining livestock or livestock product prices that are typically based on forward-looking prices from an official exchange. LPI is comparable to a put option and allows a producer to establish a floor price while keeping upside price potentials but with the advantage compared to options of not requiring a minimum contract size and margin accounts. LPI exists in the USA under LRP (see below) and in Canada through the WLPIP.

Under LPI, an indemnity occurs if the actual ending price value at the expiry of the insurance contract, with a minimal duration of a calendar month, is below the coverage price. The coverage price includes the coverage level which is selected by the policyholder relative to the expected ending value determined when insurance is purchased. Expected ending values are typically established from futures contracts of the relevant livestock species or livestock product and therefore represent anticipated prices at the end of the policy period. Pricing of LPI products follows the concepts of financial option pricing where livestock future prices are modelled through the Black–Scholes Option Pricing Model or Geometric Brownian Motion, in the same way as crop prices are simulated for crop revenue insurance (Section 6.6).

LIVESTOCK GROSS MARGIN INSURANCE

Livestock gross margin insurance (LGMI) provides indemnity against declining livestock or livestock product prices (e.g. milk) and increasing costs of main feed commodities as offered by current market conditions. LGMI provides most value when feed costs increase and livestock or livestock product prices decrease and lead to lower margins. LGMI is similar in buying both a call option to limit higher feed costs and a put option to set a floor on livestock or livestock product prices. LGMI contracts are most useful for livestock operators which purchase and use feed on an as-needed basis. LGMI products are available in the USA (see below) and are piloted in China for gross margins of pork producers (see below).

Advantages of LGMI compared with forward contracts, futures and options include (i) the combination of livestock prices and feed costs are more closely related to profits than livestock or livestock product and feed prices alone, (ii) costs for insurance are typically lower than costs for individual options covering livestock or livestock product prices and different key commodities used for feed, (iii) insurance does not require the maintenance of margin accounts, (iv) there is more beneficial tax treatment as insurance can be recorded as a cost, and (v) there are potential government premium subsidies for insurance lowering the costs for a producer. Further, LGMI contracts can be tailored to any production size, unlike options which require a fixed contract size.

Main Insurance Terms

To qualify for LGMI, producers need to submit past production achievements including sales receipts and a forward-looking marketing plan. The sum insured is established through livestock numbers or livestock product quantities that are expected to be produced over given time intervals (typically calendar months). Producers can typically select the policy duration, coverage and deductible levels and the sum insured. The policy period can range from a single month to several months but with the first month typically not being covered to avoid adverse selection. A study of dairy LGMI contracts in the USA found that total optimal coverage increased significantly with the level of risk aversion of producers at lower deductibles, but when deductibles increased, the risk aversion had a lesser impact on total optimal coverage.[33]

Under LGMI, gross margins are parameterized through livestock or livestock product prices and feed costs, which are a function of different feed components that are listed on futures market and typically include a combination of corn and soybean meal. While LGMI provides a standardised feed mix ratio, some insurance programmes allow producers to modify the ratio within predefined boundaries. As some feed components are not represented at commodity exchanges (e.g. oats) but are important, insurers or government agencies provide conversion ratios to compute corn or soybean meal equivalents. Weight factors and feed ratios are used to convert prices into live weights and gross margins vary per livestock type, feed composition, type of operation and area in case regional futures prices are used (Figure 7.4).

The expected gross margin (EGM) is calculated at the time when insurance is purchased and is based on futures market prices for livestock or products and feed and is typically an average over the most recent few days. For a swine LGMI contract in the USA, the EGM_t at a given time t for a farrow-to-finish operation is:[34]

$$EGM_t = 0.74 \cdot 2.6 \cdot FPswine_t - 12 \cdot FPcorn_{t-3} - \left(138.55 / 2000 \cdot FPsbm_{t-3}\right)$$

---

[33] Valvekar, M. et al., 2011: Revenue risk management, risk aversion and the use of Livestock Gross Margin for dairy cattle insurance. *Agric. Syst.*, 104, 671–78.
[34] www.rma.usda.gov/help/faq/lgmswine.html (accessed December 2017).

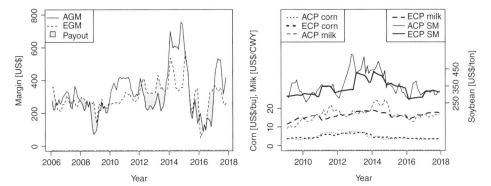

FIGURE 7.4 Left: Livestock gross margin (LGM) insurance in Iowa (USA) for cattle (contract 0803) calf finishing (807) for an insurance period of January to November with expected monthly gross margins (EGM) and actual monthly gross margins (AGM) and insurance payouts (grey areas), 2006–2017. Right: LGM in Illinois (USA) for milk from dairy cattle (contract 0847) including expected monthly prices (ECP) and actual monthly prices (ACP) of corn, soybean meal (SM) and milk for an insurance period of January to November, 2009–2017.
Data source: RMA.

with a weight factor of 2.6 per hundredth weight (CWT), a yield factor of 0.74 to convert the futures price to live weights, and the expected feed costs three months before the time t when the swine is marketed composed of 12 bushels of corn at the futures price for corn $FPcorn_{t-3}$ and 138.55 pounds per 2000 pounds per ton at the futures price for soybean meal $FPsbm_{t-3}$. The three-month lag time aligns the price with the median point in the feed cycle. In comparison to an LGMI contract for farrow-to-finish operators, EGM_t for a finish feeder operation is:

$$EGM_t = 0.74{\cdot}2.6{\cdot}FPswine_t - 9{\cdot}FPcorn_{t-2} - \left(82\,/\,2000{\cdot}FPsbm_{t-2}\right)$$

with a weight factor of 2.6 CWT, a yield factor of 0.74 and the expected feed costs two months before the time t when the swine is marketed consisting of nine bushels of corn at a futures price for corn $FPcorn_{t-2}$ and 82 pounds per 2000 pounds per ton at the futures price for soybean meal $FPsbm_{t-2}$. For a LGM dairy contract in the USA, EGM_t is defined through:

$$EGM_t = FPmilk_t - 0.5{\cdot}FPcorn_t - 0.002{\cdot}FPsbm_t$$

with $FPmilk_t$ as the futures price for milk, $FPcorn_t$ as the futures price for corn, $FPsbm_t$ as the futures price for soybean meal, based on default feeding values of 0.5 bushels of corn and 0.002 tons of soybean meal per CWT.

The actual gross margin (AGM) is a weighted average of futures prices over a prespecified period (e.g. a month) for livestock or livestock products and livestock feed calculated at the end of the contract period. As such, the AGM is determined in the same way as the EGM but uses actual weighted futures prices for livestock or livestock products and feed ingredients.

Indemnity Function

Under LGMI, an indemnity occurs if there is a difference between the AGM and the EGM which is guaranteed under the insurance contract (Figure 7.4). Shown at the example of a 10-month LGMI dairy contract that is bought in a month i and computed at differences between monthly AGMs and monthly EGMs, the Indemnity (I_i) is defined as:[35]

$$I_i = \max\left\{ \sum_{j=i+2}^{i+12} EGM_{ij} - AGM_i, 0 \right\}$$

with EGM_{ij} for the purchase month i and coverage month j as:

$$EGM_{ij} = \alpha \cdot \left(p_{ij}^{milk} - \beta p_{ij}^{corn} - \gamma p_{ij}^{soymeal} - Deductible \right)$$

with p as the futures prices of the relevant commodity (i.e. milk, corn and soybean meal), α as the coverage level and β and γ as coefficients.

Pricing Approaches

LGMI pricing requires the establishment of a joint probability distribution for livestock or livestock product prices and prices of commodities used for feed, which is similar to the approach under crop revenue insurance where joint probability distributions of crop yield and commodity prices are developed (Section 6.6).

While LGMI contracts often include a temporal lag of feed prices relative to livestock prices (e.g. two to three months prior) as the feed is anticipated to be used to raise the livestock to a marketable size, a negative correlation is often observed between feed prices (e.g. corn) and livestock prices (e.g. live cattle) and increases the variance of gross margins, i.e. a percentage increase in livestock prices results into a percentage decrease in feed prices and represents a reduction in costs and an increase in gross margin.

Pricing approaches for LGMI products include the use of jointly lognormally distributed livestock and feed prices, Monte Carlo simulations and option pricing methods that consider LGMI as Asian options, look-back options and barrier options.[36] The jointly lognormally distributed livestock and feed prices assume that prices follow Geometric Brownian motions (random walks) and net revenues and resulting gross margins are approximately normally distributed. Similarly, the Monte Carlo approach requires prices to follow Geometric Brownian motions with futures contracts prices as inputs.

LIVESTOCK REVENUE INSURANCE IN THE USA

LRP and LGM insurance were introduced in 2002 but were pulled from the market in December 2003 following the discovery of BSE. Both products were reintroduced in October 2004, with substantial modifications. LRP and LGM are administered by the

---

[35] Burdine, K.H. et al., 2014: Livestock Gross Margin – dairy: an assessment of its effectiveness as a risk management tool and its potential to induce supply expansion. *J. Agr. Appl. Econ.*, 46(2), 245–56.

[36] Turvey, C., 2006: Conceptual issues with livestock insurance. In Koontz, S.R. et al. (ed), The Economics of Livestock Disease Insurance. CABI Publishing, Wallingford, 272p.

RMA and benefit from government premium subsidies, contribution to administrative expenses and reinsurance.

Livestock Risk Protection

LRP protects against declining national livestock prices from futures markets for swine, feeder cattle (calves, steers, heifers, Brahman cattle and dairy cattle), fed cattle and lambs. LRP is sold daily and once bought, endorsements can be added, including the number of livestock expected to be marketed at an expected weight towards the end of the insurance period. As there are no futures market prices for lamb, a model is used to forecast prices which are used under LRP products.

The livestock producer can select a coverage price ranging between 70% and 100% of the expected ending value for swine, feed and fed cattle and 80–95% for lamb. LRP policies are limited over a crop year (1 July–30 June) to (i) an annual limit of 4000 fed cattle, (ii) 2000 feeder cattle in weight classes of 600–900 pounds and below 600 pounds, (iii) 10 000 hogs with an annual limit of 32 000 hogs, and (iv) 2000 lambs with an annual limit of 28 000 heads. The policy duration varies per livestock species and typically ranges between 13 and 52 weeks. LRP benefits from average government premium subsidies of 13%.

A loss occurs when the actual ending value is below the coverage price and is based on the number of heads expected to be marked multiplied by the expected weight. Actual ending values are based on average weighted prices as reported by the Chicago Mercantile Exchange (CME). Adjustment values are used for the expected and actual ending values of different sub livestock species (e.g. heifers and dairy cattle under the LRP feeder cattle contracts).

Livestock Gross Margin

LGM provides protection against a decline of the expected margin for cattle, swine and dairy, defined as (i) cattle price minus the cost of feeder cattle and corn, (ii) lean hog price less the cost of corn and soybean meal, and (iii) milk price net of the cost of corn, soybean meal and other equivalent feeds. The default feeding rates can be adjusted within predefined bounds to allow for specific production needs. LGM policies can be bought on the last business Friday of the month and cover a period of 11 months for cattle and dairy and six months for swine but with the first month not covered. The insurance policy covers monthly intervals for the time it takes to raise the livestock.

Government premium subsidies are available for dairy if a policy period of at least two months is chosen and reached 18% of the premium rate for LGM at zero deductible and up to 50% subsidies for higher deductibles.

LIVESTOCK REVENUE INSURANCE PILOT IN CHINA

Cyclical variations of hog prices have severe financial implications for producers and consumers. To more proactively manage hog price volatility, the government introduced an intervention programme in 2009.[37] The main purpose of this programme is

---

[37]Gale, F. et al., 2012: China's Volatile Pork Industry. USDA Economic Research Service Report LDP-M-211-01, 30p.

for the government to buy pork for reserves to increase demand when prices are falling and to sell pork to stimulate supply when prices are high, while at the same time stabilising hog inventories.

Triggers for pork sales and purchases are largely based on a hog–corn price ratio, which is considered normal for values between $6:1$ and $9:1$. For ratios below $5.5:1$, pork is purchased for reserves, interest on loans of large meat processors are subsidised to encourage increased pork processing, live hogs kept in reserve are increased and direct payments are dispersed to hog farmers to encourage production. The hog–corn price ratio is often considered as a primary indicator of profitability with a break-even point of $6:1$, below which producers typically reduce pig numbers until hog prices increase.

Hog Revenue Insurance Pilot

While SLI for hog mortality is available in China through the National Agricultural Insurance Program (Section 5.2), a hog revenue insurance pilot was implemented. Weekly hog prices, corn prices and hog–corn price ratios are regularly published by the government. Under hog revenue insurance, an indemnity occurs if average hog–corn price ratios over the period of insurance fall below guaranteed levels, which is typically a ratio of $6:1$. The insurance period typically varies from three to 12 months but can reach up to three years under some policies.

Terms of hog–corn price insurance vary by insurer and by province. Based on the trigger of the hog–corn price *(HC$_t$)*, the actual hog–corn price *(HC$_a$)*, the corn price *(C)* and an average hog weight *(W)*, the indemnity *(I)* is determined through one of the following ways:[38]

$$I = \begin{cases} (HC_t - HC_a) \times C \times W \\ (HC_t - HC_a) / HC_t \times C \times W \\ (HC_t - HC_a) \times Ratio\ of\ Sum\ Insured \end{cases}$$

Volatility of hog prices is the driving factor of the performance of hog revenue insurance and pricing is based on historical data as the lean meat pork price index exists only since 2017.[39] The government supports the programme through premium subsidies of up to 80% and approves the triggers and premium rate levels. The availability of hog futures prices will allow hog revenue insurance to be improved through forward-looking prices and will enable larger and more sophisticated producers to actively hedge against price volatility in hog and corn prices.

---

[38] Hu, S., 2015: Agricultural Underwriting: A Cautionary Tale. *Hong Kong Actuaries*, 3, 12–15.
[39] In March 2017, the Dalian Commodity Exchange (DCE) has released the lean meat pork price index, which is based on nine large pork processors over 16 regions, representing 32% of national supply and plans to develop hog future contracts.

BIBLIOGRAPHY

Battaglia, R.A. (2006). *Handbook of Livestock Management*, 4e. Pearson Publishing, 656p.

FAO (2016). Livestock-related Interventions During Emergencies. FAO Animal Production and Health Manual 18, Rome, 260p.

Gerber, P., Mooney, H.A., Dijkman, J. et al. (2010). *Livestock in a Changing Landscape: Experiences and Regional Perspectives*, vol. 2. Washington: Island Press, 2010p.

Greer, R. (2018). *Livestock Management: Breeding and Raising Healthy Animals*. Syrawood Publishing, 250p.

Pieterse, E., Swarts, I.C., and Hoffman, L.C. (2009). The effect of porcine somatotropin (pST) and gender on production parameters and tissue yield of pigs slaughtered at 135 kg live weight. *S. Afr. J. Anim. Sci.* 39 (4): 286–295.

Robinson, T.P., Thornton, P.K., Franceschini, G. et al. (2011). *Global Livestock Production Systems*. Nairobi: International Livestock Research Institute (ILRI), 152p.

Steinfeld, H., Mooney, H.A., Schneider, F., and Neville, L.E. (2010). *Livestock in a Changing Landscape: Drivers, Consequences and Responses*, vol. 1. Washington DC: Island Press, 450p.

Swiss Re, 2017: Closing the Insurance Gap for Livestock. Publication 1507280, Zurich, 28p.

Wahlberg, M., 2004: Market Beef Planning Guide. Virginia Corporative Extension, 4p.

CHAPTER 8

Aquaculture Insurance

8.1 INTRODUCTION

Due to overfishing, aquaculture production has grown rapidly to meet the shortfall in the demand for aquatic animals and plants. This has been achieved through intensified production methods and consistent risk management of a large range of risks in different aquaculture systems. Aquaculture is a relatively new industry, with considerable fragmentation ranging from small-scale farms to vertically integrated global firms that produce some of the most economically valuable species. Aquaculture is one of the most efficient ways to produce easily digested, high-quality proteins and while it is the fastest growing food producing sector, it carries some of the greatest risks. Future growth of aquaculture to provide for the increasing demand for seafood is potentially limited due to environmental restrictions, dependence on wild fish for feed and competition for space in suitable locations.

Despite the large growth and industrialisation of large parts of the aquaculture sector, insurance penetration remains low due to limited experience with emerging aquaculture techniques and new species, limited data, fragmentation of the industry, non-standardisation of production methods and diverse perils that impact production. Aquaculture insurance is a highly specialised domain and certainly is the most challenging of all agricultural production assets to insure.

This chapter provides an overview of aquaculture production systems and trends in production. Key risks are presented, with a focus on production risks, and the main concepts of all-risk mortality, named-peril insurance and index covers are discussed.

8.2 SECTOR TRENDS

Production from capture fisheries remains the main source of fishery products but has been static since the late 1980s (Figure 8.1). The share of wild fish stocks within biologically sustainable levels decreased from 90% in 1974 to 68% in 2013, which means that effectively 32% of fish stocks are fished at a biologically unsustainable level (overfishing).[1]

---

[1] FAO, 2016: The State of the World Fisheries and Aquaculture. Contributing to food security and nutrition for all. Rome, 204p.

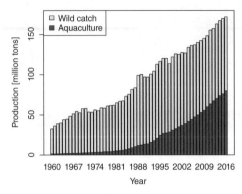 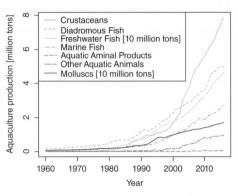

FIGURE 8.1 Left: Global wild catch and aquaculture production (excluding aquatic plants), 1960–2014. Right: Global aquaculture production (excluding aquatic plants) for crustaceans (includes shrimp, lobsters, crabs), diadromous fish (eels, salmon, shads, sturgeon), freshwater fish (carp, barbels, tilapias), marine fish (cod, flounders, tunas), aquatic animal products (pearl, shells), other aquatic animals (amphibians, urchins, turtles) and molluscs, 1960–2016.
Data source: FAO Fisheries Statistical Collections.

The *blue revolution* as aquaculture is often called has grown at annual rates of 3.2% (1961–2013), and while it provided only 7% of fish for human consumption in 1974, that figure increased to 44% in 2014. The livelihoods of 12% of the world's population depend on fisheries and aquaculture and the industry provided over 3.1 billion people with 17% of average per capita intake of animal protein and 7% of all consumed proteins. Fish is one of the most traded food commodities, with 78% of seafood products estimated to be exposed to international trade competition.

AQUACULTURE PRODUCTION SYSTEMS

Due to a different production intensity, culture systems and farmed species, a large diversity exists in aquaculture production systems that operate in fresh, brackish and salt water environments. Despite the high diversity, production systems are mostly classified through the level of production intensity and the scale of production.

Definition of Aquaculture

Aquaculture or aquafarming refers to the managed farming of aquatic animals and plants using techniques designed to increase productivity beyond the natural capacity of the environment through some form of intervention in the rearing process, stocking, feeding and the introduction of risk management. Mariculture is a subcategory of aquaculture and relates to farming of aquatic species in the marine environment. The typical phases of aquaculture include bloodstock holding, hatchery production of fish seed, nursing systems, grow-out systems and quarantining systems. Aquaculture includes the production of species that live in cold water, cool water, warm water and tropical water. In 2014, the FAO recorded 580 different farmed species, including 362 finfish species, 104 molluscs, 62 crustaceans and 37 aquatic plant types.

Classification According to Intensity of Production

Aquaculture systems are classified according to production intensity that is often a function of the extent of human intervention in the production processes and the stocking densities into open systems (extensive), semi-closed systems, closed systems (intensive) and hybrid systems (highly intensive).[2]

Open Systems (Offshore and Near-Shore)

These systems rely on natural waterbodies to provide oxygenated water, waste removal and nutrients and include (i) bivalve cultures, which are marine and freshwater molluscs that are grown in floats, rafts and trays, (ii) cages used for finfish and crustaceans in fenced compounds in shallow water or with net bottoms that are suspended off the bottom by flotation, and (iii) net pens, which are large netted cages that are mainly used offshore. The productivity of open systems is variable but can reach $1500 \, tons \, ha^{-1}$ for highly productive salmon farms. While open systems include natural water exchange and relatively low rates of diseases, these systems are exposed to predators (e.g. sealions, birds), algal blooms, tsunamis and storms as well as pollution.

Semi-Closed Systems (Onshore)

As with open systems, semi-closed systems rely on the natural environment for water, temperature and waste removal but with man-made structures and high protein feed. These systems optimise water depth, temperature and oxygen levels and allow water replacement and facilitate early detection of diseases and deteriorating water quality. Common semi-closed structures include (i) raceways that add fresh water through troughs and flush out waste, and (ii) ponds where oxygen is provided by photosynthetic phytoplankton and complemented by mechanical aeration and where heterotrophic bacteria decompose most of the solid wastes and algae absorb the released nitrate. In heavily fertilised ponds, plankton blooms are likely to develop and reduce photosynthesis in lower parts of the pond, which can lead to high stock mortality.

Closed Systems (Onshore)

Production in closed systems, also called recirculating aquaculture systems, reuses and disinfects water and generally optimises the production environment, including permanent monitoring of feed consumption and conversion ratios. In biofilter systems, waste is removed through mechanical filters where large cultures of nitrifying bacteria decompose waste. In heterotrophic systems, bacteria live with the aquatic stock and directly consume organic wastes. Often, eggs, larvae and juveniles that are sold to aquaculture producers as broodstock are grown in closed systems.

Hybrid Systems (Onshore)

These systems combine elements of open, semi-closed and closed systems. Aquaponic systems operate in water-constraint environments where biofilters are replaced by saleable plants (e.g. vegetables) that assimilate the nitrogenous waste products. In-pond raceways are systems where water constantly flows through raceways and through cages. The partitioned aquaculture system is a modified pond structure that circulates

---

[2] Tidwell, J.H., 2012: Aquaculture Production Systems. Wiley-Blackwell, Oxford, 434p.

TABLE 8.1 Annual production in function of aquaculture systems (ponds and cages), hydraulic detention time and density for different farmed fish species.

System	Application	HDT[a] (d)	Density (kg m^{-3})	Annual Production (kg ha^{-1})	Species
Ponds	Unfed in monoculture	100–300	0.03–0.05	300–500	Channel catfish
	Fertilised in polyculture	100–300	0.5–0.7	5000–7000	Chinese carp
	Fed without aeration	100–300	0.2–0.3	2000–3000	Channel catfish
	Fed with aeration	100–200	0.3–1.0	3000–10 000	Channel catfish
Cages	Freshwater	0.02–0.04	100–200	2000–3000	Channel catfish
	Marine water	0.008–0.1	50–100	2 000 000	Salmon

[a]Hydraulic detention time measured in days (d).
Source: After Colt (1991).

water through narrow channels so that the entire water column in the pond obtains sufficient sunlight for photosynthesis. Hybrid systems require high investments and are not suitable for all aquatic animals and plants.

Production Factors
The production value of aquatic stock depends on the species and production environment in terms of areal and volumetric density of stock, water loading (closed systems), exchange rate of water, hydraulic detention time and cumulative oxygen consumption (Table 8.1).[3] That means that the same aquatic species can produce different yields according to the production system, stocking density and hydraulic detention time, while the types of feed and feeding rates are additional components that determine growth. This generates a high diversity of production levels even among neighbouring farms that produce the same species.

Classification According to Scale of Production
Aquaculture production varies largely among smallholders (artisanal production) and industrialised operators that produce aquatic animals and plants at large scale.[4]

Smallholder Production
Most aquaculture in low- and most middle-income countries is produced by smallholders with subsistent and semi-organised production, for local consumption. Nearly 90% of the global farmed fish comes from Asia, with over 80% of fish farmers operating at

---

[3] Colt, J., 1991: Aquacultural production systems. *J Anim. Sci.*, 69, 4183–92.
[4] OECD, 2010: Globalisation in Fisheries and Aquaculture Opportunities and Challenges. OECD Publishing, Paris, 162p.

small scale and often in or near fragile ecosystems. In smallholder systems, production is extensive, with low levels of technology and infrastructure; some of the main fish species include carp, shrimps and tilapia. Fertilisation of pond systems has dramatically increased productivity but caused environmental concerns, particularly in shrimp farming. A future increase in production in smallholder systems will require improved access to finance and risk management (including insurance), knowledge transfer and better access to export markets.

Industrial Production

Industrial aquaculture production dominates in high-income countries where high-value aquatic stock (e.g. salmon, eels, tuna, oysters) is produced for export. Most industrial production is vertically integrated in that all processes from hatching to rearing, harvesting, marketing and often feed production are managed by one company. Industrial producers have expanded internationally to benefit from the availability of space, reduced labour costs, improved access to raw materials (feed and stock) and lower transportation costs through proximity to markets. For example, Marine Harvest (Norway) is the largest producer of salmon, with operations in 24 countries including Norway, Chile, Canada, Scotland and Ireland and several Asian countries. Nippon Suisan (Japan) operates salmon farms in Chile and eel farms in China, and Maruha (Japan) owns subsidiaries involved in tuna farming in Spain and shrimp in Madagascar.

TRENDS IN AQUACULTURE PRODUCTION AND CONSUMPTION

Intensive production in managed open and semi-closed systems generated significant increases in productivity but has led to an overuse of antibiotics and polluted waste waters that favour the spread of diseases, environmental destruction and degradation (e.g. mangroves). The introduction of biosecurity frameworks, environmental laws and sustainable production certificates has led to improved production standards in some markets.

Development of Aquaculture Production

Aquatic animal production increased 50 times from 1.6 million tons in 1960 to 80 million tons in 2016, a rapid growth that mainly was driven by the adaptation of new production methods in the 1990s and the expansion of farmed areas (Figure 8.1). In 2014, aquaculture produced 101 million tons, including 73.8 million tons from aquatic animals worth US$160 billion and 27.2 million tons of aquatic plants. Around 64% of the production of aquatic animals stems from inland production and 36% from marine and coastal environments.

In 2016, freshwater fish (carp, barbels, tilapias) were the most farmed species, with a share of 58%, followed by molluscs (21%) and crustaceans (shrimp, lobsters, crabs) with a 10% share (Figure 8.1). Salmon is among the most economically successful species, with an increase in production of 8000 tons in 1980 to 2.4 million tons in 2016.

In 2014, Asia contributed 89% to the total aquaculture production for human consumption. China was by far the largest producer with a 58% share, followed by Indonesia (14%), India (5%), Vietnam (3%) and the Philippines (2%). The largest

25 aquaculture producering countries contributed a share of the global production of 96.3% for aquatic animals and 99.3% of aquatic plants.

Growth rates in aquaculture production are expected to slow due to constraints in water availability and accessibility, competition from alternative uses of land suitable for aquaculture, accessibility of high quality broodstock and the cost of feed. Low- and middle-income countries are projected to maintain a share of 95% of global production, with Asia likely to produce 86% of the total by 2025. Driven by higher local demand and economic wealth, aquaculture production is bound to increase in Latin America (particularly Brazil) and in African countries. Future increases in aquaculture production need to come from more restrained land suitable for fish farming, a lower dependence on feed from wild catches, less pollution and a better integration into international regulatory frameworks.[5]

Development of Feed Production

Fishmeal and fish oil are the most nutritious and digestible ingredients for fed fish in farms. In 2014, some 15% of the total capture fisheries were used for fishmeal, including large amounts of anchovies caught along the coasts of Chile and Peru. Fishmeal production is managed through quota to prevent the industry falling into the *fish meal trap* where aquaculture's demand for fishmeal from limited wild stock is driving certain marine fish species close to extinction. Volatile quantities of anchovies driven by climate oscillations such as El Niño have led to increasing fishmeal prices. Efforts have been made to supplement fish feed with soybean and sunflower seeds to use only 25% of the fish feed in the form of protein from wild catches.

Development of Demand

The global per capita fish consumption increased from 9.9 kg (1960s) to 19.7 kg (2013) and is expected to reach well over 20 kg in the coming years. The demand for fish from capture fisheries and aquaculture is projected to grow to 196 million tons in 2025, which represents an increase of 17% relative to averages of 2013–2015. Most of the demand is anticipated to come from low- and middle-income countries, particularly in Asia. The Global Aquaculture Alliance has estimated that US$100 billion of new investment might be necessary to meet the global food security and rural development objectives set out for aquaculture.

Driven by consumers and retailers, several fishery and aquaculture production certificates (eco-labels) have been developed to promote sustainable production and improve the traceability of products. The Marine Stewardship Council (fisheries), the Aquaculture Stewardship Council (aquaculture), Friend of the Sea (fisheries and aquaculture) and Hazard Analysis and Critical Control Point (aquaculture farming process) are some of the main labels.[6]

---

[5] OECD, 2015: Green Growth in Fisheries and Aquaculture. OECD Green Growth Studies, Paris, 116p.
[6] OECD, 2011: Fisheries and Aquaculture Certification. OECD Publishing, Paris, 105p.

KEY RISKS IN AQUACULTURE

Aquaculture production assets are exposed to variety of risks that are often linked to both environmental and economic factors.

Generally, the main risks for aquaculture producers include (i) pathogen risks where harmful pathogens from imported aquatic stock, feed or equipment spread in the form of disease in the domestic stock, (ii) food safety and public health risks which result from new pathogens, (iii) ecological risks including escapes and spread of diseases from non-native species into the natural environment, (iv) genetic risks through the use of genetic methods to improve aquatic stocks that can lead to loss of local adaptation and introgression of new genetics by native species, (v) environmental risks through contaminated water and ecosystems (e.g. mangroves), (vi) regulatory risks, (vii) financial risks related to price volatility, changes in production costs and input supplies (e.g. juvenile stock, feed, fuel), and (viii) production risks with reduced yield or mass mortality due to environmental conditions and diseases.[7] Pathogen risk, food safety risks and genetic risks are typically addressed by regulation. Financial and production risks are key risks that need to be managed by individual operators.

Financial Risks

While price risk is actively managed for many grain and livestock commodities, the development of price risk management systems for seafood and aquaculture has been challenging. Efforts to provide exchanges for some of the main seafood products have mostly failed due to insufficient trading volume, lack of product homogeneity, limited price transparency, the presence of numerous types of products, small markets, and fish usually being sold in a fresh form and being perishable. A successful case is the Fish Pool ASA exchange in Norway that started to trade salmon futures contracts in 2005 and has over 200 members.[8]

Production Risks

Production risks include mortality and low yield of aquatic stock related to environmental conditions (water temperature, oxygen levels, pollution), cannibalism, algal bloom, outbreaks of diseases, natural perils, predators and several types of accidents. Besides preventative measures, risk transfer to (re)insurance markets is the main approach to manage production risks.

Environmental Conditions

Large temperature fluctuations can have lethal consequences as fish can adjust only slowly to temperature changes as new enzymes need to be produced for the temperature adjustment. Abrupt changes in water temperature often result from storms and floods, equipment failure (e.g. pond heaters) and warm water released from nearby nuclear powerplants or geothermal industries. The capacity of water to dissolve oxygen is negatively correlated to temperature and abrupt increases in temperature typically lead to reduced oxygen levels. Although aquatic animals can adapt to a certain

---

[7] Arthur, J.R. et al., 2009: Understanding and Applying Risk Analysis in Aquaculture. FAO Technical Paper 519/1. Rome, 113p.

[8] Ankamah-Yeboah, I. et al., 2017: Price formation of the salmon aquaculture futures market. *Aquacult. Econ. Manage.*, 21(3), 376–99.

range of oxygen concentrations, low oxygen levels lead to stress and higher mortality. Low oxygen levels are often caused by failure of aerators related to power cuts.

The breakdown of protein-based fish feed creates ammonia, which in higher concentrations is toxic for most aquatic species. Waste water removal through water movements (e.g. offshore cages), decomposition by algae or bacteria (onshore ponds) or filtering (closed systems) is essential to keep ammonia levels at minimal levels.

Cannibalism
For predatory fish species such as catfish, pikes and salmonids, cannibalism occurs in different growth stages and can lead to severe losses. Mortality ratios from cannibalism can reach from 1.5–12% (perch) to 40% (dorade) in larval stages. The intensity of cannibalism is often a function of stock density, genetic predispositions and abiotic factors including the availability of feed, feeding schedules, water temperature and clarity, and light intensity.[9] Aquaculture producers address cannibalism through frequent monitoring, adapting rearing conditions (feeding schedules, physical and chemical characteristics of feed) and size-sorting at different growth stages to disrupt dominance hierarchies.

Algal Blooms
Natural waterbodies contain phytoplankton and algae that are essential for the ecosystem through the production of oxygen. Large concentrations of phytoplankton and algae, known as algal blooms, occasionally occur along coastal areas and discolour the water red, brown or green. Algal blooms deplete oxygen levels through excessive respiration or decomposition and can produce toxic substances in harmful algal bloom (HAB). Among the thousands of phytoplankton and algae species, 144 seawater and 35 predominately freshwater species are considered harmful for aquatic animals and humans.[10] Algae can clog gills of filter-feeding animals and turn shellfish toxic, causing high mortality in aquaculture systems. For example, the 2016 algal bloom in Chile reduced the country's salmon production by 25%, produced a financial loss of US$800 million and as a direct consequence of Chile being the second largest salmon producer, global salmon prices increased by 40%.

Conditions that favour the development of HAB include nutrient enrichment that leads to increased plant growth (eutrophication), large-scale hydrometeorological changes, upwelling of nutrient rich bottom water along coasts and coastal pollution, especially from sewage. The 2016 algal bloom in Chile is thought to have been the result of high nitrogen contents in coastal water from livestock production and 2–4°C higher sea surface temperatures related to the 2016 El Niño event.

Many countries operate mandatory monitoring programmes which are based on field observations (sampling) and satellite imagery of chlorophyll concentrations in near surface waters. To project the development of HABs and provide early warning, different models have been developed using ocean currents for transport, eco-system models that use equations based on physical (transport) and biological (growth, bloom, mortality) characteristics as well as coupled observational modelling systems.[11]

---

[9] Naumowicz, K. et al., 2017: Intracohort cannibalism and methods for its mitigation in cultured freshwater fish. *Rev. Fish Biol. Fisheries*, 27, 193–208.
[10] http://www.marinespecies.org/hab/index.php (accessed January 2018).
[11] Davidson, K. et al., 2016: Forecasting the risk of harmful algal blooms. *Harmful Algae*, 53, 1–7.

Diseases

Intensive aquaculture production is prone to outbreaks of viral, bacterial, fungal and parasite diseases, some of which are epidemic in that the majority of or all stock is affected within a short time. Diseases can spread rapidly through water and affect a larger number of aquaculture production sites, particularly in offshore cage systems and onshore pond structures that use the same water resources (Section 3.11). Some of the most damaging diseases for the aquaculture industry include the white spot syndrome virus, which can affect all aquatic crustaceans, and the infectious salmon anaemia (Section 3.11). While vaccinations are available for some diseases, sustainable stock densities, well-functioning biosecurity plans and diagnostic laboratories are essential to manage disease outbreaks.

Natural Perils

Depending on the location, aquaculture operations are exposed to natural perils including (i) tropical and extratropical cyclones that damage infrastructure through high wind-speed and waves and can lead to the disappearance of aquatic stock, (ii) tsunamis that cause damage similar to that of tropical cyclones, (iii) freeze that causes ice formation in the cells of aquatic stock and ice floating, (iv) flooding that impacts onshore pond systems and causes declining water temperature, pollution and disappearance of stock, and (v) droughts that impact water availability and increase temperature in open- and semi-closed production systems. Aquaculture producers have been relying on early warning systems to mitigate losses (e.g. moving offshore cages ahead of a tropical cyclone).

8.3 OVERVIEW OF RISK TRANSFER SOLUTIONS

With 40 years of experience, aquaculture is a relatively new and highly specialised industry with a large range of species farmed under different structural, technical and managerial approaches and a high fragmentation and concentration of production. Aquaculture risks are the most complex risks in agricultural insurance. The global aquaculture insurance premium reached US$161 million in 2017, which consisted of 0.5% of the total agricultural premium of US$30.7 billion. It is estimated that around 5% of the global aquaculture production is currently insured.

AQUACULTURE INSURANCE MARKETS

Globally, aquaculture insurance has developed as a function of the size of operations into (i) insurance for industrialised aquaculture, with tailor-made covers that are based on detailed inventories and typically includes several sites, and (ii) insurance for small-scale producers with standardised products and underwriting based on limited data.

Industrialised Aquaculture

Insurance for industrialised aquaculture has developed in Europe (particularly in Norway and the Mediterranean) and expanded to Latin America (mainly Chile), Canada and the Middle East where large-scale production has rapidly expanded. Norway is the largest market with a premium volume of US$45 million, followed by Canada (US$20 million) and Chile (US$15 million), and salmon contributes most of the exposure and premium in the industrialised aquaculture insurance segment. Aquaculture premium in the USA is estimated at US$15 million and includes several insurance products that have been piloted for clams (Section 8.4) and trout and a recent attempt to provide gross margin insurance for catfish (Section 8.5). In Spain, Agroseguro extended government-subsidised insurance to aquaculture farms and Tarsim covers some larger aquaculture risks in Turkey under a pool arrangement.

Main Insurance Products
The main covers include all-risk mortality insurance and named-peril insurance with tailor-made covers to individual sites or aquaculture portfolios that include several sites in a region or farms in different countries. Industrial producers often use captives to procure catastrophe covers from reinsurance markets for global production portfolios. These policies typically contain per event and per risk deductibles as well as annual aggregated deductibles before indemnity occurs. Industrialised producers maintain detailed records of stock control plans and inventories, which has become a standard for species such as salmon, tuna, sea bass and sea bream, for which aquaculture insurance was first developed. Often, banks that finance production have mandated stock mortality insurance, as is often the case in Norway for salmon producers.

As the market is limited and highly specialised and insurance typically does not benefit from government premium subsidies, covers can be expensive and limited and the insurance penetration remains low. For example, Marine Harvest, the largest salmon producer in the world, states that it is not possible currently to obtain insurance for certain diseases or only at a premium considered uneconomical and that the number of insurers involved in fish farm insurance is small while insured values may be positively or negatively related to book values.[12] As margins in aquaculture are thin, producers often consider insurance as not affordable and struggle to comply with frequently updating inventories. A survey among salmon producers in Norway showed moderate risk aversity.[13]

Small-Scale Aquaculture
Insurance for small-scale aquaculture originated in Asia, which is the main producer of global aquaculture products and includes large numbers of smallholder operators that have grown production from initially open systems to semi-closed production with feed, aeration and fertilisation of ponds. Small-scale producers often lack access to cooperative systems or farmer groups that would increase economy of scale and facilitate services such as insurance. Further, smallholders often do not keep consistent records and stock inventories, which is a fundamental requirement for aquaculture insurance. With smallholder structures, providing proof of losses that shows the size, number and value of stock lost is challenging. Operationally, commercial aquaculture insurance for smallholders is difficult to implement due to large numbers of small units and affordability is often a main constraint besides lacking data, moral hazard, adverse selection and large diversity of operational and risk management standards. Smallholder aquaculture insurance promoted by governments with products issued through government networks, cooperatives and farmer groups exists in South Korea through

---

[12] Marine Harvest ASA, 2013: Voluntary offer to acquire all issued and outstanding shares of Cermaq ASA. Bergen, 185p.
[13] Bergfjord, O.J., 2009: Risk perception and risk management in Norwegian aquaculture. *J. Risk Res.*, 12(1), 91–104.

the National Federation of Fisheries Cooperatives (NFFC), in China with the China Fishery Mutual Insurance Association (CFMIA), and has been piloted in Vietnam.

Southeast Asia
In Vietnam, a government-supported aquaculture insurance pilot reached 8000 smallholder shrimp farmers, produced US$8.7 million in premium but incurred a loss ratio of 306% driven by large losses from early mortality syndrome (EMS), which led to the discontinuation of the pilot.[14] Following severe losses to Thailand's shrimp industry from EMS, the Thai National Farmers Council is developing an initiative to group smallholders into shrimp clusters to better benefit from services including shrimp mortality insurance.[15] Thailand has a disaster relief programme for aquaculture farmers, including shrimp, finfish and crabs, which could be complemented through insurance. In Indonesia, larger aquaculture farms have been buying aquaculture insurance but with low penetration.

China
Aquaculture is of increasing importance in China, which is by far the largest global producer. In 2013, aquaculture insurance was integrated into the National Agricultural Insurance Program (Section 5.2) and benefits from government premium subsidies ranging between 20% and 80% to provide financial incentives for insurance take-up. In 2016, the premium volume reached US$49 million and made China the largest single market for aquaculture insurance globally.

Aquaculture has developed as (i) commercial insurance which is provided by eight insurers and targets industrialised aquaculture operators through indemnity- and index-based covers, (ii) mutual insurance that covers members that farm the same aquatic species under similar practices, and (iii) insurance for cooperatives with a policy issued per cooperative and indemnities passed on to members.[16] The CFMIA is the largest mutual and while having traditionally covered fishing vessels against accidents, insurance has been offered to aquaculture farms since 2012 through regional associations. The associations share risks with CFMIA and private insurers to protect against large losses from disease outbreaks and natural disasters.

Indemnity-based insurance covers stock mortality or production loss from storms (typhoon, windstorm, rainstorm), flooding, low temperature, frost and diseases as well as the disappearance of stock from pond collapse and overflows. Index insurance is based on hydrological, wind speed (seaweed, oyster) and temperature for sea cucumber, freshwater crab and mitten crab (Section 8.5).

Challenges of Aquaculture Insurance
Due to severe losses in the past, aquaculture insurance is often considered to be unprofitable and insurers are typically reluctant to offer coverage for different reasons, including (i) exposure to both high-frequency losses (e.g. sea lice) and low-frequency–high-severity

---

[14] FAO, 2016: Aquaculture Insurance in Viet Nam: Experiences from the Pilot Program. FAO Circular 1133, Rome, 29p.
[15] FAO, 2017: Workshop on Development of Aquaculture Insurance System for Small-Scale Farmers. FAO Report 1177, Rome, 45p.
[16] FAO, 2017: Fishery and Aquaculture Insurance in China. FAO Circular 1139, Rome, 41p.

damage (e.g. algae bloom, natural perils, epidemic diseases), (ii) high natural mortality from broodstock to marketable stock that varies per species and production system, (iii) high-risk concentrations and fragmented markets that limit efficient risk pooling, (iv) lack of reliable data on inventories and loss experience that prevents the development of risk-adequate rates, (v) large difference in management standards and dependence on government biosecurity regulations that include culling and movement restrictions, (vi) specific veterinary and pathologic expertise for loss adjustment that needs to be outsourced, and (vii) high moral hazard and adverse selection in a highly fragmented industry. Further, limited loss experience exists for newly farmed aquatic species while production methods are constantly evolving. Additionally, price data that are necessary to determine values at risk are limited and generally not publicly reported.

AQUACULTURE INSURANCE PRODUCTS

Aquaculture insurance products can be distinguished into (i) all-risk insurance, which covers all possible perils that result in stock mortality and damage to equipment (Section 8.4), (ii) named-peril insurance that provides coverage only of certain well-defined perils that are typically those covered under all-risk insurance (Section 8.4), and (iii) index-based insurance for production risks, with the feasibility of gross margin insurance being investigated (Section 8.5).

8.4 ALL-RISK STOCK MORTALITY AND NAMED-PERIL AQUACULTURE INSURANCE

All-risk insurance, also called biomass insurance, covers all possible perils that result in stock mortality subject to exclusions stated in the policy wording, which typically include natural mortality, unexplained losses, cannibalism, mysterious disappearance and unexplained shortages, sexual maturing, intentional slaughter ordered by authorities and damage related to nuclear risks, sonic bangs, war, strikes, riots, civil commotion and terrorism. All-risk policies include a provision subject to individual deductibles and acceptable receipts and invoices to indemnity against extra expenses to (i) minimise or avert a loss but excluding the cost for routine veterinary examination, medication and vaccines, and (ii) destroy and dispose of dead stock. In a few markets (e.g. Norway), all-risk mortality insurance provides for losses from government slaughter orders for notifiable diseases (e.g. infectious salmon anaemia) and indemnifies a predefined percentage (e.g. 50%) of the lost value of aquatic stock after substantial deductibles. In contrast to all-risk mortality covers, named-peril insurance covers only individual well-defined perils that are typically those covered under all-risk insurance.

INSURED PERILS

Insured perils vary according to the production system, location and in function of government biosecurity plans. Commonly, insured perils differ between offshore production systems (cages) and onshore systems such as ponds and closed systems. For named-peril insurance particularly but also for all-risk mortality covers where different perils include a particular deductible or a loss limit, insurable events are defined in terms of duration.

Offshore Perils

Offshore production is typically covered for stock mortality resulting from natural perils including storm, lightning, tsunami, freezing and ice damage. Further, coverage is provided for accidents such as collisions, damage to equipment (floating equipment, cages, feed barges), predation from sharks, sealions, jellyfish or birds, algal blooms and named diseases that often include epidemic diseases. In some markets, theft, malicious acts and pollution as well as deteriorating water quality through changes in temperature, chemical compositions of the water and deoxygenation are insured. Sometimes, transit of aquatic stock and broodstock between farm sites or from hatcheries is included additionally.

Onshore Perils

Onshore aquaculture production is insured for stock mortality that is related to natural perils such as flood, earthquake, tsunami, tidal waves, storm, freezing, drought and diseases. Additionally, damage from equipment failure is covered and typically includes mechanical breakdown, electrical interruption including electrocution, and breakages of the water supply system. Deterioration of water quality through temperature changes, deoxygenation from increased microbiological activity and generally changes to the normal chemical composition of the water (including supersaturation with dissolved gases and changes in pH and salinity) is often included in coverage. Losses related to predators, theft and transit are additionally insurable.

Event Definitions

Most natural perils include a clear event definition and a duration, e.g. storm is typically defined as an event occurring within 72 hours and flood within 168 hours. Disease events are typically defined through a duration of 45 days but can range from 30 to 90 days depending on the disease and the market.

Transit Covers

Harvested stock is typically transported alive by ships or specially equipped trucks with the stock in water that is aerated, temperature-controlled and free of diseases and pollutants. Transit insurance covers risks such as collision during transit, excessive vibrations and changes in water conditions that result in stock mortality. Typically, a loss limit in monetary amounts and a deductible as a percentage of the value or a predefined amount is applied for each transit or in the annual aggregate. Mortality of broodstock in transit from hatcheries to aquaculture sites is usually the responsibility of the hatchery until the broodstock has been accepted by the aquaculture operator.

INSURANCE TERMS

Insurance terms for industrial aquaculture policies are typically tailor-made for each site and can vary among producers of the same species and area as a function of loss experience and perils selected by the policyholder to be included. Terms for small-scale aquaculture insurance are typically predefined, with some adjustments according to management standards but with little option for the policyholder to select deductibles and perils to be insured.

Preconditions for Insurance

At inception, the insured typically warrants that the aquatic stock is free of diseases, equipment is functional and is regularly serviced, and structures such as cages, fences and dykes are frequently controlled and repaired. Further, assurance is required that monthly stock declarations are accurate and recorded (including harvested amount, dead amount, intake of stock, natural mortality). Further, the policyholder assures that action is immediately taken in the presence of a disease including water sampling and that material changes in the stock are immediately reported to the insurer. The operator makes sure that workers on the aquaculture farm have adequate expertise and are trained professionals.

Inventory Methods

Aquaculture insurance relies on the determination of inventories when new stock is delivered from hatcheries to production sites and during the growth cycle until the stock has reached a marketable size. Inventories form an integral part of the insurance proposal form that is required to evaluate risks and define exposure. The inventory is calculated as a function of the stock placed and feed conversion rates and is adjusted by mortalities. Industrialised producers establish monthly inventories through predefined sampling procedures (fish-in and fish-out), including beginning numbers, average weights, fish per unit and ending numbers. It is good industry practice to extract and count dead fish from the production system and to determine the cause of mortality.

Inventory for Fish
The quantification of fish stock relies on manual or machine counting where fish pass through a channel to other units, with accuracies in counting in the range of 2–3%. However, machine counting has led to fish missing or being double counted and manual counting is prone to human errors through fatigue. The displacement of fish, which is necessary for counting, increases stress levels and operators therefore keep counting to a minimum, which however, leaves losses from escapes and predation largely undetected.

Alternatively, a fish inventory can be estimated through sub-samples where the average weight and the surface or volume of the sample are used to estimate overall production. Additionally, feed consumption rates have been used as indicators of biomass; however, this depends on satiation (excess feed supply) as feed consumption ratios can appear high (overfeeding) while wasted feed is flushed out of the production site and leads to overestimation of aquatic stock. Additionally, ill fish consume less feed, which can lead to underestimation of aquatic stock. The development of an inventory is more difficult in systems (e.g. carp farming) that raise multiple batches at the same time where a pond already includes a fish population to which new stock is added.

Inventory for Molluscs and Crustaceans
After seeding stages and stocking, molluscs and crustaceans live on the bottom of ponds and are partly submerged in sediments or raised in bag cultures. Counting molluscs and crustaceans in bottom cultures relies on volumetric sampling at different locations of a production site and extracting substrate and aquatic stock through a tube of a known size to determine stock numbers, sizes and weights, which are used to extrapolate the total cubic volume of production. For bag cultures, individual bags are sampled, and the obtained number of stock and sizes is estimated for the site. Shrimp

numbers are established through feed nets at random locations but at set times, based on which biomass is estimated from the sampled averages.

Survival Factors

The survival factor represents the rate at which aquatic stock survives from broodstock to marketable stock and reveals natural mortality. Survival factors largely depend on the species, the production system and the environment as well as management practices. For salmon, the normal survival rate is 90%, for catfish around 80%, for clams 60–70%, while for shrimp it is only 50%. For most species, survival rates increase after the initial growth stages. As insurance is based on monthly inventory values submitted by the policyholder, the correct application of survival factors is essential and insurers have developed standard survival factor tables, based on which monthly stock values are agreed with the insured producer.

Site Surveys

For industrialised operators, insurers commission site surveys by a trained professional to investigate (i) the physical installations, including the mooring of cages (offshore) and electrical/mechanical installations for aeration and water management (onshore), (ii) stock densities and production processes from broodstock to marketable sizes of aquatic stock, access and availability of medicine and vaccines, (iii) past inventory reports and stock losses per cause, and (iv) projected monthly stock inventories, including the application of survival factors. For smaller operators, site surveys are not economical and insurers often rely on indications of regional production levels by government agencies to derive an average production per insured unit.

Sum Insured

For the insurance of aquatic stock, insurers request producers to provide past inventories and monthly projected numbers and biomass of aquatic stock. Based on the projected inventories, the sum insured is determined for each month of the production cycle based on costs incurred to acquire the broodstock and to grow the stock until a marketable size. When predefined market values are used as sum insured, moral hazard is likely to increase as dead stock can be worth more under insurance provisions than in the market. The sum insured for equipment is typically based on replacement costs using depreciation factors over time.

As biomass significantly varies per month and naturally deviates from the initial inventory projections, insurers use the highest monthly value multiplied by the survival ratio to obtain agreed values, which are estimates and can be adjusted over the policy duration to reflect current values. Over time, insurers have established standardised valuation tables that provide expected production as a function of species and stocking densities and costs incurred. While aquatic stock has a certain residual value after a loss event, and dead fish can be used to produce fish oil or feed, the salvage potential is minimal.

Premium Rates

Premium rates for aquaculture risks largely depend on the species, the production system (e.g. offshore cages, onshore ponds, raceways, closed systems), the location and the perils insured. Premium rates for all-risk insurance range between 1% and 12% of sum insured but largely depend on the deductible structures and the presence of loss limits.

Base rates for named-peril insurance range from 0.1% to 6% of sum insured, to which further rate percentages are added for each additional peril that is insured (Table 8.2). A deposit premium is calculated based on the provisional monthly sum insured (agreed values) and a premium adjustment clause serves to adjust the actual premium at expiry of the insurance policy in function of the actual monthly sum insured.

Deductibles

Deductibles are based on the value at risk at the time of the loss and vary between 10–20% per culture unit and 20–30% for a site that contains different units. Insurance covers for industrialised agriculture with several sites in different regions or countries typically contain an annual aggregate deductible and cover losses up to a monetary limit.

Indemnity

An indemnity occurs when a loss has been confirmed by a competent loss adjustor based on onsite inspection and confirmation of a diagnostic laboratory has been obtained in case of diseases. The indemnity typically applies for individual growth

TABLE 8.2 Overview of premium rates for different perils for different fish species in offshore and onshore production systems.

| | Premium Rates (%) | | | | |
| | Offshore Production | | Onshore Production | | |
Rate Components	Salmon	Brass/Bream	Juvenile Salmon	Trout (ponds)	Closed Systems
Base rate	4.50	3.65	5.20	4.40	6.10
Base deductible (site value)	20	20	20	15	20
Pollution	0.50	0.40	0.40	0.60	0.40
Theft, malicious damage	0.20	0.25	0.20	0.70	0.20
Predators	0.40	0.30	Included in theft, malicious damage		
Flood, tidal waves			0.40	0.50	0.30
Storm, structural failure	0.90	0.80	0.60	0.40	0.60
Drought, fire			0.25	0.30	0.40
Freezing	0.50	0.10	0.25	0.40	0.30
Mechanical breakdown			0.80	0.20	1.00
Electrical breakdowns			0.70	0.10	0.50
Deoxygenation	0.80	0.60	0.40	0.20	0.80
Water chemistry change	0.50	0.50	0.40	0.20	0.80
Disease	0.75	0.70	0.80	0.50	0.60
Total rate	9.25	7.50	10.60	8.65	12.20

Source: After Secretan (2003).

stages as a function of increasing values. For some species (e.g. shrimp), the indemnity decreases after a predefined marketable size that is a function of the time spent in ponds is reached to avoid operators keeping the stock and waiting for higher market prices when the risk of disease outbreak significantly increases due to high biomass densities. Some aquaculture policies contain a provision for the insurer to replace affected stock if it is more economical than paying an indemnity.

Clam Insurance in the USA

Clam production has three distinct growth stages: (i) the hatchery phase, where mature clams spawn and fertilised eggs are placed in static culture tanks where they develop into swimming larvae which are provided to aquaculture producers, (ii) the nursery phase in plastic tanks and the transfer to indoor raceway systems, and (iii) the growout phase with transfer to bottom or bag cultures in the sea. The production cycle takes between 20 months (southern USA) and four years (northern USA). Key risks for clam production in the USA include abrupt changes in water temperature and salinity, high turbidity (e.g. during tidal waves and storm surges) that causes suffocation, predators and the Quahog parasite (QPX).

Aquaculture Dollar Amount of Insurance

The first federal aquaculture insurance programme was the Aquaculture Dollar Amount of Insurance (ADAI), which started for cultivated claims in 2000 and is available in Massachusetts, South Carolina and Virginia.[17] ADAI covers clams in the growout phase for different phases against stock mortality related to oxygen depletion, decrease in salinity, diseases, freeze, hurricane, tidal wave, storm surge and ice floe. The survival factor for clams is 60–70% during the growout phase and is applied to the projected inventory of the insured to obtain the insurable values. Indemnities are based on reductions of inventory values (after application of the survival factor) as submitted by the producer, net of a deductible. Clam farmers can choose coverage level between 50% and 75%, with the 50% level benefiting from 100% government-subsidised premium but with indemnity at the 55% level of the established price per clam at the time of the loss. Government premium subsidy levels range from 67% for a coverage level of 50% to 55% at coverage level of 75%. ADAI includes an annual deductible as well as occurrence-based deductibles. Veterinarians and shellfish pathologists verify cause of losses due to diseases.

Performance of ADAI

In 2005, 551 policies were sold for a total premium of US$2.2 million and a loss ratio of 184%. Subsequent increases in premium rates and changes in coverage levels led to reduced interest among clam producers and a reduction in the number of policies to 41 in 2017 for a premium of US$367 000, with 304 million clams insured. The long-term average loss ratio of ADAI stands at 154% (2000–2017) and shows increased volatility in recent years. The performance of ADAI demonstrates the difficulty of insuring aquatic stock and achieving a balance between insurance terms and participation rates, despite substantial government premium subsidies.

---

[17] Beach, R.H. and Viator, C.L., 2008: The economics of aquaculture insurance: An overview of the U.S. pilot insurance program for cultivated clams. *Aquacult. Econ. Manage.*, 12(1), 25–38.

PRICING

Given the high diversity of farmed species, production systems and management standards and the general lack of claims data, pricing of aquaculture risks is mainly based on the experience of the underwriter. A first step consists in the establishment of a base rate for a given site, to which subsequently rate loadings are applied for additional covers including pollution, predators, natural perils, equipment failure, abrupt changes in water conditions and diseases. For pollution, the distance of the site to potential pollution sources is estimated, and through water currents, expected losses are estimated and compared to loss experience at the site or surrounding sites. Predator losses are mainly determined from government statistics and industry reports. Loss potentials from natural perils are assessed from past damage reports or through scenarios where, for example, storm frequency and severity are related to an assumed vulnerability of offshore cages to windspeed and waves. Equipment failure and changes in water quality are difficult to estimate and often experience from sites with loss records is taken as a benchmark. Disease losses are most challenging to establish as loss experience is limited and loss potentials are large. Insurers often task aquaculture research institutions with providing scenario-based estimates that are based on past events projected onto current production systems or on outputs of epidemic diseases models (Section 3.11).

LOSS ADJUSTMENT

Loss adjustment of aquatic stock requires expertise in marine biology and insurers often commission specialised third parties that use systematic methods to determine lost stock value at the time of a confirmed loss. Mortality of aquatic stock is difficult to measure as dead fish cannot easily be observed (particularly in ponds) and molluscs and crustaceans are submerged in sediments in bottom cultures. In raceway systems, dead and ailing fish are easily observed as they naturally move towards the filters and can therefore be removed for examination and counting. For disease losses, samples need to be collected and sent for histological examination to a competent laboratory where the type of disease is confirmed.

For a unit that reported a loss, the loss adjustor determines the value of the inventory for the day before the loss and applies the pre-agreed survival factor from the stocking stage until the time of the loss. The method to determine numbers, sizes and weights of stock corresponds to approaches taken to establish inventories. Loss adjustors additionally check feed records to establish changes in stock over time and the occurrence of non-insured losses as well as natural mortality that occurred prior to the loss that is adjusted.

8.5 AQUACULTURE INDEX INSURANCE

Aquaculture index insurance is a new product and has been considered in several countries but is only implemented China to (i) cover perils that are otherwise difficult or expensive to insure through indemnity-based products, and (ii) cover offshore sites that are difficult to access. Current index products in aquaculture are based on weather indices, particularly wind speed and temperature, that closely relate to expected stock mortalities. Following the concept of livestock revenue insurance, gross margin covers have recently been investigated in the USA for catfish producers (see below).

AQUACULTURE WEATHER INDEX INSURANCE

Weather index insurance for aquaculture covers stock mortality or production losses from storms (typhoon, windstorm, rainstorm), flooding, low temperature and the disappearance of stock from pond dyke collapse and overflows related to weather events. Most indices are based on indices that are composed of wind speed (seaweed, oyster) and temperature (sea cucumber, freshwater crab and mitten crab). China has been most active in the development of weather indices for aquaculture, with a heatwave index as one of the first products. While weather index products for aquaculture risks have significant potential, limited data on actual production, basis risk and the producers' understanding of the concept are factors that are liekly to limit growth.

Mitten Crab Temperature Index Insurance in China

In autumn of every year, the Chinese crave for the mitten crab (also called the hairy crab), which is widely regarded as a culinary delicacy. Due to overfishing and habitat destruction in the 1960s, the Chinese mitten crab (CMC) became increasingly rare and efforts were undertaken to cultivate the crabs in aquaculture farms in the 1980s. Today, CMC aquaculture is worth US$70 million, with the main production concentrated in the provinces of Jiangsu, Zhejiang and Liaoning. Wholesale prices depend on supply and demand and range from US$1.50 to US$50 for one crab.

The production of marketable CMCs takes two years and the crab is most sensitive to abrupt increases in water temperature. The CMC can tolerate air temperatures up to 35°C and water temperatures of up to 28°C; however, mortality rates increase significantly during heatwaves with consecutive days of air temperatures over 35°C. In 2013, the province of Jiangsu experienced a heatwave with temperatures above 40°C which caused CMC losses of 30%, with many farms reporting total losses. Besides losses in production, CMC producers incurred additional costs as employees obtain mandatory compensation from employers for heat days that are defined as temperatures above 37°C. The severe losses in Jiangsu together with an increasing awareness of potential impacts of climate change led to demand for an insurance product.

Heat Day Index Product
As a response to the devastating losses, a leading Chinese insurer, with the support of an international reinsurer, structured a high temperature weather index for CMC farmers in the Taihu region of Jiangsu. The index is based on a consecutive number of heat days when the maximum air temperature is equal to or above 37.5°C during the summer months and provides indemnity after three consecutive heat days have been experienced. The sum insured covers production costs including broodstock, feed and labour. CMC production data are available from the Aquaculture Bureau for historical years and served to evaluate basis risk for the indices. The municipal government supports the programme with a premium subsidy of 25%. In 2014, around 3000 ha of CMC farms were insured for a total sum insured of US$30 million. The product received positive acceptance for CMC farmers and was expanded to more areas in 2015.

AQUACULTURE REVENUE INSURANCE

Although revenue insurance for aquaculture has been investigated, such products have not been implemented, despite the interest of some large and fully integrated aquaculture producers. Recently, the feasibility of a gross margin insurance for catfish has been investigated in the USA.[18] Revenue insurance for aquatic stock would follow the methodologies used for livestock insurance where volatility of gross margins is covered based on livestock or livestock product prices and prices of main feed ingredients such as grains and oilseeds, as are used in the USA and China (Section 7.6). A pre-condition for revenue insurance is the availability of (i) publicly reported spot market prices, based on which forward-looking prices or forward contract prices can be developed, and (ii) main components of feed for which prices are publicly available from forward contracts or can be projected from spot market data. However, forward contracts exist only for salmon through the Fish Pool ASA (Norway); for other species, forward-looking prices for gross margin insurance would need to be developed through models in a similar way as for LGM insurance of lamb in the USA. Further, feed components have highly complex ingredients and while the ratio of wild catch fish is decreasing, and the share of plant-based commodities are increasing in fish feed, it will be challenging to correlate commodity prices to fish feed costs.

While revenue products for aquaculture have potential, more research and feasibility studies are required to explore commercial opportunities. The feasibility study of catfish gross margin insurance in the USA offers valuable insights into the complexities.

Catfish Margin Insurance in the USA

As livestock producers currently benefit from LGM programmes that cover loss in the difference between livestock market prices and the cost of key feed ingredients (mainly corn and soybean meal), the 2014 Farm Bill initiated the investigation of a similar product for catfish operators for which government premium subsidies would be available.

Catfish Market
Catfish is the most economically important aquaculture finfish industry in the USA with annual sales of US$400 million and with 700 predominantly small-scale operators. Farm sizes and stocking densities are highly variable, while rearing cycles for catfish in pond systems range from 18 to 36 months. Feed conversation ratios depend on the growth stage and range between 1.9 and 2.4, with an average of 2.2. The overall survival rate from egg to marketable catfish is about 45%, with natural mortality of 10–20% in growout ponds. Catfish operators are exposed to a number of risks, including power outage of aerators in ponds, diseases, volatility in feed costs, predation from birds and the timing of selling of catfish in function of available processing capacities. As the cost of feed consists on average of 60% of production costs, some operators typically lock in feed costs through specific agreements with feed mills. Further, catfish can be carried over to the next season in case market conditions are not commercially attractive.

---

[18]RMA, 2016: Insurance Program Development for Catfish Margin Protection. Report D15PD00514, Agralytica, Alexandria, 149p.

Catfish Margin Insurance

For a margin insurance product to be feasible, catfish forward-looking prices or reliable price projections need to be available along with future market prices of main feed components. As catfish are not traded, futures markets and prices do not exist. The use of past catfish prices to establish future prices for 6- and 12-month windows contained substantial errors, with overestimation of price levels. The development of an econometric model to predict future price expectations did not provide satisfying results and could not simulate import dynamics of catfish. Catfish feed is complex but includes large quantities of plant-based commodities (e.g. soybean meal, corn, peanut meal, cottonseed meal, canola meal) for which futures prices exist and a composite index produced reliable results relative to past feed cost. Although valuable correlations exist between futures prices of a basket of commodities that are used in catfish feed and historical catfish prices, the 18–36-month growth cycle of catfish requires prices for these time periods, which, however, are not available and are difficult to the extent that a reliable insurance product can be developed.

Due to the inability to predict catfish prices, a general lack of data and actuarial limitations, and concerns that an insurance product could distort the catfish market, it was decided that a catfish gross margin insurance was not feasible at this stage.

BIBLIOGRAPHY

Alday, V. (2010). Aquaculture insurance: the need for evaluation of disease risk for the sustainability of a company. *Trébol* 53: 4–13.

Asche, F. (2015). *Aquaculture: Opportunities and Challenges*, 24. Geneva: International Centre for Trade and Sustainable Development (ICTSD).

Coble, K.H., Hanson, T.R., Sempier, S. et al. (2006). Investigating the feasibility of livestock disease insurance: a case study in aquaculture. In: *The Economics of Livestock Disease Insurance* (ed. S.R. Koontz, D.L. Hoag, D. Thilmany, et al.), 272. Wallingford: CABI Publishing.

FAO, 2016: Aquaculture Big Numbers. Technical Paper 601, Rome, 80p.

FAO, 2009: Understanding and Applying Risk Analysis in Aquaculture. Technical Paper 519/1, Rome, 128p.

Fotedar, R.K. and Phillips, B.F. (2011). *Recent Advances and New Species in Aquaculture*, 424. Oxford: Wiley-Blackwell.

Jackson, A. (2009). Fish in-fish out: ratios explained. *Aquaculture Europe* 34 (3): 5–10.

Lekang, O.I. (2013). *Aquaculture Engineering*, 2e, 432. Oxford: Wiley-Blackwell.

Nash, C.E. (2011). *The History of Aquaculture*, 227. Oxford: Wiley-Blackwell.

Secretan, P.A.D. (2003). *The Availability of Aquaculture Crop (Stock Mortality) Insurance. National Risk Management Feasibility Program for Aquaculture*, 73. Starkville: Mississippi State University.

Secretan, P.A.D. Bueno, P.B., van Anrooy, R. et al., 2007: Guidelines to meet insurance and other risk management needs in developing aquaculture in Asia. FAO Technical Paper 496, Rome, 148p.

CHAPTER 9

Forest Insurance

9.1 INTRODUCTION

Forests play a vital role as ecosystems, provide a large range of raw materials and serve as carbon sinks. While the global forest area has decreased in recent decades, planted forests have grown considerably and led to demand for risk transfer of production risks including physical losses from natural perils and carbon reversal under emission trading schemes in some markets. At the same time, government agencies' increasing costs to fight wildfires has led to some insurance transactions. Insurance is one of the main risk management approaches for production risks, mainly through named-peril insurance, with some applications of index-based insurance.

This chapter provides first an overview of trends in the forest sector and discusses different definitions of *forest* and its interpretation. An introduction to insurance approaches and products including key perils are provided thereafter. Plantation insurance as the main product is discussed, followed by an overview of concepts of carbon reversal insurance and firefighting cost covers. An outlook for index-based forest insurance and its potential use is then given.

9.2 SECTOR TRENDS

While the global forest area has been slightly decreasing for the main benefits to develop agricultural land, the area of planted forests under different production systems has been growing to satisfy the demand for timber products. Financial and production risks remain key challenges for small-scale and industrialised timber plantations.

FOREST PRODUCTION SYSTEMS

The definition, assessment and valuation of forests depend on the point of view, which varies among forest conservation initiatives, forest management strategies, climate-change initiatives (carbon sinks) and social-ecological and economical systems.

Definition of Forest

Different definitions and classifications of forest areas and lands are used.[1] The FAO defines a forest as land with tree crown cover (or equivalent stocking level) of more than 10% and area of more than 0.5 ha, with trees reaching a minimum height of 5 m at maturity. Under the definition of the United Nations Framework Convention on Climate Change (UNFCCC), a forest is defined as a minimum area of land of 0.05–1.0 ha with a tree crown cover (or equivalent stocking level) of more than 10–30%, with trees of the potential to reach a minimum height of 2–5 m at maturity. The Convention on Biological Diversity (CBD) defines a forest as a land area of more than 0.5 ha, with a tree canopy cover of more than 10%, which is not primarily under agricultural or other specific non-forest land use and with trees capable of reaching a height of 5 m. These different definitions have resulted in some confusion and different assessments of the global forest land surface.

Measurement of Forest Areas

Large differences can occur in forest areas between surveyed areas and estimates based on satellite imagery as remote-sensing devices (i) incur difficulties in differentiating between tree covers in agricultural production systems (e.g. palm oil plantations) and tree covers over land that are under agricultural and urban land use, (ii) measure areas that have been temporarily removed as part of management schemes or lost from natural disturbances (e.g. wildfire, storm) but will be replanted as lost area, and (iii) encounter difficulties in detecting newly established forests. While remote sensing provides valuable information on forest ecosystem developments and provides spatially and temporally consistent estimates, including the assessment of tree species and canopy cover, the determination of deforestation rates and the status of the global forests relies on forest surveys such as the FAO's Forest Resources Information Management System.

Classification According to Forest Composition

Forests are classified into (i) natural forests, including primary forest which consists of native species with undisturbed ecological processes and no human interference and are typically owned by governments, and modified natural forests with naturally regenerated native species and with human interference, typically government-owned, and (ii) planted forests, including semi-natural forests which consist of native species that have been established through planting, seeding or assisted natural regeneration, productive forest plantations, which are primarily established for the production of timber, fibre and industrial tree crops, and protective forest plantations, whose purpose is to conserve soil and water and to provide a protective ecosystem service function.[2] Industrial plantations are referred to as large-scale, intensively managed, even-aged monocultures, mostly exotic trees like fast-growing eucalyptus, pine and acacia species, destined for industrial processes that produce pulp and paper as well as rubber and oil palm products.[3]

---

[1] Chazdon, R.L. et al., 2016: When is a forest a forest? Forest concepts and definitions in the era of forest and landscape restoration. *Ambio*, 45, 538–50.
[2] FAO, 2016: Global Forest Resources Assessment. 2nd edition. Rome, 54p.
[3] Borges, J.G. et al., 2014: The Management of Industrial Forest Plantations Theoretical Foundations and Applications – Theoretical Foundations and Applications. Springer, Dordrecht, 544p.

Classification According to Ownership

Forests can be classified according to ownership structures into (i) non-industrial private forest owners (NIPFOs), which include individuals that own and manage forests, (ii) industrial private forest owners (IPFOs), including institutional forest land owners, timber investment management organisations (TIMOs) and real estate investment trusts (REITs), and (iii) public ownership by governments, which can include some form of private–public ownerships.[4]

TIMOs are management entities that support institutional investors to manage and expand timberland investment portfolios using outsourced services for forest management and harvesting to achieve maximum investment returns.[5] Investments under TIMOs are owned as illiquid direct investments, partnership shares or through pooled funds and investors include pension funds, financial institutions, foundations, universities, endowments and wealthy individual investors. REITs are privately or publicly owned companies that own and, in some cases, operate income-producing real estate including timberlands. REITs distribute most profits to the shareholders in the form of dividends.

TRENDS IN FOREST AREAS AND WOOD PRODUCTION

While the global forest land has been decreasing, particularly in tropical ecosystems, the area of planted forests has been increasing. At the same time, wood production has rapidly increased to satisfy growing demand for timber products.

Development of Forest Land and Area

Based on the FAO definition of forest, the global forest land in 2015 consisted of 24% primary forests (961 million ha), 69% modified natural forests (2734 million ha) and 7% planted forests, including semi-natural forests, production and protective forest plantations (291 million ha).[6] In 2015, the 10 largest countries – among them Russia, Brazil, Canada, the USA, China and the Democratic Republic of the Congo – contributed 67% of the global forest land. Most of the forests that have been converted to other land uses are in tropical areas, led by Brazil, Indonesia and Myanmar, while China and Australia show the highest gains in forest areas. Commercial agriculture accounts for about 40% of the reasons for deforestation in the tropics, local subsistence agriculture for 3%, infrastructure for 10%, urban expansion for 10% and mining for some 7%.[7]

Between 1990 and 2015, the global forest land decreased by 3%, with the largest loss in forest area in Africa and Latin America, but with increases in Asia driven by China, North America and Europe (Figure 9.1). In recent years, planted forests have been increasing at annual rates of 3.3 million ha. China has the highest area of planted forests (77 million ha), followed by the USA (25 million ha), Russia (17 million ha) and Japan (10 million ha).

---

[4] Zhang, D. and Stenger, A., 2014: Timber insurance: perspectives from a legal case and a preliminary review of practices throughout the world. *NZ J. For. Sci.*, 44, 1–7.

[5] Fernholz, K. et al., 2007: TIMOs & REITs: What, Why & How They Might Impact Sustainable Forestry. Dovetail Partners, Minneapolis, 14p.

[6] FAO, 2016: Global Forest Resources Assessment. 2nd edition. Rome, 54p.

[7] FAO, 2016: State of the World's Forests. Forests and agriculture: land-use challenges and opportunities, Rome, 126p.

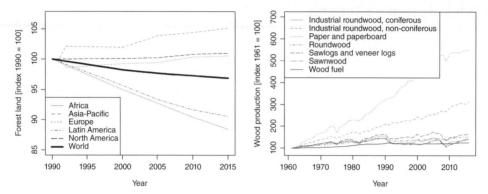

FIGURE 9.1   Left: Indexed (1990) forest land (FAO definition) by geographical region, 1990–2015.
Right: Indexed production (1961) of the main forestry products, 1961–2016.
Data source: FAOSTAT.

Most forests are publicly owned, but the proportion of privately owned forests increased from 15% (1990) to 18% (2010), particularly through management rights of public forests held by private companies. Western and Central Africa show by far the highest proportion of public ownership (99%), followed by Western and Central Asia (9%) and South and Southeast Asia (9%); the highest private ownership was reported for East Asia and Oceania (42%) and North America (33%). A continued decrease in net forest loss rates in the tropics, an increased demand for conversion of forests due to population growth, and with some increases in the temperate and boreal areas, the global forest area is likely to continue to decrease and gradually level out.

Development of Wood Production

In the past 50 years, wood production has nearly doubled, from of 6.5 million m³ (1961) to 11.7 million m³ (2016), with an increase in all main wood products (Figure 9.1). It is estimated that global consumption of industrial roundwood as well as paper and paperboard products is increasing gradually.

To promote sustainability, independent certification of forest management was introduced in the 1990s under the Forest Stewardship Council (FSC) and the Programme for the Endorsement of Forest Certification (PEFC) as the largest international programmes. As a result, the forest area under the FSC and the PEFC increased from 14 million ha (2000) to over 438 million ha (2014) and has demonstrated the fast adaptation of voluntary sustainability certificates.

KEY PERILS

Forests are exposed to a large range of production risks, including (i) natural perils such as wildfire triggered by lightning and following earthquakes, tropical and extratropical cyclones (thunderstorms and winter storms), hail, snow, frost, volcanic eruption, (ii) biotic perils associated with pests and diseases, which are often more prominent following damage from natural perils, and (iii) man-made perils including fire (arson), pollution and contamination. Additionally, regulatory and political risks can cause significant socio-economic changes in how forests are managed and forest products are used.

Financial Risks

In some of the key producing markets lumber, which is timber that is sawed or split into planks or boards, is traded through exchanges to facilitate active price management. The first futures contracts for lumber and lumber products were established at the CME in 1969. The most important CME lumber futures are standardised contracts set at units of 100 000 board feet for 2 inch × 4 inch lumber that is between 8 ft and 20 ft long and includes three quality grades at predefined moisture levels and with spruce, pine and fir as the deliverable timber species. The CME further provides futures contracts for soft pulp and hardwood pulp.

However, as lumber futures contracts are traded in standard units and are available for only a limited number of timber species and products in the main markets, smaller forest owners are exposed to the high volatilities of timber spot market prices.

Production Risks

Insurance remains the main form to protect against production risks, particularly for natural perils. Increasingly, lending institutions and timber investment funds require active management of production risks through insurance, including insurance of carbon reversal under emissions trading schemes (ETSs) in the most advanced markets.

Storm and wildfire damage are the most severe risks to forests on a global scale and have caused considerable losses in the past decades. A series of snowstorms caused financial losses of US$8.4 billion to China's forestry sector in 2008 and winter storm Lothar in 1999 caused damage of over US$6 billion to the forestry sectors of several European countries (Section 3.8). From historical records, one of the worst wildfire damage to forests occurred during in 1939 during the Black Friday Fires in Australia, with US$750 million worth of damage, and the 1987 Black Dragon Fire in Northeast China, with US$700 million of damage (Section 3.9).

Government Disaster Compensation Programmes
Forest owners have been relying on government compensation, tax credits and subsidised low-interest loans for ex-post management of disasters to forests. However, such payments are often available only for the most damaging and large-scale events, while most wildfire and storm events have local impacts. Further, government compensation typically covers only a fraction of the losses, e.g. following storm Gudrun in 2005, the Danish government provided public assistance of €20 million (50% of the total damage) and the Swedish government compensated €2 million relative to the total damage of €940 million.[8] In general, it has been argued that public aid for private forest owners impacted by natural disasters has discouraged the development of private sector forest insurance and reduced incentives for risk management.

9.3 OVERVIEW OF RISK TRANSFER SOLUTIONS

Forest insurance has developed as a function of market demand and consists mainly of private sector products that are tailored to the needs to cover production risks

---

[8] Brunette, M. and Couture, S., 2008: Public compensation for windstorm damage reduces incentives for risk management investments. *Forest Policy Econ.*, 10(7), 491–99.

of NIPFOs, IPFOs and publicly owned forests. The global forest insurance premium reached an estimated US$557 million in 2017, 1.8% of the total agricultural premium of US$30.7 billion.

FOREST INSURANCE PRODUCT TYPES

Insurance products for forest assets include (i) indemnity-based plantation insurance that covers named-perils through basic and enhanced coverage, (ii) firefighting cost insurance, and (iii) index-based insurance for named perils (Table 9.1).

FOREST INSURANCE MARKETS

Forest insurance exists in most countries with large timber sectors. While plantation insurance is offered to NIPFOs with standardised coverage, IPFOs benefit from tailor-made plantation insurance that is often purchased through captives.

Non-industrial Private Forest Owners

NIPFOs are typically self-financed and manage forest assets as part of a wider portfolio of agricultural activities. Plantation insurance for NIPFOs typically works through a facility that offers standardised terms and coverage, particularly when production management and exposure to natural perils are comparable. Due to long rotation cycles, NIPFOs are believed to be risk-neutral in being indifferent between a guaranteed outcome and the same outcome with higher variability.[9] NIPFOs often perceive a higher value in investing in fire breaks, using controlled burning and fencing properties to mitigate the risk from wildfires and arson rather than buying insurance. Because of limited coverage, risk neutral forest owners and high premium rates that are necessary to insure high exposure to wildfire and storms in a limited market, plantation insurance generally had limited success, with low penetration ratios and issues with adverse selection and moral hazard. As forest insurance is offered in most markets as a private sector proposition and compared with most crop and livestock insurance does not benefit from government-premium subsidies, high premium rates have been another limiting reason for poor insurance penetration ratios.

North America

In the USA, forest insurance was first proposed as early as the 1930s but attracted limited interest among forest owners and resulted in low insurance penetrations, with a premium volume estimated at US$8 million in 2017. For example, the expectation of an insurance premium rate in the USA is 0.3% while the mortality rate for all forests is 0.8%,[10] which led to insurance of only 3% of privately owned forests.

---

[9] Manley, B. and Watt, R., 2009: Forestry Insurance, Risk Pooling and Risk Minimisation Options. Ministry of Agriculture and Forestry, University of Canterbury, New Zealand, 54p.
[10] Smith, W.D. et al., 2009: Forest Resources of the United States, 2007. USDA/FS General Technical Report WO-78, Washington.

TABLE 9.1 Overview of the main types of forest insurance products.

Type of Product	Characteristics	Perils Covered	Advantages	Disadvantages	Most Suitable Application
Plantation insurance Section 9.4	▪ Farm-based insurance covering entire plantations or individual sub-sections ▪ Loss assessment at level of plantation or sub-section ▪ Sum insured based on agreed values or replanting costs ▪ Indemnity based on full values, net-of-salvage values or replanting costs ▪ Loss limits per event and in the annual aggregate	*Basic coverage* Total and partial losses from physical damage to standing tree stands from: ▪ Wildfire of natural (mainly lightning) and human (mainly accidents, arson) causes ▪ Windstorm (tropical and extratropical cyclones) ▪ Drought, hail, flood, freeze, snow ▪ Pests and diseases (only in some markets) covering treatment costs only *Extended coverage (non-exhaustive)* ▪ Third-party liability ▪ Onsite harvested timber ▪ Re-establishment costs ▪ Claims preparation costs ▪ Loss mitigation expenses (including additional fire-fighting costs) ▪ Business interruption for industrial tree crops for asset losses ▪ Carbon reversal (Section 9.5)	▪ Tailor-made covers with numerous options for policyholders (deductibles, franchises, premium discounts in function of loss mitigation measures) ▪ Covers most types of plantations and concept easily understood by policyholders ▪ Surveys and questionnaire for larger plantation to identify site-specific risks and management/ mitigation standards	▪ Adverse selection and moral hazard ▪ High costs for administration, distribution and loss adjustment ▪ Valuation of non-standard forests can be complex and costly ▪ Standard insurance conditions can be limited for small farms that are insured through facilities ▪ Successful salvage strategies lead to loss recovery but can be costly ▪ Not suitable for larger public forest areas (mixed stands and age profiles)	▪ Smaller farms insured through facilities or at aggregated level ▪ Industrial plantations through individual coverage in well-developed forestry production systems (e.g. North America, Europe, Latin America, Australia/New Zealand and parts of Asia and Africa)

(Continued)

TABLE 9.1 *(Continued)*

Type of Product	Characteristics	Perils Covered	Advantages	Disadvantages	Most Suitable Application
Firefighting cost insurance Section 9.6	▪ Indemnity-based insurance based on third-party audited expenditure ▪ Index-based insurance based on triggers that closely relate to expenditures (e.g. number of fires, area burnt, fire weather indices) ▪ Annual or multiyear policies with forest areas clearly defined	▪ Large or numerous wildfires causing increased ▪ Suppression costs (e.g wages, transportation, equipment, services, supplies) ▪ Prevention costs (e.g. patrols, surveillance)	▪ Stability in firefighting budgets of government agencies ▪ Fast payouts particularly for index-based products	▪ Basis risk of index-based solutions ▪ Unexpected non-defined expenses are not covered	▪ Large continuous forest areas (natural forests and plantations) under the responsibility for fire suppression of a dedicated (government) agency
Index-based forest insurance Section 9.7	▪ Portfolio-based insurance with aggregate payout based on satellite-detected area burnt above a pre-agreed level ▪ Compensation of pre-agreed value per burnt area ▪ Annual or multi-year policies	▪ Wildfire defined through area burnt as detected by satellite ▪ Aspects of business interruption can be included based on pre-agreed values per area burnt	▪ No adverse selection and moral hazard as losses are determined from satellite data ▪ Lower cost compared to indemnity-based insurance	▪ Short data series of high-resolution area burnt data from satellites (1 km or smaller) ▪ Basis risk and errors in fire classifications by satellites (hot spot) and corresponding area burnt	▪ Large corporate forest owners which are prepared to retain substantial risk and provide comprehensive geo-coded maps with forests under production

Europe

In Spain, only 1.25% of forests are insured against replanting costs following fire, despite Spain having one of the highest exposure to fires and the government promoting forest insurance.[11] The main policy covers replanting costs following wildfires, with loss to timber production being covered for only some tree species, and produced a premium volume of US$7.5 million in 2017. In France, where half of all forests are privately owned and forests of NIPFOs consist of 4%, only 250 000 ha are insured for fire and/or storm risk for a premium volume of US$4.5 million in 2017. With the cancellation of the French government disaster support for private forest owners in 2017 and an area of over 1 million ha owned by NIPFOs, the demand for plantation insurance is expected to increase. Around 2% of the privately owned forests in Germany are insured for fire.

Insurance penetration is highest in Scandinavian countries, where forest insurance is arranged through (i) dedicated mutual insurers like Skogbrand Forest Insurance, with penetration ratios of 35% of all forest area, (ii) landowner associations in Sweden, with 95% of the NIPFOs forest area insured for a premium volume of US$35 million (2017), and Finland, with 40% of NIPFO areas covered under a premium volume of US$6 million (2017). In Denmark, the government made forest insurance a precondition to obtain additional government disaster payments in case of storm and fire losses.

Asia-Pacific

In Japan, government forest insurance started in 1937 and was subsequently combined with an insurance programme managed by the National Federation of Forest Owners' Cooperative Association (Zenmoriren) to provide insurance to NIPFOs, which own about 70% of Japan's forest areas. The annual premium generated from forest insurance is estimated at US$20 million.

Forest insurance in China started in 1982 and increased to a premium volume of US$375 million (2017) after natural woodlands and timber plantations were integrated into the National Agricultural Insurance Program (Section 5.2) in 2009. Different levels of government provide premium subsidies between 30% and 50% to cover reforestation costs from fire only or additional perils including windstorm, hail, landslide, drought and certain pests and diseases. Premium rates are typically applied at province level and vary between 0.1% for fire-only cover and 1.1% for comprehensive insurance, while rates tend to be higher for plantations than for natural woodlands.

In Australia, NIPFOs can buy forest insurance through the Australian Forest Growers Association (AFG) and similarly in New Zealand, Standsure provides coverage for small and middle-sized forest owners. Insurance for NIFPOs in Southeast Asia remains in its infancy.[12]

---

[11] Barreal, J. et al., 2014: On insurance as a tool for securing forest restoration after wildfires. *Forest Policy Econ.*, 42, 15–23.

[12] Cottle, P., 2007: Insuring Southeast Asian commercial forests: Fire risk analysis and the potential for use of data in risk pricing and reduction of forest fire risk. *Mitig. Adapt. Strat. Glob. Change*, 12, 181–201.

Australian Forest Growers Plantation Insurance Scheme
In 2011, Australia reported a forest area of 125 million ha, equivalent to 16% of the
land area, which included (i) 123 million ha of native forests, of which 91.9 million
(66.8%) are privately managed, and, (ii) 2 million ha of industrial plantations, with
31% owned by institutional investors, 24% by managed investment schemes and
21% under private ownership, including farm foresters, timber industry companies
and other private entities.[13] In 2015, the Australian forestry industry was valued at
AU$9.6 billion, its key export markets being China and Japan.

Australia's forests are exposed to cyclones (northern Australia), wildfires, drought
as well as pests and diseases, with climate change likely to increase annual timber
losses. The demand for plantation insurance is high among private forest owners and
commercial timber plantations, but coverage is limited and available from only a few
insurers. To provide standardised and affordable coverage, the AFG, as the national
association representing over 500 smaller private forest owners and private forest companies, has been offering plantation insurance since 1984.

The AFG Plantation Insurance Scheme provides coverage for AFG members for
total and partial losses from fire, lightning, hail, windstorm, cyclone and aircraft damage on the basis of agreed values.[14] Extended coverage is provided for public liability,
claims preparation costs, loss mitigation expenses up to a maximum of AU$100 000
and debris removal costs of up to 10% of sum insured or AU$250 000. Each pol-
icy contains a maximum loss limit of AU$12 million. Standard valuation tables are
used for the main tree species (*Pinus radiata* and *Eucalyptus globulus*) and experts are
committed to approving valuations for other tree species. Insureds have the option to
agree to a net-of-salvage option for older pine plantations or to insure replanting costs
only. The insurance scheme functions on automatic acceptance based on standard rates
that vary by region, tree species and age, with certain standard management standards
required (e.g. fire breaks). Premium rates are tailored to risk levels and are a function of
plantation management standards. The insurance scheme has provided private forest
owners continuous insurance protection and through high participation and geographical spread, premium rates are kept at reasonable levels.

Industrial Private Forest Owners

Insurance of timber assets of IPFOs is available in most markets with larger-scale
commercial timber production.[15] IPFOs typically own geographically diversified forests and in some cases production assets in different regions or countries. Insurance
is therefore tailored to specific risks and often covers entire production portfolios,
with large first loss limits and deductibles per loss event. Some IPFOs own captives
(Section 2.3) through which facultative reinsurance protection is purchased from international markets. In New Zealand, around 59% of the total forest area is owned by

---

[13] ABARES, 2014: Australia's State of the Forests Report 2013. Five-yearly Report, Executive
Summary, 16p.
[14] http://www.afg.asn.au/insurance/features-of-the-scheme (accessed December 2017).
[15] Examples of IFPOs that have or are buying plantation insurance for natural perils include
Arauco, Forestal Bio and CMPC (Chile), Sinoforest (China), Asia Pulp & Paper (Indonesia),
Weyerhauser and Hancock (Australia/New Zealand), Sappi and Mondi (South Africa) and the
Navigator Company (Portugal).

timber companies with areas under management of above 10 000 ha where insurance penetration for windstorm insurance has reached 36% and 19% for fire respectively.

However, the corporate forestry segment, particularly operations with geographically well-diversified assets, considers the risk of production losses small and manageable through cash reserves, while insurance is perceived to be expensive and limited in coverage. Increasingly, investors require plantation insurance for integrative risk management, particularly for concentrated timber assets, where insurers offer tailor-made plantation insurance products for aggregated risks.

Public Forest Owners

Publicly owned forests tend to be uninsured and losses are absorbed through government budgets. An exception is Sveaskog, which is owned by the Swedish government and manages 4 million ha of Sweden's forest land or a 14% share of the total forest land. To avoid unexpected costs from storm damage to standing timber that is valued at US$3.5 billion, Sveaskog has been buying forestry reinsurance for its captive to cover increased cost of up to US$220 million.[16] In China, state-owned forests are directly insured as natural woodlands covering pre-agreed reforestation costs following damage from fire only or comprehensive named-peril forest insurance. In some countries, government agencies buy insurance for increased costs and budget volatility due to fighting particularly large forest fires (Section 9.6).

CHALLENGES OF FOREST INSURANCE

The insurance of forest assets is challenging due to the (i) presence of systemic perils such as windstorm (Section 3.8) and wildfire (Section 3.9), which cause rare but high losses at large scale and disrupt the dynamics of entire timber markets, (ii) complexity of valuation of different age and species compositions that cover large geographical areas under long rotation cycles of 20–80 years, (iii) different management standards and interdependence of risks, e.g. well-managed plantations beside neglected forests incur higher risks from fire, (iv) high reliance on authorities for mitigation (e.g. firefighting), (v) general lack of or difficult access to forest loss data and models to calculate loss severity and frequency of different perils, (vi) initial high investment costs in technical capabilities including monitoring, administration and loss adjustment, and (vii) reputation risk in markets where illegal logging occurs and timber certification requirements are not met. Other challenges include long claims settlement processes, particularly when salvage of damaged timber needs to be established. As with other agricultural insurance products, forest insurance schemes have suffered from moral hazard and adverse selection where inaccurate rates lead to an accumulation of high risks and insurance terms perceived to be uneconomical.

9.4 PLANTATION INSURANCE

Planted forests (plantations) typically include higher-valued tree species in monocultures that have 10–40 years of rotation cycles and with several plots that have a

---

[16] Sveaskog, 2018: Annual Report and Sustainability Report 2017. Stockholm, 112p.

uniform tree age, high concentration of values and large risk exposure. Increasingly, the demand for plantation insurance is driven by timber investment funds and in some markets carbon certificates to protect forest assets against unforeseeable damage from natural perils. Plantation insurance provides basic coverage and extended coverage to NIPFOs and IPFOs, in function of market requirements and the size of the plantations. NIPFOs, with smaller plantations, tend to be insured in schemes with standard coverage and insurance terms while IPFOs benefit from tailor-made insurance structures.

INSURANCE TERMS

Planation insurance provides basic coverage while extended coverage is available in some markets in addition to basic coverage (endorsements) or as standalone products. The valuation of forest assets forms the basis to define insured values, while potential salvage after loss events is a key element in the definition of insurance terms.

Requirements for Insurance

Forest insurance policies typically require the insurance of all plantations that are within a certain distance of the main location in a dedicated schedule that states location (i.e., administrative area or geo-coordinates), tree species, age class and total agreed values. Insurers often request a forest management plan and maps showing the forests to be insured. The insured warrants to comply with standard forest management approaches that include compliance with (i) fire plans as required by legislation, including maintenance of fire breaks and firefighting equipment, (ii) thinning plans as common market practice, (iii) controlled burning where the insurer needs to be notified, and (iv) maintenance of records including events that did not lead to an insurance claim. The insurer often asks the insured to provide details on (i) public access to the plantations by roads or foot, and public recreational activities in or near the plantations (e.g. camping), (ii) powerlines running through or at the edges of the plantation and maintenance of the interface with the plantation (regularity of trimming), and (iii) management of fuel loads in the plantation and availability of on-site fire fighting equipment.

As timber plantations have been flagged for sustainability in the context of establishments on prime forest resources, insurers, to minimise reputational risks, often request sustainable forest management including a certificate label such as those from the Forest Stewardship Council (FSC) and the Programme for the Endorsement of Forest Certification Schemes (PEFC).

Basic Insurance Coverage

Plantation insurance basic coverage includes direct total or partial damage from windstorm, fire and hail as well as lightning and aircraft impact for standing timber of different age classes. In some markets, partial or total losses from snow pressure, flooding, volcanic eruption (ashfall and mudflows) as well as the occurrence of named pests and diseases are insured. In some countries (e.g. UK and Ireland), third-party liability is provided under basic coverage. Plantation insurance policies typically contain an annual aggregate limit and often have event limits of 72 hours for windstorm, 72–168 hours for wildfire, depending on the market, and 72 hours for volcanic eruption.

Standard exclusions of plantation insurance include (i) felled, damaged or dead timber or timber without a commercial value as observed at inception of insurance,

(ii) stored timber unless explicitly covered, (iii) damage from pest, diseases, fungi, insects, wild animals and rodents, (iv) nuclear risks related to ionising radiations, contamination and radioactivity, and (v) acts of terrorism that are officially recognised by a competent authority. Some of the excluded perils are insurable under extensions of plantation insurance.

Extended Insurance Coverage

Extended coverage under planation insurance typically includes (i) third-party liability for cases when a fire started on the policyholder's property and damaged other property, (ii) re-establishment costs, (iii) claims preparation costs for e.g. aerial mapping, and (iv) loss mitigation expenses. Re-establishment costs include expenses for clearing and land preparation (debris removal), repairing/replacing fences, repairing bridges and firefighting reservoirs, purchasing new seedlings and initial replanting. As environmental conditions (e.g. a drought) can considerably delay re-establishment and increase overall costs, insurers impose a time limit for re-establishment (e.g. until the next growing season). While firefighting is typically the responsibility of government agencies, which often prioritise large fires near urban areas (Section 9.6), forest owners' costs can be significant for supressing smaller fires in or near plantations. In some cases, additional firefighting costs and charges to contribute to government funds for fire suppression are insurable under extended covers. Felled logs that are stored on the policyholder's property are insured in some countries. Extended coverage is mostly sub-limited for each type of coverage through an annual aggregate limit or a limit per area unit of insurance (e.g. a block). Carbon insurance is typically offered as a standalone product in markets with active ETSs.

Valuation of Forest Assets

Forest owners periodically value forest production assets according to standardised valuation methods, which often form the basis for determining the sum insured under plantation insurance covers. Forest valuation is used to establish fair market value for the purpose of government levies on harvested timber and forestry property taxes.

Forest Valuation Methods
Governments typically recommend certain forest valuation methods for tax assessments of NIPFOs and commercial timber companies and provide software to support the determination of timber values.

The three most common valuation methods for plantations and natural forests are (i) the market value method, which relies on quoted or average historical log prices and mainly is used for forests with short rotation cycles (5–20 years), (ii) the historical cost method, where incurred costs for input supplies and management are used for newly established plantations up to an age of 4–5 years, and (iii) the net present value method, which is based on anticipated future cash flows and costs (maintenance, thinning, transport) discounted to present value and is used in the absence of reliable quoted market prices and for slow growing forests.[17] The net present value method

---

[17] PricewaterhouseCoopers, 2009: Forest Industry: Application review of IAS 41, Agriculture: The Fair Value of Standing Timber, 26p.

relies on modification of the original Faustmann formula where the value of a forest (VF_s) with trees of a given age s is calculated for a first rotation as:[18]

$$VF_s = \left[v(t) + \sum_{j=s=1}^{t} A_j e^{r(t-j)} + LEV \right] e^{-r(t-s)}$$

with $v(t)$ as the stumpage value of the stand at the end of the first rotation, A_j as the intermediate incomes or expenses for a year j, r as the interest rate for the first rotation, LEV as the land value at the end of the first rotation and s as the tree age with $0 \le s \le t$. The Faustmann formula can be generalised to any rotation.

Forest Yield Tables

Yield tables are important elements for forest valuation to calculate the expected harvested timber volume as a function of tree species, age profile, stand density, management practices and site conditions (e.g. soil types). Site conditions are typically expressed through a site index that measures the average height of the tallest 20 trees per surface unit. Typically, naturally regenerated stands show higher timber volume than plantation stands at the same site index; however, plantations contain larger log diameters (Figure 9.2). Management practices such as thinning from below or above have an impact on yield, and while intensive thinning reduces the overall yield per surface unit, it maximises log diameters (Figure 9.2). Natural forests are more complex to

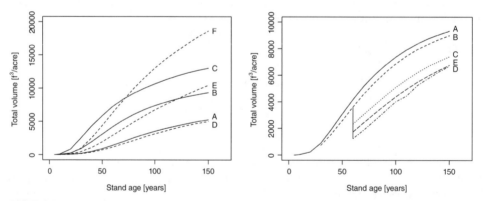

FIGURE 9.2 Left: Yield curves in function of stand age for (i) Douglas fir (solid lines) with <500 trees/acre and no thinning at site index 50 (A), 70 (B) and 90 (C = most productive), and (ii) naturally regenerated stands in a fir ecosystem (dashed lines) at site index 50 (D) and 70 (E) and 90 (F = most productive) for inland forests in the Northwest of the USA. Right: Yield curves in function of stand age for a Douglas fir stand with <500 trees/acre with no thinning (A), thinning from below to 250 trees at age 20 (B), thinning at age 20 from below to 100 trees at age 50 (C), thinning at age 20 from above to 100 trees at age 50 (D) and thinning at age 20 and to 100 trees at age 50 so that mean diameters at breast height stays the same (E) for inland forests in the Northwest of the USA. *Data source*: USDA/Forest Service.

---

[18] Chang, S.J., 2014: Forest valuation under the generalized Faustmann formula. *Can. J. For. Res.*, 44, 56–63.

valuate as they typically contain a mixture of tree species, age profiles and management standards.

Sum Insured

Plantation insurance uses established timber valuation practices and the policyholder submits details to the insurer in a schedule attached to the insurance proposal. The sum insured is based on agreed values, which are determined at inception of insurance as a function of tree species, age, location and management standards according to a standard valuation methodology and approved valuation tables that rely on productivity estimates and include annual cubic metre values per surface units, tree species and sites.

The basis of agreed values is defined as (i) full value that reflects the valuation of the plantation at market terms, (ii) net-of-salvage value, which deducts potential salvage values of damaged timber after an insured loss, or (iii) replanting costs that represent a portion of the initial costs to establish a plantation and are typically applied to younger tree stands. In some markets, full value coverage is limited by a predefined monetary amount. A typical sum insured for planation insurance ranges from US$1000 to US$3000 per hectare. For industrial tree crops, insured value can reach over US$250 per tree.

Indemnity

An indemnity occurs based on loss assessment of the volume of damaged timber relative to the volume of insured timber net of any deductible and up to the maximum loss limit, if any. In some markets (e.g. China), losses are determined according to damage ratios where (i) partial losses are compensated for certain perils (e.g. storm damage) for broken branches, and (ii) total losses are paid for severe damage to stems and crowns as well as uprooting. Under extended coverage, indemnity is provided based on actual incurred costs (e.g. claims preparation costs, loss mitigation expenses) or estimated costs (e.g. re-establishment) net of deductibles and up to pre-agreed limits.

Deductibles are typically applied for each and every loss amount as a percentage of sum insured or a monetary value, whichever is the greater. Larger plantation risks that include several distinct geographical locations often include an annual aggregate deductible.

Salvage Evaluation

Uprooted trees are exposed to sap-staining fungi (e.g. blue stain), which cause large losses if logs are not salvaged and stored within a reasonable time. Generally, wood quality is longest preserved in hardwood tree species (e.g. oak) and logs destined for veneer wood have the highest devaluation from wood staining. A damaged tree contains a certain residual value, called salvage value, that depends on the age, the intended use of the timber, the damage extent and cause as well as the processing capacity of sawmills and market conditions. For example, fire-damaged *P. radiata* logs can have salvage potentials of up to 50% at 20 years of age and 80% at 30 years.

Following large-scale damage, local timber markets are often oversupplied, which causes a decline in timber prices, results in saw mills refusing to accept further timber for processing and can put the entire industry in economic downturn. In the longer term, an initial decrease in timber prices due to oversupply can result in higher prices due to undersupply of the initially damaged standing timber inventory. Models have been developed to determine the optimum timing and amount to salvage storm- and fire-damaged timber for private forests that consist of monocultures; however, this is challenging for public forests due to different interest groups and motivations relative to salvage.[19]

Storage of Salvaged Timber
Options to store salvaged timber while preventing significant wood decay include (i) in-situ storage through live conservation or drying by transpiration of trees which are still alive and have sufficient root contact, (ii) wet storage using water sprinklers or immersion in fresh water like a lake, (iii) drying in covered cross-pile storages, (iv) storage under humid conditions in piles covered with plastic, and (v) conservation under oxygen exclusion which is used for high-value timber. The costs of each methods depend on the circumstances and some methods require special site-specific conditions. As salvage potential can be considerable, salvage is carefully assessed by forestry experts to outweigh the increased costs for storage and transportation.

Salvage Potentials Under Plantation Insurance
For plantation insurance policies that are based on full value, the insurer has the right to commission salvage and store the timber at its own expense and is the ultimate beneficiary from potential loss recoveries from sales of salvaged logs. However, salvage operations are often expensive and loss recovery can take months and in some cases years, particularly when logs need to be exported as domestic markets are oversupplied or logs need to be stored in lakes that are in environmental protection zones. Equally, the determination of salvage under net-of-salvage policies, where salvage is the duty of the policyholder, can take a long time. To provide indemnity before final values are established, some net-of-salvage insurance policies include pre-agreed salvage tables.

Premium Rates
Premium rates are expressed in function of the sum insured of the plantation (agreed values) and depend on the location, age of the forest, perils covered and management standards, with different options in function of event and annual aggregate limits and deductibles. Plantation premium rates are typically in the permilles (e.g. 0.2% for fire and 0.4% for storm) but can reach up to 3% for all risk insurance, as in Sweden for example. While rates are applied individually for large plantations, smaller plantations that are covered under plantation schemes are often based on risk zones classified as low, medium and high risk. Typical premium rates for plantation insurance range from 0.2% (fire only) to 3% (all disaster damage) with regional differences, e.g. 1.5–2.6% (fire only) in South Africa and 0.8% for all damage up to full reforestation cost in China.

Plantation insurance typically includes a non-claims bonus in the form of a discount on premium rates for the next season relative to the current season, with a

---

[19] Prestemon. J.P. et al., 2006: Wildfire, timber salvage, and the economics of expediency. *Forest Policy Econ.*, 8, 312–22.

maximum discount defined after a period of several years of loss-free records (e.g. a no-claims bonus of 30% after 10 years).

PRICING

Forest insurance is often loss free but can show catastrophe losses from wildfire and storm in some years, which makes underwriting and pricing based on historical insurance losses a challenge in most markets. As historical insurance claims are not consistently available, stand compositions vary over rotation cycles, forest management practices change over time, loss mitigation measures (e.g. fire breaks) are not always maintained at the same level, and forest owners hardly buy insurance over subsequent years, standardising historical insurance claims, as is common practice under crop insurance programmes, is hardly possible.

Use of Loss Proxies for Pricing

The most common approach for pricing forestry risks is the use of loss proxies, which are typically available through forest surveys from government agencies and include, for a given administrative area (e.g. a county) or forest exploitation zone, peril-specific area damaged per season or year (e.g. number of fires, area burnt, area damaged by windstorm). In some cases, loss proxies provide additional information on (i) loss scales, e.g. area burnt from small, large and very large fires, (ii) loss severity split into total losses and partial losses, and (iii) loss occurrence where losses for each individual fire are based on fire observation reports. Loss proxies are generally available in tabular form, but in some countries (e.g. the USA), area damaged by peril is available for each year in the form of maps or geo-referenced polygons for individual loss events. Loss proxies typically cover larger areas and longer time frames (>20 years) than data from single plantations and are therefore more likely to include large and catastrophe-type losses. It has to be noted that some of the largest losses to plantations have occurred in recent years and that forest–urban interfaces have changed significantly over time.

For wider risk analyses, fire danger indices,[20] which rely on observed meteorological parameters and environmental conditions (Section 3.9), have been used for wildfires to derive numbers of fires of a given severity that are likely to occur, with consistent time series reaching back 40–60 years. Besides fire danger indices, standard precipitation indices (Section 3.3) and heating degree days (Section 6.9) have been applied as proxies to represent environmental conditions that are conducive for large wildfires. Further, satellite-based analyses of area burnt can be used to assess spatial fire patterns on different time scales for at least 10–15 years (Section 4.3.2).

Modelling of Damage Ratios

Based on loss proxies, vulnerability profiles are established and risk rates determined according to plantation-specific parameters, including loss mitigation measures and the level of access of the public. Damage ratio can be approximated through an empirical

---

[20] For example, the Canadian Forest Fire Weather Index (Canada), Orieux (France), IREPI (Italy), the Fire Danger Rating System (USA) and the Monte Alegre Formula (Brazil).

probability distribution $F_n(t)$ for a forest stand of age t with areas of age classes assumed to be uniformly distributed through:[21]

$$F_n(t) = \sum_{i < t} \frac{\hat{f}}{\hat{f}_i}$$

with $\hat{f} = \sum_{i=1}^{k} \hat{f}_i$ and $\hat{f}$ as the total expected population proportion of a destruction occurrence within the sample areas and $\hat{f}_i$ as the population proportion of the expected destroyed areas in a particular age class i.

Often, the Weibull distribution is chosen as the empirical distribution for a specific peril as well as a combination of perils.[22] The Weibull distribution has found to be well suited to model windstorm severity and the inverse Gaussian distribution for fire severity. For extreme wildfire and windstorm events, the Generalised Extreme Value distribution and the Generalised Pareto distribution have been proposed.[23] Further, spatio-temporal autoregressive models based on historical loss proxies have been suggested as viable models to determine forest insurance terms.[24]

In cases where the forest area can be damaged by only one peril, which is often the case for combined fire and windstorm occurrence, which happen in different seasons, probabilities are summed up over the perils to obtain the total damage expectation. However, when each peril can occur at any time and even simultaneously (e.g. forest fire, drought and hail, which tend to occur in the same season), a joint probabilities function needs to be developed. In practice, loss expectations of secondary perils such as hail are often added to the expected loss from main perils such as fire and windstorm. For forest insurance structures where indemnity is defined for a single rather than the sum of annual events, loss frequency and loss severity modelling is commonly applied and subsequently combined through an aggregate loss model (Section 2.4).

LOSS ADJUSTMENT

Loss adjustment for insurance purposes establishes the (i) volume of damaged timber in relation to timber volumes before a loss event, or (ii) damage ratios in terms of partial and total losses. Most forest insurance policies require intensive surveys to be undertaken within 30 days of a claim notification, which can be challenging in large-scale forests and inaccessible terrain. Forestry loss adjusters and salvage specialists provide an overview of salvage options, which is essential for policies that are based on full values and where salvage is to the benefit of the insurer.

---

[21] Holecy, J. and Hanewinkel, M., 2006: A forest management risk insurance model and its application to coniferous stands in southwest Germany. *Forest Policy Econ.*, 8, 161–74.

[22] Brunette, M. et al., 2015: An actuarial model of forest insurance against multiple natural hazards in fir (*Abies alba* Mill.) stands in Slovakia. *Forest Policy Econ.*, 55, 46–57.

[23] Lin, X.G. et al., 2011: Estimate of Maximum Insurance Loss due to Bushfires. 19th International Congress on Modelling and Simulation, Perth, Australia, 12–16 December 2011, 7p. and Bengtsson, A. and Nilsso, C., 2007: Extreme value modelling of storm damage in Swedish forests. *Nat. Haz. Earth Syst. Sci.*, 7, 515–21.

[24] Chen, X. et al., 2013: Is timber insurable? A study of wildfire risks in the U.S. forest sector using spatio-temporal models. *Amer. J. Agr. Econ.*, 96(1), 213–31.

The estimation of losses on forest stands relies on (i) general surveys that establish the area damaged from aerial photography (helicopters, airplanes and increasing from drones) and satellite images, and (ii) intensive surveys where damage is assessed through site inspections to determine damaged timber volume, partial and total losses. For larger damage areas, intensive surveys are undertaken through transects and loss extents are extrapolated to wider areas using general survey techniques. Some coordinative efforts have been undertaken to provide real-time information on damage extents in forests for actuarial modelling and loss adjustment in the European Union.[25]

Constructive total losses (CTLs) are declared for areas when remaining trees will continue to grow but the area is cleared as the remaining trees are considered uneconomical to manage until maturity. Such managed felling of remaining trees is relatively common for wind-damaged stands. Standard plantation insurance either (i) excludes CTLs or (ii) covers CTLs based on pre-agreed damage thresholds, e.g. 75% of trees damaged to such an extent that the area is judged to be non-economical.

Loss Adjustment of Storm Damage

For storm damage, loss surveys identify damage ratios including (i) stem breakage, which requires pruning or felling, (ii) twisted trunks, (iii) uprooted trees, which need to be salvaged, and (iv) bent trees, with taller trees to be removed and younger trees likely to straighten naturally.[26] Heavy rainfall from tropical cyclones can cause (i) flooding in forest stands where the loss of soil oxygen leads to root mortality and tree death, and (ii) saltwater intrusion in coastal areas, which causes forest stands to turn brown and show reduced growth, though they usually recover after time.

Forest stands with (i) light damage (broken branches, tree bending <45°) will typically recover naturally, (ii) moderate damage (>25% of stems broken, bent or uprooted) require salvage through removal of trees that are unlikely to survive, and a partial loss is recognised, (iii) severe damage (>30% of stems broken, tree tops broken, uprooted trees and tree bending >45°) require salvage through clear-cutting, and a total loss is recognised, and (iv) catastrophic damage (>50% broken stems, large number of blown down trees and broken tree tops, uprooted trees and tree bending >45°) are salvaged through clear-cutting, and a total loss is recognised.[27]

Loss Adjustment of Wildfire Damage

For wildfires, loss surveys identify (i) crown scorch, which are needles that were exposed to lethal temperatures which leave bare branches on trees, (ii) stem char line, which refers to the blackened portion of the stem that was exposed to flames and leaves permanent stains in the wood, (iii) crown consumption, which reveals the portion of the crown and living needles directly burnt by crown fires, and (iv) burnt roots, which occurs from slow burning fires and leads to tree mortality. Typically, severely burned stands (>70% stem char) are immediately salvaged and stands with light damage

---

[25] For example, Forest Loss Assessment through Remote Evaluation (FLARE, https://business. esa.int/projects/flare).

[26] Barry, P.J. et al., 1993: How to evaluate and manage storm-damaged forest areas. USDA/FS Management Bulletin R8-MB 63, Washington, 18p.

[27] Bates, C. et al., 2017: Timber impact assessment. Georgia Forestry Commission, GFC Timber Impacts Assessment, 7p.

(<30% stem char) are left to survive, while forests with moderate damage are left to survive or are salvaged, depending on site-specific and market conditions.

9.5 CARBON REVERSAL INSURANCE

The absorption of greenhouse gases (GHGs) by forests has been recognised in efforts to combat climate change and investigations into carbon offsetting and trading schemes started following the Kyoto Protocol in 1997. Under the Kyoto Protocol, countries can trade GHG emissions in the form of certificates from projects that are based on biological sequestration, renewable energy, industrial gases, methane capturing, energy efficiency and fuel switching. The financial liabilities of the risk of reversal of carbon credits through physical damage to forests have led to the development of carbon insurance in markets like New Zealand with active carbon ETSs.

CARBON EMISSIONS TRADING SCHEMES

The Kyoto Protocol has led to the establishment of several ETSs and exchanges (e.g. the European Climate Exchange, the Chicago Climate Exchange) for the benefit of governments and corporations. Emission trading schemes can be distinguished into (i) projects-based markets, where a baseline for a business is defined as the usual activity and credits are granted for emitting less relative to the baseline, and (ii) allowance markets, which follow a cap-and-trade system where specific limits are imposed and permits are issued for reductions of emissions to equal permits issued or additional permits bought. Different mechanisms that offset carbon, including forests under the biological sequestration category, have been identified, with a basic unit of carbon off-set defined as one ton of carbon dioxide equivalent (tCO_2e) that has not been emitted into the atmosphere.

Carbon Offset Markets

Carbon offset markets can be split into (i) compliance markets, where government agencies set the rules on permitted offsets (e.g. the California cap-and-trade scheme), and (ii) voluntary markets, where corporations purchase carbon offsets for emissions caused under rules set by voluntary standard bodies. In 2016, voluntary markets offset carbon of 63.4 million tCO_2e for a value of US\$191.3 million at an average price of US\$3.0/tCO_2e, which was a reduction from a peak at 134.5 million tCO_2e in 2012.[28] In 2013, voluntary forest carbon markets offset 29 million tCO_2e and compliance forest carbon markets 4 million tCO_2e, mainly in California, Australia and New Zealand.[29] The implementation of the 2015 Paris Agreement, where most governments made a commitment to enhance GHG mitigation, is likely to increase the supply and demand for carbon offsets.

---

[28] Hamrick, K. and Gallant, M., 2017: Unlocking Potential State of the Voluntary Carbon Markets 2017 - Overview. Forest Trends Publication, Washington DC, 20p.
[29] Goldstein, A. and Gonzalez, G., 2014: Turning over a New Leaf: State of the Forest Carbon Markets 2014. Forest Trends report, Washington DC, 110p.

Carbon Sequestration in Forests

Carbon sequestration by forest land falls under the Land Use, Land-Use Change and Forestry (LULUCF) activities and includes projects that (i) avoid emissions through conservation of existing carbon stock, which are called reduced deforestation and degradation (REDD), (ii) increase carbon storage by sequestration through afforestation and reforestation, and (iii) enhance carbon storage through improved forest management. Such projects are eligible for carbon credits through ETSs. For a forest activity to obtain a carbon credit, the offset must be real, permanent (i.e. 100 years), verifiable by a third party and have a clear ownership.

The amount of carbon sequestrated in forests is determined by in-field assessment as a function of tree species, age and region or is available in some markets through standardised look-up tables. Look-up tables are pre-calculated average values of carbon stock in forests, in function of forest types, age and region. These tables reveal the amount of CO_2 removed from the atmosphere and stored in a forest, as well as the carbon that would be released back into the atmosphere from harvest (Figure 9.3).

Carbon Credits and Risk of Reversal

Carbon credits can be grouped in (i) ex-ante, where forests receive certificates on reductions that are planned or forecasted but have not yet been achieved, and (ii) ex-post, in that forests obtain certificates based only on reductions that have already occurred and where quantities are certain. Ex-ante certificates bear the risk of non-performance from the destruction of forests by natural perils or human causes, which leads to a reversal and premature rendering of carbon credits as the carbon is released into the atmosphere. Additional risks with carbon credits of forest projects include (i) anthropogenic factors such as encroachment, fires, theft, harvesting, land management, (ii) political risks including non-enforcement, non-compliance, expropriation, uncertain property rights, policy changes, (iii) economic risks such as fluctuations in exchange and interest

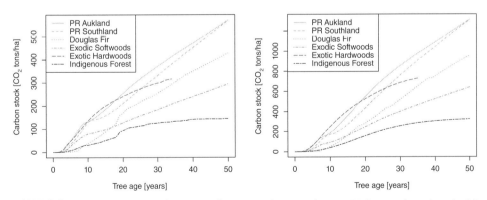

FIGURE 9.3 Carbon stock in function of tree age for *P. radiata* (PR) in two locations in New Zealand and other main tree species as well as indigenous forests for Left: the first rotation, and Right: harvested residues of the previous rotation (above-ground wood and in roots) and carbon stock in the second (or later) rotation with <10 years after the previous forest was cleared or harvested.

Data source: Ministry of Primary Industries of New Zealand.

rates, and changes in opportunity costs of land, and (iv) financial, market and institutional risks.[30]

Reversals are classified as (i) avoidable, which include inadequate forest management practices that lead to overharvesting, and (ii) unavoidable, which includes damage caused by natural perils such as drought, fire, storm, and pests and diseases. It is typically the responsibility of the seller of the carbon credit (i.e. the owner of the forest asset) to compensate for reversals in carbon credits. To manage potential liabilities from carbon reversals, sellers, either individually or through a buffer pool, set aside forest areas that can be replaced by the areas that are under carbon certificates and have incurred a reversal.

CARBON REVERSAL INSURANCE

In markets where forest activities obtain carbon credits, liabilities from the risk of reversals have triggered demand for risk transfer through insurance. Carbon insurance covers the value of sequestered carbon up to the time of the reversal and operates as a cover for additional value under an endorsement to plantation insurance, which insures the same trees that are certified for carbon sequestration against physical damage. Loss costs for reversals of carbon from natural perils would be like those for plantation insurance. For example, the premium for carbon insurance has been calculated to reach US$0.64/ton of carbon for a project that sequestrates annually 3 tons of carbon over 10 years at an annual premium rate of 0.7% of carbon value and a carbon credit value of US$30/ton at a discount rate of 8%.[31]

The risk of carbon reversals and related liabilities is seen as a key entrance barrier to voluntary carbon schemes and risk transfer or mitigation solutions will significantly contribute in managing liabilities arising from natural perils and will lead to growth in the forest segment in ETSs. New Zealand is the best known and probably the only market where private forest owners can insure unavoidable reversals of carbon credits in the form of standardised insurance.

Challenges with Carbon Reversal Insurance

Despite demand to manage the risk of carbon reversal, insurers are often reluctant to cover the risk of reversals of carbon credits as (i) forest insurance is complex in itself and plantation owners are considered as risk neutral, (ii) there are long lead times, with tree rotation cycles of 30–50 years and carbon credit durations of up to 100 years, (iii) it can be difficult to understand carbon valuation approaches of different forest types and access relevant data, (iv) it can be difficult to evaluate loss potentials and price risks based on little historical experience, (v) there is high historical volatility of carbon prices (500% in some markets), (vi) there is potential accumulation in exposure from insuring the same plantation under traditional forestry schemes, and (vii) there

---

[30] Wong-Leung, J.P. and Dutschke, M., 2003: Can Permanence be Insured? Consideration of some Technical and Practical Issues of Insuring Carbon Credits from Afforestation and Reforestation. HWWA Discussion Paper 235, Hamburg, 22p.

[31] Subak, S., 2003: Replacing carbon lost from forests: An assessment of insurance, reserves, and expiring credits. *Climate Policy*, 3, 107–22.

is exposure to changes in regulation of carbon credits and carbon trading schemes. Additionally, the implementation of ETSs is slow as new regulation, carbon eligibility rules, valuation scales and accounting rules need to be defined and most markets have seen high volatilities of carbon prices in past years.

The Insurability of Carbon Credits for Forests in New Zealand

The forestry sector in New Zealand generates an annual gross income of NZ$5 billion and contributes 3% to the country's GDP. New Zealand consists of 7.8 million ha of natural forests and 1.7 million ha of planted forests, with *P. radiata* covering over 90% of the plantation areas. Around 60% of forests are publicly owned and 40% belong to private owners, while 95% of the planted forests are privately owned.

Carbon Initiatives

New Zealand ratified the Kyoto Protocol in 2002 and entered into binding international obligations to meet its commitments, with the estimated requirement for 45.5 million carbon credits by the end of 2012, and established the Permanent Forest Sinks Initiative (PFSI), the Afforestation Grant Scheme (AGS) and ETSs. PFSI offers owners of planted forests that are permanently established since 1990 emission units for the carbon absorbed by forests. AGS aims to establish 15 000 ha of new forests in New Zealand (2015–2020).

Forestry was the first sector to enter the ETS in 2008, with voluntary participation of owners with post-1989 forest land and mandatory participation for owners with pre-1990 forests that have been deforested. Under ETS, owners of post-1989 forests are liable for emissions due to all disturbances and are obliged to submit carbon stock assessments to record changes in carbon stock due to harvesting and growth. To determine the value of carbon per region, tree species and age class, owners of smaller forests (<100 ha) use look-up tables provided by the government that are based on past field evaluations. Owners of larger forests (>100 ha) follow a field measurement approach for sample plots selected by the government, based on which owner-specific look-up tables are created.

Carbon Reversal Insurance

For forest owners under PFSI, the government has suggested self-insurance in the form of a buffer pool of certificates as the cost of forest carbon credit insurance from the private market was judged to be most likely uneconomical. For forests committed under ETS, private insurers have been offering coverage for unavoidable reversals of carbon credits as an extension to plantation insurance since 2010. As a recent amendment in the ETS legislation removed liabilities for carbon losses due to natural causes if forest re-establishment was not possible after the event, carbon insurance focuses on liabilities of carbon reversals that are not re-established.

9.6 FIREFIGHTING COST INSURANCE

In years with particularly numerous and/or large wildfires, government agencies that are charged to suppress fires regularly incur increased costs that are to be covered through additional budgets. Prolonged wildfire seasons as a possible effect of global warming and changes in urban–forest interfaces are likely to increase the risk for wild-fires and related firefighting expenses.

Costs from wildfires can be considerable for government agencies and can be grouped into (i) prevention costs, including fire detection, training of crew, enforcement (patrols) and firefighting equipment, (ii) mitigation costs, including fuel management, insurance and disaster assistance, (iii) suppression costs, including costs for labour and equipment, and (iv) other costs related to regulation and legal requirements, research and development. Direct costs for fire suppression include expenditures for wages, transportation, equipment, services and supplies, which exponentially increase in the case of particularly large and catastrophic wildfires when additional resources and equipment are required. With changes from volunteer to professional fire departments and the occurrence of more and larger wildfires, firefighting costs have increased sig-nificantly in many countries and have become a concern. For example, the US Forest Service and other local, state and federal government spend US$1–2 billion annually for fire suppression and an average US$1.4 billion per year to mitigate losses through timber salvage.[32]

Firefighting cost insurance provides stability to firefighting budgets through indemnity-based and index-based products.

INDEMNITY-BASED FIREFIGHTING EXPENSE INSURANCE

As indemnity-based firefighting expense insurance is based on actual expenditure, which is only known after a fire season and needs to be verified by an independent third party, considerable time can pass until indemnity payments can be made.

The Oregon Department of Forestry (ODF) in the state of Oregon (USA) was one of the first government agencies to buy indemnity-based insurance against increased firefighting costs since 1973. The Municipal Insurance Association of British Columbia has been providing insurance for fire control costs for member communities through the Fire Fighting Expenses Endorsement under the Liability Protection Agreement with a maximum coverage of CA$2 million per loss event and member. In the Canadian province of Manitoba, increased costs under the Manitoba Wildfire Program for flights to suppress wildfires were compensated for fires that occurred above a certain fire danger index as pre-agreed costs per flight minute and area bombed.

Firefighting Expense Insurance in Oregon (USA)

While federal and state government agencies have jurisdiction over most of Oregon's forest lands, around one third of forest land is privately owned and the forestry indus-try and the government collaborate to manage the cost for wildfire suppression. The ODF overlooks wildfire management and firefighting and receives funding for fire pre-vention, education and firefighting from (i) private forest land owners, who pay timber taxes and land assessment levies into the Oregon Forest Land Protection Fund (OFLPF),

---

[32] Zybach, B. et al., 2009: US Wildfire Cost-Plus-Loss Economics Project: The 'One-Pager' Check-list. Wildland Fire Lessons Learned Center, Advances in Fire Practices, 9p.

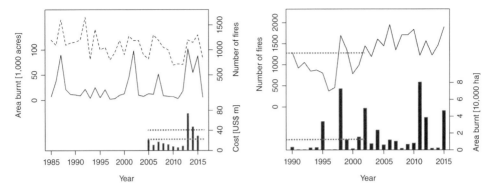

FIGURE 9.4   Left: Area burnt (left axis, solid line), number of fires (right axis, dashed line) and firefighting costs of the Oregon Department of Forestry (right axis, columns) in the state of Oregon (USA), 1985–2016, with the insurance cover of US$25 million in excess of US$20 million (dotted lines). Right: Number of fires (left axis, solid line) and area burnt (right axis columns) in the province of Alberta (Canada), 1990–2015, with the triggers of the insurance cover in terms of number of fires and area burnt (dotted lines).
Data source: Oregon Department of Forestry (left plot) and Government of Alberta (right plot).

with an average contribution of US$11 million per year and fees depending on the region and type of land, and (ii) the General State Fund, which is used to mobilise additional resources in case of extreme fires.

In a normal year, the ODF through OFLPF spends below US$10 million on firefighting and OFLPF has covered 80% of the fire suppression costs over the past 20 years. However, large and extreme wildfires incur costs that require the support of the state government. For example, firefighting costs reached US$50 million in 2002, while in 2013, the ODF spent over US$73 million on firefighting, with US$42 million for the Big Windy fire and US$16 million for the Douglas Complex fire (Figure 9.4).

Development of Firefighting Costs

The ODF's main concern is that a series of particularly large wildfires causes costs that are beyond the financial means of its fund. Long-term droughts, high temperatures and limited snow pack have increased the fire danger period. While the average annual number of fires reached 1083, with 20 500 ha burnt (1985–2012), 2013, 2014 and 2015 were above these averages (Figure 9.4). The ODF's firefighting costs (2005–2015) are more related to the area burnt (correlation coefficient of 0.84) than to the number of fires (0.48) and the main cause of fire is from human activity – lightning causes only 10% of fires on average.

Long-term climate projections indicate that the mean annual temperature across most of the western USA will increase by 2050, causing loss of moisture from soils and vegetation. Further, a shift in the range and type of vegetation and a general reduction in snow cover is likely to occur, with the forestry ecosystem becoming drier with higher fuel loads, particularly in less intensively managed state forests. These changes are likely to increase the overall fire risk, frequency and severity as well as wildfire suppression costs.

Firefighting Expense Insurance
Being aware of the potential fire suppression costs from large wildfires and uncertainty about the level of financial support from federal and state funds, the ODF has been insuring OFLPF through non-proportional insurance since 1973. The cover provides indemnity for US$25 million in excess of US$20 million per occurrence and in the annual aggregate against the ODF's expenditures for firefighting and operational costs (depreciation, taxes, licences and all direct cost of maintenance, repairs and administration). The actual expenses of the ODF are audited annually by an independent third party.

Performance of the Firefighting Expense Insurance
A series of particularly large fires between 2013 and 2015 led to consecutive insurance payouts but left the ODF with uncovered costs above the limit of the insurance policy, e.g. in 2013, it incurred costs of US$29 million after the US$25 million recovery from insurance and required a credit from the Oregon treasury. In 2015, the insurance structure was adjusted to US$25 million in excess of US$50 million, which represents the US$20 million OFLPF fund and US$30 million contributed from the General State Fund. At the same time, a multiyear insurance agreement was considered and a sublayer of US$30 million in excess of US$20 million was investigated based on weather indices or area burnt derived from satellite data.

INDEX-BASED FIREFIGHTING EXPENSE INSURANCE

Index-based firefighting expense insurance aims to provide faster payouts than indemnity-based covers. Parametric firefighting expense covers rely on one or several triggers that can include (i) fire frequency expressed as number of fires in a season or fires above a certain size, (ii) fire severity in terms of area burnt in a season, (iii) actual firefighting and related expenses, and (iv) fire weather indices. The Forest Protection Division (FPD) in province of Alberta (Canada) was probably the first government agency to buy index-based insurance protection to manage the financial burden of high firefighting expenses in 2002.

Firefighting Expense Insurance in Alberta (Canada)
The province of Alberta has two distinct forest fire regimes, in (i) an arboreal regime where fires can occur at any time, with a peak in occurrence in spring, and (ii) a slope regime, with most fires in late summer when dry organic matter forms an ideal combustible fuel. Lightning is the main cause of fires, particularly in remote forests, and warming temperatures have been stated to contribute to an earlier melting of snow covers, which leaves soil and vegetation drier and leads to an earlier start of the fire season. In some years, exceptionally large forest fires cause high fire suppression expenses for the FPD, which is exclusively responsible for monitoring and suppressing wildfires in the province of Alberta.

Wildfire Management
The FPD incurs different types of expenses for administrating, preventing, detecting, pre-suppressing and supressing wildfires. Pre-suppression efforts rely on a fire hazard index where monitored fuel conditions and weather data are combined in an index

ranging from 1 (low) to 6 (very severe) – Level 4 and above require the mobilisation of firefighting equipment (e.g. helicopters, bulldozers) and resources in the area. Most of FPD's expenditure is related to fires that occur with fire hazard indices between Levels 4 and 6. As an index of Level 4 requires mobilisation of resources and equipment, the FPD incurs a minimum cost independent of its size. Therefore, the average cost per hectare burnt decreases with the size of the fire, i.e. the cost per hectare to suppress a small fire is the highest. Close to 98% of fires are typically extinguished before 2 ha are reached; the FPD's highest costs occur for particularly large fires, which additional budget required from government sources. Large fires occur as a combination of dry conditions, strong wind and large amounts of combustible biomass when groundfires develop into crown fires and get out of control. The FPD relies for fire detection on (i) planned detection agents, including aerial patrols, fire outlooks, ground and water patrols, and (ii) unplanned detection agents through the public (free phone number to report a fire) and government employees. The FPD further uses satellite images to monitor fires. The FPD has a history of each fire in terms of location (geo-coordinates), size and area burnt since 1961.

Large Fire Events and Years
On average, 1273 fires occur annually in Alberta, with 170 000 ha burnt (1990–2015); however, some years have seen significantly more fires and a greater area burnt. In 2011, a fire in a remote part of northern Alberta grew to more than 700 000 ha; in 2015, a fire developed from an initial size of 1200 ha within days to over 220 000 ha. The Fort McMurray wildfire of 2016 reached a size of 590 000 ha and lasted nearly two months. One of the largest fires on record occurred in 1951, with over 1.4 million ha burnt, one of the largest reported fires in North America. Between 1990 and 2015, the largest annual area burnt reached 806 000 ha from 1218 fires (2011) and the highest number of fires occurred in 2015, with 1898 fires and 466 000 ha burnt (Figure 9.4). As particularly large fires influence the total area burnt, the number of fires correlates to only 0.32 with the area burnt (1990–2015).

Index-Based Fire Suppression Cost Insurance
In 2002, the FPD bought an index-based fire suppression cost insurance from the Agriculture Financial Services Cooperation (AFSC) for large and very large wildfires, with aggregate excess of loss (AXOL) reinsurance from international markets. Up to 2001, Alberta recorded annually an average of 955 fires and 121 000 ha burnt (1990–2001). The AXOL covered the FPD's expenditures for administrating, preventing, detecting, pre-suppressing and supressing wildfires (ultimate net loss) in the forest protection area in Alberta for a period of 12 months. The structure of the AXOL was defined as CA$80 million ultimate net loss in excess of CA$175 million ultimate net loss with a coinsurance of AFSC of 10%.

Under the AXOL, an indemnity occurred if the following four criteria were all fulfilled: (i) FPD expenditures (ultimate net loss) of a minimum of CA$175 million, (ii) occurrence of a minimum of 1350 fires as officially reported by the FPD, (iii) minimum of 150 000 ha burnt as determined from the number of fires and the size per fire, and (iv) minimum of 25% of days with a fire hazard index between 4 and 6. An indemnity schedule was defined where the payout per hectare burnt was limited according to bands of area burnt area and decreased with increasing total area burnt, matching the expenses of the FPD. An independent auditor was appointed to verify the records of the FPD in terms of expenditures, number of fires and area burnt.

Performance of the Index-Based Fire Suppression Cost Insurance
In 2002, an exceptionally mild winter with below normal snow cover and spring melt was followed by a dry summer, which is a typical pattern for the onset of an El Niño event in Alberta. As a result, Alberta experienced above normal wildfire activity and all four triggers of the AXOL were reached: (i) 1447 fires, (ii) 496 000 ha burnt, (iii) fire hazard index above Level 4 reached in 29% of the days, and (iv) FPD expenses of CA\$230 million for fire suppression. The loss to the AXOL reached close to CA\$55 million of the CA\$80 million total limit and provided the FPD with immediate funding. At renewal, the triggers for the area burnt and the suppression expenses were increased and the indemnity schedule was adjusted, with lower payouts per hectare burnt.

As one of the first index-based fire suppression covers, the concept found interest in other countries, while advances in monitoring wildfires and fire propagation near real time will facilitate the implementation of similar structures.

9.7 INDEX-BASED FOREST INSURANCE

Index-based forest insurance hardly exists in the market despite several applications having been discussed with industrial timber corporations and reflections on possible concepts in the literature. Index-based products could cover individual natural perils (e.g. wildfire or storm) or general yield reduction in forest areas. The reason for the non-existence of index-based products is probably related to the same reasons why plantation insurance has low penetration ratios (Section 9.3), including (i) fragmented markets with heterogeneous timber production as a mixture of different species, age classes and management strategies, (ii) random occurrence of systemic perils (e.g. wildfire, storm) that cause substantial losses and prevent efficient risk pooling, (iii) lack of data that reflect past losses of a given peril or yield reduction in general, and (iv) limited availability of lumber futures prices. As indemnity-based plantation insurance incurs high costs with adverse selection, moral hazard and shows low insurance penetrations in most markets, index-based forest insurance has been suggested as a viable solution.[33] Possible forms of index insurance could include area-based fire and area-based yield insurance; more theoretical investigations would be necessary to determine the viability of such products in real market environments.

AREA-BASED FIRE INDEX INSURANCE

Area-based forest fire index insurance could be based on historical seasonal or annual area burnt statistics that are available in some markets through government agencies, and the total forest area, based on which a burnt forest area ratio can be

---

[33] Chen, X. et al., 2013: Is timber insurable? A study of wildfire risks in the U.S. forest sector using spatio-temporal models. *Amer. J. Agr. Econ.*, 96(1), 213–31.

computed for a given area (e.g. a county). As certain trees species are more resilient to wildfire, and considerable salvage potential exists depending on the species and destined use, area burnt ratios could be adjusted historically to reflect current forest compositions. Similarly, the area burnt ratios could be adjusted according to forest management practices. As an alternative to historical area burnt statistics, area burnt analyses (Section 4.3) could be explored to develop burnt area ratios, with the knowledge that satellite-derived burnt areas induce additional basis risk as smaller fires tend to be underrepresented due to difficulties in detection and resolution.

As with corresponding crop insurance products, an area-based fire index cover for forests would let the insured choose the level of (i) the sum insured relative to a benchmark and defined as agreed values, actual values or fire prevention costs, (ii) the timber price relative to a benchmark in case the sum insured is based on actual values, and (iii) the coverage level relative to the burnt area ratio of recent years.

Recently, a large timber corporation in Southeast Asia enquired about a satellite-based fire index cover to protect against large-scale losses to forest areas. The index was developed based on MODIS fire scars within forest areas that were provided in the form of geo-referenced maps, with an overall indemnity in function of actual satellite-based burnt areas at the end of the fire season.

AREA-YIELD INDEX INSURANCE

An extension to an area-based fire index would be an area-yield index covering all possible causes of lower timber yields in a given area (e.g. county, sub-district). The concept would closely follow the corresponding area-yield indices used for crop insurance (Section 6.8) and could be applied in forest production systems with relatively homogeneous forest areas.

Forest owners and industrial timber companies regularly assess timber volumes to derive timber yield for tax purposes and government levy fees. The net present value method that relies on timber yield curves (Section 9.4) could provide reliable estimates of expected timber values in an area as long as forest stands are relatively uniform in terms of tree species and age. As with the corresponding crop insurance products, an area-yield index cover for forests would require regular yield assessment or estimations by a competent government agency at an acceptable resolution such as a county. A main constraint would certainly be the high level of heterogeneity among forest producers in terms of size of production, tree species and age profiles in stands, management practices (e.g. rotation cycles, thinning methods) and risk mitigation approaches (e.g. fire breaks, presence of firefighting equipment).

BIBLIOGRAPHY

Borges, J.G. et al. (2014). *The Management of Industrial Forest Plantations Theoretical Foundations and Applications*. Dordrecht: Springer, 544p.

Chenost, C. et al. (2010). *Bringing Forest Carbon Projects to the Market*. ONF International, 165p.

Gardiner, B. et al. (2013). *Living with Sorm Damage to Forests*. Joensuu: European Forest Institute, 132p.

Hanewinkel, M. et al. (2011). Assessing natural hazards in forestry for risk management: a review. *Eur. J. Forest Res.* 130: 329–351.

Lowell, E.C. et al., 2010: Effects of Fire, Insect, and Pathogen Damage on Wood Quality of Dead and Dying Western Conifers. USDA General Technical Report PNW-GTR-816, Washington, 80p.

Pischedda, D. (2004). *Technical Guide on Harvesting and Conservation of Storm Damaged Timber*. Paris: STODAFOR, 103p.

Schelhaas, M. (2008). *Impact of Natural Disturbances on the Development of European Forest Resources*. Wageningen: Alterra Scientific Contributions 23, Alterra, 171p.

Swiss Re, 2015: Forestry Insurance: A Largely Untapped Potential. Publication 1506240, Zurich, 20p.

CHAPTER 10

Risk Transfer to Reinsurance Markets

10.1 INTRODUCTION

While the reinsurance industry remains the main form of risk transfer for insurers, capital markets are gaining in importance and provided 12% of the global reinsurance capacity in 2016, mainly through insurance-linked securities (Chapter 11). Reinsurance has a long tradition and is a fundamental pillar of the insurance supply chain. Reinsurance risk management, underwriting and pricing follow broadly the same concepts as are used for insurance risks (Chapter 2), but with the main difference that reinsurance typically covers peak risks on entire insurance portfolios. Agricultural risks are mainly reinsured through facultative covers (single risks), proportional treaties (quota shares and rarely surpluses) and nonproportional structures (stop-loss (SL) and rarely per risk/event excess of loss (XOL)). Agricultural reinsurance used to be provided by a few companies with dedicated specialists but has rapidly evolved and now most reinsurers underwrite some agricultural exposure. As with agricultural insurance, the fastest growth in agricultural reinsurance has occurred in emerging markets, particularly in Asia, driven by China and India.

This chapter provides a brief overview of the global reinsurance industry and agricultural reinsurance. The main concepts of reinsurance and reinsurance forms are then discussed, with a focus on agricultural risks. The chapter also introduces the key methodologies to price facultative and treaty reinsurance and includes special sections on agricultural risks.

10.2 GLOBAL REINSURANCE MARKET

Reinsurance is a global business that seeks to diversify risks through different geographies and lines of insurance business. In 2016, the life and non-life reinsurance premium of the largest 10 reinsurers was reported at US$154 billion.[1] Global non-life

---

[1] AM Best, 2017: 2017 Reinsurance market briefing. Monte Carlo Reinsurance Rendez-Vous, AM Best Presentation, 31p.

reinsurance premiums reached US$160 billion, with 74% from mature and 26% from emerging markets. In 2016, the total capacity from traditional sources (reinsurance) amounted to US$514 billion, with an additional US$81 billion contributed by alternative capital, which includes direct institutional investors, reinsurance-sponsored managers and insurance-linked securities managers.[2]

GLOBAL REINSURANCE MARKETS

The main professional reinsurers, those fully dedicated to reinsurance, can be grouped into the European Big 4 (Munich Re, Swiss Re, Hannover Re and SCOR), the USA and Bermuda markets as well as Lloyds in London, which is a consortium of different syndicates. Today, the reinsurance market consists of over 200 reinsurers and most of them are professional reinsurers.

In some countries, state-owned reinsurers service the domestic market and are often operated under a monopoly with compulsory reinsurance cessions. National reinsurers exist in most Asian countries (e.g. China Re, Vina Re, Korea Re, GIC Re, Pakistan Re), in parts of the former Soviet Union (e.g. Russia Re), in some European countries (e.g. CCR in France, Milli Re in Turkey), in Latin America (e.g. IRB in Brazil) and in Africa (e.g. Africa Re for the African Union, Uganda Re, Kenya Re). Some national reinsurers have expanded to underwrite global reinsurance business besides domestic reinsurance.

AGRICULTURAL REINSURANCE MARKETS

Agricultural reinsurance is highly specialised and is dominated by a small group of leading large international reinsurers and in some markets national reinsurers. Today, most reinsurers underwrite agricultural risks, which is driven by the large growth of agricultural insurance and the opportunity to diversify reinsurance portfolios. In 2016, reinsurance cession reached around 25% (US$7.2 billion) and reveals the share of the global agricultural insurance premium volume that was transferred by insurers to international and national reinsurers.

Government-owned GIC Re in India was the largest reinsurer in agriculture in 2016, with a premium income of US$1.5 billion, and Munich Re was the largest international reinsurer, with a premium of US$930 million (Table 10.1). The share of agricultural reinsurance to the total reinsurance premium of the largest seven reinsurers ranged between 1.7% (Lloyd's) and 11.6% (Partner Re). The China Agricultural Reinsurance Pool (CARP) is a fully specialised agricultural reinsurance pool that provides reinsurance capacity to Chinese insurers, with a premium volume of US$850 million. The share of the largest seven international reinsurers and the three largest national reinsurers of the total agricultural reinsurance premium reached 89% in 2016.

---

[2] Aon, 2018: Reinsurance Market Outlook. Aon Publication, 22p.

TABLE 10.1 Overview of the largest seven international and three national reinsurers in agriculture, including gross written premium and total gross written premium (life- and non-life reinsurance), ranked by the agriculture reinsurance premium volume in 2016.

	Company	Head Office	Agricultural Reinsurance Premium 2016 (US$m)	Total Reinsurance Premium 2016 (US$m)	Ratio Agricultural Premium (%)
International reinsurer (top seven in agriculture)	Munich Re	Munich, Germany	930	31 839	2.9
	Swiss Re	Zurich, Switzerland	880	33 570	2.6
	Hannover Re	Hannover, Germany	650	15 363	4.2
	Partner Re	Bermuda	620	5357	11.6
	SCOR	Paris, France	350	13 231	2.6
	Mapfre Re	Madrid, Spain	280	3731[a]	7.5
	Lloyd's	London, UK	150	8959	1.7
National reinsurer (top three in agriculture)	GIC Re	Mumbai, India	1550	5038	30.8
	CARP	Beijing, China	850	850	100.0
	IRB	Rio de Janeiro, Brazil	149	1568	9.5
Total			6409	119 506	5.4
Total market[b]			7197		

Data source: Annual reports, S&P reinsurance industry reports.
[a] Data from 2015.
[b] Assumed at a reinsurance cession of 25% of the total agricultural insurance premium of US$28.78 billion in 2016.

10.3 KEY CONCEPTS OF REINSURANCE

Insurers often carry large liabilities that exceed their capitalisation in case of systemic loss events. Insurers have the option to transfer part of the liability to (i) other insurers under co-insurance agreements (also called reciprocity), (ii) to reinsurers which assume liability of ceded business under traditional reinsurance agreements, or (iii) to capital markets through insurance-linked securities (Chapter 11). Driven by demand and supply of capacity, reinsurance markets are cyclical, going through soft- and hard-market cycles. Reinsurance regulation has become more important, particularly for certain reinsurance products and structures where risk transfer tests have to be undertaken.

The overall benefits of reinsurance include risk transfer to stabilise insurers' financial results from unexpected major losses through global diversification, financing, as reinsurance can be a cost-effective substitute for equity and debt, and knowledge transfer, where reinsurers support insurers in pricing and managing risks in general. Reinsurance further provides insurers certain tax benefits and access to services including product development and market intelligence.

Current trends in reinsurance include globalisation of risks, innovations including more advanced models, digitalisation, big data algorithms and distribution via the internet and smart phones, and the availability of alternative capital. The reinsurance industry is likely to continue developing towards higher commoditisation and increased retentions of insurers of standard risks and greater use of innovative risk transfer. To gain efficiency, the entire insurance value chain targets a direct interaction with the policyholder, with insurers by definition being more advantaged than reinsurers and capital markets.

REINSURANCE PRINCIPLES

Reinsurance is a contractual arrangement between an insurer and a reinsurer to cede liabilities against the payment of a premium. In other words, reinsurance is insurance for an insurer. Although reinsurance can be seen as a particular form of insurance and includes several common features, it is different from insurance in that it deals typically with large risks, uses aggregated data for underwriting and pricing, and diversifies risk at a global scale. Like insurance, reinsurance relies on a high level of trust between the reinsurer and the insurer as the reinsurer is bound to follow the settlement of the insurer. Reinsurance is mainly a long-term relationship that covers different lines of insurance with the same insurer. Reinsurers are subject to the same types and sources of risk, including the random occurrence of large and catastrophic losses and fluctuations in the size and number of claims. Therefore, reinsurance principles follow closely concepts of insurance (Chapter 2). A reinsurer may buy reinsurance through retrocession, where the ceding reinsurer that requires protection (retrocedent) passes on risks to a capacity-providing reinsurer (retrocessionaire) against the payment of a premium. Additionally, reinsurers transfer peak risks that are difficult to cede to retrocession markets, to capital markets through insurance-linked securities (Chapter 11).

Reinsurance Cycles
Reinsurance markets, more than insurance markets, are cyclic in that extreme industry-wide losses cause a shift in the frequency and severity of losses and impact the availability and cost of reinsurance capital.

Hard Markets
In a hard market, reinsurance capacity is limited while reinsurance prices increase because a larger part of the industry has experienced catastrophic losses. Due to capital depletion, failure of insurance companies and shortages of reinsurance capacity, new equity capital is typically provided for the establishment of new reinsurers to fill the gap. Hard markets occurred in the 1980s based on the commercial liability insurance crisis, the early 1990s following Hurricane Andrew (1992) and the Northridge earthquake (1994), and the early 2000s as a result of the World Trade Center terrorist attacks (2001) and Hurricane Katrina (2005).

Soft Markets
In a soft market, reinsurance capacity is abundant and leads to gradual declines in reinsurance prices. The current soft market started in early 2007 and has seen numerous mergers and acquisitions among reinsurers as well as large inflows of alternative capital from investment and pension funds seeking higher returns compared with lower performing financial markets. With substantial losses of US\$136 billion from catastrophes in 2017, reinsurance terms slightly hardened for the affected lines of business and particularly for property reinsurance in the USA but did not turn into a hard market.

Reinsurance Placement Process
The placement of insurance business with a reinsurer is called a cession and the non-ceded risk that remains on the insurer's balance sheet is the retention. Under a reinsurance contract, a reinsurer is liable only for the exposure under the cession. Reinsurance is ceded directly to the reinsurer or through intermediaries such as reinsurance brokers. In most cases, insurers cede their own business to reinsurers. However, in some cases, fronting agreements are arranged where another insurer issues policies and transfers risks to reinsurers for a specified fee and typically with a small retention.

Reinsurers analyse data provided by the insurer or the reinsurance broker through a reinsurance submission and prepare a quotation, which includes the reinsurance terms and a share the quoting reinsurer is willing to assume at the quoted terms. Following the review of quotations from different reinsurers, the insurer nominates a lead reinsurer, which is usually one with a satisfying credit rating and a larger share. The terms of the lead reinsurer are then accepted by following reinsurers until the reinsurance placement is complete. The reinsurance contract may specifically empower the lead reinsurer to bind following reinsurers to limited changes or enhancements in the reinsurance contract. For particularly desirable risks, the reinsurance placement can be over-subscribed when shares of individual reinsurers are (often proportionally) reduced.

A placement slip is signed between the insurer and reinsurers and acts as a temporary agreement of reinsurance terms and conditions (including risk, cover period, premium, shares and some exclusions or other specific terms) until a formal reinsurance contract is issued. The reinsurance contract includes a reinsurance wording with general clauses and a schedule with the specific terms and conditions.

An insurer's assessment of the creditworthiness of a reinsurer relies on ratings provided by independent rating agencies such as Standard & Poor's and A.M. Best and is a key factor for an insurer in selecting a reinsurer. Additional important criteria in the view of an insurer include the overall reputation of the reinsurer, local reinsurance licences, technical expertise and ease to pay claims.

Reinsurance Intermediaries

Reinsurance brokers are intermediaries between the insurer and the reinsurers and are appointed by an insurer for two to five-year terms. Reinsurance brokers act on behalf of the insurer and provide a range of services, including (i) analytical and modelling capabilities to define risk-adequate reinsurance structures and solvency requirements, (ii) selection of reinsurers according to financial strength and reputation, (iii) preparation of a reinsurance submission and contract, and (iv) negotiation of shares and terms with reinsurers. Reinsurance brokers further administrate the payments of reinsurance premiums and the collection of claims payments.

Reinsurance brokers receive a brokerage, which is defined as a percentage of ceded premium under proportional reinsurance and as a percentage of the non-proportional reinsurance premium. Often several reinsurance brokers collaborate on a placement, each with a list of approved reinsurers. In markets where regulation requires the collaboration of international and local reinsurance brokers (e.g. India), joint ventures are typically formed.

Reinsurance Intermediaries in Agriculture

The main international reinsurance brokers for agricultural risks include Guy Carpenter, Aon Benfield, Willis Towers Watson and JLT Re, all of which over time have established specialist agricultural teams. In some markets (e.g. India and increasingly China), local reinsurance brokers are involved in agricultural reinsurance placements. For specialised agricultural business, dedicated brokerage firms have been established and in addition to standard services provide risk surveys and loss adjustment. For agricultural reinsurance, a typical reinsurance brokerage ranges between 2% and 5% (often 2.5%) of proportional reinsurance cessions and between 10% and 15% (often 10%) of the reinsurance premium under non-proportional agreements.

REINSURANCE REGULATION

Reinsurers require a licence to operate and are generally regulated in the same way as insurers to ensure sufficient solvency to compensate future indemnities. Unlike financial instruments, reinsurance agreements need to transfer risks as stated by accounting standards and regulatory rules. With the emergence of financial reinsurance in the late 1990s, the assessment of the level of risk transfer has become an essential part of reinsurance underwriting, with implications for financial reporting of reinsurance companies. While traditional reinsurance focuses on the transfer of insurance risk, financial reinsurance (also called finite reinsurance) transfers some extent of risk in combination with purely financial objectives that target capital management, solvency relief and financing as well as smoothing profits and losses under multi-year agreements.

Reinsurance regulation and international accounting guidelines such as the International Financial Reporting Standards (IFRS) and the United States Generally Accepted Accounting Principles (US-GAAP) require separate treatments of traditional reinsurance (reinsurance accounting) and financial reinsurance (deposit accounting) for the purpose of statutory financial reporting.[3]

---

[3] Gurenko, E.N. et al., 2012: Insurance Risk Transfer and Categorization of Reinsurance Contracts. World Bank Policy Research Working Paper 6299, Washington DC, 41p.

RISK TRANSFER TESTS

To establish the presence of risk transfer, a common practice is to examine a reinsurance contract for reasonably self-evident features. Reinsurance agreements that are likely to lack reasonably self-evident features and therefore require risk transfer testing include (i) risk limiting features such as premium levels of a per risk/event XOL treaty that approach the present value of the coverage and include profit commissions, (ii) multi-year reinsurance contracts, particularly with a sharing of negative and positive experiences, and (iii) quota share contracts with loss ratio caps, loss corridors and certain types of sliding scale commissions. The most common quantitative risk transfer tests include the 10-10 rule and the expected reinsurer's deficit (ERD).

The 10-10 Rule

The 10-10 rule states that the reinsurer is required to face a reasonable possibility of a significant loss and a contract contains significant risk transfer if there is at least a 10% probability of an at least 10% loss relative to the cash inflows (usually reinsurance premiums) of the reinsurer. While simple to implement, some forms of reinsurance do not fulfil the 10-10 rule although there is risk transfer and include (i) non-proportional catastrophe covers where top layers contain less than a 10% chance of loss due to the infrequencies of catastrophes, and (ii) proportional treaties that are based on high-frequency but low-severity losses that might not create a loss of at least 10% relative to the cash inflow of the reinsurer. In practice, both cases are usually considered as reinsurance contracts with risk transfer.

Expected Reinsurer's Deficit

ERD addresses low-frequency and high-severity events (right tail distribution) and high-frequency and low-severity losses based on realistic loss distributions and a threshold defined for risk transfer. Each reinsurance contract that fulfils the 10-10 rule also transfers risks under ERD at the 1% threshold, which is a 10% loss multiplied by a 10% probability.

Risk Transfer Tests for Agriculture

Most agricultural reinsurance contracts qualify for risk transfer under reasonably self-evident criteria, particularly if systemic perils are covered. However, quota share treaties that cover high-frequency and low-severity losses with very stable loss ratios over time (e.g. pet insurance portfolios) are likely to require risk transfer testing. While the 10-10 rules is straightforward for agricultural risks, the application of ERD can be complex, particularly for the reinsurance of portfolios that contain revenue insurance policies where combined loss distributions need to be developed for crop yield and commodity prices.

10.4 FORMS OF REINSURANCE

Over time, different forms of reinsurance have developed to cover both single and portfolio risks under annual and multi-year agreements. Strategic reinsurance is a newer domain of reinsurance and includes financial reinsurance, which provides highly customised risk transfer solutions for capital optimisation, earnings volatility, regulatory risks and solvency margins. The optimum reinsurance structure for an insurer depends broadly on the exposure and composition of the insurance portfolio, capitalisation levels, solvency requirements, the budget to purchase reinsurance and the reinsurance market environment. For agriculture, most reinsurance is structured as facultative covers (single risks) and as proportional and non-proportional treaties which include large numbers of individual risks in portfolios.

REINSURANCE STRATEGY

The optimum reinsurance strategy and contracts have been widely researched from an insurer's and a reinsurer's point of view.[4] The ideal reinsurance protection for an insurer is typically a compromise between reducing exposure to large losses, smoothing earnings, creating surplus capital and coverage, structure and reinsurance price. The reinsurance buying strategy of an insurer largely depends on its capitalisation, solvency requirements as defined by insurance regulators, and modelled losses in terms of maximum event retention and minimum capital requirements. Through reinsurance, the insurer aims to maximise the amount claimable for a given value at risk while minimising the overall loss amount, which is often achieved through traditional reinsurance in combining proportional and non-proportional reinsurance structures. Typically, insurers buy non-proportional reinsurance in layers which covers (i) the insurer's retention of specific underlying risks or the entire insurance portfolio after proportional reinsurance, or (ii) the entire net-retained risks or portfolio. The optimal combination of reinsurance structures is determined through risk metrics such as the variance, value at risk and conditional tail expectation.[5] The price of reinsurance is an important factor and insurers tend to buy more reinsurance in soft reinsurance cycles.

Reinsurance Strategy in Agriculture

In most markets, agricultural insurers purchase proportional reinsurance capacity (mainly quota share) and protect the retention through non-proportional treaties (mainly SL). In markets with long experience and well-capitalised insurers, SL treaties are the dominant form of reinsurance where the conditional tail expectation has been explored to derive optional reinsurance layering.[6]

The principle of reinsurance relies on the interests of the insurer and the reinsurer being aligned, particularly under proportional treaties, where ceding commissions are to cover the costs of the insurer to produce the business, with profit commissions as an incentive for profitable underwriting results. In several markets, insurers have managed to cede a majority of the risks to quota share reinsurance markets and use a portion of the obtained ceding commission to fund SL reinsurance to then aggressively underwrite

---

[4] Huang, F. and Honglin, Y., 2018: Optimal reinsurance: A reinsurer's perspective. *Annal. Actuar. Sci.*, 12(1), 147–84.

[5] Cai, J. et al., 2008: Optional reinsurance under VaR and CTE risk measures. *Insur. Math. Econ.*, 43, 185–96.

[6] Porth, L. et al., 2013: Optimal reinsurance analysis from a crop insurer's perspective. *Agr. Finance Rev.*, 73(2), 310–28.

business at below risk-adequate levels. For combined quota share and SL programmes, reinsurers analyse the level of gearing of the insurer and try to avoid situations where the insurer can purchase SL reinsurance from the quota share commission and incurs a net loss at significantly higher losses than the reinsurer. Insurance regulators upon pressure from reinsurers have been trying to introduce minimum cession limits under agricultural quota share agreements in some markets.

FACULTATIVE REINSURANCE

Facultative reinsurance covers single large risks such as large hotels and commercial buildings, refineries, satellites, industrialised livestock operations or large commercial forests. The term facultative refers to the fact that the arrangement is optional in that neither the insurer nor the reinsurer is obliged to offer or accept the business.

Facultative contracts tend to carry large liabilities that the insurer cannot or does not want to carry on its balance sheet. Due to the large size of these risks, significant exposure and different management and maintenance practices, it is difficult to cover single large risks under reinsurance treaties, which pool large numbers of similar-sized risks. Facultative covers offer the necessary flexibility in providing special conditions compared with a reinsurance treaty where more standardised terms are applied. Often, facultative risks require on-site inspections by a risk surveyor to establish a risk assessment report that captures risk management and loss mitigation standards that form an integral part of underwriting.

Facultative reinsurance involves some level of adverse selection for the reinsurer and is generally expensive as a function of large exposure, uncertainty and perils covered as well as administrative costs incurred by the reinsurer to administrate and execute each risk individually. Reinsurers often see facultative reinsurance as accommodating business to treaties underwritten from the same insurer.

Forms of Facultative Reinsurance

Facultative reinsurance can be proportional in that the premium and losses are shared equally between the insurer and the reinsurer, or non-proportional, where the liability of the reinsurer is defined in monetary terms net of each-and-every loss deductibles and/or annual aggregate deductibles. In some markets and for some lines of business, similar-sized large risks are reinsured through facultative facilities with a case by case acceptance by the reinsurer. Alternatively, a facultative obligatory treaty gives the insurer the option to cede single large risks, with the reinsurer accepting these risks under a treaty arrangement. A facultative obligatory treaty can be associated with a surplus reinsurance treaty when the treaty reinsurance capacity is exhausted and the remaining risks still need to be transferred.

Facultative Reinsurance in Agriculture

Single agricultural risks that are either too large or too complex to be covered under a reinsurance treaty are placed as facultative risks. Examples include large crop farms (e.g. >10 000 ha), industrialised livestock production enterprises, large aquaculture farms, greenhouse complexes and corporate timber plantations. Further, high-value breeding animals (e.g. cattle) and individual racing or show jumping horses tend to be reinsured on a facultative basis.

Facultative agreements are also used to cover a single-source risk aggregator, e.g. a cooperative or an input supplier which buys agricultural insurance for its members or contract farmers and with a payout from reinsurance to the aggregator. Typically, most risk transfer with agribusinesses is of a facultative nature and most reinsurance business from captives of agricultural corporates takes a facultative form. In developing markets where agricultural reinsurance treaties are not yet established, larger agricultural risks are often first insured facultatively and based on larger demand and experience gained, insurers transition the risks into a facultative facility or a reinsurance treaty.

Facultative obligatory treaties are rare in agriculture, as large risks are covered by individual facultative placements; however, they exist for greenhouses and crop insurance in markets with a large number of similar-sized farms and a few very large farms. For example, large broadacre farms in Australia (e.g. the 96 000 ha Cubbie Station) are covered against hail and fire damage under a surplus reinsurance treaty, with the exceeding risk being transferred into a facultative obligatory treaty.

TREATY REINSURANCE

Under treaty reinsurance, the insurer agrees in advance to the form of reinsurance, including terms and conditions. Almost all treaty reinsurance is obligatory in that the insurer agrees to cede all or part of the risks of a certain category and the reinsurer accepts all ceded risks. Before inception, a reinsurance treaty is agreed and defines the type of perils and lines of business covered, geographic locations, the coverage period and the way claims are to be recognised under the treaty. Generally, adverse selection is less likely to occur under treaties compared with facultative reinsurance, particularly if the insurer seeks to establish a long-term business relationship with a reinsurer.

Recognition of Claims

The way in which claims are recognised under a reinsurance treaty defines which losses are covered. Risk attaching refers to the underwriting year basis, with an attachment defined as the effective or renewal date of the original policy, i.e. any losses that occur on policies written or renewed with inception or renewal dates during the term of the reinsurance contract are covered irrespective of when the loss occurred. Loss occurring relates to the accident year where the attachment is the date of the loss of the original policy, i.e. any losses occurring during the term of the reinsurance contract on policies that are in force, written or renewed are covered. Losses occurring on risks attaching refers to an attachment for losses from original policies which incepted during the term of the reinsurance contract and for losses that occur only during the term of reinsurance.

Types of Reinsurance Treaties

Reinsurance treaties are divided into (i) proportional reinsurance, which is also called pro-rata reinsurance and obligatory reinsurance, where premiums and losses are shared proportionally between the insurer and the reinsurer; it includes quota share and surplus treaties, and (ii) non-proportional reinsurance, where only losses above a certain threshold are reinsured; it includes per risk/event XOL, aggregated excess

TABLE 10.2 Overview of the basic mechanism of quota share, surplus, excess of loss, aggregate excess of loss and stop-loss reinsurance treaties.

Treaty Form	Risk	Premium	Claim
Quota share	Total	$P = \sum_{i=1}^{n} P_i$	$L = \sum_{i=1}^{n} L_i$
	Retained	$Q \times P$	$Q \times L$
	Ceded	$(1-Q) \times P$	$(1-Q) \times L$
Surplus	Total	$P = \sum_{i=1}^{n} P_i$	$L = \sum_{i=1}^{n} L_i$
	Retained	$\sum_{i=1}^{n} Q_i P_i$	$\sum_{i=1}^{n} Q_i L_i$
	Ceded	$\sum_{i=1}^{n} (1-Q_i) P_i$	$\sum_{i=1}^{n} (1-Q_i) L_i$
Excess of loss	Total	$P = \sum_{i=1}^{n} P_i$	$L = \sum_{i=1}^{n} L_i$
	Retained	$(1-Q) \times P$	$\sum_{i=1}^{n} \sum_{i=1}^{Ni} (\min(Y_{ij}, b_i) + (Y_{ij}, -b_i - a_i))$
	Ceded	$Q \times P$	$\sum_{i=1}^{n} \sum_{i=1}^{Ni} \min(Y_{ij}, b_i), a_i$
Aggregate excess of loss	Total	$P = \sum_{i=1}^{n} P_i$	$L = \sum_{i=1}^{n} L_i$
	Retained	$(1-Q) \times P$	$\min(L, T) + (S - T - U)$
	Ceded	$Q \times P$	$\min((L-T), U)$
Stop-loss	Total	$P = \sum_{i=1}^{n} P_i$	$L = \sum_{i=1}^{n} L_i$
	Retained	$(1-Q) \times P$	$\min(L, T \times P) + (L - T \times P - U \times P)$
	Ceded	$Q \times P$	$\min((L - T \times P), U \times P)$

With P as the premium, Q as the retention and $1-Q$ as the cession rate.
With a as the limit, b as the priority for excess of loss; note that a loss event less than b will not trigger a loss payment and an event that exceeds $(a+b)$ is the insurer's liability.
With U as the limit and T the priority for aggregate excess of loss and stop-loss.
Source: Adapted from Deelstra and Plantin (2015).

of loss (AEXOL) and SL treaties (Table 10.2). For non-proportional reinsurance, the frequency and severity of losses determine the reinsurance structure to cover losses for a certain event and risk (per event/risk XOL) or compensate for losses over the entire reinsurance period (AEXOL or SL).

Quota Share Treaty

Under quota share reinsurance, the insurer and reinsurer share the premium, the administrative expenses and losses through a pre-agreed percentage (Figure 10.1). Quota share reinsurance is most suited for a pool of similar-sized risks for a single or for multiple lines of insurance business. A reinsurer's share of a quota share is expressed as a ratio of the total underlying insurance portfolio, e.g. 3% of 100%, or of the reinsurance cession, e.g. 10% share of 30% cession of the 100% underlying portfolio, which is equivalent to 3% of 100%.

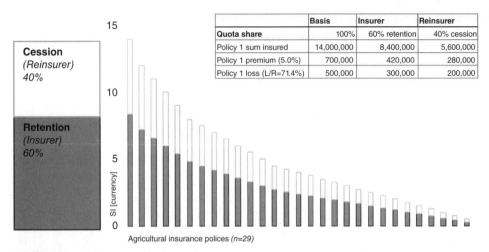

		Basis	Insurer	Reinsurer
Quota share		100%	60% retention	40% cession
Policy 1 sum insured		14,000,000	8,400,000	5,600,000
Policy 1 premium (5.0%)		700,000	420,000	280,000
Policy 1 loss (L/R=71.4%)		500,000	300,000	200,000

FIGURE 10.1 Schematic overview of a quota share reinsurance contract with an example of agricultural insurance Policy 1, how sum insured (SI), premium and losses are shared between the insurer (60% retention) and the reinsurer (40% cession).
Source: Adapted from Swiss Re (2010).

Ceding Commissions
To compensate the insurer for its expenses in producing the business, the reinsurer pays a ceding commission that can be defined as a (i) fixed commission with or without a profit commission, or (ii) sliding scale commission. In some cases, an overrider is paid in addition to the ceding commission to compensate the insurer or third parties such as general managing agents for any other types of expenses.

A fixed ceding commission is a percentage of the premium, which depending on the expected profitability ranges between 15% and 25%. To incentivise the insurer for good performance, a profit commission is often granted in addition to the fixed commission if losses including loss adjustment expenses, brokerage and a pre-agreed allowance for the reinsurer's own costs (also called management expenses) are below the premium income and a profit occurs. Often, losses under profit commission structures are carried forward and counted against future profits for a pre-defined number of years or until extinction.

Under a sliding scale commission, the level of commission is inversely related in a linear or non-linear way to the loss extent established at the end of the treaty period. The reinsurer pays a preliminary commission, which tends to be the commission foreseen around the level of the average expected loss ratio, with a final commission adjustment at the end of the treaty period when underwriting results are known.

Loss Controlling Measures
In the case of deteriorating loss experience over time, or a new and potentially more risky line of business being introduced to an existing quota share, the reinsurer is likely to impose a loss cap or a loss corridor. A loss cap is expressed in terms of loss ratio above which the reinsurer is not liable to pay losses. A loss corridor includes a band defined in terms of loss ratios (a corridor) between which the reinsurer assumes a lower share of the losses compared with the cession rate. In markets with highly

concentrated risks and large growth potential, reinsurers impose underwriting limits where an insurer is allowed to write exposure only up to a certain monetary limit that is typically applied per region and/or type of products.

Quota Share Reinsurance in Agriculture

The typical duration of a quota share for agricultural risks is 12 months, while often the risk period is less than 12 months, with the advantage that results of the previous season are largely known at reinsurance renewal. In markets where insurers tender for business with the government (e.g. India) and portfolio compositions are therefore highly variable between crop seasons, quota share terms need to be agreed by insurance regulation at the beginning of the crop season, which can lead to significant changes between assumed and actual portfolios. Most quota shares renew after each contract period, but in some markets (e.g. the USA, India, Turkey), multi-year quota share agreements with profit commission features are agreed, particularly when reinsurers assist on product development or support the turn-around in a portfolio.

Commission and Loss Sharing Structures

Typically, newer quota shares include fixed commissions that gradually include profit commissions and ultimately sliding scale commissions as the underwriting experience increases over time. Loss caps are often agreed for newer portfolios where the insurer obtains proportional reinsurance capacity up to the loss cap for a duration of one to three years. On some occasions, insurers introduce loss caps on new business to obtain proportional reinsurance capacity, e.g. a leading Chinese insurer introduced a 170% loss ratio cap on its new livestock portfolio to provide comfort to reinsurers. Loss corridors are used when proportional reinsurance capacity is required but the loss experience has been deteriorating, e.g. reinsurers imposed loss corridors on Italian crop hail portfolios over several years. Similarly, following several unprofitable seasons for crop insurance in India, loss corridors were introduced to provide the required quota share capacity for the fast-growing underlying portfolios. In several markets, governments provide loss caps on retained business of insurers to limit losses to the insurance industry and to prevent market failure in case of catastrophic losses. Examples of markets with agricultural insurance programmes with government loss caps include China, South Korea, the USA and Poland.

Cash Flows

As most agricultural insurance programmes benefit from government premium subsidies, the timing of the insurer's receipt of the subsidies determines the cash flow of the insurer and the ceded premium to the reinsurer. While some quota shares provide premium to reinsurers at or close to the time of inception (e.g. China), there are markets (e.g. Italy, USA) where the reinsurer receives the net of the premium and the losses only well after the end of the reinsurance term. Quota shares of private sector insurance programmes (e.g. crop hail) contain a real cash flow for the reinsurer.

Surplus Treaty

A surplus treaty works as a quota share but with the difference that the cession is determined on a risk-by-risk basis once the risk is underwritten by the insurer. The insurer has the right to decide the retention of each risk, which is defined in monetary terms and is called a *line*. The reinsurer accepts risks for a capacity expressed in

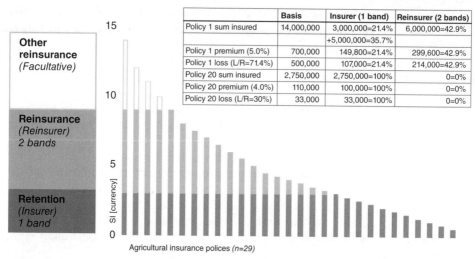

	Basis	Insurer (1 band)	Reinsurer (2 bands)
Policy 1 sum insured	14,000,000	3,000,000=21.4%	6,000,000=42.9%
		+5,000,000=35.7%	
Policy 1 premium (5.0%)	700,000	149,800=21.4%	299,600=42.9%
Policy 1 loss (L/R=71.4%)	500,000	107,000=21.4%	214,000=42.9%
Policy 20 sum insured	2,750,000	2,750,000=100%	0=0%
Policy 20 premium (4.0%)	110,000	100,000=100%	0=0%
Policy 20 loss (L/R=30%)	33,000	33,000=100%	0=0%

FIGURE 10.2 Schematic overview of a surplus reinsurance contract with an example of agricultural insurance Policy 1 and Policy 20, how sum insured (SI), premium and losses are shared between the insurer (1 Band) and the reinsurer (2 Bands).
Source: Adapted from Swiss Re (2010).

terms of numbers of lines relative to the retention of the insurer and pays its share of the losses in the same proportion as the premium is shared (Figure 10.2). The cession rate typically increases with higher surplus lines as risk increases. Surplus treaties bear high costs as each risk needs to be administrated separately and insurers share the development of the portfolio at regular intervals (e.g. on a quarterly basis) in the form of bordereaux, which are detailed lists of the underwritten risks. Reinsurance commissions of surplus treaties operate in the same way as under quota share agreements, but due to higher levels of adverse selection, tend to be considerably lower.

Surplus treaties are mainly used for large commercial and industrial risks that have various sizes of exposures and require large capacity. A surplus provides an insurer with a homogeneous portfolio in the retention and cedes an over-proportionally higher share of exposed (and often less performing) risks to reinsurers. In some cases, several surplus treaties are needed to cover the largest individual risk exposure. Once the limit expressed as the number of bands of the first surplus treaty is exceeded, a second or even a third surplus is established when the capacity of several risks is exhausted. When only a few risks exceed the first surplus, these risks are typically reinsured on an individual basis through facultative placements or collectively through a facultative obligatory treaty.

Surplus Reinsurance in Agriculture

As most agricultural insurance portfolios contain comparable sizes of risks, surplus treaties are relatively rare. However, there can be cases when a larger number of large risks cannot be placed facultatively but fulfil the standardised conditions for a reinsurance treaty. For example, in the Australian broadacre market, landholdings of farmers and corporate farms vary significantly but are insured under comparable standards and coverage through a surplus treaty. In some markets, insurers use surplus treaties to increase underwriting limits per region and risk type.

Excess of Loss Treaty

Under XOL reinsurance treaties, indemnity occurs only if losses have exceeded a pre-defined retention of the insurer. The insurer's retention and the reinsurer's liability (limit) are defined in monetary terms. The XOL structure is therefore written as reinsurance liability in excess of (abbreviated as xs) the insurer's retention. The premium for XOL structures is defined as a percentage of the subject premium base, which can be (i) the gross net premium income (GNPI) for loss occurring policies or (ii) gross net written premium income (GNWPI) for risks attaching policies. Layered reinsurance programmes tend to be more expensive compared with a one-layer programme as the reinsurer needs to charge for administrative expenses of each layer. Some reinsurers apply minimum and fixed administrative expenses for non-proportional reinsurance.

Layering of XOL Treaties
XOL treaties are often layered for the insurer to obtain more competitive terms and for reinsurers to participate with different shares on different layers. An XOL structure of US$8 million xs US$2 million can be layered for example as US$3 million xs US$2 million (Layer 1) and US$5 million xs US$5 million (Layer 2). Layered structures typically build on each other in a consistent and progressive way. The attachment basis of the underlying policies is defined on a loss occurring basis, i.e. any loss during the term of the XOL reinsurance agreement is covered independent of the inception and termination date of the individual insurance policies.

A common term in XOL reinsurance is the rate on line (ROL), from which the payback period is derived – it facilitates a better understanding of the exposure from working, middle layers and catastrophe layers. ROL is calculated as the ratio of the premium for a layer (P_{Layer}) and the limit of the same layer (L_{Layer}) as:

$$ROL = \frac{P_{Layer}}{L_{Layer}} = \frac{1}{Payback}$$

ROL decreases from working layers (typically >15%) to middle layers (4–15%) and top (catastrophe) layers (<4%). For very high layers, where from a risk point of view reinsurance protection would not necessarily be required, reinsurers have internal criteria for the ROL not to be below a certain minimum level, which is often set at 1%. The payback reveals the frequency of losses to the layer and the number of years the reinsurer needs to earn reinsurance premiums to cover a full loss to the layer.

Per Risk/Event Excess of Loss Reinsurance

A risk excess of loss (RXOL) treaty applies for losses of each individual risk separately while for an event excess of loss (EXOL), a loss refers to a predefined event that impacts several risks. RXOL and EXOL provide an insurer with protection against large and catastrophe-type losses. A RXOL requires a precise definition on an individual risk covered and an EXOL needs a clear definition of an event that is measurable and will trigger an indemnity both in terms of spatial (e.g. the geographical scope of the underlying portfolio) and the temporal extent (e.g. within 72 hours for tropical cyclones or 168 hours for floods). In return for reinsurance protection, the insurer pays the reinsurer a premium that is a function of the diversification of the underlying risks (geographically and by products), perils covered and the amount of reinsurance capacity required. The reinsurance premium is expressed as a percentage of the underlying exposure. As exposure varies during the reinsurance contract period, a deposit premium or a minimum deposit premium (MDP) is paid in several instalments, with a final adjustment at the end of the contract period.

Reinstatements

As individual risks covered by a ROXL and the insurance portfolio protected by an EXOL can incur several consecutive losses during the reinsurance period, insurers often require continued coverage. Continued coverage is based on reinstatement provisions that restore the reinsurance limit to its full amount after the first loss. Most reinstatements are defined for a predefined number of subsequent events for which an additional premium for each reinstatement is calculated for the amount used (pro rata amount) and/or the remaining time of the reinsurance period (pro-rated time). Some XOL treaties include unlimited reinstatements where the used capacity of a loss is automatically reinstated. In the event an insurer did not buy reinstatements or has exhausted the agreed number of reinstatements, a reinstatement cover can be bought seperately.

Excess of Loss Reinsurance in Agriculture

RXOL and EXOL structures are relatively rare for agricultural risks, as it is difficult to define a particular event in terms of temporal and spatial extent and to establish losses from such an event relative to losses from other non-insured incidents. Under crop insurance, the final loss at harvest is a function of several perils and events, while favourable growth conditions can lead to a partial or total recovery of the crop. Further, some perils are difficult to define in terms of duration, e.g. droughts are gradually developing and therefore cannot be limited within a defined temporal timeframe. Similarly, the duration of an epidemic livestock disease outbreak can last from several weeks to several months and loss extents largely depend on contingency measures of the affected farmer and the government (e.g. emergency culling, vaccination, quarantine). Perils that cause large losses to agricultural assets and can be defined in terms of temporal duration would include frost, winter kill, cyclones and to some extent flooding and wildfires.

Catastrophe risks in agriculture typically affect a large number of policies at the same time and the duration and intensity of an event (e.g. a drought) are critical to the final loss outcome. Therefore, catastrophe risks in agriculture tend to be reinsured through SL treaties rather than through XOL structures.

Examples of RXOL and EXOL

An example of a combined RXOL/EXOL reinsurance in agriculture is for severe winter storms (blizzards) for feedlots in the USA. Blizzards are clearly identifiable events with a direct cause of loss for feedlot cattle, which are kept in large numbers in outdoor fences. During blizzards, the cattle crowd to conserve body heat, which in turn can cause high mortality through suffocation and can affect several farms at the same time. US insurers are reinsuring feedlots through a combined RXOL/EXOL structure to protect against large losses at individual feedlots (RXOL) and against accumulated mortality from individual events that occur within 72 hours over several feedlots (EXOL). Another example where RXOL is commonly used are losses from mortality and infertility in equine portfolios that are composed of horses of values of US$0.5–1.5 million.

In the early years of crop insurance in South Korea, insurers bought typhoon EXOLs to cover horticulture exposure that included mainly apples and pears. While typhoon is a clearly identifiable event in terms of wind speed, temporal duration and area impacted, loss extents to horticulture proved difficult to establish due to other causes of loss such as hail and frost before typhoon damage and led to several disputes between insurers and reinsurers. As a result, the EXOL structure was not renewed and the exposure transferred under an SL agreement.

Aggregate Excess of Loss and Stop-Loss Reinsurance

AEXOL and SL are special forms of excess of loss reinsurance in that the structures protect insurance portfolio losses during a specific period, which is usually 12 months (Figure 10.3). The insurer's retention is called priority or attachment point and the reinsurer's liability is termed limit. For an AEXOL, an indemnity occurs when losses exceed a pre-agreed monetary amount while a SL defines losses in function of a pre-agreed percentage of the underlying premium volume or exposure. The basis of the AEXOL and the SL is usually losses occurring. In some cases, a co-insurance factor is used for AEXOL and SL layers where the insurer retains a certain portion of the losses (e.g. 10%), or in other words where only a portion of the layer limit (e.g. 90%) is ceded to the reinsurance market.

An umbrella stop-loss (USL) provides coverage of different underlying reinsured and retained risks in an insurance portfolio to provide catastrophe risk protection in the case of individual or several underlying structures incurring a loss above the respective

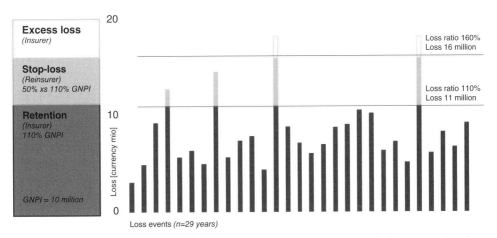

FIGURE 10.3 Schematic overview of a stop-loss reinsurance contract including a stop-loss layer expressed in terms of GNPI and in monetary terms.

expected liability of the insurer net of reinsurance recoverable. As USLs cover under-lying reinsurance structures, losses in the underlying business influence the loss of the over-spanning umbrella structure, which is defined in function of how losses to the underlying treaties are recognised in (i) inuring to the benefit of the reinsurer if losses of the underlying treaties are absorbed by the underlying reinsurance structures before impacting the umbrella structure, or (ii) inuring to the benefit of the insurer when losses to the underlying treaties are disregarded and directly impact the umbrella cover.

Priorities and Monetary Limits

Most SL covers are based on the underlying premium, which is a direct function of insurance terms and therefore exposes the SL reinsurer to changes in premium rates and deductibles of the original policies. For new markets and volatile portfolios, reinsurers prefer SL structures that are based on exposure (sum insured) and therefore do not depend on underlying insurance terms. For SL covers that are based on GNPI, reinsurers limit the maximum downside and a minimum priority through buffers. Buffers guarantee adequate coverage in case the actual reinsured portfolio contains a lower premium volume than expected in that a lower priority is expressed (usually 70–90% of GNPI). To limit the SL capacity for larger than expected growth, buffers allow an upper monetary limit (usually 110–130% of GNPI). The typical formulation of a GNPI-based SL layer with a buffer of ±20% and a GNPI of US$10 million is expressed as '50% of GNPI but with a maximum of US$6.0 million in excess of 110% of GNPI but with a minimum of US$8.8 million'.

Reinsurance Premium

The reinsurance premium that is due from the insurer is expressed as a percentage of the underlying GNPI or the sum insured. As the underlying portfolio develops over the period of reinsurance, reinsurers charge the insurer an MDP with a final adjustment in function of the final GNPI or sum insured at the end of the contract period. The MDP is owed to the reinsurer independent of the development of the underlying portfolio that is protected by the SL. Some SL agreements include a pre-agreed percentage of the reinsurance premium that is returned after the treaty period to the insurer in the form of a (i) no claims bonus in case the reinsurance structure did not incur a loss, and/or (ii) a low claims bonus depending on the loss extent incurred by the SL.

Stop-Loss Reinsurance in Agriculture

SL reinsurance is widely used for agricultural risks to protect against large and catastrophe-type losses. The vast majority of SL programmes are based on GNPI, but there are some exceptions where SL structures relate to sum insured. Typically, agri-cultural insurers buy SL treaties over the entire portfolio which can include different products for a line of business (e.g. crop hail, MPCI) or various agricultural exposures (e.g. crop, livestock, forestry, greenhouses). Most SL treaties are based on 12-month periods but there are cases (e.g. India) where a SL covers one crop season as crop types and portfolio changes between the seasons make risk compositions of the portfo-lios difficult to estimate in advance. Multi-year SL programmes exist in some markets which can be driven by insurers trying to benefit from favourable reinsurance terms in soft reinsurance cycles. Multi-year SL covers usually contain a clause for reinsurance premium adjustments and renegotiation of terms in case losses and material changes in exposure occur. Multi-year SL programmes typically include no claims bonus provisions for a loss to individual or to all layers.

Umbrella Stop-Loss Programmes
USL structures that cover different lines of agricultural business and underlying reinsurance structures are rare. The only larger market where USLs are common is China, where the larger insurers maintain different quota share cessions per province, cover retentions by SL agreements at province level or retain all business in certain provinces and USLs provide for losses that exceed the underlying SL covers and absorb losses from uncovered retentions. Underwriting these USL programmes is challenging as the underlying cession ratios per province and line of business need to be understood and details of the underlying SL programmes need to be known. Further, loss distributions need to be aggregated in preserving spatial correlations and correlations among different products and lines of business while realistic scenarios that trigger USL layers need to be developed for reinsurance pricing.

STRATEGIC REINSURANCE

Strategic reinsurance is a newer term and includes the concepts of financial reinsurance, structured reinsurance and alternative risk transfer. Strategic reinsurance has developed from insurers' increasing need for customised risk transfer solutions for capital optimisation, earnings volatility, regulatory risks and solvency margins. For mutual insurers which do not have access to other capital, strategic reinsurance is often a preferred way to build capital through retained earnings of their policyholder members.

Retrospective solutions transfer current and future loss obligations through loss portfolio transfer and adverse development covers. These solutions support an insurer in ring-fencing a certain business and preparing an exit of a certain line of business or territory. Prospective solutions enhance the efficiency of risk mitigation to protect against volatility in net retained risks and to optimise corporate capital through different ways of risk transfer. These solutions include holistic covers that combine loss events in integrated multi-year, multi-line or multi-trigger reinsurance structures and parametric solutions are used when traditional solutions are costly, complex or when losses are difficult to measure (e.g. pandemics, disaster relief).[7]

While a large part of the reinsurance market is based on traditional risk transfer, the increasing complexity and the global scope of certain risks (e.g. cyber, climate change, terrorism, supply chain business interruption), along with more risk-based capital requirements from regulators, are likely to increase the demand for strategic reinsurance.

Strategic Reinsurance in Agriculture

Prospective solutions, and particularly holistic covers, allow agricultural insurers to buy cost-efficient longer-term reinsurance that is tailor made and supports efficient capital management. Further, holistic covers enable agribusinesses to combine insurances of non-correlated risks in a cost-effective way. United Grain Growers, a Canadian grain handling company, was probably the first to benefit from such solutions to combine property, liability, marine and grain volume insurance to manage earning volatility (Section 6.8).

Compliance with solvency requirements from insurance regulators is of high importance for insurers, and monoline insurers, including many specialist agricultural insurers, are mandated to maintain high solvency margins for required liquidity levels in case of natural disasters. While traditional reinsurance structures such as SL provide loss protection, regulatory risk solutions can contribute further capacity when required but need to be financially competitive with conventional forms of capital rising.

10.5 BASICS OF REINSURANCE PRICING

Reinsurance pricing uses essentially the same concepts as actuarial insurance pricing (Section 2.4), with elements of exposure and experience pricing but with a larger focus on large losses (tail risk) and data that are geographically aggregated and summarised per type of insurance product. Therefore, reinsurance pricing is more uncertain than insurance pricing and makes the variance of the losses typically a more important parameter than the average of the losses. Uncertainty increases when reinsurers need to undertake as-if adjustments to restate loss amounts to current insurance conditions and develop unearned premiums and claims. Reinsurance pricing approaches depend largely on the pricing philosophy of the reinsurer, the complexity of the risk transfer structure, the time available to perform the pricing, the experience of the actuary and the level of details of data received from the underlying risks. As reinsurance is a long-term relationship between a reinsurer and an insurer, reinsurance costing turns actuarial pricings into commercially viable reinsurance terms considering the competitiveness of the market and the overall relationship with a particular insurer.

ADJUSTMENT OF HISTORICAL INSURANCE DATA (AS-IF ANALYSES)

The preparation of historical insurance data, which are often at portfolio or sub-portfolio level, includes consistency analyses, identifying catastrophe-type losses and adjusting historical claims and premiums according to changes of the main underlying insurance conditions. While the reinsurer receives detailed information for single risks (facultative reinsurance), portfolio-level data are typically used for treaties and include the historical performance per line of business and product type at a larger geographical unit (e.g. district, province). Although most insurers have developed detailed databases of past claims at policy level, these data remain proprietary to the insurer and are hardly shared with reinsurers.

Data of Reinsurance Submissions in Agriculture

For facultative reinsurance that covers larger livestock, forestry and aquaculture risks on a single risk basis, reinsurers receive a detailed submission including the location of the risk (often on a map), a risk survey report that describes management and loss mitigation standards, and past losses per cause. For treaty reinsurance, the standard information includes exposure (sum insured), written premium, losses incurred and outstanding losses at the resolution of the portfolio or sub-portfolios (e.g. province) and risk types (e.g. crop types) for the last 10–15 years. Often, the submission includes a summary of the main changes in insurance terms, including premium rates, franchises, deductibles, exclusions and government support in the form of premium subsidies and risk sharing

---

[7] Swiss Re, 2016: Strategic reinsurance and insurance: the increasing trend of customised solutions. Swiss Re Publication Sigma No 5/2016, 39p.

structures. Occasionally, the number of written policies and the number of policies per sum insured band and area (crop insurance) or heads (livestock insurance) insured is available. The submission usually provides a forward-looking underwriting plan that outlines anticipated shifts in product types by geography and sometimes includes an overview of past reinsurance structures and loss experiences.

Data Consistency Analysis

At least five years of insurance loss histories should be available, including a good understanding of changes in insurance terms and conditions, geographical and product scope, and causes of large losses, preferably through a list of key events and loss extent per event. Reinsurers have developed benchmark data for certain lines of business, product types and geographies which allow comparisons of a particular portfolio to the performance of a major part of the industry, and facilitates the identification of data inconsistencies.

Catastrophe Losses

Agricultural portfolios are likely to include large or catastrophe-type losses from systemic perils such as drought, flood, cyclones, large-scale forest fires and epidemic livestock and aquaculture diseases. As catastrophe losses are rare but costly events, reinsurance pricings are highly sensitive to outliers in loss experiences. An inadequate assessment of catastrophe losses can lead to under- or overestimation of future risk and may have significant impacts on the profitability expectations of reinsurance treaties. Large losses are typically left in the data while catastrophe losses are assessed for realistic return periods relative to the portfolio based on catastrophe risk reports and outputs of catastrophe risk models (Section 2.5).

As-If Adjustments

Adjusting historical claims data is challenging with actuarial methods alone, particularly if programmes have been fast expanding and do not include catastrophe-type losses that would trigger non-proportional reinsurance structures. For treaty reinsurance, the typical approach includes the adjustment of (i) the written premium based on changes in the underlying average premium rate of the last available year, and (ii) losses based on the most recent level of franchises, deductibles and loss limits. In markets with government loss sharing structures, relevant adjustments need to be made to the losses. If experience data are available per sub-region and/or per risk type, the as-if adjustment is performed at this higher resolution and aggregated thereafter over the portfolio in function of the reinsurance structure. Further, the way losses are realised in the underlying insurance policies has to be matched to how losses are accounted under the reinsurance treaty on the basis of losses occurring or risk attaching. In some cases, insurers provide reinsurers with as-if adjusted data, which facilitates reinsurance pricing and should lead to more consistent pricings among reinsurers as fewer assumptions need to be taken to adjust historical data.

Example of an As-If Analysis of an Agricultural Insurance Portfolio

The standard as-if analysis is demonstrated through a crop insurance portfolio that contains 16 years (2002–2017) of premium, exposure and average premium rates (Table 10.3). The portfolio experienced significant growth, from a premium of

TABLE 10.3 Example of a crop insurance portfolio with 16 years of experience (2002–2017) including number of districts and crop types insured, sum insured, premium volume, average premium rate and losses. The As-If Analysis includes adjustments for premium volumes and translates the 2017 premium volume through the as-if loss ratios into weighted losses (Loss Today).

Year	Districts	Crop Types	Sum Insured	Premium	Premium Rate	Loss	L/R	As-If Analysis			
								Premium	Loss	L/R	Loss Today
2002	4	3	148,601,149	8,539,228	5.75%	8,397,500	98%	16,613,608	8,397,500	51%	48,626,755
2003	4	4	166,901,493	10,014,256	6.00%	9,742,045	97%	18,659,587	9,742,045	52%	50,227,011
2004	4	4	205,255,668	14,398,000	7.01%	11,585,340	80%	22,947,584	11,585,340	50%	48,569,214
2005	5	5	229,465,634	19,867,530	8.66%	14,465,105	73%	25,654,258	14,465,105	56%	54,243,961
2006	6	5	228,354,645	20,959,572	9.18%	19,109,147	91%	25,530,049	19,109,147	75%	72,007,695
2007	5	6	237,063,648	24,112,950	10.17%	53,982,162	224%	26,503,716	53,982,162	204%	195,944,355
2008	7	6	620,673,106	79,598,000	12.82%	45,568,755	57%	69,391,253	45,568,755	66%	63,175,936
2009	8	7	638,812,004	83,083,614	13.01%	43,643,954	53%	71,419,182	43,643,954	61%	58,789,324
2010	9	7	713,660,087	90,931,814	12.74%	55,666,688	61%	79,787,198	55,666,688	70%	67,119,919
2011	9	7	535,592,383	69,284,580	12.94%	23,714,316	34%	59,879,228	23,714,316	40%	38,099,884
2012	11	8	498,290,601	64,815,388	13.01%	37,122,123	57%	55,708,889	37,122,123	67%	64,105,834
2013	13	9	660,327,773	75,402,853	11.42%	88,079,686	117%	73,824,645	88,079,686	119%	114,779,318
2014	15	10	547,220,448	60,551,050	11.07%	37,898,507	63%	61,179,246	37,898,507	62%	59,594,644
2015	15	10	612,886,902	68,030,446	11.10%	44,219,790	65%	68,520,756	44,219,790	65%	62,084,585
2016	18	10	717,077,676	79,954,161	11.15%	75,956,453	95%	80,169,284	75,956,453	95%	91,147,743
2017	20	10	860,493,211	96,203,141	11.18%	58,683,916	61%	96,203,141	58,683,916	61%	58,683,916
Average							73%			74%	

US$8.5 million (2002) to US$96 million (2017), driven by the expansion in the number of districts and crop types. At the same time, the average premium rates increased significantly.

For reinsurance pricing, the premium volume is adjusted for all years in function of the premium rate of the most recent year (as-if premiums) and as premium rate levels used to be low in earlier years, as-if premium volumes increase as more premium would have been charged at current premium rates. Based on the as-if premiums and the observed losses, a loss ratio (as-if loss ratio) is computed and losses are weighted at the most recent year's premium volume (loss today), which forms the basis for experience-based reinsurance pricing. In this example, the as-if adjustments led to an increase in the average loss ratio from 73% (historical series) to 74% (as-if adjusted series), while the loss ratio in the year 2007 decreased from 224% to 204% through the as-if adjusted premium volumes.

While the as-if adjusted data are more presentative of today's insurance conditions, portfolio-level data (as used in this example) do not allow a regional analysis and adjustments for the additional crop types that have been insured over time. If regional and crop specific data are available, as-if adjustments should be undertaken at higher resolutions and would lead to more accurate adjustments and risk-adequate reinsurance terms. In case average deductibles and franchises are known at the portfolio or sub-portfolio level, historical losses can be adjusted in (i) proportional scaling when the sizes of individual risks have been comparable over time, or (ii) developing functions that describe loss distributions.

FLAT-RATE PRICING

The flat-rate approach is the most pragmatic pricing method that uses the present value of the expected loss and different costs related with the reinsurance transaction to determine the premium rate (PR) as:[8]

$$PR = \frac{PV\big[E(L)\big]}{(1-EE)\times(1-IE)\times(1-TER)}$$

with $PV\big[E(L)\big]$ as the present value of the expected loss, EE as external expenses that typically include brokerage, ceding commission and taxes, IE as the internal expenses of the reinsurer and TER as the targeted economic return of the reinsurer, which is a complex function of the target return on equity and the relative risk level of the particular reinsurance contract. The flat-rate approach assumes that there are no commission or premium adjustments.

For short-tail business like most agricultural insurances, where losses are rapidly known after occurrence and require little to no development of losses and unearned premium, $PV\big[E(L)\big]$ can be substituted by the expected loss cost. While actuarial and catastrophe modelling concepts provide premium rates, market forces, the reinsurer's growth strategy as well as the overall business relationships between the reinsurer and the insurer determine the costing approach to derive competitive reinsurance terms.

FACULTATIVE REINSURANCE PRICING

Standard facultative risks are typically priced through exposure curves, rating schedules and rating factors that are based on industry experience. However, exposure curves may not exist for larger and more complex risk where underwriting experience is used to derive reinsurance rates. Experience from other countries with large losses to similar risks support the development of PML and MFL scenarios. For catastrophe-exposed risks, pricing is based on (i) scenarios that derive loss frequency and severity distributions which are combined in an aggregated model, or (ii) outputs of catastrophe risk models (Section 2.5) where locations of single risk are entered and physical models generate probabilistic losses in function of the location and risk characteristics for modelled perils and markets. While underwriters often estimate premium rates for non-proportional facultative covers through standardised tables (sometimes called Lloyd's tables) as a factor of the primary rate, more actuarially sound methods express the expected loss as a percentage of the total expected loss.

Facultative Reinsurance Pricing in Agriculture

Exposure curves for facultative agricultural risks hardly exist as unlike property risk classes, large single crop farms, livestock operators, aquaculture production sites or timber plantations vary widely in exposure, management standards and loss expectations. Underwriting experience and international best-practise is used for facultative covers that exclude natural catastrophes, while scenario-based frequency and severity modelling is applied for catastrophe-exposed single risks. Often, risk survey reports for large single risks include an estimate from the policyholder about loss potentials and serve as a basis to benchmark loss frequency and severity assumptions.

TREATY REINSURANCE PRICING

Reinsurance pricing of treaties relies on aggregated data that reflect historical and projected exposure and premium volume on an insurance portfolio or for a sub-portfolio with more detailed data per region and for the main product types. Additional important information for pricing are original policy wordings per product type, and deductibles and limits that are applied by the insurer. Based on as-if adjusted historical insurance data, either aggregated models or loss-frequency models are applied to establish reinsurance terms for proportional and non-proportional structures. The pricing approach largely depends on the granularity of the historical insurance data, the presence or absence of catastrophe-type losses and the reinsurance structure.

Aggregate Loss Modelling

Aggregate models are used for reinsurance structures when little information is available on individual losses and historical insurance data from the insurer are obtained in aggregated form, which is typically the case for quota share and SL reinsurance.

---

[8] Patrik, G.S., 2001: Reinsurance. In Foundations of Casualty Actuarial Science. 4th edition. Casualty Actuarial Society, Arlington, USA, 142p.

Pricing input data			
Year	Premium today	Losses today	L/R
2002	98,956,719	48,626,755	49%
2003	98,956,719	50,227,011	51%
2004	98,956,719	48,569,214	49%
2005	98,956,719	54,243,961	55%
2006	98,956,719	72,007,695	73%
2007	98,956,719	195,944,355	198%
2008	98,956,719	63,175,936	64%
2009	98,956,719	58,789,324	59%
2010	98,956,719	67,119,919	68%
2011	98,956,719	38,099,884	39%
2012	98,956,719	64,105,834	65%
2013	98,956,719	114,779,318	116%
2014	98,956,719	59,594,644	60%
2015	98,956,719	62,084,585	63%
2016	98,956,719	91,147,743	92%
2017	98,956,719	58,683,916	59%

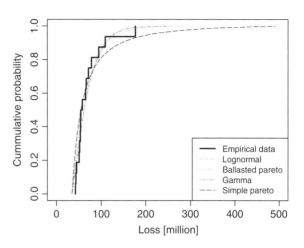

FIGURE 10.4 Example of an experience-based stop-loss pricing with Left: Pricing input data including premiums and losses adjusted at the 2017 portfolio (as-if analysis) and Right: Empirical losses and losses simulated through different PDFs.

Based on as-if adjusted claims, premium and exposure, either a historical burning rate approach is used to determine the average expected loss or statistical models with PDFs are fitted to claims data.

Historical Burning Rate Approach
The HBR approach essentially follows the concept used by insurers (Section 2.4) and allows fast computation of burning costs for different reinsurance structures. For a non-proportional reinsurance structure, HBR compares the losses to a layer XL_j to the premium obtained for the same layer in a year t $(t = 1, 2, ..., T-1)$ and derives the burning cost (BC) as:[9]

$$BC = \frac{\sum_{t=1}^{T-1}\sum_{k_t=1}^{n_t}\min\left(L - A; \left(\max\left(0; C_{t,k_t} - A\right)\right)\right)}{\sum_{t=1}^{T-1}P_t}$$

with L as the limit of the layer, A as the attachment point of the layer, C_t as a claim with n_t as the total number of claims for the year t and P_t as the premium. For a quota share and SL programme, insurers typically report the claims as the total over the reinsurance period, which is typically 12 months. The claims C_{t,k_t} can be indexed for the cost of reconstruction of buildings. While the HBR method provides burning costs for lower layers (working layers) that contain historical loss experiences, the burning cost for higher (catastrophe) layers might be equal to zero when no historical (observed or adjusted) claims have occurred (Figure 10.4).

---

[9]Desmedt, S. et al., 2012: Experience and exposure rating for property per risk excess of loss reinsurance revisited. *ASTIN Bull.*, 42(1), 233–70.

Statistical Models

To increase the range of possible loss outcomes, actuarial pricing uses statistical functions for the aggregated loss severity that are fitted to the (observed or adjusted) claims to determine average losses for proportional reinsurance structures and loss costs for different layers of non-proportional covers. Experienced actuaries usually know a priori which PDF is most suitable for a certain type of risk and geography. The goodness of fit of a PDF is investigated visually and through statistical fitting tests. When none of the PDFs fits the claims well and might inaccurately reflect the loss potential to high layers, often several PDFs are used for pricing with weighting different distributions. Commonly used PDFs for aggregate models include gamma, lognormal, Weibull and different forms of the Pareto distribution (Section 2.4).

Loss Frequency and Severity Modelling

When individual claims data are available, or at least large claims above a certain threshold, which is typically the case in submissions of RXOL and EXOL structures, loss frequency and severity modelling can be applied to obtain a joint loss distribution through an aggregate model. The process of obtaining the loss frequency and severity distributions closely follows the concept used by insurers (Section 2.4). For the loss frequency, the Poisson, the binomial or the negative binomial distribution is applied while distributions such as gamma, lognormal, Weibull and different forms of the Pareto distribution are often used to describe the loss severity.

Exposure Modelling

When historical insurance data limit experience rating through aggregate or loss-frequency/severity modelling for non-proportional structures, exposure rating is applied. Exposure rating is based on risk profiles and standardised exposure curves from industry experience that allow pricing of risks of similar sum insured and PMLs under the assumptions that risks are homogeneously distributed in certain exposure bands.[10]

Catastrophe risk models support the probabilistic modelling on current exposure in deriving losses from physical modelling, vulnerability functions and financial models (Section 2.5). Vendor models and in-house models of larger reinsurers allow the modelling of different catastrophe perils in key insurance markets. Increasingly, catastrophe models are available for specialised insurance business, including marine, cyber and agriculture.

Treaty Reinsurance Pricing in Agriculture

As most agricultural reinsurance is in the form of treaties, particularly as quota shares and SL covers, pricing relies largely on experience-based approaches through aggregate loss models. Often, the same pricing model is used for quota share and SL reinsurance structures that form part of the same reinsurance submission. Frequency–severity models are applied for RXOL and EXOL treaties based on available individual historical claims. Some reinsurers have developed in-house exposure pricing models, which relate regional exposure to publicly available proxies (e.g. weather and crop yield data) to derive loss amounts based on vulnerabilities. For some of the main agricultural insurance markets, catastrophe risk models simulate probabilistic losses to agricultural exposure including combinations of yield reductions and commodity price volatilities (Section 2.5).

Aggregate Modelling

When individual loss events are difficult to define and are not required by reinsurance structures such as quota shares and SLs, an aggregate loss model is used for pricing based on as-if adjusted premium and loss data. Based on as-if adjusted claims and premium volumes, the main pricing approaches use (i) an HBR approach for longer time series and when large and catastrophe-type losses are judged to be adequately represented in the data, or (ii) statistical models where PDFs are fitted to the claims data. Frequently used PDFs for agricultural risk include the lognormal, left truncated normal, gamma and generalised Pareto distributions.

A particular difficulty arises when historical claims include catastrophe losses that are magnitudes higher than usual claims. The return period of a catastrophe loss might not be adequately represented in the historical years and can lead to an (i) overestimation of risk if the return period of the catastrophe loss is longer than the insurance experience (e.g. a 50-year drought occurred in 10 years of insurance loss experience), or (ii) underestimation of the loss potential when the catastrophe loss has a shorter return period than the claims records (e.g. a 10-year flood occurred in a 30-year insurance loss time series). A pragmatic approach is to adjust the return period (frequency) of the catastrophe loss from data and information of catastrophe loss reports, the research community or outputs of catastrophe models. However, the return period of the physical event is not necessarily the same as the insurance loss and varies among different portfolios, e.g. a drought with a climatological return period of 50 years can cause a five-year loss on one insurance portfolio but a 100-year loss on another portfolio, depending on the geographical distribution of the insured exposure and the composition of the insurance products in a portfolio. Increasingly, open source proxies such as weather data and drought indices are used to quantify meteorological events (Chapter 3), satellite imagery supports the spatial assessment of flood extents, and area-burnt analyses allow an estimation of frequencies of large wildfires (Section 4.3). In some markets, catastrophe risk models allow probabilistic modelling on agricultural (re)insurance portfolios (Section 2.5).

Example of Stop-Loss Pricing for an Agricultural Portfolio

The standard SL pricing approach is demonstrated through a crop insurance portfolio that contains 16 years of as-if adjusted premium and losses with a GNPI of 98.9 million that reflect the current underwritten business (Figure 10.4). For illustration purposes, a GNPI-based SL with four layers as 50% xs 100%, 50% xs 150%, 100% xs 200% and 100% xs 300% is priced using a burning cost analysis based on the empirical data and different PDFs including gamma, lognormal, ballasted Pareto and simple Pareto.

The burning cost analysis uses simply the as-if adjusted losses and provides risk rates only for the first two SL layers, with the first layer having experienced one total loss (L/R 198%) and a partial loss (L/R 116%) in the last 16 years (Table 10.4). The gamma and lognormal distribution produce similar risk rates for all SL layers but estimate low risk for the higher two SL layers. The ballasted Pareto distribution includes more weights on the tail risk and therefore provides higher risk rates for all SL layers. The highest risk rates for the upper layers are obtained through the simple Pareto distribution (Table 10.4).

---

[10] Bernegger S., 1997: The Swiss Re exposure curves and the MBBEFD distribution class 1. *ASTIN Bull.*, 27(1), 99–111.

TABLE 10.4 Risk premium rates for four stop-loss layers based on the portfolio used in Figure 10.4 based on the burning cost approach as well as four distributions.

	Risk Premium Rates			
	50% xs 100%	50% xs 150%	100% xs 200%	200% xs 100%
Burning cost	9.38%	1.81%	0.00%	0.00%
Gamma	3.82%	0.61%	0.10%	0.00%
Lognormal	3.32%	0.56%	0.13%	0.01%
Ballasted Pareto	4.54%	1.15%	0.36%	0.03%
Simple Pareto ($\alpha = 1.51$)	6.94%	3.75%	3.72%	1.96%

In practice, a weighting between the different distributions would be chosen. This example shows the sensitivity of choosing an appropriate distribution function and that a pure burning cost analysis underestimates tail risks in this case.

Loss Frequency and Severity Modelling

For RXOL and EXOL reinsurance structures where indemnity is based on individual events that are measurable and quantifiable and reinsurers receive detailed claims statistics, loss frequency and severity distributions are combined in an aggregated model. Although rare, XOL treaties are used for certain livestock risks, forestry exposure (storm and fire), bloodstock and greenhouse complexes, where losses can be clearly differentiated and allocated to a particular event that is quantifiable in terms of occurrence and severity.

Exposure Modelling

Exposure curves as they are used in property reinsurance to determine rates of non-proportional structures are hardly available for agricultural risks. Instead, leading reinsurers have developed exposure models for crop insurance in large markets such as the USA, China, India and Brazil. Exposure models link exposure and insurance conditions as provided by insurers and/or published by government agencies to proxies such as yield and weather data on which the insurance products are based. Exposure models are essentially large databases and often include features that allow the spatial disaggregation of aggregated exposure to smaller units (e.g. from a province to a district or a calculation grid) through land use cover masks or area-planted statistics. Further, loss proxies such as disaster-declared areas per peril are used to complement the analyses and identify catastrophe events where little experience exists. For markets with revenue crop insurance, some reinsurers have correlated historical commodity prices to yield data and developed joint yield-price simulations to obtain losses in a similar way to crop insurers (Section 6.6).

As such, exposure modelling replicates the pricing work of an insurer but typically with less detailed data, more assumptions and higher uncertainties. Exposure modelling for agricultural risks contains some elements of catastrophe risk modelling (Section 2.5) and provides the reinsurer with a historical event catalogue that is as long as loss proxies are available, e.g. 20–40 years for crop yield data and 40–60 years for weather records. Exposure modelling has several advantages compared with aggregate modelling in that regional changes in the underlying portfolio are considered, changes in risk types and new risks are modelled as far as there is supporting data, and large as well as catastrophe losses of past years are applied on the current portfolio compositions and (average) insurance terms. Increasingly, catastrophe risk models are available from vendors for agricultural assets and currently include probabilistic models for the USA (MPCI, hail), Canada (hail), China (crop, livestock, forestry) and India (crop).

BIBLIOGRAPHY

Albrecher, H., Beirlant, J., and Teugels, J.L. (2017). *Reinsurance: Actuarial and Statistical Aspects*, 357. Oxford: Wiley.

Boyer, M.M. and Dupont-Courtade, T. (2015). The Structure of Reinsurance Contracts. *The Geneva Papers* 40: 474–492.

Clark, D.R. (2014). *Basics of Reinsurance Pricing*. Actuarial study note, 52. CAS.

Deelstra, G. and Plantin, G. (2015). *Risk Theory and Reinsurance*, 85. London: Springer.

Re, M. (2010). *Reinsurance: A Basic Guide to Facultative and Treaty Reinsurance*, 80. Munich: Munich Re Publication.

Reily, K. (2012). *Reinsurance: The Nuts and Bolts*, 3e, 269. Witherby Seamanship International.

Swiss Re, 2004: Exposure Rating. Publication 1501264_04_en, Zurich, 32p.

Swiss Re, 2010: The Essential Guide to Reinsurance. Publication 1504240_10, Zurich, 51p.

Swiss Re, 2016: Strategic reinsurance and insurance: the increasing trend of customised solutions. Sigma No. 5, Zurich, 39p.

Wehrhahn, R., 2009: Introduction to Reinsurance. World Bank Primer Series on Insurance Issue 2, Washington DC, 43p.

CHAPTER 11

Risk Transfer to Capital Markets

11.1 INTRODUCTION

Alternative capital providers such as hedge funds, pension funds, sovereign wealth funds, mutual funds and specialised catastrophe-oriented funds are of increasing importance in providing capital for insurance risks. In 2016, a capital of US$81 billion, or 12% of the global reinsurance capacity, was provided by alternative capital markets. While mainly used by (re)insurers to expand the basis of protection of highly correlated events such as natural catastrophes, government entities and state funds increasingly engage in non-traditional risk transfer.

While traditional reinsurance capacity is available in all markets and placements are often oversubscribed, insurance-linked securities (ILS) offer interesting opportunities for the agricultural sector, particularly when conventional solutions are not available due to systemic risks and concentrations of high exposures. Catastrophe bonds can play a vital role for governments in transferring peak risks in low- and middle-income countries that are highly dependent on agriculture and have little developed insurance and finance markets that can absorb systemic losses in an undiversified economy. Recent efforts to develop catastrophe risk models for agricultural risk classes support non-traditional risk transfer.

This chapter first introduces the main terminologies of capital market risk transfer and provides an overview of the current market. The main ILS products, including collateralised reinsurance, sidecars, catastrophe bonds and industry loss warranties, are then discussed, including examples where these products are or could be used for agricultural risks.

11.2 GLOBAL INSURANCE-LINKED SECURITIES MARKETS

Since capital market-based risk transfer became available for insurance risks in the 1990s, different terminologies have been introduced, including alternative capital, collateralisation, securitisation through ILS, with the main products including catastrophe bonds (cat bonds), sidecars, industry loss warranties and collateralised reinsurance.

ALTERNATIVE CAPITAL AND COLLATERALISATION

Alternative capital refers to counterparties such as hedge funds, pension funds, sovereign wealth funds, mutual funds and specialised catastrophe-oriented funds, which are commonly called capital market investors. As alternative capital providers are not rated for insurance risks, they are to provide letters of credit from a commercial bank or put collateral into a trust fund to back potential liabilities and mitigate credit risk. Typically, collateralisation covers the full reinsurance limit net of premiums charged but varies in function of the underlying insurance risks.

(Re)insurance risks allow alternative capital providers attractive returns in the current prevailing low-interest investment environment and add to diversification of investments as catastrophe risk has little correlation to the performance of financial markets.

SECURITISATION AND INSURANCE-LINKED SECURITIES

Capital market risk transfer refers to securitisation, which is a financial technique that pools assets and turns them into tradable securities. Securitisations have focused on life insurance risks, including true risk transfer and monetisation of future profits, non-life risks and particularly catastrophe exposure, and collateralised debt obligations to cover the funding request of the insurance industry. Generally, securitisation in insurance aims to reduce required capital for peak risks. It started as catastrophe bonds after Hurricane Andrew (1992) when reinsurance capacity was limited and expensive. Securitisation provides insurers with an alternative form of reinsurance and reinsurers with additional retrocession markets.

ILS, also called risk-linked securities, are financial instruments that cede insurance risks to capital markets. For non-life risks, ILS instruments typically include catastrophe bonds, catastrophe swaps, industry loss warranties, contingent capital and sidecars. Further forms of ILS comprise weather derivatives and, under some definitions, the general transformation of capital market risks into reinsurance. Some types of ILS can be traded among investors and on the secondary market.

ALTERNATIVE CAPITAL MARKETS

ILS markets increased from US$22 billion in 2007 to US$81 billion in 2016 and compare to US$514 billion capacity from traditional sources (reinsurance). Of the total alternative capital in 2016, 60% was allocated to collateralised reinsurance, 29% for cat bonds, 7% to sidecars and 4% to industry loss warranties (Figure 11.1). Following large natural catastrophe losses in the USA in 2017, US$11.3 billion new cat bonds have been issued, the highest volume since 2008.

11.3 OVERVIEW OF KEY PRODUCTS

ILS products are developing continuously and the main products can be distinguished as collateralised reinsurance, sidecars, catastrophe bonds and industry loss warranties. While all products differ in the way loss events are recognised, risk is transferred and alternative capital providers participate in the risk, collateralisation is required for all products.

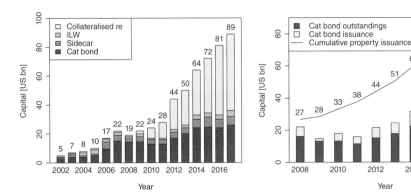

FIGURE 11.1 Left: Alternative capital per product type, 2002–2016, with half-yearly figures for 2017. Right: Issued and outstanding cat bonds and cumulative cat bond issuance for property exposure, 2008–2017.
Data source: Aon Securities.

COLLATERALISED REINSURANCE

Collateralised reinsurance (CRe) provides alternative capital providers which are typically non-rated and licensed for insurance risks to participate in individual reinsurance transactions. CRe can be placed through fully funded trusts established in the (re) insurer's name to cover reinsurance liabilities that are typically fully collateralised for non-proportional structures and collateralised up to a PML for proportional reinsurance covers. Alternatively, a placement can be undertaken through a rated fronting provider, which is typically a highly rated (re)insurer, where investors provide collateral directly to the fronter, or through a cell company. Under CRe, capital providers receive premiums from a (re)insurer as a return, net of commissions and/or overriders for the (re)insurer. The cost of collateralisation through letters of credits can be considerable and is borne by the alternative capital provider.

There are no known cases where collateralised reinsurance was set up specifically for agricultural risks but it might have been included in collateralised agreements.

REINSURANCE SIDECARS

Sidecars are a special form of CRe and became prominent following large losses from Hurricane Katrina (2005) as agreements between (re)insurers and capital markets to increase capacity and for investors to participate in potential profits based on anticipated increases of (re)insurance prices following large industry-wide losses. Sidecars saw a second growth after the 9/11 World Trade Center event. Sidecars are typically off-balance-sheet transactions for short-tail (re)insurance business for a duration of one to two years. Sidecars are special-purpose vehicles (SPVs) that are established by the sponsor to allow investors to participate through preferred shares in a private placement. The capital needs of the SPV, default probabilities and expected losses are derived from outputs of catastrophe risk models. While some sidecars are capitalised to full aggregate limits, others might not be adequately capitalised for tail risks, a risk that is borne by the (re)insurer as the financial liability of the investors is limited to the funds in the SPV.

The SPV receives investment from the securities, collects premium income from the (re)insurer under quota share agreements, pays the trust dividends and pays claims to the (re)insurer. The financial performance of the sidecar closely follows the underwriting results of the (re)insurer. The (re)insurer obtains a ceding commission for originating, underwriting and managing the book of business relevant for the sidecar and often a profit commission is provided for good underwriting results. Most sidecars have been established in Bermuda, which offers favourable regulatory and tax systems.

Reinsurance Sidecars in Agriculture

As agriculture insurance risks are short-tail and in most cases diversify property catastrophe books, they have been included in some sidecar agreements. One example is Lorenz Re, which was established by Partner Re in 2013 and includes a US$50 million retrocession quota share for US crop insurance business within two segregated cells.

CAT BONDS

A catastrophe bond (cat bond) is a risk-linked security that transfers predefined risks that are generally natural catastrophes from a sponsor (e.g. a (re)insurer) to investors. Cat bonds were created in the early 1990s following large-scale losses in the reinsurance industry from Hurricane Andrew and the Northridge earthquake, with the first transaction in 1994. Through the depth and strength of capital markets, cat bonds provide efficient coverage for peak risks and therefore complement traditional reinsurance markets. Non-life (re)insurers are using cat bonds to hedge against low-frequency but high-severity losses from hurricanes, earthquakes, winter storms and flood, with most applications for property risks. As risk diversification decreases with correlated peak risks, the cost of maintaining risk-adequate capital becomes uneconomical for a (re)insurer.

Over time, costs and the minimum size of a bond to justify the expenses have been reduced to provide smaller (re)insurers access to alternative capital, including transactions through cat bond-lite platforms. Multi-year cat bonds allow sponsors to spread the fixed costs of issuing the bonds over several years and to reduce costs on an annualised basis. Cat bond prices in low- and middle-income countries tend to be lower than in high-income countries as cat bond portfolios tend to be weighted towards US hurricane and earthquake exposure and investors welcome geographical diversification.[1]

Cat Bond Structures

A typical cat bond includes an SPV, which is specifically set up for administration and the issuance of securities to investors. The SPV collects the premium from the sponsor and the principal from the investors, to be held in a trust or collateral account with investments into highly rated money market funds and fixed-income products.

---

[1] Cummins, J.D. and Mahul, O., 2009: Catastrophe risk financing in developing countries: principles for public intervention. World Bank Publication, Washington DC, 299p.

A cat bond can be structured in that premiums and generated investment income are used to pay investors a regular coupon. The coupon is defined as a spread over the interbank offered rates (often LIBOR), with the spread typically ranging from 3% to 20% depending on the duration and structure of the bond. In case of the absence of triggering losses before maturity of the bond, the principal is returned to the investors and the coupon becomes payable. In case of a loss, the SPV covers the losses and the investors obtain the remaining balance of principal in accordance with the seniority of the cat bond.

Alternatively, the bond can be structured as a zero-coupon bond, which is sold at a discount and the investor's return is the difference between the purchase price and the face value. In case of a loss, the indemnity at the time of maturity (I_T) is defined through:

$$I_T = \begin{cases} A \times F, & \text{if} & L > T \\ F, & \text{if} & L \leq T \end{cases}$$

with F as the face value of the bond, L as the loss relative to the predefined trigger T and A as the proportion of the face value returned to the investor with $0 \leq A < 1$.

Most cat bonds are structured as floating-rate bonds where the principal is lost if specified trigger conditions occur. Some bonds include principal-protected tranches that guarantee the return of the principal and a triggering loss event but lower or reduce the interest and spread payments as well as the time when the principal is repaid. Cat bonds have a typical duration of three to five years and are considered risky investments, being rated by rating agencies such as Standard & Poor's, A.M. Best and Fitch as BB. The rating is based on the assessment of probabilities of triggering losses, full exhaustion of the principal and expected losses from catastrophe risk models.

A cat bond can be structured to cover individual events (event-linked bonds) or losses from events that have occurred over a certain time period in an aggregated form. Some cat bonds include multi-loss triggers where payments occur only after several subsequent events have occurred. MultiCat bonds cover events from different catastrophe risks (e.g. hurricane and earthquake) on the same underlying portfolio and the same or different geographies.

Indemnity Triggers
Indemnity triggers are based on actual losses of the sponsor based on ultimate net losses and are therefore directly linked to the performance of the underlying (re)insurance portfolio. Extensive legal documentation is required to define the underlying book of business, the loss event and the peril. Indemnity-based cat bonds include moral hazard for the investor as the (re)insurer could relax underwriting standards after bond issuance. Further, information asymmetries occur as investors typically don't have access to detailed portfolio information. The settlement of contracts with indemnity triggers can take a considerable time until all underlying losses are determined through loss adjustment. Indemnity triggers have become increasingly popular with insurers as they do not contain basis risk and investors become more comfortable with potential moral hazard and information asymmetries as sponsors provide more detailed portfolio information for risk modelling.

Parametric Triggers

Parametric triggers use indices based on actual reported physical parameters such as windspeed or earthquake magnitude. The benefit for the sponsor is that portfolio details do not have to be disclosed, and for the investor, the risk is easier to quantify while the securities are more liquid and tradable.

A basic form of a parametric trigger is a catastrophe-in-the-box (CIB) product. A CIB is tailor-made for a particular type of natural peril (cat) and depends on physical parameters that occur in a predefined geographical area (box), defined by a box which is typically a polygon or a circle. For example, in the case of earthquake, physical criteria that trigger a CIB payout are based on the location of the epicentre, the magnitude and the depth of the actual fault rupture. For tropical cyclones, payout triggers are established as predefined wind speeds that need to be exceeded when the storm enters the designated area (box). For CIB products, intensities of an event must be publicly reported and verified by independent third parties without vested interests, such as catastrophe modelling firms or universities. The CIB payout function is either defined as binary (step function) in that a predefined amount is payable in full once the structure is triggered, or scaled where algebraic functions are used to define the indemnity as a function of intensity and/or distance of a location to the origin or maximum intensity of a triggering event. CIB structures pay out rapidly, are transparent as both the data and payout functions are public, but as with all parametric risk transfer products, induce basis risk.

CIB products have been used by corporates for natural disasters in the energy off-shore industry where oil platforms have to be shut down during hurricanes and consequently this leads to significant physical damage and business interruption. Further, CIB solutions have covered damage from cyclones to overland power transmission lines, which otherwise would be difficult to insure through conventional insurance products. Government agencies have bought multiCat parametric products that are based on CIB concepts to provide payment for emergency expenses after disaster impact.[2] For example, Fonden, a disaster fund of the Mexican government, has been using multiCat bonds since 2006. The 2012 structure for Fonden that was placed as a cat bond for a three-year term included (i) a US$140 million notional for earthquakes of predefined magnitude and depths in five regions, (ii) US$75 million coverage for Atlantic hurricanes in two zones with a central pressure <920 millibar, and (iii) a US$100 million capacity for Pacific hurricanes in one zone with pressures of 920–931 millibar (50% payout) and <920 millibar (full payout).[3]

Industry Loss Index Triggers

Industry loss index triggers are based on indices of estimated industry-wide losses that are determined through an independent party such as Property Claims Services (PCS) in the USA or PERILS in Europe. These triggers induce basis risk for the sponsor when individual insurance portfolios do not perfectly correlate to the industry.

---

[2] Michel-Kerjan, E. et al., 2011: Catastrophe Financing for Governments: Learning from the 2009–2012 Multi-cat Program in Mexico. OECD Working Papers on Finance, Insurance and Private Pensions, No. 9, Paris, 64p.
[3] World Bank, 2013: Mexico Multi-cat Bond. GFDDR Publication, Washington DC, 2p.

Modelled Loss Triggers

Modelled loss triggers use actual physical measurements that are entered into an agreed catastrophe risk model on a predefined (escrowed) portfolio of risks on which event losses are simulated for pricing and loss settlement of events that occur during the contract period. For some cat bonds, the sponsor has the right to modify the predefined portfolio during the period of the bond. Modelled loss trigger and indexes include model risk in that models over- or underestimate risk of an event is based on assumptions taken in catastrophe risk models.

Hybrid Triggers

Hybrid triggers combine two or more different types of triggers (e.g. modelled loss triggers and industry loss indices) and were developed in an effort to reduce basis risk and eliminate potential moral hazard in cat bond transactions.

Cat Bonds in Agriculture

While parametric covers are very common in agricultural insurance and results of theoretical studies of cat bonds are encouraging, cat bonds so far have not been implemented for agricultural production risks. This is probably related to the current abundance of reinsurance capacity, lower loss potentials for the insurance industry compared with property and infrastructure exposure, large costs to set up a cat bond, basis risk and the general unfamiliarity of agricultural insurers and government entities with the concept.

The use of cat bonds for agricultural risks has been explored theoretically, with the suggestion that such structures can complement or substitute reinsurance in markets where reinsurance capacity is limited or not available. One of the first investigations included the design of an annual zero-coupon cat bond for crop insurers that cover cotton in Georgia (USA) based on realised yield losses measured as a percentage deviation of actual from the long-term average state yield.[4] A further study designed a three-year cat bond for drought risk in Kenya, with dual triggers for rainfall in two seasons.[5] The feasibility of a cat bond between an insurer and a hedge fund was investigated at the example of low temperature triggers and agricultural losses in two locations in Iran.[6] As losses to agriculture assets from extreme droughts cannot be entirely absorbed by the (re)insurance industry, it has been suggested that such risks should be securitised through weather indices to capital markets in the form of famine bonds.[7] Besides cat bonds, the use of commodity-linked bonds, which are issued under option or option-like structures linked to the price of a specific commodity, has been explored to cover catastrophe risks in agriculture.[8]

---

[4] Vedenov, D.V. et al., 2006: Designing catastrophe bonds to securitize systemic risks in agriculture: The case of Georgia cotton. *J. Agric. Resour. Econ.*, 31 318–38.

[5] Sun, L. et al., 2015: Designing catastrophic bonds for catastrophic risks in agriculture. *Agric. Finance Rev.*, 22, 523–45.

[6] Karagiannis, N. et al., 2016: Modelling and pricing of catastrophe risk bonds with a temperature-based agricultural application. *Quant. Financ.*, 16 (12), 1949–59.

[7] Chantarat, S. et al., 2008: Improving humanitarian response to slow-onset disasters using temperature-based, weather derivatives. *Agr. Finance Rev.*, 68(1), 169–95.

[8] Turvey, C.G., 2006: Managing food industry business and financial risks with commodity-linked credit instruments. *Agribusiness*, 22, 523–45.

Example of a Possible Cat-in-the-Box Product for Banana Production in Australia

Banana production is the largest single horticultural industry in Australia, with a farmgate value of AU$600 million and an annual contribution to the economy of AU$1.3 billion in 2017. Bananas are produced on 650 farms on 12 000 ha, with Queensland as the key producer (94% of production), followed by New South Wales (4%) and Western Australia (2%). Most bananas are of the Cavendish variety (95% market share) and achieve a wholesale price of AU$5–25 per carton and a gross margin of AU$6000 per hectare. Around 12 months are required after planting to the first harvest, with subsequent harvests every eight–10 months thereafter.

In Queensland, most production is concentrated in Northern Queensland over a 160 km coastal strip including the towns of Tully, Innisfail and Kennedy, where mostly the Cavendish variety is produced. Northern Queensland experiences tropical cyclones during the summer months, which cause significant damage to banana production and interruption of supplies in the domestic market. Landfalling cyclones cause significant devastation to banana plantations through defoliation, stem breakage and flooding, with additional damage to infrastructure. The worst devastation typically occurs within 100 km of the cyclone's centre and with wind speeds >70 km h^{-1}, while wet soils and soft grounds before cyclone impact increase the number of blown-over banana plants.

Cyclone Damage to Banana Production

Since 1984, the key banana growing area in Northern Queensland has been impacted by three severe cyclones: (i) cyclone Winifred (1986, cat 3), which caused a loss of AU$35 million to a developing banana industry, (ii) cyclone Larry (2006, cat 4), which destroyed over 90% of the crops and caused a production loss of over AU$300 million, and (iii) cyclone Yasi (2011, cat 5), which devastated over 80% of plantations worth AU$400 million (Figure 11.2). As the production surface has increased from 2500 ha (1986) to over 11 500 ha (2016), the loss of earlier cyclones like Winifred and Larry would cause significantly higher losses today.

For banana growers, cyclones result in a lack of income from production losses, increased costs related to replanting and higher labour costs for canopy removal as a loss reducing measure before cyclone impact. As Australia does not allow imports of fresh bananas due to biosecurity risks, a shortfall of domestic banana production leads to limited supply and large price increases in the wholesale and retail markets, which can last as long as 10 months. For example, following cyclone Larry (2006), banana prices increased 3.6 times and cyclone Yasi (2011) saw 3.9 times higher prices at AU$7.5/kg compared with normal price levels of AU$2/kg. Furthermore, the simultaneous replanting of large areas that were devastated by cyclones led to oversupplies and decreasing prices in the mid run.

Despite interest among Queensland's banana producers, natural disaster insurance is not available as insurers judge exposure to be highly concentrated, loss potential to be significant and insurance products to be simply too costly. In the absence of insurance solutions, banana growers rely on government disaster compensation to cover immediate financial needs and apply pre-cyclone loss mitigation strategies, including diversifying farm location and destroying growing bunches as well as reducing canopy areas to reduce the surface exposed to strong wind.[9]

---

[9] Queensland Government, 2012: Scheduling Banana Production after Tropical Cyclones, 69p.

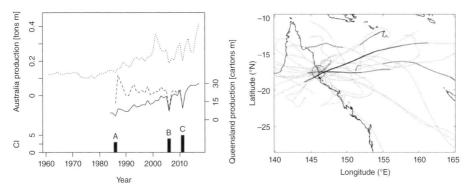

FIGURE 11.2 Left: Banana production in Australia (left axis, dotted line), 1961–2017, banana production in Queensland (right axis, solid line) and detrended production (right axis, dashed line), 1984–2017, and cyclone intensity (left axis, columns) for cat 3 cyclone Winifred (A), cat 4 cyclone Larry (B) and cat 5 cyclone Yasi (C). Right: Historical cyclone tracks over Northeast Australia with intensities of cat 1 and cat 2 (dotted), cat 3 and cat 4 (grey) and cat 5 (black) and a circle of a radius of 60 miles centred over Innisfail in the heart of the banana growing industry in Northern Queensland, 1970–2016.
Source: Banana Industry Annual Report and Australian Banana Growers' Council (left plot) and Swiss Re with permission (right plot).

Cat-In-The-Box Product

The systemic nature of cyclone damage and reoccurring high losses in geographically concentrated areas are conditions in which CIB solutions can provide coverage for the entire North Queensland banana industry. As used for property and infrastructure, a CIB structure for banana plantations could provide indemnity as soon as a cyclone of a predefined category enters a pre-agreed area (circle) located around the main production area. The indemnity function can be defined as follows:

- Trigger. Cyclone of an intensity of a category equal to or above three on the Australian cyclone intensity scale as reported by the Australian Bureau of Meteorology (BOM)[10] enters a circle with a radius of 60 miles located over Innisfail, Northern Queensland (Trigger Area).
- Indemnity function. Binary indemnity for a payout (P) defined as $P = I_{BOM \geq 3} \times AU\$50$ million with $I_{BOM \geq 3}$ as the reported cyclone intensity of category 3 and above in the Trigger Area for each cyclone category.

Between 1970 and 2016, a total of 18 tropical storms and cyclones entered the Trigger Area, including six cat 1 cyclones, one cat 2, one cat 3 (Winifred, 1986), one cat 4 (Larry, 2006) and one cat 5 (Yasi, 2011). Since 1970, the CIB structure would have provided the following payouts: AU\$150 million in 1986, AU\$200 million in 2006 and AU\$250 million in 2011, which approximately represents 54% of the value of the North Queensland banana production the year before cyclone Yasi, 45% in the case of cyclone Larry and 60% for cyclone Winifred.

---

[10] BOM defines tropical cyclone intensity as the maximum mean 10-minute wind speed over open flat land or water in five scales from categories 1 to 5.

The beneficiary of the payout could be the Australian Banana Growers' Council, which includes most banana growers, with funds to be used to provide payments to individual growers in function of damage extent on ground. Alternatively, the Queensland government could use the indemnity to compensate against disaster payments that are provided to banana growers for immediate relief after cyclone impact. A risk transfer product based on the CIB concept can be structured as a cat bond or could take the form of index-based insurance.

CAT FUTURES AND OPTIONS

As to finance future catastrophes, CBOT launched catastrophe futures in 1992 followed by catastrophe call and put options that were based on aggregated catastrophe loss indexes compiled by PCS for the USA. However, due to a lack of trading volume and of interest among insurers driven by high perceived basis risk, the contracts were later withdrawn. In 2007, the CME introduced futures and options contracts for US hurricanes that allow trading of intensities of landed hurricanes in six regions of the USA.[11]

Cat-E-Puts

Catastrophe equity puts (Cat-E-Puts) are options where the writer of the option receives a premium and the (re)insurer obtains the option to issue preferred stock at a pre-agreed price once a qualified loss has occurred. Cat-E-Puts allow the (re)insurer to raise equity at pre-agreed prices immediately after a major catastrophe and at a time when share prices are likely to be low. However, Cat-E-Puts are not collateralised and include counterparty credit risks.

Cat Swaps

Catastrophe risk swaps are agreements to exchange catastrophe risks between two parties with similar exposure and are facilitated by an exchange such as the Catastrophic Risk Exchange (CATEX). CATEX allows (re)insurers to find a counterparty to swap catastrophe-type risks. Often, parametric triggers are used to define payouts in a way that expected losses calculated from catastrophe risk models are comparable for both parties in the swap. Swap agreements do not include premium payments and can be annual or may cover multiple seasons or years. The indemnity function can be defined through a scale, with a full payout in case of severe events and partial payouts for less severe events. The main advantage of swaps is that a (re)insurer obtains risk diversification in swapping some risk for risks that complement the current portfolio, while efficiently managing equity capital. Swaps include basis risk and model risks and are complex to implement.

---

[11] Perrakis, S. and Boloorforoosh, A., 2018: Catastrophe futures and reinsurance contracts: An incomplete markets approach. *J. Futures Markets*, 38(1), 104–28.

INDUSTRY LOSS WARRANTIES

An ILW is a contract that allows one party to obtain protection from an individual or a series of events based on the total insured loss experienced by the industry or physical indices. Occurrence-based ILWs cover individual events; aggregate ILWs include cumulative events (e.g. over 12 months) and use monetary loss amounts for each event.

ILW contracts contain a specific limit which defines the amount per geographical area that the beneficiary obtains and in return the beneficiary pays a predefined premium to the counterparty. ILWs are typically priced as aggregate excess of loss contracts and use actuarial concepts to establish industry loss distributions.[12] Alternatively, catastrophe risk models are applied for natural perils in the main insurance markets.

Compared with traditional reinsurance, ILWs incur lower costs and limited moral hazard and information asymmetries as the indemnity is based on the entire industry rather than on an individual insurance portfolio. ILWs provide an alternative to traditional reinsurance and catastrophe bonds when insurers with portfolios that reflect general market performance aim at smoothing results from the impact of catastrophe events. Further, ILWs are often a cost-efficient approach for retrocession. However, ILWs contain basis risk as the industry loss is not fully correlated with losses on individual insurance portfolios. Basis risk tends to be lower for portfolios that closely follow the market, such as those of larger national insurers.

Forms of Industry Loss Warranties

ILWs can be derivative contracts or reinsurance agreements, in which case an ultimate net clause is required where the beneficiary needs to demonstrate that a specified loss amount, which is typically set at a minimum level, has occurred. ILW derivatives can be traded and facilitating brokers publish estimated bid and offer levels. Live-Cat ILWs are traded while an event is developing and Dead-Cat ILWs are purchased and traded immediately after the occurrence of an event but before final loss amounts are known. Back-up ILWs are available after an event and cover consequential losses such as fire after earthquakes. Most ILWs are executed in reinsurance form, while ILW risk transfer between funds often takes a derivative form.

Indemnity Functions

Under a derivative form, the indeminty (I) of an ILW can reach up to a limit (L) if a predefined trigger (T) based on an industry loss (L_I) has been reached, written as:[13]

$$I = \begin{cases} L, & if \quad L_I \geq T \\ 0, & if \quad L_I < T \end{cases}$$

---

[12] Gatzert, N. and Schmeiser, H., 2012: Industry loss warranties: Contract features, pricing, and central demand factors. *J. Risk Finance*, 13(1), 13–31.

[13] Zeng, L., 2000: On the basis risk of industry loss warranties. *J. Risk Finance*, 1(4), 27–32.

Under an indemnity-based ILW contract (reinsurance), a claim is paid up to the beneficiary's own actual loss (L_A) up to the limit in case the industry loss exceeds the trigger, written as:

$$I = \begin{cases} \min(L, L_A), & if \quad L_I \geq T \\ 0, & if \quad L_I < T \end{cases}$$

Industry losses are established by a competent third party such as PCS for property losses in the USA or the RMA for US crop insurance losses.

Industry Loss Warranties in Agriculture

A precondition for ILWs for agricultural insurance risks is the existence of an independent, reliable and widely accepted organisation that regularly and transparently establishes industry-wide losses – typically these are government agencies or industry associations. Markets where government agencies determine insurance conditions (e.g. US MPCI, Canada MPCI, China's National Agricultural Insurance Program) and aggregate industry loss statistics form an ideal basis for the development of ILWs. To limit basis risk under an ILW, individual insurance portfolios need to be reasonably comparable and diversified in order for basis risk to be manageable and for the ILW to be an acceptable risk transfer mechanism.

ILW for Multi-Peril Crop Insurance in the USA

After the severe 2012 drought in the USA (Section 3.3), retrocession capacity for MPCI portfolios was temporarily limited. In response, an ILW contract was established for 2013 with a payout in case the net loss ratio, excluding government reinsurance protection, of the US MPCI insurance industry exceeds 100% at national level and over all insurable crop types in a given underwriting year. MPCI business is clearly defined by the RMA, which also publishes the net industry loss ratio. Under the MPCI ILW, the net loss ratio (LR_{Net}) is defined as:

$$LR_{Net} = 1 - \frac{UWR_{Net}}{RP_{Net}}$$

with UWR_{Net} as the industry underwriting result in terms of gains or losses and RP_{Net} as the net retained premium of all admitted crop insurers after cessions to government risk funds as published by the RMA.[14] The ILW that was issued for 2016 included different layers that were defined in terms of LR_{Net}, ranging from 5% xs 100% to 25% xs 100%. At present, the USA remains the only agricultural market with ILWs.

BIBLIOGRAPHY

Albertini, L. and Barrieu, P. (2009). *The Handbook of Insurance-Linked Securities*. Wiley, 398p.
Ishaq, A. (2005). *Reinsuring for Catastrophes through Industry Loss Warranties – A Practical Approach*. Arlington: Casualty Actuarial Society Forum, 18p.

---

[14] https://prodwebnlb.rma.usda.gov/apps/ReinsuranceReports (accessed December 2017).

Lane, M. and Mahul, O., 2008: Catastrophe Risk Pricing-An Empirical Analysis. World Bank Policy Research Working Paper 4765, Washington DC, 26p.

Pompella, M. and Scordis, N.A. (2017). *The Palgrave Handbook of Unconventional Risk Transfer*. Palgrave Macmillan, 583p.

Swiss Re, 2009: The role of indices in transferring insurance risks to capital markets. Sigma 4/2009, Zurich, 48p.

Swiss Re, 2011: The fundamentals of Insurance-Linked Securities. Publication 1498744_11_en, Zurich, 40p.

Weber, C. (2011). *Insurance Linked Securities. The Role of the Banks*. Wiesbaden: Gabler/Springer Fachmedien, 367p.

Acronyms and Abbreviations

ORGANISATIONS AND INSTITUTIONS

ADB	Asian Development Bank
CBH	Co-operative Bulk Handling (Australia)
CBOT	Chicago Board of Trade (USA)
CME	Chicago Mercantile Exchange (USA)
CRED	Centre for Research on the Epidemiology of Disasters
ECMWF	European Centre of Midrange Weather Forecasting (UK)
EM-DAT	Emergency Events Database, Université Catholique de Louvain (Belgium)
EU	European Union
FAO	Food and Agriculture Organization
FCIC	Federal Crop Insurance Corporation (USA)
GFMC	Global Fire Monitoring Centre
IFAD	International Fund for Agricultural Development
IFC	International Finance Corporation (World Bank Group)
IFPRI	International Food Policy Research Institute
ILRI	International Livestock Research Institute
IPCC	Intergovernmental Panel on Climate Change
NASA	National Aeronautics and Space Administration (USA)
NASS	National Agricultural Statistics Service (USA)
NCAR	National Center for Atmospheric Research (USA)
NCIS	National Crop Insurance Services (USA)
NOAA	National Oceanic and Atmospheric Administration (USA)
OECD	Organisation for Economic Co-operation and Development
OIE	World Organisation for Animal Health
PCS	Property Claims Services (USA)
RMA	Risk Management Agency (USA)
USDA	United States Department of Agriculture
USGS	United States Geological Survey
WMO	World Meteorological Organization
WTO	World Trade Organization

CONCEPTS AND PRODUCTS

AAL	average annual loss
AEP	aggregate exceedance probability
AET	actual evapotranspiration
ARIMA	autoregressive integrated moving average
AVHRR	advanced very high resolution radiometer
BSE	bovine spongiform encephalopathy
CRESTA	catastrophe risk evaluation and standardizing target accumulations
ELC	expected loss calculation
ELR	expected loss ratio
ELT	event loss table
ENSO	El Niño southern oscillation
EP	exceedance probability
ERM	enterprise risk management
fAPAR	fraction of absorbed photosynthetically active radiation
fCover	vegetation cover fraction
FMD	foot and mouth disease
GDD	growing degree day
GDP	gross domestic product
GHG	greenhouse gas
GNPI	gross net written premium income
GWP	gross written premium
HBR	historical burn rate
IBNR	incurred but not reported
IDW	inverse distance weighting
ILS	insurance-linked securities
ILW	industry loss warranties
ISA	infectious salmon anemia
LCR	loss cost ratio
LR	loss ratio
MFL	maximum foreseeable loss
MGA	managing general agent
MODIS	moderate resolution imaging spectroradiometer
MPCI	multi-peril crop insurance
NDVI	normalised difference vegetation index
NWFM	numerical weather forecast model
OEP	occurrence exceedance probability
PDF	probability density function
PET	potential evapotranspiration
PML	probable maximum loss
PPP	private-public partnership
PRRS	porcine reproductive and respiratory syndrome
SAR	synthetic aperture radar
SPI	standardized precipitation index
SPOT	satellite pour l'observation de la terre
TVaR	tail value at risk
VaR	value at risk
VI	vegetation index (based on satellite data)
WRSI	water requirement satisfaction index
WSSV	white spot syndrome virus

Index

Note: Page references followed by 'f' refer to Figures; those followed by 't' refer to Tables

10-10 rule (risk transfer) 369

A.M. Best 397
absorbed PAR (APAR) 121
accident and infertility insurance (livestock) 290
actual production history (APH) 54, 199
actual revenue history (ARH) 54
actuarial insurance pricing 30–5
adjusted gross revenue (AGR, USA) 221
adjusted gross revenue lite (AGR-Lite, USA) 221
adjusted historical claims data (insurance) 27, 31
Advanced Very High Resolution Radiometer (AVHRR) 120, 123, 263
adverse selection 25, 174
AFG Plantation Insurance Scheme (Australia) 342
Africa, agricultural insurance 167–9
  developing markets 167–8
  established markets 167
  innovative distribution channels 168–9
  livestock insurance 284
  macro-insurance 168
  microinsurance 168
Africa, WRSI Drought Indices 266–8
  Africa Risk View Software 267–8
  droughts in Africa 266–7
  insurance through African Risk Capacity (ARC) 267
Africa Rainfall (RFE2) (NOAA) 109
Africa Rainfall Climatology Version 2.0 (ARC2) (NOAA) 109
African Rainfall Estimate Climatology 267
African Risk Capacity (ARC) 168, 266
aggregate exceedance probability (AEP) 37
aggregate excess of loss (AXOL) 372–3, 373t, 379–80, 379f
  contract 245
  priorities and monetary limits 380
  reinsurance 359, 360
  reinsurance premium 380

aggregate loss modelling 33–4, 386–8, 389
  historical burning rate approach 387, 387f
  statistical models 388
aggregate-yield index insurance 242–5
AgInsure (Canada) 159, 180, 234–5
agribusinesses, major risks for 12, 13–15t
agricultural indices 56
agricultural insurance markets 156–7, 156f, 156t, 158t
agricultural insurance operations 184–6
agricultural insurance products 152, 153–5t
agricultural insurance systems 178–84
  private sector system 179
  private–public sector system 182–4
  public sector system 179–81
agricultural insurance, benefits of 169–72
  government benefits 170
  producer benefits 169
  supply chain benefits 170
agricultural insurance, challenges of 172–8
  affordability of premiums 176
  empirical evidence 176–7
  insurance demand and affordability 175–7
  insurance distribution 178
  loss adjustment 177–8
  operations, administration and distribution 177–8
  systemic risks 173–5
  underwriting and pricing 177
  value attached to insurance 175–6
agricultural insurance, credits and guarantees link to 170–2
Agricultural Production Systems Simulator (APSIM) 131
agricultural reinsurance markets 364
agricultural reinsurance pricing 382–5
  adjustment of historical insurance data (as-if analyses) 382–5
  reinsurance submissions data 382–3

data consistency analysis 383
catastrophe losses 383
as-if adjustments 383–5, 384t
agricultural sector 1–6
    availability of natural resources and
        investments 4
    supply challenges 3–6
    climate change 5–6
    conflicts and poverty 5
    productivity 3–4
    rising demand 2–3
    risk management in 6–19
    structural changes 3
    supply chains 4–5
agricultural surveys 127–9
    aggregation issues 128
    quality of yields from agricultural surveys 129
    yield surveys in the USA 127–8
Agriculture Financial Services Corporation (AFSC,
    Canada) 159, 264, 359
Agriculture Income Disaster Assistance (AIDA,
    Canada) 234
Agriculture Insurance Company of India Limited
    (AICI) 237
AgriInsure (Canada) 234–5, 282
AgriInvest (Canada) 159, 234–5
AgriStability (Canada) 159, 233, 234, 235. 236
Agroasemex (Mexico) 166, 300
Agroseguro (Spain) 160, 185, 320
AIR Multi-Peril Crop Insurance Model
    40–3, 42f, 42t
    financial module 40–1
    hazard and vulnerability module 40
    model applications 41
    model validations 41
Alberta, Canada
    expenses of the Forest Protection Division 358–9
    firefighting cost insurance in (Canada) 358–60
    index-based fire suppression cost
        insurance 359–60
    large fire events and years 359
    performance of the index-based fire suppression
        cost insurance 360–1
    satellite yield insurance 264
    satellite-based pasture insurance 264
algal blooms 318
Algeria: Caisse Nationale de la Mutualité Agricole
    (Algeria) 167
all-risk insurance (aquaculture) 322
all-risk stock mortality insurance
    (aquaculture) 322–8
alternative capital 394
ANAGSA schemes (Mexico) 166, 180
anthrax 295
Aon Benfield 368
APH (crop insurance) 214

apiculture insurance (USA) 107–8
Aquacrop 131
aquaculture 4
    definition of 312
    diseases of 319
    key risks in 317–19
aquaculture index insurance 328–31
aquaculture insurance 311–28
    challenges of 321–2
    risk transfer solutions 319–22
    sector trends 311–19, 312f
aquaculture insurance markets 319–22
    industrialised aquaculture 319–20
    main insurance products 320
    small-scale aquaculture 320–1
aquaculture insurance products 322
aquaculture production certificates 316
aquaculture production systems 312–15
    classification according to intensity of
        production 313–14
    classification according to scale of
        production 314–15
    closed systems 313
    development of aquaculture production 315–16
    development of demand 316
    development of feed production 316
    hybrid systems 313–14
    industrial production 315
    open systems 313
    production factors 314, 314t
    semi-closed systems 313
    smallholder production 314–15
    trends in aquaculture production and
        consumption 315–16
aquaculture revenue insurance 330–1
aquaculture surveys 145–7
aquaculture weather index insurance 329
area burnt analyses (forestry) 124–5
area revenue protection (ARP) 240
area revenue with harvest price exclusion
    (ARPwHPE) 240
area-based fire index insurance (forestry) 360–1
area-based mortality index insurance
    (AMII) 278t, 295
area-yield index insurance (AYII) 191, 195t,
    199, 236–48
    challenges of 240
    for forests 361
    insurance terms 241–2
    markets 237–41
area-yield index insurance pricing 245–8
    example of 246–8
    risk rates based on observed yield 247–8,
        247f, 248f
    with yield time series 245–6
area-yield indices 125, 268

area-yield production (AYP) 240
Argentina
    agricultural insurance in 167
    La Segunda 185
    Sancor Seguros 185
artificial neural network (ANN) models 60
Asian options 306
Asian Precipitation – Highly-Resolved
    Observational Data Integration Towards
    Evaluation of Water Resources (Aphrodite)
    (Japan Meteorological Agency) 106
Asia-Pacific
    agricultural insurance 161–4
    livestock insurance 282–3
    multi-peril crop insurance 216
    non-industrial private forest owners 341
    revenue insurance 223
as-if adjustments 383–5, 384t
Assurance Récolte Sahel 168
Atkinson–Holiday model 83
Aujeszky's disease 295
AusSpread 94
Australia
    agricultural insurance in 165
    Black Friday fires 337
    Bureau of Meteorology (BoM) 107
Australian Banana Growers' Council 402
Australian Barley Board 245
Australian Forest Growers Association (AFG) 341
Australian Forest Growers Plantation Insurance
    Scheme 342
Autoregressive Integrated Moving Average
    (ARIMA) 60, 117, 137, 259
average annual losses (AALs) 37
avian influenza 89, 91, 93, 94 294, 295

back-up ILWs 403
ballasted Pareto distribution 389
Barnes approach 115
barrier options 306
basis risk 224, 251, 403
Bayesian analysis 31
Beijing Municipal Government (BMG) 18
Berkeley Earth Surface Temperature (BEST) 106
Best Track Data 85
beta distribution 139
binomial distribution 34t
biomass insurance (aquaculture) 322
biophysical indices 118, 121, 265
biosecurity plans (livestock) 90–1
Black–Scholes Option Pricing Model 226, 227, 303
Black–Scholes with copula functions 229t
blockchain 29
bonus-malus systems 27
bovine spongiform encephalopathy (BSE)
    91, 93, 295

bovine tuberculosis 89, 295
Brazil
    Agricultural Fund for Natural Disasters 166
    agricultural insurance 165–6
    Bank of Brazil 165
    CADENA 166
    National Agricultural Insurance Company
        (CNSA) 165
    Natural Disaster Fund (FONDEN) 166
    ProAgro 166, 180
    Reinsurance Institute of Brazil (IRB) 165
    revenue insurance 223
    Rural Insurance Premium Subsidy
        Program (PSR) 165
    Rural Stability Fund 165
British Columbia
    Fire Fighting Expenses Endorsement 356
    Liability Protection Agreement 356
brucellosis 89, 91
Bühlmann credibility method (insurance) 31
burning cost analyses 290
burning cost ratio 32
Burr distributions 139
business interruption insurance
    (livestock) 292, 295

CAIS (Canada) 234
Caisse Nationale d'Assurances Mutuelles Agricoles
    (Tunisia) 167, 185
Caisse Nationale de la Mutualité Agricole
    (Algeria) 167
calamity data 143–4
    area-affected data 143–4
    crop insurance pricing in China 143–4
    limitations of area-affected data 144
calamity-based crop insurance (CBCI) 191, 192t,
    198, 210–12
call options 10
Canada
    aggregate crop shortfall insurance 243–5
    agricultural insurance 159
    Co-operative Hail Insurance Company
        185
    Federal Agriculture Improvement and
        Reform Act 221
    firefighting cost insurance (Alberta) 358–60
    Gross Revenue Insurance Program (GRIP)
        220
    income insurance 233–4
    livestock insurance 282
    multi-peril crop insurance 180, 215, 404
    Poultry Insurance Exchange (PIE) 282
    revenue insurance 220–1
    satellite yield insurance (Alberta) 264
    satellite-based pasture insurance (Alberta)
        264

United Grain Growers (UGG) 243–5, 244f
Western Livestock Price Insurance Program
   (WLPIP) 159, 282
Canadian Agricultural Income Stabilization
   (CAIS) 233
Canadian Egg Industry Reciprocal Alliance
   (CEIRA), 282
Canadian Farm Income Program (CFIP)
   233, 234
Canadian Wildland Fire Information System 89
cannibalism (aquaculture) 318
canopy wind speed (CWS) 84
capital market investors 394
captives 29–30
carbon credits (forestry) 353–4
carbon emissions trading schemes 352
carbon offset markets 352
   compliance markets 352
   voluntary markets 352
carbon reversal insurance (forestry) 352–5
carbon sequestration in forests 353, 353f
Caribbean agricultural insurance 165–7
cat bond-lite platforms 396
cat bonds 393, 394, 396–402
   for agriculture 399
   structures 396–9
   triggers 397–9
cat futures 402
cat options 402
cat swaps 402
catastrophe bonds see cat bonds
catastrophe equity puts (Cat-E-Puts) 402
catastrophe insurance (CAT, USA) 213
catastrophe loading 214, 217, 260
Catastrophe Risk Evaluation and Standardizing
   Target Accumulations (CRESTA) 37
catastrophe risk modelling 27, 36–41, 388
   applications of 38
   challenges in modelling biological systems 38–9
   for agricultural risks 38–43
   input into 37
   main modules of 36–8
   output of 37
   uncertainties in 37–8
catastrophe risk swaps 402
Catastrophic Risk Exchange (CATEX) 402
cat-in-the-box product 398, 401–2
   for banana production 400
censored normal distribution 226
Center for Satellite Applications and Research
   (STAR) (NOAA) 120
Centre for Research on the Epidemiology of
   Disasters (CRED) 143
Chicago Board of Trade (CBOT) 11
Chicago Climate Exchange 352
Chile, infectious Salmon Anaemia outbreak in 100

chilling degree hours 254t
China
   agricultural insurance 161–4, 163t
   Agricultural Insurance Act 164
   Agricultural Insurance Program 162
   Agriculture Reinsurance Pool (CARP)
      162, 185, 364
   Animal Epidemic Prevention Law 283
   Black Dragon fire (1987), 337
   Crop insurance products 162
   Fishery Mutual Insurance Association
      (CFMIA) 321
   future developments of agricultural
      insurance 164
   government risk transfer for agricultural
      risks in 18–19
   heat day index product (aquaculture) 329
   Insurance Regulation Commission (CIRC) 162
   livestock insurance 283
   livestock revenue insurance 308
   mitten crab temperature index insurance 329
   National Agricultural Insurance Program 161–2,
      283, 308, 321, 341, 404
   natural disaster fund 19
   sovereign risk transfer 19
   Sunlight Agricultural Mutual Insurance 185
China Snow Disaster (2008) 74–5
   damage to agriculture 75
   damage to forests 75
   development of the disaster 75
CICS High-Resolution Optimally Interpolated
   Microwave Precipitation from Satellites
   (CHOMPS) (Cooperative Institute for Climate
   Studies) 109
classical swine fever 91, 94, 295
climate change 5–6
   climatological disasters 5
   impacts on crop production 5–6
   impacts on livestock, aquaculture and forestry
      6
climate data 103–18
   detrending 115–17
   discontinuities in 114, 114f
   erroneous 114
   gridded 105–7
   missing 115
   open source 105
   probability density functions for
      precipitation 117
   probability density functions for
      temperature 117
   reanalysis 111–12
   satellite-based 108–11
   sources of 104–8
   treatment of 113
   weather station data 104

Climate Hazards Group InfraRed Precipitation
   with Station data (CHIRPS) (USGS) 109
climate models 112–13
   climate scenarios 113
   climate model outputs 113
climate variability and agriculture 48–51
Climatic Research Unit (CRU) (University of East
   Anglia) 106
climatological disasters 5
CMORPH (CPC MORPHing technique)
   (NOAA) 109
coastal aquaculture systems 6
co-insurance pools 185–6
collateralisation 393, 394
collateralised reinsurance 393, 394, 395
combine harvesters 129–30
combined named-peril crop insurance 160
commodity price management instruments 9–10
Common Agricultural Policy (CAP, Europe) 233
conflicts and agriculture 5
consequential livestock loss insurance 292, 294–5
constructive total losses (forestry) 351
contagious bovine pleuropneumonia 91
contingent business interruption insurance
   (livestock) 292
contingent claim 226
contingent debt contracts 17
contract farming 10–11
Convective Available Potential Energy (CAPE) 67
cooperative insurers 184–5
Copernicus 64
Copernicus Emergency Management Service 89
copula functions 117, 230
credibility theory 31
credit guarantee programmes 172
credit guarantee systems 172
credit-linked insurance programmes 171
Cressman method 115
crop calendars 255, 255f
crop growth phases 255–6
crop hail insurance 189, 198–207
   definition of sum insured 201–2
   franchises and deductibles 202
   insurance terms 201–2
   loss adjustment 205–7
   loss mitigation measures 204–5
   pricing 202–5
   pricing based on insurance claims 203–4
   pricing without insurance claims 205
   standardising insurance claims 202–3, 204t
   in Switzerland 200–1
   in the USA 199–200
crop insurance 189–269
   overview of products 191–8
   products 191–8, 192–6t
   sector trends 189–90, 190f

crop models 130–2
   mechanistic 131–2
   types of 130–1
crop moisture index 57t, 59
crop revenue coverage (CRC, USA)
   221
crop yield data 125–40
   definition of yield 125–6
   discontinuities 133–4, 134f
   missing yield data 134
   sources of 126–7
   time trends in crop yields 135–8, 135f
   treatment of 132–3
crop yield distributions 138–40
   importance of detrending 140, 141f
   non-parametric methods 140
   parametric methods 139–40
Cropping System Model (CSM)
   132
CROPSYS model 131
cumulative rainfall 253t
cyclone damage to agriculture 81–2
   to banana production 400, 401f
   damage to crops 81
   damage to forests 82, 82t
Cyclone Larry (2006) 400
cyclone models 83–4
   air pressure models 83
   open source tropical cyclone track data
      85
   satellite imagery 83–4
   windstorm models for forestry 84–5
Cyclone Olivia (1996) 78
Cyclone Winifred (1986) 400
Cyclone Yasi (2011) 400
cyclones 76–85
   cyclone losses 78–82
   development conditions 77
   extratropical cyclones 77
   intensity scales 78
   Super Typhoon Haiyan 78–81, 80f
   tropical cyclones 77–8, 79t
   types of 77–8

Daily Surface Weather and Climatological
   Summaries (Daymet) (NASA) 107
Dartmouth Flood Observatory 64
data uncertainty factor 261
Daymet 106
Dead-Cat ILWs 403
Decision Support System for Agrotechnology
   Transfer (DSSAT) 131–2
deductibles (insurance) 27
deficit rainfall 253t
deposit premium (reinsurance) 378
derivative 26

detrending climate data 115–17
  non-parametric detrending 116–17
  parametric detrending 116
  seasonality in temperature data 117
detrending crop yield data 136
  importance for risk transfer products 138, 139f
  piecewise linear trends 137–8
digitalisation of information 29
disaster assistance programmes 16
disaster and calamity data 140–4
disaster declaration process 141–3
  government response 142
  key indicators for disasters 142
  risk statements 142–3
disaster risk financing programmes 16–18
discontinuities (climate data) 114
disease conductive days 254t
distribution functions (loss modelling) 34t
downscaling of climate model 113
drought 51–60
  definition 51
  damage to agriculture 52, 52t
  losses 52–5
  models 60
  types of 51–2
drought indices 56–9, 57–8t
  use of, for risk transfer 59
Duvorak pressure-wind model 83
dynamic risks 23

early mortality syndrome (EMS) 321
early warning and forecast systems of ENSO
  50–1
Earthdata (NASA) 89
economic yield 126
El Niño 6, 48, 50, 51, 316
El Niño Southern Oscillation (ENSO)
  45, 48–9, 133
  impacts on crop production 49–50
  classifications of events 48–9, 49t
Emergency Event Database (EM-Dat) 143
emissions trading schemes (ETSs) 337
eMODIS (USGS) 120
enterprise risk management (ERM) 12
environmental conditions, aquaculture
  317–18
Environmental Policy Integrated Climate
  (EPIC) model 131
enzootic bovine leucosis 294
epidemic aquaculture diseases 95–101
  epidemic disease losses 96–100, 97–8t, 99t
  epidemic diseases models 100–1
  types of 95–6
epidemic disease losses
  aquaculture 96–100, 97–8t, 99t
  livestock 93

epidemic disease models
  aquaculture 100–1
  livestock 94–5
epidemic livestock disease insurance 290–5
  business interruption insurance 292, 295
  consequential livestock loss insurance
    292, 294–5
  contingent business interruption insurance
    292
  government compensation schemes
    291–2, 294–5
  pricing of 293
epidemic livestock diseases 89–95, 92t
  biosecurity plans and disease response 90–1
  disease reporting and sanitary statuses 91
  epidemic disease losses 93
  epidemic disease models 94–5
  government response to 89–91
  international monitoring of diseases 91
  large historical losses 93
ERA-Interim (ECMWF) 112
Europe
  crop insurance 160–1
  income insurance 233
  livestock insurance 275–81
  multi-peril crop insurance 215
  non-industrial private forest owners 341
  revenue insurance 223
European Climate Assessment Dataset
  (ECAD) 105, 107
European Climate Exchange 352
European Flood Awareness System (EFAS) 64
event excess of loss reinsurance (EXOL)
  377–8, 388
  examples 378–9
event loss tables (ELTs) 37
ex-ante disaster financing instruments 17
exceedance probability (EP) curves 37
excess of loss treaty (reinsurance) 373t, 377
  in agriculture 378–9
  layering of 377
  reinstatements 378
  risk/event excess of loss reinsurance
    377–8, 378–9
excess rainfall 253t
expected loss calculation (ELC) 30, 33, 259
expected reinsurer's deficit 369
expected utility function 175
experience rating 32–5
ex-post disaster financing instruments 16–17
exposure modelling 388, 390–1
exposure rating 35
extended livestock insurance 290–5, 276t
  accident and infertility insurance 290
  epidemic disease insurance 290–5
extreme value theory 33

facultative reinsurance 371–2
facultative reinsurance pricing 386
Famine Early Warning Systems Network
   (FEWS-NET) 266
farm risk management 12
FarSite 88
Faustmann formula (forestry) 346
Federal Fire Occurrence Website (USA) 89
field crops, Loss Adjustment of 206–7, 206f
financial instruments 11
financial services providers 170
fire danger indices 349
fire weather indices 86
firefighting cost insurance 340t, 355–60
   indemnity-based firefighting expense
      insurance 356–8
   index-based firefighting expense
      insurance 358–60
Fish Pool ASA (Norway) 317, 330
flash floods 61–2
flat-rate pricing 385–6
flood 60–4
   types of 61–2
flood damage to agriculture 62–3, 62t
flood losses 62–3
flood models 63–4
   physical flood models 63
   remote sensing 63–4
foot and mouth disease 89, 91, 93, 94
forage production indices 265
forest areas and wood production 335–6
   development of forest land and area
      335–6, 336f
   development of wood production 336
forest insurance 333–61
   challenges of 343
   government disaster compensation
      programmes 337
   product types 338, 339–40t
   risk transfer solutions 337–43
   sector trends 333–7
forest insurance markets 338–43
   industrial private forest owners 342–3
   non-industrial private forest owners 338–42
   public forest owners 343
forest management certification 336
forest production systems 333–5
   classification according to forest
      composition 334
   classification according to forest ownership 335
   financial risks 337
   key perils 336–7
   measurements of forest areas 334
   production risks 337
Forest Resources Information Management
   System (FAO) 334

forest surveys 147
   natural disaster data 147–8
   historical fire data 148
ForestGales 84
forestry data 147–8
forests
   cyclone damage to 82, 82t
   definition of forest 334
   snow damage to 74, 75
   wildfire damage to 86–7
forward contracts 9–10
fraction of absorbed PAR (fAPAR) 121
France: satellite-based pasture insurance 265
franchises (insurance) 27
frost 67–73
   damage to crops 68–72
   frost models 72–3
   frost sensitivity of summer crops 69
   frost sensitivity of winter crops 69–72
   lethal minimum temperature 69, 69t
   minimum temperature models 72
   types of 68
frost days 73, 209
frost insurance 189, 208–10
   insurance terms 208
   loss adjustment 209–10, 209t
   pricing 208–9
fundamental insurance equation 26
futures contracts 10

gamma distribution 33, 34t, 117, 139, 388
generalised extreme value 117
generalised extreme value distribution 350
generalised Pareto distribution 33, 350
generalised skew logistic distribution 117
Geometric Brownian Motion 226, 277–8, 303
Geometric Brownian Motion with copula
   functions 229t
Geo-WRSI 266
Germany: consequential livestock loss
   insurance 294–5
Global Agricultural Monitoring Production
   System (NASA) 120
global agriculture insurance markets 150–69
   developing agricultural markets 151
   development of agricultural insurance 150–2
   from public sector programmes to private–
      public partnerships 150–1
   future developments of agricultural
      insurance 151–2
   mature agricultural markets 151
Global Aquaculture Alliance 316
Global Fire Emissions Database (GFED) 125
Global Fire Monitoring Center (GFMC) 89, 124
Global Historical Climatology Network
   (GHCN) 105

Global Index Insurance Facility (GIIF) 168
global insurance market 21–2
    overview 22, 22t
global insurance-linked securities markets 393–4
Global Surface Summary of the Day (GSOD) 105
global warming 5
government compensation for livestock diseases 91, 291–2, 294–5
government disaster compensation programmes 337
government risk management 16–19
grain elevators 130
gridded climate data 105–7
    gridding techniques 106
    open source gridded climate data 106–7
gross net premium income (GNPI) 377
gross net written premium income (GNWPI) 377
gross written premium (GWP) 21, 22
group risk income protection (GRIP, USA) 240
group risk plan (GRP, USA) 240
growing degree days256
Gumbel 117
Guy Carpenter 368

hail 64–7
    examples of severe hail losses in the USA (2014) 67
    formation 64–5
    hail damage time series (hail days) 65–6
    hail damage to crops 66–7
    hail models 67
    measurement of 65–6
Hannover Re 364
hardening (or acclimation) 68
harmful algal bloom 318
hedge funds 394
hematopoietic virus 96
hepatopancreatic parvovirus 96
highest monthly average daily wind speed 254t
historical burn rate method 32–3, 35, 387, 387f
historical claims data 30
Holland Formula (cyclone models) 83
horticulture crops, Loss Adjustment of 207, 207t
hotspots (forest fires) 122, 123
Hurricane Andrew (1992) 367, 396
HURricane DATabase (HURDAT) 85
Hurricane Katrina (2005) 367, 395
HWIND 84
hybrid triggers (cat bond) 399
hydrological indices 56
hypodermal viruses 96

ICICI Lombard 249
IFFCO Tokio General Insurance 249
IFRS 368

income insurance 189, 194t, 232–6
    accounting rules and adjustments 235
    calculating programme margins 235–6
    income insurance markets 233–5
    insurance terms 235–6
    pricing 236
indemnity function 256–7, 401, 403–4
indemnity triggers (cat bond) 397
indemnity-based crop insurance 191–8
index-based crop insurance 198
index-based forest insurance 340t, 360–1
    area-based fire index insurance 360–1
    area-yield index insurance 361
India
    agricultural insurance 164
    area-yield index insurance 237–40
    Comprehensive Crop Insurance Scheme (CCIS) 237
    Farm Income Insurance Scheme (FIIS) 233
    General Insurance Corporation of India (GIC) 237
    livestock insurance 283
    Meteorological Department (IMD) 107
    Modified National Agriculture Insurance Scheme (mNAIS) 238–9
    National Agricultural Insurance Scheme (NAIS) 237–8
    Pradhan Mantri Fasal Bima Yojana (PMFBY) 164, 237, 250
    Weather-Based Crop Insurance Scheme (WBCIS) 164, 249, 250
Indian Ocean Dipole (IOD) 48, 50
industrial private forest owners 335
industry loss index triggers (cat bond) 398
industry loss warranties 393, 394, 403–4
    in agriculture 404
    forms of 403
infectious salmon anaemia (ISA) 96, 99–100
    outbreak in Chile 100
infertility insurance (livestock) 290
insurability of agricultural risks 25, 173
insurability of risks 25
insurable interest 26
insurance 11
    definition 23
    key concepts 23–30
insurance operations 28–30
    information flows 29
    special forms of 29–30
    technology and29
insurance policy, key components 26–7
insurance risk management frameworks 24–6
insurance-linked securities (ILS) 393, 394
    markets 394, 395f
Intergovernmental Panel on Climate Change (IPCC) 47

International Best Track Archive for Climate
  Stewardship (IBTrACS) 85
International Finance Corporation (IFC)
  110, 111, 168
inverse distance weighting 106, 115
inverse Gaussian distribution 350
Israel: Kanat 167

Japan
  Agricultural Disaster Compensation Act 180
  agricultural insurance 161
  agricultural risk management in 180
  Crop Insurance Act 180
  Food, Agriculture and Rural Areas Basis Act 181
  government agricultural insurance in 180–1
  Income Security Program for Farmers 181
  Livestock Insurance Act 180
  National Federation of Forest Owners'
    Cooperative Association 341
  National Mutual Insurance Federation of
    Agricultural Cooperatives 185
  Nogyo Kyosai Seido (NOSAI) 180, 181
  Program for Stabilisation of Management
    Income 181
JLT Re 368

Kenya
  Hunger Safety Net Program 302
  index-based livestock insurance in 301–2
  Index-Based Livestock Insurance Pilot
    (IBLIP) 168, 301
  Kenya Livestock Insurance Program 168, 263, 302
  Kenya National Agriculture Program
    (KNAP), 168
  Kenya National Safety Net Program 302
Kernel estimator 117, 138
Kernel smoothing 134
kriging 106, 115, 134
Kyoto Protocol 352

La Niña, classification of events 48–9, 49t, 50, 51
Land Use, Land-Use Change and Forestry
  (LULUCF) activities 353
LANDFIRE 88, 89
LANDSAT 122, 124, 300
Latin America
  agricultural insurance 165–7
  livestock insurance 283–4
  multi-peril crop insurance 215
law of large numbers (insurance) 25
layering of risks 18
LGMI (livestock) 306
liability management (insurance) 27–8
Light Detection and Ranging (LiDAR) 205
Live-Cat ILWs 403

livestock gross margin insurance (LGMI)
  281, 303–6
  indemnity function 306
  main insurance terms 304–5, 305f
  pricing approaches 306
livestock index insurance 295–309
  area-based mortality index insurance 296–9
  satellite-based livestock mortality index
    insurance 299–302
livestock indicators 145,146t
livestock insurance 271–90
  challenges of 284–5
  livestock production systems 272–3
  product types 275, 276–80t
  sector trends 271–4
  standard 285–90
livestock insurance markets 275–85
livestock mortality 145
livestock price insurance 303
livestock production systems 272–3
  challenges per production system 273
  development of livestock feed requirements 274
  development of livestock production 273, 274f
  projections of livestock demand 274
  trends in livestock production and
    consumption 273
livestock revenue insurance 280t, 302–3
livestock state-transition models 94–5
  disease stages 94–5
  infection rates 95
livestock surveys 144–5
Lloyd's tables (reinsurance) 386
loess regression 117
logistic function 231
lognormal distribution 33, 34t, 388
long-tail business 27
look-back options 306
Lorenz Re 396
loss adjustment of field crops 206–7, 206f
  defoliation 206
  ear damage 206
  stalk damage 206
  stand reduction 206
loss adjustment of horticulture crops 207, 207t
loss cap (reinsurance) 374
loss corridor (reinsurance) 374
loss cost 34
loss cost ratio 32, 203
loss frequency modelling 33, 388, 390
loss ratio 374
loss reduction 24
loss reserves (insurance) 27–8
loss severity modelling 33, 388, 390

managing general agents (MGAs) 29
Manitoba Wildfire Program 356

Marine Harvest (Norway) 315, 320
market risk management 9–11
maximum foreseeable loss (MFL) 24, 386
MEaSUREs 76
mechanistic crop models 39, 131–2, 268–9
  performance of 132, 133f
meteorological indices 56
Mexico
  agricultural insurance 166
  Fondos de Aseguramiento (Fondos) 185
  index-based livestock insurance 300–1
  livestock insurance 284
minimum deposit premium (reinsruance) 378
model-based index insurance 197t, 266–9
modelled loss triggers (cat bond) 399
modelling biological systems 38–9
  changing vulnerabilities 39
  dynamic exposure changes 39
Moderate Resolution Imaging
  Spectroradiometer see MODIS
Modern-Era Retrospective Analysis for Research
  and Applications (MERRA) 112
modified National Agricultural Insurance Scheme
  (mNAIS, India) 237, 238
MODIS 64, 109, 120, 122, 262, 300
  area burned product 124–5
  hotspot product 123–4
  fire scars 361
Mongolia
  agricultural insurance 165
  Agricultural Reinsurance Company 299
  dzuds 296, 297–8, 297f
  extreme livestock mortality 297–8, 297f
  Index-Based Livestock Insurance Program
  (IBLIP) in 296–9
monodon baculovirus 96
Monsoon Asia Integrated Regional Study
  (MAIRS) 109, 110
Monte Carlo simulations 34, 230, 306
moral hazard (insurance) 25, 174–5
Morocco: Mutuelle Agricole Marocaine
  d'Assurance 167
Mozambique: weather index insurance in 110–11
MultiCat bonds 397
multi-peril crop insurance 28, 125, 150, 189, 193t,
  198, 213–20, 268
  challenges with 216
  insurance terms 216
  loss adjustment 220
  markets 213–16
  premium rates 216, 217t
  pricing 217–20, 219f
  pricing with historical claims data 217–18
  pricing with yield time series 218–19
multivariate pricing 30
Munich Re 364

Municipal Insurance Association of British
  Columbia 356
mutual insurers 184–5

named-peril aquaculture insurance 192t, 322–8
  deductibles 326
  event definitions 323
  indemnity 326–7
  insurance terms 323–7
  insured perils 322–3
  inventory for fish 324
  inventory for molluscs and crustaceans 324–5
  inventory methods 324–5
  loss adjustment 328
  offshore perils 323
  onshore perils 323
  preconditions for insurance 324
  premium rates 325–6, 326t
  pricing 328
  site surveys 325
  sum insured 325
  survival factors 325
  transit covers 323
named-peril crop insurance 189, 191, 198–212
  calamity-based 210–12
  frost insurance 208–10
  hail insurance 198–207
NASA Power 109
National Agricultural Insurance Scheme (NAIS,
  India) 180, 237, 238
National Agricultural Statistics Service
  (NASS, USA) 127
  agricultural yield survey 128
  objective yield survey 128
National Snowfall Analysis (USA) 76
national weather services 104
natural disasters and agriculture 47–8, 48f
  trends in global disasters relevant for 47–8
Net Income Stabilisation Accounts (Canada) 233
New Zealand
  Afforestation Grant Scheme 355
  agricultural insurance 165
  carbon initiatives 355
  carbon reversal insurance 355
  ETSs 355
  insurability of carbon credits for forests in 355
  Permanent Forest Sinks Initiative 355
  Standsure 341
Newcastle disease 94
NOAA-AVHRR 122
Nogyo Kyosai Seido (NOSAI, Japan) 161
non-industrial private forest owners 335
non-proportional reinsurance 372
normal distribution 33
normalised difference vegetation index (NDVI)
  58t, 59, 65, 119–20, 168, 205, 262, 263, 300

North America
  agricultural insurance 157–9
  livestock insurance 281–2
  non-industrial private forest owners 338
North American Animal Disease Spread Model 94
North American Regional Reanalysis (NARR) 112
North Atlantic Oscillation (NAO) 48, 50
Northridge earthquake (1994) 367, 396
numerical weather forecast model (NWFM) 111

obligatory reinsurance 372
occurrence exceedance probability (OEP) 37
open source climate data 105
open source drought data 60, 64
open source gridded climate data 106–7
open source hotspot and area burnt data 124–5
open source reanalysis climate data 112
open source satellite-based climate data 108–9
open source tropical cyclone track data 85
open source vegetation indices 120
open source wildfire data 88–9
option pricing methods 306
Oregon Forest Land Protection Fund (OFLPF) 356
Oxfam 168

Palmer drought severity index (PDSI) 56, 57t, 142
Parameter-elevation Regressions on Independent
  Slopes Model (PRISM) 106
parametric insurance 198
parametric triggers (cat bond) 398
Pareto distribution 33, 34t, 388
pasture vegetation index 264
Penman–Monteith equation 59
per risk/event XOL (reinsurance) 372
perils for agriculture 46–51
  biological perils 47
  classification of 46–7
  climate variability and 48–51
  natural disasters 47–8, 48f
  natural perils 46–7
peste des petits ruminants 91
phenological observations 255, 255f
Philippines
  Crop Insurance Corporation (PCIC) 80,
    81, 164, 180
  Land Bank of the Philippines (LBP), 80
Philippines: Super Typhoon Haiyan 78–81, 80f
  crop insurance 80–1
  development of 78
  impact 78–80
  losses to agriculture 80
photosynthetically active radiation (PAR) 120–1
physical (or mechanistic) fire spread models 88
plantation insurance 339t, 343–52
  basic insurance coverage 344–5
  extended insurance coverage 345

forest valuation methods 345–6
forest yield tables 346–7, 346f
indemnity 347
insurance terms 344–9
loss adjustment 350–2
loss adjustment of storm damage 351
loss adjustment of wildfire damage 351–2
modelling of damage ratios 349–50
premium rates 348–9
pricing 349–50
requirements for insurance 344
salvage evaluation 347–8
salvage potentials under plantation
  insurance 348
storage of salvaged timber 348
sum insured 347
use of loss proxies for pricing 349–50
valuation of forest assets 345–7
PMFBY (India) 250
Poisson distribution 34t
potential evapotranspiration (PET) 51
precipitation data 117
  simulation of 117–18
Precipitation Estimation from Remotely Sensed
  Information using Artificial Neural Networks-
  Climate Data Record (PERSIANN-CDR)
  (CHRS) 109
preventative culling (livestock) 90
price volatility, calculation of 226
principal component analyses (PCA) 117–18
PRISM High-Resolution Spatial Climate
  Data (USA) 107
private sector system 179
private–public partnerships 149, 150, 151,
  152, 223, 335
private–public sector system 182–4
  forms of 182
  government intervention 182–3
  government subsidies 183–4
probabilistic risk models 39
probability density functions 30, 133
probable maximum loss (PML) 24, 386
production risk management 11
production risks in aquaculture 317–19
Prometheus 88
Property Claims Services (PCS, USA) 398
proportional reinsurance, 372
pro-rata reinsurance 372
pseudorabies 94
public sector system 179–81
put option 10, 236, 256

quota share treaty (reinsurance) 373–4, 373t, 374f
  cash flows 375
  ceding commissions 374
  commission and loss sharing structures 375

in agriculture 375
loss controlling measures 374–5

R4 Rural Resilience Initiative 168
radiation use efficiency (RUE) 121
Rainfall Index Insurance Plan (RIIP, USA) 107
rate on line (ROL) 377
real estate investment trusts (REITs) 335
reanalysis climate data 111–12
    numerical weather forecast models 111–12
    open source reanalysis climate data 112
    use of reanalysis data 112
reduced deforestation and degradation (REDD) 353
reinsurance cycles 366–7
reinsurance intermediaries 368
reinsurance markets 363–91
    agricultural reinsurance markets 364
    global 363–5, 365t
    national reinsurers 364
reinsurance placement process 367
reinsurance regulation 368
reinsurance sidecars 395–6
reinsurance strategy 370–1
reinsurance
    forms of 369–82
    hard markets 367
    key concepts 366–9
    reinsurance cycles 366–7
    reinsurance principles 366–8
    soft markets 367
remote sensing 63–4, 87
remote sensing-based indices 56
Remote Sensing-Based Information and Insurance
    for Crops in Emerging Economies (RIICE)
    project 121–2
revenue assurance (RA, USA) 221
revenue insurance 189, 194t, 220–32
    calculation of price volatility 226
    calculation of yield volatility 225–6
    calculation of yield-price correlations 228–30, 229t
    challenges of revenue insurance 223
    example of revenue insurance pricing 230–2
    geographical downward adjustments 230
    insurance terms 224
    price volatility indices 225
    pricing 224–32
    revenue insurance markets 220–3
    sources of commodity prices 225
revenue insurance pricing 224–32
    joint yield-price simulations 231–2, 232t
    pricing price volatility 231
    pricing yield volatility 231
    risk premium rates 232
revenue protection (RP, USA) 54, 220, 230
ring culling (livestock) 90
risk adversity 24–5

risk assessment, 24
risk control 24
risk excess of loss reinsurance 377–8
    examples 378–9
risk excess of loss (RXOL) treaty
    (reinsurance) 377–78
risk financing 24
risk identification 24
risk layering in agriculture 8, 8f
Risk Management Agency (RMA, USA) 41,
    159, 199, 214
risk management in agriculture 6–19
    farm risk management 12
    government risk management 16–19
    market risk management 9–11
    production risk management 11
    risk management strategies 7–9
    supply chain risk management 12–16
risk measurement 24
risk perception 24–5
risk premium 34
risk strategies in agriculture 7–8
risk terminologies (insurance) 23–4
risk transfer in agriculture 8–9
risk transfer tests (reinsurance) 369
risk types (insurance) 23–4
risk/event excess of loss (XOL) 363
risk-linked securities 394
river flooding 61
RP-HPE 230

satellite data 118–25
satellite-based climate data 108–11
    estimation of meteorological parameters 108–9
    open source satellite-based climate data 108–9
satellite-based index insurance 197t, 262–5
satellite-based livestock mortality index insurance
    279t, 299–302
    challenges with NDVI for Insurance
        Applications 300
satellite-based mortality index insurance 295
Satellite Pour l'Observation de la Terre
    (SPOT) 120, 122
schedule rating (insurance) 31–2
SCOR 364
scrapie 295
securitisation 393, 394
short-tail business 27
sidecars 393, 394
SL see Stop-Loss
smoothing in yield time series 129
snow 73–6
    China snow disaster (2008) 74–5
    damage to agriculture 74–5
    damage to forests 74
    definition of 73–4

measurement of 73–4
open source snow cover data 76
snow depth 74
snow models 76
Snow Cover Product (MODIS) 76
SnowFrost 76
snowMAUS 76
soil moisture deficit index (SMDI) 58t
Soil Plant System Simulation Model (DAISY) 131
South Africa: multi-peril crop insurance 215
South Korea
  National Agricultural Cooperative
    Federation 164
  National Federation of Fisheries Cooperatives
    164, 320–1
Southeast Asia
  agricultural insurance 164
  agricultural risk pool 185
  small-scale aquaculture 321
Spatiotemporal Epidemiological Modeler 94
special-purpose vehicles (SPVs) 395
standard livestock insurance 276t, 285–90
  identification of livestock 285–6
  indemnity 288
  individual animal valuation methods 286, 287f
  insurance terms 285–8
  livestock mortality ratios 288–9, 289t
  loss adjustment 290
  overall valuation methods 286
  premium rates 288
  pricing 288–90
  pricing livestock mortality 289–90
  requirements for insurance 286–7
  sum insured 287
  valuation of livestock for inventories 286
standard precipitation evapotranspiration index
  (SPEI) 56, 57, 60
standard precipitation index (SPI) 56, 57t,
  59, 60, 142
standard risk theoretic model 34
Statplan (USA) 31
stochastic modelling 30
stochastic risk model 39
stop-loss pricing 389–90, 390t
stop-loss reinsurance 373t, 379–80, 379f
  in agriculture 380–1
  priorities and monetary limits 380
  reinsurance premium 380
  umbrella stop-loss programmes 381
storm damage, loss adjustment, plantation
  insurance 351
Storm Gudrun (2005) 337
storm surge 62
strategic reinsurance 381–2
supply chain risk management 12–16
Surface Dynamics Modeling Lab 64

surplus reinsurance 373t, 375–6, 376f
  surplus reinsurance in agriculture 376–7
swaps 10
Swiss Re 364
Switzerland
  crop hail insurance in 200–1
  Swiss Hail Insurance Company 185, 200
synthetic aperture radar (SAR) 121
systemic risks 173–5

tail value at risk (TVaR) 37
Taura syndrome virus 96
temperature data 117
  simulation of 117–18
term sheets (weather index insurance) 257, 258–9f
Thailand
  Bank for Agriculture and Agricultural
    Cooperatives 164, 211
  calamity data 212
  calamity-based rice insurance in 210–12
  performance of the rice insurance
    scheme 211–12
  pricing with calamity data 212
  rice insurance programme 211
thin-plate smoothing splines 106
timber investment management organisations
  (TIMOs) 335
transboundary animal diseases (TADs) 90
treaty reinsurance 372–81
  recognition of claims 372
  types 372–3, 374t
treaty reinsurance pricing 386–91
  aggregate modelling 389
  exposure modelling 390–1
  loss frequency and severity modelling 390
  stop-loss pricing for 389–90, 390t
Tropical Applications of Meteorology
  (TAMSAT) 109, 267
Tropical Ocean Global Atmosphere
  Program (TOGA)105
Tropical Rainfall Measuring Mission
  (TRMM) 109
Tunisia: Caisse Nationale d'Assurances Mutuelles
  Agricoles 167, 185
Turkey
  agricultural insurance pool in 186
  Agricultural Insurance Act 186
  TARSIM 185, 186, 320
Typhoon Haiyan (Philippines) 78

uberrima fides (insurance) 28
Ukraine, winterkill in 70–2
umbrella stop-loss 379
unearned premium (insurance) 27–8
Unified Gauge-Based Analysis of Global Daily
  Precipitation 106

UNISYS 85
United Grain Growers (UGG) 242
USA
    agricultural insurance 157–9
    apiculture insurance 107–8
    Aquaculture Dollar Amount of Insurance
        (ADAI) 327
    area-yield index insurance 240–1
    catfish margin insurance 330–1
    clam insurance 327
    crop hail insurance 199–200
    Crop Production Plan 199
    drought (2012) 53–5, 55t
    drought monitor (USDM) 58t
    Federal Crop Insurance Act 159, 213
    Federal Crop Insurance Corporation
        (FCIC) 157, 213
    Firefighting Expense Insurance (Oregon)
        356–8, 357f
    hail losses (2014) in 67
    livestock gross margin 307
    livestock insurance 281–2
    livestock revenue insurance 306–7
    livestock risk protection 307
    livestock risk protection programme 281
    multi-peril crop insurance 213–15, 404
    revenue insurance 221
    Whole-Farm Revenue Protection (WFRP)
        221–2, 281
USAID Famine Early Warning Systems
    Network 110
utility theory 25

value at risk 26, 37
vegetation condition index (VCI) 58
vegetation cover fraction (fCover) 121, 265
vegetation indices 103, 118, 119–21, 124, 263–4
    crop yield estimations from 120–1
    land use classification from 120
vegetation monitoring 118

WAHIS 91
WAHIS-Wild 91
water requirement satisfaction index (WRSI) 58t,
    59, 60, 110, 168, 266–8
weather index insurance 191, 196t, 248–62
    basis risk 251
    challenges of 251
    in Mozambique 110–11
    weather index insurance markets 249–51
weather index insurance pricing 259–62
    corn growth phases and weather parameters 262
    correlation analysis 262
    example of weather index insurance
        pricing 261–2

expected loss calculation 260
    historical burn rate calculation 260
weather indices 191, 252–6
    crop growth phases 255–6
    cumulative indices 252
    index structures 252–5
    insurance terms 256–7
    multicover indices 252–5
    multiphase indices 252
weather radars 66
weather satellites 66
Weibull distribution 33, 34t, 117, 350, 388
White Spot Syndrome Virus (WSSV) in
    shrimp 96–9
wildfire models 87–8
    physical fire models 88
    spatial and temporal fire models 88
    statistical fire models 88
wildfires 85–9, 87t
    definition and cause of 85–6
    detection 123–4
    monitoring 122–3
    plantation insurance 351–2
    wildfire indices 86
    wildfire losses 86–7
    wildfire damage to forests 86–7
Willis Re 368
windstorm models for forestry 84–5
winter freeze 71
winterkill 69–70
    in the Ukraine (2002-2003) 70–2, 71f
    insurance 70–2
World Animal Health Information System
    (WAHIS) 91
World Food Programme (WFP) 168
World Food Studies (WOFOST) model 131
World Meteorological Organization (WMO) 57t
World Organisation for Animal Health (OIE)
    90, 91, 143
World Trade Organization (WTO) 91, 149
    rules for agricultural insurance subsidies
        183–4

XOL reinsurance treaties (reinsurance) 377

yellow-head virus 96
yield gap 126
yield protection (YP, USA) 54
yield-price correlations, calculation of
    228–30, 229t
    additive methods and simple simulations 230
    copula functions 230
yield volatility, calculation of 225–6

zero-coupon bond 397